Part IV Study Aids for *The Urantia Book*

Urantia Foundation
533 Diversey Parkway
Chicago, Illinois 60614

All direct quotes are from:
The Urantia Book

ISBN: 978–0–911560–60–2
Imprint: Urantia Foundation

Originally Prepared By:

Ruth E. Renn

Originally published: 1975

Updated 2020:
Content and formatting: Rick Lyon
Cover design: Susan Lyon
CosmicCreations.BIZ

"Thanksgiving and adoration to the Son
who made possible our sonship career."
Ruth E. Renn

"Jesus' earthly life was devoted to one great purpose—doing the Father's will,
living the human life religiously and by faith."
196:0.14 (2090.1)

PART IV of
THE URANTIA BOOK

The Life and Teachings of Jesus

The midway creatures, not visible to mortal man, are permanent citizens of Urantia. They work unceasingly for the uplifting of mankind. Having been on this world since their origin at the time of the Planetary Prince, they have records of happenings during the time of Jesus' life on Urantia.

Parts I—III of *The Urantia Book* provides a framework for Part IV which explains Jesus' bestowal on Urantia and the two concepts potential in his human-divine self.

Because of the relevance of Paper 119—"The Bestowals Of Christ Michael" to Part IV, we have included it as part of this study aid. It serves as both introduction and prelude to Part IV.

References to quotes from *The Urantia Book* are shown as this example: 196:1.3 (2090.4). This style of referencing quotes indicates: Paper 196: Section 1. Paragraph 3 (Page 2090. paragraph 4). Use these references to locate complete quotes in *The Urantia Book.*

The original "Part IV Study Aids of *The Urantia Book*" was published by Ruth Renn in 1975. With this revision, we have done our best to remain true to the original work while modernizing the format and expanding the content. We have attempted to be as thorough as possible but as with the original, this is only a sampling of the text from *The Urantia Book*. Complete answers or descriptions may only be found there.

Jane Allen, Ruth Renn, and Marjorie Bales
In the garden of the Hales' home; June 1948

Ruth E. Renn, the original author of this publication, became a Forum member in 1925 when Dr. Sadler invited her, as one of his patients, to attend a meeting at his home and offices located at 533 Diversey Parkway, Chicago, IL. USA

In April of 1958, Urantia Brotherhood reported that the first class for teaching *The Urantia Book* to children had started at the home of the teacher Mrs. Ruth Renn. She found her nine young charges, ranging in ages from 6 to 13, to be very space-minded, and intensely interested in what she taught them. They decided themselves to call their group the "Junior Urantia Class."

In 1972, Mrs. Renn and Mrs. Sylvia Sunderland created cassette tape recordings of *The Urantia Book*.

On November 18, 1975, Urantia Foundation published "*Study Aids for Part IV of The Urantia Book—The Life and Teachings of Jesus*" prepared by Mrs. Renn. Approximately 500 printed copies were mailed out that first day, and through the years orders have continued to come in at a steady pace. It has proven to be a very valuable study aid for students of "*The Urantia Book*." The original publication was 103 pages and remained available until 2019. Mrs. Renn graduated from this world in 1997; no doubt with full honors for a job well done. We dedicate this revision of the "Part IV Study Aids" to Mrs. Renn.

As we produced this revision, we were able to take advantage of the online PDF version of *The Urantia Book*. Using Ruth's page references, we scrolled through the document, highlighted the paragraph, and then with a couple of clicks of the keyboard, copy and pasted the text from the PDF into the new document. When we could not find the referenced paragraph or if we wanted to add more information, we simply typed in the keyword to the search bar and like magic all the places that word is used in the 2096 pages of *The Urantia Book* appeared before us.

It occurred to us that in 1975 nobody had even dreamed of a personal desktop computer that almost everyone has nowadays. The internet was something found only in a basement of some college campus. We imagined how Ruth had to do this same process. Her knowledge of *The Urantia Book* had to be vast. To find the quote she wanted required a lot of reading just to find one quote. Then, that quote had to be typed—on a typewriter—using White Out to fix typos rather than the back button. We spent many hours copying Ruth's original work. Just imagine the months she spent creating it.

We sought to remain as true to the original work of Ruth Renn as possible while, with the benefit of computer age tools, enhancing and expanding upon her work. May this work bring a smile to her face and honor to her memory.

Rick and Susan Lyon

The Study of Jesus' Life

On page 1729 of *The Urantia Book* we are told that the most thrilling and inspiring of all possible human experiences is the personal quest for truth, and that the supreme adventure of all human existence is man seeking God, and finding him.

> *"Of all human knowledge, that which is of greatest value is to know the religious life of Jesus and how he lived it."* 196:1.3 (2090:4)

Where could we find greater truths than in "The Life and Teachings of Jesus", Part IV of *The Urantia Book*? Where could we find a greater adventure than the story of Jesus' life and how he lived it?

There is no conceivable practical problem that we may face in our human life and no deeper questions about the eternal mystery of God that the human intellect may ask, for which the religion of Jesus does not have some words of wisdom, hope, and comfort. Jesus' life was not intended to be an example of how we should live our life in our day and age but rather a standard of spiritual living for all ages. His life, the greatest mortal life ever lived on Urantia, is an inspiration for us and shows what is possible for our own life and by our own choosing. His death and resurrection proved that what he taught about our own potential resurrection and eternal life is true.

In reading about Jesus' journeys, his talks with the apostles and the people he met as he passed by, and his teaching and preaching to his followers and disciples, we learn that the greatest truth mortal man can ever hear is the living gospel of the Fatherhood of God and the brotherhood of man. He taught the truth that we are all children of God, our Paradise Father. It is revealed to us that part of God dwells within us, that we are gradually becoming perfect even as our Father in heaven is perfect. Jesus declared that the Paradise Father, at the center of the universe, is truly attainable by every mortal creature who accepts sonship with God. Someday we will surely stand before Him and hear these words we all long to hear: "Well done , good and *faithful* servant."

Jesus, the creator of a vast universe of 10 million worlds with the responsibility of a universe upon his shoulders, attended cheerfully to all the everyday duties of family life. For several years he was planning to leave the family, but he did not neglect the little things of life as he prepared for the big things of a universe.

Jesus did for religion what no other human being ever could. He translated eternal truths into everyday language. The common people heard him gladly. Jesus was the first teacher who talked to people and told them the highest truths of the universe.

Ruth Renn

Part IV Study Aids Table of Contents

The Source of Part IV of The Urantia Book

Acting under the supervision of a commission of twelve members of the United Brotherhood of Urantia Midwayers, conjointly sponsored by the presiding head of our order and the Melchizedek of record, I am the secondary midwayer of onetime attachment to the Apostle Andrew, and I am authorized to place on record the narrative of the life transactions of Jesus of Nazareth as they were observed by my order of earth creatures, and as they were subsequently partially recorded by the human subject of my temporal guardianship. Knowing how his Master so scrupulously avoided leaving written records behind him, Andrew steadfastly refused to multiply copies of his written narrative. A similar attitude on the part of the other apostles of Jesus greatly delayed the writing of the Gospels. 121:0.1 (1332.1)

[Acknowledgment: In carrying out my commission to restate the teachings and retell the doings of Jesus of Nazareth, I have drawn freely upon all sources of record and planetary information. My ruling motive has been to prepare a record which will not only be enlightening to the generation of men now living, but which may also be helpful to all future generations. From the vast store of information made available to me, I have chosen that which is best suited to the accomplishment of this purpose. As far as possible I have derived my information from purely human sources. Only when such sources failed, have I resorted to those records which are superhuman. When ideas and concepts of Jesus' life and teachings have been acceptably expressed by a human mind, I invariably gave preference to such apparently human thought patterns. Although I have sought to adjust the verbal expression the better to conform to our concept of the real meaning and the true import of the Master's life and teachings, as far as possible, I have adhered to the actual human concept and thought pattern in all my narratives. I well know that those concepts which have had origin in the human mind will prove more acceptable and helpful to all other human minds. When unable to find the necessary concepts in the human records or in human expressions, I have next resorted to the memory resources of my own order of earth creatures, the midwayers. And when that secondary source of information proved inadequate, I have unhesitatingly resorted to the superplanetary sources of information. 121:8.12 (1343.1)

The memoranda which I have collected, and from which I have prepared this narrative of the life and teachings of Jesus—aside from the memory of the record of the Apostle Andrew—embrace thought gems and superior concepts of Jesus' teachings assembled from more than two thousand human beings who have lived on earth from the days of Jesus down to the time of the inditing of these revelations, more correctly restatements. The revelatory permission has been utilized only when the human record and human concepts failed to supply an adequate thought pattern. My revelatory commission forbade me to resort to extrahuman sources of either information or expression until such a time as I could testify that I had failed in my efforts to find the required conceptual expression in purely human sources. 121:8.13 (1343.2)

While I, with the collaboration of my eleven associate fellow midwayers and under the supervision of the Melchizedek of record, have portrayed this narrative in accordance with my concept of its effective arrangement and in response to my choice of immediate expression, nevertheless, the majority of the ideas and even some of the effective expressions which I have thus utilized had their origin in the minds of the men of many races who have lived on earth during the intervening generations, right on down to those who are still alive at the time of this undertaking. In many ways I have served more as a collector and editor than as an original narrator. I have unhesitatingly appropriated those ideas and concepts, preferably human, which would enable me to create the most effective portraiture of Jesus' life, and which would qualify me to restate his matchless teachings in the most strikingly helpful and universally uplifting phraseology. In behalf of the Brotherhood of the United Midwayers of Urantia, I most gratefully acknowledge our indebtedness to all sources of record and concept which have been hereinafter utilized in the further elaboration of our restatement of Jesus' life on earth.] 121:8.14 (1343.3)

Year and Jesus' Age by Paper

08 B.C.		Paper 122:0
07 B.C	Birth	Paper 122:2
06 B.C.	Age 1	Paper 122:3
05 B.C.	Age 2	Paper 122:3
04 B.C.	Age 3	Paper 123:0
03 B.C.	Age 4	Paper 123:1
02 B.C.	Age 5	Paper 123:2
01 B.C.	Age 6	Paper 123:3
01 A.D.	Age 7	Paper 123:4
02 A.D.	Age 8	Paper 123:6
03 A.D.	Age 9	Paper 124:1
04 A.D.	Age 10	Paper 124:2
05 A.D.	Age 11	Paper 124:3
06 A.D.	Age 12	Paper 124:4
07 A.D.	Age 13	Paper 124:5
08 A.D.	Age 14	Paper 126:0
9 A.D.	Age 15	Paper 126:3
10 A.D.	Age 16	Paper 127:0
11 A.D.	Age 17	Paper 127:2
12 A.D.	Age 18	Paper 127:3
13 A.D.	Age 19	Paper 127:4
14 A.D.	Age 20	Paper 127:6
15 A.D.	Age 21	Paper 128:0
16 A.D.	Age 22	Paper 128:2
17 A.D.	Age 23	Paper 128:3
18 A.D.	Age 24	Paper 128:5
19 A.D.	Age 25	Paper 128:6
20 A.D.	Age 26	Paper 128:7
21 A.D.	Age 27	Paper 129:0
22 A.D.	Age 28	Paper 129:2
23 A.D.	Age 29	Paper 129:3
24 A.D.	Age 30	Paper 134:0
25 A.D.	Age 31	Paper 134:7
26 A.D.	Age 32	Paper 135:8
27 A.D.	Age 33	Paper 138:10
28 A.D.	Age 34	Paper 144:9
29 A.D.	Age 35	Paper 150:0
30 A.D.	Died 04/09/30	Paper 165:0

Specific Dates of Events in Part IV

NOTE: Years separated by lines

DECEMBER 31, ~198,066 B.C.
The Lucifer manifesto was issued at the annual conclave of Satania on the sea of glass, in the presence of the assembled hosts of Jerusem, on the last day of the year, about two hundred thousand years ago, Urantia time. 53:4.1 (604.3)

MARCH 25, 7 B.C.
JOHN the Baptist was born March 25, 7 B.C., in accordance with the promise that Gabriel made to Elizabeth in June of the previous year. 135:0.1 (1496.1)

APRIL 2, 7 B.C.
Zacharias and Elizabeth rejoiced greatly in the realization that a son had come to them as Gabriel had promised, and when on the eighth day they presented the child for circumcision, they formally christened him John. 122:2.7 (1346.2)

MAY 29, 7 B.C.
The beautiful legend of the star of Bethlehem originated in this way: Jesus was born August 21 at noon, 7 B.C. On May 29, 7 B.C., there occurred an extraordinary conjunction of Jupiter and Saturn in the constellation of Pisces. 122:8.7 (1352.3)

AUGUST 18, 7 B.C.
Mary, being large with child, rode on the animal with the provisions while Joseph walked, leading the beast. And so this Jewish couple went forth from their humble home early on the morning of August 18, 7 B.C., on their journey to Bethlehem. 122:7.4 (1350.6)

AUGUST 19, 7 B.C.
Bright and early the morning of August 19, Joseph and Mary were again on their way. They partook of their noontide meal at the foot of Mount Sartaba, overlooking the Jordan valley, and journeyed on, making Jericho for the night, where they stopped at an inn on the highway in the outskirts of the city. 122:7.6 (1351.2)

AUGUST 20, 7 B.C.
Early in the morning of August 20 they [Joseph and Mary] resumed their journey, reaching Jerusalem before noon, visiting the temple, and going on to their destination, arriving at Bethlehem in midafternoon. 122:7.6 (1351.2)

AUGUST 21, 7 B.C.
By the break of day the pangs of childbirth were well in evidence, and at noon, August 21, 7 B.C., with the help and kind ministrations of women fellow travelers, Mary was delivered of a male child. Jesus of Nazareth was born into the world, 122:8.1 (1351.5)

AUGUST 22, 7 B.C.
The next day after the birth of Jesus, Joseph made his enrollment.... That afternoon they moved up to the inn, where they lived for almost three weeks until they found lodgings in the home of a distant relative of Joseph. 122:8.3 (1351.7)

AUGUST 23, 7 B.C.
The second day after the birth of Jesus, Mary sent word to Elizabeth that her child had come and received word in return inviting Joseph up to Jerusalem to talk over all their affairs with Zacharias. 122:8.4 (1351.8)

AUGUST 29, 7 B.C.
In just the same manner as all babies before that day and since have come into the world, the promised child was born; and on the eighth day, according to the Jewish practice, he was circumcised and formally named Joshua (Jesus). 122:8.2 (1351.6)

Zacharias knew the day Joseph and Mary were expected to appear at the temple with Jesus, and he had prearranged with Simeon and Anna to indicate, by the salute of his upraised hand, which one in the procession of first-born children was Jesus.... For this occasion Anna had written a poem which Simeon proceeded to sing, much to the astonishment of Joseph, Mary, 122:9.3 (1353.2)

SEPTEMBER 29, 7 B.C.
On May 29, 7 B.C., there occurred an extraordinary conjunction of Jupiter and Saturn in the constellation of Pisces. And similar conjunctions occurred on September 29 and December 5 of the same year. 122:8.7 (1352.3)

OCTOBER 2, 4 B.C.
Joseph and Mary departed from Bethlehem for Nazareth, going by way of Lydda and Scythopolis. They started out early one Sunday morning, Mary and the child riding on their newly acquired beast of burden. 123:0.6 (1356.3)

APRIL 2, 3 B.C.
The next important event in the life of this Nazareth family was the birth of the second child, James, in the early morning hours of April 2, 3 B.C. Jesus was thrilled by the thought of having a baby brother. 123:1.5 (1357.2)

FEBRUARY 11, 2 B.C.
Jesus arrived at the age of his first personal and wholehearted moral decision; and there came to abide with him a Thought Adjuster, a divine gift of the Paradise Father, which had aforetime served with Machiventa Melchizedek. 123:2.1 (1357.5)

JULY 11, 2 B.C.
In this year, 2 B.C., a little more than one month before his fifth birthday anniversary, Jesus was made very happy by the coming of his sister Miriam, who was born on the night of July 11. 123:2.3 (1357.7)

JULY 12, 2 B.C.
During the evening of the following day Jesus had a long talk with his father concerning the manner in which various groups of living things are born into the world as separate individuals. The most valuable part of Jesus' early education was secured from his parents in answer to his thoughtful and searching inquiries. 123:2.3 (1357.7)

JANUARY 22 A.D. 1
This was, indeed, an eventful year in Jesus' life. Early in January a great snowstorm occurred in Galilee. Snow fell two feet deep, the heaviest snowfall Jesus saw during his lifetime and one of the deepest at Nazareth in a hundred years. 123:4.1 (1361.1)

MARCH 16 A.D. 1
The fourth member of the Nazareth family, Joseph, was born Wednesday morning, March 16, A.D. 1. 123:4.9 (1362.1)

JANUARY 24 A.D. 2
[Jesus'] first week's sojourn on his uncle's farm (since infancy) was in January of this year; 123:6.2 (1364.5)

APRIL 14 A.D. 2
Jesus' third brother, Simon, was born on Friday evening, April 14, of this year, A.D. 2. 123:6.7 (1365.2)

SEPTEMBER 13 A.D. 3
Jesus' second sister, Martha, was born Thursday night, September 13. 124:1.7 (1367.3)

OCTOBER 5 A.D. 3
Three weeks after the coming of Martha, Joseph started the building of an addition to their house, a combined workshop and bedroom. A small workbench was built for Jesus, and for the first time he possessed tools of his own. 124:1.7 (1367.3)

JULY 5 A.D. 4
It was the fifth of July, the first Sabbath of the month, when Jesus, while strolling through the countryside with his father, first gave expression to feelings and ideas which indicated that he was becoming self-conscious of the unusual nature of his life mission. 124:2.1 (1368.3)

JUNE 24 A.D. 5
On Wednesday evening, June 24, A.D. 5, Jude was born. Complications attended the birth of this, the seventh child. Mary was so very ill for several weeks that Joseph remained at home. 124:3.4 (1370.2)

JANUARY 9 A.D. 7
On Sunday night, January 9, A.D. 7, his [Jesus'] baby brother, Amos, was born. 124:5.2 (1373.2)

MARCH 18 A.D. 7
Friday of the week before [Jesus graduated], Joseph had come over from Sepphoris, where he was in charge of the work on a new public building, to be present on this glad occasion. Jesus' teacher confidently believed that his alert and diligent pupil was destined to some outstanding career, some distinguished mission. 124:5.5 (1373.5)

MARCH 20 A.D. 7
On the first day of the week, March 20, A.D. 7, Jesus graduated from the course of training in the local school connected with the Nazareth synagogue. This was a great day in the life of any ambitious Jewish family, the day when the first-born son was pronounced a "son of the commandment" 124:5.4 (1373.4)

APRIL 5 A.D. 7
Jesus was qualified to proceed to Jerusalem with his parents to participate with them in the celebration of his first Passover. A considerable company (103) made ready to depart from Nazareth early Monday morning for Jerusalem. 124:6.1 (1374.1)

APRIL 7 A.D. 7
On the day before the Passover Sabbath, flood tides of spiritual illumination swept through the mortal mind of Jesus and filled his human heart to overflowing with affectionate pity for the spiritually blind and morally ignorant multitudes assembled for the celebration of the ancient Passover commemoration. 124:6.15 (1376.1)

APRIL 8 A.D. 7
Joseph found time to take his son around to visit the academy where it had been arranged for him to resume his education two years later, as soon as he reached the required age of fifteen. Joseph was truly puzzled when he observed how little interest Jesus evinced in all these carefully laid plans. 124:6.13 (1375.7)

APRIL 17 A.D. 9

On Wednesday evening, April 17, A.D. 9, Ruth, the baby of the family, was born, and to the best of his ability Jesus endeavored to take the place of his father in comforting and ministering to his mother during this trying and peculiarly sad ordeal. 126:3.2 (1389.5)

AUGUST 24 A.D. 9

With the coming of his fifteenth birthday, Jesus could officially occupy the synagogue pulpit on the Sabbath day. And when all the faithful in Nazareth had assembled, the young man stood up and began to read: "The spirit of the Lord God is upon me, for the Lord has anointed me; he has sent me to bring good news to the meek, 126:4.1 (1391.5)

DECEMBER 3 A.D. 12

On Saturday afternoon, December 3, of this year, death for the second time struck at this Nazareth family. Little Amos, their baby brother, died after a week's illness with a high fever. 127:3.13 (1400.5)

APRIL 26 A.D. 22

Jesus and the two natives from India — Gonod and his son Ganid — left Jerusalem on a Sunday morning, April 26, A.D. 22. 130:0.1 (1427.1)

AUGUST 17 A.D. 22

On August 17, A.D. 22, when John [the Baptist] was twenty-eight years of age, his mother suddenly passed away. 135:4.1 (1499.1)

DECEMBER 10 A.D. 23

Jesus said good-bye to Gonod and his son Ganid in the city of Charax on the Persian Gulf on the 10th of December the following year, A.D. 23. 130:0.1 (1427.1)

MARCH 6 A.D. 24

Jesus, followed by his disciples, left Nazareth this Sunday morning, and traveling by different routes, they all finally assembled at Bethsaida by noon on Thursday, March 10. They came together as a sober and serious group of disillusioned preachers of the gospel150:9.5. (1687.2)

APRIL 1 A.D. 24

It was the first of April, A.D. 24, when Jesus left Nazareth on the caravan trip to the Caspian Sea region. The caravan which Jesus joined as its conductor was going from Jerusalem by way of Damascus and Lake Urmia through Assyria, Media, and Parthia to the southeastern Caspian Sea region. 134:2.1 (1484.5)

APRIL 6 A.D. 24

On Sunday morning, Jesus and the apostles went down to Jerusalem; and this was the first time the Master and all of the twelve had been there together. (1595.7) 141:9.3

SEPTEMBER 21 A.D. 25

Both of them [Jesus and John] were present at the solemn services of the day of atonement. John was much impressed by the ceremonies of this day of all days in the Jewish religious ritual, but Jesus remained a thoughtful and silent spectator. To the Son of Man this performance was pitiful and pathetic. 134:9.3 (1494.6)

JANUARY 13 A.D. 26

Just before the noon rest, Jesus laid down his tools, removed his work apron, and merely announced to the three workmen in the room with him, "My hour has come." 135:8.3 (1504.1)

JANUARY 14 A.D. 26
John was atremble with emotion as he made ready to baptize Jesus of Nazareth in the Jordan at noon on Monday, January 14, A.D. 26. Thus did John baptize Jesus and his two brothers James and Jude. 135:8.6 (1504.4)

FEBRUARY 23 A.D. 26
It was early on the morning of Sabbath, February 23, that the company of John, engaged in eating their morning meal, looked up toward the north and beheld Jesus coming to them. As he approached them, John stood upon a large rock and, lifting up his sonorous voice, said: "Behold the Son of God, the deliverer of the world!" 135:9.7 (1505.7)

FEBRUARY 24 A.D. 26
Sunday morning, February 24, A.D. 26, Jesus took leave of John the Baptist by the river near Pella, never again to see him in the flesh. [Jesus and 6 apostles] all remained overnight with Joseph in Jesus' boyhood home. 137:2.1 (1526.1)

FEBRUARY 25 A.D. 26
The next day Jesus sent his apostles on to Cana, since all of them were invited to the wedding of a prominent young woman of that town, while he prepared to pay a hurried visit to his mother at Capernaum, stopping at Magdala to see his brother Jude. 137:3.1 (1527.4)

FEBRUARY 26 A.D. 26
On the next day, Tuesday, they all journeyed over to Cana for the wedding of Naomi, which was to take place on the following day. 137:3.6 (1527.9)

FEBRUARY 27 A.D. 26
Near at hand stood six waterpots of stone, filled with water, holding about twenty gallons apiece. The commotion of the servants about these huge stone vessels, under the busy direction of his mother, attracted Jesus' attention, and going over, he observed that they were drawing wine out of them by the pitcherful. 137:4.11 (1530.3)

FEBRUARY 28 A.D. 26
Though many of the guests remained for the full week of wedding festivities, Jesus, with his newly chosen disciple-apostles — James, John, Andrew, Peter, Philip, and Nathaniel — departed very early the next morning for Capernaum, going away without taking leave of anyone. 137:5.1 (1531.5)

MARCH 1 A.D. 26
The next morning Jesus joined his friends at breakfast, but they were a cheerless group. He visited with them and at the end of the meal gathered them about him, saying: "It is my Father's will that we tarry hereabouts for a season. 137:5.4 (1532.2)

MARCH 2 A.D. 26
Jesus' first public appearance following his baptism was in the Capernaum synagogue on Sabbath, March 2, A.D. 26. The synagogue was crowded to overflowing. The story of the baptism in the Jordan was now augmented by the fresh news from Cana about the water and the wine. 137:6.1 (1532.3)

MARCH 3 A.D. 26
Since Jesus had gone north into Galilee, John felt led to retrace his steps southward. Accordingly, on Sunday morning, March 3, John and the remainder of his disciples began their journey south. 135:10.1 (1506.3)

JUNE 12 A.D. 26
Herod Antipas, very early in the morning of June 12, before the multitude arrived to hear the preaching and witness the baptizing, the agents of Herod placed John under arrest. 135:10.3 (1506.5)

JUNE 18 A.D. 26
Jesus did his last work at the carpenter bench on this Tuesday, June 18, A.D. 26. Jesus laid down his tools once more, removed his apron, and said to Peter: "The Father's hour has come." 137:8.3 (1535.9)

JUNE 19 A.D. 26
Jesus sent his brother James to ask for the privilege of speaking in the synagogue the coming Sabbath day. And the ruler of the synagogue was much pleased that Jesus was again willing to conduct the service. 137:8.3 (1535.9)

JUNE 20 A.D. 26
A few days before the preaching of this sermon on "The Kingdom," as Jesus was at work in the boat shop, Peter brought him the news of John's arrest. Jesus laid down his tools once more, removed his apron, and said to Peter: "The Father's hour has come." 137:8.2 (1535.8)

JUNE 22 A.D. 26
On Sabbath, June 22, shortly before they went out on their first preaching tour and about ten days after John's imprisonment, Jesus occupied the synagogue pulpit for the second time since bringing his apostles to Capernaum, preaching a sermon on "The Kingdom." 137:8.1 (1535.7)

JUNE 23 A.D. 26
The next day, Sunday, June 23, A.D. 26, Jesus imparted his final instructions to the six. He directed them to go forth, two and two, to teach the glad tidings of the kingdom. Jesus purposed to make their first tour entirely one of personal work. 138:1.1 (1538.3)

JANUARY 12 A.D. 27
Just before noon on Sunday, January 12, A.D. 27, Jesus called his disciple- apostles together and formally ordained them as ambassadors of the kingdom and preachers of its glad tidings. 138:10.11 (1547.11)

JANUARY 19 A.D. 27
ON THE first day of the week, January 19, A.D. 27, Jesus and the twelve apostles made ready to depart from their headquarters in Bethsaida. Just before leaving, the apostles missed the Master, and Andrew went out to find him. After a brief search he found Jesus sitting in a boat down the beach, and he was weeping. 141:0.1 (1587.1)

JANUARY 20 A.D. 27
The first day Jesus and the apostles only journeyed as far as Tarichea, where they rested for the night. The next day they traveled to a point on the Jordan near Pella where John had preached about one year before, and where Jesus had received baptism. 141:1.2 (1587.4)

JANUARY 21 A.D. 27
Jesus did no public preaching. Andrew divided the multitude and assigned the preachers for the forenoon and afternoon assemblies; after the evening meal Jesus talked with the twelve. He taught them nothing new but reviewed his former teaching and answered their many questions. 141:1.3 (1588.1)

JUNE 28 A.D. 27
On Tuesday, June 28, the Master and his associates left Sidon, going up the coast to Porphyreon and Heldua. They were well received by the gentiles, and many were added to the kingdom during this week of teaching and preaching. 156:3.1 (1736.6)

NOVEMBER 2 A.D. 27
Two months and a half from this time John was executed, and throughout this period the apostles of John remained with Jesus and the twelve. The Gilboa camp was broken up on November 2, A.D. 27. 144:6.13 (1626.1)

JANUARY 10 A.D. 28
John the Baptist was executed by order of Herod Antipas on the evening of January 10, A.D. 28. 144:9.1 (1627.6)

JANUARY 11 A.D. 28
The next day a few of John's disciples who had gone to Machaerus heard of his execution and, going to Herod, made request for his body, which they put in a tomb, later giving it burial at Sebaste, the home of Abner. 144:9.1 (1627.6)

JANUARY 12 A.D. 28
Jesus said: "John is dead. The hour has come to proclaim the kingdom openly and with power. Tomorrow we go into Galilee." 144:9.1 (1627.6)

JANUARY 14 AD 28
Wednesday, Thursday, and Friday [January 14,15,16] Jesus spent at the Zebedee house instructing his apostles preparatory to their first extensive public preaching tour. 145:0.2 (1628.2)

JANUARY 17 A.D. 28
That Sabbath was a great day in the earth life of Jesus, yes, in the life of a universe. In a moment of time 683 men, women, and children were made whole. Such a scene was never witnessed on earth before that day, nor since. 145:3.4 (1632.3)

JANUARY 18 A.D. 28
Jesus and the apostles started out upon their first really public and open preaching tour of the cities of Galilee. On this first tour they preached the gospel of the kingdom in many cities, but they did not visit Nazareth. 145:5.8 (1636.1)

MARCH 18 A.D. 28
THE first public preaching tour of Galilee began on Sunday, January 18, A.D. 28, and continued for about two months, ending with the return to Capernaum on March 17. 146:0.1 (1637.1)

MAY 1 A.D. 28
They [Jesus and the twelve] did not move toward home until early Sabbath morning, the first day of May. The Jerusalem spies were sure they would now secure their first charge against Jesus — that of Sabbath breaking — since he had presumed to start his journey on the Sabbath day. 147:6.3 (1654.2)

MAY 3 A.D. 28
It was around noon on Monday, May 3, when Jesus and the twelve came to Bethsaida by boat from Tarichea. They traveled by boat in order to escape those who journeyed with them. But by the next day [May 4] the others, including the official spies from Jerusalem, had again found Jesus. 147:7.1 (1655.3)

MAY 3 TO OCTOBER 3, A.D. 28, an enormous camp was maintained by the seaside near the Zebedee residence, which had been greatly enlarged to accommodate the growing family of Jesus. This tented city was under the general supervision of David Zebedee, assisted by the Alpheus twins. 148:0.1 (1657.1)

OCTOBER 1 A.D. 28
On Friday afternoon, October 1, there occurred one of the strangest and most unique episodes of all Jesus' earth life – the healing of the Paralytic. 148:9.1 (1666.5)

OCTOBER 3 A.D. 28
THE second public preaching tour of Galilee began on Sunday, October 3, A.D. 28, and continued for almost three months, ending on December 30. On this tour they visited Gadara, Ptolemais, Japhia, Dabaritta, Megiddo, Jezreel, Scythopolis, Tarichea, Hippos, Gamala, Bethsaida-Julias, and many other cities and villages. 149:0.1 (1668.1)

JANUARY 16 A.D. 29
Of all the daring things which Jesus did in connection with his earth career, the most amazing was his sudden announcement on the evening of January 16: "On the morrow we will set apart ten women for the ministering work of the kingdom." 150:1.1 (1678.5)

FEBRUARY 20 A.D. 29
After spending two or three days with one group of twelve evangelists, Jesus would move on to join another group, being informed as to the whereabouts and movements of all these workers by David's messengers. 150:6.2 (1683.4)

FEBRUARY 21 A.D. 29
For months the people of Nazareth had discussed Jesus much, but their opinions were, on the whole, unfavorable to him. 150:7.2 (1684.1)

MARCH 4 A.D. 29
This Friday afternoon Jesus walked about Nazareth quite unobserved and wholly unrecognized. He passed by the home of his childhood and the carpenter shop and spent a half hour on the hill which he so much enjoyed when a lad. 150:7.1 (1683.6)

MARCH 5 A.D. 29
Thus did the Master find himself in the midst of, not a welcome homecoming, but a decidedly hostile and hypercritical atmosphere. But this was not all. His enemies, had hired numerous rough and uncouth men to harass him and in every way possible make trouble. 150:7.3 (1684.2)

MARCH 26 A.D. 29
Jesus continued to teach the people by day while he instructed the apostles and evangelists at night. On Friday [yesterday] he declared a furlough of one week that all his followers might go home or to their friends for a few days before preparing to go up to Jerusalem for the Passover. 152:2.1 (1700.2)

MARCH 27 A.D. 29
The Master had so little rest over the Sabbath that on Sunday morning, March 27, he sought to get away from the people. 152:2.1 (1700.2)

MARCH 28 A.D. 29
Monday afternoon the multitude had increased to more than three thousand. And still—way into the evening—the people continued to flock in, bringing all manner of sick folks with them. 152:2.4 (1700.5)

MARCH 30 A.D. 29
Jesus took up the loaves in his hands, and after he had given thanks, he broke the bread and gave to his apostles, who passed it on to their associates, who in turn carried it to the multitude. Jesus in like manner broke and distributed the fishes. And this multitude did eat and were filled. 152:2.9 (1701.4)

APRIL 24 A.D. 29
On Sunday, April 24, Jesus and the apostles left Jerusalem for Bethsaida, going by way of the coast cities of Joppa, Caesarea, and Ptolemais. 152:7.3 (1706.4)

APRIL 29 A.D. 29
Jesus dispatched Andrew to ask of the ruler of the synagogue permission to speak the next day, that being the Sabbath, at the afternoon service. And Jesus well knew that that would be the last time he would ever be permitted to speak in the Capernaum synagogue. 152:7.3 (1706.4)

MAY 1–7 A.D. 29
From May 1 to May 7 Jesus held intimate counsel with his followers at the Zebedee house. Only the tried and trusted disciples were admitted to these conferences. 154:1.1 (1717.4)

MAY 7 A.D. 29
The last of the seaside meetings was held on Sabbath afternoon, May 7. Jesus talked to less than one hundred and fifty who had assembled at that time. This Saturday night marked the time of the lowest ebb in the tide of popular regard for Jesus and his teachings. 154:1.3 (1718.1)

MAY 8 A.D. 29
Sunday, May 8, A.D. 29, at Jerusalem, the Sanhedrin passed a decree closing all the synagogues of Palestine to Jesus and his followers. 154:2.1 (1718.2)

MAY 16 A.D. 29
On May 16 the second conference at Tiberias between the authorities at Jerusalem and Herod Antipas was convened. Both the religious and the political leaders from Jerusalem were in attendance. A new effort was made to have Herod place Jesus under arrest, but he refused to do their bidding. 154:3.1 (1719.2)

MAY 21 A.D. 29
On Saturday night, May 21, just before midnight of this day, Herod signed the decree which authorized the officers of the Sanhedrin to seize Jesus within Herod's domains and forcibly to carry him to Jerusalem for trial. 154:3.2 (1719.3)

MAY 22 A.D. 29
May 22 was an eventful day in the life of Jesus. On this Sunday morning, before daybreak, one of David's messengers arrived in great haste from Tiberias, bringing the word that Herod had authorized, the arrest of Jesus by the officers of the Sanhedrin. 154:5.1 (1720.4)

MAY 23 A.D. 29
On Monday morning, May 23, Jesus directed Peter to go over to Chorazin with the twelve evangelists while he, with the eleven, departed for Caesarea-Philippi, where they tarried and taught for two weeks. 155:2.1 (1726.4)

MAY 24 A.D. 29
On Monday morning, May 23, Jesus directed Peter to go over to Chorazin with the twelve evangelists while he, with the eleven, departed for Caesarea-Philippi… They arrived during the afternoon of Tuesday, May 24. 155:2.1 (1726.4)

JUNE 7 A.D. 29
When it appeared that no more people were minded to seek entrance into the kingdom, Peter, on Tuesday, June 7, called his associates together and departed for Caesarea-Philippi to join Jesus and the apostles. 155:2.3 (1726.6)

JUNE 8 A.D. 29
Peter and his associates arrived [Caesarea-Philippi] about noontime on Wednesday and spent the entire evening in rehearsing their experiences among the unbelievers of Chorazin. 155:2.3 (1726.6)

JUNE 9 A.D. 29
On Thursday morning, June 9, after receiving word regarding the progress of the kingdom brought by the messengers of David from Bethsaida, this group of twenty-five teachers of truth left Caesarea- Philippi to begin their journey to the Phoenician coast. 155:4.1 (1728.1)

JUNE 10 A.D. 29
While pausing for lunch near Luz, Jesus delivered one of the most remarkable addresses which his apostles ever listened to throughout all their years of association with him – the discourse on true religion. 155:4.2 (1728.2)

JUNE 11 A.D. 29
There lived near the home of Karuska, where the Master lodged, a Syrian woman who had heard much of Jesus as a great healer and teacher, came over, bringing her little daughter who was afflicted with a grievous nervous disorder. To Peter's entreaties she replied only: "I will not depart until I have seen your Master." 156:1.1 (1734.3)

JULY 6 A.D. 29
On Wednesday, July 6, they [Jesus and the Apostles] all returned to Sidon and tarried at the home of Justa until Sunday morning, when they departed for Tyre, going south along the coast by way of Sarepta, arriving at Tyre on Monday, July 11. 156:3.2 (1737.1)

JULY 11 A.D. 29
From July 11 to July 24 they taught in Tyre. Each of the apostles took with him one of the evangelists, and thus two and two they taught and preached in all parts of Tyre and its environs. The polyglot population of this busy seaport heard them gladly, and many were baptized into the outward fellowship of the kingdom. 156:4.1 (1737.2)

JULY 20 A.D. 29
The Master spoke in Tyre only once, on the afternoon of July 20, when he taught the believers concerning the Father's love for all mankind and the mission of the Son to reveal the Father to all races of men. Jesus first told the story of the white lily which rears its pure and snowy head high into the sunshine while its roots are grounded in the slime and muck of the darkened soil beneath. 156:4.2 (1737.3)

JULY 23 A.D. 29
The day before Jesus left Tyre for the return to the region of the Sea of Galilee, he called his associates together and directed the twelve evangelists to go back by a route different from that which he and the twelve apostles were to take. And after the evangelists left Jesus, they were never again so intimately associated with him. 156:5.23 (1740.10)

JULY 24 A.D. 29
About noon on Sunday, July 24, Jesus and the twelve left the home of Joseph, south of Tyre, going down the coast to Ptolemais. 156:6.1 (1741.1)

JULY 25 A.D. 29
Jesus and the twelve tarried for a day, speaking words of comfort to the company of believers resident there [Ptolemais]. Peter preached to them on the evening of July 25. 156:6.1 (1741.1)

JULY 26 A.D. 29
On Tuesday Jesus and his associates left Ptolemais, going east inland to near Jotapata by way of the Tiberias road. 156:6.2 (1741.2)

JULY 27 A.D. 29
Wednesday Jesus and his associates stopped at Jotapata and instructed the believers further in the things of the kingdom. 156:6.2 (1741.2)

JULY 28 A.D. 29
Thursday Jesus and his associates left Jotapata, going north on the Nazareth-Mount Lebanon trail to the village of Zebulun, by way of Ramah. 156:6.2 (1741.2)

JULY 29 A.D. 29
Jesus and his associates held meetings at Ramah on Friday and remained over the Sabbath. 156:6.2 (1741.2)

JULY 31 A.D. 29
Jesus and his associates reached Zebulun on Sunday, the 31st, holding a meeting that evening and departing the next morning. 156:6.2 (1741.2)

AUGUST 1 A.D. 29
During a brief conference with David they learned that many leaders were then gathered together on the opposite side of the lake near Kheresa, that very evening a boat took them across. 156:6.4 (1741.4)

AUGUST 2 A.D. 29
...the Master returned from the Phoenician mission and began the reorganization of his scattered, tested, and depleted forces for this last and eventful year of his mission on earth. 156:6.9 (1742.1)

AUGUST 3 A.D. 29
Jesus and his associates rested for three days and held daily conferences, which were attended by about fifty men and women resident in Capernaum and its environs. 156:6.4 (1741.4)

AUGUST 7 A.D. 29
BEFORE Jesus took the twelve for a short sojourn in the vicinity of Caesarea-Philippi, he arranged through the messengers of David to go over to Capernaum on Sunday, August 7, for the purpose of meeting his family. 157:0.1 (1743.1)

AUGUST 8 A.D. 29
On Monday, while Jesus and the twelve apostles were encamped in Magadan Park, near Bethsaida-Julias, more than one hundred believers, the evangelists, the women's corps, and others interested in the establishment of the kingdom, came over from Capernaum for a conference. 157:2.1 (1744.4)

AUGUST 9 A.D. 29
Early Tuesday morning Jesus and the twelve apostles left Magadan Park for Caesarea-Philippi, the capital of the Tetrarch Philip's domain. He [Jesus] asked this surprising question, "Who do men say that I am?" 157:3.1 (1745.2)

AUGUST 12 A.D. 29
Accordingly, on the morning of Friday, August 12, Jesus said to the twelve: "Lay in provisions and prepare yourselves for a journey to yonder mountain, where the spirit bids me go to be endowed for the finish of my work on earth." 157:7.5 (1751.4)

AUGUST 13 A.D. 29
Jesus and his associates reached the foot of Mount Hermon. And here they sojourned for two days in spiritual preparation for the events so soon to follow. 158:0.1 (1752.1)

AUGUST 15 A.D. 29
Early on the morning of Monday, August 15, Jesus and the three apostles began the ascent of Mount Hermon, and this was six days after the memorable noontide confession of Peter by the roadside under the mulberry trees. (1752.3) 158:1.1

AUGUST 16 A.D. 29
The anxious father of the afflicted lad stepped forward and, kneeling at Jesus' feet, said: "About noon yesterday, seeking for you, I caught up with your disciples, and while we were waiting, your apostles sought to cast out this demon, but they could not do it. And now, Master, will you do this for us, will you heal my son?" 158:5.1 (1757.1)

SEPTEMBER 16 A.D. 29
On Friday, September 16, the entire corps of workers assembled by prearrangement at Magadan Park. 159:6.2 (1771.3)

SEPTEMBER 17 A.D. 29
On the Sabbath day a council of more than one hundred believers was held at which the future plans for extending the work of the kingdom were fully considered. 159:6.2 (1771.3)

SEPTEMBER 18 A.D. 29
ON SUNDAY morning, September 18, Andrew announced that no work would be planned for the coming week. All of the apostles, except Nathaniel and Thomas, went home to visit their families or to sojourn with friends. 160:0.1 (1772.1)

SEPTEMBER 19 A.D. 29
Early Monday morning, Rodan began a series of ten addresses to Nathaniel, Thomas, and a group of some two dozen believers who chanced to be at Magadan. 160:1.1 (1772.2)

OCTOBER 20 A.D. 29
On the evening of the next to the last day of the feast, when the scene was brilliantly illuminated by the lights of the candelabras and the torches, Jesus stood up in the midst of the assembled throng and said: "I am the light of the world." 162:5.1 (1794.4)

OCTOBER 21 A.D. 29
On the last day, the great day of the feast, as the procession from the pool of Siloam passed through the temple courts, and just after the water and the wine had been poured down upon the altar by the priests, Jesus, standing among the pilgrims, said: "If any man thirst, let him come to me and drink." 162:6.1 (1795.5)

OCTOBER 22 A.D. 29
The day following the close of the feast, Jesus had departed for Bethany, and he did not again teach in the temple during this visit to Jerusalem. 162:9.1 (1798.2)

OCTOBER 30 A.D. 29
On Sunday, October 30, Jesus and his associates left the city of Ephraim, where he had been resting in seclusion for a few days, and, going by the west Jordan highway directly to Magadan Park, arrived late on the afternoon of Wednesday, November 2. 162:9.6 (1798.7)

NOVEMBER 4 A.D. 29
Jesus and the twelve began a course of intensive training for this special group of believers, and from this aggregation of disciples the Master subsequently chose the seventy teachers. This regular instruction began on Friday, November 4, and continued until Sabbath, November 19. 163:0.1 (1800.1)

NOVEMBER 19 A.D. 29
The seventy were ordained by Jesus on Sabbath afternoon, November 19, at the Magadan Camp, and Abner was placed at the head of these gospel preachers and teachers. 163:1.1 (1800.3)

NOVEMBER 20 A.D. 29
Early the next morning Abner sent the seventy messengers into all the cities of Galilee, Samaria, and Judea. And these thirty-five couples went forth preaching and teaching for about six weeks, all of them returning to the new camp near Pella, in Perea, on Friday, December 30. 163:1.6 (1801.3)

DECEMBER 6 A.D. 29
On Tuesday, December 6, the entire company of almost three hundred started out at daybreak with all their effects to lodge that night near Pella by the river at the same site John the Baptist occupied years before. 163:5.1 (1806.2)

DECEMBER 7 A.D. 29
After the breaking up of the Magadan Camp, David Zebedee returned to Bethsaida and began immediately to curtail the messenger service. 163:5.2 (1806.3)

DECEMBER 18 A.D. 29
Accordingly, on Sunday, December 18, David, with the help of his messenger corps, loaded on to the pack animals the camp equipage, then stored in his father's house, with which he had formerly conducted the camp of Bethsaida by the lake. Bidding farewell to Bethsaida for the time being, 163:5.2 (1806.3)

DECEMBER 19 A.D. 29
David Zebedee proceeded down the lake shore and along the Jordan to a point about one-half mile north of the apostolic camp; and in less than a week he was prepared to offer hospitality to almost fifteen hundred pilgrim visitors. 163:5.2 (1806.3)

DECEMBER 27 A.D. 29
The next day being the Sabbath, Jesus went apart with the seventy and said to them: "I did indeed rejoice with you when you came back bearing the good tidings of the reception of the gospel of the kingdom by so many people scattered throughout Galilee, Samaria, and Judea. 163:6.6 (1807.5)

DECEMBER 30 A.D. 29
On Friday, December 30, At last Jesus was able to see men going out to spread the good news without his personal presence. The Master now knew that he could leave this world without seriously hindering the progress of the kingdom. 163:6.1 (1806.5)

JANUARY 28 A.D. 30
By the end of January the Sabbath-afternoon multitudes numbered almost three thousand. On Saturday, January 28, Jesus preached the memorable sermon on "Trust and Spiritual Preparedness." 165:3.1 (1819.9)

JANUARY 29 A.D. 30
And this was the end of a full and busy Sabbath day. On the morrow [today] Jesus and the twelve went into the cities of northern Perea to visit with the seventy, who were working in these regions under Abner's supervision. 165:6.4 (1824.7)

FEBRUARY 18 A.D. 30
On Sabbath, February 18, Jesus was at Ragaba, where there lived a wealthy Pharisee named Nathaniel; and since quite a number of his fellow Pharisees were following Jesus and the twelve around the country, he made a breakfast for all of them, about twenty in number, and invited Jesus as the guest of honor. 166:1.1 (1825.3)

FEBRUARY 19 A.D. 30
The next day Jesus went with the twelve over to Amathus, near the border of Samaria, and as they approached the city, they encountered a group of ten lepers who sojourned near this place. Nine of this group were Jews, one a Samaritan. 166:2.1 (1827.6)

FEBRUARY 22 A.D. 30
Jesus and the ten apostles arrived at Philadelphia on Wednesday, February 22, and spent Thursday and Friday resting from their recent travels and labors. That Friday night James spoke in the synagogue, and a general council was called for the following evening. 167:0.3 (1833.3)

MARCH 6 A.D. 30
LATE on Monday evening, Jesus and the ten apostles arrived at the Pella camp. This was the last week of Jesus' sojourn there, and he was very active in teaching the multitude and instructing the apostles. 169:0.1 (1850.1)

MARCH 9 A.D. 30
On Thursday afternoon Jesus talked to the multitude about the "Grace of Salvation." In the course of this sermon he retold the story of the lost sheep and the lost coin and then added his favorite parable of the prodigal son. 169:1.1 (1850.8)

MARCH 11 A.D. 30
SATURDAY afternoon, March 11, Jesus preached his last sermon at Pella. This was among the notable addresses of his public ministry, embracing a full and complete discussion of the kingdom of heaven. 170:0.1 (1858.1)

MARCH 12 A.D. 30
THE day after the memorable sermon on "The Kingdom of Heaven," Jesus announced that on the following day he and the apostles would depart for the Passover at Jerusalem, visiting numerous cities in southern Perea on the way. 171:0.1 (1867.1)

MARCH 13 A.D. 30
On the forenoon of Monday, March 13, Jesus and his twelve apostles took final leave of the Pella encampment, starting south on their tour of the cities of southern Perea, where Abner's associates were at work. 171:1.1 (1868.3)

MARCH 15 A.D. 30
Acting on the instructions of the Apostle Andrew, David Zebedee closed the visitors' camp at Pella on Wednesday, March 15. At this time almost four thousand visitors were in residence. 171:1.4 (1868.6)

APRIL 4 A.D. 30
It was just before midnight on this Tuesday, April 4, A.D. 30, that the Sanhedrin, as then constituted, officially and unanimously voted to impose the death sentence upon both Jesus and Lazarus. 175:3.1 (1909.4)

APRIL 5 A.D. 30
The Master spent this last day of quiet on earth visiting with this truth- hungry youth and talking with his Paradise Father. This event has become known as "the day which a young man spent with God in the hills." 177:1.3 (1921.1)

APRIL 6 A.D. 30
Jesus said: "Take this cup and divide it among yourselves and, when you partake of it, realize that I shall not again drink with you the fruit of the vine since this is our last supper." 179:2.2 (1938.1)

APRIL 9 A.D. 30
Sunday morning, at two minutes past three o'clock, this Sunday morning, April 9, A.D. 30, the resurrected morontia form and personality of Jesus of Nazareth came forth from the tomb. 189:1.1 (2020.4)

APRIL 10 A.D. 30
The next day, Monday, was spent wholly with the morontia creatures then present on Urantia. About midnight of this Monday the Master's morontia form was adjusted for transition to the second stage of morontia progression. 191:3.1 (2040.4)

APRIL 11 A.D. 30
The tenth morontia manifestation of Jesus occurred a short time after eight o'clock at Philadelphia, where he showed himself to Abner and Lazarus and some one hundred and fifty of their associates, including more than fifty of the evangelistic corps of the seventy. 191:4.1 (2041.4)

APRIL 12 A.D. 30
Early the next morning, even while the apostles tarried in Jerusalem awaiting the emotional recovery of Thomas, these believers at Philadelphia went forth proclaiming that Jesus of Nazareth had risen from the dead. 191:4.6 (2042.3)

APRIL 13 A.D. 30
The next day, Wednesday, Jesus spent without interruption in the society of his morontia associates, and during the midafternoon hours he received visiting morontia delegates from the mansion worlds of every local system of inhabited spheres throughout the constellation of Norlatiadek. 191:4.7 (2042.4)

APRIL 14 A.D. 30
Jesus made the transit to the third stage of morontia on Friday, April 14 A.D. 30; 191:3.3 (2041.2)

APRIL 15 A.D. 30
Thomas spent a lonesome week alone with himself in the hills around about Olivet. It was about nine o'clock on Saturday, April 15, when the two apostles found him and took him back with them to their rendezvous at the Mark home. 191:5.1 (2042.5)

APRIL 16 A.D. 30
Thomas said: "I will not believe unless I see the Master with my own eyes and put my finger in the mark of the nails." As they thus sat at supper, the morontia Master suddenly appeared inside the curvature of the table and, standing directly in front of Thomas. . . 191:5.2 (2042.6)

APRIL 18 A.D. 30
While the eleven apostles were on the way to Galilee, drawing near their journey's end, on Tuesday evening, at about half past eight o'clock, Jesus appeared to Rodan and some 80 other believers, in Alexandria. This was the Master's 12th appearance in morontia form. (2044.2) 191:6.1

APRIL 20 A.D. 30
The apostles arrived at Bethsaida very late on Wednesday night. It was noontime on [this] Thursday before they were all awake and ready to partake of breakfast. 192:0.5 (2045.5)

APRIL 21 A.D. 30
About six o'clock Friday morning, April 21, the morontia Master made his thirteenth appearance, the first in Galilee, to the ten apostles as their boat drew near the shore close to the usual landing place at Bethsaida. 192:1.1 (2045.6)

APRIL 22 A.D. 30
At noon on Saturday, April 22, the eleven apostles assembled by appointment on the hill near Capernaum, and Jesus appeared among them. This was the Master's fourteenth morontia manifestation. 192:3.1 (2050.1)

APRIL 27 A.D. 30
Jesus made the transit to the third stage of morontia on Friday, April 14; to the fourth stage on Monday, the 17th; to the fifth stage on Saturday, the 22nd; to the sixth stage on Thursday, the 27th; . . . 191:3.3 (2041.2)

MAY 2 A.D. 30
Jesus made the transit to the third stage of morontia on April 14; to the fourth stage on the 17th; to the fifth stage on the 22nd; to the sixth stage on the 27th; to the seventh stage on Tuesday, May 2. 191:3.3 (2041.2)

MAY 3 A.D. 30
Sunday, April 30, the [11 Apostles] left Bethsaida for Jerusalem. They did considerable teaching and preaching on the way down the Jordan, arriving at the home of the Marks in Jerusalem until late on May 3. 192:4.4 (2051.1)

MAY 5 A.D. 30
THE sixteenth morontia manifestation of Jesus occurred on Friday, May 5, in the courtyard of Nicodemus, about nine o'clock at night. On this evening the Jerusalem believers had made their first attempt to get together since the resurrection. 193:0.1 (2052.1)

MAY 13 A.D. 30
About four o'clock on Sabbath afternoon, May 13, the Master appeared to Nalda and about 75 Samaritan believers near Jacob's well, at Sychar. The believers were in the habit of meeting at this place, near where Jesus had spoken to Nalda concerning the water of life. 193:1.1 (2053.3)

MAY 14 A.D. 30
Jesus entered the embrace of the Most Highs of Edentia on Sunday, the 14th. 191:3.3 (2041.2)

MAY 16 A.D. 30
The Master's 18th morontia appearance was at Tyre, on Tuesday, May 16, at a little before nine o'clock in the evening. 193:2.1 (2054.2)

MAY 17 A.D. 30
ABOUT one o'clock, as the one hundred and twenty believers were engaged in prayer, they all became aware of a strange presence in the room. Peter stood up and declared that this must be the coming of the Spirit of Truth which the Master had promised them and proposed that they go to the temple and begin the proclamation of the good news committed to their hands. 194:0.1 (2059.1)

MAY 18 A.D. 30
It was almost half past seven o'clock when Jesus arrived on the western slope of Mount Olivet with his eleven silent and somewhat bewildered apostles. Jesus now prepared to say his last farewell to the apostles before he took leave of Urantia. 193:5.1 (2057.3)

It was about seven forty-five this morning when the morontia Jesus disappeared from the observation of his eleven apostles to begin the ascent to the right hand of his Father, there to receive formal confirmation of his completed sovereignty of the universe of Nebadon. 193:5.5 (2057.7)

It is at the enthronement of the Creator Son as a Master Son, at the jubilee of jubilees, that the Universe Spirit, before the assembled hosts, first makes public and universal acknowledgment of subordination to the Son, pledging fidelity and obedience. This event occurred in Nebadon at the time of Michael's return to Salvington after the Urantian bestowal. 33.3.5 (368.5)

NOVEMBER 21 A.D. 74

Abner lived to be 89 years old, dying at Philadelphia on the 21st day of November, A.D. 74. And to the very end he was a faithful believer in, and teacher of, the gospel of the heavenly kingdom. 166:5.7 (1832.3)

OTHER IMPORTANT DATES:

Paper 1 of *The Urantia Book, The Universal Father* was received March 1–15, 1925

The first 56 papers of *The Urantia Book* were indited and put in English language in the year A.D. 1934

Papers 57 to 119 were indited and put in English language in the year A.D. 1935

The last meeting of the Forum was held on May 31st, 1942.

Dr. Sadler officially disbanded the Forum: June 7, 1942.

Urantia Foundation was created on January 11, 1950.

The Urantia Book first published October 12, 1955.

Table of Contents of Part IV of *The Urantia Book*

The Structure of Part IV of *The Urantia Book*

Paper Number and Title	Pages	Year
Paper 119—The Bestowals of Christ Michael	1308–1319	NA
A review of the six previous incarnations and post-bestowal status of Christ Michael. These papers were authorized by a Nebadon commission of twelve under the direction of Mantutia Melchizedek, who indited these papers in the English language, by a technique authorized by their superiors, in the year A.D. 1935. Author: Gavalia, Chief of the Evening Stars of Nebadon.		
Paper 120—The Bestowal of Michael on Urantia	1323–1331	NA
Prebestowal charge of Immanuel to Michael who subsequently became Jesus of Nazareth on Urantia. The one Paper in Part IV not written by a midwayer. Author: the Melchizedek director of the revelatory commission		
Paper 121—The Times of Michael's Bestowal	1332–1343	NA
The narrative of the life transactions of Jesus of Nazareth as they were observed by the secondary midwayer of onetime attachment to the Apostle Andrew and subsequently partially recorded by the apostle Andrew. Description of people and culture at the time of Jesus's birth. Origin of four gospels.		
Paper 122—Birth and Infancy of Jesus	1344–1354	8 B.C.–5 B.C.
Choosing of Joseph and Mary and their heritage. Birth and infancy of Jesus.		
Paper 123—The Early Childhood of Jesus	1355–1365	4 B.C.–A.D. 2
The early years of Jesus' helpless infancy and childhood spans from 1 to 8 years of age, including his life in Alexandria and the trip back home to Nazareth. Section 5 is about school days in Nazareth.		
Paper 124—The Later Childhood of Jesus	1366–1376	A.D. 3–A.D. 7
During this period, Jesus suffered some of the minor ailments of childhood. He dared to challenge the chazan at school regarding the teaching that all images, pictures, and drawings were idolatrous in nature. Martha, Jesus' second sister, was born. Jesus saw ice for the first time. It was the fifth of July, A.D. 4, when Jesus first gave expression to feelings and ideas which indicated that he was becoming self-conscious of the unusual nature of his life mission. Jesus was startled by his father's display of emotion when Jesus suggested the building of an amphitheater at Nazareth. Jesus' first trip to Jerusalem for Passover. This was one of the most extraordinary days in the life of Jesus when there appeared to him a messenger from Salvington, commissioned by Immanuel, who said: "The hour has come. It is time that you began to be about your Father's business."		
Paper 125—Jesus at Jerusalem	1377–1385	A.D. 7
No incident in all Jesus' eventful earth career was more engaging, more humanly thrilling, than this, his first remembered visit to Jerusalem. The profanation of the temple fully aroused all his youthful indignation, and he did not hesitate to express himself freely to Joseph. Joseph and Mary departed Jerusalem not knowing that Jesus was left behind to spend four days in the temple where he deftly sparred with the expounders of the law		

Paper Number and Title	Pages	Year
Paper 126—The Two Crucial Years	1386–1394	A.D. 8–A.D. 9
Two crucial years—ages 14 and 15 years. The death of Joseph. Jesus takes firm grasp of managing his family. He gave his first sermon in the synagogue. Jesus adopts as his inaugural title "the Son of Man." The beginning of financial hardships.		
Paper 127—The Adolescent Years	1395–1406	A.D. 10–A.D. 14
Jesus attained his full physical growth. He decided that after rearing his family he would enter publicly upon his work as a teacher of truth and as a revealer of the heavenly Father. The Zealots came to see Jesus. All the family property, except the home and garden, was disposed of. Jesus takes James to the Passover. Little Amos, their baby brother, died. John [the future John the Baptist] visited Jesus at his home in Nazareth. The love of Rebecca.		
Paper 128—Jesus' Early Manhood	1407–1418	A.D. 15–A.D. 20
Early manhood—21st through 26th year. Jesus began the task of completing the experience of mastering the knowledge of the life of Urantia mortals, thereby finally and fully earning the right of unqualified rulership of his self-created universe. He entered upon this stupendous task fully realizing his dual nature. But he had already effectively combined these two natures into one—Jesus of Nazareth. 23rd year: The Damascus episode: one of the greatest temptations that Jesus ever faced in the course of his purely human career. 24th year: Jesus' first year of comparative freedom from family responsibility. 25th year: Jesus took Jude to Passover. Jude was taken to the military prison. 26th year: Jesus became strongly conscious that he possessed a wide range of potential power. A double wedding.		
Paper 129—The Later Adult Life of Jesus	1419–1426	A.D. 21–A.D. 23
Personal ministry and last of private life. Jesus separated himself from the management of the Nazareth family. Jesus took unceremonious leave of his family going over to Tiberias and then on to visit other cities about the Sea of Galilee. Jesus worked with John Zebedee only a little more than one year, but during that time he created a new style of boat and established entirely new methods of boatbuilding. A.D. 22: In March, Jesus took leave of Capernaum. Salome, Zebedee's wife, introduced him to the former high priest, Annas. A.D. 23: The whole of Jesus' twenty-ninth year was spent finishing up the tour of the Mediterranean world. When this paper ends Jesus is not only a Son of Man.		
Paper 130—On the Way to Rome	1427–1441	A.D. 23
Jesus travels to Caesarea, Alexandria, Crete, Carthage, Naples, and Rome. All new material, previously unknown on Urantia. *Discourse on Jonah, Discourse on Reality, The Young Man Who Was Afraid,* and *Discourse on Time and Space.* Jesus bought fruit and changed the life of a small boy, a fruit vendor, whom he fed the bread of life.		

Paper Number and Title	Pages	Year
Paper 131—The World's Religions	1442–1454	A.D. 23
Jesus and Ganid study religious writings at Alexandria. They studied Cynicism, Judaism, Buddhism, Hinduism, Zoroastrianism, Suduanism (Jainism), Shinto, Taoism, Confucianism. Ganid produces a summary of "Our Religion."		
Paper 132—The Sojourn at Rome	1455–1467	A.D. 23
Jesus gained intimate knowledge of all races and classes of men who lived the largest and most cosmopolitan city of the world. He had an all-night talk with Angamon, the leader of the Stoics, about true values. Jesus conversed with Mardus, leader of the Cynics, about good and evil. He discussed truth and faith with Nabon the leader of the Mithraic cult. A rich man asked Jesus' what he would do with wealth if he had it. He spent several hours restoring a lost child to his anxious mother. Jesus, Gonod, and Ganid made five trips away from Rome including northern Italy, and Switzerland. "*When man goes in partnership with God, great things may, and do, happen.*"		
Paper 133—The Return from Rome	1468–1482	A.D. 23
Discussion on mercy and justice. A man mistreating his wife. Two public women. Personal work in Corinth. Discourses on science. Discourse on the soul at Ephesus. Discourse on mind. A visit to wicked Antioch. Thus ended that chapter in the life of the Son of Man which might be termed: *The mission of Joshua the teacher.*		
Paper 134—The Transition Years	1483–1495	A.D. 24—A.D. 25
After taking leave of Gonod and Ganid at Charax (in December of A.D. 23), Jesus returned by way of Ur to Babylon, where he joined a desert caravan on its way to Damascus. On his return, Jesus gave twenty-four lectures: The Urmia lectures. This is the year of Jesus' solitary wanderings through Palestine and Syria. After spending some time in the vicinity of Caesarea-Philippi, Jesus proceeded along the Damascus road to a village sometime known as Beit Jenn in the foothills of Mount Hermon. For long years this transformation of mind and spirit had been in progress, and it was finished during the eventful [40 days] sojourn on Mount Hermon. Rumors came to Capernaum of one John who was preaching while baptizing penitents in the Jordan, and John preached: "The kingdom of heaven is at hand; repent and be baptized."		
Paper 135—John the Baptist	1496–1508	A.D. 25—A.D. 26
The life of John the Baptist. March A.D. 25 John begins to preach: "The kingdom of heaven is at hand; repent and be baptized." Jesus is baptized by John. The death of John the Baptist.		
Paper 136—Baptism and the Forty Days	1509–1523	A.D. 26
Just before noon, Jesus laid down his tools, removed his work apron, and announced to the three workmen in the room with him, "My hour has come." He went out to his brothers James and Jude, repeating, "My hour has come—let us go to John." January 14th, Jesus was baptized by John and began a forty day retreat in the hills producing six decisions about his mission.		

The Structure of Part IV of *The Urantia Book*

<table>
<tr><th>Paper Number and Title</th><th>Pages</th><th>Year</th></tr>
<tr><td>Paper 137—Tarrying Time in Galilee</td><td>1524–1537</td><td>A.D. 26</td></tr>
<tr><td colspan="3">First six apostles chosen. Cana wedding; changing water to wine. March 2, A.D. 26, Jesus first sermon after baptism. June 22nd, Jesus gave sermon on the Kingdom, the first pretentious effort of his public career.</td></tr>
<tr><td>Paper 138—Training the Kingdom's Messengers</td><td>1538–1547</td><td>A.D. 26–A.D. 27</td></tr>
<tr><td colspan="3">Jesus calls the six apostles together to disclose his plans for visiting the cities around and about the Sea of Galilee. Choosing the last six apostles. Training, testing, and organization of the twelve apostles. Another disappointment. The first work of the twelve.</td></tr>
<tr><td>Paper 139—The Twelve Apostles</td><td>1548–1567</td><td>A.D. 27</td></tr>
<tr><td colspan="3">Detailed introduction of the twelve apostles.</td></tr>
<tr><td>Paper 140—The Ordination of the Twelve</td><td>1568–1586</td><td>A.D. 27</td></tr>
<tr><td colspan="3">Picks up story where PAPER 138 left off. Sunday, January 12, A.D. 27, Jesus called the apostles together for their ordination as public preachers of the gospel of the kingdom. Presentation and elaboration of the Ordination Sermon, also known as the "Sermon on the Mount."</td></tr>
<tr><td>Paper 141—Beginning the Public Work</td><td>1587–1595</td><td>A.D. 27</td></tr>
<tr><td colspan="3">Andrew found Jesus weeping. This entire year was spent taking over John's work in Perea and Judea. Jesus gives the apostles instructions on God's Law and the Father's Will. At Amathus, Jesus spent much time instructing the apostles in the new concept that God is a Father, not a great and supreme bookkeeper who is chiefly engaged in making damaging entries against his erring children on earth. Jesus began to teach the twelve more fully concerning their mission "to comfort the afflicted and minister to the sick." The Master taught them much about the whole man—the union of body, mind, and spirit to form the individual man or woman. Simon Zelotes brought to Jesus one Teherma, a Persian doing business at Damascus. Jesus, his apostles, and a large group of followers journeyed down the Jordan to the ford near Bethany in Perea. On Sunday, April 6, Jesus and the apostles went to Jerusalem; the first time the Master and all of the twelve had been there together.</td></tr>
<tr><td>Paper 142—The Passover at Jerusalem</td><td>1596–1605</td><td>A.D. 27</td></tr>
<tr><td colspan="3">April A.D. 27: Teaching in the Temple. God's Wrath. The concepts of God. Ten commandments of Israelites. Six phases of growth of God idea. Discourse on Assurance. Jesus meets Flavius and Nicodemus. The lesson on true family founded on seven facts.</td></tr>
<tr><td>Paper 143—Going Through Samaria</td><td>1607–1616</td><td>A.D. 27</td></tr>
<tr><td colspan="3">Covers two months of time. "But who told you that my gospel was intended only for slaves and weaklings? Lessons on Self-Mastery, Diversion and Relaxation, and Prayer and Worship. Nalda at Jacob's well.</td></tr>
</table>

Paper Number and Title	Pages	Year
Paper 144—At Gilboa and in the Decapolis	1617–1627	A.D. 27–A.D. 28
Covers a little over 4 months. Entire month of September devoted to theme of Prayer and Worship. Apostles of Jesus and John worked out a method of working without friction. During these September weeks they rested, visited, recounted their experiences since Jesus first called them to service, and engaged in an earnest effort to co-ordinate what the Master had so far taught them. Discourse on Prayer with the Believer's Prayer and prayers from other inhabited worlds. Jesus paused to say to John's friends: "Go back and tell John that he is not forgotten. Tell him what you have seen and heard, that the poor have good tidings preached to them." Death of John the Baptist.		
Paper 145—Four Eventful Days at Capernaum	1628–1636	A.D. 28
Start of aggressive work. The Draft of Fishes. Jesus preached his sermon on "The Will of the Father in Heaven." Healing at sundown. Departure for first preaching tour.		
Paper 146—First Preaching Tour of Galilee	1637–1646	A.D. 28
Two months visiting and teaching. January 18 to March 17, A.D. 28. Nain and the widow's son. Discussion at Ramah with Greek teacher. Preaching at Rimmon, Jotapata, Ramah, Iron, Cana.		
Paper 147—The Interlude Visit to Jerusalem	1647–1656	A.D. 28
Healing the Centurion's servant. John and Jesus at the pool of Bethesda. The Rule of Living. Visiting Simon the Pharisee. The Feast of Spiritual Goodness.		
Paper 148—Training Evangelists at Bethsaida	1657–1667	A.D. 28
A new school of the Prophets. The Bethsaida Hospital. Evil, Sin, and Iniquity. The purpose of Affliction. Discourse on Job. The man with the withered hand. Healing the Paralytic.		
Paper 149—The Second Preaching Tour	1668–1677	A.D. 28
The widespread fame of Jesus. Religious leaders at Jerusalem became increasingly alarmed and antagonistic. A question about anger and the desirability of possessing well-balanced characters. Lesson regarding contentment. The "Fear of the Lord."		
Paper 150—The Third Preaching Tour	1678–1687	A.D. 29
Formation of the Women's Evangelistic Corps. Sending the Apostles out Two and Two. What Must I Do to be Saved. The Nazareth Rejection. Enemies almost threw Jesus off cliff.		
Paper 151—Tarrying and Teaching by the Seaside	1688–1697	A.D. 29
Parable of the Sower. Discussion of Parables. Parables by the Sea. "The kingdom of heaven is like a grain of mustard seed which a man sowed in his field. The Kheresa Lunatic.		

Paper Number and Title	Pages	Year
Paper 152—Events Leading up to the Capernaum Crisis	1698–1706	A.D. 29
At Jairus's house. "Your daughter is not dead; she is only asleep." Feeding the five thousand. The king-making episode. Simon Peter's night vision. During this sojourn at Jerusalem the twelve learned how bitter the feeling was becoming toward their Master.		
Paper 153—Crisis at Capernaum	1707–1716	A.D. 29
The Master comprehended that he faced the immediate declaration of open warfare by his increasing enemies, and he elected boldly to assume the offensive. At the feeding of the five thousand he had challenged their ideas of the material Messiah; now he chose again openly to attack their concept of the Jewish deliverer. The epochal sermon: "I am this bread of life." "You know who I am; come out of him; and I charge one of your loyal fellows to see that you do not return." And this is the first case where Jesus really cast an "evil spirit" out of a human being. "How can Satan cast out Satan?" Crisis of apostles' life began here and ended with crucifixion.		
Paper 154—Last Days at Capernaum	1717–1724	A.D. 29
All synagogues refused to allow Jesus to preach. His family arrives to take Jesus home. "I have no mother; I have no brothers. Behold my mother and behold my brethren! For whosoever does the will of my Father who is in heaven, the same is my mother, my brother, and my sister." Hasty flight May 22, A.D. 29.		
Paper 155—Fleeing Through Northern Galilee	1725–1733	A.D. 29
Two discourses on "True Religion." 'Why do the heathen rage? Never forget there is only one adventure which is more satisfying and thrilling than the attempt to discover the will of the living God, and that is the supreme experience of honestly trying to do that divine will.		
Paper 156 The Sojourn at Tyre and Sidon	1734–1742	A.D. 29
Norana replied: "Yes, teacher, I understand your words. I am only a dog in the eyes of the Jews, but as concerns your Master, I am a believing dog." Teaching in Tyre and Sidon. Nathaniel asked Jesus: "Master, why do we pray that God will lead us not into temptation when we well know from your revelation of the Father that he never does such things?"		
Paper 157—At Caesarea-Philippi	1743–1751	A.D. 29
The true record of Peter's catching a fish with a shekel in its mouth. Said Jesus, "How is it that you so well know how to discern the face of the heavens but are so utterly unable to discern the signs of the times?" After his return from Phoenicia, Jesus for the first time declared himself the Son of God. "Who do men say that I am?" "But who say you that I am?" There was a moment of tense silence. The twelve never took their eyes off the Master, and then Simon Peter, springing to his feet, exclaimed: "You are the Deliverer, the Son of the living God." And now Jesus would take his apostles along with him to Mount Hermon, where he had appointed to inaugurate his fourth phase of earth ministry as the Son of God.		

Paper Number and Title	Pages	Year
Paper 158—The Mount of Transfiguration	1752–1761	A.D. 29
Peter asked the Master, "How long do we remain on this mountain away from our brethren?" And Jesus answered: "Until you shall see the glory of the Son of Man and know that whatsoever I have declared to you is true." Peter erroneously conjectured that the beings with Jesus were Moses and Elijah; in reality, they were Gabriel and the Father Melchizedek. The Apostles had so recently reaffirmed their faith in Jesus as the Deliverer, the Son of God, and they had just beheld him transfigured in glory before their very eyes, and now he began to talk about "rising from the dead"!		
Paper 159—The Decapolis Tour	1762–1771	A.D. 29
Four weeks tour. Sermon on forgiveness. The Strange Preacher. Instructions for Teachers and Believers. Talk with Nathaniel about scriptures. The positive nature of Jesus' religion.		
Paper 160—Rodan of Alexandria	1772–1782	A.D. 29
A series of ten addresses by the Greek philosopher Rodan to Nathaniel, Thomas and a group of some two dozen believers. The Art of Living. The Lure of Maturity		
Paper 161—Further Discussions with Rodan	1783–1787	A.D. 29
Further discussion with Rodan. Personality of God. Divine nature of Jesus. Jesus' human and divine minds.		
Paper 162—At the Feast of Tabernacles	1788–1799	A.D. 29
Woman taken in adultery. Feast of the Tabernacles. Sermon on the Light of the World. Water of Life. Spiritual Freedom. Abner and his eleven fellows cast their lot with Jesus and the twelve and labored with them as one organization right on down to the crucifixion.		
Paper 163—Ordination of the Seventy at Magadan	1800–1808	A.D. 29
Over fifty disciples who sought ordination and appointment to membership in the seventy were rejected by the committee appointed by Jesus to select these candidates. No man can serve two masters. And I declare that it is as easy for this camel to go through the needle's eye as for these self- satisfied rich ones to enter the kingdom of heaven." The seventy were ordained by Jesus on Sabbath afternoon, November 19, at the Magadan Camp, and Abner was placed at the head of these gospel preachers and teachers. Farewell to Seventy.		
Paper 164—At the Feast of Dedication	1809–1816	A.D. 29
"Teacher, I would like to ask you just what I should do to inherit eternal life?" Story of the Good Samaritan. "Who is my neighbor?" Jesus went to the feast of the dedication to give the Sanhedrin and the Jewish leaders another chance to see the light. The principal event of these few days in Jerusalem occurred on Friday night at the home of Nicodemus. Healing the blind Josiah as an open challenge to the Sanhedrin. Solomon's Porch:		

Paper Number and Title	Pages	Year
Paper 165—The Perean Mission Begins	1817–1824	A.D. 30
Perean Mission. Sermon on the Good Shepard. memorable sermon on "Trust and Spiritual Preparedness." "My son, what shall it profit you if you gain the whole world and lose your own soul?" Discussion about wealth.		
Paper 166—Last Visit to Northern Perea	1825–1832	A.D. 30
Northern Perea. The Master took his seat at the left of Nathaniel without going to the water basins to wash his hands. Healing the ten lepers. "Lord, will there be few or many really saved?" Born again—born of the spirit. Accidents: the angels and other spirit beings are able to prevent accidents." What happened at Philadelphia. Why nothing is heard of Abner and his work in the Gospel records of the New Testament.		
Paper 167—The Visit to Philadelphia	1833–1841	A.D. 30
Visiting the Pharisees at Philadelphia. "Lord, he whom you love is very sick." Jesus refused to be drawn into a controversy with the Pharisees concerning divorce, he did proclaim a positive teaching of the highest ideals regarding marriage. He exalted marriage as the most ideal and highest of all human relationships. "Suffer little children to come to me; forbid them not, for of such is the kingdom of heaven." Talk about Angels.		
Paper 168—The Resurrection of Lazarus	1842–1849	A.D. 30
"I am the resurrection and the life; he who believes in me, though he dies, yet shall he live. In truth, whosoever lives and believes in me shall never really die. Jesus regretted having to summon his friend back to experience the bitter persecution which he well knew Lazarus would have to endure as a result of being the subject of the greatest of all demonstrations of the divine power of the Son of Man. Jesus' answers to many questions about prayer.		
Paper 169—Last Teaching at Pella	1850–1857	A.D. 30
The Pharisees and the chief priests had begun to formulate their charges and to crystallize their accusations. Parable of the lost son. Parable of the Shrewd Steward. Parable of the rich man and the beggar. Jesus never called the Father a king, and he very much regretted that the Jewish hope for a restored kingdom and John's proclamation of a coming kingdom made it necessary for him to denominate his proposed spiritual brotherhood the kingdom of heaven.		
Paper 170—The Kingdom of Heaven	1858–1866	A.D. 30
Summary of Jesus's teaching on the Kingdom. Later ideas and concepts of the kingdom and a prophetic forecast of the kingdom as it may evolve in the age to come.		
Paper 171—On the way to Jerusalem	1867–1877	A.D. 30
Counting the Cost. For more than two weeks Jesus and the twelve journeyed about in Perea, visiting all of the towns wherein the seventy labored. Jesus once more plainly the Apostles that he will be put to death but declared that on the third day he shall rise. Blind man of Jericho. As Jesus Passed By. Parable of the Pounds.		

Paper Number and Title	Pages	Year
Paper 172—Going into Jerusalem	1878–1887	A.D. 30
Mary the sister of Lazarus proceeded to open a large alabaster cruse of very rare and costly ointment; and after anointing the Master's head, she began to pour it upon his feet as she took down her hair and wiped them with it. Jesus would not enter Jerusalem as a man on horseback, but he was willing to enter peacefully and with good will as the Son of Man on a donkey. Palm Sunday. The Apostles' Attitude.		
Paper 173—Monday in Jerusalem	1888–1896	A.D. 30
The one absorbing thought of Judas was: What shall I do? Shall I go on with Jesus and my associates, or shall I withdraw? And if I am going to quit, how shall I break off? Jesus drove the animals from the temple. He strode majestically before the thousands assembled in the temple court to the farthest cattle pen and proceeded to open the gates of every stall and to drive out the imprisoned animals. The assembled pilgrims were electrified, and with uproarious shouting they began to overturn the tables of the money-changers. When his authority to teach was questioned, Jesus asked: "I would also like to ask you one question which, if you will answer me, I likewise will tell you by what authority I do these works. The baptism of John, whence was it? Did John get his authority from heaven or from men?" Parable of the Two sons; the Absent Landlord; the Marriage Feast;		
Paper 174—Tuesday Morning in the Temple	1897–1904	A.D. 30
This morning he greeted each of the twelve with a personal salutation. James and Simon Peter take their debate about forgiveness to Jesus. Jewish rulers harassment and questioning of Jesus. "Master, I am a lawyer, and I would like to ask you which, in your opinion, is the greatest commandment?" Philip was accosted by a delegation of strangers, a group of believing Greeks from Alexandria, Athens, and Rome,		
Paper 175—The Last Temple Discourse	1905–1911	A.D. 30
Jesus, accompanied by eleven apostles, Joseph of Arimathea, the thirty Greeks, and certain other disciples, arrived at the temple and began the delivery of his last address in the courts of the sacred edifice. This discourse was intended to be his last appeal to the Jewish people and the final indictment of his vehement enemies and would-be destroyers—the scribes, Pharisees, Sadducees, and the chief rulers of Israel.		
Paper 176—Tuesday Evening on Mount Olivet	1912–1919	A.D. 30
Jesus makes remarks depicting the destruction of the sacred temple. Nathaniel asked: "Tell us, Master, how shall we know when these events are about to come to pass?" Jesus had made statements which led his hearers to infer that, while he intended presently to leave this world, he would most certainly return to consummate the work of the heavenly kingdom.		
Paper 177—Wednesday, the Rest Day	1920–1928	A.D. 30
The day which a young man spent with God in the hills. Judas decides to abandon Jesus and his fellow apostles. He was presented to Caiaphas and the Jewish rulers by his cousin. This Wednesday evening was the low-tide mark of the Apostles spiritual status up to the actual hour of the Master's death.		

Paper Number and Title	Pages	Year
Paper 178—Last Day at the Camp	1929–1935	A.D. 30
Discourse on Sonship and Citizenship. Arrangements for Last Supper.		
Paper 179—The Last Supper	1936–1943	A.D. 30
The Last Supper. Desire for Preference. Washing the Apostles feet. "Do you really understand what I have done to you? Now has my hour come, but it was not required that one of you should betray me into the hands of my enemies." Establishing the Remembrance Supper.		
Paper 180—The Farewell Discourse	1944–1952	A.D. 30
A new commandment: That you "love one another even as I have loved you." The enmity of the world. The new helper which Jesus promised to send into the hearts of believers, to pour out upon all flesh, is the *Spirit of Truth.* Necessity for Leaving.		
Paper 181—Final Admonitions and Warnings	1953–1962	A.D. 30
After the conclusion of the farewell discourse, Jesus visited informally with the Apostles and recounted many experiences with them as a group and as individuals. At last it was beginning to dawn upon these Galileans that their friend and teacher was going to leave them. Jesus gave each apostle a personal farewell admonition.		
Paper 182—In Gethsemane	1963–1970	A.D. 30
Jesus prayed their last group prayer. He said: "I am the bread of life." Jesus sent a message to Abner at Philadelphia saying that the hour has come when he will be delivered into the hands of his enemies, who will put him to death, but that he will rise from the dead and appear to you shortly, before he goes to the Father, and that he will then give you guidance to the time when the new teacher shall come to live in your hearts.'" Just before the greatest of all the revelations of Jesus' divinity, his resurrection, must now come the greatest proofs of his mortal nature, his humiliation and crucifixion. Jesus experienced that natural ebb and flow of feeling which is common to all human experience.		
Paper 183—The Betrayal and Arrest of Jesus	1971–1977	A.D. 30
The Father in heaven had nothing whatever to do with instigating the barbarous behavior of those supposedly civilized human beings who so brutally tortured the Master and so horribly heaped successive indignities upon his nonresisting person. Doings of Judas. The arrest of Jesus and the journey to the palace of Annas.		
Paper 184—Before the Sanhedrin Court	1978–1986	A.D. 30
Jesus before the Jewish Court. Peter in the courtyard denies knowing Jesus. At 3 a.m. Friday morning, Chief Priest Caiaphas called the Sanhedrist court to order beginning the formal trial of Jesus. What is this trait in man which leads him to want to insult and physically assault that which he cannot spiritually attain or intellectually achieve?		

Paper Number and Title	Pages	Year
Paper 185—The Trial Before Pilate	1987–1996	A.D. 30
Shortly after six o'clock on this Friday morning, April 7, A.D. 30, Jesus was brought before Pilate, the Roman procurator, bound and accompanied by about fifty of his accusers, including the Sanhedrist court, Judas Iscariot, the high priest Caiaphas, and by the Apostle John. Pilate was afraid of a tumult or a riot during the Passover. He ordered a basin and some water, washed his hands, saying: "I am innocent of the blood of this man.		
Paper 186—Just Before the Crucifixion	1997–2003	A.D. 30
The humiliation, guilt, and the end of Judas Iscariot. Although Jesus lived and died on Urantia, his whole human career, from first to last, was a spectacle designed to influence and instruct the entire universe of his creation and unceasing upholding. Throughout this tragic day, until the message finally went forth that the Master had been laid in the tomb, David Zebedee sent messengers about every half hour with reports to the apostles, the Greeks, and Jesus' earthly family, assembled at the home of Lazarus in Bethany.		
Paper 187—The Crucifixion	2004–2011	A.D. 30
Jesus said: "The Father loves and sustains me because I am willing to lay down my life. But I will take it up again. No one takes my life away from me—I lay it down of myself. I have authority to lay it down, and I have authority to take it up." Jesus' only words, as they nailed him to the crossbeam, were, "Father, forgive them, for they know not what they do." Jesus did not for one moment entertain the slightest doubt that he had lived in accordance with the Father's will; and he never doubted that he was now laying down his life in the flesh in accordance with his Father's will. He did not feel that the Father had forsaken him. Jesus died royally—as he had lived. He freely admitted his kingship and remained master of the situation throughout the tragic day.		
Paper 188—The Time of the Tomb	2012–2019	A.D. 30
The burial of Jesus. Meaning of Death on the Cross. Urantia has become known as the "World of the Cross." Though it is hardly proper to speak of Jesus as a sacrificer, a ransomer, or a redeemer, it is wholly correct to refer to him as a *savior.* The cross of Jesus portrays the full measure of the supreme devotion of the true shepherd for even the unworthy members of his flock. It forever places all relations between God and man upon the family basis. God is the Father; man is his son. Love becomes the central truth in the relations of Creator and creature.		
Paper 189—The Resurrection	2020–2028	A.D. 30
At two minutes past three o'clock, this Sunday morning, April 9, A.D. 30, the resurrected morontia form and personality of Jesus came forth from the tomb. The dissolution of Jesus' material body. Michael appeared before Gabriel, saying: "let the roll call of the planetary resurrection begin." Discovery of the empty tomb and the first two Morontia appearances; first to Mary then Peter and John.		
Paper 190—Morontia Appearances of Jesus	2029–2036	A.D. 30
The resurrected Jesus now prepares to spend a short period on Urantia for the purpose of experiencing the ascending morontia career of a mortal of the realms. Although this time of the morontia life is to be spent on the world of his mortal incarnation, it will, however, be in all respects the counterpart of the experience of Satania mortals who pass through the progressive morontia life of the seven mansion worlds of Jerusem. David Zebedee's heralds of the Resurrection. Third through seventh Morontia appearances: Bethany-first to James and then to his family and friends, the home of Joseph of Arimathea, the home of Flavius, at Emmaus,		

<table>
<tr><th>Paper Number and Title</th><th>Pages</th><th>Year</th></tr>
<tr><td>Paper 191—Appearances to the Apostles and Other Leaders</td><td>2037–2044</td><td>A.D. 30</td></tr>
<tr><td colspan="3">Resurrection Sunday was a terrible day in the lives of the apostles. It was near half past eight o'clock this Sunday evening when Jesus appeared to Simon Peter in the garden of the Mark home. Shortly after nine o'clock, as the apostles were in the upper chamber with all the doors bolted, the Master, suddenly appeared saying: "Peace be upon you." Jesus spent the next day wholly with the morontia creatures then present on Urantia. The tenth morontia manifestation of Jesus occurred a short time after eight o'clock on Tuesday, April 11, at Philadelphia, where he showed himself to Abner and Lazarus and some one hundred and fifty of their associates, including more than fifty of the evangelistic corps of the seventy. On Sunday, April 16th, the Apostles were having their evening meal a little after six o'clock, when the doubting apostle said: "I will not believe unless I see the Master with my own eyes and put my finger in the mark of the nails." As they thus sat at supper, and while the doors were securely shut and barred, the morontia Master suddenly appeared inside the curvature of the table. On Tuesday evening, April 18, at about half past eight o'clock, Jesus appeared to Rodan and some eighty other believers, in Alexandria.</td></tr>
<tr><td>Paper 192—Appearances in Galilee</td><td>2045–2051</td><td>A.D. 30</td></tr>
<tr><td colspan="3">About six o'clock Friday morning, April 21, the morontia Master made his thirteenth appearance, the first in Galilee, to the ten apostles as their boat drew near the shore close to the usual landing place at Bethsaida. Talking with the Apostles two and two.

At noon on Saturday, April 22, the eleven apostles assembled by appointment on the hill near Capernaum at the site of their ordination ceremony, and Jesus appeared among them.

On Saturday, April 29, at three o'clock, more than five hundred believers at Bethsaida to hear Peter preach his first public sermon since the resurrection. Just as he finished making this declaration of faith, there by his side, in full view of all these people, the Master appeared in morontia form and, speaking to them in familiar accents, said, "Peace be upon you, and my peace I leave with you." When he had thus appeared and had so spoken to them, he vanished from their sight. This was the fifteenth morontia manifestation of the risen Jesus.</td></tr>
<tr><td>Paper 193—Final Appearances and Ascension</td><td>2052–2058</td><td>A.D. 30</td></tr>
<tr><td colspan="3">The sixteenth morontia manifestation of Jesus occurred on Friday, May 5, in the courtyard of Nicodemus, about nine o'clock at night. About four o'clock on Sabbath afternoon, May 13, the Master appeared to Nalda and about seventy-five Samaritan believers near Jacob's well, at Sychar. The Master's eighteenth morontia appearance was at Tyre, on Tuesday, May 16, at a little before nine o'clock in the evening. Early Thursday morning, May 18, Jesus made his last appearance on earth as the eleven apostles were about to sit down to breakfast in the upper chamber of Mary Mark's home, Jesus appeared to them. It was about seven forty-five this morning when the morontia Jesus disappeared from the observation of his eleven apostles to begin the ascent to the right hand of his Father, there to receive formal confirmation of his completed sovereignty of the universe of Nebadon. The downfall of Judas.</td></tr>
<tr><td>Paper 194—Bestowal of the Spirit of Truth</td><td>2059–2068</td><td>A.D. 30</td></tr>
<tr><td colspan="3">About one o'clock, the one hundred and twenty believers were engaged in prayer, became aware of a strange presence in the room. At the same time these disciples all became conscious of a new and profound sense of spiritual joy, security, and confidence. This new consciousness of spiritual strength was followed by a strong urge to publicly proclaim the gospel of the kingdom and the good news that Jesus had risen from the dead. Peter stood up and declared that this must be the coming of the Spirit of Truth which the Master had promised them Bestowal of Spirit of Truth. The significance of Pentecost. Beginnings of Christian Church.</td></tr>
</table>

Paper Number and Title	Pages	Year
Paper 195—After Pentecost	2069–2086	A.D. 30
Peter was the real founder of the Christian church; Paul carried the Christian message to the gentiles, and the Greek believers carried it to the whole Roman Empire. At first, Christianity won as converts only the lower social and economic strata. But by the beginning of the second century the very best of Greco-Roman culture was increasingly turning to this new order of Christian belief, this new concept of the purpose of living and the goal of existence. The Romans bodily took over Greek culture, putting representative government in the place of government by lot. And presently this change favored Christianity in that Rome brought into the whole Western world a new tolerance for strange languages, peoples, and even religions. Christianity came with refreshing comfort and liberating power to a spiritually hungry people whose language had no word for "unselfishness." That which gave greatest power to Christianity was the way its believers lived lives of service and even the way they died for their faith during the earlier times of drastic persecution. "The kingdom of God is within you" was probably the greatest pronouncement Jesus ever made, next to the declaration that his Father is a living and loving spirit.		
Paper 196—The Faith of Jesus.	2087–2097	A.D. 30
Jesus enjoyed a sublime and wholehearted faith in God. He experienced the ordinary ups and downs of mortal existence, but he never religiously doubted the certainty of God's watchcare and guidance. The human Jesus saw God as being holy, just, and great, as well as being true, beautiful, and good. Jesus' great contribution to the values of human experience was that he so magnificently and humanly demonstrated a new and higher type of *living faith in God.* Never on all the worlds of this universe, in the life of any one mortal, did God ever become such a *living reality* as in the human experience of Jesus of Nazareth. No matter how great the fact of the sovereignty of Michael, you must not take the human Jesus away from men. To "follow Jesus" means to personally share his religious faith and to enter into the spirit of the Master's life of unselfish service for man. One of the most important things in human living is to find out what Jesus believed, to discover his ideals, and to strive for the achievement of his exalted life purpose. Of all human knowledge, that which is of greatest value is to know the religious life of Jesus and how he lived it. When all is said and done, the Father idea is still the highest human concept of God.		

The Organization of Part IV of *The Urantia Book*

The Organization of Part IV of *The Urantia Book*

MORTAL EPOCHS OF JESUS' LIFE			
Phase of Mortal Epoch	Phase Description	Related Paper	Paper Number
MORTAL CAREER			
Introduction	Universe	Bestowal of Michael on Urantia	120
	Planetary	Times of Michael's Bestowal	121
	Familial	Birth and Infancy of Jesus	122
GROWTH			
Growth	Childhood	Early Childhood of Jesus	123
		Later Childhood of Jesus	124
	Crisis	Jesus at Jerusalem	125
		The Two Crucial Years	126
	Maturity	The Adolescent Years	127
		Jesus' Early Manhood (21st-26th yrs.)	128
Joshua, The Tutor	General	Later Adult Life of Jesus (27th yr.)	129
	Rome	On the Way to Rome	130
		The World's Religions	131
		Sojourn at Rome	132
		Return from Rome	133
	Transition	The Transition Years	134
PUBLIC WORK (The Son of Man)			
Baptism	Preparing the way	John the Baptist	135
		Baptism and the 40 days	136
Training The Twelve	The teachers, the message, and the methods	Tarrying Time in Galilee	137
		Training the Kingdom's Messengers	138
		The Twelve Apostles	139
		Ordination of the Twelve	140

The Organization of Part IV of *The Urantia Book*

MORTAL EPOCHS OF JESUS' LIFE			
Phase of Mortal Epoch	Phase Description	Related Paper	Paper Number
Early Public Works	Beginnings	Beginning of Public Work	141
		Passover at Jerusalem	142
		Going Through Samaria	143
		At Gilboa and the Decopolis	144
		Four Eventful Days at Capernaum	145
	First Preaching Tour	First Preaching Tour of Galilee	146
		Interlude Visit to Jerusalem	147
	Second Preaching Tour	Training Evangelists at Bethsaida	148
		Second Preaching Tour	149
	Third Preaching Tour	Third Preaching Tour	150
		Tarrying and Teaching by the Seaside	151
The Crisis	Capernaum	Events Leading up to Capernaum Crisis	152
		The Crisis at Capernaum	153
		Last Days at Capernaum	154
	Phoenicia	Fleeing Through Northern Galilee	155
		Sojourn at Tyre and Sidon	156
PUBLIC WORK			
Transfiguration	Confirmation	At Caesarea-Philippi	157
		Mount of Transfiguration	158
Later Ministry	Decapolis	Decapolis Tour	159
	Rodan	Rodan of Alexandria	160
		Further Discussion with Rodan	161

The Organization of Part IV of *The Urantia Book*

Later Ministry Continued:	Pre-Perean Ministry	At Feast of Tabernacles	162
		Ordination of the Seventy at Magadan	163
		At Feast of Dedication	164
	Perean Ministry	Perean Mission Begins	165
		Last Visit to Northern Perea	166
		Visit to Philadelphia	167
		Resurrection of Lazarus	168
		Last Teaching at Pella	169
	Summary	The Kingdom of Heaven	170
Final Teachings	Jerusalem	On the Way to Jerusalem	171
		Going into Jerusalem	172
		Monday in Jerusalem	173
		Tuesday Morning in the Temple	174
		Last Temple Discourse	175
		Tuesday Evening on Mount Olivet	176
	At Camp	Wednesday, the Rest Day	177
		Last Day at Camp	178
	Last Supper	The Last Supper	179
		Farewell Discourse	180
		Final Admonitions and Warnings	181
Betrayal and Death	Arrest	In Gethsemane	182
		Betrayal and Arrest of Jesus	183
	Trial	Before the Sanhedrin Court	184
		Trial Before Pilate	185
	Crucifixion	Just Before the Crucifixion	186
		The Crucifixion	187

The Organization of Part IV of *The Urantia Book*

MORTAL EPOCHS OF JESUS' LIFE			
POST MORTAL CAREER			
The Resurrection	The greatest story ever told	The Time of the Tomb	188
		The Resurrection	189
Morontia Appearances	The proof	Morontia Appearances of Jesus	190
		Appearances to Apostles and Others	191
		Appearances in Galilee	192
		Final Appearances and Ascension	193
After Jesus Left	The future	Bestowal of Spirit of Truth	194
		After Pentecost	195
		The Faith of Jesus	196

The Fourth Epochal Revelation of Truth

The Fourth Epochal Revelation of Truth

FACT	TRUTH
	Said Jesus: "I am the living way," and so he is the living way from the material level of self-consciousness to the spiritual level of God-consciousness. 117:3.3 (1281:5)
	Jesus lived his earth life on Urantia, not to set a personal example of mortal living for the men and women of this world, but rather to create a high spiritual and inspirational ideal for all mortal beings on all worlds. 140:10.3 (1585.1)
Jesus of Nazareth A Creator Son, Michael. Sometimes Called Christ Michael:	THE Creator Sons are the makers and rulers of the local universes of time and space. These universe creators and sovereigns are of dual origin, embodying the characteristics of God the Father and God the Son. But each Creator Son is different from every other; each is unique in nature as well as in personality; each is the "only-begotten Son" of the perfect deity ideal of his origin. 21:0.1 (234.1)
	These primary Paradise Sons are personalized as Michaels. As they go forth from Paradise to found their universes, they are known as Creator Michaels. When settled in supreme authority, they are called Master Michaels. Sometimes we refer to the sovereign of your universe of Nebadon as Christ Michael. Always and forever do they reign after the "order of Michael," that being the designation of the first Son of their order and nature. 21:0.3 (234.3)
	Our Creator Son is the personification of the 611,121st original concept of infinite identity of simultaneous origin in the Universal Father and the Eternal Son. The Michael of Nebadon is the "only-begotten Son" personalizing this 611,121st universal concept of divinity and infinity. His headquarters is in the threefold mansion of light on Salvington. And this dwelling is so ordered because Michael has experienced the living of all three phases of intelligent creature existence: spiritual, morontial, and material. Because of the name associated with his seventh and final bestowal on Urantia, he is sometimes spoken of as Christ Michael. 33:1.1 (366.2)
Six Bestowals:	In the course of each of these preceding bestowals Michael not only acquired the finite experience of one group of his created beings, but he also acquired an essential experience in Paradise co-operation which would, in and of itself, further contribute to constituting him the sovereign of his self-made universe. At any moment throughout all past local universe time, Michael could have asserted personal sovereignty as a Creator Son and as a Creator Son could have ruled his universe after the manner of his own choosing. In such an event, Immanuel and the associated Paradise Sons would have taken leave of the universe. But Michael did not wish to rule Nebadon merely in his own isolated right, as a Creator Son. He desired to ascend through actual experience in co-operative subordination to the Paradise Trinity to that high place in universe status where he would become qualified to rule his universe and administer its affairs with that perfection of insight and wisdom of execution which will sometime be characteristic of the exalted rule of the Supreme Being. He aspired not to perfection of rule as a Creator Son but to supremacy of administration as the embodiment of the universe wisdom and the divine experience of the Supreme Being. 120:0.3 (1323.3)

The Fourth Epochal Revelation of Truth

Michael Selects Urantia:	The public announcement that Michael had selected Urantia as the theater for his final bestowal was made shortly after we learned about the default of Adam and Eve. And thus, for more than thirty-five thousand years, your world occupied a very conspicuous place in the councils of the entire universe. There was no secrecy (aside from the incarnation mystery) connected with any step in the Urantia bestowal. From first to last, up to the final and triumphant return of Michael to Salvington as supreme Universe Sovereign, there was the fullest universe publicity of all that transpired on your small but highly honored world. 119:7.2 (1316.5) While we believed that this would be the method, we never knew, until the time of the event itself, that Michael would appear on earth as a helpless infant of the realm. Theretofore had he always appeared as a fully developed individual of the personality group of the bestowal selection, and it was a thrilling announcement which was broadcast from Salvington telling that the babe of Bethlehem had been born on Urantia. 119:7.3 (1316.6)
Jesus' Two-Fold Purpose in Coming to Urantia:	1. The mastering of the experience of living the full life of a human creature in mortal flesh, the completion of his sovereignty in Nebadon. 128:0.3 (1407.3) 2. The revelation of the Universal Father to the mortal dwellers on the worlds of time and space and the more effective leading of these same mortals to a better understanding of the Universal Father. 128:0.4 (1407.4) All other creature benefits and universe advantages were incidental and secondary to these major purposes of the mortal bestowal. 128:0.5 (1407.5)
Immanuel's Counsel to Guide Jesus' Divine Mission During His Sojourn in the Flesh:	"And that you may know with assurance that I am empowered to do all that I am now promising (knowing full well that I am the assurance of all Paradise for the faithful performance of my word), I announce to you that there has just been communicated to me a mandate of the Ancients of Days on Uversa which will prevent all spiritual jeopardy in Nebadon throughout the period of your voluntary bestowal. From the moment you surrender consciousness, upon the beginning of the mortal incarnation, until you return to us as supreme and unconditional sovereign of this universe of your own creation and organization, nothing of serious import can happen in all Nebadon. In this interim of your incarnation, I hold the orders of the Ancients of Days which unqualifiedly mandate the instantaneous and automatic extinction of any being guilty of rebellion or presuming to instigate insurrection in the universe of Nebadon while you are absent on this bestowal. My brother, in view of the authority of Paradise inherent in my presence and augmented by the judicial mandate of Uversa, your universe and all its loyal creatures will be secure during your bestowal. You may proceed upon your mission with but a single thought—the enhanced revelation of our Father to the intelligent beings of your universe. 120:1.5 (1326.2) "1. In accordance with the usages and in conformity with the technique of Sonarington—in compliance with the mandates of the Eternal Son of Paradise—I have provided in every way for your immediate entrance upon this mortal bestowal in harmony with the plans formulated by you and placed in my keeping by Gabriel. You will grow up on Urantia as a child of the realm, complete your human education—all the while subject to the will of your Paradise Father—live your life on Urantia as you have determined, terminate your planetary sojourn, and prepare for ascension to your Father to receive from him the supreme sovereignty of your universe. 120:2.1 (1327.1)

Immanuel's Counsel to Guide Jesus' Divine Mission During His Sojourn in the Flesh: (Continued)	"2. Apart from your earth mission and your universe revelation, but incidental to both, I counsel that you assume, after you are sufficiently self-conscious of your divine identity, the additional task of technically terminating the Lucifer rebellion in the system of Satania, and that you do all this as the Son of Man; thus, as a mortal creature of the realm, in weakness made powerful by faith-submission to the will of your Father, I suggest that you graciously achieve all you have repeatedly declined arbitrarily to accomplish by power and might when you were so endowed at the time of the inception of this sinful and unjustified rebellion. I would regard it as a fitting climax of your mortal bestowal if you should return to us as the Son of Man, Planetary Prince of Urantia, as well as the Son of God, supreme sovereign of your universe. As a mortal man, the lowest type of intelligent creature in Nebadon, meet and adjudicate the blasphemous pretensions of Caligastia and Lucifer and, in your assumed humble estate, forever end the shameful misrepresentations of these fallen children of light. Having steadfastly declined to discredit these rebels through the exercise of your creator prerogatives, now it would be fitting that you should, in the likeness of the lowest creatures of your creation, wrest dominion from the hands of these fallen Sons; and so would your whole local universe in all fairness clearly and forever recognize the justice of your doing in the role of mortal flesh those things which mercy admonished you not to do by the power of arbitrary authority. 120:2.2 (1327.2) "3. When you have succeeded in terminating the Urantia secession, as you undoubtedly will, I counsel you to accept from Gabriel the conference of the title of 'Planetary Prince of Urantia' as the eternal recognition by your universe of your final bestowal experience; and that you further do any and all things, consistent with the purport of your bestowal, to atone for the sorrow and confusion brought upon Urantia by the Caligastia betrayal and the subsequent Adamic default. 120:2.3 (1327.3) "4. In accordance with your request, Gabriel and all concerned will co-operate with you in the expressed desire to end your Urantia bestowal with the pronouncement of a dispensational judgment of the realm, accompanied by the termination of an age, the resurrection of the sleeping mortal survivors, and the establishment of the dispensation of the bestowed Spirit of Truth. 120:2.4 (1328.1) "5. As concerns the planet of your bestowal and the immediate generation of men living thereon at the time of your mortal sojourn, I counsel you to function largely in the role of a teacher. Give attention, first, to the liberation and inspiration of man's spiritual nature. Next, illuminate the darkened human intellect, heal the souls of men, and emancipate their minds from age-old fears. And then, in accordance with your mortal wisdom, minister to the physical well-being and material comfort of your brothers in the flesh. Live the ideal religious life for the inspiration and edification of all your universe. 120:2.5 (1328.2) "6. On the planet of your bestowal, set rebellion-segregated man spiritually free. On Urantia, make a further contribution to the sovereignty of the Supreme, thus extending the establishment of this sovereignty throughout the broad domains of your personal creation. In this, your material bestowal in the likeness of the flesh, you are about to experience the final enlightenment of a time-space Creator, the dual experience of working within the nature of man with the will of your Paradise Father. In your temporal life the will of the finite creature and the will of the infinite Creator are to become as one, even as they are also uniting in the evolving Deity of the Supreme Being. Pour out upon the planet of your bestowal the Spirit of Truth and

Immanuel's Counsel to Guide Jesus' Divine Mission During His Sojourn in the Flesh: (Continued)	thus make all normal mortals on that isolated sphere immediately and fully accessible to the ministry of the segregated presence of our Paradise Father, the Thought Adjusters of the realms. 120:2.6 (1328.3) "7. In all that you may perform on the world of your bestowal, bear constantly in mind that you are living a life for the instruction and edification of all your universe. You are bestowing this life of mortal incarnation upon Urantia, but you are to live such a life for the spiritual inspiration of every human and superhuman intelligence that has lived, now exists, or may yet live on every inhabited world which has formed, now forms, or may yet form a part of the vast galaxy of your administrative domain. Your earth life in the likeness of mortal flesh shall not be so lived as to constitute an example for the mortals of Urantia in the days of your earthly sojourn nor for any subsequent generation of human beings on Urantia or on any other world. Rather shall your life in the flesh on Urantia be the inspiration for all lives upon all Nebadon worlds throughout all generations in the ages to come. 120:2.7 (1328.4) "8. Your great mission to be realized and experienced in the mortal incarnation is embraced in your decision to live a life wholeheartedly motivated to do the will of your Paradise Father, thus to reveal God, your Father, in the flesh and especially to the creatures of the flesh. At the same time you will also interpret, with a new enhancement, our Father, to the supermortal beings of all Nebadon. Equally with this ministry of new revelation and augmented interpretation of the Paradise Father to the human and the superhuman type of mind, you will also so function as to make a new revelation of man to God. Exhibit in your one short life in the flesh, as it has never before been seen in all Nebadon, the transcendent possibilities attainable by a God-knowing human during the short career of mortal existence, and make a new and illuminating interpretation of man and the vicissitudes of his planetary life to all the superhuman intelligences of all Nebadon, and for all time. You are to go down to Urantia in the likeness of mortal flesh, and living as a man in your day and generation, you will so function as to show your entire universe the ideal of perfected technique in the supreme engagement of the affairs of your vast creation: The achievement of God seeking man and finding him and the phenomenon of man seeking God and finding him; and doing all of this to mutual satisfaction and doing it during one short lifetime in the flesh. 120:2.8 (1328.5) "9. I caution you ever to bear in mind that, while in fact you are to become an ordinary human of the realm, in potential you will remain a Creator Son of the Paradise Father. Throughout this incarnation, although you will live and act as a Son of Man, the creative attributes of your personal divinity will follow you from Salvington to Urantia. It will ever be within your power-of-will to terminate the incarnation at any moment subsequent to the arrival of your Thought Adjuster. Prior to the arrival and reception of the Adjuster I will vouch for your personality integrity. But subsequent to the arrival of your Adjuster and concomitant with your progressive recognition of the nature and import of your bestowal mission, you should refrain from the formulation of any superhuman will-to-attainment, achievement, or power in view of the fact that your creator prerogatives will remain associated with your mortal personality because of the inseparability of these attributes from your personal presence. But no superhuman repercussions will attend your earthly career apart from the will of the Paradise Father unless you should, by an act of conscious and deliberate will, make an undivided decision which would terminate in whole-personality choice. 120:2.9 (1329.1)

The Fourth Epochal Revelation of Truth

FACT	TRUTH
Joshua Ben Joseph (Jesus) Born Unto This World:	Certain wise men of earth knew of Michael's impending arrival. Through the contacts of one world with another, these wise men of spiritual insight learned of the forthcoming bestowal of Michael on Urantia. And the seraphim did, through the midway creatures, make announcement to a group of Chaldean priests whose leader was Ardnon. These men of God visited the newborn child in the manger. The only supernatural event associated with the birth of Jesus was this announcement to Ardnon and his associates by the seraphim of former attachment to Adam and Eve in the first garden. 119:7.6 (1317.2)
	All that night Mary was restless so that neither of them slept much. By the break of day the pangs of childbirth were well in evidence, and at noon, August 21, 7 B.C., with the help and kind ministrations of women fellow travelers, Mary was delivered of a male child. Jesus of Nazareth was born into the world, was wrapped in the clothes which Mary had brought along for such a possible contingency, and laid in a near-by manger. 122:8.1 (1351:5)
What Jesus' Coming Did for Mortal Man:	And this was his true and supreme purpose. He did not come down to live on Urantia as the perfect and detailed example for any child or adult, any man or woman, in that age or any other. True it is, indeed, that in his full, rich, beautiful, and noble life we may all find much that is exquisitely exemplary, divinely inspiring, but this is because he lived a true and genuinely human life. Jesus did not live his life on earth in order to set an example for all other human beings to copy. He lived this life in the flesh by the same mercy ministry that you all may live your lives on earth; and as he lived his mortal life in his day and as he was, so did he thereby set the example for all of us thus to live our lives in our day and as we are. You may not aspire to live his life, but you can resolve to live your lives even as, and by the same means that, he lived his. Jesus may not be the technical and detailed example for all the mortals of all ages on all the realms of this local universe, but he is everlastingly the inspiration and guide of all Paradise pilgrims from the worlds of initial ascension up through a universe of universes and on through Havona to Paradise. Jesus is the new and living way from man to God, from the partial to the perfect, from the earthly to the heavenly, from time to eternity. 129:4.7 (1425.6) By the end of the twenty-ninth year Jesus of Nazareth had virtually finished the living of the life required of mortals as sojourners in the flesh. He came on earth the fullness of God to be manifest to man; he had now become well-nigh the perfection of man awaiting the occasion to become manifest to God. And he did all of this before he was thirty years of age. 129:4.8 (1426.1)
What Jesus' Coming Did for this Planet:	Urantia is comparatively isolated on the outskirts of Satania, your solar system, with one exception, being the farthest removed from Jerusem, while Satania itself is next to the outermost system of Norlatiadek, and this constellation is now traversing the outer fringe of Nebadon. You were truly among the least of all creation until Michael's bestowal elevated your planet to a position of honor and great universe interest. Sometimes the last is first, while truly the least becomes greatest. 41:10.5 (466.4)

What Jesus' Coming did for this Planet: (Continued)	Misfortune has not, however, been the sole lot of Urantia; this planet has also been the most fortunate in the local universe of Nebadon. Urantians should count it all gain if the blunders of their ancestors and the mistakes of their early world rulers so plunged the planet into such a hopeless state of confusion, all the more confounded by evil and sin, that this very background of darkness should so appeal to Michael of Nebadon that he selected this world as the arena wherein to reveal the loving personality of the Father in heaven. It is not that Urantia needed a Creator Son to set its tangled affairs in order; it is rather that the evil and sin on Urantia afforded the Creator Son a more striking background against which to reveal the matchless love, mercy, and patience of the Paradise Father. 76:5.7 (853.1)
	And all these speculations associated with the certainty of future appearances of both Magisterial and Trinity Teacher Sons, in conjunction with the explicit promise of the Creator Son to return sometime, make Urantia a planet of future uncertainty and render it one of the most interesting and intriguing spheres in all the universe of Nebadon. It is altogether possible that, in some future age when Urantia is approaching the era of light and life, after the affairs of the Lucifer rebellion and the Caligastia secession have been finally adjudicated, we may witness the presence on Urantia, simultaneously, of Machiventa, Adam, Eve, and Christ Michael, as well as either a Magisterial Son or even Trinity Teacher Sons. 93:10.8 (1025.4)
What Jesus Does for Us Today:	If your own mind does not serve you well, you can exchange it for the mind of Jesus of Nazareth, who always serves you well. 48:6.26 (553.7)
	Jesus was the perfectly unified human personality. And today, as in Galilee, he continues to unify mortal experience and to co-ordinate human endeavors. He unifies life, ennobles character, and simplifies experience. He enters the human mind to elevate, transform, and transfigure it. It is literally true: "If any man has Christ Jesus within him, he is a new creature; old things are passing away; behold, all things are becoming new." 100:7.18(1103.6)
	"The Son of Man experienced those wide ranges of human emotion which reach from superb joy to profound sorrow. He was a child of joy and a being of rare good humor; likewise was he a "man of sorrows and acquainted with grief." In a spiritual sense, he did live through the mortal life from the bottom to the top, from the beginning to the end. From a material point of view, he might appear to have escaped living through both social extremes of human existence, but intellectually he became wholly familiar with the entire and complete experience of humankind. 129:4.4 (1425.3) Jesus knows about the thoughts and feelings, the urges and impulses, of the evolutionary and ascendant mortals of the realms, from birth to death. He has lived the human life from the beginnings of physical, intellectual, and spiritual selfhood up through infancy, childhood, youth, and adulthood—even to the human experience of death. He not only passed through these usual and familiar human periods of intellectual and spiritual advancement, but he also fully experienced those higher and more advanced phases of human and Adjuster reconciliation which so few Urantia mortals ever attain. And thus he experienced the full life of mortal man, not only as it is lived on your world, but also as it is lived on all other evolutionary worlds of time and space, even on the highest and most advanced of all the worlds settled in light and life. 129:4.5 (1425.4)

What Jesus Does for Us Today: (Continued)	But the greatest mistake was made in that, while the human Jesus was recognized as having a religion, the divine Jesus (Christ) almost overnight became a religion. Paul's Christianity made sure of the adoration of the divine Christ, but it almost wholly lost sight of the struggling and valiant human Jesus of Galilee, who, by the valor of his personal religious faith and the heroism of his indwelling Adjuster, ascended from the lowly levels of humanity to become one with divinity, thus becoming the new and living way whereby all mortals may so ascend from humanity to divinity. Mortals in all stages of spirituality and on all worlds may find in the personal life of Jesus that which will strengthen and inspire them as they progress from the lowest spirit levels up to the highest divine values, from the beginning to the end of all personal religious experience. 196:2.4 (2092.2)
Jesus So Revealed the Father's Name to the World, that He, Who Was the Father Incarnate, Could Truly Say:	"I am the bread of life. "I am the living water. "I am the light of the world. "I am the desire of all ages. "I am the open door to eternal salvation. "I am the reality of endless life. "I am the good shepherd. "I am the pathway of infinite perfection. "I am the resurrection and the life. "I am the secret of eternal survival "I am the way, the truth, and the life. "I am the infinite Father of my finite children. "I am the true vine; you are the branches. "I am the hope of all who know the living truth. "I am the living bridge from one world to another. "I am the living link between time and eternity." "Thus did Jesus enlarge the living revelation of the name of God to all generations." 182:1.10–26 (1965: 4–20)
Jesus Was Referred to Variously As:	The first century after Christ. As a religious teacher, Jesus of Nazareth started out with the cult which had been established by John the Baptist and progressed as far as he could away from fasts and forms. 92:5.13 (1010.1)
	This is the year of Jesus' solitary wanderings through Palestine and Syria. Throughout this year of travel he was known by various names in different parts of the country: the carpenter of Nazareth, the boatbuilder of Capernaum, the scribe of Damascus, and the teacher of Alexandria. 134:7.2 (1492.2)
	At Antioch the Son of Man lived for over two months, working, observing, studying, visiting, ministering, and all the while learning how man lives, how he thinks, feels, and reacts to the environment of human existence. For three weeks of this period he worked as a tentmaker. He remained longer in Antioch than at any other place he visited on this trip. Ten years later, when the Apostle Paul was preaching in Antioch and heard his followers speak of the doctrines of the Damascus scribe, he little knew that his pupils had heard the voice, and listened to the teachings, of the Master himself. 134:7.3 (1492.3)

Jesus Was Referred to Variously As: (Continued)	Jesus of Nazareth was indeed a strong and forceful personality; he was an intellectual power and a spiritual stronghold. His personality not only appealed to the spiritually minded women among his followers, but also to the educated and intellectual Nicodemus and to the hardy Roman soldier, the captain stationed on guard at the cross, who, when he had finished watching the Master die, said, "Truly, this was a Son of God." And red-blooded, rugged Galilean fishermen called him Master. 141:3.5 (1589.6)
	Jesus is the spiritual lens in human likeness which makes visible to the material creature Him who is invisible. He is your elder brother who, in the flesh, makes known to you a Being of infinite attributes whom not even the celestial hosts can presume fully to understand. 169:4.13 (1857.4)
	"Do you really understand what I have done to you? You call me Master, and you say well, for so I am." 179:3.8 (1939.6)
What Jesus Earned By the Life He Lived On Urantia:	On an afternoon in late summer, amid the trees and in the silence of nature, Michael of Nebadon won the unquestioned sovereignty of his universe. On that day he completed the task set for Creator Sons to live to the full the incarnated life in the likeness of mortal flesh on the evolutionary worlds of time and space. The universe announcement of this momentous achievement was not made until the day of his baptism, months afterward, but it all really took place that day on the mountain. And when Jesus came down from his sojourn on Mount Hermon, the Lucifer rebellion in Satania and the Caligastia secession on Urantia were virtually settled. Jesus had paid the last price required of him to attain the sovereignty of his universe, which in itself regulates the status of all rebels and determines that all such future upheavals (if they ever occur) may be dealt with summarily and effectively. Accordingly, it may be seen that the so- called "great temptation" of Jesus took place sometime before his baptism and not just after that event. 134:8.9 (1494.2)
	Jesus had endured the great temptation of his mortal bestowal before his baptism when he had been wet with the dews of Mount Hermon for six weeks. There on Mount Hermon, as an unaided mortal of the realm, he had met and defeated the Urantia pretender, Caligastia, the prince of this world. That eventful day, on the universe records, Jesus of Nazareth had become the Planetary Prince of Urantia. And this Prince of Urantia, so soon to be proclaimed supreme Sovereign of Nebadon, now went into forty days of retirement to formulate the plans and determine upon the technique of proclaiming the new kingdom of God in the hearts of men. 136:3.1 (1512.5)
	While wandering about in the hills, seeking a suitable shelter, Jesus encountered his universe chief executive, Gabriel, the Bright and Morning Star of Nebadon. Gabriel now re-established personal communication with the Creator Son of the universe; they met directly for the first time since Michael took leave of his associates on Salvington when he went to Edentia preparatory to entering upon the Urantia bestowal. Gabriel, by direction of Immanuel and on authority of the Uversa Ancients of Days, now laid before Jesus information indicating that his bestowal experience on Urantia was practically finished so far as concerned the earning of the perfected sovereignty of his universe and the termination of the Lucifer rebellion. The former

What Jesus Earned By the Life He Lived On Urantia: (Continued)	was achieved on the day of his baptism when the personalization of his Adjuster demonstrated the perfection and completion of his bestowal in the likeness of mortal flesh, and the latter was a fact of history on that day when he came down from Mount Hermon to join the waiting lad, Tiglath. Jesus was now informed, upon the highest authority of the local universe and the superuniverse, that his bestowal work was finished in so far as it affected his personal status in relation to sovereignty and rebellion. He had already had this assurance direct from Paradise in the baptismal vision and in the phenomenon of the personalization of his indwelling Thought Adjuster. 136:3.4 (1513.1)
When Jesus Had Finished His Earth Life:	And having thus by your bestowal established the possibility of the sovereignty of the Supreme in Nebadon, you will in effect have brought to a close the unadjudicated affairs of all preceding insurrections, notwithstanding the greater or lesser time lag involved in the realization of this achievement. By this act the pending dissensions of your universe will be in substance liquidated. And with the subsequent endowment of supreme sovereignty over your universe, similar challenges to your authority can never recur in any part of your great personal creation. 120:2.2 (1327.2)
Sovereign of Local Universe:	Urantia belongs to a local universe whose sovereign is the God-man of Nebadon, Jesus of Nazareth and Michael of Salvington. And all of Michael's plans for this local universe were fully approved by the Paradise Trinity before he ever embarked upon the supreme adventure of space. 32:0.3 (357.3)
	Salvington is the personal headquarters of Michael of Nebadon, but he will not always be found there. While the smooth functioning of your local universe no longer requires the fixed presence of the Creator Son at the capital sphere, this was not true of the earlier epochs of physical organization. A Creator Son is unable to leave his headquarters world until such a time as gravity stabilization of the realm has been effected through the materialization of sufficient energy to enable the various circuits and systems to counterbalance one another by mutual material attraction. 32:2.5 (359.2)
	Michael of Nebadon is the "only-begotten Son" personalizing this 611,121st universal concept of divinity and infinity. His headquarters is in the threefold mansion of light on Salvington. And this dwelling is so ordered because Michael has experienced the living of all three phases of intelligent creature existence: spiritual, morontial, and material. Because of the name associated with his seventh and final bestowal on Urantia, he is sometimes spoken of as Christ Michael. 33:1.1 (366.2)
One of the Most Important Things in Human Living:	To "follow Jesus" means to personally share his religious faith and to enter into the spirit of the Master's life of unselfish service for man. One of the most important things in human living is to find out what Jesus believed, to discover his ideals, and to strive for the achievement of his exalted life purpose. Of all human knowledge, that which is of greatest value is to know the religious life of Jesus and how he lived it. 196:1.3 (2090.4)

The Seven Bestowals of Christ Michael

The Seven Bestowals of Christ Michael

The First Bestowal Mission	
Appeared as:	Emergency Melchizedek Son
Went to:	Melchizedek sphere of Salvington
Leaving Salvington:	After sending this farewell broadcast, Michael appeared on the dispatching field of Salvington, just as on many previous occasions when preparing for departure to Uversa or Paradise except that he came alone. He concluded his statement of departure with these words: "I leave you but for a short season. Many of you, I know, would go with me, but whither I go you cannot come. That which I am about to do, you cannot do. I go to do the will of the Paradise Deities, and when I have finished my mission and have acquired this experience, I will return to my place among you." And having thus spoken, Michael of Nebadon vanished from the sight of all those assembled and did not reappear for twenty years of standard time. 119:1.2 (1309.3)
Mission:	Not until the third day after Michael's departure was any message of significance received. On this day a communication was registered on Salvington from the Melchizedek sphere, the headquarters of that order in Nebadon, which simply recorded this extraordinary and never-before-heard-of transaction: "At noon today there appeared on the receiving field of this world a strange Melchizedek Son, not of our number but wholly like our order. He was accompanied by a solitary omniaphim who bore credentials from Uversa and presented orders addressed to our chief, derived from the Ancients of Days and concurred in by Immanuel of Salvington, directing that this new Melchizedek Son be received into our order and assigned to the emergency service of the Melchizedeks of Nebadon. And it has been so ordered; it has been done." 119:1.3 (1309.4) And this is about all that appears on the records of Salvington regarding the first Michael bestowal. Nothing more appears until after one hundred years of Urantia time, when there was recorded the fact of Michael's return and unannounced resumption of the direction of universe affairs. But a strange record is to be found on the Melchizedek world, a recital of the service of this unique Melchizedek Son of the emergency corps of that age. This record is preserved in a simple temple which now occupies the foreground of the home of the Father Melchizedek, and it comprises the narration of the service of this transitory Melchizedek Son in connection with his assignment to twenty- four missions of universe emergency. And this record, which I have so recently reviewed, ends thus: 119:1.4 (1310.1)
Return to Salvington:	"And at noon on this day, without previous announcement and witnessed by only three of our brotherhood, this visiting Son of our order disappeared from our world as he came, accompanied only by a solitary omniaphim; and this record is now closed with the certification that this visitor lived as a Melchizedek, in the likeness of a Melchizedek he worked as a Melchizedek, and he faithfully performed all of his assignments as an emergency Son of our order. By universal consent he has become chief of Melchizedeks, having earned our love and adoration by his matchless wisdom, supreme love, and superb devotion to duty. He loved us, understood us, and served with us, and forever we are his loyal and devoted fellow Melchizedeks, for this stranger on our world has now eternally become a universe minister of Melchizedek nature." 119:1.5 (1310.2)

The Seven Bestowals of Christ Michael

The Second Bestowal Mission	
Appeared as:	Primary Lanonandek Son, successor of the deposed Lutentia
Went to:	System 11 of constellation 37
Leaving Salvington:	For almost one hundred and fifty million years after the Melchizedek bestowal of Michael, all went well in the universe of Nebadon, when trouble began to brew in system 11 of constellation 37. This trouble involved a misunderstanding by a Lanonandek Son, a System Sovereign, which had been adjudicated by the Constellation Fathers and approved by the Faithful of Days, the Paradise counselor to that constellation, but the protesting System Sovereign was not fully reconciled to the verdict. After more than one hundred years of dissatisfaction he led his associates in one of the most widespread and disastrous rebellions against the sovereignty of the Creator Son ever instigated in the universe of Nebadon, a rebellion long since adjudicated and ended by the action of the Ancients of Days on Uversa. 119:2.1 (1310.4) This rebel System Sovereign, Lutentia, reigned supreme on his headquarters planet for more than twenty years of standard Nebadon time; whereupon, the Most Highs, with approval from Uversa, ordered his segregation and requisitioned the Salvington rulers for the designation of a new System Sovereign to assume direction of that strife-torn and confused system of inhabited worlds. 119:2.2 (1311.1) Simultaneously with the reception of this request on Salvington, Michael initiated the second of those extraordinary proclamations of intention to be absent from the universe headquarters for the purpose of "doing the bidding of my Paradise Father," promising to "return in due season" and concentrating all authority in the hands of his Paradise brother, Immanuel, the Union of Days. 119:2.3 (1311.2) And then, by the same technique observed at the time of his departure in connection with the Melchizedek bestowal, Michael again took leave of his headquarters sphere. Three days after this unexplained leave-taking there appeared among the reserve corps of the primary Lanonandek Sons of Nebadon, a new and unknown member. This new Son appeared at noon, unannounced and accompanied by a lone tertiaphim who bore credentials from the Uversa Ancients of Days, certified by Immanuel of Salvington, directing that this new Son be assigned to system 11 of constellation 37 as the successor of the deposed Lutentia and with full authority as acting System Sovereign pending the appointment of a new sovereign. 119:2.4 (1311.3)
Mission:	For more than seventeen years of universe time this strange and unknown temporary ruler administered the affairs and wisely adjudicated the difficulties of this confused and demoralized local system. No System Sovereign was ever more ardently loved or more widespreadly honored and respected. In justice and mercy this new ruler set the turbulent system in order while he painstakingly ministered to all his subjects, even offering his rebellious predecessor the privilege of sharing the system throne of authority if he would only apologize to Immanuel for his

Second Bestowal Mission: (Continued)	indiscretions. But Lutentia spurned these overtures of mercy, well knowing that this new and strange System Sovereign was none other than Michael, the very universe ruler whom he had so recently defied. But millions of his misguided and deluded followers accepted the forgiveness of this new ruler, known in that age as the Savior Sovereign of the system of Palonia. 119:2.5 (1311.4)
Return to Salvington:	And then came that eventful day on which there arrived the newly appointed System Sovereign, designated by the universe authorities as the permanent successor of the deposed Lutentia, and all Palonia mourned the departure of the most noble and the most benign system ruler that Nebadon had ever known. He was beloved by all the system and adored by his fellows of all groups of the Lanonandek Sons. His departure was not unceremonious; a great celebration was arranged when he left the system headquarters. Even his erring predecessor sent this message: "Just and righteous are you in all your ways. While I continue in rejection of the Paradise rule, I am compelled to confess that you are a just and merciful administrator." 119:2.6 (1311.5) And then did this transient ruler of a rebellious system take leave of the planet of his short administrative sojourn, while on the third day thereafter Michael appeared on Salvington and resumed the direction of the universe of Nebadon. 119:2.7 (1312.1)
The Third Bestowal Mission	
Appeared as:	Material Son acting Planetary Prince
Went to:	Planet 217 in system 87 in constellation 61
Leaving Salvington:	The supreme council on Salvington had just finished the consideration of the call of the Life Carriers on planet 217 in system 87 in constellation 61 for the dispatch to their assistance of a Material Son. Now this planet was situated in a system of inhabited worlds where another System Sovereign had gone astray, the second such rebellion in all Nebadon up to that time. 119:3.1 (1312.2) Upon the request of Michael, action on the petition of the Life Carriers of this planet was deferred pending its consideration by Immanuel and his report thereon. This was an irregular procedure, and I well remember how we all anticipated something unusual, and we were not long held in suspense. Michael proceeded to place universe direction in the hands of Immanuel, while he intrusted command of the celestial forces to Gabriel, and having thus disposed of his administrative responsibilities, he took leave of the Universe Mother Spirit and vanished from the dispatching field of Salvington precisely as he had done on two previous occasions. 119:3.2 (1312.3)
Mission:	And, as might have been expected, on the third day thereafter there appeared, unannounced, on the headquarters world of system 87 in constellation 61, a strange Material Son, accompanied by a lone seconaphim, accredited by the Uversa Ancients of Days, and certified by Immanuel of Salvington. 119:3.3 (1312.4)

Third Bestowal Mission: (Continued)	Thus did this unique Material Son begin his difficult career on a quarantined world of secession and rebellion, located in a beleaguered system without any direct communication with the outside universe, working alone for one whole generation of planetary time. This emergency Material Son effected the repentance and reclamation of the defaulting Planetary Prince and his entire staff and witnessed the restoration of the planet to the loyal service of the Paradise rule as established in the local universes. 119:3.4 (1312.5) I regret that I do not have permission to narrate the patience, fortitude, and skill with which this Material Son met the trying situations on this confused planet. The reclamation of this isolated world is one of the most beautifully touching chapters in the annals of salvation throughout Nebadon. By the end of this mission it had become evident to all Nebadon as to why their beloved ruler chose to engage in these repeated bestowals in the likeness of some subordinate order of intelligent being. 119:3.5 (1312.6) Never, since this marvelous bestowal as the Planetary Prince of a world in isolation and rebellion, have any of the Material Sons or Daughters in Nebadon been tempted to complain of their assignments or to find fault with the difficulties of their planetary missions. For all time the Material Sons know that in the Creator Son of the universe they have an understanding sovereign and a sympathetic friend, one who has in "all points been tried and tested," even as they must also be tried and tested. 119:3.7 (1313.2)
Third Bestowal Return to Salvington:	In due time a Material Son and Daughter arrived on this rejuvenated and redeemed world, and when they had been duly installed as visible planetary rulers, the transitory or emergency Planetary Prince took formal leave, disappearing at noon one day. On the third day thereafter, Michael appeared in his accustomed place on Salvington, and very soon the superuniverse broadcasts carried the fourth proclamation of the Ancients of Days announcing the further advancement of the sovereignty of Michael in Nebadon. 119:3.4 (1312.5)
The Fourth Bestowal Mission	
Appeared as:	Seraphim: seraphic teaching counselor
Went to:	Seraphic headquarters of Nebadon but served on 22 worlds
Leaving Salvington:	It was at the end of one of the periodic millennial roll calls of Uversa that Michael proceeded to place the government of Nebadon in the hands of Immanuel and Gabriel; and, of course, recalling what had happened in times past following such action, we all prepared to witness Michael's disappearance on his fourth mission of bestowal, and we were not long kept waiting, for he shortly went out upon the Salvington dispatching field and was lost to our view. 119:4.1 (1313.4)
Mission:	On the third day after this bestowal disappearance we observed, in the universe broadcasts to Uversa, this significant news item from the seraphic headquarters of Nebadon: "Reporting the unannounced arrival of an unknown seraphim, accompanied by a solitary supernaphim and Gabriel of Salvington. This unregistered seraphim qualifies as of the Nebadon order and bears credentials

The Fourth Bestowal—Mission: (Continued)	from the Uversa Ancients of Days, certified by Immanuel of Salvington. This seraphim tests out as belonging to the supreme order of the angels of a local universe and has already been assigned to the corps of the teaching counselors." 119:4.2 (1313.5) Michael was absent from Salvington during this, the seraphic bestowal, for a period of over forty standard universe years. During this time he was attached as a seraphic teaching counselor, what you might denominate a private secretary, to twenty-six different master teachers, functioning on twenty-two different worlds. His last or terminal assignment was as counselor and helper attached to a bestowal mission of a Trinity Teacher Son on world 462 in system 84 of constellation 3 in the universe of Nebadon. 119:4.3 (1313.6) Never, throughout the seven years of this assignment, was this Trinity Teacher Son wholly persuaded as to the identity of his seraphic associate. True, all seraphim during that age were regarded with peculiar interest and scrutiny. Full well we all knew that our beloved Sovereign was abroad in the universe, disguised as a seraphim, but never could we be certain of his identity. Never was he positively identified until the time of his attachment to the bestowal mission of this Trinity Teacher Son. But always throughout this era were the supreme seraphim regarded with special solicitude, lest any of us should find that we had unawares been host to the Sovereign of the universe on a mission of creature bestowal. And so it has become forever true, concerning angels, that their Creator and Ruler has been "in all points tried and tested in the likeness of seraphic personality." 119:4.4 (1314.1) Now has Michael passed through the bestowal experience of three orders of his created universe Sons: the Melchizedeks, the Lanonandeks, and the Material Sons. Next he condescends to personalize in the likeness of angelic life as a supreme seraphim before turning his attention to the various phases of the ascending careers of his lowest form of will creatures, the evolutionary mortals of time and space. 119:4.6 (1314.3)
Return to Salvington:	Not given
The Fifth Bestowal Mission	
Appeared as:	Eventod, ascending son
Went to:	Uversa, headquarters of the superuniverse of Orvonton
Leaving Salvington:	A little over three hundred million years ago, as time is reckoned on Urantia, we witnessed another of those transfers of universe authority to Immanuel and observed the preparations of Michael for departure. This occasion was different from the previous ones in that he announced that his destination was Uversa, headquarters of the superuniverse of Orvonton. In due time our Sovereign departed, but the broadcasts of the superuniverse never made mention of Michael's arrival at the courts of the Ancients of Days. Shortly after his departure

Leaving Salvington: (Continued)	from Salvington there did appear in the Uversa broadcasts this significant statement: "There arrived today an unannounced and unnumbered ascendant pilgrim of mortal origin from the universe of Nebadon, certified by Immanuel of Salvington and accompanied by Gabriel of Nebadon. This unidentified being presents the status of a true spirit and has been received into our fellowship." 119:5.1 (1314.4)
Mission:	If you should visit Uversa today, you would hear the recounting of the days when Eventod sojourned there, this particular and unknown pilgrim of time and space being known on Uversa by that name. And this ascending mortal, at least a superb personality in the exact likeness of the spirit stage of the ascending mortals, lived and functioned on Uversa for a period of eleven years of Orvonton standard time. This being received the assignments and performed the duties of a spirit mortal in common with his fellows from the various local universes of Orvonton. In "all points he was tested and tried, even as his fellows," and on all occasions he proved worthy of the confidence and trust of his superiors, while he unfailingly commanded the respect and loyal admiration of his fellow spirits. 119:5.2 (1314.5)
Return to Salvington:	On Salvington we followed the career of this spirit pilgrim with consummate interest, knowing full well, by the presence of Gabriel, that this unassuming and unnumbered pilgrim spirit was none other than the bestowed ruler of our local universe. This first appearance of Michael incarnated in the role of one stage of mortal evolution was an event which thrilled and enthralled all Nebadon. We had heard of such things but now we beheld them. He appeared on Uversa as a fully developed and perfectly trained spirit mortal and, as such, continued his career up to the occasion of the advancement of a group of ascending mortals to Havona; whereupon he held converse with the Ancients of Days and immediately, in the company of Gabriel, took sudden and unceremonious leave of Uversa, appearing shortly thereafter in his accustomed place on Salvington. 119:5.3 (1315.1)
The Sixth Bestowal Mission	
Appeared as:	A morontia mortal of evolutionary ascension
Went to:	Endantum
Leaving Salvington:	Now that all Salvington was familiar with the preliminaries of an impending bestowal, Michael called the sojourners on the headquarters planet together and, for the first time, unfolded the remainder of the incarnation plan, announcing that he was soon to leave Salvington for the purpose of assuming the career of a morontia mortal at the courts of the Most High Fathers on the headquarters planet of the fifth constellation. And then we heard for the first time the announcement that his seventh and final bestowal would be made on some evolutionary world in the likeness of mortal flesh. 119:6.1 (1315.4) Before leaving Salvington for the sixth bestowal, Michael addressed the assembled inhabitants of the sphere and departed in full view of everyone, accompanied by a lone seraphim and the Bright and Morning Star of Nebadon. While the direction of the universe had again been intrusted to Immanuel, there was a wider distribution of administrative responsibilities. 119:6.2 (1315.5)

The Seven Bestowals of Christ Michael

Mission:	Michael appeared on the headquarters of constellation five as a full-fledged morontia mortal of ascending status. I regret that I am forbidden to reveal the details of this unnumbered morontia mortal's career, for it was one of the most extraordinary and amazing epochs in Michael's bestowal experience, not even excepting his dramatic and tragic sojourn on Urantia. But among the many restrictions imposed upon me in accepting this commission is one which forbids my undertaking to unfold the details of this wonderful career of Michael as the morontia mortal of Endantum. 119:6.3 (1315.6)
Sixth Bestowal Return to Salvington:	When Michael returned from this morontia bestowal, it was apparent to all of us that our Creator had become a fellow creature, that the Universe Sovereign was also the friend and sympathetic helper of even the lowest form of created intelligence in his realms. We had noted this progressive acquirement of the creature's viewpoint in universe administration before this, for it had been gradually appearing, but it became more apparent after the completion of the morontia mortal bestowal, even still more so after his return from the career of the carpenter's son on Urantia. 119:6.4 (1316.1) We were informed in advance by Gabriel of the time of Michael's release from the morontia bestowal, and accordingly we arranged a suitable reception on Salvington. Millions upon millions of beings were assembled from the constellation headquarters worlds of Nebadon, and a majority of the sojourners on the worlds adjacent to Salvington were gathered together to welcome him back to the rulership of his universe. In response to our many addresses of welcome and expressions of appreciation of a Sovereign so vitally interested in his creatures, he only replied: "I have simply been about my Father's business. I am only doing the pleasure of the Paradise Sons who love and crave to understand their creatures." 119:6.5 (1316.2)
The Seventh Bestowal Mission	
Appeared as:	A Mortal in the flesh
Went to:	Urantia
Leaving Salvington:	The public announcement that Michael had selected Urantia as the theater for his final bestowal was made shortly after we learned about the default of Adam and Eve. And thus, for more than thirty-five thousand years, your world occupied a very conspicuous place in the councils of the entire universe. There was no secrecy (aside from the incarnation mystery) connected with any step in the Urantia bestowal. From first to last, up to the final and triumphant return of Michael to Salvington as supreme Universe Sovereign, there was the fullest universe publicity of all that transpired on your small but highly honored world. 119:7.2 (1316.5) While we believed that this would be the method, we never knew, until the time of the event itself, that Michael would appear on earth as a helpless infant of the realm. Theretofore had he always appeared as a fully developed individual of the personality group of the bestowal selection, and it was a thrilling announcement which was broadcast from Salvington telling that the babe of Bethlehem had been born on Urantia. 119:7.3 (1316.6)

Leaving Salvington: (Continued)	We then not only realized that our Creator and friend was taking the most precarious step in all his career, apparently risking his position and authority on this bestowal as a helpless infant, but we also understood that his experience in this final and mortal bestowal would eternally enthrone him as the undisputed and supreme sovereign of the universe of Nebadon. For a third of a century of earth time all eyes in all parts of this local universe were focused on Urantia. All intelligences realized that the last bestowal was in progress, and as we had long known of the Lucifer rebellion in Satania and of the Caligastia disaffection on Urantia, we well understood the intensity of the struggle which would ensue when our ruler condescended to incarnate on Urantia in the humble form and likeness of mortal flesh. 119:7.4 (1316.7)
Mission:	Joshua ben Joseph, the Jewish baby, was conceived and was born into the world just as all other babies before and since except that this particular baby was the incarnation of Michael of Nebadon, a divine Son of Paradise and the creator of all this local universe of things and beings. And this mystery of the incarnation of Deity within the human form of Jesus, otherwise of natural origin on the world, will forever remain unsolved. Even in eternity you will never know the technique and method of the incarnation of the Creator in the form and likeness of his creatures. That is the secret of Sonarington, and such mysteries are the exclusive possession of those divine Sons who have passed through the bestowal experience. 119:7.5 (1317.1)
Seventh Bestowal Return to Salvington:	"Among yourselves, here, you share the knowledge that I have risen from the dead, but that is not strange. I have the power to lay down my life and to take it up again; the Father gives such power to his Paradise Sons. You should the rather be stirred in your hearts by the knowledge that the dead of an age entered upon the eternal ascent soon after I left Joseph's new tomb. I lived my life in the flesh to show how you can, through loving service, become God- revealing to your fellow men even as, by loving you and serving you, I have become God-revealing to you. I have lived among you as the Son of Man that you, and all other men, might know that you are all indeed the sons of God. Therefore, go you now into all the world preaching this gospel of the kingdom of heaven to all men. Love all men as I have loved you; serve your fellow mortals as I have served you. Freely you have received, freely give. Only tarry here in Jerusalem while I go to the Father, and until I send you the Spirit of Truth. He shall lead you into the enlarged truth, and I will go with you into all the world. I am with you always, and my peace I leave with you." 193:0.5 (2053.1) When the Master had spoken to them, he vanished from their sight. It was near daybreak before these believers dispersed; all night they remained together, earnestly discussing the Master's admonitions and contemplating all that had befallen them. James Zebedee and others of the apostles also told them of their experiences with the morontia Master in Galilee and recited how he had three times appeared to them. 193:0.6 (2053.2)

The Seven Bestowals of Christ Michael

Results of the Bestowals

The bestowals of Michael as a Melchizedek Son, then as a Lanonandek Son, and next as a Material Son are all equally mysterious and beyond explanation. In each instance he appeared suddenly and as a fully developed individual of the bestowal group. The mystery of such incarnations will never be known except to those who have access to the inner circle of the records on the sacred sphere of Sonarington. 119:3.6 (1313.1)

Each of these missions was followed by an age of increasing service and loyalty among all celestial intelligences of universe origin, while each succeeding bestowal age was characterized by advancement and improvement in all methods of universe administration and in all techniques of government. Since this bestowal no Material Son or Daughter has ever knowingly joined in rebellion against Michael; they love and honor him too devotedly ever consciously to reject him. Only through deception and sophistry have the Adams of recent times been led astray by higher types of rebel personalities. 119:3.8 (1313.3)

These various will aspects of the Deities are eternally personalized in the differing natures of the Seven Master Spirits, and each of Michael's bestowals was peculiarly revelatory of one of these divinity manifestations. On his Melchizedek bestowal he manifested the united will of the Father, Son, and Spirit, on his Lanonandek bestowal the will of the Father and the Son; on the Adamic bestowal he revealed the will of the Father and the Spirit, on the seraphic bestowal the will of the Son and the Spirit; on the Uversa mortal bestowal he portrayed the will of the Conjoint Actor, on the morontia mortal bestowal the will of the Eternal Son; and on the Urantia material bestowal he lived the will of the Universal Father, even as a mortal of flesh and blood. 119:8.4 (1318.3)

The completion of these seven bestowals resulted in the liberation of Michael's supreme sovereignty and also in the creation of the possibility for the sovereignty of the Supreme in Nebadon. On none of Michael's bestowals did he reveal God the Supreme, but the sum total of all seven bestowals is a new Nebadon revelation of the Supreme Being. 119:8.5 (1318.4)

Michael's Postbestowal Status

After Michael's final and successful bestowal on Urantia he was not only accepted by the Ancients of Days as sovereign ruler of Nebadon, but he was also recognized by the Universal Father as the established director of the local universe of his own creation. Upon his return to Salvington this Michael, the Son of Man and the Son of God, was proclaimed the settled ruler of Nebadon. From Uversa came the eighth proclamation of Michael's sovereignty, while from Paradise came the joint pronouncement of the Universal Father and the Eternal Son constituting this union of God and man sole head of the universe and directing the Union of Days stationed on Salvington to signify his intention of withdrawing to Paradise. The Faithfuls of Days on the constellation headquarters were also instructed to retire from the councils of the Most Highs. But Michael would not consent to the withdrawal of the Trinity Sons of counsel and co-operation. He assembled them on Salvington and personally requested them forever to remain on duty in Nebadon. They signified their desire to comply with this request to their directors on Paradise, and shortly thereafter there were issued those mandates of Paradise divorcement which forever attached these Sons of the central universe to the court of Michael of Nebadon. 119:8.1 (1317.5)

The Seven Bestowals of Christ Michael

In completing his creature bestowals, Michael was not only establishing his own sovereignty but also was augmenting the evolving sovereignty of God the Supreme. In the course of these bestowals the Creator Son not only engaged in a descending exploration of the various natures of creature personality, but he also achieved the revelation of the variously diversified wills of the Paradise Deities, whose synthetic unity, as revealed by the Supreme Creators, is revelatory of the will of the Supreme Being. 119:8.3 (1318.2)

The completion of these seven bestowals resulted in the liberation of Michael's supreme sovereignty and also in the creation of the possibility for the sovereignty of the Supreme in Nebadon. On none of Michael's bestowals did he reveal God the Supreme, but the sum total of all seven bestowals is a new Nebadon revelation of the Supreme Being. 119:8.5 (1318.4)

In the experience of descending from God to man, Michael was concomitantly experiencing the ascent from partiality of manifestability to supremacy of finite action and finality of the liberation of his potential for absonite function. Michael, a Creator Son, is a time-space creator, but Michael, a sevenfold Master Son, is a member of one of the divine corps constituting the Trinity Ultimate. 119:8.6 (1318.5)

Urantia is the sentimental shrine of all Nebadon, the chief of ten million inhabited worlds, the mortal home of Christ Michael, sovereign of all Nebadon, a Melchizedek minister to the realms, a system savior, an Adamic redeemer, a seraphic fellow, an associate of ascending spirits, a morontia progressor, a Son of Man in the likeness of mortal flesh, and the Planetary Prince of Urantia. And your record tells the truth when it says that this same Jesus has promised sometime to return to the world of his terminal bestowal, the World of the Cross. 119:8.8 (1319.1)

The Lineage of Jesus

The Lineage of Jesus

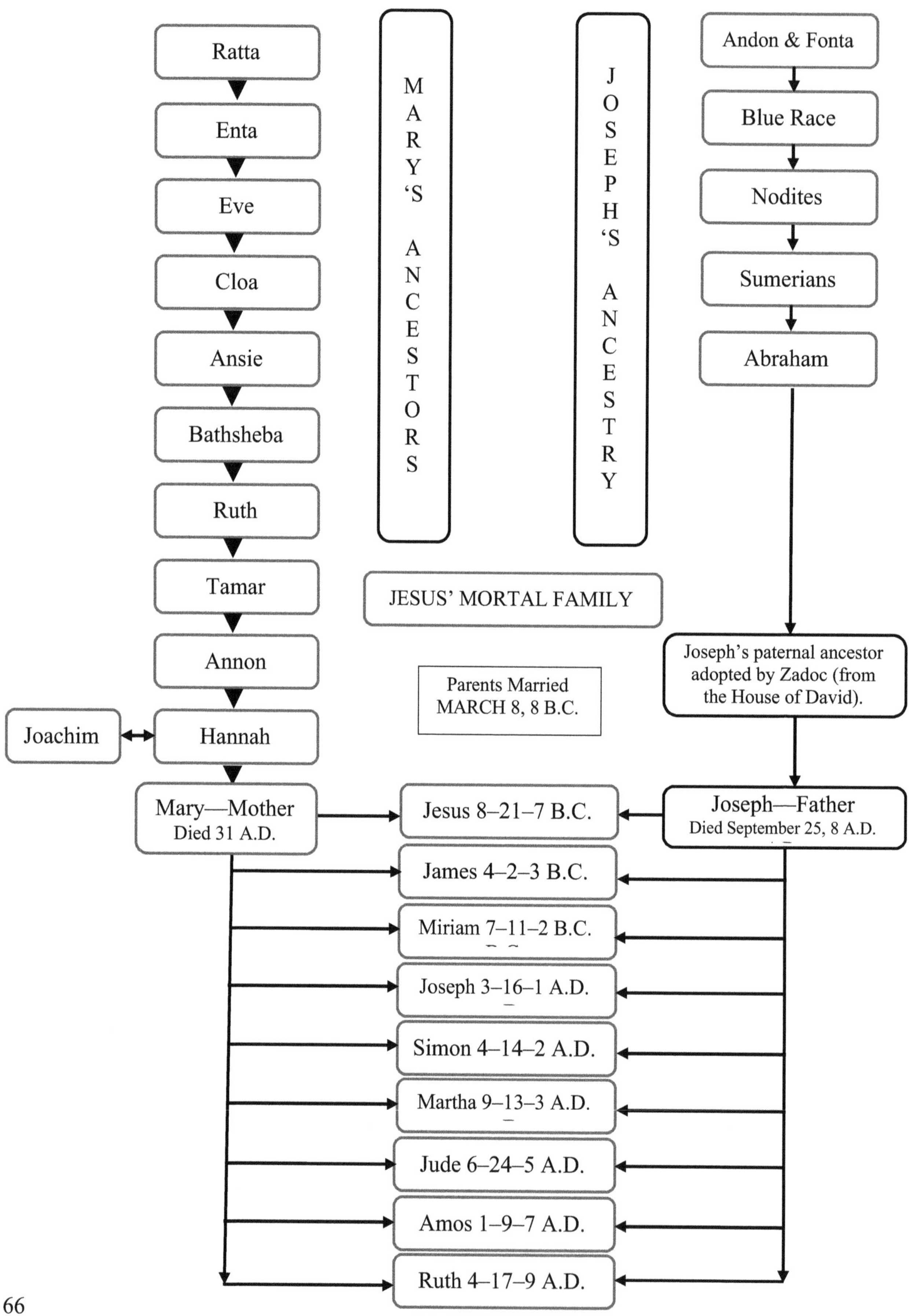

The Lineage of Jesus

Why Joseph and Mary?	IT WILL hardly be possible fully to explain the many reasons which led to the selection of Palestine as the land for Michael's bestowal, and especially as to just why the family of Joseph and Mary should have been chosen as the immediate setting for the appearance of this Son of God on Urantia. 122:0.1 (1344.1) Michael finally chose Urantia as the planet whereon to enact his final bestowal. Subsequent to this decision Gabriel made a personal visit to Urantia, and, as a result of his study of human groups and his survey of the spiritual, intellectual, racial, and geographic features of the world and its peoples, he decided that the Hebrews possessed those relative advantages which warranted their selection as the bestowal race. Upon Michael's approval of this decision, Gabriel appointed and dispatched to Urantia the Family Commission of Twelve—selected from among the higher orders of universe personalities—which was intrusted with the task of making an investigation of Jewish family life. When this commission ended its labors, Gabriel was present on Urantia and received the report nominating three prospective unions as being, in the opinion of the commission, equally favorable as bestowal families for Michael's projected incarnation. 122:0.2 (1344.2) From the three couples nominated, Gabriel made the personal choice of Joseph and Mary, subsequently making his personal appearance to Mary, at which time he imparted to her the glad tidings that she had been selected to become the earth mother of the bestowal child. 122:0.3 (1344.3)
Joseph: Human Father of Jesus:	Joseph, the human father of Jesus (Joshua ben Joseph), was a Hebrew of the Hebrews, albeit he carried many non-Jewish racial strains which had been added to his ancestral tree from time to time by the female lines of his progenitors. The ancestry of the father of Jesus went back to the days of Abraham and through this venerable patriarch to the earlier lines of inheritance leading to the Sumerians and Nodites and, through the southern tribes of the ancient blue man, to Andon and Fonta. David and Solomon were not in the direct line of Joseph's ancestry, neither did Joseph's lineage go directly back to Adam. Joseph's immediate ancestors were mechanics—builders, carpenters, masons, and smiths. Joseph himself was a carpenter and later a contractor. His family belonged to a long and illustrious line of the nobility of the common people, accentuated ever and anon by the appearance of unusual individuals who had distinguished themselves in connection with the evolution of religion on Urantia. 122:1.1 (1344.4)
	Joseph was not of the line of King David. Mary had more of the Davidic ancestry than Joseph. True, Joseph did go to the City of David, Bethlehem, to be registered for the Roman census, but that was because, six generations previously, Joseph's paternal ancestor of that generation, being an orphan, was adopted by one Zadoc, who was a direct descendant of David; hence was Joseph also accounted as of the "house of David." 122:4.3 (1347.5)
	Joseph was a mild-mannered man, extremely conscientious, and in every way faithful to the religious conventions and practices of his people. He talked little but thought much. The sorry plight of the Jewish people caused Joseph much sadness. As a youth, among his eight brothers and sisters, he had been more cheerful, but in

Joseph: Human Father of Jesus: (Continued)	the earlier years of married life (during Jesus' childhood) he was subject to periods of mild spiritual discouragement. These temperamental manifestations were greatly improved just before his untimely death and after the economic condition of his family had been enhanced by his advancement from the rank of carpenter to the role of a prosperous contractor. 122:5.1 (1348.1)
	All did go well until that fateful day of Tuesday, September 25, when a runner from Sepphoris brought to this Nazareth home the tragic news that Joseph had been severely injured by the falling of a derrick while at work on the governor's residence. The messenger from Sepphoris had stopped at the shop on the way toJoseph's home, informing Jesus of his father's accident, and they went together to the house to break the sad news to Mary. Jesus desired to go immediately to his father, but Mary would hear to nothing but that she must hasten to her husband's side. She directed that James, then ten years of age, should accompany her to Sepphoris while Jesus remained home with the younger children until she should return, as she did not know how seriously Joseph had been injured. But Joseph died of his injuries before Mary arrived. They brought him to Nazareth, and on the following day he was laid to rest with his fathers. 126:2.1 (1388.1)
Mary: Human Mother of Jesus:	Mary, the earth mother of Jesus, was a descendant of a long line of unique ancestors embracing many of the most remarkable women in the racial history of Urantia. Although Mary was an average woman of her day and generation, possessing a fairly normal temperament, she reckoned among her ancestors such well-known women as Annon, Tamar, Ruth, Bathsheba, Ansie, Cloa, Eve, Enta, and Ratta. No Jewish woman of that day had a more illustrious lineage of common progenitors or one extending back to more auspicious beginnings. Mary's ancestry, like Joseph's, was characterized by the predominance of strong but average individuals, relieved now and then by numerous outstanding personalities in the march of civilization and the progressive evolution of religion. Racially considered, it is hardly proper to regard Mary as a Jewess. In culture and belief she was a Jew, but in hereditary endowment she was more a composite of Syrian, Hittite, Phoenician, Greek, and Egyptian stocks, her racial inheritance being more general than that of Joseph. 122:1.2 (1345.1)
	Mary's temperament was quite opposite to that of her husband. She was usually cheerful, was very rarely downcast, and possessed an ever-sunny disposition. Mary indulged in free and frequent expression of her emotional feelings and was never observed to be sorrowful until after the sudden death of Joseph. And she had hardly recovered from this shock when she had thrust upon her the anxieties and questionings aroused by the extraordinary career of her eldest son, which was so rapidly unfolding before her astonished gaze. But throughout all this unusual experience Mary was composed, courageous, and fairly wise in her relationship with her strange and little-understood first-born son and his surviving brothers and sisters. 122:5.2 (1348.2)
	And so John and Jude led Mary away from Golgotha. John took the mother of Jesus to the place where he tarried in Jerusalem and then hastened back to the scene of the crucifixion. After the Passover Mary returned to Bethsaida, where she lived at John's

Mary: Human Mother of Jesus: (Continued)	home for the rest of her natural life. Mary did not live quite one year after the death of Jesus. 187:4.7 (2009.6)
	By ten thirty, one hundred and twenty of the foremost disciples of Jesus living in Jerusalem had forgathered to hear the report of the farewell message of the Master and to learn of his ascension. Among this company was Mary the mother of Jesus. She had returned to Jerusalem with John Zebedee when the apostles came back from their recent sojourn in Galilee. Soon after Pentecost she returned to the home of Salome at Bethsaida. 193:6.1 (2057.8)
	Both the mother and brother of Jesus were present among the one hundred and twenty believers, and as members of this common group of disciples, they also received the outpoured spirit. They received no more of the good gift than did their fellows. No special gift was bestowed upon the members of Jesus' earthly family. 194:3.15 (2065.3)
Joseph and Mary as Parents:	Jesus derived much of his unusual gentleness and marvelous sympathetic understanding of human nature from his father; he inherited his gift as a great teacher and his tremendous capacity for righteous indignation from his mother. In emotional reactions to his adult-life environment, Jesus was at one time like his father, meditative and worshipful, sometimes characterized by apparent sadness; but more often he drove forward in the manner of his mother's optimistic and determined disposition. All in all, Mary's temperament tended to dominate the career of the divine Son as he grew up and swung into the momentous strides of his adult life. In some particulars Jesus was a blending of his parents' traits; in other respects he exhibited the traits of one in contrast with those of the other. 122:5.3 (1348.3) From Joseph Jesus secured his strict training in the usages of the Jewish ceremonials and his unusual acquaintance with the Hebrew scriptures; from Mary he derived a broader viewpoint of religious life and a more liberal concept of personal spiritual freedom. 122:5.4 (1348.4) The families of both Joseph and Mary were well educated for their time. Joseph and Mary were educated far above the average for their day and station in life. He was a thinker; she was a planner, expert in adaptation and practical in immediate execution. Joseph was a black-eyed brunet; Mary, a brown-eyed well-nigh blond type. 122:5.5 (1349.1) Had Joseph lived, he undoubtedly would have become a firm believer in the divine mission of his eldest son. Mary alternated between believing and doubting, being greatly influenced by the position taken by her other children and by her friends and relatives, but always was she steadied in her final attitude by the memory of Gabriel's appearance to her immediately after the child was conceived. 122:5.6 (1349.2) Mary was an expert weaver and more than averagely skilled in most of the household arts of that day; she was a good housekeeper and a superior homemaker. Both Joseph and Mary were good teachers, and they saw to it that their children were well versed in the learning of that day. 122:5.7 (1349.3)

Joseph and Mary as Parents (Continued):	When Joseph was a young man, he was employed by Mary's father in the work of building an addition to his house, and it was when Mary brought Joseph a cup of water, during a noontime meal, that the courtship of the pair who were destined to become the parents of Jesus really began. 122:5.8 (1349.4) Joseph and Mary were married, in accordance with Jewish custom, at Mary's home in the environs of Nazareth when Joseph was twenty-one years old. This marriage concluded a normal courtship of almost two years' duration. Shortly thereafter they moved into their new home in Nazareth, which had been built by Joseph with the assistance of two of his brothers. The house was located near the foot of the near-by elevated land which so charmingly overlooked the surrounding countryside. In this home, especially prepared, these young and expectant parents had thought to welcome the child of promise, little realizing that this momentous event of a universe was to transpire while they would be absent from home in Bethlehem of Judea. 122:5.9 (1349.5) The larger part of Joseph's family became believers in the teachings of Jesus, but very few of Mary's people ever believed in him until after he departed from this world. Joseph leaned more toward the spiritual concept of the expected Messiah, but Mary and her family, especially her father, held to the idea of the Messiah as a temporal deliverer and political ruler. Mary's ancestors had been prominently identified with the Maccabean activities of the then but recent times. 122:5.10 (1349.6) Joseph held vigorously to the Eastern, or Babylonian, views of the Jewish religion; Mary leaned strongly toward the more liberal and broader Western, or Hellenistic, interpretation of the law and the prophets. 122:5.11 (1349.7)

Educational Experience of Jesus

Educational Experience of Jesus

TIME PERIOD	EDUCATIONAL EXPERIENCE
Before Third Birthday:	Throughout the two years of their sojourn at Alexandria, Jesus enjoyed good health and continued to grow normally. Aside from a few friends and relatives no one was told about Jesus' being a "child of promise." One of Joseph's relatives revealed this to a few friends in Memphis, descendants of the distant Ikhnaton, and they, with a small group of Alexandrian believers, assembled at the palatial home of Joseph's relative-benefactor a short time before the return to Palestine to wish the Nazareth family well and to pay their respects to the child. On this occasion the assembled friends presented Jesus with a complete copy of the Greek translation of the Hebrew scriptures. But this copy of the Jewish sacred writings was not placed in Joseph's hands until both he and Mary had finally declined the invitation of their Memphis and Alexandrian friends to remain in Egypt. These believers insisted that the child of destiny would be able to exert a far greater world influence as a resident of Alexandria than of any designated place in Palestine. These persuasions delayed their departure for Palestine for some time after they received the news of Herod's death. 123:0.3 (1355:3)
The Fourth Year:	Jesus was about three years and two months old at the time of their return to Nazareth. He had stood all these travels very well and was in excellent health and full of childish glee and excitement at having premises of his own to run about in and to enjoy. But he greatly missed the association of his Alexandrian playmates. 123:1.2 (1356:5)
	Jesus' entire fourth year was a period of normal physical development and of unusual mental activity. Meantime he had formed a very close attachment for a neighbor boy about his own age named Jacob. Jesus and Jacob were always happy in their play, and they grew up to be great friends and loyal companions. 123:1.4 (1357:1)
	The next important event in the life of this Nazareth family was the birth of the second child, James, in the early morning hours of April 2, 3 B.C. Jesus was thrilled by the thought of having a baby brother, and he would stand around by the hour just to observe the baby's early activities. 123:1.5 (1357.2)
	It was midsummer of this same year that Joseph built a small workshop close to the village spring and near the caravan tarrying lot. After this he did very little carpenter work by the day. He had as associates two of his brothers and several other mechanics, whom he sent out to work while he remained at the shop making yokes and plows and doing other woodwork. He also did some work in leather and with rope and canvas. And Jesus, as he grew up, when not at school, spent his time about equally between helping his mother with home duties and watching his father work at the shop, meanwhile listening to the conversation and gossip of the caravan conductors and passengers from the four corners of the earth. 123:1.6 (1357.3) In July of this year, one month before Jesus was four years old, an outbreak of malignant intestinal trouble spread over all Nazareth from contact with the

Educational Experience of Jesus

The Fourth Year: (Continued)	caravan travelers. Mary became so alarmed by the danger of Jesus being exposed to this epidemic of disease that she bundled up both her children and fled to the country home of her brother, several miles south of Nazareth on the Megiddo road near Sarid. They did not return to Nazareth for more than two months; Jesus greatly enjoyed this, his first experience on a farm. 123:1.7 (1357.4)
The Fifth Year:	In something more than a year after the return to Nazareth the boy Jesus arrived at the age of his first personal and wholehearted moral decision; and there came to abide with him a Thought Adjuster, a divine gift of the Paradise Father, which had aforetime served with Machiventa Melchizedek, thus gaining the experience of functioning in connection with the incarnation of a supermortal being living in the likeness of mortal flesh. This event occurred on February 11, 2 B.C. 123:2.1 (1357:5)
	It was the custom of the Galilean Jews for the mother to bear the responsibility for a child's training until the fifth birthday, and then, if the child were a boy, to hold the father responsible for the lad's education from that time on. This year, therefore, Jesus entered upon the fifth stage of a Galilean Jewish child's career, and accordingly on August 21, 2 B.C., Mary formally turned him over to Joseph for further instruction. 123:2.13 (1358.10) Though Joseph was now assuming the direct responsibility for Jesus' intellectual and religious education, his mother still interested herself in his home training. She taught him to know and care for the vines and flowers growing about the garden walls which completely surrounded the home plot. She also provided on the roof of the house (the summer bedroom) shallow boxes of sand in which Jesus worked out maps and did much of his early practice at writing Aramaic, Greek, and later on, Hebrew, for in time he learned to read, write, and speak, fluently, all three languages. 123:2.14 (1358.11)
	In this year, 2 B.C., a little more than one month before his fifth birthday, Jesus was made very happy by the coming of his sister Miriam, who was born on the night of July 11. During the evening of the following day Jesus had a long talk with his father concerning the manner in which various groups of living things are born into the world as separate individuals. The most valuable part of Jesus' early education was secured from his parents in answer to his thoughtful and searching inquiries. Joseph never failed to do his full duty in taking pains and spending time answering the boy's numerous questions. From the time Jesus was five years old until he was ten, he was one continuous question mark. 123:2.3 (1357.7)
The Sixth Year:	Already, with his mother's help, Jesus had mastered the Galilean dialect of the Aramaic tongue; and now his father began teaching him Greek. The textbook for the study of the Greek language was the copy of the Hebrew scriptures—a complete version of the law and the prophets, including the Psalms—which had been presented to them on leaving Egypt. There were only two complete copies of the Scriptures in Greek in all Nazareth, and the possession of one of them by the carpenter's family made Joseph's home a much-sought place and enabled Jesus, as he grew up, to meet an almost endless procession of earnest students and sincere truth seekers. 123:3.1 (1359:2)

Educational Experience of Jesus

The Sixth Year: (Continued)	The first great shock of Jesus' young life occurred when he was not quite six years old. It had seemed to the lad that his father—at least his father and mother together—knew everything. Imagine, therefore, the surprise of this inquiring child, when he asked his father the cause of a mild earthquake which had just occurred, to hear Joseph say, "My son, I really do not know." Thus began that long and disconcerting disillusionment in the course of which Jesus found out that his earthly parents were not all-wise and all-knowing. 123:3.2 (1359.3)
	Having met John, who came from near Jerusalem, Jesus began to evince an unusual interest in the history of Israel and to inquire in great detail as to the meaning of the Sabbath rites, the synagogue sermons, and the recurring feasts of commemoration. His father explained to him the meaning of all these seasons. 123:3.5 (1359.6)
	This year Jesus made great progress in adjusting his strong feelings and vigorous impulses to the demands of family co-operation and home discipline. Mary was a loving mother but a fairly strict disciplinarian. In many ways, however, Joseph exerted the greater control over Jesus as it was his practice to sit down with the boy and fully explain the real and underlying reasons for the necessity of disciplinary curtailment of personal desires in deference to the welfare and tranquility of the entire family. 123:3.9 (1360:4)
	Much of his spare time—when his mother did not require his help about the house—was spent studying the flowers and plants by day and the stars by night. He evinced a troublesome penchant for lying on his back and gazing wonderingly up into the starry heavens long after his usual bedtime in this well-ordered Nazareth household. 123:3.10 (1360:5)
The Seventh Year:	The play life of Jewish children in the times of Jesus was rather circumscribed; all too often the children played at the more serious things they observed their elders doing. They played much at weddings and funerals, ceremonies which they so frequently saw and which were so spectacular. They danced and sang but had few organized games, such as children of later days so much enjoy. 123:4.2 (1361:2)
	Jesus was now seven years old, the age when Jewish children were supposed to begin their formal education in the synagogue schools. Accordingly, in August of this year he entered upon his eventful school life at Nazareth. Already this lad was a fluent reader, writer, and speaker of two languages, Aramaic and Greek. He was now to acquaint himself with the task of learning to read, write, and speak the Hebrew language. And he was truly eager for the new school life which was ahead of him. 123:5.1 (1362.2) For three years—until he was ten—he attended the elementary school of the Nazareth synagogue. For these three years he studied the rudiments of the Book of the Law as it was recorded in the Hebrew tongue. For the following three years he studied in the advanced school and committed to memory, by the method of repeating aloud, the deeper teachings of the sacred law. 123:5.2 (1362.3)

<table>
<tr><td rowspan="3">The Seventh Year: (Continued)</td><td>At Nazareth the pupils sat on the floor in a semicircle, while their teacher, the chazan, an officer of the synagogue, sat facing them. Beginning with the Book of Leviticus, they passed on to the study of the other books of the law, followed by the study of the Prophets and the Psalms. The Nazareth synagogue possessed a complete copy of the Scriptures in Hebrew. Nothing but the Scriptures was studied prior to the twelfth year. In the summer months the hours for school were greatly shortened. 123:5.3 (1362.4)

Jesus early became a master of Hebrew, and as a young man, when no visitor of prominence happened to be sojourning in Nazareth, he would often be asked to read the Hebrew scriptures to the faithful assembled in the synagogue at the regular Sabbath services. 123:5.4 (1362.5)

These synagogue schools, of course, had no textbooks. In teaching, the chazan would utter a statement while the pupils would in unison repeat it after him. When having access to the written books of the law, the student learned his lesson by reading aloud and by constant repetition. 123:5.5 (1362.6)

Next, in addition to his more formal schooling, Jesus began to make contact with human nature from the four quarters of the earth as men from many lands passed in and out of his father's repair shop. When he grew older, he mingled freely with the caravans as they tarried near the spring for rest and nourishment. Being a fluent speaker of Greek, he had little trouble in conversing with the majority of the caravan travelers and conductors. 123:5.6 (1362.7)</td></tr>
<tr><td>Jesus received his moral training and spiritual culture chiefly in his own home. He secured much of his intellectual and theological education from the chazan. But his real education—that equipment of mind and heart for the actual test of grappling with the difficult problems of life—he obtained by mingling with his fellow men. It was this close association with his fellow men, young and old, Jew and gentile, that afforded him the opportunity to know the human race. Jesus was highly educated in that he thoroughly understood men and devotedly loved them. 123:5.8 (1363.1)

Throughout his years at the synagogue he was a brilliant student, possessing a great advantage since he was conversant with three languages. The Nazareth chazan, on the occasion of Jesus' finishing the course in his school, remarked to Joseph that he feared he "had learned more from Jesus' searching questions" than he had "been able to teach the lad." 123:5.9 (1363.2)

Throughout his course of study Jesus learned much and derived great inspiration from the regular Sabbath sermons in the synagogue. It was customary to ask distinguished visitors, stopping over the Sabbath in Nazareth, to address the synagogue. As Jesus grew up, he heard many great thinkers of the entire Jewish world expound their views, and many also who were hardly orthodox Jews since the synagogue of Nazareth was an advanced and liberal center of Hebrew thought and culture. 123:5.10 (1363.3)</td></tr>
<tr><td>When entering school at seven years (at this time the Jews had just inaugurated a compulsory education law), it was customary for the pupils to choose their</td></tr>
</table>

The Seventh Year: (Continued)	"birthday text," a sort of golden rule to guide them throughout their studies, one upon which they often expatiated at their graduation when thirteen years old. The text which Jesus chose was from the Prophet Isaiah: "The spirit of the Lord God is upon me, for the Lord has anointed me; he has sent me to bring good news to the meek, to bind up the brokenhearted, to proclaim liberty to the captives, and to set the spiritual prisoners free." 123:5.11 (1363.4)
	When they did not climb the heights to view the distant landscape, they strolled through the countryside and studied nature in her various moods in accordance with the seasons. Jesus' earliest training, aside from that of the home hearth, had to do with a reverent and sympathetic contact with nature. 123:5.14 (1364.2) Before he was eight years of age, he was known to all the mothers and young women of Nazareth, who had met him and talked with him at the spring, which was not far from his home, and which was one of the social centers of contact and gossip for the entire town. This year Jesus learned to milk the family cow and care for the other animals. During this and the following year he also learned to make cheese and to weave. When he was ten years of age, he was an expert loom operator. It was about this time that Jesus and the neighbor boy Jacob became great friends of the potter who worked near the flowing spring; and as they watched Nathan's deft fingers mold the clay on the potter's wheel, many times both of them determined to be potters when they grew up. Nathan was very fond of the lads and often gave them clay to play with, seeking to stimulate their creative imaginations by suggesting competitive efforts in modeling various objects and animals. 123:5.15 (1364.3)
The Eighth Year:	This was an interesting year at school. Although Jesus was not an unusual student, he was a diligent pupil and belonged to the more progressive third of the class, doing his work so well that he was excused from attendance one week out of each month. This week he usually spent either with his fisherman uncle on the shores of the Sea of Galilee near Magdala or on the farm of another uncle (his mother's brother) five miles south of Nazareth. 123:6.1 (1364:4)
	About this time Jesus met a teacher of mathematics from Damascus, and learning some new techniques of numbers, he spent much time on mathematics for several years. He developed a keen sense of numbers, distances, and proportions. 123:6.3 (1364.6) Jesus began to enjoy his brother James very much and by the end of this year had begun to teach him the alphabet. 123:6.4 (1364.7)
	This year Jesus made arrangements to exchange dairy products for lessons on the harp. He had an unusual liking for everything musical. Later on he did much to promote an interest in vocal music among his youthful associates. By the time he was eleven years of age, he was a skillful harpist and greatly enjoyed entertaining both family and friends with his extraordinary interpretations and able improvisations. 123:6.5 (1364:8)

Educational Experience of Jesus

<table>
<tr><td>The Ninth Year:</td><td>Jesus continued to grow physically, intellectually, socially, and spiritually. His trips away from home did much to give him a better and more generous understanding of his own family, and by this time even his parents were beginning to learn from him as well as to teach him. Jesus was an original thinker and a skillful teacher, even in his youth. He was in constant collision with the so-called "oral law," but he always sought to adapt himself to the practices of his family. He got along fairly well with the children of his age, but he often grew discouraged with their slow-acting minds. Before he was ten years old, he had become the leader of a group of seven lads who formed themselves into a society for promoting the acquirements of manhood—physical, intellectual, and religious. Among these boys Jesus succeeded in introducing many new games and various improved methods of physical recreation. 124:1.13 (1368:2)</td></tr>
<tr><td rowspan="2">The Tenth Year:</td><td>He entered the advanced school of the synagogue in August. At school he was constantly creating trouble by the questions he persisted in asking. Increasingly he kept all Nazareth in more or less of a hubbub. His parents were loath to forbid his asking these disquieting questions, and his chief teacher was greatly intrigued by the lad's curiosity, insight, and hunger for knowledge. 124:2.2 (1368:4)</td></tr>
<tr><td>This year he began to show a marked preference for the company of older persons. He delighted in talking over things cultural, educational, social, economic, political, and religious with older minds, and his depth of reasoning and keenness of observation so charmed his adult associates that they were always more than willing to visit with him. Until he became responsible for the support of the home, his parents were constantly seeking to influence him to associate with those of his own age, or more nearly his age, rather than with older and better-informed individuals for whom he evinced such a preference. 124:2.6 (1369.2)

Late this year he had a fishing experience of two months with his uncle on the Sea of Galilee, and he was very successful. Before attaining manhood, he had become an expert fisherman. 124:2.7 (1369.3)</td></tr>
<tr><td rowspan="2">The Eleventh Year:</td><td>Jesus spent considerable time at the caravan supply shop, and by conversing with the travelers from all parts of the world, he acquired a store of information about international affairs that was amazing, considering his age. This was the last year in which he enjoyed much free play and youthful joyousness. From this time on difficulties and responsibilities rapidly multiplied in the life of this youth. 124:3.3 (1370:1)</td></tr>
<tr><td>The chazan spent one evening each week with Jesus, helping him to master the Hebrew scriptures. He was greatly interested in the progress of his promising pupil; therefore was he willing to assist him in many ways. This Jewish pedagogue exerted a great influence upon this growing mind, but he was never able to comprehend why Jesus was so indifferent to all his suggestions regarding the prospects of going to Jerusalem to continue his education under the learned rabbis. 124:3.5 (1370:3)</td></tr>
</table>

Educational Experience of Jesus

The Twelfth Year:	This year Jesus paid more attention than ever to music, and he continued to teach the home school for his brothers and sisters. It was at about this time that the lad became keenly conscious of the difference between the viewpoints of Joseph and Mary regarding the nature of his mission. He pondered much over his parents' differing opinions, often hearing their discussions when they thought he was sound asleep. 124:4.5 (1372:2)
	During his last year at school, when he was twelve years old, Jesus remonstrated with his father about the Jewish custom of touching the bit of parchment nailed upon the doorpost each time on going into, or coming out of, the house and then kissing the finger that touched the parchment. As a part of this ritual it was customary to say, "The Lord shall preserve our going out and our coming in, from this time forth and even forevermore." Joseph and Mary had repeatedly instructed Jesus as to the reasons for not making images or drawing pictures, explaining that such creations might be used for idolatrous purposes. Though Jesus failed fully to grasp their proscriptions against images and pictures, he possessed a high concept of consistency and therefore pointed out to his father the essentially idolatrous nature of this habitual obeisance to the doorpost parchment. And Joseph removed the parchment after Jesus had thus remonstrated with him. 124:4.7 (1372:4)
The Thirteenth Year:	He graduated from this school of the synagogue during his thirteenth year and was turned over to his parents by the synagogue rulers as an educated "son of the commandment"—henceforth a responsible citizen of the commonwealth of Israel, all of which entailed his attendance at the Passovers in Jerusalem; accordingly, he attended his first Passover that year in company with his father and mother. 123:5.2 (1362.3)
	On the first day of the week, March 20, A.D. 7, Jesus graduated from the course of training in the local school connected with the Nazareth synagogue. This was a great day in the life of any ambitious Jewish family, the day when the first-born son was pronounced a "son of the commandment" and the ransomed first-born of the Lord God of Israel, a "child of the Most High" and servant of the Lord of all the earth. 124:5.4 (1373:4)
	They now passed down to the priests' court beneath the rock ledge in front of the temple, where the altar stood, to observe the killing of the droves of animals and the washing away of the blood from the hands of the officiating slaughter priests at the bronze fountain. The bloodstained pavement, the gory hands of the priests, and the sounds of the dying animals were more than this nature-loving lad could stand. The terrible sight sickened this boy of Nazareth; he clutched his father's arm and begged to be taken away. They walked back through the court of the gentiles, and even the coarse laughter and profane jesting which he there heard were a relief from the sights he had just beheld. 125:1.4 (1378.6)

Educational Experience of Jesus

The Thirteenth Year: (Continued)	At the second conference Jesus had made bold to ask questions, and in a very amazing way he participated in the temple discussions but always in a manner consistent with his youth. Sometimes his pointed questions were somewhat embarrassing to the learned teachers of the Jewish law, but he evinced such a spirit of candid fairness, coupled with an evident hunger for knowledge, that the majority of the temple teachers were disposed to treat him with every consideration. But when he presumed to question the justice of putting to death a drunken gentile who had wandered outside the court of the gentiles and unwittingly entered the forbidden and reputedly sacred precincts of the temple, one of the more intolerant teachers grew impatient with the lad's implied criticisms and, glowering down upon him, asked how old he was. Jesus replied, "thirteen years lacking a trifle more than four months." "Then," rejoined the now irate teacher, "why are you here, since you are not of age as a son of the law?" And when Jesus explained that he had received consecration during the Passover, and that he was a finished student of the Nazareth schools, the teachers with one accord derisively replied, "We might have known; he is from Nazareth." But the leader insisted that Jesus was not to be blamed if the rulers of the synagogue at Nazareth had graduated him, technically, when he was twelve instead of thirteen; and notwithstanding that several of his detractors got up and left, it was ruled that the lad might continue undisturbed as a pupil of the temple discussions. 125:4.3 (1382.1)
The Fourteenth Year:	He continued to carry on his advanced courses of reading under the synagogue teachers, and he also continued with the home education of his brothers and sisters as they grew up to suitable ages. 126:1.3 (1387:3)
	The improved economic condition of the Nazareth family was reflected in many ways about the home and especially in the increased number of smooth white boards which were used as writing slates, the writing being done with charcoal. Jesus was also permitted to resume his music lessons; he was very fond of playing the harp. 126:1.6 (1387.6)
The Fifteenth Year:	On Wednesday evening, April 17, A.D. 9, Ruth, the baby of the family, was born, and to the best of his ability Jesus endeavored to take the place of his father in comforting and ministering to his mother during this trying and peculiarly sad ordeal. For almost a score of years (until he began his public ministry) no father could have loved and nurtured his daughter any more affectionately and faithfully than Jesus cared for little Ruth. And he was an equally good father to all the other members of his family. 126:3.2 (1389.5)
	While turning all these problems over in his mind, he found in the synagogue library at Nazareth, among the apocalyptic books which he had been studying, this manuscript called "The Book of Enoch"; and though he was certain that it had not been written by Enoch of old, it proved very intriguing to him, and he read and reread it many times. There was one passage which particularly impressed him, a passage in which this term "Son of Man" appeared. The writer of this so-called Book of Enoch went on to tell about this Son of Man, describing the work

The Fifteenth Year: (Continued)	he would do on earth and explaining that this Son of Man, before coming down on this earth to bring salvation to mankind, had walked through the courts of heavenly glory with his Father, the Father of all; and that he had turned his back upon all this grandeur and glory to come down on earth to proclaim salvation to needy mortals. As Jesus would read these passages (well understanding that much of the Eastern mysticism which had become admixed with these teachings was erroneous), he responded in his heart and recognized in his mind that of all the Messianic predictions of the Hebrew scriptures and of all the theories about the Jewish deliverer, none was so near the truth as this story tucked away in this only partially accredited Book of Enoch; and he then and there decided to adopt as his inaugural title "the Son of Man." And this he did when he subsequently began his public work. Jesus had an unerring ability for the recognition of truth, and truth he never hesitated to embrace, no matter from what source it appeared to emanate. 126:3.8 (1390.3)
The Sixteenth Year:	This physically strong and robust youth also acquired the full growth of his human intellect, not the full experience of human thinking but the fullness of capacity for such intellectual development. He possessed a healthy and well-proportioned body, a keen and analytical mind, a kind and sympathetic disposition, a somewhat fluctuating but aggressive temperament, all of which were becoming organized into a strong, striking, and attractive personality. 127:1.3 (1395:7)
The Seventeenth Year:	Jesus, then scarcely seventeen years of age, was confronted with one of the most delicate and difficult situations of his early life. Patriotic issues, especially when complicated by tax-gathering foreign oppressors, are always difficult for spiritual leaders to relate themselves to, and it was doubly so in this case since the Jewish religion was involved in all this agitation against Rome. 127:2.6 (1397.4)
The Eighteenth Year:	For four years their standard of living had steadily declined; year by year they felt the pinch of increasing poverty. By the close of this year they faced one of the most difficult experiences of all their uphill struggles. James had not yet begun to earn much, and the expenses of a funeral on top of everything else staggered them. But Jesus would only say to his anxious and grieving mother: "Mother-Mary, sorrow will not help us; we are all doing our best, and mother's smile, perchance, might even inspire us to do better. Day by day we are strengthened for these tasks by our hope of better days ahead." His sturdy and practical optimism was truly contagious; all the children lived in an atmosphere of anticipation of better times and better things. And this hopeful courage contributed mightily to the development of strong and noble characters, in spite of the depressiveness of their poverty. 127:3.14 (1400.6) Jesus possessed the ability effectively to mobilize all his powers of mind, soul, and body on the task immediately in hand. He could concentrate his deep-thinking mind on the one problem which he wished to solve, and this, in connection with his untiring patience, enabled him serenely to endure the trials of a difficult mortal existence— to live as if he were "seeing Him who is invisible." 127:3.15 (1400.7)

Educational Experience of Jesus

The Nineteenth Year:	Jesus began wise discipline upon his brothers and sisters at such an early age that little or no punishment was ever required to secure their prompt and wholehearted obedience. The only exception was Jude, upon whom on sundry occasions Jesus found it necessary to impose penalties for his infractions of the rules of the home. On three occasions when it was deemed wise to punish Jude for self-confessed and deliberate violations of the family rules of conduct, his punishment was fixed by the unanimous decree of the older children and was assented to by Jude himself before it was inflicted. 127:4.3 (1401:3)
The Twentieth Year:	As a child he accumulated a vast body of knowledge; as a youth he sorted, classified, and correlated this information; and now as a man of the realm he begins to organize these mental possessions preparatory to utilization in his subsequent teaching, ministry, and service in behalf of his fellow mortals on this world and on all other spheres of habitation throughout the entire universe of Nebadon. 127:6.14 (1405.6)
	And now as a full-grown man—an adult of the realm—he prepares to continue his supreme mission of revealing God to men and leading men to God. 127:6.16 (1406:1)
22 A.D. Jesus' 28th Year:	The real purpose of his trip around the Mediterranean basin was to know men. He came very close to hundreds of humankind on this journey. He met and loved all manner of men, rich and poor, high and low, black and white, educated and uneducated, cultured and uncultured, animalistic and spiritual, religious and irreligious, moral and immoral. 129:3.8 (1424.3) On this Mediterranean journey Jesus made great advances in his human task of mastering the material and mortal mind, and his indwelling Adjuster made great progress in the ascension and spiritual conquest of this same human intellect. By the end of this tour Jesus virtually knew—with all human certainty—that he was a Son of God, a Creator Son of the Universal Father. The Adjuster more and more was able to bring up in the mind of the Son of Man shadowy memories of his Paradise experience in association with his divine Father ere he ever came to organize and administer this local universe of Nebadon. Thus did the Adjuster, little by little, bring to Jesus' human consciousness those necessary memories of his former and divine existence in the various epochs of the well-nigh eternal past. The last episode of his prehuman experience to be brought forth by the Adjuster was his farewell conference with Immanuel of Salvington just before his surrender of conscious personality to embark upon the Urantia incarnation. And this final memory picture of prehuman existence was made clear in Jesus' consciousness on the very day of his baptism by John in the Jordan. 129:3.9 (1424.4)

Timetable of Personal Ministry of Jesus

Timetable of Personal Ministry of Jesus

Time Period	Personal Ministry Activity	Reference
A.D. 22 Jesus' 28th Year:	This fascinating period of Jesus' personal ministry was conducted by the human Jesus, the Son of Man.	129:4.1 (1424:5)
	Most of the 28th and the entire 29th year of Jesus' life was spent on tour of the Roman world. Throughout this tour he was known as the "Damascus scribe."	129:3.3 (1423:5)
	On Sunday morning, April 26, Jesus and two natives from India, Gonod and his son, Ganid, left Jerusalem.	130:0.1 (1427:1)
	AT JOPPA: • Talk with Gadiah, a Philistine interpreter, about Jonah.	130:1.1 (1428:1)
	AT CAESAREA: • (The living of heavenly life while on earth...) • Talk at inn with merchant from Mongolia • Jesus talks to Ganid about human will.	130:2.1 (1429:3) 130:2.2 (1429:4) 130:2.7 (1431:2)
	AT ALEXANDRIA: (IN EGYPT) • Approaching the city's harbor Jesus remarked to Ganid about the lighthouse. Jesus and Ganid visited Alexandria library (greatest in world then). • Ganid made a collection of the world's religions about God and his relation to mortal man. • Visit with one of government professors at the university. • Discourse on Reality.	130:3.2 (1432:2) 130:3.5 (1432:5) 130:4.1 (1433:6)
	ON THE ISLAND OF CRETE: • Talk with Gonod about religion. • Visit to Fair Havens. Personal encounter with drunken degenerate and slave girl. • Jesus' talk with Fortune, the young man who was afraid.	130:5.2 (1436:3) 130:5.4 (1436:5) 130:6.1 (1437:1)
	TWO-DAY STOP AT CYRENE: • First aid to a lad, Rufus.	130:6.6 (1438:3)
	AT CARTHAGE: • Jesus tells Ganid what one could do to make friends. • Talk with Mithraic priest. • Discourse on time and space.	130:7.2 (1438:5) 130:7.3 (1439:1) 130:7.4 (1439:2)
	STOP AT ISLAND OF MALTA: • Talk with discouraged young man named Claudus.	130:8.1 (1440:1)

Timetable of Personal Ministry of Jesus

A.D. 22 Jesus' 28th Year: (Continued)	AT SYRACUSE: (Spent full week here) • Rehabilitation of Ezra, the backslidden Jew.	130:8.2 (1440:2)
	ONE DAY AT MESSINA: • Changing life of small boy, a fruit vendor.	130:8.3 (1440:3)
	AT NAPLES: • Contact with street beggar who had no capacity for sonship • Jesus spread good cheer with many smiles upon hundreds of men, women, and children.	130:8.4 (1440:4) 130:8.5 (1441:1)
	THREE DAYS AT CAPUA:	130:8.6 (1441:2)
	THE SOJOURN AT ROME: • Jesus, Gonod, and Ganid appeared before Tiberius, the Roman ruler with greetings from the Prince of India. After chatting with the trio, the emperor made the great statement regarding Jesus. • The most valuable of all experiences in his six months' sojourn in Rome was contact with, and influence upon, the religious leaders. He made acquaintance of worthwhile leaders of the Cynics, the Stoics, the mystery cults, in particular, the Mithraic group. • All-night talk with Angamon, leader of the Stoics. • Day after day Mardus, a leader of the Cynics, conversed with Jesus. Discussion about good and evil. • Discussion of truth and faith with Nabon, a Greek Jew and foremost among leaders of the Mithraic mystery cult.	132:0.1 (1455:1) 132:0.4 (1455 :4) 132:1.1 (1456:7) 132:2.1 (1457:4) 132:3.1 (1459:1)
	JESUS' PERSONAL MINISTRY: • During Jesus' sojourn in Rome he came in personal contact with more than 500 mortals of the realm. • Talk with Roman senator. • Talk with Claudius, wealthy slaveholder. • Visit with Greek physician. • Talk with Roman soldier. • To speaker at the forum. • Superb address in behalf of poor man, falsely accused. • Counseling the rich man.	132:4.3 (1461.1) 132:4.5 (1461:3) 132:4.6 (1461:4) 132:4.7 (1461:5) 132:4.8 (1462:1) 132:5.1 (1462:2
	SOCIAL MINISTRY: • Restoring a lost child to his anxious mother. • Comforting a widow with five children.	132:6.1 (1465 :5) 132:6.2 (1465:6)
	TO NORTHERN ITALIAN LAKES: • Man not hungry for truth.	132:7.1 (1466:1)

Timetable of Personal Ministry of Jesus

A.D. 22 Jesus' 28th Year: (Continued)	VISIT TO SWITZERLAND: • All day talk about Buddhism. • Jesus says that religions are not made. They grow. • The three travelers walked leisurely across Italy over the Appian Way. • Halfway to Tarentum Jesus answers Ganid and talks about Indian caste system.	132:7.3 (1466:3) 133:0.2 (1468:2) 133:0.3 (1468.3)
	NEARING TARENTUM: • On roadside Jesus assists assaulted youth. • Talk to Ganid about Mercy ministry and justice.	133:1.1 (1468:4) 133:1.2 (1469:1)
	EMBARKING AT TARENTUM: • Man mistreating his wife.	133:2.1 (1470:2)
	SEVERAL DAYS AT NICOPOLIS: • Lodged in home of Jeramy, a Greek proselyte of the Jewish faith.	133:2.5 (1471:4)
	AT CORINTH: (Two months) • Meeting of Crispus, the chief ruler of the synagogue, his wife and five children. • In Jewish home of Justus. • Two public women taken to home of Justus; plan of new and better life.	133:3.1 (1471:5) 133:3.5 (1472:4) 133:3.6 (1472:5)
	Jesus enjoyed many talks with a large number of hungry souls. Among a few of them: • Meeting Gaius. • Jesus teaches the miller. • Talked to Roman centurion. • Talk with Epicurean teacher. • Talk with Greek contractor. • Talk with Roman Judge. • Talk with mistress of Greek inn. • Visits with Chinese merchant. • Talk with traveler from Britain. • Talk to runaway lad. • Talk to condemned criminal.	133:3.11 (1473:4) 133:4.2 (1474:2) 133:4.3 (1474:3) 133:4.5 (1474:5) 133:4.6 (1474:6) 133:4.7 (1474:7) 133:4.8 (1475:1) 133:4.9 (1475:2) 133:4.10 (1475:3) 133:4.11 (1475:4) 133:4.12 (1475:5)
	AT ATHENS: • Discussion on science with a Greek philosopher.	133:5.3 (1476:5)
	AT EPHESUS: • Talk with a discouraged young Phoenician. • Talk about the soul with a learned Greek at the school of philosophy.	133:6.2 (1478:1) 133:6.4 (1478:3)

Timetable of Personal Ministry of Jesus

A.D. 22 Jesus' 28th Year (Continued) :	SOJOURN AT CYPRESS: • Discourse on mind. • Ganid taken grievously ill.	133:7.3 (1479:3)
	AT ANTIOCH: • Ganid helped a man connected to his father's business.	133:8.3 (1481:1)
	IN MESOPOTAMIA: • Caravan trip across desert. • Jesus interested in Ur and in ruins of Susa.	133:9.1 (1481:3) 133:9.2 (1481:4)
A.D. 23 Jesus' 29th Year:	AT CHARAX ON THE PERSIAN GULF: • On December 10, the Master said good-bye to his friends from India. • Thus ended "The mission of Joshua, the teacher." • Jesus returned by way of Ur to Babylon. He joined a desert caravan that was on the way to Damascus.	133:9.4 (1481:6) 133:9.6 (1482:1) 134:1.1 (1483:3)
	STAY OF A FEW WEEKS AT NAZARETH:	134:1.3 (1483:5)
A.D. 24 Jesus' 30th Year:	CARAVAN TRIP TO THE CASPIAN: • On April 1st, Jesus left Nazareth as a conductor of a caravan. He spent a full year on caravan trip to Caspian Sea region. • This trip was another adventure of personal ministry. Scores of men, women, and children along the route lived richer lives as a result of their contact with Jesus.	134:2.1 (1484:5) 134:2.2 (1484.6)
	AT URMIA: (PERSIAN CITY ON SHORES OF LAKE URMIA) • Here Jesus gave up direction of caravan and tarried for two weeks. • Concerning lectures and discourses in school of religion.	134:2.5 (1485:2) 134:3.3 (1485:5)
	SOVEREIGNTY—DIVINE AND HUMAN:	134:4.1 (1486.4)
	POLITICAL SOVEREIGNTY:	134:5.1 (1487.8)
	LAW, LIBERTY, AND SOVEREIGNTY: • Global government and world peace.	134:6.1 (1490:4)
A.D. 25 Jesus' 31st Year:	JESUS RETURNED FROM CASPIAN SEA JOURNEY: • In April he left for Tyre. This was the year of Jesus' solitary wanderings through Palestine and Syria.	134:7.1 (1492:1) 134:7.2 (1492:2)
	AT ANTIOCH: • Two months of working, observing, visiting and ministering.	134:7.3 (1492:3)

Timetable of Public Ministry of Jesus

Timetable of Public Ministry of Jesus

Time Period	Public Ministry Activity	Reference
BAPTISM AND CHOOSING AND TRAINING THE APOSTLES		
A.D. 26 Jesus' 32nd Year:	January 14: Jesus baptism by John the Baptist, near Pella.	135:8.4 (1504.2)
	February 23 and 24: first six apostles are chosen.	137:1.1 (1524.2)
	February 22: wedding at Cana; turning water into wine.	137:4.1 (1528.4)
	March through June: four months of training at Zebedee home. Long conferences with the six and Jesus' brother, James.	137:7.1 (1533.5)
	June 23 to July 5: practice teaching in nearby towns.	138:1.1 (1538.3)
	Early July: six more apostles chosen	138:2.1 (1539.4)
	July 10–17: A week of intensive training for new recruits.	
	August through December: five long months of training for all twelve.	138:7.1 (1543.4)
	Alternate periods of fishing and training: personal work in villages.	138:7.6 (1544.5)
	Organization of the twelve.	138:10.1 (1547.1)
ORDINATION OF THE TWELVE. A YEAR-LONG TRIP TO JERUSALEM. QUIETLY TAKING OVER THE WORK OF JOHN THE BAPTIST		
A.D. 27 Jesus' 33rd Year:	January 12: Ordination of twelve in highlands north of Capernaum. The ordination sermon (the "Sermon on the Mount")	140:0.1 (1568.1) 140:3.1 (1570.2)
	January 18: Consecration charge: "Go into all the world."	140:9.2 (1584.1)
	BEGINNING THE PUBLIC WORK	
	January 19 to March 31: Journey to Jerusalem (two and a half months). Two weeks at Pella; three weeks at Amathus; four weeks at Bethany Ford.	141:0.1 (1587.1)– 141:9.3 (1595.7)
	April, May, June: In Jerusalem and vicinity (three months). In Jerusalem, Hebron, Bethlehem, and Engedi.	142:0.1 (1596.1)– 142:8.5 (1606.2)

Timetable of Public Ministry of Jesus

A.D. 27 Jesus' 33rd Year: (Continued)	July Through December: Return Trip Through Samaria And Decapolis. (six months)	
	July and August: Archelais (weaklings), Sychar (Nalda), etc.	143:1.1 (1607.3)
	September through December: Camp Gilboa and the Decapolis.	144:0.1 (1617.1)– 144:7.4 (1626.5)
FIRST AND SECOND PREACHING TOURS—EVANGELISTS TRAINED		
A.D. 28 Jesus' 34th Year:	January 10: death of John the Baptist. "Tomorrow we go into Galilee." (from Pella)	144:9.1 (1627.6)
	January 17: healing at sundown, Zebedee home, Capernaum. 683 afflicted persons healed.	145:3.1 (1631.6) 145:3.10 (1633.1)
	January 18 to March 17: first preaching tour (two months). Jesus, his twelve apostles and twelve of John's, visited nearby towns.	146:0.1 (1637.1)
	March 17 to March 30: apostles taught for two more weeks at Bethsaida headquarters.	147:0.1 (1647.1)
	Most of April: Jesus and his apostolic party of twenty-four made the trip to Jerusalem for the Passover.	147:2.1 (1648.3)
	Six Sanhedrin spies followed Jesus to Capernaum.	147:6.2 (1654.1)
	May 3 to October 3: five months' school for evangelists at Bethsaida. Tent city for 1500 with David Zebedee in charge. Elman was physician. In forenoons, apostles taught evangelists. In afternoons, evangelists taught multitudes.	148:0.1 (1657.1)
	October 3 to December 30: second preaching tour. Worked in groups of one apostle and twelve evangelists. Of 117 evangelists in second preaching tour, only 75 survived the test of experience.	149:0.1 (1668.1) 149:7.3 (1677.4)
THIRD PREACHING TOUR—TRANSFIGURATION. DECAPOLIS TOUR.		
A.D. 29 Jesus' 35th Year:	January 18 to March 4: third preaching tour (seven weeks). Participants: John's twelve, tested evangelists, and women's corps. Jesus' apostles to Jews only.	150:0.3 (1678.3)– 150:4.1 (1681.8)
	March 5: mounting opposition seen in the following events: Nazareth rejection after synagogue sermon.	150:9.1 (1686.4)

Timetable of Public Ministry of Jesus

A.D. 29 Jesus' 35th Year: (Continued)	March 30: Feeding 5000. King making episode.	152:2.1 (1700.2)
	April 30: crisis at Capernaum synagogue.	153:0.1 (1707.1)
	May 8: Sanhedrin closes all synagogues to Jesus.	154:2.1 (1718:2)
	May 22: flight from Galilee.	154:7.1 (1723.4)
	Son-of-man ministry lasted three and a half years. Son-of-God ministry began—lasted less than nine months.	
	August 9: Peter's confession.	157:3.1 (1745.2)
	August 15: the transfiguration.	158:0.1 (1752.1)
	August 18 to September 16: Decapolis tour from Magadan Park. Evangelists and apostles in groups visited cities. Rodan gave series of ten addresses.	159:0.2 (1762.2)
	September 18: discussion with Nathaniel and Thomas.	160:0.1 (1772.1)
	October: Feast of Tabernacles, Jesus taught boldly.	162:1.1 (1788.5)
	November 19: ordination of seventy, at Magadan.	163:1.1 (1800.3)
	November 20: Abner sent 70 to Galilee, Samaria, and Judea.	163:1.6 (1801.3)
	December 30: return of 70 to new camp at Pella.	163:6.1 (1806.5)
	Late December: meanwhile, Jesus, Nathaniel, Thomas, attended Feast of Dedication, Jerusalem.	164:0.1 (1809.1)
PEREAN MISSION. JESUS' FINAL WEEK. THE RESURRECTION. MORONTIA APPEARANCES.		
A.D. 30 Jesus' 36th Year:	After January 3: Perean mission (almost three months). The 70 and the women's corps in field. Jesus and apostles taught camp multitudes, up to 4000.	165:0.1 (1817.1)
	March 2: the resurrection of Lazarus at Bethany.	168:2.1 (1845.7)
	March 13: last teaching at Pella. Final departure.	171:1.1 (1868.3)

Timetable of Public Ministry of Jesus

	Jesus' Last Days In Jerusalem:	
A.D. 30 Jesus' 36th and Final Year: (Continued)	April 2—early Sunday afternoon: triumphal entry.	172:3.1 (1880.7)
	April 3—Monday 9:00 a.m.: cleansing the temple.	173:0.3 (1888.3)
	April 3—Monday 2:00 p.m.: "By what authority?"	173:2.1 (1891.2)
	April 4—Tuesday: "Render unto Caesar" The Great Commandment. Temple Discourse. Destruction of Jerusalem. "Truth is living;..." The Master's second coming.	174:2.2 (1899.2) 174:4.1 (1901.1) 175:1.1 (1905.3) 176:1.1 (1912.3) 176:1-3 (1912–1917) 176:2.1 (1914.2)
	April 5—daytime Wednesday: Jesus talk to John Mark. Evening, talks with Greeks, later with apostles. Judas makes his choice. The last social hour.	177:1.1 (1920.5) 177:5.1 (1927.2)
	April 6—forenoon Thursday: "Sonship and Citizenship." Dusk to 10:00 p.m. The Last Supper in upper chamber. A new commandment. A promised helper. Farewell discourse, personal farewells. After 10:00 p.m.: In Gethsemane—prayers—arrest. Late night, in Palace of Annas, on Olivet 3 hours.	178:1.1 (1929.2) 179:0.1 (1936.1) 180:0.1 (1944.1) 180:4.1 (1948.2) 181:2.1 (1955.2) 182:0.1 (1963.1)

John the Baptist

<table>
<tr><th colspan="2">John the Baptist</th></tr>
<tr><td rowspan="2">Born:</td><td>It was late in the month of June, 8 B.C., about three months after the marriage of Joseph and Mary, that Gabriel appeared to Elizabeth at noontide one day, just as he later made his presence known to Mary. Said Gabriel: 122:2.2 (1345.4)

"While your husband, Zacharias, stands before the altar in Jerusalem, and while the assembled people pray for the coming of a deliverer, I, Gabriel, have come to announce that you will shortly bear a son who shall be the forerunner of this divine teacher, and you shall call your son John. He will grow up dedicated to the Lord your God, and when he has come to full years, he will gladden your heart because he will turn many souls to God, and he will also proclaim the coming of the soul-healer of your people and the spirit-liberator of all mankind. Your kinswoman Mary shall be the mother of this child of promise, and I will also appear to her." 122:2.3 (1345.5)</td></tr>
<tr><td>JOHN the Baptist was born March 25, 7 B.C., in accordance with the promise that Gabriel made to Elizabeth in June of the previous year. For five months Elizabeth kept secret Gabriel's visitation; and when she told her husband, Zacharias, he was greatly troubled and fully believed her narrative only after he had an unusual dream about six weeks before the birth of John. Excepting the visit of Gabriel to Elizabeth and the dream of Zacharias, there was nothing unusual or supernatural connected with the birth of John the Baptist. 135:0.1 (1496.1)</td></tr>
<tr><td rowspan="2">Parents:</td><td>Jesus' lifework on Urantia was really begun by John the Baptist. Zacharias, John's father, belonged to the Jewish priesthood, while his mother, Elizabeth, was a member of the more prosperous branch of the same large family group to which Mary the mother of Jesus also belonged. Zacharias and Elizabeth, though they had been married many years, were childless. 122:2.1 (1345.3)</td></tr>
<tr><td>Zacharias and Elizabeth had a small farm on which they raised sheep. They hardly made a living on this land, but Zacharias received a regular allowance from the temple funds dedicated to the priesthood. 135:0.5 (1496.5)

After their return from Nazareth John's parents began the systematic education of the lad. There was no synagogue school in this little village; however, as he was a priest, Zacharias was fairly well educated, and Elizabeth was far better educated than the average Judean woman; she was also of the priesthood, being a descendant of the "daughters of Aaron." Since John was an only child, they spent a great deal of time on his mental and spiritual training. Zacharias had only short periods of service at the temple in Jerusalem so that he devoted much of his time to teaching his son. 135:0.4 (1496.4)</td></tr>
</table>

John the Baptist

Childhood:	On the eighth day John was circumcised according to the Jewish custom. He grew up as an ordinary child, day by day and year by year, in the small village known in those days as the City of Judah, about four miles west of Jerusalem. 135:0.2 (1496.2) The most eventful occurrence in John's early childhood was the visit, in company with his parents, to Jesus and the Nazareth family. This visit occurred in the month of June, 1 B.C., when he was a little over six years of age. 135:0.3 (1496.3)
The Concept of a Herald of the Messiah:	National egotism, false faith in a misconceived promised Messiah, and the increasing bondage and tyranny of the priesthood forever silenced the voices of the spiritual leaders (excepting Daniel, Ezekiel, Haggai, and Malachi); and from that day to the time of John the Baptist all Israel experienced an increasing spiritual retrogression. But the Jews never lost the concept of the Universal Father; even to the twentieth century after Christ they have continued to follow this Deity conception. 97:10.3 (1075.8) From Moses to John the Baptist there extended an unbroken line of faithful teachers who passed the monotheistic torch of light from one generation to another while they unceasingly rebuked unscrupulous rulers, denounced commercializing priests, and ever exhorted the people to adhere to the worship of the supreme Yahweh, the Lord God of Israel. 97:10.4 (1076.1)
	In order to understand John's message, account should be taken of the status of the Jewish people at the time he appeared upon the stage of action. For almost one hundred years all Israel had been in a quandary; they were at a loss to explain their continuous subjugation to gentile overlords. Had not Moses taught that righteousness was always rewarded with prosperity and power? Were they not God's chosen people? Why was the throne of David desolate and vacant? In the light of the Mosaic doctrines and the precepts of the prophets the Jews found it difficult to explain their long-continued national desolation. 135:5.1 (1500.1) About one hundred years before the days of Jesus and John a new school of religious teachers arose in Palestine, the apocalyptists. These new teachers evolved a system of belief that accounted for the sufferings and humiliation of the Jews on the ground that they were paying the penalty for the nation's sins. They fell back onto the well-known reasons assigned to explain the Babylonian and other captivities of former times. But, so taught the apocalyptists, Israel should take heart; the days of their affliction were almost over; the discipline of God's chosen people was about finished; God's patience with the gentile foreigners was about exhausted. The end of Roman rule was synonymous with the end of the age and, in a certain sense, with the end of the world. These new teachers leaned heavily on the predictions of Daniel, and they consistently taught that creation was about to pass into its final stage; the kingdoms of this world were about to become the kingdom of God. To the Jewish mind of that day this was the meaning of that phrase—the kingdom of heaven—which runs throughout the teachings of both John and Jesus. To the Jews of Palestine the phrase "kingdom of heaven" had but one meaning: an absolutely righteous state in which God (the Messiah) would

	rule the nations of earth in perfection of power just as he ruled in heaven—"Your will be done on earth as in heaven." 135:5.2 (1500.2) In the days of John all Jews were expectantly asking, "How soon will the kingdom come?" There was a general feeling that the end of the rule of the gentile nations was drawing near. There was present throughout all Jewry a lively hope and a keen expectation that the consummation of the desire of the ages would occur during the lifetime of that generation. 135:5.3 (1500.3) While the Jews differed greatly in their estimates of the nature of the coming kingdom, they were alike in their belief that the event was impending, near at hand, even at the door. Many who read the Old Testament literally looked expectantly for a new king in Palestine, for a regenerated Jewish nation delivered from its enemies and presided over by the successor of King David, the Messiah who would quickly be acknowledged as the rightful and righteous ruler of all the world. Another, though smaller, group of devout Jews held a vastly different view of this kingdom of God. They taught that the coming kingdom was not of this world, that the world was approaching its certain end, and that "a new heaven and a new earth" were to usher in the establishment of the kingdom of God; that this kingdom was to be an everlasting dominion, that sin was to be ended, and that the citizens of the new kingdom were to become immortal in their enjoyment of this endless bliss. 135:5.4 (1500.4)
The Concept of a Herald of the Messiah: (Continued)	All were agreed that some drastic purging or purifying discipline would of necessity precede the establishment of the new kingdom on earth. The literalists taught that a world-wide war would ensue which would destroy all unbelievers, while the faithful would sweep on to universal and eternal victory. The spiritists taught that the kingdom would be ushered in by the great judgment of God which would relegate the unrighteous to their well-deserved judgment of punishment and final destruction, at the same time elevating the believing saints of the chosen people to high seats of honor and authority with the Son of Man, who would rule over the redeemed nations in God's name. And this latter group even believed that many devout gentiles might be admitted to the fellowship of the new kingdom. 135:5.5 (1500.5) Some of the Jews held to the opinion that God might possibly establish this new kingdom by direct and divine intervention, but the vast majority believed that he would interpose some representative intermediary, the Messiah. And that was the only possible meaning the term Messiah could have had in the minds of the Jews of the generation of John and Jesus. Messiah could not possibly refer to one who merely taught God's will or proclaimed the necessity for righteous living. To all such holy persons the Jews gave the title of prophet. The Messiah was to be more than a prophet; the Messiah was to bring in the establishment of the new kingdom, the kingdom of God. No one who failed to do this could be the Messiah in the traditional Jewish sense. 135:5.6 (1501.1) Who would this Messiah be? Again the Jewish teachers differed. The older ones clung to the doctrine of the son of David. The newer taught that, since the new kingdom was a heavenly kingdom, the new ruler might also be a

The Concept of a Herald of the Messiah: (Continued)	divine personality, one who had long sat at God's right hand in heaven. And strange as it may appear, those who thus conceived of the ruler of the new kingdom looked upon him not as a human Messiah, not as a mere man, but as "the Son of Man"—a Son of God—a heavenly Prince, long held in waiting thus to assume the rulership of the earth made new. Such was the religious background of the Jewish world when John went forth proclaiming: "Repent, for the kingdom of heaven is at hand!" 135:5.7 (1501.2) It becomes apparent, therefore, that John's announcement of the coming kingdom had not less than half a dozen different meanings in the minds of those who listened to his impassioned preaching. But no matter what significance they attached to the phrases which John employed, each of these various groups of Jewish-kingdom expectants was intrigued by the proclamations of this sincere, enthusiastic, rough-and-ready preacher of righteousness and repentance, who so solemnly exhorted his hearers to "flee from the wrath to come." 135:5.8 (1501.3)
Becoming John the Baptist:	John had no school from which to graduate at the age of fourteen, but his parents had selected this as the appropriate year for him to take the formal Nazarite vow. Accordingly, Zacharias and Elizabeth took their son to Engedi, down by the Dead Sea. This was the southern headquarters of the Nazarite brotherhood, and there the lad was duly and solemnly inducted into this order for life. After these ceremonies and the making of the vows to abstain from all intoxicating drinks, to let the hair grow, and to refrain from touching the dead, the family proceeded to Jerusalem, where, before the temple, John completed the making of the offerings which were required of those taking Nazarite vows. 135:1.1 (1496.6) John took the same life vows that had been administered to his illustrious predecessors, Samson and the prophet Samuel. A life Nazarite was looked upon as a sanctified and holy personality. The Jews regarded a Nazarite with almost the respect and veneration accorded the high priest, and this was not strange since Nazarites of lifelong consecration were the only persons, except high priests, who were ever permitted to enter the holy of holies in the temple. 135:1.2 (1496.7) John returned home from Jerusalem to tend his father's sheep and grew up to be a strong man with a noble character. 135:1.3 (1497.1) When sixteen years old, John, as a result of reading about Elijah, became greatly impressed with the prophet of Mount Carmel and decided to adopt his style of dress. From that day on John always wore a hairy garment with a leather girdle. At sixteen he was more than six feet tall and almost full grown. With his flowing hair and peculiar mode of dress he was indeed a picturesque youth. And his parents expected great things of this their only son, a child of promise and a Nazarite for life. 135:1.4 (1497.2) Along the valley of this little brook John built no less than a dozen stone shelters and night corrals, consisting of piled-up stones, wherein he could watch over and safeguard his herds of sheep and goats. John's life as a shepherd afforded him a great deal of time for thought. He talked much with

	Ezda, an orphan lad of Beth-zur, whom he had in a way adopted, and who cared for the herds when he made trips to Hebron to see his mother and to sell sheep, as well as when he went down to Engedi for Sabbath services. John and the lad lived very simply, subsisting on mutton, goat's milk, wild honey, and the edible locusts of that region. This, their regular diet, was supplemented by provisions brought from Hebron and Engedi from time to time. 135:3.1 (1497.7)
Becoming John the Baptist: (Continued)	Elizabeth kept John posted about Palestinian and world affairs, and his conviction grew deeper and deeper that the time was fast approaching when the old order was to end; that he was to become the herald of the approach of a new age, "the kingdom of heaven." This rugged shepherd was very partial to the writings of the Prophet Daniel. He read a thousand times Daniel's description of the great image, which Zacharias had told him represented the history of the great kingdoms of the world, beginning with Babylon, then Persia, Greece, and finally Rome. John perceived that already was Rome composed of such polyglot peoples and races that it could never become a strongly cemented and firmly consolidated empire. He believed that Rome was even then divided, as Syria, Egypt, Palestine, and other provinces; and then he further read "in the days of these kings shall the God of heaven set up a kingdom which shall never be destroyed. And this kingdom shall not be left to other people but shall break in pieces and consume all these kingdoms, and it shall stand forever." "And there was given him dominion and glory and a kingdom that all peoples, nations, and languages should serve him. His dominion is an everlasting dominion, which shall not pass away, and his kingdom never shall be destroyed." "And the kingdom and dominion and the greatness of the kingdom under the whole heaven shall be given to the people of the saints of the Most High, whose kingdom is an everlasting kingdom, and all dominions shall serve and obey him." 135:3.2 (1498.1)
	John was never able completely to rise above the confusion produced by what he had heard from his parents concerning Jesus and by these passages which he read in the Scriptures. In Daniel he read: "I saw in the night visions, and, behold, one like the Son of Man came with the clouds of heaven, and there was given him dominion and glory and a kingdom." But these words of the prophet did not harmonize with what his parents had taught him. Neither did his talk with Jesus, at the time of his visit when he was eighteen years old, correspond with these statements of the Scriptures. Notwithstanding this confusion, throughout all of his perplexity his mother assured him that his distant cousin, Jesus of Nazareth, was the true Messiah, that he had come to sit on the throne of David, and that he (John) was to become his advance herald and chief support. 135:3.3 (1498.2)
	From all John heard of the vice and wickedness of Rome and the dissoluteness and moral barrenness of the empire, from what he knew of the evil doings of Herod Antipas and the governors of Judea, he was minded to believe that the end of the age was impending. It seemed to this rugged and noble child of nature that the world was ripe for the end of the age of man and the dawn of the new and divine age—the kingdom of heaven. The feeling grew in John's heart that he was to be the last of the old prophets and the first of the new.

	And he fairly vibrated with the mounting impulse to go forth and proclaim to all men: "Repent! Get right with God! Get ready for the end; prepare yourselves for the appearance of the new and eternal order of earth affairs, the kingdom of heaven." 135:3.4 (1498.3)
	On August 17, A.D. 22, when John was twenty-eight years of age, his mother suddenly passed away. Elizabeth's friends, knowing of the Nazarite restrictions regarding contact with the dead, even in one's own family, made all arrangements for the burial of Elizabeth before sending for John. When he received word of the death of his mother, he directed Ezda to drive his herds to Engedi and started for Hebron. 135:4.1 (1499.1)
	On returning to Engedi from his mother's funeral, he presented his flocks to the brotherhood and for a season detached himself from the outside world while he fasted and prayed. John knew only of the old methods of approach to divinity; he knew only of the records of such as Elijah, Samuel, and Daniel. Elijah was his ideal of a prophet. Elijah was the first of the teachers of Israel to be regarded as a prophet, and John truly believed that he was to be the last of this long and illustrious line of the messengers of heaven. 135:4.2 (1499.2)
	For two and a half years John lived at Engedi, and he persuaded most of the brotherhood that "the end of the age was at hand"; that "the kingdom of heaven was about to appear." And all his early teaching was based upon the current Jewish idea and concept of the Messiah as the promised deliverer of the Jewish nation from the domination of their gentile rulers. 135:4.3 (1499.3)
Becoming John the Baptist: (Continued)	Throughout this period John read much in the sacred writings which he found at the Engedi home of the Nazarites. He was especially impressed by Isaiah and by Malachi, the last of the prophets up to that time. He read and reread the last five chapters of Isaiah, and he believed these prophecies. Then he would read in Malachi: "Behold, I will send you Elijah the prophet before the coming of the great and dreadful day of the Lord; and he shall turn the hearts of the fathers toward the children and the hearts of the children toward their fathers, lest I come and smite the earth with a curse." And it was only this promise of Malachi that Elijah would return that deterred John from going forth to preach about the coming kingdom and to exhort his fellow Jews to flee from the wrath to come. John was ripe for the proclamation of the message of the coming kingdom, but this expectation of the coming of Elijah held him back for more than two years. He knew he was not Elijah. What did Malachi mean? Was the prophecy literal or figurative? How could he know the truth? He finally dared to think that, since the first of the prophets was called Elijah, so the last should be known, eventually, by the same name. Nevertheless, he had doubts, doubts sufficient to prevent his ever calling himself Elijah. 135:4.4 (1499.4)
	It was the influence of Elijah that caused John to adopt his methods of direct and blunt assault upon the sins and vices of his contemporaries. He sought to dress like Elijah, and he endeavored to talk like Elijah; in every outward aspect he was like the olden prophet. He was just such a stalwart and picturesque child of nature, just such a fearless and daring preacher of righteousness. John was not illiterate, he did well know the Jewish sacred writings, but he was hardly cultured. He was a clear thinker, a powerful

Becoming John the Baptist: (Continued)	speaker, and a fiery denunciator. He was hardly an example to his age, but he was an eloquent rebuke. 135:4.5 (1499.5) At last he thought out the method of proclaiming the new age, the kingdom of God; he settled that he was to become the herald of the Messiah; he swept aside all doubts and departed from Engedi one day in March of A.D. 25 to begin his short but brilliant career as a public preacher. 135:4.6 (1499.6)
Role:	John the Baptist, the forerunner of Michael's mission on Urantia and, in the flesh, distant cousin of the Son of Man. 45:4.17 (514.7)
	Jesus' lifework on Urantia was really begun by John the Baptist. 122:2.1 (1345.3)
What John the Baptist Taught:	From Moses to John the Baptist there extended an unbroken line of faithful teachers who passed the monotheistic torch of light from one generation to another while they unceasingly rebuked unscrupulous rulers, denounced commercializing priests, and ever exhorted the people to adhere to the worship of the supreme Yahweh, the Lord God of Israel. 97:10.4 (1076.1)
	Early in the month of March, A.D. 25, John journeyed around the western coast of the Dead Sea and up the river Jordan to opposite Jericho, the ancient ford over which Joshua and the children of Israel passed when they first entered the promised land; and crossing over to the other side of the river, he established himself near the entrance to the ford and began to preach to the people who passed by on their way back and forth across the river. This was the most frequented of all the Jordan crossings. 135:6.1 (1501.4) It was apparent to all who heard John that he was more than a preacher. The great majority of those who listened to this strange man who had come up from the Judean wilderness went away believing that they had heard the voice of a prophet. No wonder the souls of these weary and expectant Jews were deeply stirred by such a phenomenon. Never in all Jewish history had the devout children of Abraham so longed for the "consolation of Israel" or more ardently anticipated "the restoration of the kingdom." Never in all Jewish history could John's message, "the kingdom of heaven is at hand," have made such a deep and universal appeal as at the very time he so mysteriously appeared on the bank of this southern crossing of the Jordan. 135:6.2 (1501.5) He came from the herdsmen, like Amos. He was dressed like Elijah of old, and he thundered his admonitions and poured forth his warnings in the" spirit and power of Elijah." It is not surprising that this strange preacher created a mighty stir throughout all Palestine as the travelers carried abroad the news of his preaching along the Jordan. 135:6.3 (1502.1) There was still another and a new feature about the work of this Nazarite preacher: He baptized every one of his believers in the Jordan "for the remission of sins." Although baptism was not a new ceremony among the Jews, they had never seen it employed as John now made use of it. It had long been the practice thus to baptize the gentile proselytes into the fellowship of the outer court of the temple, but never had the Jews themselves been asked

What John the Baptist Taught: (Continued)	to submit to the baptism of repentance. Only fifteen months intervened between the time John began to preach and baptize and his arrest and imprisonment at the instigation of Herod Antipas, but in this short time he baptized considerably over one hundred thousand penitents. 135:6.4 (1502.2) John preached four months at Bethany ford before starting north up the Jordan. Tens of thousands of listeners, some curious but many earnest and serious, came to hear him from all parts of Judea, Perea, and Samaria. Even a few came from Galilee. 135:6.5 (1502.3) In May of this year, while he still lingered at Bethany ford, the priests and Levites sent a delegation out to inquire of John whether he claimed to be the Messiah, and by whose authority he preached. John answered these questioners by saying: "Go tell your masters that you have heard 'the voice of one crying in the wilderness,' as spoken by the prophet, saying, 'make ready the way of the Lord, make straight a highway for our God. Every valley shall be filled, and every mountain and hill shall be brought low; the uneven ground shall become a plain, while the rough places shall become a smooth valley; and all flesh shall see the salvation of God.'" 135:6.6 (1502.4) John was a heroic but tactless preacher. One day when he was preaching and baptizing on the west bank of the Jordan, a group of Pharisees and a number of Sadducees came forward and presented themselves for baptism. Before leading them down into the water, John, addressing them as a group said: "Who warned you to flee, as vipers before the fire, from the wrath to come? I will baptize you, but I warn you to bring forth fruit worthy of sincere repentance if you would receive the remission of your sins. Tell me not that Abraham is your father. I declare that God is able of these twelve stones here before you to raise up worthy children for Abraham. And even now is the ax laid to the very roots of the trees. Every tree that brings not forth good fruit is destined to be cut down and cast into the fire." (The twelve stones to which he referred were the reputed memorial stones set up by Joshua to commemorate the crossing of the "twelve tribes" at this very point when they first entered the promised land. 135:6.7 (1502.5) John conducted classes for his disciples, in the course of which he instructed them in the details of their new life and endeavored to answer their many questions. He counseled the teachers to instruct in the spirit as well as the letter of the law. He instructed the rich to feed the poor; to the tax gatherers he said: "Extort no more than that which is assigned you." To the soldiers he said: "Do no violence and exact nothing wrongfully—be content with your wages." While he counseled all: "Make ready for the end of the age—the kingdom of heaven is at hand." 135:6.8 (1502.6) John still had confused ideas about the coming kingdom and its king. The longer he preached the more confused he became, but never did this intellectual uncertainty concerning the nature of the coming kingdom in the least lessen his conviction of the certainty of the kingdom's immediate appearance. In mind John might be confused, but in spirit never. He was in no doubt about the coming kingdom, but he was far from certain as to whether or not Jesus was to be the ruler of that kingdom. As long as John held to the idea of the restoration of the throne of David, the teachings of his

What John the Baptist Taught: (Continued)	parents that Jesus, born in the City of David, was to be the long-expected deliverer, seemed consistent; but at those times when he leaned more toward the doctrine of a spiritual kingdom and the end of the temporal age on earth, he was sorely in doubt as to the part Jesus would play in such events. Sometimes he questioned everything, but not for long. He really wished he might talk it all over with his cousin, but that was contrary to their expressed agreement. 135:7.1 (1503.1) As John journeyed north, he thought much about Jesus. He paused at more than a dozen places as he traveled up the Jordan. It was at Adam that he first made reference to "another one who is to come after me" in answer to the direct question which his disciples asked him, "Are you the Messiah?" And he went on to say: "There will come after me one who is greater than I, whose sandal straps I am not worthy to stoop down and unloose. I baptize you with water, but he will baptize you with the Holy Spirit. And his shovel is in his hand thoroughly to cleanse his threshing floor; he will gather the wheat into his garner, but the chaff will he burn up with the judgment fire." 135:7.2 (1503.2) In response to the questions of his disciples John continued to expand his teachings, from day to day adding more that was helpful and comforting compared with his early and cryptic message: "Repent and be baptized." By this time throngs were arriving from Galilee and the Decapolis. Scores of earnest believers lingered with their adored teacher day after day. 135:7.3 (1503.3)
	A future hope—when the kingdom would be realized in fullness upon the appearance of the Messiah. This is the kingdom concept which John the Baptist taught. 170:1.3 (1858.5) These teachings cover the expanded idea of the kingdom which was taught by Jesus. This great concept was hardly embraced in the elementary and confused kingdom teachings of John the Baptist. 170:2.9 (1860.4)
Significant Events:	Just before the noon rest, Jesus laid down his tools, removed his work apron, and merely announced to the three workmen in the room with him, "My hour has come." He went out to his brothers James and Jude, repeating, "My hour has come—let us go to John." And they started immediately for Pella, eating their lunch as they journeyed. This was on Sunday, January 13. They tarried for the night in the Jordan valley and arrived on the scene of John's baptizing about noon of the next day. 135:8.3 (1504.1) John had just begun baptizing the candidates for the day. Scores of repentants were standing in line awaiting their turn when Jesus and his two brothers took up their positions in this line of earnest men and women who had become believers in John's preaching of the coming kingdom. John had been inquiring about Jesus of Zebedee's sons. He had heard of Jesus' remarks concerning his preaching, and he was day by day expecting to see him arrive on the scene, but he had not expected to greet him in the line of baptismal candidates. 135:8.4 (1504.2)

	Being engrossed with the details of rapidly baptizing such a large number of converts, John did not look up to see Jesus until the Son of Man stood in his immediate presence. When John recognized Jesus, the ceremonies were halted for a moment while he greeted his cousin in the flesh and asked, "But why do you come down into the water to greet me?" And Jesus answered, "To be subject to your baptism." John replied: "But I have need to be baptized by you. Why do you come to me?" And Jesus whispered to John: "Bear with me now, for it becomes us to set this example for my brothers standing here with me, and that the people may know that my hour has come." 135:8.5 (1504.3) There was a tone of finality and authority in Jesus' voice. John was atremble with emotion as he made ready to baptize Jesus of Nazareth in the Jordan at noon on Monday, January 14, A.D. 26. Thus did John baptize Jesus and his two brothers James and Jude. And when John had baptized these three, he dismissed the others for the day, announcing that he would resume baptisms at noon the next day. As the people were departing, the four men still standing in the water heard a strange sound, and presently there appeared for a moment an apparition immediately over the head of Jesus, and they heard a voice saying, "This is my beloved Son in whom I am well pleased." A great change came over the countenance of Jesus, and coming up out of the water in silence he took leave of them, going toward the hills to the east. And no man saw Jesus again for forty days. 135:8.6 (1504.4)
Significant Events: (Continued)	Near the village of Adam, John tarried for several weeks, and it was here that he made the memorable attack upon Herod Antipas for unlawfully taking the wife of another man. By June of this year (A.D. 26) John was back at the Bethany ford of the Jordan, where he had begun his preaching of the coming kingdom more than a year previously. In the weeks following the baptism of Jesus the character of John's preaching gradually changed into a proclamation of mercy for the common people, while he denounced with renewed vehemence the corrupt political and religious rulers. 135:10.2 (1506.4)
	Herod Antipas, in whose territory John had been preaching, became alarmed lest he and his disciples should start a rebellion. Herod also resented John's public criticisms of his domestic affairs. In view of all this, Herod decided to put John in prison. Accordingly, very early in the morning of June 12, before the multitude arrived to hear the preaching and witness the baptizing, the agents of Herod placed John under arrest. As weeks passed and he was not released, his disciples scattered over all Palestine, many of them going into Galilee to join the followers of Jesus. 135:10.3 (1506.5)
	Late that evening, James, John, Andrew, and Simon held converse with John the Baptist, and with tearful eye but steady voice the stalwart Judean prophet surrendered two of his leading disciples to become the apostles of the Galilean Prince of the coming kingdom. 137:1.8 (1525.5) Sunday morning, February 24, A.D. 26, Jesus took leave of John the Baptist by the river near Pella, never again to see him in the flesh. 137:2.1 (1526.1)

John the Baptist

What John Said About Jesus:	John had a lonely and somewhat bitter experience in prison. Few of his followers were permitted to see him. He longed to see Jesus but had to be content with hearing of his work through those of his followers who had become believers in the Son of Man. He was often tempted to doubt Jesus and his divine mission. If Jesus were the Messiah, why did he do nothing to deliver him from this unbearable imprisonment? For more than a year and a half this rugged man of God's outdoors languished in that despicable prison. And this experience was a great test of his faith in, and loyalty to, Jesus. Indeed, this whole experience was a great test of John's faith even in God. Many times was he tempted to doubt even the genuineness of his own mission and experience. 135:11.1 (1506.6) After he had been in prison several months, a group of his disciples came to him and, after reporting concerning the public activities of Jesus, said: "So you see, Teacher, that he who was with you at the upper Jordan prospers and receives all who come to him. He even feasts with publicans and sinners. You bore courageous witness to him, and yet he does nothing to effect your deliverance." But John answered his friends: "This man can do nothing unless it has been given him by his Father in heaven. You well remember that I said, 'I am not the Messiah, but I am one sent on before to prepare the way for him.' And that I did. He who has the bride is the bridegroom, but the friend of the bridegroom who stands near by and hears him rejoices greatly because of the bridegroom's voice. This, my joy, therefore is fulfilled. He must increase but I must decrease. I am of this earth and have declared my message. Jesus of Nazareth comes down to the earth from heaven and is above us all. The Son of Man has descended from God, and the words of God he will declare to you. For the Father in heaven gives not the spirit by measure to his own Son. The Father loves his Son and will presently put all things in the hands of this Son. He who believes in the Son has eternal life. And these words which I speak are true and abiding." 135:11.2 (1507.1)
What Jesus Said About John:	The latter part of December they all went over near the Jordan, close by Pella, where they again began to teach and preach. Both Jews and gentiles came to this camp to hear the gospel. It was while Jesus was teaching the multitude one afternoon that some of John's special friends brought the Master the last message which he ever had from the Baptist. 144:8.1 (1626.6) John had now been in prison a year and a half, and most of this time Jesus had labored very quietly; so it was not strange that John should be led to wonder about the kingdom. John's friends interrupted Jesus' teaching to say to him: "John the Baptist has sent us to ask—are you truly the Deliverer, or shall we look for another?" 144:8.2 (1626.7) Jesus paused to say to John's friends: "Go back and tell John that he is not forgotten. Tell him what you have seen and heard, that the poor have good tidings preached to them." And when Jesus had spoken further to the messengers of John, he turned again to the multitude and said: "Do not think that John doubts the gospel of the kingdom. He makes inquiry only to assure his disciples who are also my disciples. John is no weakling. Let me ask you who heard John preach before Herod put him in prison: What did you behold in John—a reed shaken with the wind? A man of changeable moods and

What Jesus Said About John: (Continued)	clothed in soft raiment? As a rule they who are gorgeously appareled and who live delicately are in kings' courts and in the mansions of the rich. But what did you see when you beheld John? A prophet? Yes, I say to you, and much more than a prophet. Of John it was written: 'Behold, I send my messenger before your face; he shall prepare the way before you.' 144:8.3 (1626.8) "Verily, verily, I say to you, among those born of women there has not arisen a greater than John the Baptist; yet he who is but small in the kingdom of heaven is greater because he has been born of the spirit and knows that he has become a son of God." 144:8.4 (1627.1)
	Peter shuddered at the thought of the Master's dying—it was too disagreeable an idea to entertain—and fearing that James or John might ask some question relative to this statement, he thought best to start up a diverting conversation and, not knowing what else to talk about, gave expression to the first thought coming into his mind, which was: "Master, why is it that the scribes say that Elijah must first come before the Messiah shall appear?" And Jesus, knowing that Peter sought to avoid reference to his death and resurrection, answered: "Elijah indeed comes first to prepare the way for the Son of Man, who must suffer many things and finally be rejected. But I tell you that Elijah has already come, and they received him not but did to him whatsoever they willed." And then did the three apostles perceive that he referred to John the Baptist as Elijah. Jesus knew that, if they insisted on regarding him as the Messiah, then must John be the Elijah of the prophecy. 158:2.2 (1754.2)
Final Instructions:	These disciples were amazed at John's pronouncement, so much so that they departed in silence. John was also much agitated, for he perceived that he had uttered a prophecy. Never again did he wholly doubt the mission and divinity of Jesus. But it was a sore disappointment to John that Jesus sent him no word, that he came not to see him, and that he exercised none of his great power to deliver him from prison. But Jesus knew all about this. He had great love for John, but being now cognizant of his divine nature and knowing fully the great things in preparation for John when he departed from this world and also knowing that John's work on earth was finished, he constrained himself not to interfere in the natural outworking of the great preacher-prophet's career. 135:11.3 (1507.2) This long suspense in prison was humanly unbearable. Just a few days before his death John again sent trusted messengers to Jesus, inquiring: "Is my work done? Why do I languish in prison? Are you truly the Messiah, or shall we look for another?" And when these two disciples gave this message to Jesus, the Son of Man replied: "Go back to John and tell him that I have not forgotten but to suffer me also this, for it becomes us to fulfill all righteousness. Tell John what you have seen and heard—that the poor have good tidings preached to them—and, finally, tell the beloved herald of my earth mission that he shall be abundantly blessed in the age to come if he finds no occasion to doubt and stumble over me." And this was the last word John received from Jesus. This message greatly comforted him and did much to stabilize his faith and prepare him for the tragic end of his life in the flesh which followed so soon upon the heels of this memorable occasion. 135:11.4 (1507.3)

The Death of John the Baptist:	In celebration of his birthday Herod made a great feast in the Machaerian palace for his chief officers and other men high in the councils of the government of Galilee and Perea. Since Herodias had failed to bring about John's death by direct appeal to Herod, she now set herself to the task of having John put to death by cunning planning. 135:12.5 (1508.5) In the course of the evening's festivities and entertainment, Herodias presented her daughter to dance before the banqueters. Herod was very much pleased with the damsel's performance and, calling her before him, said: "You are charming. I am much pleased with you. Ask me on this my birthday for whatever you desire, and I will give it to you, even to the half of my kingdom." And Herod did all this while well under the influence of his many wines. The young lady drew aside and inquired of her mother what she should ask of Herod. Herodias said, "Go to Herod and ask for the head of John the Baptist." And the young woman, returning to the banquet table, said to Herod, "I request that you forthwith give me the head of John the Baptist on a platter." 135:12.6 (1508.6) Herod was filled with fear and sorrow, but because of his oath and because of all those who sat at meat with him, he would not deny the request. And Herod Antipas sent a soldier, commanding him to bring the head of John. So was John that night beheaded in the prison, the soldier bringing the head of the prophet on a platter and presenting it to the young woman at the rear of the banquet hall. And the damsel gave the platter to her mother. When John's disciples heard of this, they came to the prison for the body of John, and after laying it in a tomb, they went and told Jesus. 135:12.7 (1508.7)
	John the Baptist was executed by order of Herod Antipas on the evening of January 10, A.D. 28. The next day a few of John's disciples who had gone to Machaerus heard of his execution and, going to Herod, made request for his body, which they put in a tomb, later giving it burial at Sebaste, the home of Abner. The following day, January 12, they started north to the camp of John's and Jesus' apostles near Pella, and they told Jesus about the death of John. When Jesus heard their report, he dismissed the multitude and, calling the twenty-four together, said: "John is dead. Herod has beheaded him. Tonight go into joint council and arrange your affairs accordingly. There shall be delay no longer. The hour has come to proclaim the kingdom openly and with power. Tomorrow we go into Galilee." 144:9.1 (1627.6)
John After Death:	These twenty-four counselors have been recruited from the eight Urantia races, and the last of this group were assembled at the time of the resurrection roll call of Michael, nineteen hundred years ago. This Urantia advisory council is made up of the following members: 45:4.2 (513.5)
	15. John the Baptist, the forerunner of Michael's mission on Urantia and, in the flesh, distant cousin of the Son of Man. 45:4.17 (514.7)
	Since the times of Michael's bestowal on your world the general management of Urantia has been intrusted to a special group on Jerusem of twenty-four onetime Urantians. Qualification for membership on this commission is

John After Death: (Continued)	unknown to us, but we have observed that those who have been thus commissioned have all been contributors to the enlarging sovereignty of the Supreme in the system of Satania. By nature they were all real leaders when they functioned on Urantia, and (excepting Machiventa Melchizedek) these qualities of leadership have been further augmented by mansion world experience and supplemented by the training of Jerusem citizenship. Members are nominated to the twenty-four by the cabinet of Lanaforge, seconded by the Most Highs of Edentia, approved by the Assigned Sentinel of Jerusem, and appointed by Gabriel of Salvington in accordance with the mandate of Michael. The temporary appointees function just as fully as do the permanent members of this commission of special supervisors. 114:2.1 (1251.4) This board of planetary directors is especially concerned with the supervision of those activities on this world which result from the fact that Michael here experienced his terminal bestowal. They are kept in close and immediate touch with Michael by the liaison activities of a certain Brilliant Evening Star, the identical being who attended upon Jesus throughout the mortal bestowal. 114:2.2 (1251.5) At the present time one John, known to you as "the Baptist," is chairman of this council when it is in session on Jerusem. 114:2.3 (1252.1)

The Twelve Apostles of Jesus

The group who labored with Jesus in the work of establishing the new kingdom of God in the hearts of men.

"The term apostle was employed to distinguish the chosen family of Jesus' advisers from the vast multitude of believing disciples who subsequently followed him." 137:1.7 (1525.4)

The Twelve Apostles of Jesus—Andrew

Name:	**ANDREW**
Chosen:	First Apostle. 33 years of age when selected.
Born:	Andrew was born in Capernaum. 139:1.1 (1548.5)
Before Jesus:	He was the oldest child in a family of five—himself, his brother Simon, and three sisters. His father, now dead, had been a partner of Zebedee in the fish-drying business at Bethsaida, the fishing harbor of Capernaum. When he became an apostle, Andrew was unmarried but made his home with his married brother, Simon Peter. Both were fishermen and partners of James and John the sons of Zebedee. 139:1.1 (1548.5)
History:	During this Sabbath two of John's leading disciples spent much time with Jesus. Of all John's followers one named Andrew was the most profoundly impressed with Jesus; he accompanied him on the trip to Pella with the injured boy. On the way back to John's rendezvous he asked Jesus many questions, and just before reaching their destination, the two paused for a short talk, during which Andrew said: "I have observed you ever since you came to Capernaum, and I believe you are the new Teacher, and though I do not understand all your teaching, I have fully made up my mind to follow you; I would sit at your feet and learn the whole truth about the new kingdom." And Jesus, with hearty assurance, welcomed Andrew as the first of his apostles, that group of twelve who were to labor with him in the work of establishing the new kingdom of God in the hearts of men. 137:1.1 (1524.2)
	In A.D. 26, the year he was chosen as an apostle, Andrew was 33, a full year older than Jesus and the oldest of the apostles. 139:1.2 (1548.6)
Role:	Andrew was designated chairman and director general of the twelve. 138:10.2 (1547.2)
	In A.D. 26, the year he was chosen as an apostle, Andrew was 33, a full year older than Jesus and the oldest of the apostles. Jesus never gave Andrew a nickname, a fraternal designation. But even as the apostles soon began to call Jesus Master, so they also designated Andrew by a term the equivalent of Chief. 139:1.2 (1548.6)
Andrew's Personality:	Andrew would calm Peter now and then with his more seasoned and philosophic counsel. 137:7.3 (1534.2)
	He sprang from an excellent line of ancestors and was the ablest man of the twelve. Excepting oratory, he was the peer of his associates in almost every imaginable ability. 139:1.2 (1548.6)
	Andrew was a man of clear insight, logical thought, and firm decision, whose great strength of character consisted in his superb stability. His temperamental handicap was his lack of enthusiasm; he many times failed to encourage his associates by judicious commendation. And this reticence to praise the worthy accomplishments of his friends grew out of his abhorrence of flattery and insincerity. Andrew was one of those all-round, even-tempered, self-made, and successful men of modest affairs. 139:1.10 (1550.1)

The Twelve Apostles of Jesus—Andrew

Skill:	Andrew was a good organizer but a better administrator. 139:1.3 (1549.1) Although Andrew was never an effective preacher, he was an efficient personal worker, being the pioneer missionary of the kingdom in that, as the first chosen apostle, he immediately brought to Jesus his brother, Simon, who subsequently became one of the greatest preachers of the kingdom. Andrew was the chief supporter of Jesus' policy of utilizing the program of personal work as a means of training the twelve as messengers of the kingdom. 139:1.4 (1549.2) Whether Jesus privately taught the apostles or preached to the multitude, Andrew was usually conversant with what was going on; he was an understanding executive and an efficient administrator. He rendered a prompt decision on every matter brought to his notice unless he deemed the problem one beyond the domain of his authority, in which event he would take it straight to Jesus. 139:1.5 (1549.3) Andrew and Peter were very unlike in character and temperament, but it must be recorded everlastingly to their credit that they got along together splendidly. Andrew was never jealous of Peter's oratorical ability. Not often will an older man of Andrew's type be observed exerting such a profound influence over a younger and talented brother. Andrew and Peter never seemed to be in the least jealous of each other's abilities or achievements. Late on the evening of the day of Pentecost, when, largely through the energetic and inspiring preaching of Peter, two thousand souls were added to the kingdom, Andrew said to his brother: "I could not do that, but I am glad I have a brother who could." 139:1.6 (1549.4)
	Of all the apostles, Andrew was the best judge of men. ....Andrew's great service to the kingdom was in advising Peter, James, and John concerning the choice of the first missionaries who were sent out to proclaim the gospel, and also in counseling these early leaders about the organization of the administrative affairs of the kingdom. Andrew had a great gift for discovering the hidden resources and latent talents of young people. 139:1.8 (1549.6)
Significant Events:	Sunday evening, on reaching the home of Zebedee from the highlands north of Capernaum, Jesus and the twelve partook of a simple meal. Afterward, while Jesus went for a walk along the beach, the twelve talked among themselves. After a brief conference, while the twins built a small fire to give them warmth and more light, Andrew went out to find Jesus, and when he had overtaken him, he said: "Master, my brethren are unable to comprehend what you have said about the kingdom. We do not feel able to begin this work until you have given us further instruction. I have come to ask you to join us in the garden and help us to understand the meaning of your words." And Jesus went with Andrew to meet with the apostles. 140:6.1 (1576.1)
	Just before leaving, the apostles missed the Master, and Andrew went out to find him. After a brief search he found Jesus sitting in a boat down the beach, and he was weeping. The twelve had often seen their Master when he seemed to grieve, and they had beheld his brief seasons of serious preoccupation of mind, but none of them had ever seen him weep. Andrew was somewhat startled to see the Master thus affected on the eve of their departure for Jerusalem, and he ventured to approach Jesus and ask: "On this great day, Master, when we are to depart for Jerusalem to proclaim the Father's kingdom, why is it that you weep? Which of us has offended you?" And Jesus, going back with Andrew to join the twelve, answered him: "No one of you has grieved me. I am saddened only

Andrew Significant Events: (Continued)	because none of my father Joseph's family have remembered to come over to bid us Godspeed." At this time Ruth was on a visit to her brother Joseph at Nazareth. Other members of his family were kept away by pride, disappointment, misunderstanding, and petty resentment indulged as a result of hurt feelings. 141:0.2 (1587.2)
	Andrew was much occupied with the task of adjusting the constantly recurring misunderstandings and disagreements between the disciples of John and the newer disciples of Jesus. Serious situations would arise every few days, but Andrew, with the assistance of his apostolic associates, managed to induce the contending parties to come to some sort of agreement, at least temporarily. Jesus refused to participate in any of these conferences; neither would he give any advice about the proper adjustment of these difficulties. He never once offered a suggestion as to how the apostles should solve these perplexing problems. When Andrew came to Jesus with these questions, he would always say: "It is not wise for the host to participate in the family troubles of his guests; a wise parent never takes sides in the petty quarrels of his own children." 141:3.3 (1589.4)
	About this time a state of great nervous and emotional tension developed among the apostles and their immediate disciple associates. They had hardly become accustomed to living and working together. They were experiencing increasing difficulties in maintaining harmonious relations with John's disciples. The contact with the gentiles and the Samaritans was a great trial to these Jews. And besides all this, the recent utterances of Jesus had augmented their disturbed state of mind. Andrew was almost beside himself; he did not know what next to do, and so he went to the Master with his problems and perplexities. When Jesus had listened to the apostolic chief relate his troubles, he said: "Andrew, you cannot talk men out of their perplexities when they reach such a stage of involvement, and when so many persons with strong feelings are concerned. I cannot do what you ask of me—I will not participate in these personal social difficulties—but I will join you in the enjoyment of a three-day period of rest and relaxation. Go to your brethren and announce that all of you are to go with me up on Mount Sartaba, where I desire to rest for a day or two. 143:3.1 (1610.4)
	In those days the appearance of a bright and supposedly new star was regarded as a token indicating that a great man had been born on earth. Such a star having then recently been observed, Andrew asked Jesus if these beliefs were well founded. In the long answer to Andrew's question the Master entered upon a thoroughgoing discussion of the whole subject of human superstition. 150:3.2 (1680.4)
	That evening Andrew took it upon himself to hold a personal and searching conference with each of his brethren, and he had profitable and heartening talks with all of his associates except Judas Iscariot. Andrew had never enjoyed such intimate personal association with Judas as with the other apostles and therefore had not thought it of serious account that Judas never had freely and confidentially related himself to the head of the apostolic corps. But Andrew was now so worried by Judas's attitude that, later on that night, after all the apostles were fast asleep, he sought out Jesus and presented his cause for anxiety to the Master. Said Jesus: "It is not amiss, Andrew, that you have come to me with this matter, but there is nothing more that we can do; only go on placing the utmost confidence in this apostle. And say nothing to his brethren concerning this talk with me." 157:7.1 (1750.10)

The Twelve Apostles of Jesus—Andrew

Andrew Admired Jesus For:	Andrew was tremendously impressed with the human naturalness of Jesus. He never grew weary of contemplating how one who could live so near God could be so friendly and considerate of men. 137:7.3 (1534.2)
	Andrew admired Jesus because of his consistent sincerity, his unaffected dignity. 139:1.11 (1550.2)
Final Instructions:	To Andrew he said: "Be not dismayed by the events just ahead. Keep a firm hold on your brethren and see that they do not find you downcast." 174:0.2 (1897.2)
	When the Master had finished speaking to James Zebedee, he stepped around to the end of the table where Andrew sat and, looking his faithful helper in the eyes, said: "Andrew, you have faithfully represented me as acting head of the ambassadors of the heavenly kingdom. Although you have sometimes doubted and at other times manifested dangerous timidity, still, you have always been sincerely just and eminently fair in dealing with your associates. Ever since the ordination of you and your brethren as messengers of the kingdom, you have been self-governing in all group administrative affairs except that I designated you as the acting head of these chosen ones. In no other temporal matter have I acted to direct or to influence your decisions. And this I did in order to provide for leadership in the direction of all your subsequent group deliberations. In my universe and in my Father's universe of universes, our brethren-sons are dealt with as individuals in all their spiritual relations, but in all group relationships we unfailingly provide for definite leadership. Our kingdom is a realm of order, and where two or more will creatures act in co-operation, there is always provided the authority of leadership." 181:2.16 (1958.3) And now, Andrew, since you are the chief of your brethren by authority of my appointment, and since you have thus served as my personal representative, and as I am about to leave you and go to my Father, I release you from all responsibility as regards these temporal and administrative affairs. From now on you may exercise no jurisdiction over your brethren except that which you have earned in your capacity as spiritual leader, and which your brethren therefore freely recognize. From this hour you may exercise no authority over your brethren unless they restore such jurisdiction to you by their definite legislative action after I shall have gone to the Father. But this release from responsibility as the administrative head of this group does not in any manner lessen your moral responsibility to do everything in your power to hold your brethren together with a firm and loving hand during the trying time just ahead, those days which must intervene between my departure in the flesh and the sending of the new teacher who will live in your hearts, and who ultimately will lead you into all truth. As I prepare to leave you, I would liberate you from all administrative responsibility which had its inception and authority in my presence as one among you. Henceforth I shall exercise only spiritual authority over you and among you. 181:2.17 (1959.1) "If your brethren desire to retain you as their counselor, I direct that you should, in all matters temporal and spiritual, do your utmost to promote peace and harmony among the various groups of sincere gospel believers. Dedicate the remainder of your life to promoting the practical aspects of brotherly love among your brethren. Be kind to my brothers in the flesh when they come fully to believe this gospel; manifest loving and impartial devotion to the Greeks in the West and to Abner in the East. Although these, my apostles, are soon going to be scattered to the four corners of the earth, there to

Andrew Final Instructions: (Continued)	proclaim the good news of the salvation of sonship with God, you are to hold them together during the trying time just ahead, that season of intense testing during which you must learn to believe this gospel without my personal presence while you patiently await the arrival of the new teacher, the Spirit of Truth. And so, Andrew, though it may not fall to you to do the great works as seen by men, be content to be the teacher and counselor of those who do such things. Go on with your work on earth to the end, and then shall you continue this ministry in the eternal kingdom, for have I not many times told you that I have other sheep not of this flock?" 181:2.18 (1959.2) When they returned to the others, Jesus went for a walk and talk with Andrew and James. When they had gone a short distance, Jesus said to Andrew, "Andrew, do you trust me?" And when the former chief of the apostles heard Jesus ask such a question, he stood still and answered, "Yes, Master, of a certainty I trust you, and you know that I do." Then said Jesus: "Andrew, if you trust me, trust your brethren more—even Peter. I once trusted you with the leadership of your brethren. Now must you trust others as I leave you to go to the Father. When your brethren begin to scatter abroad because of bitter persecutions, be a considerate and wise counselor to James my brother in the flesh when they put heavy burdens upon him which he is not qualified by experience to bear. And then go on trusting, for I will not fail you. When you are through on earth, you shall come to me." 192:2.7 (2048.3)
After Jesus:	Knowing how his Master so scrupulously avoided leaving written records behind him, Andrew steadfastly refused to multiply copies of his written narrative. A similar attitude on the part of the other apostles of Jesus greatly delayed the writing of the Gospels. 121:0.1 (1332.1) Very soon after Jesus' ascension on high, Andrew began the writing of a personal record of many of the sayings and doings of his departed Master. After Andrew's death other copies of this private record were made and circulated freely among the early teachers of the Christian church. These informal notes of Andrew's were subsequently edited, amended, altered, and added to until they made up a fairly consecutive narrative of the Master's life on earth. The last of these few altered and amended copies was destroyed by fire at Alexandria about one hundred years after the original was written by the first chosen of the twelve apostles. 139:1.9 (1549.7)
Death:	When the later persecutions finally scattered the apostles from Jerusalem, Andrew journeyed through Armenia, Asia Minor, and Macedonia and, after bringing many thousands into the kingdom, was finally apprehended and crucified in Patrae in Achaia. It was two full days before this robust man expired on the cross, and throughout these tragic hours he continued effectively to proclaim the glad tidings of the salvation of the kingdom of heaven. 139:1.12 (1550.3)

The Twelve Apostles of Jesus—Simon Peter

Name:	**Simon Peter**
Chosen:	Second apostle presented to Jesus by Andrew, his brother.
Born:	30 years of age when selected.
Before Jesus:	When Simon joined the apostles, he was thirty years of age. He was married, had three children, and lived at Bethsaida, near Capernaum. His brother, Andrew, and his wife's mother lived with him. Both Peter and Andrew were fisher partners of the sons of Zebedee. 139:2.1 (1550.4) The Master had known Simon for some time before Andrew presented him as the second of the apostles. 139:2.2 (1550.5)
History:	Soon after Jesus and Andrew returned to the camp, Andrew sought out his brother, Simon, and taking him aside, informed him that he had settled in his own mind that Jesus was the great Teacher, and that he had pledged himself as a disciple. He went on to say that Jesus had accepted his proffer of service and suggested that he (Simon) likewise go to Jesus and offer himself for fellowship in the service of the new kingdom. Said Simon: "Ever since this man came to work in Zebedee's shop, I have believed he was sent by God, but what about John? Are we to forsake him? Is this the right thing to do?" Whereupon they agreed to go at once to consult John. John was saddened by the thought of losing two of his able advisers and most promising disciples, but he bravely answered their inquiries, saying: "This is but the beginning; presently will my work end, and we shall all become his disciples." Then Andrew beckoned to Jesus to draw aside while he announced that his brother desired to join himself to the service of the new kingdom. And in welcoming Simon as his second apostle, Jesus said: "Simon, your enthusiasm is commendable, but it is dangerous to the work of the kingdom. I admonish you to become more thoughtful in your speech. I would change your name to Peter." 137:1.3 (1524.4)
Role:	Peter, James, and John were appointed personal companions of Jesus. They were to attend him day and night, to minister to his physical and sundry needs, and to accompany him on those night vigils of prayer and mysterious communion with the Father in heaven. 138:10.3 (1547.3)
Simon Peter's Personality:	This period of waiting and teaching was especially hard on Simon Peter. He repeatedly sought to persuade Jesus to launch forth with the preaching of the kingdom in Galilee while John continued to preach in Judea. But Jesus' reply to Peter ever was: "Be patient, Simon. Make progress. We shall be none too ready when the Father calls." 137:7.3 (1534.2) Simon Peter was a man of impulse, an optimist. He had grown up permitting himself freely to indulge strong feelings; he was constantly getting into difficulties because he persisted in speaking without thinking. This sort of thoughtlessness also made incessant trouble for all of his friends and associates and was the cause of his receiving many mild rebukes from his Master. The only reason Peter did not get into more trouble because of his thoughtless speaking was that he very early learned to talk over many of his plans and schemes with his brother, Andrew, before he ventured to make public proposals. 139:2.3 (1550.6)

The Twelve Apostles of Jesus—Simon Peter

Simon Peter's Personality: (Continued)	Simon Peter was distressingly vacillating; he would suddenly swing from one extreme to the other. First he refused to let Jesus wash his feet and then, on hearing the Master's reply, begged to be washed all over. But, after all, Jesus knew that Peter's faults were of the head and not of the heart. He was one of the most inexplicable combinations of courage and cowardice that ever lived on earth. His great strength of character was loyalty, friendship. Peter really and truly loved Jesus. And yet despite this towering strength of devotion he was so unstable and inconstant that he permitted a servant girl to tease him into denying his Lord and Master. Peter could withstand persecution and any other form of direct assault, but he withered and shrank before ridicule. He was a brave soldier when facing a frontal attack, but he was a fear-cringing coward when surprised with an assault from the rear. 139:2.6 (1551.2)
	He was the first one of the apostles to make wholehearted confession of Jesus' combined humanity and divinity and the first—save Judas—to deny him. Peter was not so much of a dreamer, but he disliked to descend from the clouds of ecstasy and the enthusiasm of dramatic indulgence to the plain and matter-of-fact world of reality. 139:2.8 (1551.4)
Skill:	Peter was a fluent speaker, eloquent and dramatic. He was also a natural and inspirational leader of men, a quick thinker but not a deep reasoner. He asked many questions, more than all the apostles put together, and while the majority of these questions were good and relevant, many of them were thoughtless and foolish. Peter did not have a deep mind, but he knew his mind fairly well. He was therefore a man of quick decision and sudden action. While others talked in their astonishment at seeing Jesus on the beach, Peter jumped in and swam ashore to meet the Master. 139:2.4 (1550.7)
	In following Jesus, literally and figuratively, he was either leading the procession or else trailing behind—"following afar off." But he was the outstanding preacher of the twelve; he did more than any other one man, aside from Paul, to establish the kingdom and send its messengers to the four corners of the earth in one generation. 139:2.9 (1551.5)
Significant Events:	We who view human activities from behind the scenes and in the light of nineteen centuries of time recognize just three factors of paramount value in the early setting of the stage for the rapid spread of Christianity throughout Europe, and they are: 132:0.5 (1456.1) 1. The choosing and holding of Simon Peter as an apostle. 132:0.6 (1456.2)
	The apostles, without their Master—sent off by themselves—entered the boat and in silence began to row toward Bethsaida on the western shore of the lake. None of the twelve was so crushed and downcast as Simon Peter. Hardly a word was spoken; they were all thinking of the Master alone in the hills. Had he forsaken them? He had never before sent them all away and refused to go with them. What could all this mean? 152:4.1 (1703.1) Darkness descended upon them, for there had arisen a strong and contrary wind which made progress almost impossible. As the hours of darkness and hard rowing

Simon Peter Significant Events: (Continued)	passed, Peter grew weary and fell into a deep sleep of exhaustion. Andrew and James put him to rest on the cushioned seat in the stern of the boat. While the other apostles toiled against the wind and the waves, Peter dreamed a dream; he saw a vision of Jesus coming to them walking on the sea. When the Master seemed to walk on by the boat, Peter cried out, "Save us, Master, save us." And those who were in the rear of the boat heard him say some of these words. As this apparition of the night season continued in Peter's mind, he dreamed that he heard Jesus say: "Be of good cheer; it is I; be not afraid." This was like the balm of Gilead to Peter's disturbed soul; it soothed his troubled spirit, so that (in his dream) he cried out to the Master: "Lord, if it really is you, bid me come and walk with you on the water." And when Peter started to walk upon the water, the boisterous waves frightened him, and as he was about to sink, he cried out, "Lord, save me!" And many of the twelve heard him utter this cry. Then Peter dreamed that Jesus came to the rescue and, stretching forth his hand, took hold and lifted him up, saying: "O, you of little faith, wherefore did you doubt?" 152:4.2 (1703.2) In connection with the latter part of his dream Peter arose from the seat whereon he slept and actually stepped overboard and into the water. And he awakened from his dream as Andrew, James, and John reached down and pulled him out of the sea. 152:4.3 (1703.3)
	It is not strange that you have a record of Peter's catching a fish with a shekel in its mouth. In those days there were current many stories about finding treasures in the mouths of fishes; such tales of near miracles were commonplace. So, as Peter left them to go toward the boat, Jesus remarked, half- humorously: "Strange that the sons of the king must pay tribute; usually it is the stranger who is taxed for the upkeep of the court, but it behooves us to afford no stumbling block for the authorities. Go hence! maybe you will catch the fish with the shekel in its mouth." 157:1.4 (1744.2)
	That which Peter, James, and John witnessed on the mount of transfiguration was a fleeting glimpse of a celestial pageant which transpired that eventful day on Mount Hermon. 158:3.1 (1755.1)
	Then said Simon Peter: "Master, if you have a new commandment, we would hear it. Reveal the new way to us." 140:6.4 (1576.4)
	Peter was so perturbed that he sought to escape contact with his accusers by going away from the fire and remaining by himself on the porch. After more than an hour of this isolation, the gate-keeper and her sister chanced to meet him, and both of them again teasingly charged him with being a follower of Jesus. And again he denied the accusation. Just as he had once more denied all connection with Jesus, the cock crowed, and Peter remembered the words of warning spoken to him by his Master earlier that same night. As he stood there, heavy of heart and crushed with the sense of guilt, the palace doors opened, and the guards led Jesus past on the way to Caiaphas. As the Master passed Peter, he saw, by the light of the torches, the look of despair on the face of his former self-confident and superficially brave apostle, and he turned and looked upon Peter. Peter never forgot that look as long as he lived. It was such a glance of commingled pity and love as mortal man had never beheld in the face of the Master. 184:2.8 (1981.2)

The Twelve Apostles of Jesus—Simon Peter

<table>
<tr><td>Admired Jesus For:</td><td>The one trait which Peter most admired in Jesus was his supernal tenderness. Peter never grew weary of contemplating Jesus' forbearance. He never forgot the lesson about forgiving the wrongdoer, not only seven times but seventy times and seven. He thought much about these impressions of the Master's forgiving character during those dark and dismal days immediately following his thoughtless and unintended denial of Jesus in the high priest's courtyard. 139:2.5 (1551.1)</td></tr>
<tr><td rowspan="3">Final Instruction:</td><td>To Peter he said: "Put not your trust in the arm of flesh nor in weapons of steel. Establish yourself on the spiritual foundations of the eternal rocks." 174:0.2 (1897.2)</td></tr>
<tr><td>Then the Master went over to Simon Peter, who stood up as Jesus addressed him: "Peter, I know you love me, and that you will dedicate your life to the public proclamation of this gospel of the kingdom to Jew and gentile, but I am distressed that your years of such close association with me have not done more to help you think before you speak. What experience must you pass through before you will learn to set a guard upon your lips? How much trouble have you made for us by your thoughtless speaking, by your presumptuous self-confidence! And you are destined to make much more trouble for yourself if you do not master this frailty. You know that your brethren love you in spite of this weakness, and you should also understand that this shortcoming in no way impairs my affection for you, but it lessens your usefulness and never ceases to make trouble for you. But you will undoubtedly receive great help from the experience you will pass through this very night. And what I now say to you, Simon Peter, I likewise say to all your brethren here assembled: This night you will all be in great danger of stumbling over me. You know it is written, 'The shepherd will be smitten and the sheep will be scattered abroad.' When I am absent, there is great danger that some of you will succumb to doubts and stumble because of what befalls me. But I promise you now that I will come back to you for a little while, and that I will then go before you into Galilee." 181:2.27 (1962.2)

Then said Peter, placing his hand on Jesus' shoulder: "No matter if all my brethren should succumb to doubts because of you, I promise that I will not stumble over anything you may do. I will go with you and, if need be, die for you." 181:2.28 (1962.3)

As Peter stood there before his Master, all atremble with intense emotion and overflowing with genuine love for him, Jesus looked straight into his moistened eyes as he said: "Peter, verily, verily, I say to you, this night the cock will not crow until you have denied me three or four times. And thus what you have failed to learn from peaceful association with me, you will learn through much trouble and many sorrows. And after you have really learned this needful lesson, you should strengthen your brethren and go on living a life dedicated to preaching this gospel, though you may fall into prison and, perhaps, follow me in paying the supreme price of loving service in the building of the Father's kingdom. 181:2.29 (1962.4)</td></tr>
<tr><td>Jesus then turned toward Peter and asked, "Peter, do you love me?" Peter answered, "Lord, you know I love you with all my soul." Then said Jesus: "If you love me, Peter, feed my lambs. Do not neglect to minister to the weak, the poor, and the young. Preach the gospel without fear or favor; remember always that God is no respecter of persons. Serve your fellow men even as I have served you; forgive your fellow mortals even as I have forgiven you. Let experience teach you the value of meditation and the power of intelligent reflection." 192:2.2 (2047.6)</td></tr>
</table>

Simon Peter Final Instruction: (Continued)	After they had walked along a little farther, the Master turned to Peter and asked, "Peter, do you really love me?" And then said Simon, "Yes, Lord, you know that I love you." And again said Jesus: "Then take good care of my sheep. Be a good and a true shepherd to the flock. Betray not their confidence in you. Be not taken by surprise at the enemy's hand. Be on guard at all times—watch and pray." 192:2.3 (2047.7) When they had gone a few steps farther, Jesus turned to Peter and, for the third time, asked, "Peter, do you truly love me?" And then Peter, being slightly grieved at the Master's seeming distrust of him, said with considerable feeling, "Lord, you know all things, and therefore do you know that I really and truly love you." Then said Jesus: "Feed my sheep. Do not forsake the flock. Be an example and an inspiration to all your fellow shepherds. Love the flock as I have loved you and devote yourself to their welfare even as I have devoted my life to your welfare. And follow after me even to the end." 192:2.4 (2047.8) Peter took this last statement literally—that he should continue to follow after him—and turning to Jesus, he pointed to John, asking, "If I follow on after you, what shall this man do?" And then, perceiving that Peter had misunderstood his words, Jesus said: "Peter, be not concerned about what your brethren shall do. If I will that John should tarry after you are gone, even until I come back, what is that to you? Only make sure that you follow me." 192:2.5 (2048.1)
After Jesus:	After his rash denials of the Master he found himself, and with Andrew's sympathetic and understanding guidance he again led the way back to the fish nets while the apostles tarried to find out what was to happen after the crucifixion. When he was fully assured that Jesus had forgiven him and knew he had been received back into the Master's fold, the fires of the kingdom burned so brightly within his soul that he became a great and saving light to thousands who sat in darkness. 139:2.10 (1551.6) After leaving Jerusalem and before Paul became the leading spirit among the gentile Christian churches, Peter traveled extensively, visiting all the churches from Babylon to Corinth. He even visited and ministered to many of the churches which had been raised up by Paul. Although Peter and Paul differed much in temperament and education, even in theology, they worked together harmoniously for the upbuilding of the churches during their later years. 139:2.11 (1551.7) But Peter persisted in making the mistake of trying to convince the Jews that Jesus was, after all, really and truly the Jewish Messiah. Right up to the day of his death, Simon Peter continued to suffer confusion in his mind between the concepts of Jesus as the Jewish Messiah, Christ as the world's redeemer, and the Son of Man as the revelation of God, the loving Father of all mankind. 139:2.13 (1552.2)
Death:	And so this man Peter, an intimate of Jesus, one of the inner circle, went forth from Jerusalem proclaiming the glad tidings of the kingdom with power and glory until the fullness of his ministry had been accomplished; and he regarded himself as the recipient of high honors when his captors informed him that he must die as his Master had died—on the cross. And thus was Simon Peter crucified in Rome. 139:2.15 (1552.4)

The Twelve Apostles of Jesus—James Zebedee

Name:	**James Zebedee**
Chosen:	Third Apostle
Born:	30 years of age when selected. (brother of John Zebedee)
Before Jesus:	James, the older of the two apostle sons of Zebedee, whom Jesus nicknamed "sons of thunder," was thirty years old when he became an apostle. He was married, had four children, and lived near his parents in the outskirts of Capernaum, Bethsaida. He was a fisherman, plying his calling in company with his younger brother John and in association with Andrew and Simon. James and his brother John enjoyed the advantage of having known Jesus longer than any of the other apostles. 139:3.1 (1552.5)
History:	Jesus was asleep when they reached his abode, but they awakened him, saying: "How is it that, while we who have so long lived with you are searching in the hills for you, you prefer others before us and choose Andrew and Simon as your first associates in the new kingdom?" Jesus answered them, "Be calm in your hearts and ask yourselves, 'who directed that you should search for the Son of Man when he was about his Father's business?'" After they had recited the details of their long search in the hills, Jesus further instructed them: "You should learn to search for the secret of the new kingdom in your hearts and not in the hills. That which you sought was already present in your souls. You are indeed my brethren—you needed not to be received by me—already were you of the kingdom, and you should be of good cheer, making ready also to go with us tomorrow into Galilee." John then made bold to ask, "But, Master, will James and I be associates with you in the new kingdom, even as Andrew and Simon?" And Jesus, laying a hand on the shoulder of each of them, said: "My brethren, you were already with me in the spirit of the kingdom, even before these others made request to be received. You, my brethren, have no need to make request for entrance into the kingdom; you have been with me in the kingdom from the beginning. Before men, others may take precedence over you, but in my heart did I also number you in the councils of the kingdom, even before you thought to make this request of me. And even so might you have been first before men had you not been absent engaged in a well-intentioned but self-appointed task of seeking for one who was not lost. In the coming kingdom, be not mindful of those things which foster your anxiety but rather at all times concern yourselves only with doing the will of the Father who is in heaven." 137:1.6 (1525.3)
Role:	Peter, James, and John were appointed personal companions of Jesus. They were to attend him day and night, to minister to his physical and sundry needs, and to accompany him on those night vigils of prayer and mysterious communion with the Father in heaven. 138:10.3 (1547.3)
James Zebedee's Personality:	This able apostle was a temperamental contradiction; he seemed really to possess two natures, both of which were actuated by strong feelings. He was particularly vehement when his indignation was once fully aroused. He had a fiery temper when once it was adequately provoked, and when the storm was over, he was always wont to justify and excuse his anger under the pretense that it was wholly a manifestation of righteous indignation. Except for these periodic upheavals of wrath, James's personality was much like that of Andrew. He did not have Andrew's discretion or insight into human nature, but he was a much better public speaker. Next to Peter, unless it was Matthew, James was the best public orator among the twelve. 139:3.2 (1552.6)

The Twelve Apostles of Jesus—James Zebedee

James Zebedee's Personality: (Continued)	Though James was in no sense moody, he could be quiet and taciturn one day and a very good talker and storyteller the next. He usually talked freely with Jesus, but among the twelve, for days at a time he was the silent man. His one great weakness was these spells of unaccountable silence. 139:3.3 (1552.7) The outstanding feature of James's personality was his ability to see all sides of a proposition. Of all the twelve, he came the nearest to grasping the real import and significance of Jesus' teaching. He, too, was slow at first to comprehend the Master's meaning, but ere they had finished their training, he had acquired a superior concept of Jesus' message. James was able to understand a wide range of human nature; he got along well with the versatile Andrew, the impetuous Peter, and his self-contained brother John. 139:3.4 (1552.8)
Skill:	He did not have Andrew's discretion or insight into human nature, but he was a much better public speaker. Next to Peter, unless it was Matthew, James was the best public orator among the twelve. 139:3.2 (1552.6)
	Of all the twelve, he came the nearest to grasping the real import and significance of Jesus' teaching. He, too, was slow at first to comprehend the Master's meaning, but ere they had finished their training, he had acquired a superior concept of Jesus' message. James was able to understand a wide range of human nature; he got along well with the versatile Andrew, the impetuous Peter, and his self-contained brother John. 139:3.4 (1552.8)
	James Zebedee was a well-balanced thinker and planner. Along with Andrew, he was one of the more level-headed of the apostolic group. He was a vigorous individual but was never in a hurry. He was an excellent balance wheel for Peter. 139:3.7 (1553.3) He was modest and undramatic, a daily server, an unpretentious worker, seeking no special reward when he once grasped something of the real meaning of the kingdom. . . . Herod Agrippa feared James above all the other apostles. He was indeed often quiet and silent, but he was brave and determined when his convictions were aroused and challenged. 139:3.8 (1553.4)
Significant Events:	Jesus was minded to go on discussing the other commandments when James Zebedee interrupted him, asking: "Master, what shall we teach the people regarding divorcement? Shall we allow a man to divorce his wife as Moses has directed?" 140:6.6 (1576.6)
	James grasped the thrilling truth that Jesus wanted his children on earth to live as though they were already citizens of the completed heavenly kingdom. 140:8.25 (1582.6)
	One of the most eventful of all the evening conferences at Amathus was the session having to do with the discussion of spiritual unity. James Zebedee had asked, "Master, how shall we learn to see alike and thereby enjoy more harmony among ourselves?" 141:5.1 (1591.6)
	But the apostles were not yet satisfied; they desired Jesus to give them a model prayer which they could teach the new disciples. After listening to this discourse on prayer, James Zebedee said: "Very good, Master, but we do not desire a form of prayer for ourselves so much as for the newer believers who so frequently beseech us, 'Teach us how acceptably to pray to the Father in heaven.'" 144:3.1 (1619.5)

The Twelve Apostles of Jesus—James Zebedee

James Zebedee Significant Events: (Continued)	That which Peter, James, and John witnessed on the mount of transfiguration was a fleeting glimpse of a celestial pageant which transpired that eventful day on Mount Hermon. 158:3.1 (1755.1)
	It was on this Sunday afternoon that Salome the mother of James and John Zebedee came to Jesus with her two apostle sons and, in the manner of approaching an Oriental potentate, sought to have Jesus promise in advance to grant whatever request she might make. But the Master would not promise; instead, he asked her, "What do you want me to do for you?" Then answered Salome: "Master, now that you are going up to Jerusalem to establish the kingdom, I would ask you in advance to promise me that these my sons shall have honor with you, the one to sit on your right hand and the other to sit on your left hand in your kingdom." 171:0.4 (1867.4) When Jesus heard Salome's request, he said: "Woman, you know not what you ask." And then, looking straight into the eyes of the two honor-seeking apostles, he said: "Because I have long known and loved you; because I have even lived in your mother's house; because Andrew has assigned you to be with me at all times; therefore do you permit your mother to come to me secretly, making this unseemly request. But let me ask you: Are you able to drink the cup I am about to drink?" And without a moment for thought, James and John answered, "Yes, Master, we are able." Said Jesus: "I am saddened that you know not why we go up to Jerusalem; I am grieved that you understand not the nature of my kingdom; I am disappointed that you bring your mother to make this request of me; but I know you love me in your hearts; therefore I declare that you shall indeed drink of my cup of bitterness and share in my humiliation, but to sit on my right hand and on my left hand is not mine to give. Such honors are reserved for those who have been designated by my Father." 171:0.5 (1867.5)
Admired Jesus For:	That characteristic of Jesus which James most admired was the Master's sympathetic affection. Jesus' understanding interest in the small and the great, the rich and the poor, made a great appeal to him. 139:3.6 (1553.2) James was astonished at how Jesus seemed to see the end from the beginning. The Master rarely appeared to be surprised. He was never excited, vexed, or disconcerted. He never apologized to any man. He was at times saddened, but never discouraged. 141:7.13 (1594.7)
Final Instructions:	To James he said: "Falter not because of outward appearances. Remain firm in your faith, and you shall soon know of the reality of that which you believe." 174:0.2 (1897.2)
	Jesus then stepped over to James Zebedee, who stood in silence as the Master addressed him, saying: "James, when you and your younger brother once came to me seeking preferment in the honors of the kingdom, and I told you such honors were for the Father to bestow, I asked if you were able to drink my cup, and both of you answered that you were. Even if you were not then able, and if you are not now able, you will soon be prepared for such a service by the experience you are about to pass through. By such behavior you angered your brethren at that time. If they have not already fully forgiven you, they will when they see you drink my cup. Whether your ministry be long or short, possess your soul in patience. When the new teacher comes, let him teach you the poise of compassion and that sympathetic tolerance which is born of sublime confidence in me and of perfect submission to the Father's

James Zebedee Final Instructions: (Continued)	will. Dedicate your life to the demonstration of that combined human affection and divine dignity of the God-knowing and Son-believing disciple. And all who thus live will reveal the gospel even in the manner of their death. You and your brother John will go different ways, and one of you may sit down with me in the eternal kingdom long before the other. It would help you much if you would learn that true wisdom embraces discretion as well as courage. You should learn sagacity to go along with your aggressiveness. There will come those supreme moments wherein my disciples will not hesitate to lay down their lives for this gospel, but in all ordinary circumstances it would be far better to placate the wrath of unbelievers that you might live and continue to preach the glad tidings. As far as lies in your power, live long on the earth that your life of many years may be fruitful in souls won for the heavenly kingdom." 181:2.15 (1958.2)
	Then Jesus turned to James, asking, "James, do you trust me?" And of course James replied, "Yes, Master, I trust you with all my heart." Then said Jesus: "James, if you trust me more, you will be less impatient with your brethren. If you will trust me, it will help you to be kind to the brotherhood of believers. Learn to weigh the consequences of your sayings and your doings. Remember that the reaping is in accordance with the sowing. Pray for tranquility of spirit and cultivate patience. These graces, with living faith, shall sustain you when the hour comes to drink the cup of sacrifice. But never be dismayed; when you are through on earth, you shall also come to be with me." 192:2.8 (2048.4)
After Jesus:	This left but six of the original twelve apostles to become actors on the stage of the early proclamation of the gospel in Jerusalem: Peter, Andrew, James, John, Philip, and Matthew. 193:6.5 (2058.4)
Death:	He was modest and undramatic, a daily server, an unpretentious worker, seeking no special reward when he once grasped something of the real meaning of the kingdom. And even in the story about the mother of James and John, who asked that her sons be granted places on the right hand and the left hand of Jesus, it should be remembered that it was the mother who made this request. And when they signified that they were ready to assume such responsibilities, it should be recognized that they were cognizant of the dangers accompanying the Master's supposed revolt against the Roman power, and that they were also willing to pay the price. When Jesus asked if they were ready to drink the cup, they replied that they were. And as concerns James, it was literally true—he did drink the cup with the Master, seeing that he was the first of the apostles to experience martyrdom, being early put to death with the sword by Herod Agrippa. James was thus the first of the twelve to sacrifice his life upon the new battle line of the kingdom. 139:3.8 (1553.4) James lived his life to the full, and when the end came, he bore himself with such grace and fortitude that even his accuser and informer, who attended his trial and execution, was so touched that he rushed away from the scene of James's death to join himself to the disciples of Jesus. 139:3.9 (1553.5)

The Twelve Apostles of Jesus—John Zebedee

Name:	**John Zebedee**
Chosen:	Fourth Apostle—a current follower of Jesus
Born:	24 years of age when selected. (brother of James Zebedee)
Before Jesus:	He was unmarried and lived with his parents at Bethsaida; he was a fisherman and worked with his brother James in partnership with Andrew and Peter. 139:4.1 (1553.6)
History:	Same as James Zebedee.
Role:	Peter, James, and John were appointed personal companions of Jesus. They were to attend him day and night, to minister to his physical and sundry needs, and to accompany him on those night vigils of prayer and mysterious communion with the Father in heaven. 138:10.3 (1547.3)
	Both before and after becoming an apostle, John functioned as the personal agent of Jesus in dealing with the Master's family, and he continued to bear this responsibility as long as Mary the mother of Jesus lived. 139:4.1 (1553.6)
John Zebedee's Personality:	John Zebedee had many lovely traits of character, but one which was not so lovely was his inordinate but usually well-concealed conceit. His long association with Jesus made many and great changes in his character. This conceit was greatly lessened, but after growing old and becoming more or less childish, this self-esteem reappeared to a certain extent, so that, when engaged in directing Nathan in the writing of the Gospel which now bears his name, the aged apostle did not hesitate repeatedly to refer to himself as the "disciple whom Jesus loved." In view of the fact that John came nearer to being the chum of Jesus than any other earth mortal, that he was his chosen personal representative in so many matters, it is not strange that he should have come to regard himself as the "disciple whom Jesus loved" since he most certainly knew he was the disciple whom Jesus so frequently trusted. 139:4.4 (1554.2) The strongest trait in John's character was his dependability; he was prompt and courageous, faithful and devoted. His greatest weakness was this characteristic conceit. He was the youngest member of his father's family and the youngest of the apostolic group. Perhaps he was just a bit spoiled; maybe he had been humored slightly too much. But the John of after years was a very different type of person than the self-admiring and arbitrary young man who joined the ranks of Jesus' apostles when he was twenty-four. 139:4.5 (1554.3)
	John was a man of few words except when his temper was aroused. He thought much but said little. As he grew older, his temper became more subdued, better controlled, but he never overcame his disinclination to talk; he never fully mastered this reticence. But he was gifted with a remarkable and creative imagination. 139:4.7 (1554.5) There was another side to John that one would not expect to find in this quiet and introspective type. He was somewhat bigoted and inordinately intolerant. In this respect he and James were much alike—they both wanted to call down fire from heaven on the heads of the disrespectful Samaritans. When John encountered some strangers teaching in Jesus' name, he promptly forbade them. But he was not the only one of the twelve who was tainted with this kind of self-esteem and superiority consciousness. 139:4.8 (1555.1)

The Twelve Apostles of Jesus—John Zebedee

Skill:	John had a cool and daring courage which few of the other apostles possessed. He was the one apostle who followed right along with Jesus the night of his arrest and dared to accompany his Master into the very jaws of death. He was present and near at hand right up to the last earthly hour and was found faithfully carrying out his trust with regard to Jesus' mother and ready to receive such additional instructions as might be given during the last moments of the Master's mortal existence. One thing is certain, John was thoroughly dependable. John usually sat on Jesus' right hand when the twelve were at meat. He was the first of the twelve really and fully to believe in the resurrection, and he was the first to recognize the Master when he came to them on the seashore after his resurrection. 139:4.10 (1555.3)
Significant Events:	Jesus well knew that his apostles were not fully assimilating his teachings. He decided to give some special instruction to Peter, James, and John, hoping they would be able to clarify the ideas of their associates. He saw that, while some features of the idea of a spiritual kingdom were being grasped by the twelve, they steadfastly persisted in attaching these new spiritual teachings directly onto their old and entrenched literal concepts of the kingdom of heaven as a restoration of David's throne and the re-establishment of Israel as a temporal power on earth. Accordingly, on Thursday afternoon Jesus went out from the shore in a boat with Peter, James, and John to talk over the affairs of the kingdom. 140:8.1 (1579.3)
	It was on this Sunday afternoon that Salome the mother of James and John Zebedee came to Jesus with her two apostle sons and, in the manner of approaching an Oriental potentate, sought to have Jesus promise in advance to grant whatever request she might make. But the Master would not promise; instead, he asked her, "What do you want me to do for you?" Then answered Salome: "Master, now that you are going up to Jerusalem to establish the kingdom, I would ask you in advance to promise me that these my sons shall have honor with you, the one to sit on your right hand and the other to sit on your left hand in your kingdom." 171:0.4 (1867.4) When Jesus heard Salome's request, he said: "Woman, you know not what you ask." And then, looking straight into the eyes of the two honor-seeking apostles, he said: "Because I have long known and loved you; because I have even lived in your mother's house; because Andrew has assigned you to be with me at all times; therefore do you permit your mother to come to me secretly, making this unseemly request. But let me ask you: Are you able to drink the cup I am about to drink?" And without a moment for thought, James and John answered, "Yes, Master, we are able." Said Jesus: "I am saddened that you know not why we go up to Jerusalem; I am grieved that you understand not the nature of my kingdom; I am disappointed that you bring your mother to make this request of me; but I know you love me in your hearts; therefore I declare that you shall indeed drink of my cup of bitterness and share in my humiliation, but to sit on my right hand and on my left hand is not mine to give. Such honors are reserved for those who have been designated by my Father." 171:0.5 (1867.5)
	John Zebedee came somewhere near understanding why Jesus did this; at least he grasped in part the spiritual significance of this so-called triumphal entry into Jerusalem. As the multitude moved on toward the temple, and as John beheld his Master sitting there astride the colt, he recalled hearing Jesus onetime quote the

John Zebedee Significant Events: (Continued)	passage of Scripture, the utterance of Zechariah, which described the coming of the Messiah as a man of peace and riding into Jerusalem on an ass. As John turned this Scripture over in his mind, he began to comprehend the symbolic significance of this Sunday-afternoon pageant. At least, he grasped enough of the meaning of this Scripture to enable him somewhat to enjoy the episode and to prevent his becoming overmuch depressed by the apparent purposeless ending of the triumphal procession. John had a type of mind which naturally tended to think and feel in symbols. 172:5.5 (1884.4)
	Until the very end of the crucifixion, John Zebedee remained, as Jesus had directed him, always near at hand, and it was he who supplied David's messengers with information from hour to hour which they carried to David at the garden camp, and which was then relayed to the hiding apostles and to Jesus' family. (1976.3) 183:4.5
	Pilate began his talk with Jesus by assuring him that he did not believe the first count against him: that he was a perverter of the nation and an inciter to rebellion. Then he asked, "Did you ever teach that tribute should be refused Caesar?" Jesus, pointing to John, said, "Ask him or any other man who has heard my teaching." Then Pilate questioned John about this matter of tribute, and John testified concerning his Master's teaching and explained that Jesus and his apostles paid taxes both to Caesar and to the temple. When Pilate had questioned John, he said, "See that you tell no man that I talked with you." And John never did reveal this matter. 185:3.1 (1991.1)
Admired Jesus For:	Those characteristics of Jesus which John most appreciated were the Master's love and unselfishness; these traits made such an impression on him that his whole subsequent life became dominated by the sentiment of love and brotherly devotion. He talked about love and wrote about love. This "son of thunder" became the "apostle of love"; and at Ephesus, when the aged bishop was no longer able to stand in the pulpit and preach but had to be carried to church in a chair, and when at the close of the service he was asked to say a few words to the believers, for years his only utterance was, "My little children, love one another." 139:4.6 (1554.4)
	John's life was tremendously influenced by the sight of Jesus' going about without a home as he knew how faithfully he had made provision for the care of his mother and family. John also deeply sympathized with Jesus because of his family's failure to understand him, being aware that they were gradually withdrawing from him. This entire situation, together with Jesus' ever deferring his slightest wish to the will of the Father in heaven and his daily life of implicit trust, made such a profound impression on John that it produced marked and permanent changes in his character, changes which manifested themselves throughout his entire subsequent life. 139:4.9 (1555.2)
Final Instructions:	To John he said: "Be gentle; love even your enemies; be tolerant. And remember that I have trusted you with many things." 174:0.2 (1897.2)
	To John, Jesus said: "You, John, are the youngest of my brethren. You have been very near me, and while I love you all with the same love which a father bestows upon his sons, you were designated by Andrew as one of the three who should always be near me. Besides this, you have acted for me and must continue so to act in many matters concerning my earthly family. And I go to the Father, John, having full confidence that you will continue to watch over those who are mine in the flesh. See to it that their present confusion regarding my mission does not in any way prevent your

Final Instructions: (Continued)	extending to them all sympathy, counsel, and help even as you know I would if I were to remain in the flesh. And when they all come to see the light and enter fully into the kingdom, while you all will welcome them joyously, I depend upon you, John, to welcome them for me. 181:2.2 (1955.3) "And now, as I enter upon the closing hours of my earthly career, remain. near at hand that I may leave any message with you regarding my family As concerns the work put in my hands by the Father, it is now finished except for my death in the flesh, and I am ready to drink this last cup. But as for the responsibilities left to me by my earthly father, Joseph, while I have attended to these during my life, I must now depend upon you to act in my stead in all these matters. And I have chosen you to do this for me, John, because you are the youngest and will therefore very likely outlive these other apostles. 181:2.3 (1955.4) "Once we called you and your brother sons of thunder. You started out with us strong-minded and intolerant, but you have changed much since you wanted me to call fire down upon the heads of ignorant and thoughtless unbelievers. And you must change yet more. You should become the apostle of the new commandment which I have this night given you. Dedicate your life to teaching your brethren how to love one another, even as I have loved you." 181:2.4 (1955.5) As John Zebedee stood there in the upper chamber, the tears rolling down his cheeks, he looked into the Master's face and said: "And so I will, my Master, but how can I learn to love my brethren more?" And then answered Jesus: "You will learn to love your brethren more when you first learn to love their Father in heaven more, and after you have become truly more interested in their welfare in time and in eternity. And all such human interest is fostered by understanding sympathy, unselfish service, and unstinted forgiveness. No man should despise your youth, but I exhort you always to give due consideration to the fact that age oftentimes represents experience, and that nothing in human affairs can take the place of actual experience. Strive to live peaceably with all men, especially your friends in the brotherhood of the heavenly kingdom. And, John, always remember, strive not with the souls you would win for the kingdom." 181:2.5 (1955.6)
	When they had finished breakfast, and while the others sat by the fire, Jesus beckoned to Peter and to John that they should come with him for a stroll on the beach. As they walked along, Jesus said to John, "John, do you love me?" And when John answered, "Yes, Master, with all my heart," the Master said: "Then, John, give up your intolerance and learn to love men as I have loved you. Devote your life to proving that love is the greatest thing in the world. It is the love of God that impels men to seek salvation. Love is the ancestor of all spiritual goodness, the essence of the true and the beautiful." 192:2.1 (2047.5)
After Jesus:	4. *The Gospel of John.* The Gospel according to John relates much of Jesus' work in Judea and around Jerusalem which is not contained in the other records. This is the so-called Gospel according to John the son of Zebedee, and though John did not write it, he did inspire it. Since its first writing it has several times been edited to make it appear to have been written by John himself. When this record was made, John had the other Gospels, and he saw that much had been omitted; accordingly, in the year A.D. 101 he encouraged his associate, Nathan, a Greek Jew from Caesarea, to begin the writing.

After Jesus: (Continued)	John supplied his material from memory and by reference to the three records already in existence. He had no written records of his own. The Epistle known as "First John" was written by John himself as a covering letter for the work which Nathan executed under his direction. 121:8.10 (1342.5) This son of Zebedee was very closely associated with Peter in the early activities of the Christian movement, becoming one of the chief supporters of the Jerusalem church. He was the right-hand support of Peter on the day of Pentecost. 139:4.11 (1555.4) Several years after the martyrdom of James, John married his brother's widow. The last twenty years of his life he was cared for by a loving granddaughter. 139:4.12 (1555.5) John was in prison several times and was banished to the Isle of Patmos for a period of four years until another emperor came to power in Rome. Had not John been tactful and sagacious, he would undoubtedly have been killed as was his more outspoken brother James. As the years passed, John, together with James the Lord's brother, learned to practice wise conciliation when they appeared before the civil magistrates. They found that a "soft answer turns away wrath." They also learned to represent the church as a "spiritual brotherhood devoted to the social service of mankind" rather than as "the kingdom of heaven." They taught loving service rather than ruling power—kingdom and king. 139:4.13 (1555.6) When in temporary exile on Patmos, John wrote the book of *Revelation*, which you now have in greatly abridged and distorted form. This book of *Revelation* contains the surviving fragments of a great revelation, large portions of which were lost, other portions of which were removed, subsequent to John's writing. It is preserved in only fragmentary and adulterated form. 139:4.14 (1555.7) John traveled much, labored incessantly, and after becoming bishop of the Asia churches, settled down at Ephesus. He directed his associate, Nathan, in the writing of the so-called "Gospel according to John," at Ephesus, when he was ninety-nine years old. Of all the twelve apostles, John Zebedee eventually became the outstanding theologian. He died a natural death at Ephesus in A.D. 103 when he was one hundred and one years of age. 139:4.15 (1555.8)
	The Apostle John told about the crucifixion as he remembered the event two thirds of a century after its occurrence. The other records were based upon the recital of the Roman centurion on duty who, because of what he saw and heard, subsequently believed in Jesus and entered into the full fellowship of the kingdom of heaven on earth. 187:4.4 (2009.3)
	All day long John upheld the idea that Jesus had risen from the dead. He recounted no less than five different times when the Master had affirmed he would rise again and at least three times when he alluded to the third day. John's attitude had considerable influence on them, especially on his brother James and on Nathaniel. John would have influenced them more if he had not been the youngest member of the group. 191:0.2 (2037.2)
Death:	He died a natural death at Ephesus in A.D. 103 when he was one hundred and one years of age. 139:4.15 (1555.8)

The Twelve Apostles of Jesus—Philip

Name:	**Philip**
Chosen:	Fifth Apostle. Led to Jesus by Peter
Born:	27 years of age when selected.
Before Jesus:	Philip was twenty-seven years of age when he joined the apostles; he had recently been married, but he had no children at this time. The nickname which the apostles gave him signified "curiosity." 139:5.2 (1556.2) Philip came from a family of seven, three boys and four girls. He was next to the oldest, and after the resurrection he baptized his entire family into the kingdom. Philip's people were fisherfolk. His father was a very able man, a deep thinker, but his mother was of a very mediocre family. 139:5.4 (1556.4)
History:	Peter took Philip to one side and proceeded to explain that they, referring to himself, Andrew, James, and John, had all become associates of Jesus in the new kingdom and strongly urged Philip to volunteer for service. Philip was in a quandary. What should he do? Here, without a moment's warning—on the roadside near the Jordan—there had come up for immediate decision the most momentous question of a lifetime. By this time he was in earnest converse with Peter, Andrew, and John while Jesus was outlining to James the trip through Galilee and on to Capernaum. Finally, Andrew suggested to Philip, "Why not ask the Teacher?" 137:2.4 (1526.4) It suddenly dawned on Philip that Jesus was a really great man, possibly the Messiah, and he decided to abide by Jesus' decision in this matter; and he went straight to him, asking, "Teacher, shall I go down to John or shall I join my friends who follow you?" And Jesus answered, "Follow me." Philip was thrilled with the assurance that he had found the Deliverer. 137:2.5 (1526.5) Philip now motioned to the group to remain where they were while he hurried back to break the news of his decision to his friend Nathaniel, who still tarried behind under the mulberry tree, turning over in his mind the many things which he had heard concerning John the Baptist, the coming kingdom, and the expected Messiah. Philip broke in upon these meditations, exclaiming, "I have found the Deliverer, him of whom Moses and the prophets wrote and whom John has proclaimed." Nathaniel, looking up, inquired, "Whence comes this teacher?" And Philip replied, "He is Jesus of Nazareth, the son of Joseph, the carpenter, more recently residing at Capernaum." And then, somewhat shocked, Nathaniel asked, "Can any such good thing come out of Nazareth?" But Philip, taking him by the arm, said, "Come and see." 137:2.6 (1526.6) Philip was the fifth apostle to be chosen, being called when Jesus and his first four apostles were on their way from John's rendezvous on the Jordan to Cana of Galilee. Since he lived at Bethsaida, Philip had for some time known of Jesus, but it had not occurred to him that Jesus was a really great man until that day in the Jordan valley when he said, "Follow me." Philip was also somewhat influenced by the fact that Andrew, Peter, James, and John had accepted Jesus as the Deliverer. 139:5.1 (1556.1)

The Twelve Apostles of Jesus—Philip

Role:	Philip was made steward of the group. It was his duty to provide food and to see that visitors, and even the multitude of listeners at times, had something to eat. 138:10.4 (1547.4)
Philip's Personality:	Philip was always wanting to be shown. He never seemed to see very far into any proposition. He was not necessarily dull, but he lacked imagination. This lack of imagination was the great weakness of his character. He was a commonplace and matter-of-fact individual. 139:5.2 (1556.2) His strongest characteristic was his methodical thoroughness; he was both mathematical and systematic. 139:5.3 (1556.3)
	The strong point about Philip was his methodical reliability; the weak point in his make-up was his utter lack of imagination, the absence of the ability to put two and two together to obtain four. He was mathematical in the abstract but not constructive in his imagination. He was almost entirely lacking in certain types of imagination. He was the typical everyday and commonplace average man. There were a great many such men and women among the multitudes who came to hear Jesus teach and preach, and they derived great comfort from observing one like themselves elevated to an honored position in the councils of the Master; they derived courage from the fact that one like themselves had already found a high place in the affairs of the kingdom. And Jesus learned much about the way some human minds function as he so patiently listened to Philip's foolish questions and so many times complied with his steward's request to "be shown." 139:5.5 (1556.5)
	There was little about Philip's personality that was impressive. He was often spoken of as "Philip of Bethsaida, the town where Andrew and Peter live." He was almost without discerning vision; he was unable to grasp the dramatic possibilities of a given situation. He was not pessimistic; he was simply prosaic. He was also greatly lacking in spiritual insight. He would not hesitate to interrupt Jesus in the midst of one of the Master's most profound discourses to ask an apparently foolish question. But Jesus never reprimanded him for such thoughtlessness; he was patient with him and considerate of his inability to grasp the deeper meanings of the teaching. Jesus well knew that, if he once rebuked Philip for asking these annoying questions, he would not only wound this honest soul, but such a reprimand would so hurt Philip that he would never again feel free to ask questions. Jesus knew that on his worlds of space there were untold billions of similar slow-thinking mortals, and he wanted to encourage them all to look to him and always to feel free to come to him with their questions and problems. After all, Jesus was really more interested in Philip's foolish questions than in the sermon he might be preaching. Jesus was supremely interested in *men,* all kinds of men. 139:5.7 (1557.1) The apostolic steward was not a good public speaker, but he was a very persuasive and successful personal worker. He was not easily discouraged; he was a plodder and very tenacious in anything he undertook. He had that great and rare gift of saying, "Come." When his first convert, Nathaniel, wanted to argue about the merits and demerits of Jesus and Nazareth, Philip's effective reply was, "Come and see."

The Twelve Apostles of Jesus—Philip

Philip Personality: (Continued)	He was not a dogmatic preacher who exhorted his hearers to "Go"—do this and do that. He met all situations as they arose in his work with "Come"—"come with me; I will show you the way." And that is always the effective technique in all forms and phases of teaching. Even parents may learn from Philip the better way of saying to their children *not* "Go do this and go do that," but rather, "Come with us while we show and share with you the better way." 139:5.8 (1557.2)
Skill:	Philip was not a man who could be expected to do big things, but he was a man who could do little things in a big way, do them well and acceptably. Only a few times in four years did he fail to have food on hand to satisfy the needs of all. Even the many emergency demands attendant upon the life they lived seldom found him unprepared. The commissary department of the apostolic family was intelligently and efficiently managed. 139:5.4 (1556.4)
Significant Events:	A question asked by Philip was typical of their difficulties. Said Philip: "Master, these Greeks and Romans make light of our message, saying that such teachings are fit for only weaklings and slaves. They assert that the religion of the heathen is superior to our teaching because it inspires to the acquirement of a strong, robust, and aggressive character. They affirm that we would convert all men into enfeebled specimens of passive nonresisters who would soon perish from the face of the earth. They like you, Master, and freely admit that your teaching is heavenly and ideal, but they will not take us seriously. They assert that your religion is not for this world; that men cannot live as you teach. And now, Master, what shall we say to these gentiles?" 143:1.2 (1607.4)
	It was at Gamala, during the evening conference, that Philip said to Jesus: "Master, why is it that the Scriptures instruct us to 'fear the Lord,' while you would have us look to the Father in heaven without fear? How are we to harmonize these teachings?" 149:6.1 (1675.2)
	This was the stage setting about five o'clock on Wednesday afternoon, when Jesus asked James Alpheus to summon Andrew and Philip. Said Jesus: "What shall we do with the multitude? They have been with us now three days, and many of them are hungry. They have no food." Philip and Andrew exchanged glances, and then Philip answered: "Master, you should send these people away so that they may go to the villages around about and buy themselves food." And Andrew, fearing the materialization of the king plot, quickly joined with Philip, saying: "Yes, Master, I think it best that you dismiss the multitude so that they may go their way and buy food while you secure rest for a season." By this time others of the twelve had joined the conference. Then said Jesus: "But I do not desire to send them away hungry; can you not feed them?" This was too much for Philip, and he spoke right up: "Master, in this country place where can we buy bread for this multitude? Two hundred denarii worth would not be enough for lunch." 152:2.6 (1701.1)
	Strange to record, the usually inexpressive Philip did much talking throughout the afternoon of this day. During the forenoon he had little to say, but all afternoon he asked questions of the other apostles. Peter was often annoyed by Philip's questions, but the others took his inquiries good-naturedly. Philip was particularly desirous of knowing, provided Jesus had really risen from the grave, whether his body would bear the physical marks of the crucifixion. 191:0.9 (2038.4)

The Twelve Apostles of Jesus—Philip

Admired Jesus For:	The one quality about Jesus which Philip so continuously admired was the Master's unfailing generosity. Never could Philip find anything in Jesus which was small, niggardly, or stingy, and he worshiped this ever-present and unfailing liberality. 139:5.6 (1556.6)
Final Instructions:	To Philip he said: "Be unmoved by the events now impending. Remain unshaken, even when you cannot see the way. Be loyal to your oath of consecration." 174:0.2 (1897.2)
	And then Jesus went over to Philip, who, standing up, heard this message from his Master: "Philip, you have asked me many foolish questions, but I have done my utmost to answer every one, and now would I answer the last of such questionings which have arisen in your most honest but unspiritual mind. All the time I have been coming around toward you, have you been saying to yourself, 'What shall I ever doif the Master goes away and leaves us alone in the world?' O, you of little faith! And yet you have almost as much as many of your brethren. You have been a good steward, Philip. You failed us only a few times, and one of those failures we utilized to manifest the Father's glory. Your office of stewardship is about over. You must soon more fully do the work you were called to do—the preaching of this gospel of the kingdom. Philip, you have always wanted to be shown, and very soon shall you see great things. Far better that you should have seen all this by faith, but since you were sincere even in your material sightedness, you will live to see my words fulfilled. And then, when you are blessed with spiritual vision, go forth to your work, dedicating your life to the cause of leading mankind to search for God and to seek eternal realities with the eye of spiritual faith and not with the eyes of the material mind. Remember, Philip, you have a great mission on earth, for the world is filled with those who look at life just as you have tended to. You have a great work to do, and when it is finished in faith, you shall come to me in my kingdom, and I will take great pleasure in showing you that which eye has not seen, ear heard, nor the mortal mind conceived. In the meantime, become as a little child in the kingdom of the spirit and permit me, as the spirit of the new teacher, to lead you forward in the spiritual kingdom. And in this way will I be able to do much for you which I was not able to accomplish when I sojourned with you as a mortal of the realm. And always remember, Philip, he who has seen me has seen the Father." 181:2.20 (1960.1)
	After this the Master talked with Matthew and Philip. To Philip he said, "Philip, do you obey me? " Philip answered, "Yes, Lord, I will obey you even with my life." Then said Jesus: "If you would obey me, go then into the lands of the gentiles and proclaim this gospel. The prophets have told you that to obey is better than to sacrifice. By faith have you become a God-knowing kingdom son. There is but one law to obey—that is the command to go forth proclaiming the gospel of the kingdom. Cease to fear men; be unafraid to preach the good news of eternal life to your fellows who languish in darkness and hunger for the light of truth. No more, Philip, shall you busy yourself with money and goods. You now are free to preach the glad tidings just as are your brethren. And I will go before you and be with you even to the end." 192:2.11 (2049.2)

The Twelve Apostles of Jesus—Philip

<table>
<tr><td rowspan="3">After Jesus:</td><td>Philip went on through the trying times of the Master's death, participated in the reorganization of the twelve, and was the first to go forth to win souls for the kingdom outside of the immediate Jewish ranks, being most successful in his work for the Samaritans and in all his subsequent labors in behalf of the gospel. 139:5.10 (1557.4)

Philip's wife, who was an efficient member of the women's corps, became actively associated with her husband in his evangelistic work after their flight from the Jerusalem persecutions. His wife was a fearless woman. She stood at the foot of Philip's cross encouraging him to proclaim the glad tidings even to his murderers, and when his strength failed, she began the recital of the story of salvation by faith in Jesus and was silenced only when the irate Jews rushed upon her and stoned her to death. Their eldest daughter, Leah, continued their work, later on becoming the renowned prophetess of Hierapolis. 139:5.11 (1557.5)</td></tr>
<tr><td>Jesus and the twelve camped on Mount Gerizim until the end of August. They preached the good news of the kingdom—the fatherhood of God—to the Samaritans in the cities by day and spent the nights at the camp. The work which Jesus and the twelve did in these Samaritan cities yielded many souls for the kingdom and did much to prepare the way for the marvelous work of Philip in these regions after Jesus' death and resurrection, subsequent to the dispersion of the apostles to the ends of the earth by the bitter persecution of believers at Jerusalem. 143:6.6 (1616.2)</td></tr>
<tr><td>This left but six of the original twelve apostles to become actors on the stage of the early proclamation of the gospel in Jerusalem: Peter, Andrew, James, John, Philip, and Matthew. 193:6.5 (2058.4)</td></tr>
<tr><td>Death:</td><td>Philip, the onetime steward of the twelve, was a mighty man in the kingdom, winning souls wherever he went; and he was finally crucified for his faith and buried at Hierapolis. 139:5.12 (1558.1)</td></tr>
</table>

The Twelve Apostles of Jesus—Nathaniel

Name:	**Nathaniel**
Chosen:	Sixth Apostle led to Jesus by Philip
Born:	25 years of age when selected.
Before Jesus:	Nathaniel, the sixth and last of the apostles to be chosen by the Master himself, was brought to Jesus by his friend Philip. He had been associated in several business enterprises with Philip and, with him, was on the way down to see John the Baptist when they encountered Jesus. 139:6.1 (1558.2) When Nathaniel joined the apostles, he was twenty-five years old and was the next to the youngest of the group. He was the youngest of a family of seven, was unmarried, and the only support of aged and infirm parents, with whom he lived at Cana; his brothers and sister were either married or deceased, and none lived there. Nathaniel and Judas Iscariot were the two best educated men among the twelve. Nathaniel had thought to become a merchant. 139:6.2 (1558.3)
History:	Philip now motioned to the group to remain where they were while he hurried back to break the news of his decision to his friend Nathaniel, who still tarried behind under the mulberry tree, turning over in his mind the many things which he had heard concerning John the Baptist, the coming kingdom, and the expected Messiah. Philip broke in upon these meditations, exclaiming, "I have found the Deliverer, him of whom Moses and the prophets wrote and whom John has proclaimed." Nathaniel, looking up, inquired, "Whence comes this teacher?" And Philip replied, "He is Jesus of Nazareth, the son of Joseph, the carpenter, more recently residing at Capernaum." And then, somewhat shocked, Nathaniel asked, "Can any such good thing come out of Nazareth?" But Philip, taking him by the arm, said, "Come and see." 137:2.6 (1526.6) Philip led Nathaniel to Jesus, who, looking benignly into the face of the sincere doubter, said: "Behold a genuine Israelite, in whom there is no deceit. Follow me." And Nathaniel, turning to Philip, said: "You are right. He is indeed a master of men. I will also follow, if I am worthy." And Jesus nodded to Nathaniel, again saying, "Follow me." 137:2.7 (1527.1)
Role:	Nathaniel watched over the needs of the families of the twelve. He received regular reports as to the requirements of each apostle's family and, making requisition on Judas, the treasurer, would send funds each week to those in need. 138:10.5 (1547.5)
Nathaniel's Personality:	Jesus did not himself give Nathaniel a nickname, but the twelve soon began to speak of him in terms that signified honesty, sincerity. He was "without guile." And this was his great virtue; he was both honest and sincere. The weakness of his character was his pride; he was very proud of his family, his city, his reputation, and his nation, all of which is commendable if it is not carried too far. But Nathaniel was inclined to go to extremes with his personal prejudices. He was disposed to prejudge individuals in accordance with his personal opinions. He was not slow to ask the question, even before he had met Jesus, "Can any good thing come out of Nazareth?" But Nathaniel was not obstinate, even if he was proud. He was quick to reverse himself when he once looked into Jesus' face. 139:6.3 (1558.4)

The Twelve Apostles of Jesus—Nathaniel

Nathaniel Personality: (Continued)	In many respects Nathaniel was the odd genius of the twelve. He was the apostolic philosopher and dreamer, but he was a very practical sort of dreamer. He alternated between seasons of profound philosophy and periods of rare and droll humor; when in the proper mood, he was probably the best storyteller among the twelve. Jesus greatly enjoyed hearing Nathaniel discourse on things both serious and frivolous. Nathaniel progressively took Jesus and the kingdom more seriously, but never did he take himself seriously. 139:6.4 (1558.5) The apostles all loved and respected Nathaniel, and he got along with them splendidly, excepting Judas Iscariot. Judas did not think Nathaniel took his apostleship sufficiently seriously and once had the temerity to go secretly to Jesus and lodge complaint against him. 139:6.5 (1558.6) Many times, when Jesus was away on the mountain with Peter, James, and John, and things were becoming tense and tangled among the apostles, when even Andrew was in doubt about what to say to his disconsolate brethren, Nathaniel would relieve the tension by a bit of philosophy or a flash of humor; good humor, too. 139:6.6 (1559.1)
Skill:	Peter, James, and John did most of the public preaching. Philip, Nathaniel, Thomas, and Simon did much of the personal work and conducted classes for special groups of inquirers; the twins continued their general police supervision, while Andrew, Matthew, and Judas developed into a general managerial committee of three, although each of these three also did considerable religious work. 141:3.2 (1589.3)
	Jesus gave a talk to this company each morning. Peter taught methods of public preaching; Nathaniel instructed them in the art of teaching; 163:0.2 (1800.2)
	Nathaniel had great confidence in Jesus' understanding of men as well as in his sagacity and cleverness in handling difficult situations. 172:5.7 (1885.2)
	More than once during the long and weary hours of this tragic day, the only sustaining influence of the group was the frequent contribution of Nathaniel's characteristic philosophic counsel. He was really the controlling influence among the ten throughout the entire day. Never once did he express himself concerning either belief or disbelief in the Master's resurrection. But as the day wore on, he became increasingly inclined toward believing that Jesus had fulfilled his promise to rise again. 191:0.7 (2038.2)
Significant Events:	Then asked Nathaniel: "Master, shall we give no place to justice? The law of Moses says, 'An eye for an eye, and a tooth for a tooth.' What shall we say?" 140:6.9 (1577.3)
	On the evening of this same Sabbath day, at Bethany, while Jesus, the twelve, and a group of believers were assembled about the fire in Lazarus's garden, Nathaniel asked Jesus this question: "Master, although you have taught us the positive version of the old rule of life, instructing us that we should do to others as we wish them to do to us, I do not fully discern how we can always abide by such an injunction. Let me illustrate my contention by citing the example of a lustful man who thus wickedly looks upon his intended consort in sin. How can we teach that this evil-intending man should do to others as he would they should do to him?" 147:4.1 (1650.2)

Nathaniel Significant Events: (Continued)	When Jesus heard Nathaniel's question, he immediately stood upon his feet and, pointing his finger at the apostle, said: "Nathaniel, Nathaniel! What manner of thinking is going on in your heart? Do you not receive my teachings as one who has been born of the spirit? Do you not hear the truth as men of wisdom and spiritual understanding? When I admonished you to do to others as you would have them do to you, I spoke to men of high ideals, not to those who would be tempted to distort my teaching into a license for the encouragement of evil-doing." 147:4.2 (1650.3)
	At another of these private interviews in the garden Nathaniel asked Jesus: "Master, though I am beginning to understand why you refuse to practice healing indiscriminately, I am still at a loss to understand why the loving Father in heaven permits so many of his children on earth to suffer so many afflictions." 148:5.1 (1661.3)
	On the evening of this same day Nathaniel asked Jesus: "Master, why do we pray that God will lead us not into temptation when we well know from your revelation of the Father that he never does such things?" 156:5.3 (1738.2)
	And then went Jesus over to Abila, where Nathaniel and his associates labored. Nathaniel was much bothered by some of Jesus' pronouncements which seemed to detract from the authority of the recognized Hebrew scriptures. Accordingly, on this night, after the usual period of questions and answers, Nathaniel took Jesus away from the others and asked: "Master, could you trust me to know the truth about the Scriptures? I observe that you teach us only a portion of the sacred writings—the best as I view it—and I infer that you reject the teachings of the rabbis to the effect that the words of the law are the very words of God, having been with God in heaven even before the times of Abraham and Moses. What is the truth about the Scriptures?" 159:4.1 (1767.3)
	On Sunday morning, September 18, Andrew announced that no work would be planned for the coming week. All of the apostles, except Nathaniel and Thomas, went home to visit their families or to sojourn with friends. This week Jesus enjoyed a period of almost complete rest, but Nathaniel and Thomas were very busy with their discussions with a certain Greek philosopher from Alexandria named Rodan. This Greek had recently become a disciple of Jesus through the teaching of one of Abner's associates who had conducted a mission at Alexandria. Rodan was now earnestly engaged in the task of harmonizing his philosophy of life with Jesus' new religious teachings, and he had come to Magadan hoping that the Master would talk these problems over with him. He also desired to secure a firsthand and authoritative version of the gospel from either Jesus or one of his apostles. Though the Master declined to enter into such a conference with Rodan, he did receive him graciously and immediately directed that Nathaniel and Thomas should listen to all he had to say and tell him about the gospel in return. 160:0.1 (1772.1)
	As the Master stood there before the blind man, engrossed in deep thought, Nathaniel, pondering the possible cause of this man's blindness, asked: "Master, who did sin, this man or his parents, that he should be born blind?" 164:3.2 (1811.3)

<table>
<tr><td rowspan="4">Nathaniel Significant Events:
(Continued)</td><td>As they journeyed up the hills from Jericho to Bethany, Nathaniel walked most of the way by the side of Jesus, and their discussion of children in relation to the kingdom of heaven led indirectly to the consideration of the ministry of angels. Nathaniel finally asked the Master this question: "Seeing that the high priest is a Sadducee, and since the Sadducees do not believe in angels, what shall we teach the people regarding the heavenly ministers?" 167:7.1 (1840.6)</td></tr>
<tr><td>It was Nathaniel who so well taught the meaning of these two parables in the after years, summing up his teachings in these conclusions: 171:8.9 (1876.6)

1. Ability is the practical measure of life's opportunities. You will never be held responsible for the accomplishment of that which is beyond your abilities. 171:8.10 (1876.7)

2. Faithfulness is the unerring measure of human trustworthiness. He who is faithful in little things is also likely to exhibit faithfulness in everything consistent with his endowments. 171:8.11 (1876.8)

3. The Master grants the lesser reward for lesser faithfulness when there is like opportunity. 171:8.12 (1876.9)

4. He grants a like reward for like faithfulness when there is lesser opportunity. 171:8.13 (1877.1)</td></tr>
<tr><td>It was about midafternoon when Nathaniel made his speech on "Supreme Desire" to about half a dozen of the apostles and as many disciples, the ending of which was: "What is wrong with most of us is that we are only halfhearted. We fail to love the Master as he loves us. If we had all wanted to go with him as much as John Mark did, he would surely have taken us all. We stood by while the lad approached the Master and offered him the basket, but when the Master took hold of it, the lad would not let go. And so the Master left us here while he went off to the hills with basket, boy, and all." 177:3.2 (1923.3)</td></tr>
<tr><td>The apostles fell asleep only because they were literally exhausted; they had been running short on sleep ever since their arrival in Jerusalem. Before they went to their separate sleeping quarters, Simon Zelotes led them all over to his tent, where were stored the swords and other arms, and supplied each of them with this fighting equipment. All of them received these arms and girded themselves therewith except Nathaniel. Nathaniel, in refusing to arm himself, said: "My brethren, the Master has repeatedly told us that his kingdom is not of this world, and that his disciples should not fight with the sword to bring about its establishment. I believe this; I do not think the Master needs to have us employ the sword in his defense. We have all seen his mighty power and know that he could defend himself against his enemies if he so desired. If he will not resist his enemies, it must be that such a course represents his attempt to fulfill his Father's will. I will pray, but I will not wield the sword." When Andrew heard Nathaniel's speech, he handed his sword back to Simon Zelotes. And so nine of them were armed as they separated for the night. 182:2.3 (1966.3)</td></tr>
</table>

The Twelve Apostles of Jesus—Nathaniel

Admired Jesus For:	Nathaniel most revered Jesus for his tolerance. He never grew weary of contemplating the broadmindedness and generous sympathy of the Son of Man. 139:6.8 (1559.3)
Final Instructions:	To Nathaniel he said: "Judge not by appearances; remain firm in your faith when all appears to vanish; be true to your commission as an ambassador of the kingdom." 174:0.2 (1897.2)
	Then went the Master over to Nathaniel. As Nathaniel stood up, Jesus bade him be seated and, sitting down by his side, said: "Nathaniel, you have learned to live above prejudice and to practice increased tolerance since you became my apostle. But there is much more for you to learn. You have been a blessing to your fellows in that they have always been admonished by your consistent sincerity. When I have gone, it may be that your frankness will interfere with your getting along well with your brethren, both old and new. You should learn that the expression of even a good thought must be modulated in accordance with the intellectual status and spiritual development of the hearer. Sincerity is most serviceable in the work of the kingdom when it is wedded to discretion. 181:2.21 (1960.2) "If you would learn to work with your brethren, you might accomplish more permanent things, but if you find yourself going off in quest of those who think as you do, in that event dedicate your life to proving that the God-knowing disciple can become a kingdom builder even when alone in the world and wholly isolated from his fellow believers. I know you will be faithful to the end, and I will someday welcome you to the enlarged service of my kingdom on high." 181:2.22 (1961.1)
	Then said the Master to Nathaniel, "Nathaniel, do you serve me?" And the apostle answered, "Yes, Master, and with an undivided affection." Then said Jesus: "If, therefore, you serve me with a whole heart, make sure that you are devoted to the welfare of my brethren on earth with tireless affection. Admix friendship with your counsel and add love to your philosophy. Serve your fellow men even as I have served you. Be faithful to men as I have watched over you. Be less critical; expect less of some men and thereby lessen the extent of your disappointment. And when the work down here is over, you shall serve with me on high." 192:2.10 (2049.1)
After Jesus:	On Thursday night the apostles had a wonderful meeting in this upper chamber and all pledged themselves to go forth in the public preaching of the new gospel of the risen Lord except Thomas, Simon Zelotes, and the Alpheus twins. Already had begun the first steps of changing the gospel of the kingdom—sonship with God and brotherhood with man—into the proclamation of the resurrection of Jesus. Nathaniel opposed this shift in the burden of their public message, but he could not withstand Peter's eloquence, neither could he overcome the enthusiasm of the disciples, especially the women believers. 192:4.7 (2051.4)
	Nathaniel's father (Bartholomew) died shortly after Pentecost, after which this apostle went into Mesopotamia and India proclaiming the glad tidings of the kingdom and baptizing believers. His brethren never knew what became of their onetime philosopher, poet, and humorist. But he also was a great man in the kingdom and did much to spread his Master's teachings, even though he did not participate in the organization of the subsequent Christian church. 193:6.4 (2058.3)

Nathaniel After Jesus: (Continued)	Nathaniel differed increasingly with Peter regarding preaching about Jesus in the place of proclaiming the former gospel of the kingdom. This disagreement became so acute by the middle of the following month that Nathaniel withdrew, going to Philadelphia to visit Abner and Lazarus; and after tarrying there for more than a year, he went on into the lands beyond Mesopotamia preaching the gospel as he understood it. 139:6.9 (1559.4)
Death:	Nathaniel died in India. 139:6.9 (1559.4)

The Twelve Apostles of Jesus—Matthew

<table>
<tr><th>Name:</th><th>Matthew</th></tr>
<tr><td>Chosen:</td><td>Seventh Apostle.</td></tr>
<tr><td>Born:</td><td>31 years of age when selected.</td></tr>
<tr><td rowspan="2">Before Jesus:</td><td>Matthew Levi, the customs collector of Capernaum, who had his office just to the east of the city, near the borders of Batanea. Matthew was married and had four children. He was the only one of any means belonging to the apostolic group. 138:2.4 1 (1539.7).</td></tr>
<tr><td>Matthew, the seventh apostle, was chosen by Andrew. Matthew belonged to a family of tax gatherers, or publicans, but was himself a customs collector in Capernaum, where he lived. He was thirty-one years old and married and had four children. He was a man of moderate wealth, the only one of any means belonging to the apostolic corps. He was a good business man, a good social mixer, and was gifted with the ability to make friends and to get along smoothly with a great variety of people. 139:7.1 (1559.5)</td></tr>
<tr><td>History:</td><td>The next day Jesus and the six went to call upon Matthew, the customs collector. Matthew was awaiting them, having balanced his books and made ready to turn the affairs of his office over to his brother. As they approached the toll house, Andrew stepped forward with Jesus, who, looking into Matthew's face, said, "Follow me." And he arose and went to his house with Jesus and the apostles. 138:3.1 (1540.4)</td></tr>
<tr><td>Role:</td><td>Matthew was the fiscal agent of the apostolic corps. It was his duty to see that the budget was balanced, the treasury replenished. If the funds for mutual support were not forthcoming, if donations sufficient to maintain the party were not received, Matthew was empowered to order the twelve back to their nets for a season. But this was never necessary after they began their public work; he always had sufficient funds in the treasurer's hands to finance their activities. 138:10.6 (1547.6)</td></tr>
<tr><td rowspan="2">Matthew's Personality:</td><td>Levi's strong point was his wholehearted devotion to the cause. That he, a publican, had been taken in by Jesus and his apostles was the cause for overwhelming gratitude on the part of the former revenue collector. However, it required some little time for the rest of the apostles, especially Simon Zelotes and Judas Iscariot, to become reconciled to the publican's presence in their midst. Matthew's weakness was his shortsighted and materialistic viewpoint of life. But in all these matters he made great progress as the months went by. He, of course, had to be absent from many of the most precious seasons of instruction as it was his duty to keep the treasury replenished. 139:7.3 (1559.7)</td></tr>
<tr><td>Though Matthew was a man with a past, he gave an excellent account of himself, and as time went on, his associates became proud of the publican's performances. He was one of the apostles who made extensive notes on the sayings of Jesus, and these notes were used as the basis of Isador's subsequent narrative of the sayings and doings of Jesus, which has become known as the Gospel according to Matthew. 139:7.5 (1560.1)</td></tr>
</table>

The Twelve Apostles of Jesus—Matthew

Skill:	The great and useful life of Matthew, the business man and customs collector of Capernaum, has been the means of leading thousands upon thousands of other business men, public officials, and politicians, down through the subsequent ages, also to hear that engaging voice of the Master saying, "Follow me." Matthew really was a shrewd politician, but he was intensely loyal to Jesus and supremely devoted to the task of seeing that the messengers of the coming kingdom were adequately financed. 139:7.6 (1560.2) The presence of Matthew among the twelve was the means of keeping the doors of the kingdom wide open to hosts of downhearted and outcast souls who had regarded themselves as long since without the bounds of religious consolation. Outcast and despairing men and women flocked to hear Jesus, and he never turned one away. 139:7.7 (1560.3) Matthew received freely tendered offerings from believing disciples and the immediate auditors of the Master's teachings, but he never openly solicited funds from the multitudes. He did all his financial work in a quiet and personal way and raised most of the money among the more substantial class of interested believers. He gave practically the whole of his modest fortune to the work of the Master and his apostles, but they never knew of this generosity, save Jesus, who knew all about it. Matthew hesitated openly to contribute to the apostolic funds for fear that Jesus and his associates might regard his money as being tainted; so he gave much in the names of other believers. During the earlier months, when Matthew knew his presence among them was more or less of a trial, he was strongly tempted to let them know that his funds often supplied them with their daily bread, but he did not yield. When evidence of the disdain of the publican would become manifest, Levi would burn to reveal to them his generosity, but always he managed to keep still. 139:7.8 (1560.4) When the funds for the week were short of the estimated requirements, Levi would often draw heavily upon his own personal resources. Also, sometimes when he became greatly interested in Jesus' teaching, he preferred to remain and hear the instruction, even though he knew he must personally make up for his failure to solicit the necessary funds. But Levi did so wish that Jesus might know that much of the money came from his pocket! He little realized that the Master knew all about it. The apostles all died without knowing that Matthew was their benefactor to such an extent that, when he went forth to proclaim the gospel of the kingdom after the beginning of the persecutions, he was practically penniless. 139:7.9 (1560.5)
Significant Events:	Matthew told Jesus of the banquet he had arranged for that evening, at least that he wished to give such a dinner to his family and friends if Jesus would approve and consent to be the guest of honor. And Jesus nodded his consent. Peter then took Matthew aside and explained that he had invited one Simon to join the apostles and secured his consent that Simon be also bidden to this feast. 138:3.2 (1540.5)
	Jesus enjoined them to devote themselves to fishing for two weeks, adding, "And then will you go forth to become fishers of men." They fished in three groups, Jesus going out with a different group each night. And they all so much enjoyed Jesus! He was a good fisherman, a cheerful companion, and an inspiring friend; the more they worked

Matthew Significant Events: (Continued)	with him, the more they loved him. Said Matthew one day: "The more you understand some people, the less you admire them, but of this man, even the less I comprehend him, the more I love him." 138:7.6 (1544.5)
	The one characteristic of Jesus' teaching was that the *morality* of his philosophy originated in the personal relation of the individual to God—this very child-father relationship. Jesus placed emphasis on the *individual,* not on the race or nation. While eating supper, Jesus had the talk with Matthew in which he explained that the morality of any act is determined by the individual's motive. Jesus' morality was always positive. The golden rule as restated by Jesus demands active social contact; the older negative rule could be obeyed in isolation. Jesus stripped morality of all rules and ceremonies and elevated it to majestic levels of spiritual thinking and truly righteous living. 140:10.5 (1185.3)
	The apostles and those who were with them, when they heard Jesus teach the people in this manner, were greatly perplexed; and after much talking among themselves, that evening in the Zebedee garden Matthew said to Jesus: "Master, what is the meaning of the dark sayings which you present to the multitude? Why do you speak in parables to those who seek the truth?" 151:1.3 (1689.1)
	Matthew was at first nonplused by this pageant performance. He did not grasp the meaning of what his eyes were seeing until he also recalled the Scripture in Zechariah where the prophet had alluded to the rejoicing of Jerusalem because her king had come bringing salvation and riding upon the colt of an ass. As the procession moved in the direction of the city and then drew on toward the temple, Matthew became ecstatic; he was certain that something extraordinary would happen when the Master arrived at the temple at the head of this shouting multitude. When one of the Pharisees mocked Jesus, saying, "Look, everybody, see who comes here, the king of the Jews riding on an ass!" Matthew kept his hands off of him only by exercising great restraint. None of the twelve was more depressed on the way back to Bethany that evening. Next to Simon Peter and Simon Zelotes, he experienced the highest nervous tension and was in a state of exhaustion by night. But by morning Matthew was much cheered; he was, after all, a cheerful loser. 172:5.8 (1885.3)
	THIS Tuesday afternoon, as Jesus and the apostles passed out of the temple on their way to the Gethsemane camp, Matthew, calling attention to the temple construction, said: "Master, observe what manner of buildings these are. See the massive stones and the beautiful adornment; can it be that these buildings are to be destroyed?" As they went on toward Olivet, Jesus said: "You see these stones and this massive temple; verily, verily, I say to you: In the days soon to come there shall not be left one stone upon another. They shall all be thrown down." 176:0.1 (1912.1)
Admired Jesus For:	It was the Master's forgiving disposition which Matthew most appreciated. He would never cease to recount that faith only was necessary in the business of finding God. He always liked to speak of the kingdom as "this business of finding God." 139:7.4 (1559.8)

	To Matthew he said: "Forget not the mercy that received you into the kingdom. Let no man cheat you of your eternal reward. As you have withstood the inclinations of the mortal nature, be willing to be steadfast." 174:0.2 (1897.2)
	When Jesus had finished speaking to Simon Zelotes, he stepped over to Matthew Levi and said: "No longer will it devolve upon you to provide for the treasury of the apostolic group. Soon, very soon, you will all be scattered; you will not be permitted to enjoy the comforting and sustaining association of even one of your brethren. As you go onward preaching this gospel of the kingdom, you will have to find for yourselves new associates. I have sent you forth two and two during the times of your training, but now that I am leaving you, after you have recovered from the shock, you will go out alone, and to the ends of the earth, proclaiming this good news: That faith-quickened mortals are the sons of God." 181:2.12 (1957.2)
Final Instructions:	Then spoke Matthew: "But, Master, who will send us, and how shall we know where to go? Will Andrew show us the way?" And Jesus answered: "No, Levi, Andrew will no longer direct you in the proclamation of the gospel. He will, indeed, continue as your friend and counselor until that day whereon the new teacher comes, and then shall the Spirit of Truth lead each of you abroad to labor for the extension of the kingdom. Many changes have come over you since that day at the customhouse when you first set out to follow me; but many more must come before you will be able to see the vision of a brotherhood in which gentile sits alongside Jew in fraternal association. But go on with your urge to win your Jewish brethren until you are fully satisfied and then turn with power to the gentiles. One thing you may be certain of, Levi: You have won the confidence and affection of your brethren; they all love you." (And all ten of them signified their acquiescence in the Master's words.) 181:2.13 (1957.3) "Levi, I know much about your anxieties, sacrifices, and labors to keep the treasury replenished which your brethren do not know, and I am rejoiced that, though he who carried the bag is absent, the publican ambassador is here at my farewell gathering with the messengers of the kingdom. I pray that you may discern the meaning of my teaching with the eyes of the spirit. And when the new teacher comes into your heart, follow on as he will lead you and let your brethren see—even all the world—what the Father can do for a hated tax-gatherer who dared to follow the Son of Man and to believe the gospel of the kingdom. Even from the first, Levi, I loved you as I did these other Galileans. Knowing then so well that neither the Father nor the Son has respect of persons, see to it that you make no such distinctions among those who become believers in the gospel through your ministry. And so, Matthew, dedicate your whole future life service to showing all men that God is no respecter of persons; that, in the sight of God and in the fellowship of the kingdom, all men are equal, all believers are the sons of God." 181:2.14 (1958.1)
	And then, speaking to Matthew, the Master asked, "Matthew, do you have it in your heart to obey me?" Matthew answered, "Yes, Lord, I am fully dedicated to doing your will." Then said the Master: "Matthew, if you would obey me, go forth to teach all

Matthew Final Instructions: (Continued)	peoples this gospel of the kingdom. No longer will you serve your brethren the material things of life; henceforth you are also to proclaim the good news of spiritual salvation. From now on have an eye single only to obeying your commission to preach this gospel of the Father's kingdom. As I have done the Father's will on earth, so shall you fulfill the divine commission. Remember, both Jew and gentile are your brethren. Fear no man when you proclaim the saving truths of the gospel of the kingdom of heaven. And where I go, you shall presently come." 192:2.12 (2049.3)
After Jesus:	Though Matthew was a man with a past, he gave an excellent account of himself, and as time went on, his associates became proud of the publican's performances. He was one of the apostles who made extensive notes on the sayings of Jesus, and these notes were used as the basis of Isador's subsequent narrative of the sayings and doings of Jesus, which has become known as the Gospel according to Matthew. 139:7.5 (1560.1) The apostles all died without knowing that Matthew was their benefactor to such an extent that, when he went forth to proclaim the gospel of the kingdom after the beginning of the persecutions, he was practically penniless. 139:7.9 (1560.5) When these persecutions caused the believers to forsake Jerusalem, Matthew journeyed north, preaching the gospel of the kingdom and baptizing believers. He was lost to the knowledge of his former apostolic associates, but on he went, preaching and baptizing, through Syria, Cappadocia, Galatia, Bithynia, and Thrace. 139:7.10 (1560.6)
Death:	And it was in Thrace, at Lysimachia, that certain unbelieving Jews conspired with the Roman soldiers to encompass his death. And this regenerated publican died triumphant in the faith of a salvation he had so surely learned from the teachings of the Master during his recent sojourn on earth. 139:7.10 (1560.6)

The Twelve Apostles of Jesus—Thomas Didymus

Name:	**Thomas Didymus**
Chosen:	Eighth Apostle. Presented by Philip
Born:	29 years of age when selected.
Before Jesus:	*Thomas Didymus,* a fisherman of Tarichea and onetime carpenter and stone mason of Gadara. He was selected by Philip. 138:2.5 (1539.8)
	When Thomas joined the apostles, he was twenty-nine years old, was married, and had four children. Formerly he had been a carpenter and stone mason, but latterly he had become a fisherman and resided at Tarichea, situated on the west bank of the Jordan where it flows out of the Sea of Galilee, and he was regarded as the leading citizen of this little village. He had little education, but he possessed a keen, reasoning mind and was the son of excellent parents, who lived at Tiberias. Thomas had the one truly analytical mind of the twelve; he was the real scientist of the apostolic group.139:8.2 (1561.2)
History:	Thomas the fisherman and Judas the wanderer met Jesus and the apostles at the fisher-boat landing at Tarichea, and Thomas led the party to his near-by home. Philip now presented Thomas as his nominee for apostleship and Nathaniel presented Judas Iscariot, the Judean, for similar honors. Jesus looked upon Thomas and said: "Thomas, you lack faith; nevertheless, I receive you. Follow me." 138:5.1 (1542.2)
Role:	Thomas was manager of the itinerary. It devolved upon him to arrange lodgings and in a general way select places for teaching and preaching, thereby insuring a smooth and expeditious travel schedule. 138:10.7 (1547.7)
Thomas' Personality:	In later times he has become known as "doubting Thomas," but his fellow apostles hardly looked upon him as a chronic doubter. True, his was a logical, skeptical type of mind, but he had a form of courageous loyalty which forbade those who knew him intimately to regard him as a trifling skeptic. 139:8.1 (1561.1)
	The early home life of Thomas had been unfortunate; his parents were not altogether happy in their married life, and this was reflected in Thomas's adult experience. He grew up having a very disagreeable and quarrelsome disposition. Even his wife was glad to see him join the apostles; she was relieved by the thought that her pessimistic husband would be away from home most of the time. Thomas also had a streak of suspicion which made it very difficult to get along peaceably with him. Peter was very much upset by Thomas at first, complaining to his brother, Andrew, that Thomas was "mean, ugly, and always suspicious." But the better his associates knew Thomas, the more they liked him. They found he was superbly honest and unflinchingly loyal. He was perfectly sincere and unquestionably truthful, but he was a natural-born faultfinder and had grown up to become a real pessimist. His analytical mind had become cursed with suspicion. He was rapidly losing faith in his fellow men when he became associated with the twelve and thus came in contact with the noble character of Jesus. This association with the Master began at once to transform Thomas's whole disposition and to effect great changes in his mental reactions to his fellow men. 139:8.3 (1561.3)

	Thomas's great strength was his superb analytical mind coupled with his unflinching courage—when he had once made up his mind. His great weakness was his suspicious doubting, which he never fully overcame throughout his whole lifetime in the flesh. 139:8.4 (1561.4)
Thomas' Personality: (Continued)	In the councils of the twelve Thomas was always cautious, advocating a policy of safety first, but if his conservatism was voted down or overruled, he was always the first fearlessly to move out in execution of the program decided upon. Again and again would he stand out against some project as being foolhardy and presumptuous; he would debate to the bitter end, but when Andrew would put the proposition to a vote, and after the twelve would elect to do that which he had so strenuously opposed, Thomas was the first to say, "Let's go!" He was a good loser. He did not hold grudges nor nurse wounded feelings. Time and again did he oppose letting Jesus expose himself to danger, but when the Master would decide to take such risks, always was it Thomas who rallied the apostles with his courageous words, "Come on, comrades, let's go and die with him." 139:8.8 (1562.2) Thomas was in some respects like Philip; he also wanted "to be shown," but his outward expressions of doubt were based on entirely different intellectual operations. Thomas was analytical, not merely skeptical. As far as personal physical courage was concerned, he was one of the bravest among the twelve. 139:8.9 (1562.3) Thomas had some very bad days; he was blue and downcast at times. The loss of his twin sister when he was nine years old had occasioned him much youthful sorrow and had added to his temperamental problems of later life. When Thomas would become despondent, sometimes it was Nathaniel who helped him to recover, sometimes Peter, and not infrequently one of the Alpheus twins. When he was most depressed, unfortunately he always tried to avoid coming in direct contact with Jesus. But the Master knew all about this and had an understanding sympathy for his apostle when he was thus afflicted with depression and harassed by doubts. 139:8.10 (1562.4) Sometimes Thomas would get permission from Andrew to go off by himself for a day or two. But he soon learned that such a course was not wise; he early found that it was best, when he was downhearted, to stick close to his work and to remain near his associates. But no matter what happened in his emotional life, he kept right on being an apostle. When the time actually came to move forward, it was always Thomas who said, "Let's go!" 139:8.11 (1562.5) Thomas is the great example of a human being who has doubts, faces them, and wins. He had a great mind; he was no carping critic. He was a logical thinker; he was the acid test of Jesus and his fellow apostles. If Jesus and his work had not been genuine, it could not have held a man like Thomas from the start to the finish. He had a keen and sure sense of *fact*. At the first appearance of fraud or deception Thomas would have forsaken them all. Scientists may not fully understand all about Jesus and his work on earth, but there lived and worked with the Master and his human associates a man whose mind was that of a true scientist—Thomas Didymus—and he believed in Jesus of Nazareth. 139:8.12 (1562.6)

The Twelve Apostles of Jesus—Thomas Didymus

Skill:	In the organization of the twelve Thomas was assigned to arrange and manage the itinerary, and he was an able director of the work and movements of the apostolic corps. He was a good executive, an excellent businessman, but he was handicapped by his many moods; he was one man one day and another man the next. He was inclined toward melancholic brooding when he joined the apostles, but contact with Jesus and the apostles largely cured him of this morbid introspection. 139:8.5 (1561.5)
Significant Events:	Jesus now recounted for them the coming of John, the baptism in the Jordan, the marriage feast at Cana, the recent choosing of the six, and the withdrawal from them of his own brothers in the flesh, and warned them that the enemy of the kingdom would seek also to draw them away. After this short but earnest talk the apostles all arose, under Peter's leadership, to declare their undying devotion to their Master and to pledge their unswerving loyalty to the kingdom, as Thomas expressed it, "To this coming kingdom, no matter what it is and even if I do not fully understand it." 138:7.3 (1544.2)
	Jesus enjoyed Thomas very much and had many long, personal talks with him. His presence among the apostles was a great comfort to all honest doubters and encouraged many troubled minds to come into the kingdom, even if they could not wholly understand everything about the spiritual and philosophic phases of the teachings of Jesus. Thomas's membership in the twelve was a standing declaration that Jesus loved even honest doubters. 139:8.6 (1561.6)
	This same evening Thomas asked Jesus: "Master, you say that we must become as little children before we can gain entrance to the Father's kingdom, and yet you have warned us not to be deceived by false prophets nor to become guilty of casting our pearls before swine. Now, I am honestly puzzled. I cannot understand your teaching." 140:10.4 (1585.2)
	In answer to Thomas's question, "Who is this God of the kingdom?" Jesus replied: "God is *your* Father, and religion—my gospel—is nothing more nor less than the believing recognition of the truth that you are his son. And I am here among you in the flesh to make clear both of these ideas in my life and teachings." 141:4.2 (1590.5)
	After the busy period of teaching and personal work of Passover week in Jerusalem, Jesus spent the next Wednesday at Bethany with his apostles, resting. That afternoon, Thomas asked a question which elicited a long and instructive answer. Said Thomas: "Master, on the day we were set apart as ambassadors of the kingdom, you told us many things, instructed us regarding our personal mode of life, but what shall we teach the multitude? How are these people to live after the kingdom more fully comes? Shall your disciples own slaves? Shall your believers court poverty and shun property? Shall mercy alone prevail so that we shall have no more law and justice?" 142:7.1 (1603.2)
	Although Jesus discoursed for several hours, Thomas was not yet satisfied, for he said: "But, Master, we do not find that the Father in heaven always deals kindly and mercifully with us. Many times we grievously suffer on earth, and not always are our prayers answered. Where do we fail to grasp the meaning of your teaching?" 142:7.16 (1605.1)

Thomas' Significant Events: (Continued)	The central theme of the discussions throughout the entire month of September was prayer and worship. After they had discussed worship for some days, Jesus finally delivered his memorable discourse on prayer in answer to Thomas's request: "Master, teach us how to pray." 144:1.9 (1618.3)
	It was the habit of Jesus two evenings each week to hold special converse with individuals who desired to talk with him, in a certain secluded and sheltered corner of the Zebedee garden. At one of these evening conversations in private Thomas asked the Master this question: "Why is it necessary for men to be born of the spirit in order to enter the kingdom? Is rebirth necessary to escape the control of the evil one? Master, what is evil?" 148:4.1 (1659.8)
	The Master permitted this confusion to pass the point of most intense expression; then he clapped his hands and called them about him. When they had all gathered around him once more, he said, "Before I tell you about this parable, do any of you have aught to say?" Following a moment of silence, Thomas spoke up: "Yes, Master, I wish to say a few words. I remember that you once told us to beware of this very thing. You instructed us that, when using illustrations for our preaching, we should employ true stories, not fables, and that we should select a story best suited to the illustration of the one central and vital truth which we wished to teach the people, and that, having so used the story, we should not attempt to make a spiritual application of all the minor details involved in the telling of the story. I hold that Peter and Nathaniel are both wrong in their attempts to interpret this parable. I admire their ability to do these things, but I am equally sure that all such attempts to make a natural parable yield spiritual analogies in all its features can only result in confusion and serious misconception of the true purpose of such a parable. That I am right is fully proved by the fact that, whereas we were all of one mind an hour ago, now are we divided into two separate groups who hold different opinions concerning this parable and hold such opinions so earnestly as to interfere, in my opinion, with our ability fully to grasp the great truth which you had in mind when you presented this parable to the multitude and subsequently asked us to make comment upon it." 151:2.5 (1690.3)
	While pausing for lunch under the shadow of an overhanging ledge of rock, near Luz, Jesus delivered one of the most remarkable addresses which his apostles ever listened to throughout all their years of association with him. No sooner had they seated themselves to break bread than Simon Peter asked Jesus: "Master, since the Father in heaven knows all things, and since his spirit is our support in the establishment of the kingdom of heaven on earth, why is it that we flee from the threats of our enemies? Why do we refuse to confront the foes of truth?" But before Jesus had begun to answer Peter's question, Thomas broke in, asking: "Master, I should really like to know just what is wrong with the religion of our enemies at Jerusalem. What is the real difference between their religion and ours? Why is it we are at such diversity of belief when we all profess to serve the same God?" 155:4.2 (1728.2)
	Early Monday morning, Rodan began a series of ten addresses to Nathaniel, Thomas, and a group of some two dozen believers who chanced to be at Magadan. These talks, condensed, combined, and restated in modern phraseology, present the following thoughts for consideration: 160:1.1 (1772.2)

The Twelve Apostles of Jesus—Thomas Didymus

Admired Jesus For:	The other apostles held Jesus in reverence because of some special and outstanding trait of his replete personality, but Thomas revered his Master because of his superbly balanced character. Increasingly Thomas admired and honored one who was so lovingly merciful yet so inflexibly just and fair; so firm but never obstinate; so calm but never indifferent; so helpful and so sympathetic but never meddlesome or dictatorial; so strong but at the same time so gentle; so positive but never rough or rude; so tender but never vacillating; so pure and innocent but at the same time so virile, aggressive, and forceful; so truly courageous but never rash or foolhardy; such a lover of nature but so free from all tendency to revere nature; so humorous and so playful, but so free from levity and frivolity. It was this matchless symmetry of personality that so charmed Thomas. He probably enjoyed the highest intellectual understanding and personality appreciation of Jesus of any of the twelve. 139:8.7 (1562.1)
Final Instructions:	And then Jesus went over to Thomas, who, standing up, heard him say: "Thomas, you have often lacked faith; however, when you have had your seasons with doubt, you have never lacked courage. I know well that the false prophets and spurious teachers will not deceive you. After I have gone, your brethren will the more appreciate your critical way of viewing new teachings. And when you all are scattered to the ends of the earth in the times to come, remember that you are still my ambassador. Dedicate your life to the great work of showing how the critical material mind of man can triumph over the inertia of intellectual doubting when faced by the demonstration of the manifestation of living truth as it operates in the experience of spirit-born men and women who yield the fruits of the spirit in their lives, and who love one another, even as I have loved you. Thomas, I am glad you joined us, and I know, after a short period of perplexity, you will go on in the service of the kingdom. Your doubts have perplexed your brethren, but they have never troubled me. I have confidence in you, and I will go before you even to the uttermost parts of the earth." 181:2.26 (1962.1)
	Jesus next talked with Thomas and Nathaniel. Said he to Thomas, "Thomas, do you serve me?" Thomas replied, "Yes, Lord, I serve you now and always." Then said Jesus: "If you would serve me, serve my brethren in the flesh even as I have served you. And be not weary in this well-doing but persevere as one who has been ordained by God for this service of love. When you have finished your service with me on earth, you shall serve with me in glory. Thomas, you must cease doubting; you must grow in faith and the knowledge of truth. Believe in God like a child but cease to act so childishly. Have courage; be strong in faith and mighty in the kingdom of God." 192:2.9 (2048.5)
After Jesus:	Thomas had a trying time during the days of the trial and crucifixion. He was for a season in the depths of despair, but he rallied his courage, stuck to the apostles, and was present with them to welcome Jesus on the Sea of Galilee. For a while he succumbed to his doubting depression but eventually rallied his faith and courage. He gave wise counsel to the apostles after Pentecost and, when persecution scattered the believers, went to Cyprus, Crete, the North African coast, and Sicily, preaching the glad tidings of the kingdom and baptizing believers. 139:8.13 (1563.1)
Death:	And Thomas continued preaching and baptizing until he was apprehended by the agents of the Roman government and was put to death in Malta. Just a few weeks before his death he had begun the writing of the life and teachings of Jesus. 139:8.13 (1563.1)

The Twelve Apostles of Jesus—James and Judas Alpheus

Name:	**James and Judas Alpheus**
Chosen:	Selected ninth and tenth. 3. *James Alpheus,* a fisherman and farmer of Kheresa, was selected by James Zebedee. 138:2.6 (1539.9) 4. *Judas Alpheus,* the twin brother of James Alpheus, also a fisherman, was selected by John Zebedee. 138:2.7 (1539.10)
Born:	26 years of age when selected.
Before Jesus:	James and Judas the sons of Alpheus, the twin fishermen living near Kheresa, were the ninth and tenth apostles and were chosen by James and John Zebedee. They were twenty-six years old and married, James having three children, Judas two. 139:9.1 (1563.2) There is not much to be said about these two commonplace fisherfolk. They loved their Master and Jesus loved them, but they never interrupted his discourses with questions. They understood very little about the philosophical discussions or the theological debates of their fellow apostles, but they rejoiced to find themselves numbered among such a group of mighty men. These two men were almost identical in personal appearance, mental characteristics, and extent of spiritual perception. What may be said of one should be recorded of the other. 139:9.2 (1563.3)
History:	On the morrow all nine of them went by boat over to Kheresa to execute the formal calling of the next two apostles, James and Judas the twin sons of Alpheus, the nominees of James and John Zebedee. The fisherman twins were expecting Jesus and his apostles and were therefore awaiting them on the shore. James Zebedee presented the Master to the Kheresa fishermen, and Jesus, gazing on them, nodded and said, "Follow me." 138:4.1 (1541.3) That afternoon, which they spent together, Jesus fully instructed them concerning attendance upon festive gatherings, concluding his remarks by saying: "All men are my brothers. My Father in heaven does not despise any creature of our making. The kingdom of heaven is open to all men and women. No man may close the door of mercy in the face of any hungry soul who may seek to gain an entrance thereto. We will sit at meat with all who desire to hear of the kingdom. As our Father in heaven looks down upon men, they are all alike. Refuse not therefore to break bread with Pharisee or sinner, Sadducee or publican, Roman or Jew, rich or poor, free or bond. The door of the kingdom is wide open for all who desire to know the truth and to find God." 138:4.2 (1541.4) That night at a simple supper at the Alpheus home, the twin brothers were received into the apostolic family. Later in the evening Jesus gave his apostles their first lesson dealing with the origin, nature, and destiny of unclean spirits, but they could not comprehend the import of what he told them. They found it very easy to love and admire Jesus but very difficult to understand many of his teachings. 138:4.3 (1541.5)
Role:	James and Judas the twin sons of Alpheus were assigned to the management of the multitudes. It was their task to deputize a sufficient number of assistant ushers to enable them to maintain order among the crowds during the preaching. 138:10.8 (1547.8)

The Twelve Apostles of Jesus—James and Judas Alpheus

Alpheus Twin's Personality:	Do not make the mistake of regarding the apostles as being altogether ignorant and unlearned. All of them, except the Alpheus twins, were graduates of the synagogue schools, having been thoroughly trained in the Hebrew scriptures and in much of the current knowledge of that day. Seven were graduates of the Capernaum synagogue schools, and there were no better Jewish schools in all Galilee. 139:0.3 (1548.3) When your records refer to these messengers of the kingdom as being "ignorant and unlearned," it was intended to convey the idea that they were laymen, unlearned in the lore of the rabbis and untrained in the methods of rabbinical interpretation of the Scriptures. They were lacking in so-called higher education. In modern times they would certainly be considered uneducated, and in some circles of society even uncultured. One thing is certain: They had not all been put through the same rigid and stereotyped educational curriculum. From adolescence on they had enjoyed separate experiences of learning how to live. 139:0.4 (1548.4)
	The twins were good-natured, simple-minded helpers, and everybody loved them. Jesus welcomed these young men of one talent to positions of honor on his personal staff in the kingdom because there are untold millions of other such simple and fear-ridden souls on the worlds of space whom he likewise wishes to welcome into active and believing fellowship with himself and his outpoured Spirit of Truth. Jesus does not look down upon littleness, only upon evil and sin. James and Judas were *little,* but they were also *faithful.* They were simple and ignorant, but they were also big-hearted, kind, and generous. 139:9.8 (1564.2)
Skill:	Andrew assigned them to the work of policing the multitudes. They were the chief ushers of the preaching hours and, in fact, the general servants and errand boys of the twelve. They helped Philip with the supplies, they carried money to the families for Nathaniel, and always were they ready to lend a helping hand to any one of the apostles. 139:9.3 (1563.4)
	James and Judas, who were also called Thaddeus and Lebbeus, had neither strong points nor weak points. The nicknames given them by the disciples were good-natured designations of mediocrity. They were "the least of all the apostles"; they knew it and felt cheerful about it. 139:9.5 (1563.6)
Significant Events:	Only once or twice in all their association with Jesus did the twins venture to ask questions in public. Judas was once intrigued into asking Jesus a question when the Master had talked about revealing himself openly to the world. He felt a little disappointed that there were to be no more secrets among the twelve, and he made bold to ask: "But, Master, when you do thus declare yourself to the world, how will you favor us with special manifestations of your goodness?" 139:9.10 (1564.4)
	It was from among such a group of depressed and disconsolate followers that Jesus went forth on this beautiful Sabbath afternoon to preach his epoch-making sermon in the Capernaum synagogue. The only word of cheerful greeting or well-wishing from any of his immediate followers came from one of the unsuspecting Alpheus twins, who, as Jesus left the house on his way to the synagogue, saluted him cheerily and said: "We pray the Father will help you, and that we may have bigger multitudes than ever." 153:0.3 (1707.3)

Alpheus Twin's Significant Events: (Continued)	Before they started, the Alpheus twins put their cloaks on the donkey and held him while the Master got on. 172:3.9 (1882.2)
	To the Alpheus twins this was a perfect day. They really enjoyed it all the way through, and not being present during the time of quiet visitation about the temple, they escaped much of the anticlimax of the popular upheaval. They could not possibly understand the downcast behavior of the apostles when they came back to Bethany that evening. In the memory of the twins this was always their day of being nearest heaven on earth. This day was the satisfying climax of their whole career as apostles. And the memory of the elation of this Sunday afternoon carried them on through all of the tragedy of this eventful week, right up to the hour of the crucifixion. It was the most befitting entry of the king the twins could conceive; they enjoyed every moment of the whole pageant. They fully approved of all they saw and long cherished the memory. 172:5.11 (1886.3)
	When Jesus had finished speaking, the Alpheus twins brought on the bread and wine, with the bitter herbs and the paste of dried fruits, for the next course of the Last Supper. 179:3.10 (1940.2)
	As the Master paused for a moment, Judas Alpheus made bold to ask one of the few questions which either he or his brother ever addressed to Jesus in public. Said Judas: "Master, you have always lived among us as a friend; how shall we know you when you no longer manifest yourself to us save by this spirit? If the world sees you not, how shall we be certain about you? How will you show yourself to us?" 180:4.4 (1948.5)
Admired Jesus For:	James Alpheus especially loved Jesus because of the Master's simplicity. These twins could not comprehend the mind of Jesus, but they did grasp the sympathetic bond between themselves and the heart of their Master. Their minds were not of a high order; they might even reverently be called stupid, but they had a real experience in their spiritual natures. They believed in Jesus; they were sons of God and fellows of the kingdom. 139:9.6 (1563.7) Judas Alpheus was drawn toward Jesus because of the Master's unostentatious humility. Such humility linked with such personal dignity made a great appeal to Judas. The fact that Jesus would always enjoin silence regarding his unusual acts made a great impression on this simple child of nature. 139:9.7 (1564.1)
Final Instructions:	To the Alpheus twins he said: "Do not allow the things which you cannot understand to crush you. Be true to the affections of your hearts and put not your trust in either great men or the changing attitude of the people. Stand by your brethren." 174:0.2 (1897.2)
	Jesus then went over to the Alpheus twins and, standing between them, said: "My little children, you are one of the three groups of brothers who chose to follow after me. All six of you have done well to work in peace with your own flesh and blood, but none have done better than you. Hard times are just ahead of us. You may not understand all that will befall you and your brethren, but never doubt that you were once called to the work of the kingdom. For some time there will be no multitudes to manage, but do not become discouraged; when your lifework is finished, I will receive you on high, where in glory you shall tell of your salvation to seraphic hosts and to

Final Instructions: (Continued)	multitudes of the high Sons of God. Dedicate your lives to the enhancement of commonplace toil. Show all men on earth and the angels of heaven how cheerfully and courageously mortal man can, after having been called to work for a season in the special service of God, return to the labors of former days. If, for the time being, your work in the outward affairs of the kingdom should be completed, you should go back to your former labors with the new enlightenment of the experience of sonship with God and with the exalted realization that, to him who is God-knowing, there is no such thing as common labor or secular toil. To you who have worked with me, all things have become sacred, and all earthly labor has become a service even to God the Father. And when you hear the news of the doings of your former apostolic associates, rejoice with them and continue your daily work as those who wait upon God and serve while they wait. You have been my apostles, and you always shall be, and I will remember you in the kingdom to come." 181:2.19 (1959.3)
	Then he walked and talked with the Alpheus twins, James and Judas, and speaking to both of them, he asked, "James and Judas, do you believe in me?" And when they both answered, "Yes, Master, we do believe," he said: "I will soon leave you. You see that I have already left you in the flesh. I tarry only a short time in this form before I go to my Father. You believe in me—you are my apostles, and you always will be. Go on believing and remembering your association with me, when I am gone, and after you have, perchance, returned to the work you used to do before you came to live with me. Never allow a change in your outward work to influence your allegiance. Have faith in God to the end of your days on earth. Never forget that, when you are a faith son of God, all upright work of the realm is sacred. Nothing which a son of God does can be common. Do your work, therefore, from this time on, as for God. And when you are through on this world, I have other and better worlds where you shall likewise work for me. And in all of this work, on this world and on other worlds, I will work with you, and my spirit shall dwell within you." 192:2.13 (2049.4)
After Jesus:	The twins served faithfully until the end, until the dark days of trial, crucifixion, and despair. They never lost their heart faith in Jesus, and (save John) they were the first to believe in his resurrection. But they could not comprehend the establishment of the kingdom. Soon after their Master was crucified, they returned to their families and nets; their work was done. 139:9.11 (1564.5)
	The Alpheus twins took little part in these serious discussions; they were fairly busy with their customary ministrations. One of them expressed the attitude of both when he said, in reply to a question asked by Philip: "We do not understand about the resurrection, but our mother says she talked with the Master, and we believe her." 191:0.11 (2038.6)
	On Thursday night the apostles had a wonderful meeting in this upper chamber and all pledged themselves to go forth in the public preaching of the new gospel of the risen Lord except Thomas, Simon Zelotes, and the Alpheus twins. 192:4.7 (2051.4)
Death:	They had not the ability to go on in the more complex battles of the kingdom. But they lived and died conscious of having been honored and blessed with four years of close and personal association with a Son of God, the sovereign maker of a universe. 139:9.11 (1564.5)

The Twelve Apostles of Jesus—Simon Zelotes

Name:	**Simon Zelotes**
Chosen:	Eleventh Apostle
Born:	28 years of age when selected.
Before Jesus:	*Simon Zelotes* was a high officer in the patriotic organization of the Zealots, a position which he gave up to join Jesus' apostles. Before joining the Zealots, Simon had been a merchant. He was selected by Peter. 138:2.8 (1540.1)
History:	Simon Zelotes, the eleventh apostle, was chosen by Simon Peter. He was an able man of good ancestry and lived with his family at Capernaum. He was twenty-eight years old when he became attached to the apostles. He was a fiery agitator and was also a man who spoke much without thinking. He had been a merchant in Capernaum before he turned his entire attention to the patriotic organization of the Zealots. 139:11.1 (1564.6)
Role:	Simon Zelotes was given charge of recreation and play. He managed the Wednesday programs and also sought to provide for a few hours of relaxation and diversion each day. 138:10.9 (1547.9)
	Simon Zelotes was given charge of the diversions and relaxation of the apostolic group, and he was a very efficient organizer of the play life and recreational activities of the twelve. 139:11.2 (1564.7)
Simon Zelotes' Personality:	He was a rebel by nature and an iconoclast by training, but Jesus won him for the higher concepts of the kingdom of heaven. He had always identified himself with the party of protest, but he now joined the party of progress, unlimited and eternal progression of spirit and truth. Simon was a man of intense loyalties and warm personal devotions, and he did profoundly love Jesus. 139:11.7 (1565.4)
Skill:	Simon's strength was his inspirational loyalty. When the apostles found a man or woman who floundered in indecision about entering the kingdom, they would send for Simon. It usually required only about fifteen minutes for this enthusiastic advocate of salvation through faith in God to settle all doubts and remove all indecision, to see a new soul born into the "liberty of faith and the joy of salvation." 139:11.3 (1564.8) Simon's great weakness was his material-mindedness. He could not quickly change himself from a Jewish nationalist to a spiritually minded internationalist. Four years was too short a time in which to make such an intellectual and emotional transformation, but Jesus was always patient with him. 139:11.4 (1565.1)
Simon Significant Events:	Although Simon was a rabid revolutionist, a fearless firebrand of agitation, he gradually subdued his fiery nature until he became a powerful and effective preacher of "Peace on earth and good will among men." Simon was a great debater; he did like to argue. And when it came to dealing with the legalistic minds of the educated Jews or the intellectual quibblings of the Greeks, the task was always assigned to Simon. 139:11.6 (1565.3)
	The Master had many talks with Simon, but he never fully succeeded in making an internationalist out of this ardent Jewish nationalist. Jesus often told Simon that it was proper to want to see the social, economic, and political orders improved, but he would always add: "That is not the business of the kingdom of heaven. We must be dedicated to the doing of the Father's will. Our business is to be ambassadors of a spiritual government on high, and we must not immediately concern ourselves with aught but

	the representation of the will and character of the divine Father who stands at the head of the government whose credentials we bear." It was all difficult for Simon to comprehend, but gradually he began to grasp something of the meaning of the Master's teaching. 139:11.9 (1565.6)
	After Jesus and Matthew had finished talking, Simon Zelotes asked, "But, Master, are *all* men the sons of God?" 140:10.7 (1585.5)
	Near the end of the last week at Amathus, Simon Zelotes brought to Jesus one Teherma, a Persian doing business at Damascus. Teherma had heard of Jesus and had come to Capernaum to see him, and there learning that Jesus had gone with his apostles down the Jordan on the way to Jerusalem, he set out to find him. Andrew had presented Teherma to Simon for instruction. Simon looked upon the Persian as a "fire worshiper," although Teherma took great pains to explain that fire was only the visible symbol of the Pure and Holy One. After talking with Jesus, the Persian signified his intention of remaining for several days to hear the teaching and listen to the preaching. 141:6.1 (1592.3) When Simon Zelotes and Jesus were alone, Simon asked the Master: "Why is it that I could not persuade him? Why did he so resist me and so readily lend an ear to you?" 141:6.2 (1592.4)
Simon Significant Events: (Continued)	About this time there arrived at the Bethsaida encampment a trance prophet from Bagdad, one Kirmeth. This supposed prophet had peculiar visions when in trance and dreamed fantastic dreams when his sleep was disturbed. He created a considerable disturbance at the camp, and Simon Zelotes was in favor of dealing rather roughly with the self-deceived pretender, but Jesus intervened and allowed him entire freedom of action for a few days. 148:8.3 (1666.2)
	When Jesus was visiting the group of evangelists working under the supervision of Simon Zelotes, during their evening conference Simon asked the Master: "Why are some persons so much more happy and contented than others? Is contentment a matter of religious experience?" 149:5.1 (1674.3)
	Jesus would have good-naturedly managed the crowd and effectively disarmed even his violent enemies had it not been for the tactical blunder of one of his own apostles, Simon Zelotes, who, with the help of Nahor, one of the younger evangelists, had meanwhile gathered together a group of Jesus' friends from among the crowd and, assuming a belligerent attitude, had served notice on the enemies of the Master to go hence. Jesus had long taught the apostles that a soft answer turns away wrath, but his followers were not accustomed to seeing their beloved teacher, whom they so willingly called Master, treated with such discourtesy and disdain. It was too much for them, and they found themselves giving expression to passionate and vehement resentment, all of which only tended to arouse the mob spirit in this ungodly and uncouth assembly. And so, under the leadership of hirelings, these ruffians laid hold upon Jesus and rushed him out of the synagogue to the brow of a near-by precipitous hill, where they were minded to shove him over the edge to his death below. But just as they were about to push him over the edge of the cliff, Jesus turned suddenly upon his captors and, facing them, quietly folded his arms. He said nothing, but his friends were more than astonished when, as he started to walk forward, the mob parted and permitted him to pass on unmolested. 150:9.3 (1686.6)

	Then came forward Simon Zelotes to remonstrate with Norana. Said Simon: "Woman, you are a Greek-speaking gentile. It is not right that you should expect the Master to take the bread intended for the children of the favored household and cast it to the dogs." But Norana refused to take offense at Simon's thrust. She replied only: "Yes, teacher, I understand your words. I am only a dog in the eyes of the Jews, but as concerns your Master, I am a believing dog. I am determined that he shall see my daughter, for I am persuaded that, if he shall but look upon her, he will heal her. And even you, my good man, would not dare to deprive the dogs of the privilege of obtaining the crumbs which chance to fall from the children's table." 156:1.5 (1735.1)
	It was late forenoon on this Wednesday when the apostles assembled in Celsus' garden for their noontime meal. During most of the night and since they had arisen that morning, Simon Peter and Simon Zelotes had been earnestly laboring with their brethren to bring them all to the point of the wholehearted acceptance of the Master, not merely as the Messiah, but also as the divine Son of the living God. The two Simons were well-nigh agreed in their estimate of Jesus, and they labored diligently to bring their brethren around to the full acceptance of their views. 157:4.2 (1746.6)
Simon Significant Events: (Continued)	As the apostles listened, Simon Zelotes and Judas Iscariot stepped into the presence of the father, saying: "We can heal him; you need not wait for the Master's return. We are ambassadors of the kingdom; no longer do we hold these things in secret. Jesus is the Deliverer, and the keys of the kingdom have been delivered to us." By this time Andrew and Thomas were in consultation at one side. Nathaniel and the others looked on in amazement; they were all aghast at the sudden boldness, if not presumption, of Simon and Judas. Then said the father: "If it has been given you to do these works, I pray that you will speak those words which will deliver my child from this bondage." Then Simon stepped forward and, placing his hand on the head of the child, looked directly into his eyes and commanded: "Come out of him, you unclean spirit; in the name of Jesus obey me." But the lad had only a more violent fit, while the scribes mocked the apostles in derision, and the disappointed believers suffered the taunts of these unfriendly critics. 158:4.6 (1756.3)
	Accordingly, when Simon Zelotes observed the Samaritan among the lepers, he sought to induce the Master to pass on into the city without even hesitating to exchange greetings with them. Said Jesus to Simon: "But what if the Samaritan loves God as well as the Jews? Should we sit in judgment on our fellow men? Who can tell? if we make these ten men whole, perhaps the Samaritan will prove more grateful even than the Jews. Do you feel certain about your opinions, Simon?" And Simon quickly replied, "If you cleanse them, you will soon find out." And Jesus replied: "So shall it be, Simon, and you will soon know the truth regarding the gratitude of men and the loving mercy of God." 166:2.3 (1827.8)
	One evening Simon Zelotes, commenting on one of Jesus' statements, said: "Master, what did you mean when you said today that many of the children of the world are wiser in their generation than are the children of the kingdom since they are skillful in making friends with the mammon of unrighteousness?" 169:2.1 (1853.4)
	Before they went to their separate sleeping quarters, Simon Zelotes led them all over to his tent, where were stored the swords and other arms, and supplied each of them with this fighting equipment. 182:2.3 (1966.3)

<table>
<tr><td rowspan="3">Simon Significant Events: (Continued)</td><td>Andrew had been released from all responsibility in the group management of his fellow apostles; accordingly, in this greatest of all crises in their lives, he was silent. After a short informal discussion, Simon Zelotes stood up on the stone wall of the olive press and, making an impassioned plea for loyalty to the Master and the cause of the kingdom, exhorted his fellow apostles and the other disciples to hasten on after the mob and effect the rescue of Jesus. The majority of the company would have been disposed to follow his aggressive leadership had it not been for the advice of Nathaniel, who stood up the moment Simon had finished speaking and called their attention to Jesus' oft-repeated teachings regarding nonresistance. 183:4.2 (1975.5)</td></tr>
<tr><td>Simon Zelotes was too much crushed to participate in the discussions. Most of the time he reclined on a couch in a corner of the room with his face to the wall; he did not speak half a dozen times throughout the whole day. His concept of the kingdom had crashed, and he could not discern that the Master's resurrection could materially change the situation. His disappointment was very personal and altogether too keen to be recovered from on short notice, even in the face of such a stupendous fact as the resurrection. 191:0.8 (2038.3)</td></tr>
<tr><td>Jesus visited with the ten apostles and John Mark for more than an hour, and then he walked up and down the beach, talking with them two and two—but not the same couples he had at first sent out together to teach. All eleven of the apostles had come down from Jerusalem together, but Simon Zelotes grew more and more despondent as they drew near Galilee, so that, when they reached Bethsaida, he forsook his brethren and returned to his home. 192:1.10 (2047.3)

Before taking leave of them this morning, Jesus directed that two of the apostles should volunteer to go to Simon Zelotes and bring him back that very day. And Peter and Andrew did so. 192:1.11 (2047.4)</td></tr>
<tr><td>Admired Jesus For:</td><td>The one thing about Jesus which Simon so much admired was the Master's calmness, his assurance, poise, and inexplicable composure. 139:11.5 (1565.2)</td></tr>
<tr><td rowspan="2">Final Instructions:</td><td>And to Simon Zelotes he said: "Simon, you may be crushed by disappointment, but your spirit shall rise above all that may come upon you. What you have failed to learn from me, my spirit will teach you. Seek the true realities of the spirit and cease to be attracted by unreal and material shadows." 174:0.2 (1897.2)</td></tr>
<tr><td>Jesus now went over to Simon Zelotes, who stood up and listened to this admonition: "You are a true son of Abraham, but what a time I have had trying to make you a son of this heavenly kingdom. I love you and so do all of your brethren. I know that you love me, Simon, and that you also love the kingdom, but you are still set on making this kingdom come according to your liking. I know full well that you will eventually grasp the spiritual nature and meaning of my gospel, and that you will do valiant work in its proclamation, but I am distressed about what may happen to you when I depart. I would rejoice to know that you would not falter; I would be made happy if I could know that, after I go to the Father, you would not cease to be my apostle, and that you would acceptably deport yourself as an ambassador of the heavenly kingdom." 181:2.7 (1956.2)</td></tr>
</table>

Final Instructions: (Continued)	Jesus had hardly ceased speaking to Simon Zelotes when the fiery patriot, drying his eyes, replied: "Master, have no fears for my loyalty. I have turned my back upon everything that I might dedicate my life to the establishment of your kingdom on earth, and I will not falter. I have survived every disappointment so far, and I will not forsake you." 181:2.8 (1956.3) And then, laying his hand on Simon's shoulder, Jesus said: "It is indeed refreshing to hear you talk like that, especially at such a time as this, but, my good friend, you still do not know what you are talking about. Not for one moment would I doubt your loyalty, your devotion; I know you would not hesitate to go forth in battle and die for me, as all these others would" (and they all nodded a vigorous approval), "but that will not be required of you. I have repeatedly told you that my kingdom is not of this world, and that my disciples will not fight to effect its establishment. I have told you this many times, Simon, but you refuse to face the truth. I am not concerned with your loyalty to me and to the kingdom, but what will you do when I go away and you at last wake up to the realization that you have failed to grasp the meaning of my teaching, and that you must adjust your misconceptions to the reality of another and spiritual order of affairs in the kingdom?" 181:2.9 (1956.4) Simon wanted to speak further, but Jesus raised his hand and, stopping him, went on to say: "None of my apostles are more sincere and honest at heart than you, but not one of them will be so upset and disheartened as you, after my departure. In all of your discouragement my spirit shall abide with you, and these, your brethren, will not forsake you. Do not forget what I have taught you regarding the relation of citizenship on earth to sonship in the Father's spiritual kingdom. Ponder well all that I have said to you about rendering to Caesar the things which are Caesar's and to God that which is God's. Dedicate your life, Simon, to showing how acceptably mortal man may fulfill my injunction concerning the simultaneous recognition of temporal duty to civil powers and spiritual service in the brotherhood of the kingdom. If you will be taught by the Spirit of Truth, never will there be conflict between the requirements of citizenship on earth and sonship in heaven unless the temporal rulers presume to require of you the homage and worship which belong only to God. 181:2.10 (1956.5) "And now, Simon, when you do finally see all of this, and after you have shaken off your depression and have gone forth proclaiming this gospel in great power, never forget that I was with you even through all of your season of discouragement, and that I will go on with you to the very end. You shall always be my apostle, and after you become willing to see by the eye of the spirit and more fully to yield your will to the will of the Father in heaven, then will you return to labor as my ambassador, and no one shall take away from you the authority which I have conferred upon you, because of your slowness of comprehending the truths I have taught you. And so, Simon, once more I warn you that they who fight with the sword perish with the sword, while they who labor in the spirit achieve life everlasting in the kingdom to come with joy and peace in the kingdom which now is. And when the work given into your hands is finished on earth, you, Simon, shall sit down with me in my kingdom over there. You shall really see the kingdom you have longed for, but not in this life. Continue to believe in me and in that which I have revealed to you, and you shall receive the gift of eternal life." 181:2.11 (1957.1)

The Twelve Apostles of Jesus—Simon Zelotes

After Jesus:	After the dispersion because of the Jerusalem persecutions, Simon went into temporary retirement. He was literally crushed. As a nationalist patriot he had surrendered in deference to Jesus' teachings; now all was lost. He was in despair, but in a few years he rallied his hopes and went forth to proclaim the gospel of the kingdom. 139:11.10 (1565.7)
Death:	He went to Alexandria and, after working up the Nile, penetrated into the heart of Africa, everywhere preaching the gospel of Jesus and baptizing believers. Thus he labored until he was an old man and feeble. And he died and was buried in the heart of Africa. 139:11.11 (1565.8)

The Twelve Apostles of Jesus—Judas Iscariot

Name:	**Judas Iscariot**
Chosen:	Judas Iscariot, the twelfth apostle, was chosen by Nathaniel. 139:12.1 (1565.9)
Born:	He was born in Kerioth, a small town in southern Judea. 139:12.1 (1565.9)
Before Jesus:	*Judas Iscariot* was an only son of wealthy Jewish parents living in Jericho. He had become attached to John the Baptist, and his Sadducee parents had disowned him. He was looking for employment in these regions when Jesus' apostles found him, and chiefly because of his experience with finances, Nathaniel invited him to join their ranks. Judas Iscariot was the only Judean among the twelve apostles. 138:2.9 (1540.2)
	Judas Iscariot, the twelfth apostle, was chosen by Nathaniel. He was born in Kerioth, a small town in southern Judea. When he was a lad, his parents moved to Jericho, where he lived and had been employed in his father's various business enterprises until he became interested in the preaching and work of John the Baptist. Judas's parents were Sadducees, and when their son joined John's disciples, they disowned him. 139:12.1 (1565.9)
History:	Thomas the fisherman and Judas the wanderer met Jesus and the apostles at the fisher-boat landing at Tarichea, and Thomas led the party to his near-by home. Philip now presented Thomas as his nominee for apostleship and Nathaniel presented Judas Iscariot, the Judean, for similar honors. Jesus looked upon Thomas and said: "Thomas, you lack faith; nevertheless, I receive you. Follow me." To Judas Iscariot the Master said: "Judas, we are all of one flesh, and as I receive you into our midst, I pray that you will always be loyal to your Galilean brethren. Follow me." 138:5.1 (1542.2)
	Nathaniel and Judas Iscariot were the two best educated men among the twelve. Nathaniel had thought to become a merchant. 139:6.2 (1558.3)
Role:	Judas Iscariot was appointed treasurer. He carried the bag. He paid all expenses and kept the books. He made budget estimates for Matthew from week to week and also made weekly reports to Andrew. Judas paid out funds on Andrew's authorization. 138:10.10 (1547.10)
Judas Iscariot's Personality:	When Nathaniel met Judas at Tarichea, he was seeking employment with a fish-drying enterprise at the lower end of the Sea of Galilee. He was thirty years of age and unmarried when he joined the apostles. He was probably the best-educated man among the twelve and the only Judean in the Master's apostolic family. Judas had no outstanding trait of personal strength, though he had many outwardly appearing traits of culture and habits of training. He was a good thinker but not always a truly *honest* thinker. Judas did not really understand himself; he was not really sincere in dealing with himself. 139:12.2 (1566.1)

Judas' Personality: (Continued)	Judas was an only son of unwise parents. When very young, he was pampered and petted; he was a spoiled child. As he grew up, he had exaggerated ideas about his self-importance. He was a poor loser. He had loose and distorted ideas about fairness; he was given to the indulgence of hate and suspicion. He was an expert at misinterpretation of the words and acts of his friends. All through his life Judas had cultivated the habit of getting even with those whom he fancied had mistreated him. His sense of values and loyalties was defective. 139:12.6 (1566.5) To Jesus, Judas was a faith adventure. From the beginning the Master fully understood the weakness of this apostle and well knew the dangers of admitting him to fellowship. But it is the nature of the Sons of God to give every created being a full and equal chance for salvation and survival. Jesus wanted not only the mortals of this world but the onlookers of innumerable other worlds to know that, when doubts exist as to the sincerity and wholeheartedness of a creature's devotion to the kingdom, it is the invariable practice of the Judges of men fully to receive the doubtful candidate. The door of eternal life is wide open to all; "whosoever will may come"; there are no restrictions or qualifications save the *faith* of the one who comes. 139:12.7 (1566.6) This is just the reason why Jesus permitted Judas to go on to the very end, always doing everything possible to transform and save this weak and confused apostle. But when light is not honestly received and lived up to, it tends to become darkness within the soul. Judas grew intellectually regarding Jesus' teachings about the kingdom, but he did not make progress in the acquirement of spiritual character as did the other apostles. He failed to make satisfactory personal progress in spiritual experience. 139:12.8 (1567.1) Judas became increasingly a brooder over personal disappointment, and finally he became a victim of resentment. His feelings had been many times hurt, and he grew abnormally suspicious of his best friends, even of the Master. Presently he became obsessed with the idea of getting even, anything to avenge himself, yes, even betrayal of his associates and his Master. 139:12.9 (1567.2) But these wicked and dangerous ideas did not take definite shape until the day when a grateful woman broke an expensive box of incense at Jesus' feet. This seemed wasteful to Judas, and when his public protest was so sweepingly disallowed by Jesus right there in the hearing of all, it was too much. That event determined the mobilization of all the accumulated hate, hurt, malice, prejudice, jealousy, and revenge of a lifetime, and he made up his mind to get even with he knew not whom; but he crystallized all the evil of his nature upon the *one* innocent person in all the sordid drama of his unfortunate life just because Jesus happened to be the chief actor in the episode which marked his passing from the progressive kingdom of light into that self-chosen domain of darkness. 139:12.10 (1567.3) The Master many times, both privately and publicly, had warned Judas that he was slipping, but divine warnings are usually useless in dealing with embittered human nature. Jesus did everything possible, consistent with man's moral freedom, to prevent Judas's choosing to go the wrong way. The great test finally came. The son of resentment failed; he yielded to the sour and sordid dictates of a proud and vengeful mind of exaggerated self-importance and swiftly plunged on down into confusion, despair, and depravity. 139:12.11 (1567.4)

	Judas then entered into the base and shameful intrigue to betray his Lord and Master and quickly carried the nefarious scheme into effect. During the outworking of his anger-conceived plans of traitorous betrayal, he experienced moments of regret and shame, and in these lucid intervals he faintheartedly conceived, as a defense in his own mind, the idea that Jesus might possibly exert his power and deliver himself at the last moment. 139:12.12 (1567.5) When the sordid and sinful business was all over, this renegade mortal, who thought lightly of selling his friend for thirty pieces of silver to satisfy his long-nursed craving for revenge, rushed out and committed the final act in the drama of fleeing from the realities of mortal existence—suicide. 139:12.13 (1567.6)
	The people of southern Samaria heard Jesus gladly, and the apostles, with the exception of Judas Iscariot, succeeded in overcoming much of their prejudice against the Samaritans. It was very difficult for Judas to love these Samaritans. The last week of July Jesus and his associates made ready to depart for the new Greek cities of Phasaelis and Archelais near the Jordan. 143:0.2 (1607.2)
Judas' Personality: (Continued)	Of all the apostles, Judas Iscariot was the most adversely affected by this processional entry into Jerusalem. His mind was in a disagreeable ferment because of the Master's rebuke the preceding day in connection with Mary's anointing at the feast in Simon's house. Judas was disgusted with the whole spectacle. To him it seemed childish, if not indeed ridiculous. As this vengeful apostle looked upon the proceedings of this Sunday afternoon, Jesus seemed to him more to resemble a clown than a king. He heartily resented the whole performance. He shared the views of the Greeks and Romans, who looked down upon anyone who would consent to ride upon an ass or the colt of an ass. By the time the triumphal procession had entered the city, Judas had about made up his mind to abandon the whole idea of such a kingdom; he was almost resolved to forsake all such farcical attempts to establish the kingdom of heaven. And then he thought of the resurrection of Lazarus, and many other things, and decided to stay on with the twelve, at least for another day. Besides, he carried the bag, and he would not desert with the apostolic funds in his possession. On the way back to Bethany that night his conduct did not seem strange since all of the apostles were equally downcast and silent. 172:5.12 (1886.4)
	As this group journeyed down Mount Olivet, Jesus led the way, the apostles following closely behind in meditative silence. There was just one thought uppermost in the minds of all save Judas Iscariot, and that was: What will the Master do today? The one absorbing thought of Judas was: What shall I do? Shall I go on with Jesus and my associates, or shall I withdraw? And if I am going to quit, how shall I break off? 173:0.2 (1888.2)
	Shortly after Jesus and John Mark left the camp, Judas Iscariot disappeared from among his brethren, not returning until late in the afternoon. This confused and discontented apostle, notwithstanding his Master's specific request to refrain from entering Jerusalem, went in haste to keep his appointment with Jesus' enemies at the home of Caiaphas the high priest. 177:4.1 (1924.5)

Judas' Personality: (Continued)	On the preceding day Judas had disclosed to some of his relatives and to certain Sadducean friends of his father's family that he had reached the conclusion that, while Jesus was a well-meaning dreamer and idealist, he was not the expected deliverer of Israel. Judas stated that he would very much like to find some way of withdrawing gracefully from the whole movement. His friends flatteringly assured him that his withdrawal would be hailed by the Jewish rulers as a great event, and that nothing would be too good for him. They led him to believe that he would forthwith receive high honors from the Sanhedrin, and that he would at last be in a position to erase the stigma of his well-meant but "unfortunate association with untaught Galileans." 177:4.2 (1924.6) Judas could not quite believe that the mighty works of the Master had been wrought by the power of the prince of devils, but he was now fully convinced that Jesus would not exert his power in self-aggrandizement; he was at last convinced that Jesus would allow himself to be destroyed by the Jewish rulers, and he could not endure the humiliating thought of being identified with a movement of defeat. 177:4.3 (1924.7) And now, as never before, Judas found himself becoming strangely resentful that Jesus had never assigned him a position of greater honor. All along he had appreciated the honor of being the apostolic treasurer, but now he began to feel that he was not appreciated; that his abilities were unrecognized. He was suddenly overcome with indignation that Peter, James, and John should have been honored with close association with Jesus, and at this time, when he was on the way to the high priest's home, he was bent on getting even with Peter, James, and John more than he was concerned with any thought of betraying Jesus. 177:4.4 (1925.1)
	And then Caiaphas looked down upon the betrayer while he said: "Judas, you go to the captain of the guard and arrange with that officer to bring your Master to us either tonight or tomorrow night, and when he has been delivered by you into our hands, you shall receive your reward for this service." When Judas heard this, he went forth from the presence of the chief priests and rulers and took counsel with the captain of the temple guards as to the manner in which Jesus was to be apprehended. 177:4.8 (1926.1) Judas returned to his associates at the camp intoxicated with thoughts of grandeur and glory such as he had not had for many a day. He had enlisted with Jesus hoping someday to become a great man in the new kingdom. 177:4.9 (1926.2) But it was ever just that way. Judas had long been engaged in this deliberate, persistent, selfish, and vengeful consciousness of progressively building up in his mind, and entertaining in his heart, these hateful and evil desires of revenge and disloyalty. Jesus loved and trusted Judas even as he loved and trusted the other apostles, but Judas failed to develop loyal trust and to experience wholehearted love in return. And how dangerous ambition can become when it is once wholly wedded to self-seeking and supremely motivated by sullen and long-suppressed vengeance! What a crushing thing is disappointment in the lives of those foolish persons who, in fastening their gaze on the shadowy and evanescent allurements of time, become blinded to the higher and more real achievements of the everlasting attainments of the eternal worlds of divine values and true spiritual realities. Judas craved worldly honor in his mind and grew to love this desire with his whole heart; the other apostles likewise craved this same worldly honor in their minds, but with their hearts they

	loved Jesus and were doing their best to learn to love the truths which he taught them. 177:4.10 (1926.3) Judas did not realize it at this time, but he had been a subconscious critic of Jesus ever since John the Baptist was beheaded by Herod. Deep down in his heart Judas always resented the fact that Jesus did not save John. 177:4.11 (1926.4)
	The dramatic appeal of this unusual scene at first touched the heart of even Judas Iscariot; but when his vainglorious intellect passed judgment upon the spectacle, he concluded that this gesture of humility was just one more episode which conclusively proved that Jesus would never qualify as Israel's deliverer, and that he had made no mistake in the decision to desert the Master's cause. 179:3.4 (1939.2)
Judas' Personality: (Continued)	As we look back upon this tragedy, we conceive that Judas went wrong, primarily, because he was very markedly an isolated personality, a personality shut in and away from ordinary social contacts. He persistently refused to confide in, or freely fraternize with, his fellow apostles. But his being an isolated type of personality would not, in and of itself, have wrought such mischief for Judas had it not been that he also failed to increase in love and grow in spiritual grace. And then, as if to make a bad matter worse, he persistently harbored grudges and fostered such psychologic enemies as revenge and the generalized craving to "get even" with somebody for all his disappointments. 193:4.2 (2055.5) This unfortunate combination of individual peculiarities and mental tendencies conspired to destroy a well-intentioned man who failed to subdue these evils by love, faith, and trust. That Judas need not have gone wrong is well proved by the cases of Thomas and Nathaniel, both of whom were cursed with this same sort of suspicion and overdevelopment of the individualistic tendency. Even Andrew and Matthew had many leanings in this direction; but all these men grew to love Jesus and their fellow apostles more, and not less, as time passed. They grew in grace and in a knowledge of the truth. They became increasingly more trustful of their brethren and slowly developed the ability to confide in their fellows. Judas persistently refused to confide in his brethren. When he was impelled, by the accumulation of his emotional conflicts, to seek relief in self-expression, he invariably sought the advice and received the unwise consolation of his unspiritual relatives or those chance acquaintances who were either indifferent, or actually hostile, to the welfare and progress of the spiritual realities of the heavenly kingdom, of which he was one of the twelve consecrated ambassadors on earth. 193:4.3 (2056.1) Judas met defeat in his battles of the earth struggle because of the following factors of personal tendencies and character weakness: 193:4.4 (2056.2) 1. He was an isolated type of human being. He was highly individualistic and chose to grow into a confirmed "shut-in" and unsociable sort of person. 193:4.5 (2056.3) 2. As a child, life had been made too easy for him. He bitterly resented thwarting. He always expected to win; he was a very poor loser. 193:4.6 (2056.4) 3. He never acquired a philosophic technique for meeting disappointment. Instead of accepting disappointments as a regular and commonplace feature of human existence, he unfailingly resorted to the practice of blaming someone in particular, or his associates as a group, for all his personal difficulties and disappointments. 193:4.7 (2056.5)

Judas' Personality: (Continued)	4. He was given to holding grudges; he was always entertaining the idea of revenge. 193:4.8 (2056.6) 5. He did not like to face facts frankly; he was dishonest in his attitude toward life situations. 193:4.9 (2056.7) 6. He disliked to discuss his personal problems with his immediate associates; he refused to talk over his difficulties with his real friends and those who truly loved him. In all the years of their association he never once went to the Master with a purely personal problem. 193:4.10 (2056.8) 7. He never learned that the real rewards for noble living are, after all, spiritual prizes, which are not always distributed during this one short life in the flesh. 193:4.11 (2056.9) As a result of his persistent isolation of personality, his griefs multiplied, his sorrows increased, his anxieties augmented, and his despair deepened almost beyond endurance. 193:4.12 (2056.10) While this self-centered and ultraindividualistic apostle had many psychic, emotional, and spiritual troubles, his main difficulties were: In personality, he was isolated. In mind, he was suspicious and vengeful. In temperament, he was surly and vindictive. Emotionally, he was loveless and unforgiving. Socially, he was unconfiding and almost wholly self-contained. In spirit, he became arrogant and selfishly ambitious. In life, he ignored those who loved him, and in death, he was friendless. 193:4.13 (2057.1) These, then, are the factors of mind and influences of evil which, taken altogether, explain why a well-meaning and otherwise onetime sincere believer in Jesus, even after several years of intimate association with his transforming personality, forsook his fellows, repudiated a sacred cause, renounced his holy calling, and betrayed his divine Master. 193:4.14 (2057.2)
Skill:	Andrew appointed Judas treasurer of the twelve, a position which he was eminently fitted to hold, and up to the time of the betrayal of his Master he discharged the responsibilities of his office honestly, faithfully, and most efficiently. 139:12.3 (1566.2)
	Judas was a good business man. It required tact, ability, and patience, as well as painstaking devotion, to manage the financial affairs of such an idealist as Jesus, to say nothing of wrestling with the helter-skelter business methods of some of his apostles. Judas really was a great executive, a farseeing and able financier. And he was a stickler for organization. None of the twelve ever criticized Judas. As far as they could see, Judas Iscariot was a matchless treasurer, a learned man, a loyal (though sometimes critical) apostle, and in every sense of the word a great success. The apostles loved Judas; he was really one of them. He must have *believed* in Jesus, but we doubt whether he really *loved* the Master with a whole heart. The case of Judas illustrates the truthfulness of that saying: "There is a way that seems right to a man, but the end thereof is death." It is altogether possible to fall victim to the peaceful deception of pleasant adjustment to the paths of sin and death. Be assured that Judas was always financially loyal to his Master and his fellow apostles. Money could never have been the motive for his betrayal of the Master. 139:12.5 (1566.4)

The Twelve Apostles of Jesus—Judas Iscariot

Admired Jesus For:	There was no special trait about Jesus which Judas admired above the generally attractive and exquisitely charming personality of the Master. Judas was never able to rise above his Judean prejudices against his Galilean associates; he would even criticize in his mind many things about Jesus. Him whom eleven of the apostles looked upon as the perfect man, as the "one altogether lovely and the chiefest among ten thousand," this self-satisfied Judean often dared to criticize in his own heart. He really entertained the notion that Jesus was timid and somewhat afraid to assert his own power and authority. 139:12.4 (1566.3)
Final Instructions:	And to Judas Iscariot he said: "Judas, I have loved you and have prayed that you would love your brethren. Be not weary in well doing; and I would warn you to beware the slippery paths of flattery and the poison darts of ridicule." 174:0.2 (1897.2)
After Jesus:	Judas was stunned, dumfounded. He rushed back to enter the hall but was debarred by the doorkeeper. He wanted to appeal to the Sanhedrin, but they would not admit him. Judas could not believe that these rulers of the Jews would allow him to betray his friends and his Master and then offer him as a reward thirty pieces of silver. He was humiliated, disillusioned, and utterly crushed. He walked away from the temple, as it were, in a trance. He automatically dropped the money bag in his deep pocket, that same pocket wherein he had so long carried the bag containing the apostolic funds. And he wandered out through the city after the crowds who were on their way to witness the crucifixions. 186:1.3 (1998.1) From a distance Judas saw them raise the cross piece with Jesus nailed thereon, and upon sight of this he rushed back to the temple and, forcing his way past the doorkeeper, found himself standing in the presence of the Sanhedrin, which was still in session. The betrayer was well-nigh breathless and highly distraught, but he managed to stammer out these words: "I have sinned in that I have betrayed innocent blood. You have insulted me. You have offered me as a reward for my service, money—the price of a slave. I repent that I have done this; here is your money. I want to escape the guilt of this deed." 186:1.4 (1998.2) When the rulers of the Jews heard Judas, they scoffed at him. One of them sitting near where Judas stood, motioned that he should leave the hall and said: "Your Master has already been put to death by the Romans, and as for your guilt, what is that to us? See you to that—and begone!" 186:1.5 (1998.3)
Death:	When the sordid and sinful business was all over, this renegade mortal, who thought lightly of selling his friend for thirty pieces of silver to satisfy his long-nursed craving for revenge, rushed out and committed the final act in the drama of fleeing from the realities of mortal existence—suicide. 139:12.13 (1567.6)
	This onetime ambassador of the kingdom of heaven on earth now walked through the streets of Jerusalem, forsaken and alone. His despair was desperate and well-nigh absolute. On he journeyed through the city and outside the walls, on down into the terrible solitude of the valley of Hinnom, where he climbed up the steep rocks and, taking the girdle of his cloak, fastened one end to a small tree, tied the other about his neck, and cast himself over the precipice. Ere he was dead, the knot which his nervous hands had tied gave way, and the betrayer's body was dashed to pieces as it fell on the jagged rocks below. 186:1.7 (1998.5)

Jesus' Manner of Teaching

Jesus' Manner of Teaching

Jesus was an original thinker and a skillful teacher, even in his youth. 124:1.13 (1368.2)
This year [Ninth Year (A.D. 3)] Jesus paid more attention than ever to music, and he continued to teach the home school for his brothers and sisters. 124:4.5 (1372.2)
By the beginning of this year [The Nineteenth Year (A.D. 13)] Jesus had fully won his mother to the acceptance of his methods of child training—the positive injunction to do good in the place of the older Jewish method of forbidding to do evil. In his home and throughout his public-teaching career Jesus invariably employed the *positive* form of exhortation. Always and everywhere did he say, "You shall do this—you ought to do that." Never did he employ the negative mode of teaching derived from the ancient taboos. He refrained from placing emphasis on evil by forbidding it, while he exalted the good by commanding its performance. 127:4.2 (1401.2)
One purpose which Jesus had in mind, when he sought to segregate certain features of his earthly experience, was to prevent the building up of such a versatile and spectacular career as would cause subsequent generations to venerate the teacher in place of obeying the truth which he had lived and taught. 128:4.6 (1413.2)
Day by day Jesus interpreted the lectures to Ganid; one day during the second week the young man exclaimed: "Teacher Joshua, you know more than these professors; you should stand up and tell them the great things you have told me; they are befogged by much thinking. I shall speak to my father and have him arrange it." Jesus smiled, saying: "You are an admiring pupil, but these teachers are not minded that you and I should instruct them. The pride of unspiritualized learning is a treacherous thing in human experience. The true teacher maintains his intellectual integrity by ever remaining a learner." 130:3.7 (1433.2)
Jesus' usual technique of social contact was to draw people out and into talking with him by asking them questions. The interview would usually begin by his asking them questions and end by their asking him questions. He was equally adept in teaching by either asking or answering questions. As a rule, to those he taught the most, he said the least. 132:4.2 (1460.6)
On their visit to the northern Italian lakes Jesus had the long talk with Ganid concerning the impossibility of teaching a man about God if the man does not desire to know God. 132:7.1 (1466.1)
In this time of waiting Jesus endeavored to teach his associates what their attitude should be toward the various religious groups and the political parties of Palestine. Jesus' words always were, "We are seeking to win all of them, but we are not *of* any of them." 137:7.5 (1534.4)
Though Jesus' public teaching mainly consisted in parables and short discourses, he invariably taught his apostles by questions and answers. He would always pause to answer sincere questions during his later public discourses. 138:8.10 (1546.1)

Jesus had little to say about the social vices of his day; seldom did he make reference to moral delinquency. He was a positive teacher of true virtue. He studiously avoided the negative method of imparting instruction; he refused to advertise evil. 140:8.21 (1582.2)

Another great handicap in this work of teaching the twelve was their tendency to take highly idealistic and spiritual principles of religious truth and remake them into concrete rules of personal conduct. Jesus would present to them the beautiful spirit of the soul's attitude, but they insisted on translating such teachings into rules of personal behavior. Many times, when they did make sure to remember what the Master said, they were almost certain to forget what he did *not* say. But they slowly assimilated his teaching because Jesus *was* all that he taught. What they could not gain from his verbal instruction, they gradually acquired by living with him. 140:10.2 (1584.5)

This new religion of Jesus was not without its practical implications, but whatever of practical political, social, or economic value there is to be found in his teaching is the natural outworking of this inner experience of the soul as it manifests the fruits of the spirit in the spontaneous daily ministry of genuine personal religious experience. 140:10.6 (1585.4)

The Master displayed great wisdom and manifested perfect fairness in all of his dealings with his apostles and with all of his disciples. Jesus was truly a master of men; he exercised great influence over his fellow men because of the combined charm and force of his personality. There was a subtle commanding influence in his rugged, nomadic, and homeless life. There was intellectual attractiveness and spiritual drawing power in his authoritative manner of teaching, in his lucid logic, his strength of reasoning, his sagacious insight, his alertness of mind, his matchless poise, and his sublime tolerance. 141:3.4 (1589.5)

The Master sought to impress upon all teachers of the gospel of the kingdom that their only business was to reveal God to the individual man as his Father—to lead this individual man to become son-conscious; then to present this same man to God as his faith son. 141:7.4 (1593.5)

He announced that he had come to function as a teacher, a teacher sent from heaven to present spiritual truth to the material mind. And this is exactly what he did; he was a teacher, not a preacher. From the human viewpoint Peter was a much more effective preacher than Jesus. Jesus' preaching was so effective because of his unique personality, not so much because of compelling oratory or emotional appeal. Jesus spoke directly to men's souls. He was a teacher of man's spirit, but through the mind. He lived with men. 141:7.10 (1594.4)

The teachers of the religion of Jesus should approach other religions with the recognition of the truths which are held in common (many of which come directly or indirectly from Jesus' message) while they refrain from placing so much emphasis on the differences. 149:2.5 (1670.6)

The Master was admired by all who met him except by those who entertained deep-seated religious prejudices or those who thought they discerned political dangers in his teachings. Men were astonished at the originality and authoritativeness of his teaching. They marveled at his patience in dealing with backward and troublesome inquirers. He inspired hope and confidence in the hearts of all who came under his ministry. Only those who had not met him feared him, and he was hated only by those who regarded him as the champion of that truth which was destined to overthrow the evil and error which they had determined to hold in their hearts at all cost. 149:2.13 (1672.2)

Jesus was a teacher who taught as the occasion served; he was not a systematic teacher. Jesus taught not so much from the law as from life, by parables. (And when he employed a parable for illustrating his message, he designed to utilize just *one* feature of the story for that purpose. Many wrong ideas concerning the teachings of Jesus may be secured by attempting to make allegories out of his parables.) 149:3.1 (1672.4)

About this time Jesus first began to employ the parable method of teaching the multitudes that so frequently gathered about him. Since Jesus had talked with the apostles and others long into the night, on this Sunday morning very few of the group were up for breakfast; so he went out by the seaside and sat alone in the boat, the old fishing boat of Andrew and Peter, which was always kept at his disposal, and meditated on the next move to be made in the work of extending the kingdom. But the Master was not to be alone for long. Very soon the people from Capernaum and near-by villages began to arrive, and by ten o'clock that morning almost one thousand were assembled on shore near Jesus' boat and were clamoring for attention. Peter was now up and, making his way to the boat, said to Jesus, "Master, shall I talk to them?" But Jesus answered, "No, Peter, I will tell them a story." And then Jesus began the recital of the parable of the sower, one of the first of a long series of such parables which he taught the throngs that followed after him. This boat had an elevated seat on which he sat (for it was the custom to sit when teaching) while he talked to the crowd assembled along the shore. 151:1.1 (1688.3)

The continued discussion of parables and further instruction as to their interpretation may be summarized and expressed in modern phraseology as follows: 151:3.2 (1692.1)

1. Jesus advised against the use of either fables or allegories in teaching the truths of the gospel. He did recommend the free use of parables, especially nature parables. He emphasized the value of utilizing the *analogy* existing between the natural and the spiritual worlds as a means of teaching truth. He frequently alluded to the natural as "the unreal and fleeting shadow of spirit realities." 151:3.3 (1692.2)

2. Jesus narrated three or four parables from the Hebrew scriptures, calling attention to the fact that this method of teaching was not wholly new. However, it became almost a new method of teaching as he employed it from this time onward. 151:3.4 (1692.3)

3. In teaching the apostles the value of parables, Jesus called attention to the following points: 151:3.5 (1692.4)

The parable provides for a simultaneous appeal to vastly different levels of mind and spirit. The parable stimulates the imagination, challenges the discrimination, and provokes critical thinking; it promotes sympathy without arousing antagonism. 151:3.6 (1692.5)

The parable proceeds from the things which are known to the discernment of the unknown. The parable utilizes the material and natural as a means of introducing the spiritual and the supermaterial. 151:3.7 (1692.6)

Parables favor the making of impartial moral decisions. The parable evades much prejudice and puts new truth gracefully into the mind and does all this with the arousal of a minimum of the self-defense of personal resentment. 151:3.8 (1692.7)

To reject the truth contained in parabolical analogy requires conscious intellectual action which is directly in contempt of one's honest judgment and fair decision. The parable conduces to the forcing of thought through the sense of hearing. 151:3.9 (1692.8)

The use of the parable form of teaching enables the teacher to present new and even startling truths while at the same time he largely avoids all controversy and outward clashing with tradition and established authority. 151:3.10 (1692.9)

The parable also possesses the advantage of stimulating the memory of the truth taught when the same familiar scenes are subsequently encountered. 151:3.11 (1693.1)

In this way Jesus sought to acquaint his followers with many of the reasons underlying his practice of increasingly using parables in his public teaching. 151:3.12 (1693.2)

Jesus taught the appeal to the emotions as the technique of arresting and focusing the intellectual attention. He designated the mind thus aroused and quickened as the gateway to the soul, where there resides that spiritual nature of man which must recognize truth and respond to the spiritual appeal of the gospel in order to afford the permanent results of true character transformations. 152:6.4 (1705.4)

Jesus continued to teach the twenty-four, saying: "The heathen are not without excuse when they rage at us. Because their outlook is small and narrow, they are able to concentrate their energies enthusiastically. Their goal is near and more or less visible; wherefore do they strive with valiant and effective execution. You who have professed entrance into the kingdom of heaven are altogether too vacillating and indefinite in your teaching conduct. 155:1.3 (1725.4)

In all his teaching Jesus unfailingly avoided distracting details. He shunned flowery language and avoided the mere poetic imagery of a play upon words. He habitually put large meanings into small expressions. For purposes of illustration Jesus reversed the current meanings of many terms, such as salt, leaven, fishing, and little children. He most effectively employed the antithesis, comparing the minute to the infinite and so on. His pictures were striking, such as, "The blind leading the blind." But the greatest strength to be found in his illustrative teaching was its naturalness. Jesus brought the philosophy of religion from heaven down to earth. He portrayed the elemental needs of the soul with a new insight and a new bestowal of affection. 159:5.17 (1771.1)

While ministering to the sick, refrain from teaching the expectation of miracles. 163:4.3 (1804.7)

Jesus was very partial to telling these three stories at the same time. He presented the story of the lost sheep to show that, when men unintentionally stray away from the path of life, the Father is mindful of such *lost* ones and goes out, with his Sons, the true shepherds of the flock, to seek the lost sheep. He then would recite the story of the coin lost in the house to illustrate how thorough is the divine *searching* for all who are confused, confounded, or otherwise spiritually blinded by the material cares and accumulations of life. And then he would launch forth into the telling of this parable of the lost son, the reception of the returning prodigal, to show how complete is the *restoration* of the lost son into his Father's house and heart. 169:1.15 (1853.2)

Jesus had long tried by direct teaching to impress upon his apostles and his disciples that his kingdom was not of this world, that it was a purely spiritual matter; but he had not succeeded in this effort. Now, what he had failed to do by plain and personal teaching, he would attempt to accomplish by a symbolic appeal. 172:3.6 (1881.4)

Said Jesus that night as they went to their rest: "Freely have you received; therefore freely should you give of the truth of heaven, and in the giving will this truth multiply and show forth the increasing light of saving grace, even as you minister it." 176:3.10 (1918.3)

In instituting this remembrance supper, the Master, as was always his habit, resorted to parables and symbols. He employed symbols because he wanted to teach certain great spiritual truths in such a manner as to make it difficult for his successors to attach precise interpretations and definite meanings to his words. In this way he sought to prevent successive generations from crystallizing his teaching and binding down his spiritual meanings by the dead chains of tradition and dogma. In the establishment of the only ceremony or sacrament associated with his whole life mission, Jesus took great pains to *suggest* his meanings rather than to commit himself to *precise definitions.* He did not wish to destroy the individual's concept of divine communion by establishing a precise form; neither did he desire to limit the believer's spiritual imagination by formally cramping it. He rather sought to set man's reborn soul free upon the joyous wings of a new and living spiritual liberty. 179:5.4 (1942.3)

[Jesus] "I have taught you much by word of mouth, and I have lived my life among you. I have done all that can be done to enlighten your minds and liberate your souls, and what you have not been able to get from my teachings and my life, you must now prepare to acquire at the hand of that master of all teachers—actual experience. And in all of this new experience which now awaits you, I will go before you and the Spirit of Truth shall be with you. Fear not; that which you now fail to comprehend, the new teacher, when he has come, will reveal to you throughout the remainder of your life on earth and on through your training in the eternal ages." 181:2.24 (1961.3)

Religion does need new leaders, spiritual men and women who will dare to depend solely on Jesus and his incomparable teachings. If Christianity persists in neglecting its spiritual mission while it continues to busy itself with social and material problems, the spiritual renaissance must await the coming of these new teachers of Jesus' religion who will be exclusively devoted to the spiritual regeneration of men. And then will these spirit-born souls quickly supply the leadership and inspiration requisite for the social, moral, economic, and political reorganization of the world. 195:9.4 (2082.9)

The Religion of Jesus

Jesus, the revelation of the highest type of religious living, proclaimed that "God is love." 92:1.5 (1004.3)

"To 'follow Jesus' means to personally share his religious faith and to enter into the spirit of the Master's life of unselfish service for man. One of the most important things in human living is to find out what Jesus believed, to discover his ideals, and to strive for the achievement of his exalted life purpose. Of all human knowledge, that which is of greatest value is to know the religious life of Jesus and how he lived it." 196:1.3 (2090.4)

The New Religion Proclaimed By Jesus:	The issues of battle are clearly drawn as the Master and his associates prepare to begin the proclamation of a new religion, the religion of the spirit of the living God who dwells in the minds of men. 156:6.10 (1742.2)
The Greatest Spiritual Treasure Ever Offered To Mortal Man:	Selfish men and women simply will not pay such a price for even the greatest spiritual treasure ever offered mortal man. Only when man has become sufficiently disillusioned by the sorrowful disappointments attendant upon the foolish and deceptive pursuits of selfishness, and subsequent to the discovery of the barrenness of formalized religion, will he be disposed to turn wholeheartedly to the gospel of the kingdom, the religion of Jesus of Nazareth. 195:9.7 (2083.3)
The Greatest Truths Mortal Man Can Ever Hear:	The hope of modern Christianity is that it should cease to sponsor the social systems and industrial policies of Western civilization while it humbly bows itself before the cross it so valiantly extols, there to learn anew from Jesus of Nazareth the greatest truths mortal man can ever hear—the living gospel of the fatherhood of God and the brotherhood of man. 195:10.21 (2086.7)
Greatest Pronouncements Jesus Ever Made:	"The kingdom of God is within you" was probably the greatest pronouncement Jesus ever made, next to the declaration that his Father is a living and loving spirit. 195:10.4 (2084.4)
No Provision for Self-Examination:	The three apostles were shocked this afternoon when they realized that their Master's religion made no provision for spiritual self-examination. 140:8.27 (1583.1)
How Religion Grows:	Religion cannot be bestowed, received, loaned, learned, or lost. It is a personal experience which grows proportionally to the growing quest for final values. Cosmic growth thus attends on the accumulation of meanings and the ever-expanding elevation of values. But nobility itself is always an unconscious growth. 100:1.7 (1095.2)
Universality of the Religion of Jesus:	The manifestations associated with the bestowal of the "new teacher," and the reception of the apostles' preaching by the men of various races and nations gathered together at Jerusalem, indicate the universality of the religion of Jesus. The gospel of the kingdom was to be identified with no particular race, culture, or language. 194:3.9 (2064.1)
The Religion of Jesus Is:	The religion of Jesus *is* salvation from self, deliverance from the evils of creature isolation in time and in eternity. 5:4.5 (67.3)
	In answer to Thomas's question, "Who is this God of the kingdom?" Jesus replied: "God is *your* Father, and religion—my gospel—is nothing more nor less than the believing recognition of the truth that you are his son. And I am here among you in the flesh to make clear both of these ideas in my life and teachings." 141:4.2 (1590.5)
	The religion of Jesus transcends all our former concepts of the idea of worship in that he not only portrays his Father as the ideal of infinite reality but positively declares that this divine source of values and the eternal center of the universe is truly and personally attainable by every mortal creature who chooses to enter the kingdom of heaven on earth, thereby acknowledging the acceptance of sonship

The Religion of Jesus Is: (Continued)	with God and brotherhood with man. That, I submit, is the highest concept of religion the world has ever known, and I pronounce that there can never be a higher since this gospel embraces the infinity of realities, the divinity of values, and the eternity of universal attainments. Such a concept constitutes the achievement of the experience of the idealism of the supreme and the ultimate. 160:5.7 (1781.3)
	The religion of Jesus is a new gospel of faith to be proclaimed to struggling humanity. This new religion is founded on faith, hope, and love. 194:3.2 (2062.11)
	To Jesus, mortal life had dealt its hardest, cruelest, and bitterest blows; and this man met these ministrations of despair with faith, courage, and the unswerving determination to do his Father's will. Jesus met life in all its terrible reality and mastered it—even in death. He did not use religion as a release from life. The religion of Jesus does not seek to escape this life in order to enjoy the waiting bliss of another existence. The religion of Jesus provides the joy and peace of another and spiritual existence to enhance and ennoble the life which men now live in the flesh. 194:3.3 (2063.1)
	If religion is an opiate to the people, it is not the religion of Jesus. 194:3.4 (2063.2)
	On the day of Pentecost the religion of Jesus broke all national restrictions and racial fetters. It is forever true, "Where the spirit of the Lord is, there is liberty." 194:3.5 (2063.3)
	The religion of Jesus fosters the highest type of human civilization in that it creates the highest type of spiritual personality and proclaims the sacredness of that person. 194:3.7 (2063.5)
	The religion of Jesus is the most powerful unifying influence the world has ever known. 194:3.17 (2065.5)
The Essence of Jesus' Teaching Was:	*Jesus of Nazareth.* Christ Michael presented for the fourth time to Urantia the concept of God as the Universal Father, and this teaching has generally persisted ever since. The essence of his teaching was *love* and *service,* the loving worship which a creature son voluntarily gives in recognition of, and response to, the loving ministry of God his Father; the freewill service which such creature sons bestow upon their brethren in the joyous realization that in this service they are likewise serving God the Father. 92:4.8 4 (1008.1)
	And this is illustrative of the way Jesus, day by day, appropriated the cream of the Hebrew scriptures for the instruction of his followers and for inclusion in the teachings of the new gospel of the kingdom. Other religions had suggested the thought of the nearness of God to man, but Jesus made the care of God for man like the solicitude of a loving father for the welfare of his dependent children and then made this teaching the cornerstone of his religion. And thus did the doctrine of the fatherhood of God make imperative the practice of the brotherhood of man. The worship of God and the service of man became the sum and substance of his religion. Jesus took the best of the Jewish religion and translated it to a worthy setting in the new teachings of the gospel of the kingdom. 159:5.7 (1769.9)

What it Means to "Follow Jesus":	To "follow Jesus" means to personally share his religious faith and to enter into the spirit of the Master's life of unselfish service for man. One of the most important things in human living is to find out what Jesus believed, to discover his ideals, and to strive for the achievement of his exalted life purpose. Of all human knowledge, that which is of greatest value is to know the religious life of Jesus and how he lived it. 196:1.3 (2090.4)
Religion of Jesus for the Individual:	Into such a generation of men, dominated by such incomplete systems of philosophy and perplexed by such complex cults of religion, Jesus was born in Palestine. And to this same generation he subsequently gave his gospel of personal religion—sonship with God. 121:5.18 (1338.3)
	The Master sought to impress upon all teachers of the gospel of the kingdom that their only business was to reveal God to the individual man as his Father—to lead this individual man to become son-conscious; then to present this same man to God as his faith son. Both of these essential revelations are accomplished in Jesus. He became, indeed, "the way, the truth, and the life." The religion of Jesus was wholly based on the living of his bestowal life on earth. When Jesus departed from this world, he left behind no books, laws, or other forms of human organization affecting the religious life of the individual. 141:7.4 (1593.5)
	Again and again would they take their troubles to Jesus, only to hear him say: "I am concerned only with your personal and purely religious problems. I am the representative of the Father to the *individual,* not to the group. 144:6.3 (1624.14)
	"No longer must you approach the Father in heaven as a child of Israel but as a *child of God.* As a group, you are indeed the children of Israel, but as individuals, each one of you is a child of God. I have come, not to reveal the Father to the children of Israel, but rather to bring this knowledge of God and the revelation of his love and mercy to the individual believer as a genuine personal experience. The prophets have all taught you that Yahweh cares for his people, that God loves Israel. But I have come among you to proclaim a greater truth, one which many of the later prophets also grasped, that God loves *you*—every one of you—as individuals. All these generations have you had a national or racial religion; now have I come to give you a personal religion. 145:2.4 (1629.5)
	It therefore is evident that the true and inner religion of the kingdom unfailingly and increasingly tends to manifest itself in practical avenues of social service. Jesus taught a living religion that impelled its believers to engage in the doing of loving service. But Jesus did not put ethics in the place of religion. He taught religion as a cause and ethics as a result. 170:3.8 (1862.5)
	This sermon was an effort on Jesus' part to make clear the fact that religion is a *personal experience.* 145:2.3 (1629.4)
	The religion of the kingdom is personal, individual; the fruits, the results, are familial, social. Jesus never failed to exalt the sacredness of the individual as contrasted with the community. But he also recognized that man develops his character by unselfish service; that he unfolds his moral nature in loving relations with his fellows. 170:3.10 (1862.7)

Religion of Jesus for the Individual: (Continued)	At last, true religion is delivered from the custody of priests and all sacred classes and finds its real manifestation in the individual souls of men. 194:3.6 (2063.4)
	The religion of Jesus fosters the highest type of human civilization in that it creates the highest type of spiritual personality and proclaims the sacredness of that person. 194:3.7 (2063.5)
	Jesus founded the religion of personal experience in doing the will of God and serving the human brotherhood; 196:2.6 (2092.4)
What the Religion of Jesus Does for Believers:	The religion of Jesus is the most dynamic influence ever to activate the human race. Jesus shattered tradition, destroyed dogma, and called mankind to the achievement of its highest ideals in time and eternity—to be perfect, even as the Father in heaven is perfect. 99:5.3 (1091.2)
	This new religion of Jesus was not without its practical implications, but whatever of practical political, social, or economic value there is to be found in his teaching is the natural outworking of this inner experience of the soul as it manifests the fruits of the spirit in the spontaneous daily ministry of genuine personal religious experience. 140:10.6 (1585.4)
	Modern men and women of intelligence evade the religion of Jesus because of their fears of what it will do *to* them—and *with* them. And all such fears are well founded. The religion of Jesus does, indeed, dominate and transform its believers, demanding that men dedicate their lives to seeking for a knowledge of the will of the Father in heaven and requiring that the energies of living be consecrated to the unselfish service of the brotherhood of man. 195:9.6 (2083.2)
	The living experience in the religion of Jesus thus becomes the sure and certain technique whereby the spiritually isolated and cosmically lonely mortals of earth are enabled to escape personality isolation, with all its consequences of fear and associated feelings of helplessness. In the fraternal realities of the kingdom of heaven the faith sons of God find final deliverance from the isolation of the self, both personal and planetary. The God-knowing believer increasingly experiences the ecstasy and grandeur of spiritual socialization on a universe scale—citizenship on high in association with the eternal realization of the divine destiny of perfection attainment. 184:4.6 (1985.1)
Jesus Promised a New Teacher:	"I have taught you much by word of mouth, and I have lived my life among you. I have done all that can be done to enlighten your minds and liberate your souls, and what you have not been able to get from my teachings and my life, you must now prepare to acquire at the hand of that master of all teachers—actual experience. And in all of this new experience which now awaits you, I will go before you and the Spirit of Truth shall be with you. Fear not; that which you now fail to comprehend, the new teacher, when he has come, will reveal to you throughout the remainder of your life on earth and on through your training in the eternal ages." 181:2.24 (1961.3)

Our Aim as Kingdom Believers Should Be:	It should not be the aim of kingdom believers literally to imitate the outward life of Jesus in the flesh but rather to share his faith; to trust God as he trusted God and to believe in men as he believed in men. Jesus never argued about either the fatherhood of God or the brotherhood of men; he was a living illustration of the one and a profound demonstration of the other. 196:1.5 (2091.1)
The Highest Religion Yet Revealed:	Religion is ever and always rooted and grounded in personal experience. And your highest religion, the life of Jesus, was just such a personal experience: man, mortal man, seeking God and finding him to the fullness during one short life in the flesh, while in the same human experience there appeared God seeking man and finding him to the full satisfaction of the perfect soul of infinite supremacy. And that is religion, even the highest yet revealed in the universe of Nebadon—the earth life of Jesus of Nazareth. 102:8.7 (1128.3)
	The religion of Jesus transcends all our former concepts of the idea of worship in that he not only portrays his Father as the ideal of infinite reality but positively declares that this divine source of values and the eternal center of the universe is truly and personally attainable by every mortal creature who chooses to enter the kingdom of heaven on earth, thereby acknowledging the acceptance of sonship with God and brotherhood with man. That, I submit, is the highest concept of religion the world has ever known, and I pronounce that there can never be a higher since this gospel embraces the infinity of realities, the divinity of values, and the eternity of universal attainments. Such a concept constitutes the achievement of the experience of the idealism of the supreme and the ultimate. 160:5.7 (1781.3)
Christianity and the Religion of Jesus:	As the original teachings of Jesus penetrated the Occident, they became Occidentalized, and as they became Occidentalized, they began to lose their potentially universal appeal to all races and kinds of men. Christianity, today, has become a religion well adapted to the social, economic, and political mores of the white races. It has long since ceased to be the religion of Jesus, although it still valiantly portrays a beautiful religion about Jesus to such individuals as sincerely seek to follow in the way of its teaching. It has glorified Jesus as the Christ, the Messianic anointed one from God, but has largely forgotten the Master's personal gospel: the Fatherhood of God and the universal brotherhood of all men. 98:7.11 (1084.9)
	These various groupings of Christians may serve to accommodate numerous different types of would-be believers among the various peoples of Western civilization, but such division of Christendom presents a grave weakness when it attempts to carry the gospel of Jesus to Oriental peoples. These races do not yet understand that there is a *religion of Jesus* separate, and somewhat apart, from Christianity, which has more and more become a *religion about Jesus.* 195:10.15 (2086.1)
	Christianity is an extemporized religion, and therefore must it operate in low gear. High-gear spiritual performances must await the new revelation and the more general acceptance of the real religion of Jesus. 195:10.18 (2086.4)

The Faith of Jesus

The Faith of Jesus

JESUS enjoyed a sublime and wholehearted faith in God. He experienced the ordinary ups and downs of mortal existence, but he never religiously doubted the certainty of God's watchcare and guidance. His faith was the outgrowth of the insight born of the activity of the divine presence, his indwelling Adjuster. His faith was neither traditional nor merely intellectual; it was wholly personal and purely spiritual. 196:0.1 (2087.1)

The human Jesus saw God as being holy, just, and great, as well as being true, beautiful, and good. All these attributes of divinity he focused in his mind as the "will of the Father in heaven." Jesus' God was at one and the same time "The Holy One of Israel" and "The living and loving Father in heaven." The concept of God as a Father was not original with Jesus, but he exalted and elevated the idea into a sublime experience by achieving a new revelation of God and by proclaiming that every mortal creature is a child of this Father of love, a son of God. 196:0.2 (2087.2)

Jesus did not cling to faith in God as would a struggling soul at war with the universe and at death grips with a hostile and sinful world; he did not resort to faith merely as a consolation in the midst of difficulties or as a comfort in threatened despair; faith was not just an illusory compensation for the unpleasant realities and the sorrows of living. In the very face of all the natural difficulties and the temporal contradictions of mortal existence, he experienced the tranquility of supreme and unquestioned trust in God and felt the tremendous thrill of living, by faith, in the very presence of the heavenly Father. And this triumphant faith was a living experience of actual spirit attainment. Jesus' great contribution to the values of human experience was not that he revealed so many new ideas about the Father in heaven, but rather that he so magnificently and humanly demonstrated a new and higher type of living faith in God. Never on all the worlds of this universe, in the life of any one mortal, did God ever become such a living reality as in the human experience of Jesus of Nazareth. 196:0.3 (2087.3)

In the Master's life on Urantia, this and all other worlds of the local creation discover a new and higher type of religion, religion based on personal spiritual relations with the Universal Father and wholly validated by the supreme authority of genuine personal experience. This living faith of Jesus was more than an intellectual reflection, and it was not a mystic meditation. 196:0.4 (2087.4)

Theology may fix, formulate, define, and dogmatize faith, but in the human life of Jesus faith was personal, living, original, spontaneous, and purely spiritual. This faith was not reverence for tradition nor a mere intellectual belief which he held as a sacred creed, but rather a sublime experience and a profound conviction which securely held him. His faith was so real and all-encompassing that it absolutely swept away any spiritual doubts and effectively destroyed every conflicting desire. Nothing was able to tear him away from the spiritual anchorage of this fervent, sublime, and undaunted faith. Even in the face of apparent defeat or in the throes of disappointment and threatening despair, he calmly stood in the divine presence free from fear and fully conscious of spiritual invincibility. Jesus enjoyed the invigorating assurance of the possession of unflinching faith, and in each of life's trying situations he unfailingly exhibited an unquestioning loyalty to the Father's will. And this superb faith was undaunted even by the cruel and crushing threat of an ignominious death. 196:0.5 (2087.5)

In a religious genius, strong spiritual faith so many times leads directly to disastrous fanaticism, to exaggeration of the religious ego, but it was not so with Jesus. He was not unfavorably affected in his practical life by his extraordinary faith and spirit attainment because this spiritual exaltation was a wholly unconscious and spontaneous soul expression of his personal experience with God. 196:0.6 (2088.1)

The Faith of Jesus

The all-consuming and indomitable spiritual faith of Jesus never became fanatical, for it never attempted to run away with his well-balanced intellectual judgments concerning the proportional values of practical and commonplace social, economic, and moral life situations. The Son of Man was a splendidly unified human personality; he was a perfectly endowed divine being; he was also magnificently co-ordinated as a combined human and divine being functioning on earth as a single personality. Always did the Master co-ordinate the faith of the soul with the wisdom-appraisals of seasoned experience. Personal faith, spiritual hope, and moral devotion were always correlated in a matchless religious unity of harmonious association with the keen realization of the reality and sacredness of all human loyalties—personal honor, family love, religious obligation, social duty, and economic necessity. 196:0.7 (2088.2)

The faith of Jesus visualized all spirit values as being found in the kingdom of God; therefore he said, "Seek first the kingdom of heaven." Jesus saw in the advanced and ideal fellowship of the kingdom the achievement and fulfillment of the "will of God." The very heart of the prayer which he taught his disciples was, "Your kingdom come; your will be done." Having thus conceived of the kingdom as comprising the will of God, he devoted himself to the cause of its realization with amazing self-forgetfulness and unbounded enthusiasm. But in all his intense mission and throughout his extraordinary life there never appeared the fury of the fanatic nor the superficial frothiness of the religious egotist. 196:0.8 (2088.3)

The Master's entire life was consistently conditioned by this living faith, this sublime religious experience. This spiritual attitude wholly dominated his thinking and feeling, his believing and praying, his teaching and preaching. This personal faith of a son in the certainty and security of the guidance and protection of the heavenly Father imparted to his unique life a profound endowment of spiritual reality. And yet, despite this very deep consciousness of close relationship with divinity, this Galilean, God's Galilean, when addressed as Good Teacher, instantly replied, "Why do you call me good?" When we stand confronted by such splendid self-forgetfulness, we begin to understand how the Universal Father found it possible so fully to manifest himself to him and reveal himself through him to the mortals of the realms. 196:0.9 (2088.4)

Jesus brought to God, as a man of the realm, the greatest of all offerings: the consecration and dedication of his own will to the majestic service of doing the divine will. Jesus always and consistently interpreted religion wholly in terms of the Father's will. When you study the career of the Master, as concerns prayer or any other feature of the religious life, look not so much for what he taught as for what he did. Jesus never prayed as a religious duty. To him prayer was a sincere expression of spiritual attitude, a declaration of soul loyalty, a recital of personal devotion, an expression of thanksgiving, an avoidance of emotional tension, a prevention of conflict, an exaltation of intellection, an ennoblement of desire, a vindication of moral decision, an enrichment of thought, an invigoration of higher inclinations, a consecration of impulse, a clarification of viewpoint, a declaration of faith, a transcendental surrender of will, a sublime assertion of confidence, a revelation of courage, the proclamation of discovery, a confession of supreme devotion, the validation of consecration, a technique for the adjustment of difficulties, and the mighty mobilization of the combined soul powers to withstand all human tendencies toward selfishness, evil, and sin. He lived just such a life of prayerful consecration to the doing of his Father's will and ended his life triumphantly with just such a prayer. The secret of his unparalleled religious life was this consciousness of the presence of God; and he attained it by intelligent prayer and sincere worship—unbroken communion with God—and not by leadings, voices, visions, or extraordinary religious practices. 196:0.10 (2088.5)

In the earthly life of Jesus, religion was a living experience, a direct and personal movement from spiritual reverence to practical righteousness. The faith of Jesus bore the transcendent fruits of the divine spirit. His faith was not immature and credulous like that of a child, but in many ways it did resemble the unsuspecting trust of the child mind. Jesus trusted God much as the child trusts a parent. He had a profound confidence in the universe—just such a trust as the child has in its parental environment. Jesus' wholehearted faith in the fundamental goodness of the universe very much resembled the child's trust in the security of its earthly surroundings. He depended on the heavenly Father as a child leans upon its earthly parent, and his fervent faith never for one moment doubted the certainty of the heavenly Father's overcare. He was not disturbed seriously by fears, doubts, and skepticism. Unbelief did not inhibit the free and original expression of his life. He combined the stalwart and intelligent courage of a full-grown man with the sincere and trusting optimism of a believing child. His faith grew to such heights of trust that it was devoid of fear. 196:0.11 (2089.1)

The faith of Jesus attained the purity of a child's trust. His faith was so absolute and undoubting that it responded to the charm of the contact of fellow beings and to the wonders of the universe. His sense of dependence on the divine was so complete and so confident that it yielded the joy and the assurance of absolute personal security. There was no hesitating pretense in his religious experience. In this giant intellect of the full-grown man the faith of the child reigned supreme in all matters relating to the religious consciousness. It is not strange that he once said, "Except you become as a little child, you shall not enter the kingdom." Notwithstanding that Jesus' faith was childlike, it was in no sense childish. 196:0.12 (2089.2)

Jesus does not require his disciples to believe in him but rather to believe with him, believe in the reality of the love of God and in full confidence accept the security of the assurance of sonship with the heavenly Father. The Master desires that all his followers should fully share his transcendent faith. Jesus most touchingly challenged his followers, not only to believe what he believed, but also to believe as he believed. This is the full significance of his one supreme requirement, "Follow me." 196:0.13 (2089.3)

Jesus' earthly life was devoted to one great purpose—doing the Father's will, living the human life religiously and by faith. The faith of Jesus was trusting, like that of a child, but it was wholly free from presumption. He made robust and manly decisions, courageously faced manifold disappointments, resolutely surmounted extraordinary difficulties, and unflinchingly confronted the stern requirements of duty. It required a strong will and an unfailing confidence to believe what Jesus believed and as he believed. 196:0.14 (2090.1)

The Faith of Jesus from Part I-III of *The Urantia Book*

The teachings of Jesus constituted the first Urantian religion which so fully embraced a harmonious co-ordination of knowledge, wisdom, faith, truth, and love as completely and simultaneously to provide temporal tranquility, intellectual certainty, moral enlightenment, philosophic stability, ethical sensitivity, God-consciousness, and the positive assurance of personal survival. The faith of Jesus pointed the way to finality of human salvation, to the ultimate of mortal universe attainment, since it provided for: 101:6.8 (1112.4)

1. Salvation from material fetters in the personal realization of sonship with God, who is spirit. 101:6.9 (1112.5)

2. Salvation from intellectual bondage: man shall know the truth, and the truth shall set him free. 101:6.10 (1112.6)

3. Salvation from spiritual blindness, the human realization of the fraternity of mortal beings and the morontian awareness of the brotherhood of all universe creatures; the service-discovery of spiritual reality and the ministry-revelation of the goodness of spirit values. 101:6.11 (1112.7)

4. Salvation from incompleteness of self through the attainment of the spirit levels of the universe and through the eventual realization of the harmony of Havona and the perfection of Paradise. 101:6.12 (1113.1)

5. Salvation from self, deliverance from the limitations of self-consciousness through the attainment of the cosmic levels of the Supreme mind and by co-ordination with the attainments of all other self-conscious beings. 101:6.13 (1113.2)
6. Salvation from time, the achievement of an eternal life of unending progression in God- recognition and God-service. 101:6.14 (1113.3)
7. Salvation from the finite, the perfected oneness with Deity in and through the Supreme by which the creature attempts the transcendental discovery of the Ultimate on the postfinaliter levels of the absonite. 101:6.15 (1113.4)

Such a sevenfold salvation is the equivalent of the completeness and perfection of the realization of the ultimate experience of the Universal Father. And all this, in potential, is contained within the reality of the faith of the human experience of religion. And it can be so contained since the faith of Jesus was nourished by, and was revelatory of, even realities beyond the ultimate; the faith of Jesus approached the status of a universe absolute in so far as such is possible of manifestation in the evolving cosmos of time and space. 101:6.16 (1113.5)

Through the appropriation of the faith of Jesus, mortal man can foretaste in time the realities of eternity. Jesus made the discovery, in human experience, of the Final Father, and his brothers in the flesh of mortal life can follow him along this same experience of Father discovery. They can even attain, as they are, the same satisfaction in this experience with the Father as did Jesus as he was. New potentials were actualized in the universe of Nebadon consequent upon the terminal bestowal of Michael, and one of these was the new illumination of the path of eternity that leads to the Father of all, and which can be traversed even by the mortals of material flesh and blood in the initial life on the planets of space. Jesus was and is the new and living way whereby man can come into the divine inheritance which the Father has decreed shall be his for but the asking. In Jesus there is abundantly demonstrated both the beginnings and endings of the faith experience of humanity, even of divine humanity. 101:6.17 (1113.6)

The Human Jesus

<table>
<tr><td>Jesus' Human Family:</td><td>Throughout this year he experienced many seasons of uncertainty, if not actual doubt, regarding the nature of his mission. His naturally developing human mind did not yet fully grasp the reality of his dual nature. The fact that he had a single personality rendered it difficult for his consciousness to recognize the double origin of those factors which composed the nature associated with that selfsame personality. 124:4.2 (1371.5)

From this time on he became more successful in getting along with his brothers and sisters. He was increasingly tactful, always compassionate and considerate of their welfare and happiness, and enjoyed good relations with them up to the beginning of his public ministry. To be more explicit: He got along with James, Miriam, and the two younger (as yet unborn) children, Amos and Ruth, most excellently. He always got along with Martha fairly well. What trouble he had at home largely arose out of friction with Joseph and Jude, particularly the latter. 124:4.3 (1371.6)</td></tr>
<tr><td rowspan="2">Young Jesus' First Passover:</td><td>No incident in all Jesus' eventful earth career was more engaging, more humanly thrilling, than this, his first remembered visit to Jerusalem. He was especially stimulated by the experience of attending the temple discussions by himself, and it long stood out in his memory as the great event of his later childhood and early youth. This was his first opportunity to enjoy a few days of independent living, the exhilaration of going and coming without restraint and restrictions. This brief period of undirected living, during the week following the Passover, was the first complete freedom from responsibility he had ever enjoyed. And it was many years subsequent to this before he again had a like period of freedom from all sense of responsibility, even for a short time. 125:0.1 (1377.1)</td></tr>
<tr><td>Everywhere Jesus went throughout the temple courts, he was shocked and sickened by the spirit of irreverence which he observed. He deemed the conduct of the temple throngs to be inconsistent with their presence in "his Father's house." But he received the shock of his young life when his father escorted him into the court of the gentiles with its noisy jargon, loud talking and cursing, mingled indiscriminately with the bleating of sheep and the babble of noises which betrayed the presence of the money-changers and the vendors of sacrificial animals and sundry other commercial commodities. 125:1.1 (1378.3).

But most of all was his sense of propriety outraged by the sight of the frivolous courtesans parading about within this precinct of the temple, just such painted women as he had so recently seen when on a visit to Sepphoris. This profanation of the temple fully aroused all his youthful indignation, and he did not hesitate to express himself freely to Joseph. 125:1.2 (1378.4)

Jesus admired the sentiment and service of the temple, but he was shocked by the spiritual ugliness which he beheld on the faces of so many of the unthinking worshipers. 125:1.3 (1378.5)

They now passed down to the priests' court beneath the rock ledge in front of the temple, where the altar stood, to observe the killing of the droves of animals and the washing away of the blood from the hands of the officiating slaughter priests at the bronze fountain. The bloodstained pavement, the gory hands of the priests, and the sounds of the dying animals were more than this nature-loving lad could stand. The terrible sight sickened this boy of Nazareth; he clutched his father's arm and begged to be taken away. They walked back through the court of the gentiles, and even the coarse laughter and profane jesting which he there heard were a relief from the sights he had just beheld. 125:1.4 (1378.6)</td></tr>
</table>

The Love Of Rebecca:	Jesus listened attentively and sympathetically to the recital of these things, first by the father, then by Rebecca herself. He made kindly reply to the effect that no amount of money could take the place of his obligation personally to rear his father's family, to "fulfill the most sacred of all human trusts—loyalty to one's own flesh and blood." Rebecca's father was deeply touched by Jesus' words of family devotion and retired from the conference. His only remark to Mary, his wife, was: "We can't have him for a son; he is too noble for us." 127:5.3 (1403.1)
	After listening attentively, he sincerely thanked Rebecca for her expressed admiration, adding, "it shall cheer and comfort me all the days of my life." He explained that he was not free to enter into relations with any woman other than those of simple brotherly regard and pure friendship. He made it clear that his first and paramount duty was the rearing of his father's family, that he could not consider marriage until that was accomplished; and then he added: "If I am a son of destiny, I must not assume obligations of lifelong duration until such a time as my destiny shall be made manifest." 127:5.5 (1403.3)
Jesus Weeping:	Just before leaving, the apostles missed the Master, and Andrew went out to find him. After a brief search he found Jesus sitting in a boat down the beach, and he was weeping. The twelve had often seen their Master when he seemed to grieve, and they had beheld his brief seasons of serious preoccupation of mind, but none of them had ever seen him weep. Andrew was somewhat startled to see the Master thus affected on the eve of their departure for Jerusalem, and he ventured to approach Jesus and ask: "On this great day, Master, when we are to depart for Jerusalem to proclaim the Father's kingdom, why is it that you weep? Which of us has offended you?" And Jesus, going back with Andrew to join the twelve, answered him: "No one of you has grieved me. I am saddened only because none of my father Joseph's family have remembered to come over to bid us Godspeed." At this time Ruth was on a visit to her brother Joseph at Nazareth. Other members of his family were kept away by pride, disappointment, misunderstanding, and petty resentment indulged as a result of hurt feelings. 141:0.2 (1587.2)
	Jesus was lighthearted and cheerful as they moved along until he came to the brow of Olivet, where the city and the temple towers came into full view; there the Master stopped the procession, and a great silence came upon all as they beheld him weeping. Looking down upon the vast multitude coming forth from the city to greet him, the Master, with much emotion and with tearful voice, said: "O Jerusalem, if you had only known, even you, at least in this your day, the things which belong to your peace, and which you could so freely have had! But now are these glories about to be hid from your eyes. You are about to reject the Son of Peace and turn your backs upon the gospel of salvation. The days will soon come upon you wherein your enemies will cast a trench around about you and lay siege to you on every side; they shall utterly destroy you, insomuch that not one stone shall be left upon another. And all this shall befall you because you knew not the time of your divine visitation. You are about to reject the gift of God, and all men will reject you." 172:3.10 (1882.3)

<table>
<tr><td>Resurrecting Lazarus:</td><td>It is difficult to explain to human minds just why Jesus wept. While we have access to the registration of the combined human emotions and divine thoughts, as of record in the mind of the Personalized Adjuster, we are not altogether certain about the real cause of these emotional manifestations. We are inclined to believe that Jesus wept because of a number of thoughts and feelings which were going through his mind at this time, such as: 168:1.2 (1844.1)

1. He felt a genuine and sorrowful sympathy for Martha and Mary; he had a real and deep human affection for these sisters who had lost their brother. 168:1.3 (1844.2)

2. He was perturbed in his mind by the presence of the crowd of mourners, some sincere and some merely pretenders. He always resented these outward exhibitions of mourning. He knew the sisters loved their brother and had faith in the survival of believers. These conflicting emotions may possibly explain why he groaned as they came near the tomb. 168:1.4 (1844.3)

3. He truly hesitated about bringing Lazarus back to the mortal life. His sisters really needed him, but Jesus regretted having to summon his friend back to experience the bitter persecution which he well knew Lazarus would have to endure as a result of being the subject of the greatest of all demonstrations of the divine power of the Son of Man. 168:1.5 (1844.4)</td></tr>
<tr><td rowspan="2">Jesus Cleansing the Temple:</td><td>As Jesus was about to begin his address, two things happened to arrest his attention. At the money table of a near-by exchanger a violent and heated argument had arisen over the alleged overcharging of a Jew from Alexandria, while at the same moment the air was rent by the bellowing of a drove of some one hundred bullocks which was being driven from one section of the animal pens to another. As Jesus paused, silently but thoughtfully contemplating this scene of commerce and confusion, close by he beheld a simple-minded Galilean, a man he had once talked with in Iron, being ridiculed and jostled about by supercilious and would-be superior Judeans; and all of this combined to produce one of those strange and periodic uprisings of indignant emotion in the soul of Jesus. 173:1.6 (1890.1)

To the amazement of his apostles, standing near at hand, who refrained from participation in what so soon followed, Jesus stepped down from the teaching platform and, going over to the lad who was driving the cattle through the court, took from him his whip of cords and swiftly drove the animals from the temple. But that was not all; he strode majestically before the wondering gaze of the thousands assembled in the temple court to the farthest cattle pen and proceeded to open the gates of every stall and to drive out the imprisoned animals. By this time the assembled pilgrims were electrified, and with uproarious shouting they moved toward the bazaars and began to overturn the tables of the money-changers. In less than five minutes all commerce had been swept from the temple. By the time the near-by Roman guards had appeared on the scene, all was quiet, and the crowds had become orderly; Jesus, returning to the speaker's stand, spoke to the multitude: "You have this day witnessed that which is written in the Scriptures: 'My house shall be called a house of prayer for all nations, but you have made it a den of robbers.'" 173:1.7 (1890.2)</td></tr>
<tr><td>This surprising act of Jesus was beyond the comprehension of his apostles. They were so taken aback by this sudden and unexpected move of their Master that they remained throughout the whole episode huddled together near the speaker's stand; they never lifted</td></tr>
</table>

Jesus Cleansing the Temple: (Continued)	a hand to further this cleansing of the temple. If this spectacular event had occurred the day before, at the time of Jesus' triumphal arrival at the temple at the termination of his tumultuous procession through the gates of the city, all the while loudly acclaimed by the multitude, they would have been ready for it, but coming as it did, they were wholly unprepared to participate. 173:1.10 (1890.5) This cleansing of the temple discloses the Master's attitude toward commercializing the practices of religion as well as his detestation of all forms of unfairness and profiteering at the expense of the poor and the unlearned. This episode also demonstrates that Jesus did not look with approval upon the refusal to employ force to protect the majority of any given human group against the unfair and enslaving practices of unjust minorities who may be able to entrench themselves behind political, financial, or ecclesiastical power. Shrewd, wicked, and designing men are not to be permitted to organize themselves for the exploitation and oppression of those who, because of their idealism, are not disposed to resort to force for self-protection or for the furtherance of their laudable life projects. 173:1.11 (1891.1)
At the Garden of Gethsemane:	The cheerful attitude of Jesus was waning. As the hour passed, he grew more and more serious, even sorrowful. The apostles, being much agitated, were loath to return to their tents even when requested to do so by the Master himself. Returning from his talk with David and John, he addressed his last words to all eleven, saying: "My friends, go to your rest. Prepare yourselves for the work of tomorrow. Remember, we should all submit ourselves to the will of the Father in heaven. My peace I leave with you." And having thus spoken, he motioned them to their tents, but as they went, he called to Peter, James, and John, saying, "I desire that you remain with me for a little while." 182:2.2 (1966.2) After all was still and quiet about the camp, Jesus, taking Peter, James, and John, went a short way up a near-by ravine where he had often before gone to pray and commune. The three apostles could not help recognizing that he was grievously oppressed; never before had they observed their Master to be so heavy-laden and sorrowful. When they arrived at the place of his devotions, he bade the three sit down and watch with him while he went off about a stone's throw to pray. And when he had fallen down on his face, he prayed: "My Father, I came into this world to do your will, and so have I. I know that the hour has come to lay down this life in the flesh, and I do not shrink therefrom, but I would know that it is your will that I drink this cup. Send me the assurance that I will please you in my death even as I have in my life." 182:3.1 (1968.2) The Master remained in a prayerful attitude for a few moments, and then, going over to the three apostles, he found them sound asleep, for their eyes were heavy and they could not remain awake. As Jesus awoke them, he said: "What! can you not watch with me even for one hour? Cannot you see that my soul is exceedingly sorrowful, even to death, and that I crave your companionship?" After the three had aroused from their slumber, the Master again went apart by himself and, falling down on the ground, again prayed: "Father, I know it is possible to avoid this cup—all things are possible with you—but I have come to do your will, and while this is a bitter cup, I would drink it if it is your will." And when he had thus prayed, a mighty angel came down by his side and, speaking to him, touched him and strengthened him. 182:3.2 (1968.3) During the years that Jesus lived among his followers, they did, indeed, have much proof of his divine nature, but just now are they about to witness new evidences of his humanity.

At the Garden of Gethsemane: (Continued)	Just before the greatest of all the revelations of his divinity, his resurrection, must now come the greatest proofs of his mortal nature, his humiliation and crucifixion. 182:3.5 (1968.6) Each time he prayed in the garden, his humanity laid a firmer faith-hold upon his divinity; his human will more completely became one with the divine will of his Father. Among other words spoken to him by the mighty angel was the message that the Father desired his Son to finish his earth bestowal by passing through the creature experience of death just as all mortal creatures must experience material dissolution in passing from the existence of time into the progression of eternity. 182:3.6 (1969.1) Earlier in the evening it had not seemed so difficult to drink the cup, but as the human Jesus bade farewell to his apostles and sent them to their rest, the trial grew more appalling. Jesus experienced that natural ebb and flow of feeling which is common to all human experience, and just now he was weary from work, exhausted from the long hours of strenuous labor and painful anxiety concerning the safety of his apostles. While no mortal can presume to understand the thoughts and feelings of the incarnate Son of God at such a time as this, we know that he endured great anguish and suffered untold sorrow, for the perspiration rolled off his face in great drops. He was at last convinced that the Father intended to allow natural events to take their course; he was fully determined to employ none of his sovereign power as the supreme head of a universe to save himself. 182:3.7 (1969.2) The assembled hosts of a vast creation are now hovered over this scene under the transient joint command of Gabriel and the Personalized Adjuster of Jesus. The division commanders of these armies of heaven have repeatedly been warned not to interfere with these transactions on earth unless Jesus himself should order them to intervene. 182:3.8 (1969.3) The experience of parting with the apostles was a great strain on the human heart of Jesus; this sorrow of love bore down on him and made it more difficult to face such a death as he well knew awaited him. He realized how weak and how ignorant his apostles were, and he dreaded to leave them. He well knew that the time of his departure had come, but his human heart longed to find out whether there might not possibly be some legitimate avenue of escape from this terrible plight of suffering and sorrow. And when it had thus sought escape, and failed, it was willing to drink the cup. The divine mind of Michael knew he had done his best for the twelve apostles; but the human heart of Jesus wished that more might have been done for them before they should be left alone in the world. Jesus' heart was being crushed; he truly loved his brethren. He was isolated from his family in the flesh; one of his chosen associates was betraying him. His father Joseph's people had rejected him and thereby sealed their doom as a people with a special mission on earth. His soul was tortured by baffled love and rejected mercy. It was just one of those awful human moments when everything seems to bear down with crushing cruelty and terrible agony. 182:3.9 (1969.4) Jesus' humanity was not insensible to this situation of private loneliness, public shame, and the appearance of the failure of his cause. All these sentiments bore down on him with indescribable heaviness. In this great sorrow his mind went back to the days of his childhood in Nazareth and to his early work in Galilee. At the time of this great trial there came up in his mind many of those pleasant scenes of his earthly ministry. And it was from these old memories of Nazareth, Capernaum, Mount Hermon, and of the sunrise and sunset on the shimmering Sea of Galilee, that he soothed himself as he made his human heart strong and ready to encounter the traitor who should so soon betray him. 182:3.10 (1969.5)

<table>
<tr><td>At the Garden of Gethsemane: (Continued)</td><td>Before Judas and the soldiers arrived, the Master had fully regained his customary poise; the spirit had triumphed over the flesh; faith had asserted itself over all human tendencies to fear or entertain doubt. The supreme test of the full realization of the human nature had been met and acceptably passed. Once more the Son of Man was prepared to face his enemies with equanimity and in the full assurance of his invincibility as a mortal man unreservedly dedicated to the doing of his Father's will. 182:3.11 (1970.1)</td></tr>
<tr><td rowspan="2">The Human Jesus:</td><td>Mark, Matthew, and Luke retain something of the picture of the human Jesus as he engaged in the superb struggle to ascertain the divine will and to do that will. John presents a picture of the triumphant Jesus as he walked on earth in the full consciousness of divinity. The great mistake that has been made by those who have studied the Master's life is that some have conceived of him as entirely human, while others have thought of him as only divine. Throughout his entire experience he was truly both human and divine, even as he yet is. 196:2.3 (2092.1)

But the greatest mistake was made in that, while the human Jesus was recognized as having a religion, the divine Jesus (Christ) almost overnight became a religion. Paul's Christianity made sure of the adoration of the divine Christ, but it almost wholly lost sight of the struggling and valiant human Jesus of Galilee, who, by the valor of his personal religious faith and the heroism of his indwelling Adjuster, ascended from the lowly levels of humanity to become one with divinity, thus becoming the new and living way whereby all mortals may so ascend from humanity to divinity. Mortals in all stages of spirituality and on all worlds may find in the personal life of Jesus that which will strengthen and inspire them as they progress from the lowest spirit levels up to the highest divine values, from the beginning to the end of all personal religious experience. 196:2.4 (2092.2)

At the time of the writing of the New Testament, the authors not only most profoundly believed in the divinity of the risen Christ, but they also devotedly and sincerely believed in his immediate return to earth to consummate the heavenly kingdom. This strong faith in the Lord's immediate return had much to do with the tendency to omit from the record those references which portrayed the purely human experiences and attributes of the Master. The whole Christian movement tended away from the human picture of Jesus of Nazareth toward the exaltation of the risen Christ, the glorified and soon-returning Lord Jesus Christ. 196:2.5 (2092.3)</td></tr>
<tr><td>You would be neither shocked nor disturbed by some of Jesus' strong pronouncements if you would only remember that he was the world's most wholehearted and devoted religionist. He was a wholly consecrated mortal, unreservedly dedicated to doing his Father's will. Many of his apparently hard sayings were more of a personal confession of faith and a pledge of devotion than commands to his followers. And it was this very singleness of purpose and unselfish devotion that enabled him to effect such extraordinary progress in the conquest of the human mind in one short life. Many of his declarations should be considered as a confession of what he demanded of himself rather than what he required of all his followers. In his devotion to the cause of the kingdom, Jesus burned all bridges behind him; he sacrificed all hindrances to the doing of his Father's will. 196:2.7 (2093.1)</td></tr>
</table>

Jesus' Examples and Teachings Concerning Prayer

"When you study the career of the Master, as concerns prayer or any other feature of the religious life, look not so much for what he taught as for what he did." 196:0.10 (2088.5)

Jesus' Examples and Teachings Concerning Prayer

The Prayers of a Young Jesus:	The Master was a pattern of reverence. The prayer of even his youth began, "Our Father who is in heaven, hallowed be your name." 100:7.16 (1103.4)
	During this year [the Sixth Year (1 B.C.)] Joseph and Mary had trouble with Jesus about his prayers. He insisted on talking to his heavenly Father much as he would talk to Joseph, his earthly father. This departure from the more solemn and reverent modes of communication with Deity was a bit disconcerting to his parents, especially to his mother, but there was no persuading him to change; he would say his prayers just as he had been taught, after which he insisted on having "just a little talk with my Father in heaven." 123:3.6 (1360.1)
	During this year [15th] Jesus first formulated the prayer which he subsequently taught to his apostles, and which to many has become known as "The Lord's Prayer." In a way it was an evolution of the family altar; they had many forms of praise and several formal prayers. After his father's death Jesus tried to teach the older children to express themselves individually in prayer—much as he so enjoyed doing—but they could not grasp his thought and would invariably fall back upon their memorized prayer forms. It was in this effort to stimulate his older brothers and sisters to say individual prayers that Jesus would endeavor to lead them along by suggestive phrases, and presently, without intention on his part, it developed that they were all using a form of prayer which was largely built up from these suggestive lines which Jesus had taught them. 126:3.3 (1389.6)
Jesus Prays for Others:	When Jesus spent whole nights on the mountain in prayer, it was mainly for his disciples, particularly for the twelve. The Master prayed very little for himself, although he engaged in much worship of the nature of understanding communion with his Paradise Father. 144:3.23 (1620.21)
	Prayer is an antidote for harmful introspection. At least, prayer as the Master taught it is such a beneficent ministry to the soul. Jesus consistently employed the beneficial influence of praying for one's fellows. The Master usually prayed in the plural, not in the singular. Only in the great crises of his earth life did Jesus ever pray for himself. 144:4.6 (1621.5)
View of Jesus' Prayer Life:	In his prayer life he appears to communicate directly with his Father. We have heard few of his prayers, but these few would indicate that he talks with God, as it were, face to face. 161:2.10 (1786.5)
Silent Prayer:	One of the reasons why Peter, James, and John, who so often accompanied Jesus on his long night vigils, never heard Jesus pray, was because their Master so rarely uttered his prayers as spoken words. Practically all of Jesus' praying was done in the spirit and in the heart—silently. 144:4.10 (1621.9)

Prayers Spoken by Jesus	
Prayer at Baptism:	When the returned and now exalted Personalized Adjuster had thus spoken, all was silence. And while the four of them tarried in the water, Jesus, looking up to the near-by Adjuster, prayed: "My Father who reigns in heaven, hallowed be your name. Your kingdom come! Your will be done on earth, even as it is in heaven." When he had prayed, the "heavens were opened," and the Son of Man saw the vision, presented by the now Personalized Adjuster, of himself as a Son of God as he was before he came to earth in the likeness of mortal flesh, and as he would be when the incarnated life should be finished. This heavenly vision was seen only by Jesus. 136:2.4 (1511.3)
Prayer at the Shore:	That evening, when they had returned to the land, before they went their way, Jesus, standing by the water's edge, prayed: "My Father, I thank you for these little ones who, in spite of their doubts, even now believe. And for their sakes have I set myself apart to do your will. And now may they learn to be one, even as we are one." 137:6.6 (1533.4)
Ordination Prayer:	Jesus now instructed the twelve mortals who had just listened to his declaration concerning the kingdom to kneel in a circle about him. Then the Master placed his hands upon the head of each apostle, beginning with Judas Iscariot and ending with Andrew. When he had blessed them, he extended his hands and prayed: 140:2.1 (1569.5) "My Father, I now bring to you these men, my messengers. From among our children on earth I have chosen these twelve to go forth to represent me as I came forth to represent you. Love them and be with them as you have loved and been with me. And now, my Father, give these men wisdom as I place all the affairs of the coming kingdom in their hands. And I would, if it is your will, tarry on earth a time to help them in their labors for the kingdom. And again, my Father, I thank you for these men, and I commit them to your keeping while I go on to finish the work you have given me to do." 140:2.2 (1569.6)
Prayer at the Return of the Seventy:	And it was at this time, just before partaking of the evening meal, that Jesus experienced one of those rare moments of emotional ecstasy which his followers had occasionally witnessed. He said: "I thank you, my Father, Lord of heaven and earth, that, while this wonderful gospel was hidden from the wise and self-righteous, the spirit has revealed these spiritual glories to these children of the kingdom. Yes, my Father, it must have been pleasing in your sight to do this, and I rejoice to know that the good news will spread to all the world even after I shall have returned to you and the work which you have given me to perform. I am mightily moved as I realize you are about to deliver all authority into my hands, that only you really know who I am, and that only I really know you, and those to whom I have revealed you. And when I have finished this revelation to my brethren in the flesh, I will continue the revelation to your creatures on high." 163:6.3 (1807.2)

Jesus' Examples and Teachings Concerning Prayer

At Lazarus' Tomb:	Jesus lifted up his eyes and said: "Father, I am thankful that you heard and granted my request. I know that you always hear me, but because of those who stand here with me, I thus speak with you, that they may believe that you have sent me into the world, and that they may know that you are working with me in that which we are about to do." And when he had prayed, he cried with a loud voice, "Lazarus, come forth!" 168:2.2 (1846.1)
Jesus Talks About Prayer:	The apostles were much stirred up in their minds and spent considerable time discussing their recent experiences as they were related to prayer and its answering. . . . All that day, again and again, they reverted to the discussion of this question of the answer to prayer. 168:4.2 (1848.2) Jesus' answers to their many questions may be summarized as follows: 168:4.3 (1848.3) 1. Prayer is an expression of the finite mind in an effort to approach the Infinite. The making of a prayer must, therefore, be limited by the knowledge, wisdom, and attributes of the finite; likewise must the answer be conditioned by the vision, aims, ideals, and prerogatives of the Infinite. There never can be observed an unbroken continuity of material phenomena between the making of a prayer and the reception of the full spiritual answer thereto. 168:4.4 (1848.4) 2. When a prayer is apparently unanswered, the delay often betokens a better answer, although one which is for some good reason greatly delayed. When Jesus said that Lazarus's sickness was really not to the death, he had already been dead eleven hours. No sincere prayer is denied an answer except when the superior viewpoint of the spiritual world has devised a better answer, an answer which meets the petition of the spirit of man as contrasted with the prayer of the mere mind of man. 168:4.5 (1848.5) 3. The prayers of time, when indited by the spirit and expressed in faith, are often so vast and all-encompassing that they can be answered only in eternity; the finite petition is sometimes so fraught with the grasp of the Infinite that the answer must long be postponed to await the creation of adequate capacity for receptivity; the prayer of faith may be so all-embracing that the answer can be received only on Paradise. 168:4.6 (1848.6) 4. The answers to the prayer of the mortal mind are often of such a nature that they can be received and recognized only after that same praying mind has attained the immortal state. The prayer of the material being can many times be answered only when such an individual has progressed to the spirit level. 168:4.7 (1848.7) 5. The prayer of a God-knowing person may be so distorted by ignorance and so deformed by superstition that the answer thereto would be highly undesirable. Then must the intervening spirit beings so translate such a prayer that, when the answer arrives, the petitioner wholly fails to recognize it as the answer to his prayer. 168:4.8 (1848.8)

Jesus Talks About prayer: (Continued)	6. All true prayers are addressed to spiritual beings, and all such petitions must be answered in spiritual terms, and all such answers must consist in spiritual realities. Spirit beings cannot bestow material answers to the spirit petitions of even material beings. Material beings can pray effectively only when they "pray in the spirit." 168:4.9 (1848.9) 7. No prayer can hope for an answer unless it is born of the spirit and nurtured by faith. Your sincere faith implies that you have in advance virtually granted your prayer hearers the full right to answer your petitions in accordance with that supreme wisdom and that divine love which your faith depicts as always actuating those beings to whom you pray. 168:4.10 (1849.1) 8. The child is always within his rights when he presumes to petition the parent; and the parent is always within his parental obligations to the immature child when his superior wisdom dictates that the answer to the child's prayer be delayed, modified, segregated, transcended, or postponed to another stage of spiritual ascension. 168:4.11 (1849.2) 9. Do not hesitate to pray the prayers of spirit longing; doubt not that you shall receive the answer to your petitions. These answers will be on deposit, awaiting your achievement of those future spiritual levels of actual cosmic attainment, on this world or on others, whereon it will become possible for you to recognize and appropriate the long-waiting answers to your earlier but ill-timed petitions. 168:4.12 (1849.3) 10. All genuine spirit-born petitions are certain of an answer. Ask and you shall receive. But you should remember that you are progressive creatures of time and space; therefore must you constantly reckon with the time-space factor in the experience of your personal reception of the full answers to your manifold prayers and petitions. 168:4.13 (1849.4)
Jesus' Help to Mortal Man in Praying:	But great sorrow later attended the misinterpretation of the Master's inferences regarding prayer. There would have been little difficulty about these teachings if his exact words had been remembered and subsequently truthfully recorded. But as the record was made, believers eventually regarded prayer in Jesus' name as a sort of supreme magic, thinking that they would receive from the Father anything they asked for. For centuries honest souls have continued to wreck their faith against this stumbling block. How long will it take the world of believers to understand that prayer is not a process of getting your way but rather a program of taking God's way, an experience of learning how to recognize and execute the Father's will? It is entirely true that, when your will has been truly aligned with his, you can ask anything conceived by that will-union, and it will be granted. And such a will-union is effected by and through Jesus even as the life of the vine flows into and through the living branches. 180:2.4 (1946.2)
Last Group Prayer:	A few moments after arriving at camp, Jesus said to them: "My friends and brethren, my time with you is now very short, and I desire that we draw apart by ourselves while we pray to our Father in heaven for strength to sustain us in this hour and henceforth in all the work we must do in his name." 182:1.1 (1963.3) When Jesus had thus spoken, he led the way a short distance up on Olivet, and in

	full view of Jerusalem he bade them kneel on a large flat rock in a circle about him as they had done on the day of their ordination; and then, as he stood there in the midst of them glorified in the mellow moonlight, he lifted up his eyes toward heaven and prayed: 182:1.2 (1963.4)
	"Father, my hour has come; now glorify your Son that the Son may glorify you. I know that you have given me full authority over all living creatures in my realm, and I will give eternal life to all who will become faith sons of God. And this is eternal life, that my creatures should know you as the only true God and Father of all, and that they should believe in him whom you sent into the world. Father, I have exalted you on earth and have accomplished the work which you gave me to do. I have almost finished my bestowal upon the children of our own creation; there remains only for me to lay down my life in the flesh. And now, O my Father, glorify me with the glory which I had with you before this world was and receive me once more at your right hand. 182:1.3 (1963.5)
Last Group Prayer: (Continued)	"I have manifested you to the men whom you chose from the world and gave to me. They are yours—as all life is in your hands—you gave them to me, and I have lived among them, teaching them the way of life, and they have believed. These men are learning that all I have comes from you, and that the life I live in the flesh is to make known my Father to the worlds. The truth which you have given to me I have revealed to them. These, my friends and ambassadors, have sincerely willed to receive your word. I have told them that I came forth from you, that you sent me into this world, and that I am about to return to you. Father, I do pray for these chosen men. And I pray for them not as I would pray for the world, but as for those whom I have chosen out of the world to represent me to the world after I have returned to your work, even as I have represented you in this world during my sojourn in the flesh. These men are mine; you gave them to me; but all things which are mine are ever yours, and all that which was yours you have now caused to be mine. You have been exalted in me, and I now pray that I may be honored in these men. I can no longer be in this world; I am about to return to the work you have given me to do. I must leave these men behind to represent us and our kingdom among men. Father, keep these men faithful as I prepare to yield up my life in the flesh. Help these, my friends, to be one in spirit, even as we are one. As long as I could be with them, I could watch over them and guide them, but now am I about to go away. Be near them, Father, until we can send the new teacher to comfort and strengthen them. 182:1.4 (1964.1)
	"You gave me twelve men, and I have kept them all save one, the son of revenge, who would not have further fellowship with us. These men are weak and frail, but I know we can trust them; I have proved them; they love me, even as they reverence you. While they must suffer much for my sake, I desire that they should also be filled with the joy of the assurance of sonship in the heavenly kingdom. I have given these men your word and have taught them the truth. The world may hate them, even as it has hated me, but I do not ask that you take them out of the world, only that you keep them from the evil in the world. Sanctify them in the truth; your word is truth. And as you sent me into this world, even so am I about to send these men into the world. For their sakes I have lived among men and have consecrated my life to your service that I might inspire them to be purified through the truth I have taught them and the love I have revealed to them. I well know, my Father, that there is no need

Last Group Prayer: (Continued)	for me to ask you to watch over these brethren after I have gone; I know you love them even as I, but I do this that they may the better realize the Father loves mortal men even as does the Son. 182:1.5 (1964.2) "And now, my Father, I would pray not only for these eleven men but also for all others who now believe, or who may hereafter believe the gospel of the kingdom through the word of their future ministry. I want them all to be one, even as you and I are one. You are in me and I am in you, and I desire that these believers likewise be in us; that both of our spirits indwell them. If my children are one as we are one, and if they love one another as I have loved them, all men will then believe that I came forth from you and be willing to receive the revelation of truth and glory which I have made. The glory which you gave me I have revealed to these believers. As you have lived with me in spirit, so have I lived with them in the flesh. As you have been one with me, so have I been one with them, and so will the new teacher ever be one with them and in them. And all this have I done that my brethren in the flesh may know that the Father loves them even as does the Son, and that you love them even as you love me. Father, work with me to save these believers that they may presently come to be with me in glory and then go on to join you in the Paradise embrace. Those who serve with me in humiliation, I would have with me in glory so that they may see all you have given into my hands as the eternal harvest of the seed sowing of time in the likeness of mortal flesh. I long to show my earthly brethren the glory I had with you before the founding of this world. This world knows very little of you, righteous Father, but I know you, and I have made you known to these believers, and they will make known your name to other generations. And now I promise them that you will be with them in the world even as you have been with me—even so." 182:1.6 (1964.3)
Prayers in Gethsemane:	After all was still and quiet about the camp, Jesus, taking Peter, James, and John, went a short way up a near-by ravine where he had often before gone to pray and commune. The three apostles could not help recognizing that he was grievously oppressed; never before had they observed their Master to be so heavy-laden and sorrowful. When they arrived at the place of his devotions, he bade the three sit down and watch with him while he went off about a stone's throw to pray. And when he had fallen down on his face, he prayed: "My Father, I came into this world to do your will, and so have I. I know that the hour has come to lay down this life in the flesh, and I do not shrink therefrom, but I would know that it is your will that I drink this cup. Send me the assurance that I will please you in my death even as I have in my life." 182:3.1 (1968.2) The Master remained in a prayerful attitude for a few moments, and then, going over to the three apostles, he found them sound asleep, for their eyes were heavy and they could not remain awake. As Jesus awoke them, he said: "What! can you not watch with me even for one hour? Cannot you see that my soul is exceedingly sorrowful, even to death, and that I crave your companionship?" After the three had aroused from their slumber, the Master again went apart by himself and, falling down on the ground, again prayed: "Father, I know it is possible to avoid this cup—all things are possible with you—but I have come to do your will, and while this is a bitter cup, I would drink it if it is your will." And when he had thus prayed, a

Prayers in Gethsemane: (Continued)	mighty angel came down by his side and, speaking to him, touched him and strengthened him. 182:3.2 (1968.3) And then, for a third time, the Master withdrew and prayed: "Father, you see my sleeping apostles; have mercy upon them. The spirit is indeed willing, but the flesh is weak. And now, O Father, if this cup may not pass, then would I drink it. Not my will, but yours, be done." And when he had finished praying, he lay for a moment prostrate on the ground. 182:3.4 (1968.5)
Jesus' Manner of Praying On the Mount of Ordination:	At this time the eleven apostles knelt in a circle about the Master and heard him repeat the charges and saw him re-enact the ordination scene even as when they were first set apart for the special work of the kingdom. And all of this was to them as a memory of their former consecration to the Father's service, except the Master's prayer. When the Master—the morontia Jesus—now prayed, it was in tones of majesty and with words of power such as the apostles had never before heard. Their Master now spoke with the rulers of the universes as one who, in his own universe, had had all power and authority committed to his hand. And these eleven men never forgot this experience of the morontia rededication to the former pledges of ambassadorship. The Master spent just one hour on this mount with his ambassadors, and when he had taken an affectionate farewell of them, he vanished from their sight. 192:3.2 (2050.2)
To Jesus Prayer Was:	When you study the career of the Master, as concerns prayer or any other feature of the religious life, look not so much for what he taught as for what he did. Jesus never prayed as a religious duty. To him prayer was a sincere expression of spiritual attitude, a declaration of soul loyalty, a recital of personal devotion, an expression of thanksgiving, an avoidance of emotional tension, a prevention of conflict, an exaltation of intellection, an ennoblement of desire, a vindication of moral decision, an enrichment of thought, an invigoration of higher inclinations, a consecration of impulse, a clarification of viewpoint, a declaration of faith, a transcendental surrender of will, a sublime assertion of confidence, a revelation of courage, the proclamation of discovery, a confession of supreme devotion, the validation of consecration, a technique for the adjustment of difficulties, and the mighty mobilization of the combined soul powers to withstand all human tendencies toward selfishness, evil, and sin. He lived just such a life of prayerful consecration to the doing of his Father's will and ended his life triumphantly with just such a prayer. The secret of his unparalleled religious life was this consciousness of the presence of God; and he attained it by intelligent prayer and sincere worship—unbroken communion with God—and not by leadings, voices, visions, or extraordinary religious practices. 196:0.10 (2088.5)

Jesus' Teachings Regarding the Kingdom of Heaven

Our Father who is in heaven,
Hallowed be your name.
Your kingdom come; your will be done
On earth as it is in heaven.

"One evening about sundown, before Joseph had returned home, Gabriel appeared to Mary by the side of a low stone table and, after she had recovered her composure, said: "I come at the bidding of one who is my Master and whom you shall love and nurture. To you, Mary, I bring glad tidings when I announce that the conception within you is ordained by heaven, and that in due time you will become the mother of a son; you shall call him Joshua, and he shall inaugurate the kingdom of heaven on earth and among men." 122:3.1 (1346.4)

Jesus' Teachings Regarding the Kingdom of Heaven

<table>
<tr><td rowspan="8">What Is the Kingdom?</td><td>The kingdom of heaven is neither a social nor economic order; it is an exclusively spiritual brotherhood of God-knowing individuals. True, such a brotherhood is in itself a new and amazing social phenomenon attended by astounding political and economic repercussions. 99:3.2 (1088.3)</td></tr>
<tr><td>The kingdom of heaven, the divine government, is founded on the fact of divine sovereignty—God is spirit. Since God is spirit, this kingdom is spiritual. The kingdom of heaven is neither material nor merely intellectual; it is a spiritual relationship between God and man. 134:4.2 (1486.5)</td></tr>
<tr><td>Spiritually, all men are equal. The kingdom of heaven is free from castes, classes, social levels, and economic groups. You are all brethren. 134:4.7 (1487.4)</td></tr>
<tr><td>While Jesus later directed that the apostles should go forth, as John had, preaching the gospel and instructing believers, he laid emphasis on the proclamation of the "good tidings of the kingdom of heaven." He unfailingly impressed upon his associates that they must "show forth love, compassion, and sympathy." He early taught his followers that the kingdom of heaven was a spiritual experience having to do with the enthronement of God in the hearts of men. 137:7.13 (1535.5)</td></tr>
<tr><td>John asked Jesus, "Master, what is the kingdom of heaven?" And Jesus answered: "The kingdom of heaven consists in these three essentials: first, recognition of the fact of the sovereignty of God; second, belief in the truth of sonship with God; and third, faith in the effectiveness of the supreme human desire to do the will of God—to be like God. And this is the good news of the gospel: that by faith every mortal may have all these essentials of salvation." 140:10.9 (1585.7)</td></tr>
<tr><td>I declare that the kingdom of heaven is the realization and acknowledgment of God's rule within the hearts of men. True, there is a King in this kingdom, and that King is my Father and your Father. We are indeed his loyal subjects, but far transcending that fact is the transforming truth that we are his sons. 141:2.1 (1588.4)</td></tr>
<tr><td>Very plainly Jesus explained that the kingdom of heaven was an evolutionary experience, beginning here on earth and progressing up through successive life stations to Paradise. In the course of the evening he definitely stated that at some future stage of kingdom development he would revisit this world in spiritual power and divine glory. 142:7.3 (1603.4)

He next explained that the "kingdom idea" was not the best way to illustrate man's relation to God; that he employed such figures of speech because the Jewish people were expecting the kingdom, and because John had preached in terms of the coming kingdom. Jesus said: "The people of another age will better understand the gospel of the kingdom when it is presented in terms expressive of the family relationship—when man understands religion as the teaching of the fatherhood of God and the brotherhood of man, sonship with God." 142:7.4 (1603.5)</td></tr>
<tr><td>"In the kingdom of heaven, which I have come to declare, there is no high and mighty king; this kingdom is a divine family. The universally recognized and unreservedly worshiped center and head of this far-flung brotherhood of intelligent beings is my Father and your Father. I am his Son, and you are also his sons. 149:6.8 (1676.2)</td></tr>
</table>

Jesus' Teachings Regarding the Kingdom of Heaven

	Notwithstanding they had many times heard the Master say that "in the kingdom of heaven there is neither rich nor poor, free nor bond, male nor female, all are equally the sons and daughters of God," they were literally stunned when he proposed formally to commission these ten women as religious teachers and even to permit their traveling about with them. 150:1.3 (1679.2)
	Jesus talked with the apostles each day, and they more clearly discerned that a new phase of the work of preaching the kingdom of heaven was now beginning. They were commencing to comprehend that the "kingdom of heaven is not meat and drink but the realization of the spiritual joy of the acceptance of divine sonship." 155:3.1 (1727.1)
	Jesus always had trouble trying to explain to the apostles that, while they proclaimed the establishment of the kingdom of God, the Father in heaven *was not a king.* At the time Jesus lived on earth and taught in the flesh, the people of Urantia knew mostly of kings and emperors in the governments of the nations, and the Jews had long contemplated the coming of the kingdom of God. For these and other reasons, the Master thought best to designate the spiritual brotherhood of man as the kingdom of heaven and the spirit head of this brotherhood as the *Father in heaven.* Never did Jesus refer to his Father as a king. 169:4.1 (1855.2)
What is the Kingdom? (Continued)	On this afternoon the Master distinctly taught a new concept of the double nature of the kingdom in that he portrayed the following two phases: 170:2.17 (1860.12)
	"The kingdom of God in heaven, the goal of mortal believers, the estate wherein the love for God is perfected, and wherein the will of God is done more divinely." 170:2.19 (1861.1)
	Jesus never gave a precise definition of the kingdom. At one time he would discourse on one phase of the kingdom, and at another time he would discuss a different aspect of the brotherhood of God's reign in the hearts of men. In the course of this Sabbath afternoon's sermon Jesus noted no less than five phases, or epochs, of the kingdom, and they were: 170:4.1 (1862.9) 1. The personal and inward experience of the spiritual life of the fellowship of the individual believer with God the Father. 170:4.2 (1862.10) 2. The enlarging brotherhood of gospel believers, the social aspects of the enhanced morals and quickened ethics resulting from the reign of God's spirit in the hearts of individual believers. 170:4.3 (1863.1) 3. The supermortal brotherhood of invisible spiritual beings which prevails on earth and in heaven, the superhuman kingdom of God. 170:4.4 (1863.2) 4. The prospect of the more perfect fulfillment of the will of God, the advance toward the dawn of a new social order in connection with improved spiritual living—the next age of man. 170:4.5 (1863.3) The kingdom in its fullness, the future spiritual age of light and life on earth. 170:4.6 (1863.4)

Jesus' Teachings Regarding the Kingdom of Heaven

Kingdom of God:	And then Thomas asked Jesus if they should "continue having everything in common." Said the Master: "Yes, my brethren, I would that we should live together as one understanding family. You are intrusted with a great work, and I crave your undivided service. You know that it has been well said: 'No man can serve two masters.' You cannot sincerely worship God and at the same time wholeheartedly serve mammon. Having now enlisted unreservedly in the work of the kingdom, be not anxious for your lives; much less be concerned with what you shall eat or what you shall drink; nor yet for your bodies, what clothing you shall wear. Already have you learned that willing hands and earnest hearts shall not go hungry. And now, when you prepare to devote all of your energies to the work of the kingdom, be assured that the Father will not be unmindful of your needs. Seek first the kingdom of God, and when you have found entrance thereto, all things needful shall be added to you. Be not, therefore, unduly anxious for the morrow. Sufficient for the day is the trouble thereof." 140:6.13 (1577.7)
	"Every earth child who follows the leading of this spirit shall eventually know the will of God, and he who surrenders to the will of my Father shall abide forever. The way from the earth life to the eternal estate has not been made plain to you, but there is a way, there always has been, and I have come to make that way new and living. He who enters the kingdom has eternal life already—he shall never perish. But much of this you will the better understand when I shall have returned to the Father and you are able to view your present experiences in retrospect." 146:3.7 (1642.3)
Entering the Kingdom:	A child has been in existence about nine months before it experiences *birth.* But the "birth" of religion is not sudden; it is rather a gradual emergence. Nevertheless, sooner or later there is a "birth day." You do not enter the kingdom of heaven unless you have been "born again"—born of the Spirit. 103:2.1 (1130.6)
	"My kingdom is not of this world. The Son of Man will not lead forth armies in battle for the establishment of a throne of power or a kingdom of worldly glory. When my kingdom shall have come, you shall know the Son of Man as the Prince of Peace, the revelation of the everlasting Father. The children of this world fight for the establishment and enlargement of the kingdoms of this world, but my disciples shall enter the kingdom of heaven by their moral decisions and by their spirit victories; and when they once enter therein, they shall find joy, righteousness, and eternal life. 137:8.7 (1536.4)
	"I have come to preach the glad tidings of the kingdom. I have not come to add to the heavy burdens of those who would enter this kingdom. I proclaim the new and better way, and those who are able to enter the coming kingdom shall enjoy the divine rest. And whatever it shall cost you in the things of the world, no matter what price you may pay to enter the kingdom of heaven, you shall receive manyfold more of joy and spiritual progress in this world, and in the age to come eternal life. 137:8.14 (1537.1) "Entrance into the Father's kingdom waits not upon marching armies, upon overturned kingdoms of this world, nor upon the breaking of captive yokes. The kingdom of heaven is at hand, and all who enter therein shall find abundant liberty and joyous salvation. 137:8.15 (1537.2)

Entering the Kingdom: (Continued)	The keys of the kingdom of heaven are: sincerity, more sincerity, and more sincerity. All men have these keys. Men use them—advance in spirit status—by decisions, by more decisions, and by more decisions. 39:4.14 (435.7)
	"John came preaching repentance to prepare you for the kingdom; now have I come proclaiming faith, the gift of God, as the price of entrance into the kingdom of heaven. If you would but believe that my Father loves you with an infinite love, then you are in the kingdom of God." 137:8.17 (1537.4)
	When Jesus began to speak, he said: "In coming here tonight to welcome Matthew and Simon to our fellowship, I am glad to witness your lightheartedness and social good cheer, but you should rejoice still more because many of you will find entrance into the coming kingdom of the spirit, wherein you shall more abundantly enjoy the good things of the kingdom of heaven. 138:3.6 (1540.9)
	That afternoon, which they spent together, Jesus fully instructed them concerning attendance upon festive gatherings, concluding his remarks by saying: "All men are my brothers. My Father in heaven does not despise any creature of our making. The kingdom of heaven is open to all men and women. No man may close the door of mercy in the face of any hungry soul who may seek to gain an entrance thereto. We will sit at meat with all who desire to hear of the kingdom. As our Father in heaven looks down upon men, they are all alike. Refuse not therefore to break bread with Pharisee or sinner, Sadducee or publican, Roman or Jew, rich or poor, free or bond. The door of the kingdom is wide open for all who desire to know the truth and to find God." 138:4.2 (1541.4)
	That night Jesus discoursed to the apostles on the new life in the kingdom. He said in part: "When you enter the kingdom, you are reborn. You cannot teach the deep things of the spirit to those who have been born only of the flesh; first see that men are born of the spirit before you seek to instruct them in the advanced ways of the spirit. Do not undertake to show men the beauties of the temple until you have first taken them into the temple. Introduce men to God and *as* the sons of God before you discourse on the doctrines of the fatherhood of God and the sonship of men. Do not strive with men—always be patient. It is not your kingdom; you are only ambassadors. Simply go forth proclaiming: This is the kingdom of heaven—God is your Father and you are his sons, and this good news, if you wholeheartedly believe it, *is* your eternal salvation." 141:6.4 (1592.6)
	Jesus endeavored to make clear that he desired his disciples, having tasted of the good spirit realities of the kingdom, so to live in the world that men, by *seeing* their lives, would become kingdom conscious and hence be led to inquire of believers concerning the ways of the kingdom. All such sincere seekers for the truth are always glad to *hear* the glad tidings of the faith gift which insures admission to the kingdom with its eternal and divine spirit realities. 141:7.3 (1593.4)

Entering the Kingdom: (Continued)	No child has aught to do with *earning* the status of son or daughter. The earth child comes into being by the will of its parents. Even so, the child of God comes into grace and the new life of the spirit by the will of the Father in heaven. Therefore must the kingdom of heaven—divine sonship—be *received* as by a little child. You earn righteousness—progressive character development—but you receive sonship by grace and through faith. 144:4.3 (1621.2)
	My Father does not require of you as the price of entering the kingdom of heaven that you should force yourself to subscribe to a belief in things which are spiritually repugnant, unholy, and untruthful. It is not required of you that your own sense of mercy, justice, and truth should be outraged by submission to an outworn system of religious forms and ceremonies. The religion of the spirit leaves you forever free to follow the truth wherever the leadings of the spirit may take you. 155:6.5 (1731.3)
The Good News of the Gospel of the Kingdom of Heaven:	Religion has little chance to function until the religious group becomes separated from all other groups—the social association of the spiritual membership of the kingdom of heaven. 99:5.4 (1091.3)
	Moral choosing is usually accompanied by more or less moral conflict. And this very first conflict in the child mind is between the urges of egoism and the impulses of altruism. The Thought Adjuster does not disregard the personality values of the egoistic motive but does operate to place a slight preference upon the altruistic impulse as leading to the goal of human happiness and to the joys of the kingdom of heaven. 103:2.7 (1131.6)
	"Be not deceived by those who come saying here is the kingdom or there is the kingdom, for my Father's kingdom concerns not things visible and material. And this kingdom is even now among you, for where the spirit of God teaches and leads the soul of man, there in reality is the kingdom of heaven. And this kingdom of God is righteousness, peace, and joy in the Holy Spirit. 137:8.9 (1536.6)
	"This kingdom is an everlasting dominion. Those who enter the kingdom shall ascend to my Father; they will certainly attain the right hand of his glory in Paradise. And all who enter the kingdom of heaven shall become the sons of God, and in the age to come so shall they ascend to the Father. And I have not come to call the would-be righteous but sinners and all who hunger and thirst for the righteousness of divine perfection. 137:8.16 (1537.3)
	"In gaining an entrance into the kingdom of heaven, it is the motive that counts. My Father looks into the hearts of men and judges by their inner longings and their sincere intentions. 140:3.19 (1571.6)
	"Happy are the poor in spirit—the humble." To a child, happiness is the satisfaction of immediate pleasure craving. The adult is willing to sow seeds of self-denial in order to reap subsequent harvests of augmented happiness. In Jesus' times and since, happiness has all too often been associated with the idea of the possession of wealth. In the story of the Pharisee and the publican praying in the temple, the one felt rich in spirit—egotistical; the other felt "poor in spirit"—humble. One was self-sufficient; the other was teachable and truth-seeking. The poor in spirit seek for goals of spiritual wealth—for God. And such seekers after truth do not have to wait for rewards in a distant future; they are rewarded *now.* They find the kingdom of heaven within their own hearts, and they experience such happiness *now.* 140:5.7 (1573.9)

The Good News of the Gospel of the Kingdom of Heaven: (Continued)	Even in the important matter of baptism, all that Jesus said was: "John did indeed baptize with water, but when you enter the kingdom of heaven, you shall be baptized with the Spirit." 141:6.5 (1593.1)
	The Master sought to impress upon all teachers of the gospel of the kingdom that their only business was to reveal God to the individual man as his Father—to lead this individual man to become son-conscious; then to present this same man to God as his faith son. Both of these essential revelations are accomplished in Jesus. He became, indeed, "the way, the truth, and the life." 141:7.4 (1593.5)
	Jesus laid great emphasis upon what he called the two truths of first import in the teachings of the kingdom, and they are: the attainment of salvation by faith, and faith alone, associated with the revolutionary teaching of the attainment of human liberty through the sincere recognition of truth, "You shall know the truth, and the truth shall make you free." Jesus was the truth made manifest in the flesh, and he promised to send his Spirit of Truth into the hearts of all his children after his return to the Father in heaven. 141:7.6 (1593.7)
	Throughout this month Jesus or one of the apostles taught daily in the temple. When the Passover crowds were too great to find entrance to the temple teaching, the apostles conducted many teaching groups outside the sacred precincts. The burden of their message was: 142:1.1 (1596.3) 1. The kingdom of heaven is at hand. 142:1.2 (1596.4) 2. By faith in the fatherhood of God you may enter the kingdom of heaven, thus becoming the sons of God. 142:1.3 (1596.5) 3. Love is the rule of living within the kingdom—supreme devotion to God while loving your neighbor as yourself. 142:1.4 (1596.6) 4. Obedience to the will of the Father, yielding the fruits of the spirit in one's personal life, is the law of the kingdom. 142:1.5 (1596.7)
	The Father in heaven. And now do we know God as our Father in heaven. Our teaching provides a religion wherein the believer *is* a son of God. That is the good news of the gospel of the kingdom of heaven. 142:3.8 (1598.9)
	"Verily, verily, I say to you, among those born of women there has not arisen a greater than John the Baptist; yet he who is but small in the kingdom of heaven is greater because he has been born of the spirit and knows that he has become a son of God." 144:8.4 (1627.1)
	On Tuesday evening Jesus was conducting one of his customary classes of questions and answers when the leader of the six spies said to him: "I was today talking with one of John's disciples who is here attending upon your teaching, and we were at a loss to understand why you never command your disciples to fast and pray as we Pharisees fast and as John bade his followers." And Jesus, referring to a statement by John, answered

	this questioner: "Do the sons of the bridechamber fast while the bridegroom is with them? As long as the bridegroom remains with them, they can hardly fast. But the time is coming when the bridegroom shall be taken away, and during those times the children of the bridechamber undoubtedly will fast and pray. To pray is natural for the children of light, but fasting is not a part of the gospel of the kingdom of heaven. Be reminded that a wise tailor does not sew a piece of new and unshrunk cloth upon an old garment, lest, when it is wet, it shrink and produce a worse rent. Neither do men put new wine into old wine skins, lest the new wine burst the skins so that both the wine and the skins perish. The wise man puts the new wine into fresh wine skins. Therefore do my disciples show wisdom in that they do not bring too much of the old order over into the new teaching of the gospel of the kingdom. You who have lost your teacher may be justified in fasting for a time. Fasting may be an appropriate part of the law of Moses, but in the coming kingdom the sons of God shall experience freedom from fear and joy in the divine spirit." 147:7.2 (1655.4)
	Let me tell you that nothing is hid in the kingdom of heaven which shall not be made manifest; neither are there any secrets which shall not ultimately be made known. 151:3.1 (1691.4)
The Good News of the Gospel of the Kingdom of Heaven: (Continued)	"Today you see this fulfilled before your eyes. But you shall not see the remainder of the Psalmist's prophecy fulfilled, for he entertained erroneous ideas about the Son of Man and his mission on earth. My kingdom is founded on love, proclaimed in mercy, and established by unselfish service. My Father does not sit in heaven laughing in derision at the heathen. He is not wrathful in his great displeasure. True is the promise that the Son shall have these so-called heathen (in reality his ignorant and untaught brethren) for an inheritance. And I will receive these gentiles with open arms of mercy and affection. All this loving-kindness shall be shown the so-called heathen, notwithstanding the unfortunate declaration of the record which intimates that the triumphant Son 'shall break them with a rod of iron and dash them to pieces like a potter's vessel.' The Psalmist exhorted you to 'serve the Lord with fear'—I bid you enter into the exalted privileges of divine sonship by faith; he commands you to rejoice with trembling; I bid you rejoice with assurance. He says, 'Kiss the Son, lest he be angry, and you perish when his wrath is kindled.' But you who have lived with me well know that anger and wrath are not a part of the establishment of the kingdom of heaven in the hearts of men. 155:1.2 (1725.3)
	Jesus continued to teach the twenty-four, saying: "The heathen are not without excuse when they rage at us. Because their outlook is small and narrow, they are able to concentrate their energies enthusiastically. Their goal is near and more or less visible; wherefore do they strive with valiant and effective execution. You who have professed entrance into the kingdom of heaven are altogether too vacillating and indefinite in your teaching conduct. The heathen strike directly for their objectives; you are guilty of too much chronic yearning. If you desire to enter the kingdom, why do you not take it by spiritual assault even as the heathen take a city they lay siege to? You are hardly worthy of the kingdom when your service consists so largely in an attitude of regretting the past, whining over the present, and vainly hoping for the future. Why do the heathen rage? Because they know not the truth. Why do you languish in futile yearning? Because you *obey* not the truth. Cease your useless yearning and go forth bravely doing that which concerns the establishment of the kingdom. 155:1.3 (1725.4)

Jesus' Teachings Regarding the Kingdom of Heaven

The Good News of the Gospel of the Kingdom of Heaven: (Continued)	Many of your brethren have minds which accept the theory of God while they spiritually fail to realize the presence of God. And that is just the reason why I have so often taught you that the kingdom of heaven can best be realized by acquiring the spiritual attitude of a sincere child. It is not the mental immaturity of the child that I commend to you but rather the *spiritual simplicity* of such an easy-believing and fully-trusting little one. It is not so important that you should know about the fact of God as that you should increasingly grow in the ability to *feel the presence of God.* 155:6.12 (1732.5)
	Jesus, knowing what it was that occupied their thoughts that day, beckoned to one of Peter's little ones and, setting the child down among them, said: "Verily, verily, I say to you, except you turn about and become more like this child, you will make little progress in the kingdom of heaven. Whosoever shall humble himself and become as this little one, the same shall become greatest in the kingdom of heaven. And whoso receives such a little one receives me. And they who receive me receive also Him who sent me. If you would be first in the kingdom, seek to minister these good truths to your brethren in the flesh. But whosoever causes one of these little ones to stumble, it would be better for him if a millstone were hanged about his neck and he were cast into the sea. If the things you do with your hands, or the things you see with your eyes give offense in the progress of the kingdom, sacrifice these cherished idols, for it is better to enter the kingdom minus many of the beloved things of life rather than to cling to these idols and find yourself shut out of the kingdom. But most of all, see that you despise not one of these little ones, for their angels do always behold the faces of the heavenly hosts." 158:8.1 (1761.2)
	The religion of Jesus transcends all our former concepts of the idea of worship in that he not only portrays his Father as the ideal of infinite reality but positively declares that this divine source of values and the eternal center of the universe is truly and personally attainable by every mortal creature who chooses to enter the kingdom of heaven on earth, thereby acknowledging the acceptance of sonship with God and brotherhood with man. That, I submit, is the highest concept of religion the world has ever known, and I pronounce that there can never be a higher since this gospel embraces the infinity of realities, the divinity of values, and the eternity of universal attainments. Such a concept constitutes the achievement of the experience of the idealism of the supreme and the ultimate. 160:5.7 (1781.3)
	Almost every human being has some one thing which is held on to as a pet evil, and which the entrance into the kingdom of heaven requires as a part of the price of admission. 163:2.7 (1802.3)
	Jesus did not teach nor countenance improvidence, idleness, indifference to providing the physical necessities for one's family, or dependence upon alms. But he did teach that the material and temporal must be subordinated to the welfare of the soul and the progress of the spiritual nature in the kingdom of heaven. 165:4.7 (1822.2)
	And when the apostles loudly rebuked these mothers, Jesus, hearing the tumult, came out and indignantly reproved them, saying: "Suffer little children to come to me; forbid them not, for of such is the kingdom of heaven. Verily, verily, I say to you, whosoever receives not the kingdom of God as a little child shall hardly enter therein to grow up to the full stature of spiritual manhood." 167:6.1 (1839.6)

Jesus' Teachings Regarding the Kingdom of Heaven

<table>
<tr><td rowspan="2">The Good News of the Gospel of the Kingdom of Heaven: (Continued)</td><td>The Master made it clear that the kingdom of heaven must begin with, and be centered in, the dual concept of the truth of the fatherhood of God and the correlated fact of the brotherhood of man. The acceptance of such a teaching, Jesus declared, would liberate man from the age-long bondage of animal fear and at the same time enrich human living with the following endowments of the new life of spiritual liberty: 170:2.1 (1859.11)

1. The possession of new courage and augmented spiritual power. The gospel of the kingdom was to set man free and inspire him to dare to hope for eternal life. 170:2.2 (1859.12)

2. The gospel carried a message of new confidence and true consolation for all men, even for the poor. 170:2.3 (1859.13)

3. It was in itself a new standard of moral values, a new ethical yardstick wherewith to measure human conduct. It portrayed the ideal of a resultant new order of human society. 170:2.4 (1859.14)

4. It taught the pre-eminence of the spiritual compared with the material; it glorified spiritual realities and exalted superhuman ideals. 170:2.5 (1859.15)

5. This new gospel held up spiritual attainment as the true goal of living. Human life received a new endowment of moral value and divine dignity. 170:2.6 (1860.1)

6. Jesus taught that eternal realities were the result (reward) of righteous earthly striving. Man's mortal sojourn on earth acquired new meanings consequent upon the recognition of a noble destiny. 170:2.7 (1860.2)

7. The new gospel affirmed that human salvation is the revelation of a far-reaching divine purpose to be fulfilled and realized in the future destiny of the endless service of the salvaged sons of God. 170:2.8 (1860.3)

These teachings cover the expanded idea of the kingdom which was taught by Jesus. 170:2.9 (1860.4)</td></tr>
<tr><td>The kingdoms of this world, being material, may often find it necessary to employ physical force in the execution of their laws and for the maintenance of order. In the kingdom of heaven true believers will not resort to the employment of physical force. The kingdom of heaven, being a spiritual brotherhood of the spirit-born sons of God, may be promulgated only by the power of the spirit. This distinction of procedure refers to the relations of the kingdom of believers to the kingdoms of secular government and does not nullify the right of social groups of believers to maintain order in their ranks and administer discipline upon unruly and unworthy members. 178:1.2 (1929.3)</td></tr>
<tr><td rowspan="2">Teaching About the Kingdom of Heaven:</td><td>To the Greek contractor and builder he said: "My friend, as you build the material structures of men, grow a spiritual character in the similitude of the divine spirit within your soul. Do not let your achievement as a temporal builder outrun your attainment as a spiritual son of the kingdom of heaven. 133:4.6 (1474.6)</td></tr>
<tr><td>"Your message to the world shall be: Seek first the kingdom of God and his righteousness, and in finding these, all other things essential to eternal survival shall be secured therewith. And now would I make it plain to you that this kingdom of my Father will not come with an outward show of power or with unseemly demonstration. You are not to go hence in the proclamation of the kingdom, saying, 'it is here' or 'it is there,' for this kingdom of which you preach is God within you. 140:1.5 (1569.2)</td></tr>
</table>

Teaching About the Kingdom of Heaven: (Continued)	"Whosoever would become great in my Father's kingdom shall become a minister to all; and whosoever would be first among you, let him become the server of his brethren. But when you are once truly received as citizens in the heavenly kingdom, you are no longer servants but sons, sons of the living God. And so shall this kingdom progress in the world until it shall break down every barrier and bring all men to know my Father and believe in the saving truth which I have come to declare. Even now is the kingdom at hand, and some of you will not die until you have seen the reign of God come in great power. 140:1.6 (1569.3)
	Jesus endeavored to make clear that he desired his disciples, having tasted of the good spirit realities of the kingdom, so to live in the world that men, by *seeing* their lives, would become kingdom conscious and hence be led to inquire of believers concerning the ways of the kingdom. All such sincere seekers for the truth are always glad to *hear* the glad tidings of the faith gift which insures admission to the kingdom with its eternal and divine spirit realities. 141:7.3 (1593.4)
	By teaching that the kingdom is within, by exalting the individual, Jesus struck the deathblow of the old society in that he ushered in the new dispensation of true social righteousness. This new order of society the world has little known because it has refused to practice the principles of the gospel of the kingdom of heaven. And when this kingdom of spiritual pre-eminence does come upon the earth, it will not be manifested in mere improved social and material conditions, but rather in the glories of those enhanced and enriched spiritual values which are characteristic of the approaching age of improved human relations and advancing spiritual attainments. 170:3.11 (1862.8)
	But doubt not, this same kingdom of heaven which the Master taught exists within the heart of the believer, will yet be proclaimed to this Christian church, even as to all other religions, races, and nations on earth—even to every individual. 170:5.8 (1864.8)
	As mortal and material men, you are indeed citizens of the earthly kingdoms, and you should be good citizens, all the better for having become reborn spirit sons of the heavenly kingdom. As faith-enlightened and spirit-liberated sons of the kingdom of heaven, you face a double responsibility of duty to man and duty to God while you voluntarily assume a third and sacred obligation: service to the brotherhood of God-knowing believers. 178:1.5 (1930.2)
	The faith of Jesus visualized all spirit values as being found in the kingdom of God; therefore he said, "Seek first the kingdom of heaven." Jesus saw in the advanced and ideal fellowship of the kingdom the achievement and fulfillment of the "will of God." The very heart of the prayer which he taught his disciples was, "Your kingdom come; your will be done." Having thus conceived of the kingdom as comprising the will of God, he devoted himself to the cause of its realization with amazing self-forgetfulness and unbounded enthusiasm. 196:0.8 (2088.3)

The Plan of Salvation

"The God-conscious mortal is certain of salvation; he is unafraid of life; he is honest and consistent. He knows how bravely to endure unavoidable suffering; he is uncomplaining when faced by inescapable hardship." 156:5.20 (1740.7)

The Plan of Salvation

What is Salvation?	"Those who are sure of salvation are forever free from lust, envy, hatred, and the delusions of wealth. While faith is the energy of the better life, nevertheless, must you work out your own salvation with perseverance. If you would be certain of your final salvation, then make sure that you sincerely seek to fulfill all righteousness. Cultivate the assurance of the heart which springs from within and thus come to enjoy the ecstasy of eternal salvation. 131:3.4 (1447.1)
	"The saving or losing of a soul has to do with whether or not the moral consciousness attains survival status through eternal alliance with its associated immortal spirit endowment. Salvation is the spiritualization of the self-realization of the moral consciousness, which thereby becomes possessed of survival value. 133:6.6 (1478.5)
	It was their belief that "it is better to die than to transgress the commandments of the elders." The spies asked this question because it had been reported that Jesus had said, "Salvation is a matter of clean hearts rather than of clean hands." But such beliefs, when they once become a part of one's religion, are hard to get away from. Even many years after this day the Apostle Peter was still held in the bondage of fear to many of these traditions about things clean and unclean, only being finally delivered by experiencing an extraordinary and vivid dream. All of this can the better be understood when it is recalled that these Jews looked upon eating with unwashed hands in the same light as commerce with a harlot, and both were equally punishable by excommunication. 153:3.6 (1713.1)
What Shall One Do to Be Saved?	Rachel asked Jesus this question: "Master, what shall we answer when women ask us, What shall I do to be saved?" When Jesus heard this question, he answered: 150:5.1 (1682.3) "When men and women ask what shall we do to be saved, you shall answer, Believe this gospel of the kingdom; accept divine forgiveness. By faith recognize the indwelling spirit of God, whose acceptance makes you a son of God. Have you not read in the Scriptures where it says, 'In the Lord have I righteousness and strength.' Also where the Father says, 'My righteousness is near; my salvation has gone forth, and my arms shall enfold my people.' 'My soul shall be joyful in the love of my God, for he has clothed me with the garments of salvation and has covered me with the robe of his righteousness.' Have you not also read of the Father that his name 'shall be called the Lord our righteousness.' 'Take away the filthy rags of self-righteousness and clothe my son with the robe of divine righteousness and eternal salvation.' It is forever true, 'the just shall live by faith.' Entrance into the Father's kingdom is wholly free, but progress—growth in grace—is essential to continuance therein. 150:5.2 (1682.4)
How is Salvation Attained?	That night Jesus discoursed to the apostles on the new life in the kingdom. He said in part: "When you enter the kingdom, you are reborn. You cannot teach the deep things of the spirit to those who have been born only of the flesh; first see that men are born of the spirit before you seek to instruct them in the advanced ways of the spirit. Do not undertake to show men the beauties of the temple until you have first taken them into the temple. Introduce men to God and *as* the sons of God before you discourse on the doctrines of the fatherhood of God and the sonship of men. Do not strive with men—always be patient. It is not your kingdom; you are only ambassadors. Simply go forth proclaiming: This is the kingdom of heaven—God is your Father and you are his sons, and this good news, if you wholeheartedly believe it, *is* your eternal salvation." 141:6.4 (1592.6)

How is Salvation Attained? (Continued)	Kingdom believers should possess an implicit faith, a whole-souled belief, in the certain triumph of righteousness. Kingdom builders must be undoubting of the truth of the gospel of eternal salvation. Believers must increasingly learn how to step aside from the rush of life—escape the harassments of material existence—while they refresh the soul, inspire the mind, and renew the spirit by worshipful communion. 156:5.12 (1739.7)
	Are your ideals sufficiently high to insure your eternal salvation while your ideas are so practical as to render you a useful citizen to function on earth in association with your mortal fellows? 156:5.16 (1740.3)
	Then Andrew brought to Jesus a certain rich young man who was a devout believer, and who desired to receive ordination. This young man, Matadormus, was a member of the Jerusalem Sanhedrin; he had heard Jesus teach and had been subsequently instructed in the gospel of the kingdom by Peter and the other apostles. Jesus talked with Matadormus concerning the requirements of ordination and requested that he defer decision until after he had thought more fully about the matter. Early the next morning, as Jesus was going for a walk, this young man accosted him and said: "Master, I would know from you the assurances of eternal life. Seeing that I have observed all the commandments from my youth, I would like to know what more I must do to gain eternal life?" In answer to this question Jesus said: "If you keep all the commandments—do not commit adultery, do not kill, do not steal, do not bear false witness, do not defraud, honor your parents—you do well, but salvation is the reward of faith, not merely of works. Do you believe this gospel of the kingdom?" And Matadormus answered: "Yes, Master, I do believe everything you and your apostles have taught me." And Jesus said, "Then are you indeed my disciple and a child of the kingdom." 163:2.4 (1801.7)
	When they had finished breakfast, and while the others sat by the fire, Jesus beckoned to Peter and to John that they should come with him for a stroll on the beach. As they walked along, Jesus said to John, "John, do you love me?" And when John answered, "Yes, Master, with all my heart," the Master said: "Then, John, give up your intolerance and learn to love men as I have loved you. Devote your life to proving that love is the greatest thing in the world. It is the love of God that impels men to seek salvation. 192:2.1 (2047.5)
Help of Our Creator Son:	When they had refreshed themselves, Jesus took the twelve apart for a season to pray with them and to instruct them in the nature and work of the Holy Spirit, but again did they largely fail to comprehend the meaning of those wonderful truths which he endeavored to teach them. One would grasp one point and one would comprehend another, but none of them could encompass the whole of his teaching. Always would they make the mistake of trying to fit Jesus' new gospel into their old forms of religious belief. They could not grasp the idea that Jesus had come to proclaim a new gospel of salvation and to establish a new way of finding God; they did not perceive that he *was* a new revelation of the Father in heaven. 138:5.2 (1542.3)

Help of Our Creator Son: (Continued)	That evening while teaching in the house, for it had begun to rain, Jesus talked at great length, trying to show the twelve what they must *be,* not what they must *do.* They knew only a religion that imposed the *doing* of certain things as the means of attaining righteousness—salvation. But Jesus would reiterate, "In the kingdom you must *be* righteous in order to do the work." Many times did he repeat, "*Be* you therefore perfect, even as your Father in heaven is perfect." All the while was the Master explaining to his bewildered apostles that the salvation which he had come to bring to the world was to be had only by *believing,* by simple and sincere faith. Said Jesus: "John preached a baptism of repentance, sorrow for the old way of living. You are to proclaim the baptism of fellowship with God. Preach repentance to those who stand in need of such teaching, but to those already seeking sincere entrance to the kingdom, open the doors wide and bid them enter into the joyous fellowship of the sons of God." But it was a difficult task to persuade these Galilean fishermen that, in the kingdom, *being* righteous, by faith, must precede *doing* righteousness in the daily life of the mortals of earth. 140:10.1 (1584.4)
	John asked Jesus, "Master, what is the kingdom of heaven?" And Jesus answered: "The kingdom of heaven consists in these three essentials: first, recognition of the fact of the sovereignty of God; second, belief in the truth of sonship with God; and third, faith in the effectiveness of the supreme human desire to do the will of God—to be like God. And this is the good news of the gospel: that by faith every mortal may have all these essentials of salvation." 140:10.9 (1585.7)
	Jesus laid great emphasis upon what he called the two truths of first import in the teachings of the kingdom, and they are: the attainment of salvation by faith, and faith alone, associated with the revolutionary teaching of the attainment of human liberty through the sincere recognition of truth, "You shall know the truth, and the truth shall make you free." Jesus was the truth made manifest in the flesh, and he promised to send his Spirit of Truth into the hearts of all his children after his return to the Father in heaven. 141:7.6 (1593.7)
	"The Father loves you, and therefore do I long for your deliverance from the bondage of prejudice and the darkness of tradition. I offer you the liberty of life and the joy of salvation. I proclaim the new and living way, the deliverance from evil and the breaking of the bondage of sin. I have come that you might have life, and have it eternally. You seek to be rid of me and my disquieting teachings. If you could only realize that I am to be with you only a little while! In just a short time I go to Him who sent me into this world. And then will many of you diligently seek me, but you shall not discover my presence, for where I am about to go you cannot come. But all who truly seek to find me shall sometime attain the life that leads to my Father's presence." 162:2.7 (1792.1)
	As Jesus stood before them at this time, he perceived the end of one dispensation and the beginning of another. Turning his attention to the Greeks, the Master said: 174:5.6 (1903.3)
	I am the open door to eternal salvation. 182:1.14 (1965.8)

	"He who believes this gospel, believes not merely in me but in Him who sent me. When you look upon me, you see not only the Son of Man but also Him who sent me. I am the light of the world, and whosoever will believe my teaching shall no longer abide in darkness. If you gentiles will hear me, you shall receive the words of life and shall enter forthwith into the joyous liberty of the truth of sonship with God. If my fellow countrymen, the Jews, choose to reject me and to refuse my teachings, I will not sit in judgment on them, for I came not to judge the world but to offer it salvation. Nevertheless, they who reject me and refuse to receive my teaching shall be brought to judgment in due season by my Father and those whom he has appointed to sit in judgment on such as reject the gift of mercy and the truths of salvation. Remember, all of you, that I speak not of myself, but that I have faithfully declared to you that which the Father commanded I should reveal to the children of men. And these words which the Father directed me to speak to the world are words of divine truth, everlasting mercy, and eternal life. 174:5.7 (1903.4)
Help of Our Creator Son: (Continued)	Jesus lived and died for a whole universe, not just for the races of this one world. While the mortals of the realms had salvation even before Jesus lived and died on Urantia, it is nevertheless a fact that his bestowal on this world greatly illuminated the way of salvation; his death did much to make forever plain the certainty of mortal survival after death in the flesh. 188:4.6 (2017.1) Though it is hardly proper to speak of Jesus as a sacrificer, a ransomer, or a redeemer, it is wholly correct to refer to him as a *savior.* He forever made the way of salvation (survival) more clear and certain; he did better and more surely show the way of salvation for all the mortals of all the worlds of the universe of Nebadon. 188:4.7 (2017.2)
	The cross forever shows that the attitude of Jesus toward sinners was neither condemnation nor condonation, but rather eternal and loving salvation. Jesus is truly a savior in the sense that his life and death do win men over to goodness and righteous survival. Jesus loves men so much that his love awakens the response of love in the human heart. Love is truly contagious and eternally creative. Jesus' death on the cross exemplifies a love which is sufficiently strong and divine to forgive sin and swallow up all evil- doing. Jesus disclosed to this world a higher quality of righteousness than justice—mere technical right and wrong. Divine love does not merely forgive wrongs; it absorbs and actually destroys them. The forgiveness of love utterly transcends the forgiveness of mercy. Mercy sets the guilt of evil-doing to one side; but love destroys forever the sin and all weakness resulting therefrom. Jesus brought a new method of living to Urantia. He taught us not to resist evil but to find through him a goodness which effectually destroys evil. The forgiveness of Jesus is not condonation; it is salvation from condemnation. Salvation does not slight wrongs; it *makes them right.* True love does not compromise nor condone hate; it destroys it. The love of Jesus is never satisfied with mere forgiveness. The Master's love implies rehabilitation, eternal survival. It is altogether proper to speak of salvation as redemption if you mean this eternal rehabilitation. 188:5.2 (2018.1) Jesus, by the power of his personal love for men, could break the hold of sin and evil. He thereby set men free to choose better ways of living. Jesus portrayed a deliverance from the past which in itself promised a triumph for the future. Forgiveness thus provided salvation. The beauty of divine love, once fully admitted to the human heart, forever destroys the charm of sin and the power of evil. 188:5.3 (2018.2)

Salvation is a Matter of Personal Choosing:	
	Revealed truth, personally discovered truth, is the supreme delight of the human soul; it is the joint creation of the material mind and the indwelling spirit. The eternal salvation of this truth-discerning and beauty-loving soul is assured by that hunger and thirst for goodness which leads this mortal to develop a singleness of purpose to do the Father's will, to find God and to become like him. There is never conflict between true knowledge and truth. There may be conflict between knowledge and human beliefs, beliefs colored with prejudice, distorted by fear, and dominated by the dread of facing new facts of material discovery or spiritual progress. 132:3.4 (1459.4)
	"Salvation is by the regeneration of the spirit and not by the self-righteous deeds of the flesh. You are justified by faith and fellowshipped by grace, not by fear and the self-denial of the flesh, albeit the Father's children who have been born of the spirit are ever and always *masters* of the self and all that pertains to the desires of the flesh. When you know that you are saved by faith, you have real peace with God. And all who follow in the way of this heavenly peace are destined to be sanctified to the eternal service of the ever-advancing sons of the eternal God. Henceforth, it is not a duty but rather your exalted privilege to cleanse yourselves from all evils of mind and body while you seek for perfection in the love of God. 143:2.6 (1610.1)
	There is a basic law of justice in the universe which mercy is powerless to circumvent. The unselfish glories of Paradise are not possible of reception by a thoroughly selfish creature of the realms of time and space. Even the infinite love of God cannot force the salvation of eternal survival upon any mortal creature who does not choose to survive. Mercy has great latitude of bestowal, but, after all, there are mandates of justice which even love combined with mercy cannot effectively abrogate. Again Jesus quoted from the Hebrew scriptures: "I have called and you refused to hear; I stretched out my hand, but no man regarded. You have set at naught all my counsel, and you have rejected my reproof, and because of this rebellious attitude it becomes inevitable that you shall call upon me and fail to receive an answer. Having rejected the way of life, you may seek me diligently in your times of suffering, but you will not find me." 146:2.5 (1638.5)
	"You also have another saying among you, and one that contains much truth: That the way which leads to eternal life is straight and narrow, that the door which leads thereto is likewise narrow so that, of those who seek salvation, few can find entrance through this door. You also have a teaching that the way which leads to destruction is broad, that the entrance thereto is wide, and that there are many who choose to go this way. And this proverb is not without its meaning. But I declare that salvation is first a matter of your personal choosing. Even if the door to the way of life is narrow, it is wide enough to admit all who sincerely seek to enter, for I am that door. And the Son will never refuse entrance to any child of the universe who, by faith, seeks to find the Father through the Son. 166:3.3 (1828.7)

Salvation is a Gift of the Father:	"Intelligent children do not fear their father in order that they may receive good gifts from his hand; but having already received the abundance of good things bestowed by the dictates of the father's affection for his sons and daughters, these much loved children are led to love their father in responsive recognition and appreciation of such munificent beneficence. The goodness of God leads to repentance; the beneficence of God leads to service; the mercy of God leads to salvation; while the love of God leads to intelligent and freehearted worship. 149:6.4 (1675.5)
	"Salvation is the gift of the Father and is revealed by his Sons. Acceptance by faith on your part makes you a partaker of the divine nature, a son or a daughter of God. By faith you are justified; by faith are you saved; and by this same faith are you eternally advanced in the way of progressive and divine perfection. By faith was Abraham justified and made aware of salvation by the teachings of Melchizedek. All down through the ages has this same faith saved the sons of men, but now has a Son come forth from the Father to make salvation more real and acceptable." 150:5.3 (1682.5)
	In summing up his final statement, Jesus said: "You cannot buy salvation; you cannot earn righteousness. Salvation is the gift of God, and righteousness is the natural fruit of the spirit-born life of sonship in the kingdom. You are not to be saved because you live a righteous life; rather is it that you live a righteous life because you have already been saved, have recognized sonship as the gift of God and service in the kingdom as the supreme delight of life on earth. When men believe this gospel, which is a revelation of the goodness of God, they will be led to voluntary repentance of all known sin. Realization of sonship is incompatible with the desire to sin. Kingdom believers hunger for righteousness and thirst for divine perfection." 150:5.5 (1683.2)
	On the way to Judea Jesus was followed by a company of almost fifty of his friends and enemies. At their noon lunchtime, on Wednesday, he talked to his apostles and this group of followers on the "Terms of Salvation," and at the end of this lesson told the parable of the Pharisee and the publican (a tax collector). Said Jesus: "You see, then, that the Father gives salvation to the children of men, and this salvation is a free gift to all who have the faith to receive sonship in the divine family. There is nothing man can do to earn this salvation. Works of self-righteousness cannot buy the favor of God, and much praying in public will not atone for lack of living faith in the heart. Men you may deceive by your outward service, but God looks into your souls. What I am telling you is well illustrated by two men who went into the temple to pray, the one a Pharisee and the other a publican. The Pharisee stood and prayed to himself: 'O God, I thank you that I am not like the rest of men, extortioners, unlearned, unjust, adulterers, or even like this publican. I fast twice a week; I give tithes of all that I get.' But the publican, standing afar off, would not so much as lift his eyes to heaven but smote his breast, saying, 'God be merciful to me a sinner.' I tell you that the publican went home with God's approval rather than the Pharisee, for every one who exalts himself shall be humbled, but he who humbles himself shall be exalted." 167:5.1 (1838.2)

	How cruel and unreasoning to compel innocent children to suffer for the sins of their progenitors, misdeeds of which they are wholly ignorant, and for which they could in no way be responsible! And to do such wicked deeds in the name of one who taught his disciples to love even their enemies! It has become necessary, in this recital of the life of Jesus, to portray the manner in which certain of his fellow Jews rejected him and conspired to bring about his ignominious death; but we would warn all who read this narrative that the presentation of such a historical recital in no way justifies the unjust hatred, nor condones the unfair attitude of mind, which so many professed Christians have maintained toward individual Jews for many centuries. Kingdom believers, those who follow the teachings of Jesus, must cease to mistreat the individual Jew as one who is guilty of the rejection and crucifixion of Jesus. The Father and his Creator Son have never ceased to love the Jews. God is no respecter of persons, and salvation is for the Jew as well as for the gentile. 175:2.3 (1909.3)
Salvation is a Gift of the Father: (Continued)	As they walked along, Jesus said to them: "How slow you are to comprehend the truth! When you tell me that it is about the teachings and work of this man that you have your discussions, then may I enlighten you since I am more than familiar with these teachings. Do you not remember that this Jesus always taught that his kingdom was not of this world, and that all men, being the sons of God, should find liberty and freedom in the spiritual joy of the fellowship of the brotherhood of loving service in this new kingdom of the truth of the heavenly Father's love? Do you not recall how this Son of Man proclaimed the salvation of God for all men, ministering to the sick and afflicted and setting free those who were bound by fear and enslaved by evil? Do you not know that this man of Nazareth told his disciples that he must go to Jerusalem, be delivered up to his enemies, who would put him to death, and that he would arise on the third day? Have you not been told all this? And have you never read in the Scriptures concerning this day of salvation for Jew and gentile, where it says that in him shall all the families of the earth be blessed; that he will hear the cry of the needy and save the souls of the poor who seek him; that all nations shall call him blessed? That such a Deliverer shall be as the shadow of a great rock in a weary land. That he will feed the flock like a true shepherd, gathering the lambs in his arms and tenderly carrying them in his bosom. That he will open the eyes of the spiritually blind and bring the prisoners of despair out into full liberty and light; that all who sit in darkness shall see the great light of eternal salvation. That he will bind up the brokenhearted, proclaim liberty to the captives of sin, and open up the prison to those who are enslaved by fear and bound by evil. That he will comfort those who mourn and bestow upon them the joy of salvation in the place of sorrow and heaviness. That he shall be the desire of all nations and the everlasting joy of those who seek righteousness. That this Son of truth and righteousness shall rise upon the world with healing light and saving power; even that he will save his people from their sins; that he will really seek and save those who are lost. That he will not destroy the weak but minister salvation to all who hunger and thirst for righteousness. That those who believe in him shall have eternal life. That he will pour out his spirit upon all flesh, and that this Spirit of Truth shall be in each believer a well of water, springing up into everlasting life. Did you not understand how great was the gospel of the kingdom which this man delivered to you? Do you not perceive how great a salvation has come upon you?" 190:5.4 (2035.1)

Salvation is a Gift of the Father: (Continued)	"Peace be upon you. You rejoice to know that I am the resurrection and the life, but this will avail you nothing unless you are first born of the eternal spirit, thereby coming to possess, by faith, the gift of eternal life. If you are the faith sons of my Father, you shall never die; you shall not perish. The gospel of the kingdom has taught you that all men are the sons of God. And this good news concerning the love of the heavenly Father for his children on earth must be carried to all the world. The time has come when you worship God neither on Gerizim nor at Jerusalem, but where you are, as you are, in spirit and in truth. It is your faith that saves your souls. Salvation is the gift of God to all who believe they are his sons. But be not deceived; while salvation is the free gift of God and is bestowed upon all who accept it by faith, there follows the experience of bearing the fruits of this spirit life as it is lived in the flesh. The acceptance of the doctrine of the fatherhood of God implies that you also freely accept the associated truth of the brotherhood of man. And if man is your brother, he is even more than your neighbor, whom the Father requires you to love as yourself. Your brother, being of your own family, you will not only love with a family affection, but you will also serve as you would serve yourself. And you will thus love and serve your brother because you, being my brethren, have been thus loved and served by me. Go, then, into all the world telling this good news to all creatures of every race, tribe, and nation. My spirit shall go before you, and I will be with you always." 193:1.2 (2053.4)
Can I Lose Salvation?	"The saving or losing of a soul has to do with whether or not the moral consciousness attains survival status through eternal alliance with its associated immortal spirit endowment. Salvation is the spiritualization of the self-realization of the moral consciousness, which thereby becomes possessed of survival value. All forms of soul conflict consist in the lack of harmony between the moral, or spiritual, self-consciousness and the purely intellectual self-consciousness. 133:6.6 (1478.5)
	"Iniquity is the willful, determined, and persistent transgression of the divine law, the Father's will. Iniquity is the measure of the continued rejection of the Father's loving plan of personality survival and the Sons' merciful ministry of salvation. 148:4.5 (1660.4)
The Benefits of Salvation:	"Entrance into the Father's kingdom waits not upon marching armies, upon overturned kingdoms of this world, nor upon the breaking of captive yokes. The kingdom of heaven is at hand, and all who enter therein shall find abundant liberty and joyous salvation. 137:8.15 (1537.2)
	The God-conscious mortal is certain of salvation; he is unafraid of life; he is honest and consistent. He knows how bravely to endure unavoidable suffering; he is uncomplaining when faced by inescapable hardship. 156:5.20 (1740.7)
	This entire idea of the ransom of the atonement places salvation upon a plane of unreality; such a concept is purely philosophic. Human salvation is *real;* it is based on two realities which may be grasped by the creature's faith and thereby become incorporated into individual human experience: the fact of the fatherhood of God and its correlated truth, the brotherhood of man. It is true, after all, that you are to be "forgiven your debts, even as you forgive your debtors." 188:4.13 (2017.8)

The Plan of Salvation

<table>
<tr><td>Finality of Human Salvation: (From Part III)</td><td>The teachings of Jesus constituted the first Urantian religion which so fully embraced a harmonious co-ordination of knowledge, wisdom, faith, truth, and love as completely and simultaneously to provide temporal tranquility, intellectual certainty, moral enlightenment, philosophic stability, ethical sensitivity, God-consciousness, and the positive assurance of personal survival. The faith of Jesus pointed the way to finality of human salvation, to the ultimate of mortal universe attainment, since it provided for: 101:6.8 (1112.4)

1. Salvation from material fetters in the personal realization of sonship with God, who is spirit. 101:6.9 (1112.5)

2. Salvation from intellectual bondage: man shall know the truth, and the truth shall set him free. 101:6.10 (1112.6)

3. Salvation from spiritual blindness, the human realization of the fraternity of mortal beings and the morontian awareness of the brotherhood of all universe creatures; the service-discovery of spiritual reality and the ministry-revelation of the goodness of spirit values. 101:6.11 (1112.7)

4. Salvation from incompleteness of self through the attainment of the spirit levels of the universe and through the eventual realization of the harmony of Havona and the perfection of Paradise. 101:6.12 (1113.1)

5. Salvation from self, deliverance from the limitations of self-consciousness through the attainment of the cosmic levels of the Supreme mind and by co-ordination with the attainments of all other self-conscious beings. 101:6.13 (1113.2)

6. Salvation from time, the achievement of an eternal life of unending progression in God-recognition and God-service. 101:6.14 (1113.3)

7. Salvation from the finite, the perfected oneness with Deity in and through the Supreme by which the creature attempts the transcendental discovery of the Ultimate on the postfinaliter levels of the absonite. 101:6.15 (1113.4)

8. Such a sevenfold salvation is the equivalent of the completeness and perfection of the realization of the ultimate experience of the Universal Father. And all this, in potential, is contained within the reality of the faith of the human experience of religion. And it can be so contained since the faith of Jesus was nourished by, and was revelatory of, even realities beyond the ultimate; the faith of Jesus approached the status of a universe absolute in so far as such is possible of manifestation in the evolving cosmos of time and space. 101:6.16 (1113.5)</td></tr>
<tr><td>Imparting Salvation to Others:</td><td>The three enjoyed a most pleasant passage to Alexandria. Ganid was delighted with the voyage and kept Jesus busy answering questions. As they approached the city's harbor, the young man was thrilled by the great lighthouse of Pharos, located on the island which Alexander had joined by a mole to the mainland, thus creating two magnificent harbors and thereby making Alexandria the maritime commercial crossroads of Africa, Asia, and Europe. This great lighthouse was one of the seven wonders of the world and was the forerunner of all subsequent lighthouses. They arose early in the morning to view this splendid lifesaving device of man, and amidst the exclamations of Ganid Jesus said: "And you, my son, will be like this lighthouse</td></tr>
</table>

	when you return to India, even after your father is laid to rest; you will become like the light of life to those who sit about you in darkness, showing all who so desire the way to reach the harbor of salvation in safety." And as Ganid squeezed Jesus' hand, he said, "I will." 130:3.2 (1432.2)
Imparting Salvation to Others: (Continued)	[Jesus said] "Ganid, the man was not hungry for truth. He was not dissatisfied with himself. He was not ready to ask for help, and the eyes of his mind were not open to receive light for the soul. That man was not ripe for the harvest of salvation; he must be allowed more time for the trials and difficulties of life to prepare him for the reception of wisdom and higher learning. Or, if we could have him live with us, we might by our lives show him the Father in heaven, and thus would he become so attracted by our lives as sons of God that he would be constrained to inquire about our Father. You cannot reveal God to those who do not seek for him; you cannot lead unwilling souls into the joys of salvation. Man must become hungry for truth as a result of the experiences of living, or he must desire to know God as the result of contact with the lives of those who are acquainted with the divine Father before another human being can act as the means of leading such a fellow mortal to the Father in heaven. If we know God, our real business on earth is so to live as to permit the Father to reveal himself in our lives, and thus will all God-seeking persons see the Father and ask for our help in finding out more about the God who in this manner finds expression in our lives." 132:7.2 (1466.2)
	"Peace be upon you. That which my Father sent me into the world to establish belongs not to a race, a nation, nor to a special group of teachers or preachers. This gospel of the kingdom belongs to both Jew and gentile, to rich and poor, to free and bond, to male and female, even to the little children. And you are all to proclaim this gospel of love and truth by the lives which you live in the flesh. You shall love one another with a new and startling affection, even as I have loved you. You will serve mankind with a new and amazing devotion, even as I have served you. And when men see you so love them, and when they behold how fervently you serve them, they will perceive that you have become faith-fellows of the kingdom of heaven, and they will follow after the Spirit of Truth which they see in your lives, to the finding of eternal salvation. 191:6.2 (2044.3)

The Will of God

"Jesus brought to God, as a man of the realm, the greatest of all offerings: the consecration and dedication of his own will to the majestic service of doing the divine will." 196:0.10 (2088.5)

The Will of God

What is the Will of God?	This was a conference which lasted well into the night, in the course of which the young man requested Jesus to tell him the difference between the will of God and that human mind act of choosing which is also called will. In substance Jesus said: The will of God is the way of God, partnership with the choice of God in the face of any potential alternative. To do the will of God, therefore, is the progressive experience of becoming more and more like God, and God is the source and destiny of all that is good and beautiful and true. The will of man is the way of man, the sum and substance of that which the mortal chooses to be and do. Will is the deliberate choice of a self-conscious being which leads to decision-conduct based on intelligent reflection. 130:2.7 (1431.2)
	The apostles all loved and respected Nathaniel, and he got along with them splendidly, excepting Judas Iscariot. Judas did not think Nathaniel took his apostleship sufficiently seriously and once had the temerity to go secretly to Jesus and lodge complaint against him. Said Jesus: "Judas, watch carefully your steps; do not overmagnify your office. Who of us is competent to judge his brother? It is not the Father's will that his children should partake only of the serious things of life. Let me repeat: I have come that my brethren in the flesh may have joy, gladness, and life more abundantly. 139:6.5 (1558.6)
	The human Jesus saw God as being holy, just, and great, as well as being true, beautiful, and good. All these attributes of divinity he focused in his mind as the "will of the Father in heaven." Jesus' God was at one and the same time "The Holy One of Israel" and "The living and loving Father in heaven." The concept of God as a Father was not original with Jesus, but he exalted and elevated the idea into a sublime experience by achieving a new revelation of God and by proclaiming that every mortal creature is a child of this Father of love, a son of God. 196:0.2 (2087.2)
Learning How to Follow the Will of God:	The highest level to which a finite creature can progress is the recognition of the Universal Father and the knowing of the Supreme. And even then such beings of finality destiny go on experiencing change in the motions of the physical world and in its material phenomena. Likewise do they remain aware of selfhood progression in their continuing ascension of the spiritual universe and of growing consciousness in their deepening appreciation of, and response to, the intellectual cosmos. Only in the perfection, harmony, and unanimity of will can the creature become as one with the Creator; and such a state of divinity is attained and maintained only by the creature's continuing to live in time and eternity by consistently conforming his finite personal will to the divine will of the Creator. Always must the desire to do the Father's will be supreme in the soul and dominant over the mind of an ascending son of God. 130:4.3 (1434.2)
	But great sorrow later attended the misinterpretation of the Master's inferences regarding prayer. There would have been little difficulty about these teachings if his exact words had been remembered and subsequently truthfully recorded. But as the record was made, believers eventually regarded prayer in Jesus' name as a sort of supreme magic, thinking that they would receive from the Father anything they asked for. For centuries honest souls have continued to wreck their faith against this stumbling block. How long will it take the world of believers to

Learning How to Follow the Will of God: (Continued)	understand that prayer is not a process of getting your way but rather a program of taking God's way, an experience of learning how to recognize and execute the Father's will? It is entirely true that, when your will has been truly aligned with his, you can ask anything conceived by that will-union, and it will be granted. And such a will-union is effected by and through Jesus even as the life of the vine flows into and through the living branches. 180:2.4 (1946.2)
Help Doing God's Will From the Spirit of Truth:	[Jesus said to James Zebedee:] "Whether your ministry be long or short, possess your soul in patience. When the new teacher comes, let him teach you the poise of compassion and that sympathetic tolerance which is born of sublime confidence in me and of perfect submission to the Father's will. 181:2.15 (1958.2)
	The coming of the Spirit of Truth purifies the human heart and leads the recipient to formulate a life purpose single to the will of God and the welfare of men. 194:3.19 (2065.7)
Relation of the Will of God to the Kingdom of Heaven:	"When you are the subjects of this kingdom, you indeed are made to hear the law of the Universe Ruler; but when, because of the gospel of the kingdom which I have come to declare, you faith-discover yourselves as sons, you henceforth look not upon yourselves as law-subject creatures of an all-powerful king but as privileged sons of a loving and divine Father. Verily, verily, I say to you, when the Father's will is your *law,* you are hardly in the kingdom. But when the Father's will becomes truly your *will,* then are you in very truth in the kingdom because the kingdom has thereby become an established experience in you. When God's will is your law, you are noble slave subjects; but when you believe in this new gospel of divine sonship, my Father's will becomes your will, and you are elevated to the high position of the free children of God, liberated sons of the kingdom." 141:2.2 (1588.5)
	To Jesus the kingdom was the sum of those *individuals* who had confessed their faith in the fatherhood of God, thereby declaring their wholehearted dedication to the doing of the will of God, thus becoming members of the spiritual brotherhood of man. 170:5.11 (1865.1)
	Sooner or later another and greater John the Baptist is due to arise proclaiming "the kingdom of God is at hand"—meaning a return to the high spiritual concept of Jesus, who proclaimed that the kingdom is the will of his heavenly Father dominant and transcendent in the heart of the believer—and doing all this without in any way referring either to the visible church on earth or to the anticipated second coming of Christ. 170:5.19 (1866.2)
	Although this gospel of the kingdom never fails to bring great peace to the soul of the individual believer, it will not bring peace on earth until man is willing to believe my teaching wholeheartedly and to establish the practice of doing the Father's will as the chief purpose in living the mortal life. 180:6.1 (1951.2)
	Jesus saw in the advanced and ideal fellowship of the kingdom the fulfillment of the "will of God." The very heart of the prayer which he taught his disciples was, "Your kingdom come; your will be done." Having thus conceived of the kingdom as comprising the will of God, he devoted himself to the cause of its realization with amazing self-forgetfulness and unbounded enthusiasm. 196:0.8 (2088.3)

	Revealed truth, personally discovered truth, is the supreme delight of the human soul; it is the joint creation of the material mind and the indwelling spirit. The eternal salvation of this truth-discerning and beauty-loving soul is assured by that hunger and thirst for goodness which leads this mortal to develop a singleness of purpose to do the Father's will, to find God and to become like him. There is never conflict between true knowledge and truth. There may be conflict between knowledge and human beliefs, beliefs colored with prejudice, distorted by fear, and dominated by the dread of facing new facts of material discovery or spiritual progress. 132:3.4 (1459.4)
	What a scene for the celestial intelligences to behold, this spectacle of the Indian lad proposing to the Creator of a universe that they make a new religion! And though the young man did not know it, they were making a new and everlasting religion right then and there—this new way of salvation, the revelation of God to man through, and in, Jesus. That which the lad wanted most to do he was unconsciously actually doing. And it was, and is, ever thus. That which the enlightened and reflective human imagination of spiritual teaching and leading wholeheartedly and unselfishly wants to do and be, becomes measurably creative in accordance with the degree of mortal dedication to the divine doing of the Father's will. When man goes in partnership with God, great things may, and do, happen. 132:7.9 (1467.5)
Benefits of Our Choosing to Do the Will of God:	Jesus portrayed to all the worlds of his vast universe the folly of creating artificial situations for the purpose of exhibiting arbitrary authority or of indulging exceptional power for the purpose of enhancing moral values or accelerating spiritual progress. Jesus decided that he would not lend his mission on earth to a repetition of the disappointment of the reign of the Maccabees. He refused to prostitute his divine attributes for the purpose of acquiring unearned popularity or for gaining political prestige. He would not countenance the transmutation of divine and creative energy into national power or international prestige. Jesus of Nazareth refused to compromise with *evil,* much less to consort with sin. The Master triumphantly put loyalty to his Father's will above every other earthly and temporal consideration. 136:8.8 (1521.3)
	"Every earth child who follows the leading of this spirit shall eventually know the will of God, and he who surrenders to the will of my Father shall abide forever. The way from the earth life to the eternal estate has not been made plain to you, but there is a way, there always has been, and I have come to make that way new and living. He who enters the kingdom has eternal life already—he shall never perish. 146:3.7 (1642.3)
	"*The spiritual level.* And then last, but greatest of all, we attain the level of spirit insight and spiritual interpretation which impels us to recognize in this rule of life the divine command to treat all men as we conceive God would treat them. That is the universe ideal of human relationships. And this is your attitude toward all such problems when your supreme desire is ever to do the Father's will. I would, therefore, that you should do to all men that which you know I would do to them in like circumstances." 147:4.9 (1651.3)

	One of the visiting Pharisees, mounting a lampstand, shouted out this question: "You tell us that you are the bread of life. How can you give us your flesh to eat or your blood to drink? What avail is your teaching if it cannot be carried out?" And Jesus answered this question, saying: "I did not teach you that my flesh is the bread of life nor that my blood is the water thereof. But I did say that my life in the flesh is a bestowal of the bread of heaven. The fact of the Word of God bestowed in the flesh and the phenomenon of the Son of Man subject to the will of God, constitute a reality of experience which is equivalent to the divine sustenance. You cannot eat my flesh nor can you drink my blood, but you can become one in spirit with me even as I am one in spirit with the Father. You can be nourished by the eternal word of God, which is indeed the bread of life, and which has been bestowed in the likeness of mortal flesh; and you can be watered in soul by the divine spirit, which is truly the water of life. The Father has sent me into the world to show how he desires to indwell and direct all men; and I have so lived this life in the flesh as to inspire all men likewise ever to seek to know and do the will of the indwelling heavenly Father." 153:3.2 (1712.2)
Benefits of Our Choosing to Do the Will of God: (Continued)	Never forget there is only one adventure which is more satisfying and thrilling than the attempt to discover the will of the living God, and that is the supreme experience of honestly trying to do that divine will. And fail not to remember that the will of God can be done in any earthly occupation. Some callings are not holy and others secular. All things are sacred in the lives of those who are spirit led; that is, subordinated to truth, ennobled by love, dominated by mercy, and restrained by fairness—justice. The spirit which my Father and I shall send into the world is not only the Spirit of Truth but also the spirit of idealistic beauty. 155:6.11 (1732.4)
	"The Father's human children have equal capacity for the reception of material blessings; therefore does he bestow things physical upon the children of men without discrimination. When it comes to the bestowal of spiritual gifts, the Father is limited by man's capacity for receiving these divine endowments. Although the Father is no respecter of persons, in the bestowal of spiritual gifts he is limited by man's faith and by his willingness always to abide by the Father's will." 166:4.11 (1831.2)
	The peace which Michael gives his children on earth is that very peace which filled his own soul when he himself lived the mortal life in the flesh and on this very world. The peace of Jesus is the joy and satisfaction of a God-knowing individual who has achieved the triumph of learning fully how to do the will of God while living the mortal life in the flesh. The peace of Jesus' mind was founded on an absolute human faith in the actuality of the divine Father's wise and sympathetic overcare. Jesus had trouble on earth, he has even been falsely called the "man of sorrows," but in and through all of these experiences he enjoyed the comfort of that confidence which ever empowered him to proceed with his life purpose in the full assurance that he was achieving the Father's will. 181:1.8 (1954.5)

<table>
<tr><td rowspan="5">Jesus' Life Consecrated to Doing the Father's Will:</td><td>Doing the Father's will. Jesus' teaching to trust in the overcare of the heavenly Father was not a blind and passive fatalism. He quoted with approval, on this afternoon, an old Hebrew saying: "He who will not work shall not eat." He pointed to his own experience as sufficient commentary on his teachings. His precepts about trusting the Father must not be adjudged by the social or economic conditions of modern times or any other age. His instruction embraces the ideal principles of living near God in all ages and on all worlds. 140:8.2 (1579.4)</td></tr>
<tr><td>Along with the faith of the creature and the life of the Creator it should also be noted that this God-man was the personified expression of the Father's will. If, in the contact of the human need and the divine power to meet it, the Father did not will otherwise, the two became one, and the healing occurred unconsciously to the human Jesus but was immediately recognized by his divine nature. The explanation, then, of many of these cases of healing must be found in a great law which has long been known to us, namely, What the Creator Son desires and the eternal Father wills IS. 149:1.7 (1669.6)</td></tr>
<tr><td>"You who would follow after me from this time on, must be willing to pay the price of wholehearted dedication to the doing of my Father's will. If you would be my disciples, you must be willing to forsake father, mother, wife, children, brothers, and sisters. If any one of you would now be my disciple, you must be willing to give up even your life just as the Son of Man is about to offer up his life for the completion of the mission of doing the Father's will on earth and in the flesh. 171:2.2 (1869.4)</td></tr>
<tr><td>"When I came into this chamber tonight, you were not content proudly to refuse to wash one another's feet, but you must also fall to disputing among yourselves as to who should have the places of honor at my table. Such honors the Pharisees and the children of this world seek, but it should not be so among the ambassadors of the heavenly kingdom. Do you not know that there can be no place of preferment at my table? Do you not understand that I love each of you as I do the others? Do you not know that the place nearest me, as men regard such honors, can mean nothing concerning your standing in the kingdom of heaven? You know that the kings of the gentiles have lordship over their subjects, while those who exercise this authority are sometimes called benefactors. But it shall not be so in the kingdom of heaven. He who would be great among you, let him become as the younger; while he who would be chief, let him become as one who serves. Who is the greater, he who sits at meat, or he who serves? Is it not commonly regarded that he who sits at meat is the greater? But you will observe that I am among you as one who serves. If you are willing to become fellow servants with me in doing the Father's will, in the kingdom to come you shall sit with me in power, still doing the Father's will in future glory." 179:3.9 (1940.1)</td></tr>
<tr><td>It was well that the Roman soldiers took possession of the Master's clothing. Otherwise, if his followers had gained possession of these garments, they would have been tempted to resort to superstitious relic worship. The Master desired that his followers should have nothing material to associate with his life on earth. He wanted to leave mankind only the memory of a human life dedicated to the high spiritual ideal of being consecrated to doing the Father's will. 187:2.9 (2008.1)</td></tr>
</table>

Jesus' Life Consecrated to Doing the Father's Will: (Continued)	Jesus' devotion to the Father's will and the service of man was even more than mortal decision and human determination; it was a wholehearted consecration of himself to such an unreserved bestowal of love. No matter how great the fact of the sovereignty of Michael, you must not take the human Jesus away from men. The Master has ascended on high as a man, as well as God; he belongs to men; men belong to him. How unfortunate that religion itself should be so misinterpreted as to take the human Jesus away from struggling mortals! Let not the discussions of the humanity or the divinity of the Christ obscure the saving truth that Jesus of Nazareth was a religious man who, by faith, achieved the knowing and the doing of the will of God; he was the most truly religious man who has ever lived on Urantia. 196:1.1 (2090.2)
	Jesus founded the religion of personal experience in doing the will of God and serving the human brotherhood; Paul founded a religion in which the glorified Jesus became the object of worship and the brotherhood consisted of fellow believers in the divine Christ. In the bestowal of Jesus these two concepts were potential in his divine-human life, and it is indeed a pity that his followers failed to create a unified religion which might have given proper recognition to both the human and the divine natures of the Master as they were inseparably bound up in his earth life and so gloriously set forth in the original gospel of the kingdom. 196:2.6 (2092.4)
Transgression of the Father's will:	"Make clear in your mind these different attitudes toward the Father and his universe. Never forget these laws of relation to the Father's will: 148:4.2 (1660.1) "Evil is the unconscious or unintended transgression of the divine law, the Father's will. Evil is likewise the measure of the imperfectness of obedience to the Father's will. 148:4.3 (1660.2) "Sin is the conscious, knowing, and deliberate transgression of the divine law, the Father's will. Sin is the measure of unwillingness to be divinely led and spiritually directed. 148:4.4 (1660.3) "Iniquity is the willful, determined, and persistent transgression of the divine law, the Father's will. Iniquity is the measure of the continued rejection of the Father's loving plan of personality survival and the Sons' merciful ministry of salvation. 148:4.5 (1660.4)
	"But, my son, you should know that the Father does not purposely afflict his children. Man brings down upon himself unnecessary affliction as a result of his persistent refusal to walk in the better ways of the divine will. Affliction is potential in evil, but much of it has been produced by sin and iniquity. Many unusual events have transpired on this world, and it is not strange that all thinking men should be perplexed by the scenes of suffering and affliction which they witness. But of one thing you may be sure: The Father does not send affliction as an arbitrary punishment for wrongdoing. The imperfections and handicaps of evil are inherent; the penalties of sin are inevitable; the destroying consequences of iniquity are inexorable. Man should not blame God for those afflictions which are the natural result of the life which he chooses to live; neither should man complain of those experiences which are a part of life as it is lived on this world. It is the Father's will that mortal man should work persistently and consistently toward the betterment of his estate on earth. Intelligent application would enable man to overcome much of his earthly misery. 148:5.3 (1661.5)

Jesus' Promises To Us

"And they found the Master's words to be true when they put his promises to the test. And since that day countless thousands also have tested and proved the surety of these same promises." 163:6.8 (1808.2)

Jesus' Promises to Us

The Promise of Eternal Life:	"All things come from, and belong to, the One God—all-wise, good, righteous, holy, resplendent, and glorious. This, our God, is the source of all luminosity. He is the Creator, the God of all good purposes, and the protector of the justice of the universe. The wise course in life is to act in consonance with the spirit of truth. God is all-seeing, and he beholds both the evil deeds of the wicked and the good works of the righteous; our God observes all things with a flashing eye. His touch is the touch of healing. The Lord is an all-powerful benefactor. God stretches out his beneficent hand to both the righteous and the wicked. God established the world and ordained the rewards for good and for evil. The all-wise God has promised immortality to the pious souls who think purely and act righteously. As you supremely desire, so shall you be. The light of the sun is as wisdom to those who discern God in the universe. 131:5.2 (1450.1)
	"And now, Simon, when you do finally see all of this, and after you have shaken off your depression and have gone forth proclaiming this gospel in great power, never forget that I was with you even through all of your season of discouragement, and that I will go on with you to the very end. You shall always be my apostle, and after you become willing to see by the eye of the spirit and more fully to yield your will to the will of the Father in heaven, then will you return to labor as my ambassador, and no one shall take away from you the authority which I have conferred upon you, because of your slowness of comprehending the truths I have taught you. And so, Simon, once more I warn you that they who fight with the sword perish with the sword, while they who labor in the spirit achieve life everlasting in the kingdom to come with joy and peace in the kingdom which now is. And when the work given into your hands is finished on earth, you, Simon, shall sit down with me in my kingdom over there. You shall really see the kingdom you have longed for, but not in this life. Continue to believe in me and in that which I have revealed to you, and you shall receive the gift of eternal life." 181:2.11 (1957.1)
	"Father, my hour has come; now glorify your Son that the Son may glorify you. I know that you have given me full authority over all living creatures in my realm, and I will give eternal life to all who will become faith sons of God. And this is eternal life, that my creatures should know you as the only true God and Father of all, and that they should believe in him whom you sent into the world. Father, I have exalted you on earth and have accomplished the work which you gave me to do. I have almost finished my bestowal upon the children of our own creation; there remains only for me to lay down my life in the flesh. And now, O my Father, glorify me with the glory which I had with you before this world was and receive me once more at your right hand. 182:1.3 (1963.5)
Jesus' Promises to His Family:	Mary endeavored to influence Joseph to permit Jesus to model in clay at home, provided he promised not to carry on any of these questionable activities at school, but Joseph felt impelled to rule that the rabbinical interpretation of the second commandment should prevail. And so Jesus no more drew or modeled the likeness of anything from that day as long as he lived in his father's house. But he was unconvinced of the wrong of what he had done, and to give up such a favorite pastime constituted one of the great trials of his young life. 124:1.5 (1367.1)

Jesus' Promises to Us

Jesus' Promises to His Family: (Continued)	Before taking up his new employment at Sepphoris, Jesus held one of his periodic family conferences and solemnly installed James, then just past eighteen years old, as acting head of the family. He promised his brother hearty support and full co-operation and exacted formal promises of obedience to James from each member of the family. From this day James assumed full financial responsibility for the family, Jesus making his weekly payments to his brother. Never again did Jesus take the reins out of James's hands. While working at Sepphoris he could have walked home every night if necessary, but he purposely remained away, assigning weather and other reasons, but his true motive was to train James and Joseph in the bearing of the family responsibility. He had begun the slow process of weaning his family. Each Sabbath Jesus returned to Nazareth, and sometimes during the week when occasion required, to observe the working of the new plan, to give advice and offer helpful suggestions. 128:2.4 (1410.3)
	And now things began to happen—marriage was in the air. James's success in gaining Jesus' assent to his marriage emboldened Miriam to approach her brother-father with her plans. Jacob, the younger stone mason, onetime self-appointed champion of Jesus, now business associate of James and Joseph, had long sought to gain Miriam's hand in marriage. After Miriam had laid her plans before Jesus, he directed that Jacob should come to him making formal request for her and promised his blessing for the marriage just as soon as she felt that Martha was competent to assume her duties as eldest daughter. 128:5.8 (1414.6)
God's Promises to Man:	The presence of the Paradise spirit in the mind of man constitutes the revelation promise and the faith pledge of an eternal existence of divine progression for every soul seeking to achieve identity with this immortal and indwelling spirit fragment of the Universal Father. 132:3.9 (1460.2)
	"By the old way you seek to suppress, obey, and conform to the rules of living; by the new way you are first *transformed* by the Spirit of Truth and thereby strengthened in your inner soul by the constant spiritual renewing of your mind, and so are you endowed with the power of the certain and joyous performance of the gracious, acceptable, and perfect will of God. Forget not—it is your personal faith in the exceedingly great and precious promises of God that ensures your becoming partakers of the divine nature. Thus by your faith and the spirit's transformation, you become in reality the temples of God, and his spirit actually dwells within you. If, then, the spirit dwells within you, you are no longer bondslaves of the flesh but free and liberated sons of the spirit. The new law of the spirit endows you with the liberty of self-mastery in place of the old law of the fear of self-bondage and the slavery of self-denial. 143:2.4 (1609.5)
	Although Jesus referred one phase of the kingdom to the future and did, on numerous occasions, intimate that such an event might appear as a part of a world crisis; and though he did likewise most certainly, on several occasions, definitely promise sometime to return to Urantia, it should be recorded that he never positively linked these two ideas together. He promised a new revelation of the kingdom on earth and at some future time; he also promised sometime to come back to this world in person; but he did not say that these two events were synonymous. From all we know these promises may, or may not, refer to the same event. 170:4.15 (1863.13)

Jesus' Promises to Us

God's Promises to Man: (Continued)	In further answer to Peter's question, Jesus said: "Why do you still look for the Son of Man to sit upon the throne of David and expect that the material dreams of the Jews will be fulfilled? Have I not told you all these years that my kingdom is not of this world? The things which you now look down upon are coming to an end, but this will be a new beginning out of which the gospel of the kingdom will go to all the world and this salvation will spread to all peoples. And when the kingdom shall have come to its full fruition, be assured that the Father in heaven will not fail to visit you with an enlarged revelation of truth and an enhanced demonstration of righteousness, even as he has already bestowed upon this world him who became the prince of darkness, and then Adam, who was followed by Melchizedek, and in these days, the Son of Man. And so will my Father continue to manifest his mercy and show forth his love, even to this dark and evil world. So also will I, after my Father has invested me with all power and authority, continue to follow your fortunes and to guide in the affairs of the kingdom by the presence of my spirit, who shall shortly be poured out upon all flesh. Even though I shall thus be present with you in spirit, I also promise that I will sometime return to this world, where I have lived this life in the flesh and achieved the experience of simultaneously revealing God to man and leading man to God. Very soon must I leave you and take up the work the Father has intrusted to my hands, but be of good courage, for I will sometime return. In the meantime, my Spirit of the Truth of a universe shall comfort and guide you. 176:2.3 (1914.4)
	Jesus promised to do two things after he had ascended to the Father, and after all power in heaven and on earth had been placed in his hands. He promised, first, to send into the world, and in his stead, another teacher, the Spirit of Truth; and this he did on the day of Pentecost. Second, he most certainly promised his followers that he would sometime personally return to this world. But he did not say how, where, or when he would revisit this planet of his bestowal experience in the flesh. On one occasion he intimated that, whereas the eye of flesh had beheld him when he lived here in the flesh, on his return (at least on one of his possible visits) he would be discerned only by the eye of spiritual faith. 176:4.3 (1918.6)
The Promise of Better Relations:	When Jacob finished speaking, Jesus replied: "Jacob, you have well stated the teachings of the olden prophets who taught the children of their generation in accordance with the light of their day. Our Father in Paradise is changeless. But the concept of his nature has enlarged and grown from the days of Moses down through the times of Amos and even to the generation of the prophet Isaiah. And now have I come in the flesh to reveal the Father in new glory and to show forth his love and mercy to all men on all worlds. As the gospel of this kingdom shall spread over the world with its message of good cheer and good will to all men, there will grow up improved and better relations among the families of all nations. As time passes, fathers and their children will love each other more, and thus will be brought about a better understanding of the love of the Father in heaven for his children on earth. Remember, Jacob, that a good and true father not only loves his family as a whole—as a family—but he also truly loves and affectionately cares for each *individual* member." 142:2.2 (1597.2)

Jesus' Promises to Us

Joy, Spiritual Progress:	"I have come to preach the glad tidings of the kingdom. I have not come to add to the heavy burdens of those who would enter this kingdom. I proclaim the new and better way, and those who are able to enter the coming kingdom shall enjoy the divine rest. And whatever it shall cost you in the things of the world, no matter what price you may pay to enter the kingdom of heaven, you shall receive manyfold more of joy and spiritual progress in this world, and in the age to come eternal life. 137:8.14 (1537.1)
On Urantia, This Gospel Will Rule:	"I have come into this world to do the will of my Father and to reveal his loving character to all mankind. That, my brethren, is my mission. And this one thing I will do, regardless of the misunderstanding of my teachings by Jews or gentiles of this day or of another generation. But you should not overlook the fact that even divine love has its severe disciplines. A father's love for his son oftentimes impels the father to restrain the unwise acts of his thoughtless offspring. The child does not always comprehend the wise and loving motives of the father's restraining discipline. But I declare to you that my Father in Paradise does rule a universe of universes by the compelling power of his love. Love is the greatest of all spirit realities. Truth is a liberating revelation, but love is the supreme relationship. And no matter what blunders your fellow men make in their world management of today, in an age to come the gospel which I declare to you will rule this very world. The ultimate goal of human progress is the reverent recognition of the fatherhood of God and the loving materialization of the brotherhood of man. 143:1.4 (1608.1)
Ask and You Shall Receive:	"Prayer is the breath of the soul and should lead you to be persistent in your attempt to ascertain the Father's will. If any one of you has a neighbor, and you go to him at midnight and say: 'Friend, lend me three loaves, for a friend of mine on a journey has come to see me, and I have nothing to set before him'; and if your neighbor answers, 'Trouble me not, for the door is now shut and the children and I are in bed; therefore I cannot rise and give you bread,' you will persist, explaining that your friend hungers, and that you have no food to offer him. I say to you, though your neighbor will not rise and give you bread because he is your friend, yet because of your importunity he will get up and give you as many loaves as you need. If, then, persistence will win favors even from mortal man, how much more will your persistence in the spirit win the bread of life for you from the willing hands of the Father in heaven. Again I say to you: Ask and it shall be given you; seek and you shall find; knock and it shall be opened to you. For every one who asks receives; he who seeks finds; and to him who knocks the door of salvation will be opened. 144:2.3 (1619.1)
Indwelling Spirit (Thought Adjuster):	"Every earth child who follows the leading of this spirit shall eventually know the will of God, and he who surrenders to the will of my Father shall abide forever. The way from the earth life to the eternal estate has not been made plain to you, but there is a way, there always has been, and I have come to make that way new and living. He who enters the kingdom has eternal life already—he shall never perish. But much of this you will the better understand when I shall have returned to the Father and you are able to view your present experiences in retrospect." 146:3.7 (1642.3)

Jesus' Promises to Us

Words of Truth:	Jesus made it clear to the twenty-four that he had not fled from Galilee because he lacked courage to confront his enemies. They comprehended that he was not yet ready for an open clash with established religion, and that he did not seek to become a martyr. It was during one of these conferences at the home of Justa that the Master first told his disciples that "even though heaven and earth shall pass away, my words of truth shall not." 156:2.5 (1736.2)
The Promise of Peace:	"It would appear that the Father in heaven has hidden some of these truths from the wise and haughty, while he has revealed them to babes. But the Father does all things well; the Father reveals himself to the universe by the methods of his own choosing. Come, therefore, all you who labor and are heavy laden, and you shall find rest for your souls. Take upon you the divine yoke, and you will experience the peace of God, which passes all understanding." 144:8.8 (1627.5)
	"And now, as I am about to leave you, I would speak words of comfort. Peace I leave with you; my peace I give to you. I make these gifts not as the world gives—by measure—I give each of you all you will receive. Let not your heart be troubled, neither let it be fearful. I have overcome the world, and in me you shall all triumph through faith. I have warned you that the Son of Man will be killed, but I assure you I will come back before I go to the Father, even though it be for only a little while. And after I have ascended to the Father, I will surely send the new teacher to be with you and to abide in your very hearts. And when you see all this come to pass, be not dismayed, but rather believe, inasmuch as you knew it all beforehand. I have loved you with a great affection, and I would not leave you, but it is the Father's will. My hour has come. 181:1.5 (1954.2)
Forgiveness of Sins:	Said Jesus: "My disciples must not only cease to do evil but learn to do well; you must not only be cleansed from all conscious sin, but you must refuse to harbor even the feelings of guilt. If you confess your sins, they are forgiven; therefore must you maintain a conscience void of offense." 156:2.7 (1736.4)
These Many Things:	When my children once become self-conscious of the assurance of the divine presence, such a faith will expand the mind, ennoble the soul, reinforce the personality, augment the happiness, deepen the spirit perception, and enhance the power to love and be loved. 159:3.12 (1766.8)
To Be With Us Through Adversity:	Teach all believers that those who enter the kingdom are not thereby rendered immune to the accidents of time or to the ordinary catastrophes of nature. Believing the gospel will not prevent getting into trouble, but it will insure that you shall be *unafraid* when trouble does overtake you. If you dare to believe in me and wholeheartedly proceed to follow after me, you shall most certainly by so doing enter upon the sure pathway to trouble. I do not promise to deliver you from the waters of adversity, but I do promise to go with you through all of them. 159:3.13 (1767.1)

Jesus' Promises to Us

Spiritual Rest For Your Soul:	"You have entered upon this great work of teaching mortal man that he is a son of God. I have shown you the way; go forth to do your duty and be not weary in well doing. To you and to all who shall follow in your steps down through the ages, let me say: I always stand near, and my invitation-call is, and ever shall be, Come to me all you who labor and are heavy laden, and I will give you rest. Take my yoke upon you and learn of me, for I am true and loyal, and you shall find spiritual rest for your souls." 163:6.7 (1808.1)
Jesus' Promises to the Father:	"But I have many other sheep not of this fold, and these words are true not only of this world. These other sheep also hear and know my voice, and I have promised the Father that they shall all be brought into one fold, one brotherhood of the sons of God. And then shall you all know the voice of one shepherd, the true shepherd, and shall all acknowledge the fatherhood of God. 165:2.9 (1819.5)
Jesus' Promise to Rise From the Dead:	Early on Thursday morning before the others were awake, Jesus called Andrew and said: "Awaken your brethren! I have something to say to them." Jesus knew about the swords and which of his apostles had received and were wearing these weapons, but he never disclosed to them that he knew such things. When Andrew had aroused his associates, and they had assembled off by themselves, Jesus said: "My children, you have been with me a long while, and I have taught you much that is needful for this time, but I would now warn you not to put your trust in the uncertainties of the flesh nor in the frailties of man's defense against the trials and testing which lie ahead of us. I have called you apart here by yourselves that I may once more plainly tell you that we are going up to Jerusalem, where you know the Son of Man has already been condemned to death. Again am I telling you that the Son of Man will be delivered into the hands of the chief priests and the religious rulers; that they will condemn him and then deliver him into the hands of the gentiles. And so will they mock the Son of Man, even spit upon him and scourge him, and they will deliver him up to death. And when they kill the Son of Man, be not dismayed, for I declare that on the third day he shall rise. Take heed to yourselves and remember that I have forewarned you." 171:4.2 (1871.4)
Fruits of the Spirit:	Then Jesus stood up again and continued teaching his apostles: "I am the true vine, and my Father is the husbandman. I am the vine, and you are the branches. And the Father requires of me only that you shall bear much fruit. The vine is pruned only to increase the fruitfulness of its branches. Every branch coming out of me which bears no fruit, the Father will take away. Every branch which bears fruit, the Father will cleanse that it may bear more fruit. Already are you clean through the word I have spoken, but you must continue to be clean. You must abide in me, and I in you; the branch will die if it is separated from the vine. As the branch cannot bear fruit except it abides in the vine, so neither can you yield the fruits of loving service except you abide in me. Remember: I am the real vine, and you are the living branches. He who lives in me, and I in him, will bear much fruit of the spirit and experience the supreme joy of yielding this spiritual harvest. If you will maintain this living spiritual connection with me, you will bear abundant fruit. 180:2.1 (1945.4)

Jesus' Promises to Us

Liberty—Joy of Salvation:	"I bear none of you ill will. The Father loves you, and therefore do I long for your deliverance from the bondage of prejudice and the darkness of tradition. I offer you the liberty of life and the joy of salvation. I proclaim the new and living way, the deliverance from evil and the breaking of the bondage of sin. I have come that you might have life, and have it eternally. You seek to be rid of me and my disquieting teachings. If you could only realize that I am to be with you only a little while! In just a short time I go to Him who sent me into this world. And then will many of you diligently seek me, but you shall not discover my presence, for where I am about to go you cannot come. But all who truly seek to find me shall sometime attain the life that leads to my Father's presence." 162:2.7 (1792.1)
Spirit is Always With You:	Throughout the vicissitudes of life, remember always to love one another. Do not strive with men, even with unbelievers. Show mercy even to those who despitefully abuse you. Show yourselves to be loyal citizens, upright artisans, praiseworthy neighbors, devoted kinsmen, understanding parents, and sincere believers in the brotherhood of the Father's kingdom. And my spirit shall be upon you, now and even to the end of the world. 178:1.17 (1932.2)
	"Peace be upon you. You rejoice to know that I am the resurrection and the life, but this will avail you nothing unless you are first born of the eternal spirit, thereby coming to possess, by faith, the gift of eternal life. If you are the faith sons of my Father, you shall never die; you shall not perish. The gospel of the kingdom has taught you that all men are the sons of God. And this good news concerning the love of the heavenly Father for his children on earth must be carried to all the world. The time has come when you worship God neither on Gerizim nor at Jerusalem, but where you are, as you are, in spirit and in truth. It is your faith that saves your souls. Salvation is the gift of God to all who believe they are his sons. But be not deceived; while salvation is the free gift of God and is bestowed upon all who accept it by faith, there follows the experience of bearing the fruits of this spirit life as it is lived in the flesh. The acceptance of the doctrine of the fatherhood of God implies that you also freely accept the associated truth of the brotherhood of man. And if man is your brother, he is even more than your neighbor, whom the Father requires you to love as yourself. Your brother, being of your own family, you will not only love with a family affection, but you will also serve as you would serve yourself. And you will thus love and serve your brother because you, being my brethren, have been thus loved and served by me. Go, then, into all the world telling this good news to all creatures of every race, tribe, and nation. My spirit shall go before you, and I will be with you always." 193:1.2 (2053.4)
Father Will Grant Petitions:	If you abide in me and my words live in you, you will be able to commune freely with me, and then can my living spirit so infuse you that you may ask whatsoever my spirit wills and do all this with the assurance that the Father will grant us our petition. Herein is the Father glorified: that the vine has many living branches, and that every branch bears much fruit. And when the world sees these fruit-bearing branches—my friends who love one another, even as I have loved them—all men will know that you are truly my disciples. 180:2.1 (1945.4)

Jesus' Promises to Us

Jesus' Promise Not to Leave Us Alone or Without Help:	Jesus continued to teach, saying: "When I have gone to the Father, and after he has fully accepted the work I have done for you on earth, and after I have received the final sovereignty of my own domain, I shall say to my Father: Having left my children alone on earth, it is in accordance with my promise to send them another teacher. And when the Father shall approve, I will pour out the Spirit of Truth upon all flesh. Already is my Father's spirit in your hearts, and when this day shall come, you will also have me with you even as you now have the Father. This new gift is the spirit of living truth. The unbelievers will not at first listen to the teachings of this spirit, but the sons of light will all receive him gladly and with a whole heart. And you shall know this spirit when he comes even as you have known me, and you will receive this gift in your hearts, and he will abide with you. You thus perceive that I am not going to leave you without help and guidance. I will not leave you desolate. Today I can be with you only in person. In the times to come I will be with you and all other men who desire my presence, wherever you may be, and with each of you at the same time. Do you not discern that it is better for me to go away; that I leave you in the flesh so that I may the better and the more fully be with you in the spirit? 180:4.1 (1948.2)
	"But I will not leave you alone in the world. Very soon, after I have gone, I will send you a spirit helper. You shall have with you one who will take my place among you, one who will continue to teach you the way of truth, who will even comfort you. 180:3.3 (1947.2)
Illuminating the Difference Between Sin and Righteousness:	"Now that I am leaving you, seeing that the hour has come when I am about to go to the Father, I am surprised that none of you have asked me, Why do you leave us? Nevertheless, I know that you ask such questions in your hearts. I will speak to you plainly, as one friend to another. It is really profitable for you that I go away. If I go not away, the new teacher cannot come into your hearts. I must be divested of this mortal body and be restored to my place on high before I can send this spirit teacher to live in your souls and lead your spirits into the truth. And when my spirit comes to indwell you, he will illuminate the difference between sin and righteousness and will enable you to judge wisely in your hearts concerning them. 180:6.2 (1951.3)
Jesus' Last Promises:	And since Jesus knew they asked these questions, he said: "Do you inquire among yourselves about what I meant when I said that in a little while I would not be with you, and that, when you would see me again, I would be on my way to the Father? I have plainly told you that the Son of Man must die, but that he will rise again. Can you not then discern the meaning of my words? You will first be made sorrowful, but later on will you rejoice with many who will understand these things after they have come to pass. A woman is indeed sorrowful in the hour of her travail, but when she is once delivered of her child, she immediately forgets her anguish in the joy of the knowledge that a man has been born into the world. And so are you about to sorrow over my departure, but I will soon see you again, and then will your sorrow be turned into rejoicing, and there shall come to you a new revelation of the salvation of God which no man can ever take away from you. And all the worlds will be blessed in this same revelation of life in effecting the overthrow of death. Hitherto have you made all your requests in my Father's name. After you see me again, you may also ask in my name, and I will hear you. 180:6.7 (1952.3)

Jesus' Promises to Us

	Then the Master went over to Simon Peter, who stood up as Jesus addressed him: "Peter, I know you love me, and that you will dedicate your life to the public proclamation of this gospel of the kingdom to Jew and gentile, but I am distressed that your years of such close association with me have not done more to help you think before you speak. What experience must you pass through before you will learn to set a guard upon your lips? How much trouble have you made for us by your thoughtless speaking, by your presumptuous self-confidence! And you are destined to make much more trouble for yourself if you do not master this frailty. You know that your brethren love you in spite of this weakness, and you should also understand that this shortcoming in no way impairs my affection for you, but it lessens your usefulness and never ceases to make trouble for you. But you will undoubtedly receive great help from the experience you will pass through this very night. And what I now say to you, Simon Peter, I likewise say to all your brethren here assembled: This night you will all be in great danger of stumbling over me. You know it is written, 'The shepherd will be smitten and the sheep will be scattered abroad.' When I am absent, there is great danger that some of you will succumb to doubts and stumble because of what befalls me. But I promise you now that I will come back to you for a little while, and that I will then go before you into Galilee." 181:2.27 (1962.2)
Jesus' Last Promises: (Continued)	"But remember my promise: When I am raised up, I will tarry with you for a season before I go to the Father. And even this night will I make supplication to the Father that he strengthen each of you for that which you must now so soon pass through. I love you all with the love wherewith the Father loves me, and therefore should you henceforth love one another, even as I have loved you." 181:2.30 (1962.5)
	"And now, my Father, I would pray not only for these eleven men but also for all others who now believe, or who may hereafter believe the gospel of the kingdom through the word of their future ministry. I want them all to be one, even as you and I are one. You are in me and I am in you, and I desire that these believers likewise be in us; that both of our spirits indwell them. If my children are one as we are one, and if they love one another as I have loved them, all men will then believe that I came forth from you and be willing to receive the revelation of truth and glory which I have made. The glory which you gave me I have revealed to these believers. As you have lived with me in spirit, so have I lived with them in the flesh. As you have been one with me, so have I been one with them, and so will the new teacher ever be one with them and in them. And all this have I done that my brethren in the flesh may know that the Father loves them even as does the Son, and that you love them even as you love me. Father, work with me to save these believers that they may presently come to be with me in glory and then go on to join you in the Paradise embrace. Those who serve with me in humiliation, I would have with me in glory so that they may see all you have given into my hands as the eternal harvest of the seed sowing of time in the likeness of mortal flesh. I long to show my earthly brethren the glory I had with you before the founding of this world. This world knows very little of you, righteous Father, but I know you, and I have made you known to these believers, and they will make known your name to other generations. And now I promise them that you will be with them in the world even as you have been with me—even so." 182:1.6 (1964.3)

Jesus' Promises to Us

Jesus' Last Promises: (Continued)	One of the brigands railed at Jesus, saying, "If you are the Son of God, why do you not save yourself and us?" But when he had reproached Jesus, the other thief, who had many times heard the Master teach, said: "Do you have no fear even of God? Do you not see that we are suffering justly for our deeds, but that this man suffers unjustly? Better that we should seek forgiveness for our sins and salvation for our souls." When Jesus heard the thief say this, he turned his face toward him and smiled approvingly. When the malefactor saw the face of Jesus turned toward him, he mustered up his courage, fanned the flickering flame of his faith, and said, "Lord, remember me when you come into your kingdom." And then Jesus said, "Verily, verily, I say to you today, you shall sometime be with me in Paradise." 187:4.1 (2008.8)
	"I bade you tarry in Jerusalem until you were endowed with power from on high. I am now about to take leave of you; I am about to ascend to my Father, and soon, very soon, will we send into this world of my sojourn the Spirit of Truth; and when he has come, you shall begin the new proclamation of the gospel of the kingdom, first in Jerusalem and then to the uttermost parts of the world. Love men with the love wherewith I have loved you and serve your fellow mortals even as I have served you. By the spirit fruits of your lives impel souls to believe the truth that man is a son of God, and that all men are brethren. Remember all I have taught you and the life I have lived among you. My love overshadows you, my spirit will dwell with you, and my peace shall abide upon you. Farewell." 193:5.2 (2057.4)
Triumph:	Jesus, by the power of his personal love for men, could break the hold of sin and evil. He thereby set men free to choose better ways of living. Jesus portrayed a deliverance from the past which in itself promised a triumph for the future. Forgiveness thus provided salvation. The beauty of divine love, once fully admitted to the human heart, forever destroys the charm of sin and the power of evil. 188:5.3 (2018.2)
To Be With You Always:	"Go, then, into all the world proclaiming this gospel of the fatherhood of God and the brotherhood of men to all nations and races and ever be wise in your choice of methods for presenting the good news to the different races and tribes of mankind. Freely you have received this gospel of the kingdom, and you will freely give the good news to all nations. Fear not the resistance of evil, for I am with you always, even to the end of the ages. And my peace I leave with you." 191:4.4 (2042.1)

The Miracles of Jesus

"Urantia mortals have varying concepts of the miraculous, but to us who live as citizens of the local universe there are few miracles, and of these by far the most intriguing are the incarnational bestowals of the Paradise Sons. The appearance in and on your world, by apparently natural processes, of a divine Son, we regard as a miracle—the operation of universal laws beyond our understanding. Jesus of Nazareth was a miraculous person." 120:4.5 (1331.5)

The Miracles of Jesus

What is a Real Miracle?	Urantia mortals have varying concepts of the miraculous, but to us who live as citizens of the local universe there are few miracles, and of these by far the most intriguing are the incarnational bestowals of the Paradise Sons. The appearance in and on your world, by apparently natural processes, of a divine Son, we regard as a miracle—the operation of universal laws beyond our understanding. Jesus of Nazareth was a miraculous person. 120:4.5 (1331.5)
	Thus did Jesus become apprised of the working out of his decision to go on living as a man among men. He had by a single decision excluded all of his attendant universe hosts of varied intelligences from participating in his ensuing public ministry except in such matters as concerned *time* only. It therefore becomes evident that any possible supernatural or supposedly superhuman accompaniments of Jesus' ministry pertained wholly to the elimination of time unless the Father in heaven specifically ruled otherwise. No miracle, ministry of mercy, or any other possible event occurring in connection with Jesus' remaining earth labors could possibly be of the nature or character of an act transcending the natural laws established and regularly working in the affairs of man as he lives on Urantia *except* in this expressly stated matter of *time.* No limits, of course, could be placed upon the manifestations of "the Father's will." The elimination of time in connection with the expressed desire of this potential Sovereign of a universe could only be avoided by the direct and explicit act of the *will* of this God-man to the effect that time, as related to the act or event in question, *should not be shortened or eliminated.* In order to prevent the appearance of apparent *time miracles,* it was necessary for Jesus to remain constantly time conscious. Any lapse of time consciousness on his part, in connection with the entertainment of definite desire, was equivalent to the enactment of the thing conceived in the mind of this Creator Son, and without the intervention of time. 136:5.5 (1517.1)
	Understanding all of this and knowing that the Master refused to work in defiance of his established laws of nature in so far as his personal conduct was concerned, you know of a certainty that he never walked on the water nor did anything else which was an outrage to his material order of administering the world; always, of course, bearing in mind that there had, as yet, been found no way whereby he could be wholly delivered from the lack of control over the element of time in connection with those matters put under the jurisdiction of the Personalized Adjuster. 136:7.3 (1519.7)
Religion and Miracles:	But religion is never enhanced by an appeal to the so-called miraculous. The quest for miracles is a harking back to the primitive religions of magic. True religion has nothing to do with alleged miracles, and never does revealed religion point to miracles as proof of authority. Religion is ever and always rooted and grounded in personal experience. And your highest religion, the life of Jesus, was just such a personal experience: man, mortal man, seeking God and finding him to the fullness during one short life in the flesh, while in the same human experience there appeared God seeking man and finding him to the full satisfaction of the perfect soul of infinite supremacy. And that is religion, even the highest yet revealed in the universe of Nebadon—the earth life of Jesus of Nazareth. 102:8.7 (1128.3)

The Miracles of Jesus

The Beliefs About Miracles in the Times of Jesus:	The Mediterranean Roman Empire, the Parthian kingdom, and the adjacent peoples of Jesus' time all held crude and primitive ideas regarding the geography of the world, astronomy, health, and disease; and naturally they were amazed by the new and startling pronouncements of the carpenter of Nazareth. The ideas of spirit possession, good and bad, applied not merely to human beings, but every rock and tree was viewed by many as being spirit possessed. This was an enchanted age, and everybody believed in miracles as commonplace occurrences. 121:7.12 (1341.1)
	By the beginning of this year both Joseph and Mary entertained frequent doubts about the destiny of their first-born son. He was indeed a brilliant and lovable child, but he was so difficult to understand, so hard to fathom, and again, nothing extraordinary or miraculous ever happened. Scores of times had his proud mother stood in breathless anticipation, expecting to see her son engage in some superhuman or miraculous performance, but always were her hopes dashed down in cruel disappointment. And all this was discouraging, even disheartening. The devout people of those days truly believed that prophets and men of promise always demonstrated their calling and established their divine authority by performing miracles and working wonders. But Jesus did none of these things; wherefore was the confusion of his parents steadily increased as they contemplated his future. 126:1.5 (1387.5)
	The Jews devoutly believed that, as Moses had delivered their fathers from Egyptian bondage by miraculous wonders, so would the coming Messiah deliver the Jewish people from Roman domination by even greater miracles of power and marvels of racial triumph. The rabbis had gathered together almost five hundred passages from the Scriptures which, notwithstanding their apparent contradictions, they averred were prophetic of the coming Messiah. And amidst all these details of time, technique, and function, they almost completely lost sight of the personality of the promised Messiah. They were looking for a restoration of Jewish national glory—Israel's temporal exaltation—rather than for the salvation of the world. It therefore becomes evident that Jesus of Nazareth could never satisfy this materialistic Messianic concept of the Jewish mind. Many of their reputed Messianic predictions, had they but viewed these prophetic utterances in a different light, would have very naturally prepared their minds for a recognition of Jesus as the terminator of one age and the inaugurator of a new and better dispensation of mercy and salvation for all nations. 136:1.3 (1509.5)
	The healing wonders which every now and then attended Jesus' mission on earth were not a part of his plan of proclaiming the kingdom. They were incidentally inherent in having on earth a divine being of well-nigh unlimited creator prerogatives in association with an unprecedented combination of divine mercy and human sympathy. But such so-called miracles gave Jesus much trouble in that they provided prejudice-raising publicity and afforded much unsought notoriety. 145:3.15 (1633.6)

<table>
<tr><td></td><td>Jesus decided that he would not utilize a single personality of this vast assemblage unless it should become evident that this was his Father's will. Notwithstanding this general decision, this vast host remained with him throughout the balance of his earth life, always in readiness to obey the least expression of their Sovereign's will. Although Jesus did not constantly behold these attendant personalities with his human eyes, his associated Personalized Adjuster did constantly behold, and could communicate with, all of them. 136:5.2 (1516.2)</td></tr>
<tr><td>Jesus' Decisions About Miracles:</td><td>The Jews were expecting a Messiah who would do even greater wonders than Moses, who was reputed to have brought forth water from the rock in a desert place and to have fed their forefathers with manna in the wilderness. Jesus knew the sort of Messiah his compatriots expected, and he had all the powers and prerogatives to measure up to their most sanguine expectations, but he decided against such a magnificent program of power and glory. Jesus looked upon such a course of expected miracle working as a harking back to the olden days of ignorant magic and the degraded practices of the savage medicine men. Possibly, for the salvation of his creatures, he might accelerate natural law, but to transcend his own laws, either for the benefit of himself or the overawing of his fellow men, that he would not do. And the Master's decision was final. 136:6.6 (1518.5)

Jesus sorrowed for his people; he fully understood how they had been led up to the expectation of the coming Messiah, the time when "the earth will yield its fruits ten thousandfold, and on one vine there will be a thousand branches, and each branch will produce a thousand clusters, and each cluster will produce a thousand grapes, and each grape will produce a gallon of wine." The Jews believed the Messiah would usher in an era of miraculous plenty. The Hebrews had long been nurtured on traditions of miracles and legends of wonders. 136:6.7 (1518.6)</td></tr>
<tr><td></td><td>The next great problem with which this God-man wrestled and which he presently decided in accordance with the will of the Father in heaven, concerned the question as to whether or not any of his superhuman powers should be employed for the purpose of attracting the attention and winning the adherence of his fellow men. Should he in any manner lend his universe powers to the gratification of the Jewish hankering for the spectacular and the marvelous? He decided that he should not. He settled upon a policy of procedure which eliminated all such practices as the method of bringing his mission to the notice of men. And he consistently lived up to this great decision. Even when he permitted the manifestation of numerous time-shortening ministrations of mercy, he almost invariably admonished the recipients of his healing ministry to tell no man about the benefits they had received. And always did he refuse the taunting challenge of his enemies to "show us a sign" in proof and demonstration of his divinity. 136:8.1 (1520.2)

Jesus very wisely foresaw that the working of miracles and the execution of wonders would call forth only outward allegiance by overawing the material mind; such performances would not reveal God nor save men. He refused to become a mere wonder-worker. He resolved to become occupied with but a single task—the establishment of the kingdom of heaven. 136:8.2 (1520.3)</td></tr>
</table>

Jesus' Decisions About Miracles: (Continued)	Throughout all this momentous dialogue of Jesus' communing with himself, there was present the human element of questioning and near-doubting, for Jesus was man as well as God. It was evident he would never be received by the Jews as the Messiah if he did not work wonders. Besides, if he would consent to do just one unnatural thing, the human mind would know of a certainty that it was in subservience to a truly divine mind. Would it be consistent with "the Father's will" for the divine mind to make this concession to the doubting nature of the human mind? Jesus decided that it would not and cited the presence of the Personalized Adjuster as sufficient proof of divinity in partnership with humanity. 136:8.3 (1520.4) Jesus was fully aware of the short cuts open to one of his powers. He knew many ways in which the attention of the nation, and the whole world, could be immediately focused upon himself. Soon the Passover would be celebrated at Jerusalem; the city would be thronged with visitors. He could ascend the pinnacle of the temple and before the bewildered multitude walk out on the air; that would be the kind of a Messiah they were looking for. But he would subsequently disappoint them since he had not come to re-establish David's throne. And he knew the futility of the Caligastia method of trying to get ahead of the natural, slow, and sure way of accomplishing the divine purpose. Again the Son of Man bowed obediently to the Father's way, the Father's will. 136:8.5 (1520.6)

Many of the occurrences believed to be miracles in the Christian Bible are not considered *real* miracles in *The Urantia Book*. In the following list, each miracle (whether real or so-called) is described according to *The Urantia Book* with any corresponding Biblical reference included at the left.

Miracle	The Urantia Book Description
Water Into Wine at Cana Wedding: Bible: John 2:1–11	But this was in no sense a miracle. No law of nature was modified, abrogated, or even transcended. Nothing happened but the abrogation of time in association with the celestial assembly of the chemical elements requisite for the elaboration of the wine. At Cana on this occasion the agents of the Creator made wine just as they do by the ordinary natural processes except that they did it independently of time and with the intervention of superhuman agencies in the matter of the space assembly of the necessary chemical ingredients. 137:4.13 (1530.5) Furthermore it was evident that the enactment of this so-called miracle was not contrary to the will of the Paradise Father, else it would not have transpired, since Jesus had already subjected himself in all things to the Father's will. 137:4.14 (1531.1)
Draught of Fishes: Bible: Luke 5:1–11	On Friday morning of this same week, when Jesus was teaching by the seaside, the people crowded him so near the water's edge that he signaled to some fishermen occupying a near-by boat to come to his rescue. Entering the boat, he continued to teach the assembled multitude for more than two hours. This boat was named "Simon"; it was the former fishing vessel of Simon Peter and had been built by Jesus' own hands. On this particular morning the boat was being used by David Zebedee and two associates, who had just come in near shore from a fruitless night of fishing on the lake. They were cleaning and mending their nets when Jesus requested them to come to his assistance. 145:1.1 (1628.4)

Draught of Fishes: (Continued) Bible: Luke 5:1–11	After Jesus had finished teaching the people, he said to David: "As you were delayed by coming to my help, now let me work with you. Let us go fishing; put out into yonder deep and let down your nets for a draught." But Simon, one of David's assistants, answered: "Master, it is useless. We toiled all night and took nothing; however, at your bidding we will put out and let down the nets." And Simon consented to follow Jesus' directions because of a gesture made by his master, David. When they had proceeded to the place designated by Jesus, they let down their nets and enclosed such a multitude of fish that they feared the nets would break, so much so that they signaled to their associates on the shore to come to their assistance. When they had filled all three boats with fish, almost to sinking, this Simon fell down at Jesus' knees, saying, "Depart from me, Master, for I am a sinful man." Simon and all who were concerned in this episode were amazed at the draught of fishes. From that day David Zebedee, this Simon, and their associates forsook their nets and followed Jesus. 145:1.2 (1628.5) But this was in no sense a miraculous draught of fishes. Jesus was a close student of nature; he was an experienced fisherman and knew the habits of the fish in the Sea of Galilee. On this occasion he merely directed these men to the place where the fish were usually to be found at this time of day. But Jesus' followers always regarded this as a miracle. 145:1.3 (1629.1)
Epileptic In Synagogue: Bible: Mark 1:21–28 Luke 4:31–37	This young man was not possessed of an unclean spirit or demon; he was a victim of ordinary epilepsy. But he had been taught that his affliction was due to possession by an evil spirit. He believed this teaching and behaved accordingly in all that he thought or said concerning his ailment. The people all believed that such phenomena were directly caused by the presence of unclean spirits. Accordingly they believed that Jesus had cast a demon out of this man. But Jesus did not at that time cure his epilepsy. Not until later on that day, after sundown, was this man really healed. Long after the day of Pentecost the Apostle John, who was the last to write of Jesus' doings, avoided all reference to these so-called acts of "casting out devils," and this he did in view of the fact that such cases of demon possession never occurred after Pentecost. 145:2.12 (1630.8) Just as Jesus finished speaking, a young man in the congregation who had been much agitated by his words was seized with a violent epileptic attack and loudly cried out. At the end of the seizure, when recovering consciousness, he spoke in a dreamy state, saying: "What have we to do with you, Jesus of Nazareth? You are the holy one of God; have you come to destroy us?" Jesus bade the people be quiet and, taking the young man by the hand, said, "Come out of it"—and he was immediately awakened. 145:2.13 (1631.1) As a result of this commonplace incident the report was rapidly spread through Capernaum that Jesus had cast a demon out of a man and miraculously healed him in the synagogue at the conclusion of his afternoon sermon. The Sabbath was just the time for the rapid and effective spreading of such a startling rumor. This report was also carried to all the smaller settlements around Capernaum, and many of the people believed it. 145:2.14 (1631.2)

Peter's Mother-In-Law: Bible: Mark 1:29–31 Luke 4:38–39 Matt 8:14–15	Peter's home was near that of Zebedee; and Jesus and his friends stopped there on the way from the synagogue because Peter's wife's mother had for several days been sick with chills and fever. Now it chanced that, at about the time Jesus stood over this sick woman, holding her hand, smoothing her brow, and speaking words of comfort and encouragement, the fever left her. Jesus had not yet had time to explain to his apostles that no miracle had been wrought at the synagogue; and with this incident so fresh and vivid in their minds, and recalling the water and the wine at Cana, they seized upon this coincidence as another miracle, and some of them rushed out to spread the news abroad throughout the city. 145:2.15 (1631.3) Amatha, Peter's mother-in-law, was suffering from malarial fever. She was not miraculously healed by Jesus at this time. Not until several hours later, after sundown, was her cure effected in connection with the extraordinary event which occurred in the front yard of the Zebedee home. 145:2.16 (1631.4)
Mass Healing at Sundown: Bible: Matt 8:16 Mark 1:32–34 Luke 4:40–41	Soon after the setting of the sun, as Jesus and the apostles still lingered about the supper table, Peter's wife heard voices in the front yard and, on going to the door, saw a large company of sick folks assembling, and that the road from Capernaum was crowded by those who were on their way to seek healing at Jesus' hands. On seeing this sight, she went at once and informed her husband, who told Jesus. 145:3.5 (1632.4) When the Master stepped out of the front entrance of Zebedee's house, his eyes met an array of stricken and afflicted humanity. He gazed upon almost one thousand sick and ailing human beings; at least that was the number of persons gathered together before him. Not all present were afflicted; some had come assisting their loved ones in this effort to secure healing. 145:3.6 (1632.5) The sight of these afflicted mortals, men, women, and children, suffering in large measure as a result of the mistakes and misdeeds of his own trusted Sons of universe administration, peculiarly touched the human heart of Jesus and challenged the divine mercy of this benevolent Creator Son. But Jesus well knew he could never build an enduring spiritual movement upon the foundation of purely material wonders. It had been his consistent policy to refrain from exhibiting his creator prerogatives. Not since Cana had the supernatural or miraculous attended his teaching; still, this afflicted multitude touched his sympathetic heart and mightily appealed to his understanding affection. 145:3.7 (1632.6) A voice from the front yard exclaimed: "Master, speak the word, restore our health, heal our diseases, and save our souls." No sooner had these words been uttered than a vast retinue of seraphim, physical controllers, Life Carriers, and midwayers, such as always attended this incarnated Creator of a universe, made themselves ready to act with creative power should their Sovereign give the signal. This was one of those moments in the earth career of Jesus in which divine wisdom and human compassion were so interlocked in the judgment of the Son of Man that he sought refuge in appeal to his Father's will. 145:3.8 (1632.7) When Peter implored the Master to heed their cry for help, Jesus, looking down upon the afflicted throng, answered: "I have come into the world to reveal the Father and establish his kingdom. For this purpose have I lived my life to this hour.

Mass Healing at Sundown: (Continued) Bible: Matt 8:16 Mark 1:32–34 Luke 4:40–41	If, therefore, it should be the will of Him who sent me and not inconsistent with my dedication to the proclamation of the gospel of the kingdom of heaven, I would desire to see my children made whole—and —" but the further words of Jesus were lost in the tumult. 145:3.9 (1632.8) Jesus had passed the responsibility of this healing decision to the ruling of his Father. Evidently the Father's will interposed no objection, for the words of the Master had scarcely been uttered when the assembly of celestial personalities serving under the command of Jesus' Personalized Thought Adjuster was mightily astir. The vast retinue descended into the midst of this motley throng of afflicted mortals, and in a moment of time 683 men, women, and children were made whole, were perfectly healed of all their physical diseases and other material disorders. Such a scene was never witnessed on earth before that day, nor since. And for those of us who were present to behold this creative wave of healing, it was indeed a thrilling spectacle. 145:3.10 (1633.1) But of all the beings who were astonished at this sudden and unexpected outbreak of supernatural healing, Jesus was the most surprised. In a moment when his human interests and sympathies were focused upon the scene of suffering and affliction there spread out before him, he neglected to bear in his human mind the admonitory warnings of his Personalized Adjuster regarding the impossibility of limiting the time element of the creator prerogatives of a Creator Son under certain conditions and in certain circumstances. Jesus desired to see these suffering mortals made whole if his Father's will would not thereby be violated. The Personalized Adjuster of Jesus instantly ruled that such an act of creative energy at that time would not transgress the will of the Paradise Father, and by such a decision—in view of Jesus' preceding expression of healing desire—the creative act was. What a Creator Son desires and his Father wills IS. Not in all of Jesus' subsequent earth life did another such en masse physical healing of mortals take place. 145:3.11 (1633.2)
The Leper at Iron: Bible: Matt 8:1–4 Mark 1:40–45 Luke 5:12–15	Late on the afternoon of the third day at Iron, as Jesus was returning from the mines, he chanced to pass through a narrow side street on his way to his lodging place. As he drew near the squalid hovel of a certain leprous man, the afflicted one, having heard of his fame as a healer, made bold to accost him as he passed his door, saying as he knelt before him: "Lord, if only you would, you could make me clean. I have heard the message of your teachers, and I would enter the kingdom if I could be made clean." And the leper spoke in this way because among the Jews lepers were forbidden even to attend the synagogue or otherwise engage in public worship. This man really believed that he could not be received into the coming kingdom unless he could find a cure for his leprosy. And when Jesus saw him in his affliction and heard his words of clinging faith, his human heart was touched, and the divine mind was moved with compassion. As Jesus looked upon him, the man fell upon his face and worshiped. Then the Master stretched forth his hand and, touching him, said: "I will—be clean." And immediately he was healed; the leprosy no longer afflicted him. 146:4.3 (1643.4)

The Miracles of Jesus

Titus the Nobleman's Son: Bible: John 4:46–54:	When this nobleman had located Jesus in Cana, he besought him to hurry over to Capernaum and heal his afflicted son. While the apostles stood by in breathless expectancy, Jesus, looking at the father of the sick boy, said: "How long shall I bear with you? The power of God is in your midst, but except you see signs and behold wonders, you refuse to believe." But the nobleman pleaded with Jesus, saying: "My Lord, I do believe, but come ere my child perishes, for when I left him he was even then at the point of death." And when Jesus had bowed his head a moment in silent meditation, he suddenly spoke, "Return to your home; your son will live." Titus believed the word of Jesus and hastened back to Capernaum. And as he was returning, his servants came out to meet him, saying, "Rejoice, for your son is improved—he lives." Then Titus inquired of them at what hour the boy began to mend, and when the servants answered "yesterday about the seventh hour the fever left him," the father recalled that it was about that hour when Jesus had said, "Your son will live." And Titus henceforth believed with a whole heart, and all his family also believed. This son became a mighty minister of the kingdom and later yielded up his life with those who suffered in Rome. Though the entire household of Titus, their friends, and even the apostles regarded this episode as a miracle, it was not. At least this was not a miracle of curing physical disease. It was merely a case of preknowledge concerning the course of natural law, just such knowledge as Jesus frequently resorted to subsequent to his baptism. 146:5.2 (1644.4)
Raising of the Widow's Son: Bible: Luke 7:11–17	When Jesus sought to leave Cana and go to Nain, a great multitude of believers and many curious people followed after him. They were bent on beholding miracles and wonders, and they were not to be disappointed. As Jesus and his apostles drew near the gate of the city, they met a funeral procession on its way to the near-by cemetery, carrying the only son of a widowed mother of Nain. This woman was much respected, and half of the village followed the bearers of the bier of this supposedly dead boy. When the funeral procession had come up to Jesus and his followers, the widow and her friends recognized the Master and besought him to bring the son back to life. Their miracle expectancy was aroused to such a high pitch they thought Jesus could cure any human disease, and why could not such a healer even raise the dead? Jesus, while being thus importuned, stepped forward and, raising the covering of the bier, examined the boy. Discovering that the young man was not really dead, he perceived the tragedy which his presence could avert; so, turning to the mother, he said: "Weep not. Your son is not dead; he sleeps. He will be restored to you." And then, taking the young man by the hand, he said, "Awake and arise." And the youth who was supposed to be dead presently sat up and began to speak, and Jesus sent them back to their homes. 146:6.2 (1645.3)
Infirm Man at Bethesda: Bible: John 5:2–9	One man who had been many years downcast and grievously afflicted by the infirmities of his troubled mind, rejoiced at Jesus' words and, picking up his bed, went forth to his home, even though it was the Sabbath day. This afflicted man had waited all these years for somebody to help him; he was such a victim of the feeling of his own helplessness that he had never once entertained the idea of helping himself which proved to be the one thing he had to do in order to effect recovery—take up his bed and walk. 147:3.5 (1649.5)

The Centurion's Servant: Bible: Matt 8:5–13 Luke 7:1–10	On the day before they made ready to go to Jerusalem for the feast of the Passover, Mangus, a centurion, or captain, of the Roman guard stationed at Capernaum, came to the rulers of the synagogue, saying: "My faithful orderly is sick and at the point of death. Would you, therefore, go to Jesus in my behalf and beseech him to heal my servant?" The Roman captain did this because he thought the Jewish leaders would have more influence with Jesus. So the elders went to see Jesus and their spokesman said: "Teacher, we earnestly request you to go over to Capernaum and save the favorite servant of the Roman centurion, who is worthy of your notice because he loves our nation and even built us the very synagogue wherein you have so many times spoken." 147:1.1 (1647.3) And when Jesus had heard them, he said, "I will go with you." And as he went with them over to the centurion's house, and before they had entered his yard, the Roman soldier sent his friends out to greet Jesus, instructing them to say: "Lord, trouble not yourself to enter my house, for I am not worthy that you should come under my roof. Neither did I think myself worthy to come to you; wherefore I sent the elders of your own people. But I know that you can speak the word where you stand and my servant will be healed. For I am myself under the orders of others, and I have soldiers under me, and I say to this one go, and he goes; to another come, and he comes, and to my servants do this or do that, and they do it." 147:1.2 (1647.4) And when Jesus heard these words, he turned and said to his apostles and those who were with them: "I marvel at the belief of the gentile. Verily, verily, I say to you, I have not found so great faith, no, not in Israel." Jesus, turning from the house, said, "Let us go hence." And the friends of the centurion went into the house and told Mangus what Jesus had said. And from that hour the servant began to mend and was eventually restored to his normal health and usefulness. 147:1.3 (1648.1)
Man With the Withered Hand: Bible: Matt 12:9–14 Mark 3:1–6 Luke 6:6–11	The leader of the spying Pharisees, as Jesus stood talking to the people, induced a man with a withered hand to approach him and ask if it would be lawful to be healed on the Sabbath day or should he seek help on another day. When Jesus saw the man, heard his words, and perceived that he had been sent by the Pharisees, he said: "Come forward while I ask you a question. If you had a sheep and it should fall into a pit on the Sabbath day, would you reach down, lay hold on it, and lift it out? Is it lawful to do such things on the Sabbath day?" And the man answered: "Yes, Master, it would be lawful thus to do well on the Sabbath day." Then said Jesus, speaking to all of them: "I know wherefore you have sent this man into my presence. You would find cause for offense in me if you could tempt me to show mercy on the Sabbath day. In silence you all agreed that it was lawful to lift the unfortunate sheep out of the pit, even on the Sabbath, and I call you to witness that it is lawful to exhibit loving-kindness on the Sabbath day not only to animals but also to men. How much more valuable is a man than a sheep! I proclaim that it is lawful to do good to men on the Sabbath day." And as they all stood before him in silence, Jesus, addressing the man with the withered hand, said: "Stand up here by my side that all may see you. And now that you may know that it is my Father's will that you do good on the Sabbath day, if you have the faith to be healed, I bid you stretch out your hand." 148:7.2 (1665.1)

Man With the Withered Hand: (Continued) Bible: Matt 12:9–14 Mark 3:1–6 Luke 6:6–11	And as this man stretched forth his withered hand, it was made whole. The people were minded to turn upon the Pharisees, but Jesus bade them be calm, saying: "I have just told you that it is lawful to do good on the Sabbath, to save life, but I did not instruct you to do harm and give way to the desire to kill." The angered Pharisees went away, and notwithstanding it was the Sabbath day, they hastened forthwith to Tiberias and took counsel with Herod, doing everything in their power to arouse his prejudice in order to secure the Herodians as allies against Jesus. But Herod refused to take action against Jesus, advising that they carry their complaints to Jerusalem. 148:7.3 (1665.2) This is the first case of a miracle to be wrought by Jesus in response to the challenge of his enemies. And the Master performed this so-called miracle, not as a demonstration of his healing power, but as an effective protest against making the Sabbath rest of religion a veritable bondage of meaningless restrictions upon all mankind. This man returned to his work as a stone mason, proving to be one of those whose healing was followed by a life of thanksgiving and righteousness. 148:7.4 (1665.3)
Paralytic in Zebedee's Front Room: Bible: Matt 9:2–8 Mark 2:1–12 Luke 5:17–26	On Friday afternoon, October 1, when Jesus was holding his last meeting with the apostles, evangelists, and other leaders of the disbanding encampment, and with the six Pharisees from Jerusalem seated in the front row of this assembly in the spacious and enlarged front room of the Zebedee home, there occurred one of the strangest and most unique episodes of all Jesus' earth life. The Master was, at this time, speaking as he stood in this large room, which had been built to accommodate these gatherings during the rainy season. The house was entirely surrounded by a vast concourse of people who were straining their ears to catch some part of Jesus' discourse. 148:9.1 (1666.5) While the house was thus thronged with people and entirely surrounded by eager listeners, a man long afflicted with paralysis was carried down from Capernaum on a small couch by his friends. This paralytic had heard that Jesus was about to leave Bethsaida, and having talked with Aaron the stone mason, who had been so recently made whole, he resolved to be carried into Jesus' presence, where he could seek healing. His friends tried to gain entrance to Zebedee's house by both the front and back doors, but too many people were crowded together. But the paralytic refused to accept defeat; he directed his friends to procure ladders by which they ascended to the roof of the room in which Jesus was speaking, and after loosening the tiles, they boldly lowered the sick man on his couch by ropes until the afflicted one rested on the floor immediately in front of the Master. When Jesus saw what they had done, he ceased speaking, while those who were with him in the room marveled at the perseverance of the sick man and his friends. Said the paralytic: "Master, I would not disturb your teaching, but I am determined to be made whole. I am not like those who received healing and immediately forgot your teaching. I would be made whole that I might serve in the kingdom of heaven." Now, notwithstanding that this man's affliction had been brought upon him by his own misspent life, Jesus, seeing his faith, said to the paralytic: "Son, fear not; your sins are forgiven. Your faith shall save you." 148:9.2 (1666.6)

Paralytic in Zebedee's Front Room: (Continued) Bible: Matt 9:2–8 Mark 2:1–12 Luke 5:17–26	When the Pharisees from Jerusalem, together with other scribes and lawyers who sat with them, heard this pronouncement by Jesus, they began to say to themselves: "How dare this man thus speak? Does he not understand that such words are blasphemy? Who can forgive sin but God?" Jesus, perceiving in his spirit that they thus reasoned within their own minds and among themselves, spoke to them, saying: "Why do you so reason in your hearts? Who are you that you sit in judgment over me? What is the difference whether I say to this paralytic, your sins are forgiven, or arise, take up your bed, and walk? But that you who witness all this may finally know that the Son of Man has authority and power on earth to forgive sins, I will say to this afflicted man, Arise, take up your bed, and go to your own house." And when Jesus had thus spoken, the paralytic arose, and as they made way for him, he walked out before them all. And those who saw these things were amazed. Peter dismissed the assemblage, while many prayed and glorified God, confessing that they had never before seen such strange happenings. 148:9.3 (1667.1)
Miscellaneous Spontaneous Healings: Bible: Mark 6:56	There began to appear about the time of this mission—and continued throughout the remainder of Jesus' life on earth—a peculiar and unexplained series of healing phenomena. In the course of this three months' tour more than one hundred men, women, and children from Judea, Idumea, Galilee, Syria, Tyre, and Sidon, and from beyond the Jordan were beneficiaries of this unconscious healing by Jesus and, returning to their homes, added to the enlargement of Jesus' fame. And they did this notwithstanding that Jesus would, every time he observed one of these cases of spontaneous healing, directly charge the beneficiary to "tell no man." 149:1.2 (1669.1) It was never revealed to us just what occurred in these cases of spontaneous or unconscious healing. The Master never explained to his apostles how these healings were effected, other than that on several occasions he merely said, "I perceive that power has gone forth from me." On one occasion he remarked when touched by an ailing child, "I perceive that life has gone forth from me." 149:1.3 (1669.2)
Stilling the Tempest: Bible: Matt 8:23–27 Mark 4:35–41 Luke 8:22–25	It was just such an evening gale that caught the boat carrying Jesus over to the other side on this Sunday evening. Three other boats containing some of the younger evangelists were trailing after. This tempest was severe, notwithstanding that it was confined to this region of the lake, there being no evidence of a storm on the western shore. The wind was so strong that the waves began to wash over the boat. The high wind had torn the sail away before the apostles could furl it, and they were now entirely dependent on their oars as they laboriously pulled for the shore, a little more than a mile and a half distant. 151:5.3 (1694.8) Meanwhile Jesus lay asleep in the stern of the boat under a small overhead shelter. The Master was weary when they left Bethsaida, and it was to secure rest that he had directed them to sail him across to the other side. These ex-fishermen were strong and experienced oarsmen, but this was one of the worst gales they had ever encountered. Although the wind and the waves tossed their boat about as though it were a toy ship, Jesus slumbered on undisturbed. Peter was at the right-hand oar near the stern. When the boat began to fill with water, he dropped his oar and, rushing over to Jesus, shook him vigorously in order to awaken him, and when he was aroused, Peter said: "Master, don't you know we are in a violent storm? If you do not save us, we will all perish." 151:5.4 (1694.9)

The Miracles of Jesus

Stilling the Tempest: (Continued) Bible: Matt 8:23–27 Mark 4:35–41 Luke 8:22–25	As Jesus came out in the rain, he looked first at Peter, and then peering into the darkness at the struggling oarsmen, he turned his glance back upon Simon Peter, who, in his agitation, had not yet returned to his oar, and said: "Why are all of you so filled with fear? Where is your faith? Peace, be quiet." Jesus had hardly uttered this rebuke to Peter and the other apostles, he had hardly bidden Peter seek peace wherewith to quiet his troubled soul, when the disturbed atmosphere, having established its equilibrium, settled down into a great calm. The angry waves almost immediately subsided, while the dark clouds, having spent themselves in a short shower, vanished, and the stars of heaven shone overhead. All this was purely coincidental as far as we can judge; but the apostles, particularly Simon Peter, never ceased to regard the episode as a nature miracle. It was especially easy for the men of that day to believe in nature miracles inasmuch as they firmly believed that all nature was a phenomenon directly under the control of spirit forces and supernatural beings. 151:5.5 (1695.1)
Kheresa Lunatic: Bible: Matt 8:28–34 Mark 5:1–20 Luke 8:26–39	This man, whose name was Amos, was afflicted with a periodic form of insanity. There were considerable spells when he would find some clothing and deport himself fairly well among his fellows. During one of these lucid intervals he had gone over to Bethsaida, where he heard the preaching of Jesus and the apostles, and at that time had become a halfhearted believer in the gospel of the kingdom. But soon a stormy phase of his trouble appeared, and he fled to the tombs, where he moaned, cried out aloud, and so conducted himself as to terrorize all who chanced to meet him. 151:6.3 (1696.1) When Amos recognized Jesus, he fell down at his feet and exclaimed: "I know you, Jesus, but I am possessed of many devils, and I beseech that you will not torment me." This man truly believed that his periodic mental affliction was due to the fact that, at such times, evil or unclean spirits entered into him and dominated his mind and body. His troubles were mostly emotional—his brain was not grossly diseased. 151:6.4 (1696.2) Jesus, looking down upon the man crouching like an animal at his feet, reached down and, taking him by the hand, stood him up and said to him: "Amos, you are not possessed of a devil; you have already heard the good news that you are a son of God. I command you to come out of this spell." And when Amos heard Jesus speak these words, there occurred such a transformation in his intellect that he was immediately restored to his right mind and the normal control of his emotions. By this time a considerable crowd had assembled from the near-by village, and these people, augmented by the swine herders from the highland above them, were astonished to see the lunatic sitting with Jesus and his followers, in possession of his right mind and freely conversing with them. 151:6.5 (1696.3) As the swine herders rushed into the village to spread the news of the taming of the lunatic, the dogs charged upon a small and untended herd of about thirty swine and drove most of them over a precipice into the sea. And it was this incidental occurrence, in connection with the presence of Jesus and the supposed miraculous curing of the lunatic, that gave origin to the legend that Jesus had cured Amos by casting a legion of devils out of him, and that these devils had entered into the herd of swine, causing them forthwith to rush headlong to their destruction in the sea

Kheresa Lunatic: (Continued) Bible: Matt 8:28–34 Mark 5:1–20 Luke 8:26–39	below. Before the day was over, this episode was published abroad by the swine tenders, and the whole village believed it. Amos most certainly believed this story; he saw the swine tumbling over the brow of the hill shortly after his troubled mind had quieted down, and he always believed that they carried with them the very evil spirits which had so long tormented and afflicted him. And this had a good deal to do with the permanency of his cure. It is equally true that all of Jesus' apostles (save Thomas) believed that the episode of the swine was directly connected with the cure of Amos. 151:6.6 (1696.4)
Woman With Issue of Blood: Bible: Matt 9:20–22 Mark 5:25–34 Luke 8:43–48	As Jesus went along with Jairus, the large crowd which had heard the father's request followed on to see what would happen. Shortly before they reached the ruler's house, as they hastened through a narrow street and as the throng jostled him, Jesus suddenly stopped, exclaiming, "Someone touched me." And when those who were near him denied that they had touched him, Peter spoke up: "Master, you can see that this crowd presses you, threatening to crush us, and yet you say 'someone has touched me.' What do you mean?" Then Jesus said: "I asked who touched me, for I perceived that living energy had gone forth from me." As Jesus looked about him, his eyes fell upon a near-by woman, who, coming forward, knelt at his feet and said: "For years I have been afflicted with a scourging hemorrhage. I have suffered many things from many physicians; I have spent all my substance, but none could cure me. Then I heard of you, and I thought if I may but touch the hem of his garment, I shall certainly be made whole. And so I pressed forward with the crowd as it moved along until, standing near you, Master, I touched the border of your garment, and I was made whole; I know that I have been healed of my affliction." 152:0.2 (1698.2) When Jesus heard this, he took the woman by the hand and, lifting her up, said: "Daughter, your faith has made you whole; go in peace." It was her faith and not her touch that made her whole. And this case is a good illustration of many apparently miraculous cures which attended upon Jesus' earth career, but which he in no sense consciously willed. The passing of time demonstrated that this woman was really cured of her malady. Her faith was of the sort that laid direct hold upon the creative power resident in the Master's person. With the faith she had, it was only necessary to approach the Master's person. It was not at all necessary to touch his garment; that was merely the superstitious part of her belief. Jesus called this woman, Veronica of Caesarea-Philippi, into his presence to correct two errors which might have lingered in her mind, or which might have persisted in the minds of those who witnessed this healing: He did not want Veronica to go away thinking that her fear in attempting to steal her cure had been honored, or that her superstition in associating the touch of his garment with her healing had been effective. He desired all to know that it was her pure and living faith that had wrought the cure. 152:0.3 (1698.3)

Raising of Jairus' Daughter: Bible: Matt 9:18–26 Mark 5:21–43 Luke 8:40–56	Jairus was, of course, terribly impatient of this delay in reaching his home; so they now hastened on at quickened pace. Even before they entered the ruler's yard, one of his servants came out, saying: "Trouble not the Master; your daughter is dead." But Jesus seemed not to heed the servant's words, for, taking with him Peter, James, and John, he turned and said to the grief-stricken father: "Fear not; only believe." When he entered the house, he found the flute-players already there with the mourners, who were making an unseemly tumult; already were the relatives engaged in weeping and wailing. And when he had put all the mourners out of the room, he went in with the father and mother and his three apostles. He had told the mourners that the damsel was not dead, but they laughed him to scorn. Jesus now turned to the mother, saying: "Your daughter is not dead; she is only asleep." And when the house had quieted down, Jesus, going up to where the child lay, took her by the hand and said, "Daughter, I say to you, awake and arise!" And when the girl heard these words, she immediately rose up and walked across the room. And presently, after she had recovered from her daze, Jesus directed that they should give her something to eat, for she had been a long time without food. 152:1.1 (1699.1) Since there was much agitation in Capernaum against Jesus, he called the family together and explained that the maiden had been in a state of coma following a long fever, and that he had merely aroused her, that he had not raised her from the dead. He likewise explained all this to his apostles, but it was futile; they all believed he had raised the little girl from the dead. What Jesus said in explanation of many of these apparent miracles had little effect on his followers. They were miracle-minded and lost no opportunity to ascribe another wonder to Jesus. 152:1.2 (1699.2)
Feeding of the Five Thousand: Bible: John 6:1–15 Matt 14:13–23 Mark 6:30–46 Luke 9:10–17	This was the stage setting about five o'clock on Wednesday afternoon, when Jesus asked James Alpheus to summon Andrew and Philip. Said Jesus: "What shall we do with the multitude? They have been with us now three days, and many of them are hungry. They have no food." Philip and Andrew exchanged glances, and then Philip answered: "Master, you should send these people away so that they may go to the villages around about and buy themselves food." And Andrew, fearing the materialization of the king plot, quickly joined with Philip, saying: "Yes, Master, I think it best that you dismiss the multitude so that they may go their way and buy food while you secure rest for a season." By this time others of the twelve had joined the conference. Then said Jesus: "But I do not desire to send them away hungry; can you not feed them?" This was too much for Philip, and he spoke right up: "Master, in this country place where can we buy bread for this multitude? Two hundred denarii worth would not be enough for lunch." 152:2.6 (1701.1) Before the apostles had an opportunity to express themselves, Jesus turned to Andrew and Philip, saying: "I do not want to send these people away. Here they are, like sheep without a shepherd. I would like to feed them. What food have we with us?" While Philip was conversing with Matthew and Judas, Andrew sought out the Mark lad to ascertain how much was left of their store of provisions. He returned to Jesus, saying: "The lad has left only five barley loaves and two dried fishes"—and Peter promptly added, "We have yet to eat this evening." 152:2.7 (1701.2)

Feeding of the Five Thousand: (Continued) Bible: John 6:1–15 Matt 14:13–23 Mark 6:30–46 Luke 9:10–17	For a moment Jesus stood in silence. There was a faraway look in his eyes. The apostles said nothing. Jesus turned suddenly to Andrew and said, "Bring me the loaves and fishes." And when Andrew had brought the basket to Jesus, the Master said: "Direct the people to sit down on the grass in companies of one hundred and appoint a leader over each group while you bring all of the evangelists here with us." 152:2.8 (1701.3) Jesus took up the loaves in his hands, and after he had given thanks, he broke the bread and gave to his apostles, who passed it on to their associates, who in turn carried it to the multitude. Jesus in like manner broke and distributed the fishes. And this multitude did eat and were filled. And when they had finished eating, Jesus said to the disciples: "Gather up the broken pieces that remain over so that nothing will be lost." And when they had finished gathering up the fragments, they had twelve basketfuls. They who ate of this extraordinary feast numbered about five thousand men, women, and children. 152:2.9 (1701.4) And this is the first and only nature miracle which Jesus performed as a result of his conscious preplanning. It is true that his disciples were disposed to call many things miracles which were not, but this was a genuine supernatural ministration. In this case, so we were taught, Michael multiplied food elements as he always does except for the elimination of the time factor and the visible life channel. 152:2.10 (1702.1)
Jesus Walking on Water: Bible: John 6:16–21 Matt 14:24–33 Mark 6:47–52	The apostles, without their Master—sent off by themselves—entered the boat and in silence began to row toward Bethsaida on the western shore of the lake. None of the twelve was so crushed and downcast as Simon Peter. Hardly a word was spoken; they were all thinking of the Master alone in the hills. Had he forsaken them? He had never before sent them all away and refused to go with them. What could all this mean? 152:4.1 (1703.1) Darkness descended upon them, for there had arisen a strong and contrary wind which made progress almost impossible. As the hours of darkness and hard rowing passed, Peter grew weary and fell into a deep sleep of exhaustion. Andrew and James put him to rest on the cushioned seat in the stern of the boat. While the other apostles toiled against the wind and the waves, Peter dreamed a dream; he saw a vision of Jesus coming to them walking on the sea. When the Master seemed to walk on by the boat, Peter cried out, "Save us, Master, save us." And those who were in the rear of the boat heard him say some of these words. As this apparition of the night season continued in Peter's mind, he dreamed that he heard Jesus say: "Be of good cheer; it is I; be not afraid." This was like the balm of Gilead to Peter's disturbed soul; it soothed his troubled spirit, so that (in his dream) he cried out to the Master: "Lord, if it really is you, bid me come and walk with you on the water." And when Peter started to walk upon the water, the boisterous waves frightened him, and as he was about to sink, he cried out, "Lord, save me!" And many of the twelve heard him utter this cry. Then Peter dreamed that Jesus came to the rescue and, stretching forth his hand, took hold and lifted him up, saying: "O, you of little faith, wherefore did you doubt?" 152:4.2 (1703.2) In connection with the latter part of his dream Peter arose from the seat whereon he slept and actually stepped overboard and into the water. And he awakened from his dream as Andrew, James, and John reached down and pulled him out of the sea. 152:4.3 (1703.3)

Youth With Unclean Spirit: Bible: Matt 12:22–28 Luke 11:14–18	In the midst of the discussions of this after meeting, one of the Pharisees from Jerusalem brought to Jesus a distraught youth who was possessed of an unruly and rebellious spirit. Leading this demented lad up to Jesus, he said: "What can you do for such affliction as this? Can you cast out devils?" And when the Master looked upon the youth, he was moved with compassion and, beckoning for the lad to come to him, took him by the hand and said: "You know who I am; come out of him; and I charge one of your loyal fellows to see that you do not return." And immediately the lad was normal and in his right mind. And this is the first case where Jesus really cast an "evil spirit" out of a human being. All of the previous cases were only supposed possession of the devil; but this was a genuine case of demoniac possession, even such as sometimes occurred in those days and right up to the day of Pentecost, when the Master's spirit was poured out upon all flesh, making it forever impossible for these few celestial rebels to take such advantage of certain unstable types of human beings. 153:4.1 (1713.3)
Norana's Twelve Year Old Daughter: Bible: Matt 15:21–28 Mark 7:24–30	Jesus had charged his associates to tell no one of his presence at the home of Karuska, explaining that he desired to have a rest. While they had obeyed their Master's instructions, the servant of Karuska had gone over to the house of this Syrian woman, Norana, to inform her that Jesus lodged at the home of her mistress and had urged this anxious mother to bring her afflicted daughter for healing. This mother, of course, believed that her child was possessed by a demon, an unclean spirit. 156:1.2 (1734.4) When Norana arrived with her daughter, the Alpheus twins explained through an interpreter that the Master was resting and could not be disturbed; whereupon Norana replied that she and the child would remain right there until the Master had finished his rest. Peter also endeavored to reason with her and to persuade her to go home. He explained that Jesus was weary with much teaching and healing, and that he had come to Phoenicia for a period of quiet and rest. But it was futile; Norana would not leave. To Peter's entreaties she replied only: "I will not depart until I have seen your Master. I know he can cast the demon out of my child, and I will not go until the healer has looked upon my daughter." 156:1.3 (1734.5) Then Thomas sought to send the woman away but met only with failure. To him she said: "I have faith that your Master can cast out this demon which torments my child. I have heard of his mighty works in Galilee, and I believe in him. What has happened to you, his disciples, that you would send away those who come seeking your Master's help?" And when she had thus spoken, Thomas withdrew. 156:1.4 (1734.6) Then came forward Simon Zelotes to remonstrate with Norana. Said Simon: "Woman, you are a Greek-speaking gentile. It is not right that you should expect the Master to take the bread intended for the children of the favored household and cast it to the dogs." But Norana refused to take offense at Simon's thrust. She replied only: "Yes, teacher, I understand your words. I am only a dog in the eyes of the Jews, but as concerns your Master, I am a believing dog. I am determined that he shall see my daughter, for I am persuaded that, if he shall but look upon her, he will heal her. And even you, my good man, would not dare to deprive the dogs of the privilege of obtaining the crumbs which chance to fall from the children's table." 156:1.5 (1735.1)

Norana's Twelve Year Old Daughter: (Continued) Bible: Matt 15:21–28 Mark 7:24–30	At just this time the little girl was seized with a violent convulsion before them all, and the mother cried out: "There, you can see that my child is possessed by an evil spirit. If our need does not impress you, it would appeal to your Master, who I have been told loves all men and dares even to heal the gentiles when they believe. You are not worthy to be his disciples. I will not go until my child has been cured." 156:1.6 (1735.2) Jesus, who had heard all of this conversation through an open window, now came outside, much to their surprise, and said: "O woman, great is your faith, so great that I cannot withhold that which you desire; go your way in peace. Your daughter already has been made whole." And the little girl was well from that hour. 156:1.7 (1735.3)
Finding a Shekel in Fish's Mouth: Bible: Matt 17:24–27	All of this had been overheard by the secret messenger of David who stood nearby, and who then signaled to an associate, fishing near the shore, to come in quickly. When Peter made ready to go out in the boat for a catch, this messenger and his fisherman friend presented him with several large baskets of fish and assisted him in carrying them to the fish merchant nearby, who purchased the catch, paying sufficient, with what was added by the messenger of David, to meet the temple tax for the three. The collector accepted the tax, foregoing the penalty for tardy payment because they had been for some time absent from Galilee. 157:1.3 (1744.1) It is not strange that you have a record of Peter's catching a fish with a shekel in its mouth. In those days there were current many stories about finding treasures in the mouths of fishes; such tales of near miracles were commonplace. So, as Peter left them to go toward the boat, Jesus remarked, half-humorously: "Strange that the sons of the king must pay tribute; usually it is the stranger who is taxed for the upkeep of the court, but it behooves us to afford no stumbling block for the authorities. Go hence! maybe you will catch the fish with the shekel in its mouth." Jesus having thus spoken, and Peter so soon appearing with the temple tax, it is not surprising that the episode became later expanded into a miracle as recorded by the writer of Matthew's Gospel. 157:1.4 (1744.2)
Fourteen Year Old Epileptic Boy Who Was Demon Possessed: Bible: Matt 17:14–20 Mark 9:14–29 Luke 9:37–43	As Jesus drew near, the nine apostles were more than relieved to welcome him, and they were greatly encouraged to behold the good cheer and unusual enthusiasm which marked the countenances of Peter, James, and John. They all rushed forward to greet Jesus and their three brethren. As they exchanged greetings, the crowd came up, and Jesus asked, "What were you disputing about as we drew near?" But before the disconcerted and humiliated apostles could reply to the Master's question, the anxious father of the afflicted lad stepped forward and, kneeling at Jesus' feet, said: "Master, I have a son, an only child, who is possessed by an evil spirit. Not only does he cry out in terror, foam at the mouth, and fall like a dead person at the time of seizure, but oftentimes this evil spirit which possesses him rends him in convulsions and sometimes has cast him into the water and even into the fire. With much grinding of teeth and as a result of many bruises, my child wastes away. His life is worse than death; his mother and I are of a sad heart and a broken spirit. About noon yesterday, seeking for you, I caught up with your disciples, and while we were waiting, your apostles sought to cast out this demon, but they could not do it. And now, Master, will you do this for us, will you heal my son?" 158:5.1 (1757.1)

Fourteen Year Old Epileptic Boy Who Was Demon Possessed: (Continued) Bible: Matt 17:14–20 Mark 9:14–29 Luke 9:37–43	When Jesus had listened to this recital, he touched the kneeling father and bade him rise while he gave the near-by apostles a searching survey. Then said Jesus to all those who stood before him: "O faithless and perverse generation, how long shall I bear with you? How long shall I be with you? How long ere you learn that the works of faith come not forth at the bidding of doubting unbelief?" And then, pointing to the bewildered father, Jesus said, "Bring hither your son." And when James had brought the lad before Jesus, he asked, "How long has the boy been afflicted in this way?" The father answered, "Since he was a very young child." And as they talked, the youth was seized with a violent attack and fell in their midst, gnashing his teeth and foaming at the mouth. After a succession of violent convulsions he lay there before them as one dead. Now did the father again kneel at Jesus' feet while he implored the Master, saying: "If you can cure him, I beseech you to have compassion on us and deliver us from this affliction." And when Jesus heard these words, he looked down into the father's anxious face, saying: "Question not my Father's power of love, only the sincerity and reach of your faith. All things are possible to him who really believes." And then James of Safed spoke those long-to-be-remembered words of commingled faith and doubt, "Lord, I believe. I pray you help my unbelief." 158:5.2 (1757.2) When Jesus heard these words, he stepped forward and, taking the lad by the hand, said: "I will do this in accordance with my Father's will and in honor of living faith. My son, arise! Come out of him, disobedient spirit, and go not back into him." And placing the hand of the lad in the hand of the father, Jesus said: "Go your way. The Father has granted the desire of your soul." And all who were present, even the enemies of Jesus, were astonished at what they saw. 158:5.3 (1757.3)
Josiah, the Blind Beggar: Bible: John 9:1–41	Jesus entered into the discussion of this case with Nathaniel and Thomas, not only because he had already decided to use this blind man as the means of that day bringing his mission once more prominently to the notice of the Jewish leaders, but also because he always encouraged his apostles to seek for the true causes of all phenomena, natural or spiritual. He had often warned them to avoid the common tendency to assign spiritual causes to commonplace physical events. 164:3.6 (1811.7) Jesus decided to use this beggar in his plans for that day's work, but before doing anything for the blind man, Josiah by name, he proceeded to answer Nathaniel's question. Said the Master: "Neither did this man sin nor his parents that the works of God might be manifest in him. This blindness has come upon him in the natural course of events, but we must now do the works of Him who sent me, while it is still day, for the night will certainly come when it will be impossible to do the work we are about to perform. When I am in the world, I am the light of the world, but in only a little while I will not be with you." 164:3.7 (1812.1) When Jesus had spoken, he said to Nathaniel and Thomas: "Let us create the sight of this blind man on this Sabbath day that the scribes and Pharisees may have the full occasion which they seek for accusing the Son of Man." Then, stooping over, he spat on the ground and mixed the clay with the spittle, and speaking of all this so that the blind man could hear, he went up to Josiah and put the clay over his sightless eyes, saying: "Go, my son, wash away this clay in the pool of Siloam, and immediately you shall receive your sight." And when Josiah had so washed in the pool of Siloam, he returned to his friends and family, seeing. 164:3.8 (1812.2)

Ten Lepers—Nine Jews and One Samaritan: Bible: Luke 17:11–19	Accordingly, when Simon Zelotes observed the Samaritan among the lepers, he sought to induce the Master to pass on into the city without even hesitating to exchange greetings with them. Said Jesus to Simon: "But what if the Samaritan loves God as well as the Jews? Should we sit in judgment on our fellow men? Who can tell? if we make these ten men whole, perhaps the Samaritan will prove more grateful even than the Jews. Do you feel certain about your opinions, Simon?" And Simon quickly replied, "If you cleanse them, you will soon find out." And Jesus replied: "So shall it be, Simon, and you will soon know the truth regarding the gratitude of men and the loving mercy of God." 166:2.3 (1827.8) Jesus, going near the lepers, said: "If you would be made whole, go forthwith and show yourselves to the priests as required by the law of Moses." And as they went, they were made whole. But when the Samaritan saw that he was being healed, he turned back and, going in quest of Jesus, began to glorify God with a loud voice. And when he had found the Master, he fell on his knees at his feet and gave thanks for his cleansing. The nine others, the Jews, had also discovered their healing, and while they also were grateful for their cleansing, they continued on their way to show themselves to the priests. 166:2.4 (1827.9) As the Samaritan remained kneeling at Jesus' feet, the Master, looking about at the twelve, especially at Simon Zelotes, said: "Were not ten cleansed? Where, then, are the other nine, the Jews? Only one, this alien, has returned to give glory to God." And then he said to the Samaritan, "Arise and go your way; your faith has made you whole." 166:2.5 (1828.1)
Dropsical Man: Bible: Luke 14:1–6	Near the end of the meal there came in from the street a man long afflicted with a chronic disease and now in a dropsical condition. This man was a believer, having recently been baptized by Abner's associates. He made no request of Jesus for healing, but the Master knew full well that this afflicted man came to this breakfast hoping thereby to escape the crowds which thronged him and thus be more likely to engage his attention. This man knew that few miracles were then being performed; however, he had reasoned in his heart that his sorry plight might possibly appeal to the Master's compassion. And he was not mistaken, for, when he entered the room, both Jesus and the self-righteous Pharisee from Jerusalem took notice of him. The Pharisee was not slow to voice his resentment that such a one should be permitted to enter the room. But Jesus looked upon the sick man and smiled so benignly that he drew near and sat down upon the floor. As the meal was ending, the Master looked over his fellow guests and then, after glancing significantly at the man with dropsy, said: "My friends, teachers in Israel and learned lawyers, I would like to ask you a question: Is it lawful to heal the sick and afflicted on the Sabbath day, or not?" But those who were there present knew Jesus too well; they held their peace; they answered not his question. 167:1.4 (1834.2) Then went Jesus over to where the sick man sat and, taking him by the hand, said: "Arise and go your way. You have not asked to be healed, but I know the desire of your heart and the faith of your soul." 167:1.5 (1834.3)

Woman With Spirit of Infirmity: Bible: Luke 13:10–17	Abner had arranged for the Master to teach in the synagogue on this Sabbath day, the first time Jesus had appeared in a synagogue since they had all been closed to his teachings by order of the Sanhedrin. At the conclusion of the service Jesus looked down before him upon an elderly woman who wore a downcast expression, and who was much bent in form. This woman had long been fear-ridden, and all joy had passed out of her life. As Jesus stepped down from the pulpit, he went over to her and, touching her bowed-over form on the shoulder, said: "Woman, if you would only believe, you could be wholly loosed from your spirit of infirmity." And this woman, who had been bowed down and bound up by the depressions of fear for more than eighteen years, believed the words of the Master and by faith straightened up immediately. When this woman saw that she had been made straight, she lifted up her voice and glorified God. 167:3.1 (1835.5)
Raising of Lazarus From the Dead: Bible: John 11:1–46	As this company of some forty-five mortals stood before the tomb, they could dimly see the form of Lazarus, wrapped in linen bandages, resting on the right lower niche of the burial cave. While these earth creatures stood there in almost breathless silence, a vast host of celestial beings had swung into their places preparatory to answering the signal for action when it should be given by Gabriel, their commander. 168:2.1 (1845.7) Jesus lifted up his eyes and said: "Father, I am thankful that you heard and granted my request. I know that you always hear me, but because of those who stand here with me, I thus speak with you, that they may believe that you have sent me into the world, and that they may know that you are working with me in that which we are about to do." And when he had prayed, he cried with a loud voice, "Lazarus, come forth!" 168:2.2 (1846.1) Though these human observers remained motionless, the vast celestial host was all astir in unified action in obedience to the Creator's word. In just twelve seconds of earth time the hitherto lifeless form of Lazarus began to move and presently sat up on the edge of the stone shelf whereon it had rested. His body was bound about with grave cloths, and his face was covered with a napkin. And as he stood up before them—alive—Jesus said, "Loose him and let him go." 168:2.3 (1846.2)
Bartimeus, the Blind Man at Jericho: Bible: Matt 20:29–34 Mark 10:46–53 Luke 18:35–43	Late on the afternoon of Thursday, March 30, Jesus and his apostles, at the head of a band of about two hundred followers, approached the walls of Jericho. As they came near the gate of the city, they encountered a throng of beggars, among them one Bartimeus, an elderly man who had been blind from his youth. This blind beggar had heard much about Jesus and knew all about his healing of the blind Josiah at Jerusalem. He had not known of Jesus' last visit to Jericho until he had gone on to Bethany. Bartimeus had resolved that he would never again allow Jesus to visit Jericho without appealing to him for the restoration of his sight. 171:5.1 (1873.1) News of Jesus' approach had been heralded throughout Jericho, and hundreds of the inhabitants flocked forth to meet him. When this great crowd came back escorting the Master into the city, Bartimeus, hearing the heavy tramping of the multitude, knew that something unusual was happening, and so he asked those

Bartimeus, the Blind Man at Jericho: (Continued) Bible: Matt 20:29–34 Mark 10:46–53 Luke 18:35–43	standing near him what was going on. And one of the beggars replied, "Jesus of Nazareth is passing by." When Bartimeus heard that Jesus was near, he lifted up his voice and began to cry aloud, "Jesus, Jesus, have mercy upon me!" And as he continued to cry louder and louder, some of those near to Jesus went over and rebuked him, requesting him to hold his peace; but it was of no avail; he cried only the more and the louder. 171:5.2 (1873.2) When Jesus heard the blind man crying out, he stood still. And when he saw him, he said to his friends, "Bring the man to me." And then they went over to Bartimeus, saying: "Be of good cheer; come with us, for the Master calls for you." When Bartimeus heard these words, he threw aside his cloak, springing forward toward the center of the road, while those nearby guided him to Jesus. Addressing Bartimeus, Jesus said: "What do you want me to do for you?" Then answered the blind man, "I would have my sight restored." And when Jesus heard this request and saw his faith, he said: "You shall receive your sight; go your way; your faith has made you whole." Immediately he received his sight, and he remained near Jesus, glorifying God, until the Master started on the next day for Jerusalem, and then he went before the multitude declaring to all how his sight had been restored in Jericho. 171:5.3 (1873.3)

The Parables of Jesus

"Jesus also resorted to the use of parables as the best possible refutation of the studied effort of the religious leaders at Jerusalem to teach that all of his work was done by the assistance of demons and the prince of devils."
151:3.14 (1693.4)

Why Jesus Spoke in Parables.

"In patience have I instructed you all this time. To you it is given to know the mysteries of the kingdom of heaven, but to the undiscerning multitudes and to those who seek our destruction, from now on, the mysteries of the kingdom shall be presented in parables. And this we will do so that those who really desire to enter the kingdom may discern the meaning of the teaching and thus find salvation, while those who listen only to ensnare us may be the more confounded in that they will see without seeing and will hear without hearing. My children, do you not perceive the law of the spirit which decrees that to him who has shall be given so that he shall have an abundance; but from him who has not shall be taken away even that which he has. Therefore will I henceforth speak to the people much in parables to the end that our friends and those who desire to know the truth may find that which they seek, while our enemies and those who love not the truth may hear without understanding. Many of these people follow not in the way of the truth. The prophet did, indeed, describe all such undiscerning souls when he said: 'For this people's heart has waxed gross, and their ears are dull of hearing, and their eyes they have closed lest they should discern the truth and understand it in their hearts.'" 151:1.4 (1689.2)

The continued discussion of parables and further instruction as to their interpretation may be summarized and expressed in modern phraseology as follows: 151:3.2 (1692.1)

1. Jesus advised against the use of either fables or allegories in teaching the truths of the gospel. He did recommend the free use of parables, especially nature parables. He emphasized the value of utilizing the *analogy* existing between the natural and the spiritual worlds as a means of teaching truth. He frequently alluded to the natural as "the unreal and fleeting shadow of spirit realities." 151:3.3 (1692.2)
2. Jesus narrated three or four parables from the Hebrew scriptures, calling attention to the fact that this method of teaching was not wholly new. However, it became almost a new method of teaching as he employed it from this time onward. 151:3.4 (1692.3)
3. In teaching the apostles the value of parables, Jesus called attention to the following points: 151:3.5 (1692.4)
   - The parable provides for a simultaneous appeal to vastly different levels of mind and spirit. The parable stimulates the imagination, challenges the discrimination, and provokes critical thinking; it promotes sympathy without arousing antagonism. 151:3.6 (1692.5)
   - The parable proceeds from the things which are known to the discernment of the unknown. The parable utilizes the material and natural as a means of introducing the spiritual and the supermaterial. 151:3.7 (1692.6)
   - Parables favor the making of impartial moral decisions. The parable evades much prejudice and puts new truth gracefully into the mind and does all this with the arousal of a minimum of the self-defense of personal resentment. 151:3.8 (1692.7)
   - To reject the truth contained in parabolical analogy requires conscious intellectual action which is directly in contempt of one's honest judgment and fair decision. The parable conduces to the forcing of thought through the sense of hearing. 151:3.9 (1692.8)
   - The use of the parable form of teaching enables the teacher to present new and even startling truths while at the same time he largely avoids all controversy and outward clashing with tradition and established authority. 151:3.10 (1692.9)
   - The parable also possesses the advantage of stimulating the memory of the truth taught when the same familiar scenes are subsequently encountered. 151:3.11 (1693.1)
   - In this way Jesus sought to acquaint his followers with many of the reasons underlying his practice of increasingly using parables in his public teaching. 151:3.12 (1693.2)

The Parables of Jesus

Jesus also resorted to the use of parables as the best possible refutation of the studied effort of the religious leaders at Jerusalem to teach that all of his work was done by the assistance of demons and the prince of devils. The appeal to nature was in contravention of such teaching since the people of that day looked upon all natural phenomena as the product of the direct act of spiritual beings and supernatural forces. He also determined upon this method of teaching because it enabled him to proclaim vital truths to those who desired to know the better way while at the same time affording his enemies less opportunity to find cause for offense and for accusations against him. 151:3.14 (1693.4)	
The Parables	
Parable of the Sower:	"A sower went forth to sow, and it came to pass as he sowed that some seed fell by the wayside to be trodden underfoot and devoured by the birds of heaven. Other seed fell upon the rocky places where there was little earth, and immediately it sprang up because there was no depth to the soil, but as soon as the sun shone, it withered because it had no root whereby to secure moisture. Other seed fell among the thorns, and as the thorns grew up, it was choked so that it yielded no grain. Still other seed fell upon good ground and, growing, yielded, some thirtyfold, some sixtyfold, and some a hundredfold." And when he had finished speaking this parable, he said to the multitude, "He who has ears to hear, let him hear." 151:1.2 (1688.4)
Parable by the Sea:	The next day Jesus again taught the people from the boat, saying: "The kingdom of heaven is like a man who sowed good seed in his field; but while he slept, his enemy came and sowed weeds among the wheat and hastened away. And so when the young blades sprang up and later were about to bring forth fruit, there appeared also the weeds. Then the servants of this householder came and said to him: 'Sir, did you not sow good seed in your field? Whence then come these weeds?' And he replied to his servants, 'An enemy has done this.' The servants then asked their master, 'Would you have us go out and pluck up these weeds?' But he answered them and said: 'No, lest while you are gathering them up, you uproot the wheat also. Rather let them both grow together until the time of the harvest, when I will say to the reapers, Gather up first the weeds and bind them in bundles to burn and then gather up the wheat to be stored in my barn.'" 151:4.1 (1693.7) After the people had asked a few questions, Jesus spoke another parable: "The kingdom of heaven is like a grain of mustard seed which a man sowed in his field. Now a mustard seed is the least of seeds, but when it is full grown, it becomes the greatest of all herbs and is like a tree so that the birds of heaven are able to come and rest in the branches thereof." 151:4.2 (1693.8) "The kingdom of heaven is also like leaven which a woman took and hid in three measures of meal, and in this way it came about that all of the meal was leavened." 151:4.3 (1694.1) "The kingdom of heaven is also like a treasure hidden in a field, which a man discovered. In his joy he went forth to sell all he had that he might have the money to buy the field." 151:4.4 (1694.2) "The kingdom of heaven is also like a merchant seeking goodly pearls; and having found one pearl of great price, he went out and sold everything he possessed that he might be able to buy the extraordinary pearl." 151:4.5 (1694.3)

Parable by the Sea: (Continued)	"Again, the kingdom of heaven is like a sweep net which was cast into the sea, and it gathered up every kind of fish. Now, when the net was filled, the fishermen drew it up on the beach, where they sat down and sorted out the fish, gathering the good into vessels while the bad they threw away." 151:4.6 (1694.4)
Parable of the Bridge:	In entering Sidon, Jesus and his associates passed over a bridge, the first one many of them had ever seen. As they walked over this bridge, Jesus, among other things, said: "This world is only a bridge; you may pass over it, but you should not think to build a dwelling place upon it." 156:2.1 (1735.5)
Parable of the Foolish Carpenter:	It was during this same sermon that Jesus made use of his first and only parable having to do with his own trade—carpentry. In the course of his admonition to "Build well the foundations for the growth of a noble character of spiritual endowments," he said: "In order to yield the fruits of the spirit, you must be born of the spirit. You must be taught by the spirit and be led by the spirit if you would live the spirit-filled life among your fellows. But do not make the mistake of the foolish carpenter who wastes valuable time squaring, measuring, and smoothing his worm-eaten and inwardly rotting timber and then, when he has thus bestowed all of his labor upon the unsound beam, must reject it as unfit to enter into the foundations of the building which he would construct to withstand the assaults of time and storm. Let every man make sure that the intellectual and moral foundations of character are such as will adequately support the superstructure of the enlarging and ennobling spiritual nature, which is thus to transform the mortal mind and then, in association with that re-created mind, is to achieve the evolvement of the soul of immortal destiny. Your spirit nature— the jointly created soul—is a living growth, but the mind and morals of the individual are the soil from which these higher manifestations of human development and divine destiny must spring. The soil of the evolving soul is human and material, but the destiny of this combined creature of mind and spirit is spiritual and divine." 156:5.2 (1738.1)
Parable of the Great Supper:	"A certain ruler gave a great supper, and having bidden many guests, he dispatched his servants at suppertime to say to those who were invited, 'Come, for everything is now ready.' And they all with one accord began to make excuses. The first said, 'I have just bought a farm, and I must needs go to prove it; I pray you have me excused.' Another said, 'I have bought five yoke of oxen, and I must go to receive them; I pray you have me excused.' And another said, 'I have just married a wife, and therefore I cannot come.' So the servants went back and reported this to their master. When the master of the house heard this, he was very angry, and turning to his servants, he said: 'I have made ready this marriage feast; the fatlings are killed, and all is in readiness for my guests, but they have spurned my invitation; they have gone every man after his lands and his merchandise, and they even show disrespect to my servants who bid them come to my feast. Go out quickly, therefore, into the streets and lanes of the city, out into the highways and the byways, and bring hither the poor and the outcast, the blind and the lame, that the marriage feast may have guests.' And the servants did as their lord commanded, and even then there was room for more guests. Then said the lord to his servants: 'Go now out into the roads and the countryside and constrain those who are there to come in that my house may be filled. I declare that none of those who were first bidden shall taste of my supper.' And the servants did as their master commanded, and the house was filled." 167:2.2 (1835.2)

Parable of the Lily:	On this Wednesday afternoon, in the course of his address, Jesus first told his followers the story of the white lily which rears its pure and snowy head high into the sunshine while its roots are grounded in the slime and muck of the darkened soil beneath. "Likewise," said he, "mortal man, while he has his roots of origin and being in the animal soil of human nature, can by faith raise his spiritual nature up into the sunlight of heavenly truth and actually bear the noble fruits of the spirit." 156:5.1 (1737.5)
Parable of the Lost Sheep:	"You have been admonished by the prophets from Samuel to John that you should seek for God—search for truth. Always have they said, 'Seek the Lord while he may be found.' And all such teaching should be taken to heart. But I have come to show you that, while you are seeking to find God, God is likewise seeking to find you. Many times have I told you the story of the good shepherd who left the ninety and nine sheep in the fold while he went forth searching for the one that was lost, and how, when he had found the straying sheep, he laid it over his shoulder and tenderly carried it back to the fold. And when the lost sheep had been restored to the fold, you remember that the good shepherd called in his friends and bade them rejoice with him over the finding of the sheep that had been lost. Again I say there is more joy in heaven over one sinner who repents than over the ninety and nine just persons who need no repentance. The fact that souls are *lost* only increases the interest of the heavenly Father. I have come to this world to do my Father's bidding, and it has truly been said of the Son of Man that he is a friend of publicans and sinners. 169:1.2 (1850.9)
Parable of the Shrewd Steward:	"You may all learn a lesson from the story of a certain rich man who had a shrewd but unjust steward. This steward had not only oppressed his master's clients for his own selfish gain, but he had also directly wasted and squandered his master's funds. When all this finally came to the ears of his master, he called the steward before him and asked the meaning of these rumors and required that he should give immediate accounting of his stewardship and prepare to turn his master's affairs over to another. 169:2.3 (1853.6) "Now this unfaithful steward began to say to himself: 'What shall I do since I am about to lose this stewardship? I have not the strength to dig; to beg I am ashamed. I know what I will do to make certain that, when I am put out of this stewardship, I will be welcomed into the houses of all who do business with my master.' And then, calling in each of his lord's debtors, he said to the first, 'How much do you owe my master?' He answered, 'A hundred measures of oil.' Then said the steward, 'Take your wax board bond, sit down quickly, and change it to fifty.' Then he said to another debtor, 'How much do you owe?' And he replied, 'A hundred measures of wheat.' Then said the steward, 'Take your bond and write fourscore.' And this he did with numerous other debtors. And so did this dishonest steward seek to make friends for himself after he would be discharged from his stewardship. Even his lord and master, when he subsequently found out about this, was compelled to admit that his unfaithful steward had at least shown sagacity in the manner in which he had sought to provide for future days of want and adversity. 169:2.4 (1853.7) "I say to you who profess to be acquiring treasure in heaven: Take lessons from those who make friends with the mammon of unrighteousness, and likewise so conduct your lives that you make eternal friendship with the forces of righteousness in order that, when all things earthly fail, you shall be joyfully received into the eternal habitations. 169:2.5 (1854.1)

Parable of the Shrewd Steward: (Continued)	"I affirm that he who is faithful in little will also be faithful in much, while he who is unrighteous in little will also be unrighteous in much. If you have not shown foresight and integrity in the affairs of this world, how can you hope to be faithful and prudent when you are trusted with the stewardship of the true riches of the heavenly kingdom? If you are not good stewards and faithful bankers, if you have not been faithful in that which is another's, who will be foolish enough to give you great treasure in your own name? 169:2.6 (1854.2)
Parable of the of the Rich Man and the Beggar:	"There was a certain rich man named Dives, who, being clothed in purple and fine linen, lived in mirth and splendor every day. And there was a certain beggar named Lazarus, who was laid at this rich man's gate, covered with sores and desiring to be fed with the crumbs which fell from the rich man's table; yes, even the dogs came and licked his sores. And it came to pass that the beggar died and was carried away by the angels to rest in Abraham's bosom. And then, presently, this rich man also died and was buried with great pomp and regal splendor. When the rich man departed from this world, he waked up in Hades, and finding himself in torment, he lifted up his eyes and beheld Abraham afar off and Lazarus in his bosom. And then Dives cried aloud: 'Father Abraham, have mercy on me and send over Lazarus that he may dip the tip of his finger in water to cool my tongue, for I am in great anguish because of my punishment.' And then Abraham replied: 'My son, you should remember that in your lifetime you enjoyed the good things while Lazarus in like manner suffered the evil. But now all this is changed, seeing that Lazarus is comforted while you are tormented. And besides, between us and you there is a great gulf so that we cannot go to you, neither can you come over to us.' Then said Dives to Abraham: 'I pray you send Lazarus back to my father's house, inasmuch as I have five brothers, that he may so testify as to prevent my brothers from coming to this place of torment.' But Abraham said: 'My son, they have Moses and the prophets; let them hear them.' And then answered Dives: 'No, No, Father Abraham! but if one go to them from the dead, they will repent.' And then said Abraham: 'If they hear not Moses and the prophets, neither will they be persuaded even if one were to rise from the dead.'" 169:3.2 (1854.6)
Parable of the Pounds:	Said Jesus: "You think that the Son of Man goes up to Jerusalem to receive a kingdom, but I declare that you are doomed to disappointment. Do you not remember about a certain prince who went into a far country to receive for himself a kingdom, but even before he could return, the citizens of his province, who in their hearts had already rejected him, sent an embassy after him, saying, 'We will not have this man to reign over us'? As this king was rejected in the temporal rule, so is the Son of Man to be rejected in the spiritual rule. Again I declare that my kingdom is not of this world; but if the Son of Man had been accorded the spiritual rule of his people, he would have accepted such a kingdom of men's souls and would have reigned over such a dominion of human hearts. Notwithstanding that they reject my spiritual rule over them, I will return again to receive from others such a kingdom of spirit as is now denied me. You will see the Son of Man rejected now, but in another age that which the children of Abraham now reject will be received and exalted. 171:8.3 (1875.8)

Parable of the Two Sons:	As the caviling Pharisees stood there in silence before Jesus, he looked down on them and said: "Since you are in doubt about John's mission and arrayed in enmity against the teaching and the works of the Son of Man, give ear while I tell you a parable: A certain great and respected landholder had two sons, and desiring the help of his sons in the management of his large estates, he came to one of them, saying, 'Son, go work today in my vineyard.' And this unthinking son answered his father, saying, 'I will not go'; but afterward he repented and went. When he had found his older son, likewise he said to him, 'Son, go work in my vineyard.' And this hypocritical and unfaithful son answered, 'Yes, my father, I will go.' But when his father had departed, he went not. Let me ask you, which of these sons really did his father's will?" 173:3.1 (1893.1) And the people spoke with one accord, saying, "The first son." And then said Jesus: "Even so; and now do I declare that the publicans and harlots, even though they appear to refuse the call to repentance, shall see the error of their way and go on into the kingdom of God before you, who make great pretensions of serving the Father in heaven while you refuse to do the works of the Father. It was not you, the Pharisees and scribes, who believed John, but rather the publicans and sinners; neither do you believe my teaching, but the common people hear my words gladly."173:3.2 (1893.2)
Parable of the Absent Landlord:	"There was a good man who was a householder, and he planted a vineyard. He set a hedge about it, dug a pit for the wine press, and built a watchtower for the guards. Then he let this vineyard out to tenants while he went on a long journey into another country. And when the season of the fruits drew near, he sent servants to the tenants to receive his rental. But they took counsel among themselves and refused to give these servants the fruits due their master; instead, they fell upon his servants, beating one, stoning another, and sending the others away empty-handed. And when the householder heard about all this, he sent other and more trusted servants to deal with these wicked tenants, and these they wounded and also treated shamefully. And then the householder sent his favorite servant, his steward, and him they killed. And still, in patience and with forbearance, he dispatched many other servants, but none would they receive. Some they beat, others they killed, and when the householder had been so dealt with, he decided to send his son to deal with these ungrateful tenants, saying to himself, 'They may mistreat my servants, but they will surely show respect for my beloved son.' But when these unrepentant and wicked tenants saw the son, they reasoned among themselves: 'This is the heir; come, let us kill him and then the inheritance will be ours.' So they laid hold on him, and after casting him out of the vineyard, they killed him. When the lord of that vineyard shall hear how they have rejected and killed his son, what will he do to those ungrateful and wicked tenants?" 173:4.2 (1893.6) And when the people heard this parable and the question Jesus asked, they answered, "He will destroy those miserable men and let out his vineyard to other and honest farmers who will render to him the fruits in their season." And when some of them who heard perceived that this parable referred to the Jewish nation and its treatment of the prophets and to the impending rejection of Jesus and the gospel of the kingdom, they said in sorrow, "God forbid that we should go on doing these things." 173:4.3 (1894.1)

Parable of the Marriage Feast:	After the scribes and rulers had withdrawn, Jesus addressed himself again to the assembled crowd and spoke the parable of the wedding feast. He said: 173:5.2 (1894.5) "The kingdom of heaven may be likened to a certain king who made a marriage feast for his son and dispatched messengers to call those who had previously been invited to the feast to come, saying, 'Everything is ready for the marriage supper at the king's palace.' Now, many of those who had once promised to attend, at this time refused to come. When the king heard of these rejections of his invitation, he sent other servants and messengers, saying: 'Tell all those who were bidden, to come, for, behold, my dinner is ready. My oxen and my fatlings are killed, and all is in readiness for the celebration of the forthcoming marriage of my son.' But again did the thoughtless make light of this call of their king, and they went their ways, one to the farm, another to the pottery, and others to their merchandise. Still others were not content thus to slight the king's call, but in open rebellion they laid hands on the king's messengers and shamefully mistreated them, even killing some of them. And when the king perceived that his chosen guests, even those who had accepted his preliminary invitation and had promised to attend the wedding feast, had finally rejected his call and in rebellion had assaulted and slain his chosen messengers, he was exceedingly wroth. And then this insulted king ordered out his armies and the armies of his allies and instructed them to destroy these rebellious murderers and to burn down their city. 173:5.1 (1894.4) "And when he had punished those who spurned his invitation, he appointed yet another day for the wedding feast and said to his messengers: 'They who were first bidden to the wedding were not worthy; so go now into the parting of the ways and into the highways and even beyond the borders of the city, and as many as you shall find, bid even these strangers to come in and attend this wedding feast.' And then these servants went out into the highways and the out-of-the-way places, and they gathered together as many as they found, good and bad, rich and poor, so that at last the wedding chamber was filled with willing guests. When all was ready, the king came in to view his guests, and much to his surprise he saw there a man without a wedding garment. The king, since he had freely provided wedding garments for all his guests, addressing this man, said: 'Friend, how is it that you come into my guest chamber on this occasion without a wedding garment?' And this unprepared man was speechless. Then said the king to his servants: 'Cast out this thoughtless guest from my house to share the lot of all the others who have spurned my hospitality and rejected my call. I will have none here except those who delight to accept my invitation, and who do me the honor to wear those guest garments so freely provided for all.'" 173:5.3 (1895.1)
Parable of the Talents:	"As individuals, and as a generation of believers, hear me while I speak a parable: There was a certain great man who, before starting out on a long journey to another country, called all his trusted servants before him and delivered into their hands all his goods. To one he gave five talents, to another two, and to another one. And so on down through the entire group of honored stewards, to each he intrusted his goods according to their several abilities; and then he set out on his journey. When their lord had departed, his servants set themselves at work to gain profits from the wealth intrusted to them. Immediately he who had received five talents began to trade with them and very soon had made a profit of another five talents. In like manner he who had received two talents soon had gained two more. And so did all of these servants make gains for

Parable of the Talents (Continued)	their master except him who received but one talent. He went away by himself and dug a hole in the earth where he hid his lord's money. Presently the lord of those servants unexpectedly returned and called upon his stewards for a reckoning. And when they had all been called before their master, he who had received the five talents came forward with the money which had been intrusted to him and brought five additional talents, saying, 'Lord, you gave me five talents to invest, and I am glad to present five other talents as my gain.' And then his lord said to him: 'Well done, good and faithful servant, you have been faithful over a few things; I will now set you as steward over many; enter forthwith into the joy of your lord.' And then he who had received the two talents came forward, saying: 'Lord, you delivered into my hands two talents; behold, I have gained these other two talents.' And his lord then said to him: 'Well done, good and faithful steward; you also have been faithful over a few things, and I will now set you over many; enter you into the joy of your lord.' And then there came to the accounting he who had received the one talent. This servant came forward, saying, 'Lord, I knew you and realized that you were a shrewd man in that you expected gains where you had not personally labored; therefore was I afraid to risk aught of that which was intrusted to me. I safely hid your talent in the earth; here it is; you now have what belongs to you.' But his lord answered: 'You are an indolent and slothful steward. By your own words you confess that you knew I would require of you an accounting with reasonable profit, such as your diligent fellow servants have this day rendered. Knowing this, you ought, therefore, to have at least put my money into the hands of the bankers that on my return I might have received my own with interest.' And then to the chief steward this lord said: 'Take away this one talent from this unprofitable servant and give it to him who has the ten talents.'176:3.4 (1916.4) "To everyone who has, more shall be given, and he shall have abundance; but from him who has not, even that which he has shall be taken away. You cannot stand still in the affairs of the eternal kingdom. My Father requires all his children to grow in grace and in a knowledge of the truth. You who know these truths must yield the increase of the fruits of the spirit and manifest a growing devotion to the unselfish service of your fellow servants. And remember that, inasmuch as you minister to one of the least of my brethren, you have done this service to me. 176:3.5 (1917.1) "And so should you go about the work of the Father's business, now and henceforth, even forevermore. Carry on until I come. In faithfulness do that which is intrusted to you, and thereby shall you be ready for the reckoning call of death. And having thus lived for the glory of the Father and the satisfaction of the Son, you shall enter with joy and exceedingly great pleasure into the eternal service of the everlasting kingdom." 176:3.6 (1917.2)

People Who Met Jesus But Did Not Recognize Him Later in His Life

People Who Met Jesus But Did Not Recognize Him Later in His Life

Stephen, a Young Hellenist:	Perhaps the most notable of all these contacts was the one with a young Hellenist named Stephen. This young man was on his first visit to Jerusalem and chanced to meet Jesus on Thursday afternoon of Passover week. While they both strolled about viewing the Asmonean palace, Jesus began the casual conversation that resulted in their becoming interested in each other, and which led to a four-hour discussion of the way of life and the true God and his worship. Stephen was tremendously impressed with what Jesus said; he never forgot his words. 128:3.5 (1411.5) And this was the same Stephen who subsequently became a believer in the teachings of Jesus, and whose boldness in preaching this early gospel resulted in his being stoned to death by irate Jews. Some of Stephen's extraordinary boldness in proclaiming his view of the new gospel was the direct result of this earlier interview with Jesus. But Stephen never even faintly surmised that the Galilean he had talked with some fifteen years previously was the very same person whom he later proclaimed the world's Savior, and for whom he was so soon to die, thus becoming the first martyr of the newly evolving Christian faith. When Stephen yielded up his life as the price of his attack upon the Jewish temple and its traditional practices, there stood by one named Saul, a citizen of Tarsus. And when Saul saw how this Greek could die for his faith, there were aroused in his heart those emotions which eventually led him to espouse the cause for which Stephen died; later on he became the aggressive and indomitable Paul, the philosopher, if not the sole founder, of the Christian religion. 128:3.6 (1411.6)
Men of Damascus:	Presently this merchant brought before Jesus a group of twelve merchants and bankers who agreed to support this newly projected school. Jesus manifested deep interest in the proposed school, helped them plan for its organization, but always expressed the fear that his other and unstated but prior obligations would prevent his accepting the direction of such a pretentious enterprise. His would-be benefactor was persistent, and he profitably employed Jesus at his home doing some translating while he, his wife, and their sons and daughters sought to prevail upon Jesus to accept the proffered honor. But he would not consent. He well knew that his mission on earth was not to be supported by institutions of learning; he knew that he must not obligate himself in the least to be directed by the "councils of men," no matter how well-intentioned. 128:4.2 (1412.5) He who was rejected by the Jerusalem religious leaders, even after he had demonstrated his leadership, was recognized and hailed as a master teacher by the businessmen and bankers of Damascus, and all this when he was an obscure and unknown carpenter of Nazareth. 128:4.3 (1412.6) He never spoke about this offer to his family, and the end of this year found him back in Nazareth going about his daily duties just as if he had never been tempted by the flattering propositions of his Damascus friends. Neither did these men of Damascus ever associate the later citizen of Capernaum who turned all Jewry upside down with the former carpenter of Nazareth who had dared to refuse the honor which their combined wealth might have procured. 128:4.4 (1412.7)
Simon of Cyrene:	The travelers were truly rested and refreshed when they made ready about noon one day to sail for Carthage in northern Africa, stopping for two days at Cyrene. It was here that Jesus and Ganid gave first aid to a lad named Rufus, who had been injured by the breakdown of a loaded oxcart. They carried him home to his mother, and his father, Simon, little dreamed that the man whose cross he subsequently bore by orders of a Roman soldier was the stranger who once befriended his son. 130:6.6 (1438.3)

People Who Met Jesus But Did Not Recognize Him Later in His Life

Jews of Alexandria:	The week following the Passover of this year a young man from Alexandria came down to Nazareth to arrange for a meeting, later in the year, between Jesus and a group of Alexandrian Jews at some point on the Palestinian coast. This conference was set for the middle of June, and Jesus went over to Caesarea to meet with five prominent Jews of Alexandria, who besought him to establish himself in their city as a religious teacher, offering as an inducement to begin with, the position of assistant to the chazan in their chief synagogue. 128:5.2 (1413.7) The spokesmen for this committee explained to Jesus that Alexandria was destined to become the headquarters of Jewish culture for the entire world; that the Hellenistic trend of Jewish affairs had virtually outdistanced the Babylonian school of thought. They reminded Jesus of the ominous rumblings of rebellion in Jerusalem and throughout Palestine and assured him that any uprising of the Palestinian Jews would be equivalent to national suicide, that the iron hand of Rome would crush the rebellion in three months, and that Jerusalem would be destroyed and the temple demolished, that not one stone would be left upon another. 128:5.3 (1414.1) Jesus listened to all they had to say, thanked them for their confidence, and, in declining to go to Alexandria, in substance said, "My hour has not yet come." They were nonplused by his apparent indifference to the honor they had sought to confer upon him. Before taking leave of Jesus, they presented him with a purse in token of the esteem of his Alexandrian friends and in compensation for the time and expense of coming over to Caesarea to confer with them. But he likewise refused the money, saying: "The house of Joseph has never received alms, and we cannot eat another's bread as long as I have strong arms and my brothers can labor." 128:5.4 (1414.2) His friends from Egypt set sail for home, and in subsequent years, when they heard rumors of the Capernaum boatbuilder who was creating such a commotion in Palestine, few of them surmised that he was the babe of Bethlehem grown up and the same strange-acting Galilean who had so unceremoniously declined the invitation to become a great teacher in Alexandria. 128:5.5 (1414.3)
Claudus:	The first stop on the way to Italy was at the island of Malta. Here Jesus had a long talk with a downhearted and discouraged young man named Claudus. This fellow had contemplated taking his life, but when he had finished talking with the scribe of Damascus, he said: "I will face life like a man; I am through playing the coward. I will go back to my people and begin all over again." Shortly he became an enthusiastic preacher of the Cynics, and still later on he joined hands with Peter in proclaiming Christianity in Rome and Naples, and after the death of Peter he went on to Spain preaching the gospel. But he never knew that the man who inspired him in Malta was the Jesus whom he subsequently proclaimed the world's Deliverer. 130:8.1 (1440.1)
Religious Leaders of Rome:	Through all their experiences, neither Stephen nor the thirty chosen ones ever realized that they had once talked with the man whose name became the subject of their religious teaching. Jesus' work in behalf of the original thirty-two was entirely personal. In his labors for these individuals the scribe of Damascus never met more than three of them at one time, seldom more than two, while most often he taught them singly. And he could do this great work of religious training because these men and women were not tradition bound; they were not victims of a settled preconception as to all future religious developments. 132:0.9 (1456.5)

People Who Met Jesus But Did Not Recognize Him Later in His Life

Paul:	Many were the times in the years so soon to follow that Peter, Paul, and the other Christian teachers in Rome heard about this scribe of Damascus who had preceded them, and who had so obviously (and as they supposed unwittingly) prepared the way for their coming with the new gospel. Though Paul never really surmised the identity of this scribe of Damascus, he did, a short time before his death, because of the similarity of personal descriptions, reach the conclusion that the "tentmaker of Antioch" was also the "scribe of Damascus." On one occasion, while preaching in Rome, Simon Peter, on listening to a description of the Damascus scribe, surmised that this individual might have been Jesus but quickly dismissed the idea, knowing full well (so he thought) that the Master had never been in Rome. 132:0.10 (1456.6) At Antioch the Son of Man lived for over two months, working, observing, studying, visiting, ministering, and all the while learning how man lives, how he thinks, feels, and reacts to the environment of human existence. For three weeks of this period he worked as a tentmaker. He remained longer in Antioch than at any other place he visited on this trip. Ten years later, when the Apostle Paul was preaching in Antioch and heard his followers speak of the doctrines of the *Damascus scribe,* he little knew that his pupils had heard the voice, and listened to the teachings, of the Master himself. 134:7.3 (1492.3)
Justus:	Jesus and Ganid were often guests in another Jewish home, that of Justus, a devout merchant, who lived alongside the synagogue. And many times, subsequently, when the Apostle Paul sojourned in this home, did he listen to the recounting of these visits with the Indian lad and his Jewish tutor, while both Paul and Justus wondered whatever became of such a wise and brilliant Hebrew teacher. 133:3.5 (1472.4)
Ganid and Gonod:	At last the day came for the separation. They were all brave, especially the lad, but it was a trying ordeal. They were tearful of eye but courageous of heart. In bidding his teacher farewell, Ganid said: "Farewell, Teacher, but not forever. When I come again to Damascus, I will look for you. I love you, for I think the Father in heaven must be something like you; at least I know you are much like what you have told me about him. I will remember your teaching, but most of all, I will never forget you." Said the father, "Farewell to a great teacher, one who has made us better and helped us to know God." And Jesus replied, "Peace be upon you, and may the blessing of the Father in heaven ever abide with you." And Jesus stood on the shore and watched as the small boat carried them out to their anchored ship. Thus the Master left his friends from India at Charax, never to see them again in this world; nor were they, in this world, ever to know that the man who later appeared as Jesus of Nazareth was this same friend they had just taken leave of—Joshua their teacher. 133:9.4 (1481.6)
Teachers at Urmia:	Cymboyton's eldest son had appealed to Abner at Philadelphia for help, but Abner's choice of teachers was most unfortunate in that they turned out to be unyielding and uncompromising. These teachers sought to make their religion dominant over the other beliefs. They never suspected that the oft-referred-to lectures of the caravan conductor had been delivered by Jesus himself. 134:6.16 (1491.9)

People Who Met Jesus But Did Not Recognize Him Later in His Life

Herod Antipas:	When Herod Antipas stopped in Jerusalem, he dwelt in the old Maccabean palace of Herod the Great, and it was to this home of the former king that Jesus was now taken by the temple guards, and he was followed by his accusers and an increasing multitude. Herod had long heard of Jesus, and he was very curious about him. When the Son of Man stood before him, on this Friday morning, the wicked Idumean never for one moment recalled the lad of former years who had appeared before him in Sepphoris pleading for a just decision regarding the money due his father, who had been accidentally killed while at work on one of the public buildings. As far as Herod knew, he had never seen Jesus, although he had worried a great deal about him when his work had been centered in Galilee. Now that he was in custody of Pilate and the Judeans, Herod was desirous of seeing him, feeling secure against any trouble from him in the future. Herod had heard much about the miracles wrought by Jesus, and he really hoped to see him do some wonder. 185:4.1 (1992.3)

Questions Asked of Jesus

One day after the evening meal Jesus and the young Philistine strolled down by the sea, and Gadiah, not knowing that this "scribe of Damascus" was so well versed in the Hebrew traditions, pointed out to Jesus the ship landing from which it was reputed that Jonah had embarked on his ill-fated voyage to Tarshish. And when he had concluded his remarks, he asked Jesus this question:

"But do you suppose the big fish really did swallow Jonah?"

Jesus perceived that this young man's life had been tremendously influenced by this tradition, and that its contemplation had impressed upon him the folly of trying to run away from duty; Jesus therefore said nothing that would suddenly destroy the foundations of Gadiah's present motivation for practical living. In answering this question, Jesus said: "My friend, we are all Jonahs with lives to live in accordance with the will of God, and at all times when we seek to escape the present duty of living by running away to far-off enticements, we thereby put ourselves in the immediate control of those influences which are not directed by the powers of truth and the forces of righteousness. The flight from duty is the sacrifice of truth. The escape from the service of light and life can only result in those distressing conflicts with the difficult whales of selfishness which lead eventually to darkness and death unless such God-forsaking Jonahs shall turn their hearts, even when in the very depths of despair, to seek after God and his goodness. And when such disheartened souls sincerely seek for God—hunger for truth and thirst for righteousness—there is nothing that can hold them in further captivity. No matter into what great depths they may have fallen, when they seek the light with a whole heart, the spirit of the Lord God of heaven will deliver them from their captivity; the evil circumstances of life will spew them out upon the dry land of fresh opportunities for renewed service and wiser living." 130:1.2 (1428.2)

Jesus' last visit with Gadiah had to do with a discussion of good and evil. This young Philistine was much troubled by a feeling of injustice because of the presence of evil in the world alongside the good. He said:

"How can God, if he is infinitely good, permit us to suffer the sorrows of evil; after all, who creates evil?"

It was still believed by many in those days that God creates both good and evil, but Jesus never taught such error. In answering this question, Jesus said: "My brother, God is love; therefore he must be good, and his goodness is so great and real that it cannot contain the small and unreal things of evil. God is so positively good that there is absolutely no place in him for negative evil. Evil is the immature choosing and the unthinking misstep of those who are resistant to goodness, rejectful of beauty, and disloyal to truth. Evil is only the misadaptation of immaturity or the disruptive and distorting influence of ignorance. Evil is the inevitable darkness which follows upon the heels of the unwise rejection of light. Evil is that which is dark and untrue, and which, when consciously embraced and willfully endorsed, becomes sin. 130:1.5 (1429.1)

"Your Father in heaven, by endowing you with the power to choose between truth and error, created the potential negative of the positive way of light and life; but such errors of evil are really nonexistent until such a time as an intelligent creature wills their existence by mischoosing the way of life. And then are such evils later exalted into sin by the knowing and deliberate choice of such a willful and rebellious creature. This is why our Father in heaven permits the good and the evil to go along together until the end of life, just as nature allows the wheat and the tares to grow side by side until the harvest." 130:1.6 (1429.2)

One of the young men who worked with Jesus one day on the steering paddle became much interested in the words which he dropped from hour to hour as they toiled in the shipyard. When Jesus intimated that the Father in heaven was interested in the welfare of his children on earth, this young Greek, Anaxand, said:

"If the Gods are interested in me, then why do they not remove the cruel and unjust foreman of this workshop?"

He was startled when Jesus replied, "Since you know the ways of kindness and value justice, perhaps the Gods have brought this erring man near that you may lead him into this better way. Maybe you are the salt which is to make this brother more agreeable to all other men; that is, if you have not lost your savor. As it is, this man is your master in that his evil ways unfavorably influence you. Why not assert your mastery of evil by virtue of the power of goodness and thus become the master of all relations between the two of you? I predict that the good in you could overcome the evil in him if you gave it a fair and living chance. There is no adventure in the course of mortal existence more enthralling than to enjoy the exhilaration of becoming the material life partner with spiritual energy and divine truth in one of their triumphant struggles with error and evil. It is a marvelous and transforming experience to become the living channel of spiritual light to the mortal who sits in spiritual darkness. If you are more blessed with truth than is this man, his need should challenge you. Surely you are not the coward who could stand by on the seashore and watch a fellow man who could not swim perish! How much more of value is this man's soul floundering in darkness compared to his body drowning in water!" 130:2.4 (1430.2)

Ganid was, by this time, beginning to learn how his tutor spent his leisure in this unusual personal ministry to his fellow men, and the young Indian set about to find out the motive for these incessant activities. He asked,

"Why do you occupy yourself so continuously with these visits with strangers?"

And Jesus answered: "Ganid, no man is a stranger to one who knows God. In the experience of finding the Father in heaven you discover that all men are your brothers, and does it seem strange that one should enjoy the exhilaration of meeting a newly discovered brother? To become acquainted with one's brothers and sisters, to know their problems and to learn to love them, is the supreme experience of living." 130:2.6 (1431.1)

A very interesting incident occurred one afternoon by the roadside as they neared Tarentum. They observed a rough and bullying youth brutally attacking a smaller lad. Jesus hastened to the assistance of the assaulted youth, and when he had rescued him, he tightly held on to the offender until the smaller lad had made his escape. The moment Jesus released the little bully, Ganid pounced upon the boy and began soundly to thrash him, and to Ganid's astonishment Jesus promptly interfered. After he had restrained Ganid and permitted the frightened boy to escape, the young man, as soon as he got his breath, excitedly exclaimed: "I cannot understand you, Teacher.

If mercy requires that you rescue the smaller lad, does not justice demand the punishment of the larger and offending youth?" In answering, Jesus said: 133:1.1 (1468.4)

"Ganid, it is true, you do not understand. Mercy ministry is always the work of the individual, but justice punishment is the function of the social, governmental, or universe administrative groups. As an individual I am beholden to show mercy; I must go to the rescue of the assaulted lad, and in all consistency I may employ sufficient force to restrain the aggressor. And that is just what I did. I achieved the deliverance of the assaulted lad; that was the end of mercy ministry. Then I forcibly detained the aggressor a sufficient length of time to enable the weaker party to the dispute to make his escape, after which I withdrew from the affair. I did not proceed to sit in judgment on the aggressor, thus to pass upon his motive—to adjudicate all that entered into his attack upon his fellow—and then undertake to execute the punishment which my mind might dictate as just recompense for his wrongdoing. Ganid, mercy may be lavish, but justice is precise. Cannot you discern that no two persons are likely to agree as to the punishment which would satisfy the demands of justice? One would impose forty lashes, another twenty, while still another would advise solitary confinement as a just punishment. Can you not see that on this world such responsibilities had better rest upon the group or be administered by chosen representatives of the group? In the universe, judgment is vested in those who fully know the antecedents of all wrongdoing as well as its motivation. In civilized society and in an organized universe the administration of justice presupposes the passing of just sentence consequent upon fair judgment, and such prerogatives are vested in the juridical groups of the worlds and in the all-knowing administrators of the higher universes of all creation." 133:1.2 (1469.1)

For days they talked about this problem of manifesting mercy and administering justice. And Ganid, at least to some extent, understood why Jesus would not engage in personal combat. But Ganid asked one last question, to which he never received a fully satisfactory answer; and that question was:

"But, Teacher, if a stronger and ill-tempered creature should attack you and threaten to destroy you, what would you do? Would you make no effort to defend yourself?"

Although Jesus could not fully and satisfactorily answer the lad's question, inasmuch as he was not willing to disclose to him that he (Jesus) was living on earth as the exemplification of the Paradise Father's love to an onlooking universe, he did say this much: 133:1.3 (1469.2)

"Ganid, I can well understand how some of these problems perplex you, and I will endeavor to answer your question. First, in all attacks which might be made upon my person, I would determine whether or not the aggressor was a son of God—my brother in the flesh—and if I thought such a creature did not possess moral judgment and spiritual reason, I would unhesitatingly defend myself to the full capacity of my powers of resistance, regardless of consequences to the attacker. But I would not thus assault a fellow man of sonship status, even in self-defense. That is, I would not punish him in advance and without judgment for his assault upon me. I would by every possible artifice seek to prevent and dissuade him from making such an attack and to mitigate it in case of my failure to abort it. Ganid, I have absolute confidence in my heavenly Father's overcare; I am consecrated to doing the will of my Father in heaven. I do not believe that *real* harm can befall me; I do not believe that my lifework can really be jeopardized by anything my enemies might wish to visit upon me, and surely we have no violence to fear from our friends. I am absolutely assured that the entire universe is friendly to me—this all-powerful truth I insist on believing with a wholehearted trust in spite of all appearances to the contrary." 133:1.4 (1469.3)

This long suspense in prison was humanly unbearable. Just a few days before his death John again sent trusted messengers to Jesus, inquiring:

"Is my work done? Why do I languish in prison? Are you truly the Messiah, or shall we look for another?"

And when these two disciples gave this message to Jesus, the Son of Man replied: "Go back to John and tell him that I have not forgotten but to suffer me also this, for it becomes us to fulfill all righteousness. Tell John what you have seen and heard—that the poor have good tidings preached to them—and, finally, tell the beloved herald of my earth mission that he shall be abundantly blessed in the age to come if he finds no occasion to doubt and stumble over me." 135:11.4 (1507.3)

Jesus was asleep when they reached his abode, but they awakened him, saying:

"How is it that, while we who have so long lived with you are searching in the hills for you, you prefer others before us and choose Andrew and Simon as your first associates in the new kingdom?"

Jesus answered them, "Be calm in your hearts and ask yourselves, 'who directed that you should search for the Son of Man when he was about his Father's business?'" After they had recited the details of their long search in the hills, Jesus further instructed them: "You should learn to search for the secret of the new kingdom in your hearts and not in the hills. That which you sought was already present in your souls. You are indeed my brethren—you needed not to be received by me—already were you of the kingdom, and you should be of good cheer, making ready also to go with us tomorrow into Galilee." John then made bold to ask, "But, Master, will James and I be associates with you in the new kingdom, even as Andrew and Simon?" And Jesus, laying a hand on the shoulder of each of them, said: "My brethren, you were already with me in the spirit of the kingdom, even before these others made request to be received. You, my brethren, have no need to make request for entrance into the kingdom; you have been with me in the kingdom from the beginning. Before men, others may take precedence over you, but in my heart did I also number you in the councils of the kingdom, even before you thought to make this request of me. And even so might you have been first before men had you not been absent engaged in a well-intentioned but self-appointed task of seeking for one who was not lost. In the coming kingdom, be not mindful of those things which foster your anxiety but rather at all times concern yourselves only with doing the will of the Father who is in heaven." 137:1.6 (1525.3)

Jesus had planned for a quiet missionary campaign of five months' personal work. He did not tell the apostles how long this was to last; they worked from week to week. And early on this first day of the week, just as he was about to announce this to his twelve apostles, Simon Peter, James Zebedee, and Judas Iscariot came to have private converse with him. Taking Jesus aside, Peter made bold to say:

"Master, we come at the behest of our associates to inquire whether the time is not now ripe to enter into the kingdom. And will you proclaim the kingdom at Capernaum, or are we to move on to Jerusalem? And when shall we learn, each of us, the positions we are to occupy with you in the establishment of the kingdom—"

and Peter would have gone on asking further questions, but Jesus raised an admonitory hand and stopped him. And beckoning the other apostles standing nearby to join them, Jesus said: "My little children, how long shall I bear with you! Have I not made it plain to you that my kingdom is not of this world? I have told you many times that I have not come to sit on David's throne, and now how is it that you are inquiring which place each of you will occupy in the Father's kingdom? Can you not perceive that I have called you as ambassadors of a spiritual kingdom? Do you not understand that soon, very soon, you are to represent me in the world and in the proclamation of the kingdom, even as I now represent my Father who is in heaven? Can it be that I have chosen you and instructed you as messengers of the kingdom, and yet you do not comprehend the nature and significance of this coming kingdom of divine pre-eminence in the hearts of men? My friends, hear me once more. Banish from your minds this idea that my kingdom is a rule of power or a reign of glory. Indeed, all power in heaven and on earth will presently be given into my hands, but it is not the Father's will that we use this divine endowment to glorify ourselves during this age. In another age you shall indeed sit with me in power and glory, but it behooves us now to submit to the will of the Father and to go forth in humble obedience to execute his bidding on earth." 138:7.1 (1543.4)

Jesus was minded to go on discussing the other commandments when James Zebedee interrupted him, asking:

"Master, what shall we teach the people regarding divorcement?

Shall we allow a man to divorce his wife as Moses has directed?" And when Jesus heard this question, he said: "I have not come to legislate but to enlighten. I have come not to reform the kingdoms of this world but rather to establish the kingdom of heaven. It is not the will of the Father that I should yield to the temptation to teach you rules of government, trade, or social behavior, which, while they might be good for today, would be far from suitable for the society of another age. I am on earth solely to comfort the minds, liberate the spirits, and save the souls of men. But I will say, concerning this question of divorcement, that, while Moses looked with favor upon such things, it was not so in the days of Adam and in the Garden."140:6.6 (1576.6)

Then asked Nathaniel:

"Master, shall we give no place to justice? The law of Moses says, 'An eye for an eye, and a tooth for a tooth.' What shall we say?"

And Jesus answered: "You shall return good for evil. My messengers must not strive with men, but be gentle toward all. Measure for measure shall not be your rule. The rulers of men may have such laws, but not so in the kingdom; mercy always shall determine your judgments and love your conduct. And if these are hard sayings, you can even now turn back. If you find the requirements of apostleship too hard, you may return to the less rigorous pathway of discipleship." 140:6.9 (1577.3)

After Jesus and Matthew had finished talking, Simon Zelotes asked,

"But, Master, are *all* men the sons of God?"

And Jesus answered: "Yes, Simon, all men are the sons of God, and that is the good news you are going to proclaim." But the apostles could not grasp such a doctrine; it was a new, strange, and startling announcement. And it was because of his desire to impress this truth upon them that Jesus taught his followers to treat all men as their brothers. 140:10.7 (1585.5)

In response to a question asked by Andrew, the Master made it clear that the morality of his teaching was inseparable from the religion of his living. He taught morality, not from the *nature* of man, but from the *relation* of man to God. 140:10.8 (1585.6)

John asked Jesus, **"Master, what is the kingdom of heaven?"**

And Jesus answered: "The kingdom of heaven consists in these three essentials: first, recognition of the fact of the sovereignty of God; second, belief in the truth of sonship with God; and third, faith in the effectiveness of the supreme human desire to do the will of God—to be like God. And this is the good news of the gospel: that by faith every mortal may have all these essentials of salvation." 140:10.9 (1585.7)

In answer to Thomas's question,

"Who is this God of the kingdom?"

Jesus replied: "God is *your* Father, and religion—my gospel—is nothing more nor less than the believing recognition of the truth that you are his son. And I am here among you in the flesh to make clear both of these ideas in my life and teachings." 141:4.2 (1590.5)

One of the most eventful of all the evening conferences at Amathus was the session having to do with the discussion of spiritual unity. James Zebedee had asked,

"Master, how shall we learn to see alike and thereby enjoy more harmony among ourselves?"

When Jesus heard this question, he was stirred within his spirit, so much so that he replied: "James, James, when did I teach you that you should all see alike? I have come into the world to proclaim spiritual liberty to the end that mortals may be empowered to live individual lives of originality and freedom before God. I do not desire that social harmony and fraternal peace shall be purchased by the sacrifice of free personality and spiritual originality. What I require of you, my apostles, is *spirit unity*—and that you can experience in the joy of your united dedication to the wholehearted doing of the will of my Father in heaven. You do not have to see alike or feel alike or even think alike in order spiritually to *be alike.* Spiritual unity is derived from the consciousness that each of you is indwelt, and increasingly dominated, by the spirit gift of the heavenly Father. Your apostolic harmony must grow out of the fact that the spirit hope of each of you is identical in origin, nature, and destiny. 141:5.1 (1591.6)

"In this way you may experience a perfected unity of spirit purpose and spirit understanding growing out of the mutual consciousness of the identity of each of your indwelling Paradise spirits; and you may enjoy all of this profound spiritual unity in the very face of the utmost diversity of your individual attitudes of intellectual thinking, temperamental feeling, and social conduct. Your personalities may be refreshingly diverse and markedly different, while your spiritual natures and spirit fruits of divine worship and brotherly love may be so unified that all who behold your lives will of a surety take cognizance of this spirit identity and soul unity; they will recognize that you have been with me and have thereby learned, and acceptably, how to do the will of the Father in heaven. You can achieve the unity of the service of God even while you render such service in accordance with the technique of your own original endowments of mind, body, and soul. 141:5.2 (1591.7)

"Your spirit unity implies two things, which always will be found to harmonize in the lives of individual believers: First, you are possessed with a common motive for life service; you all desire above everything to do the will of the Father in heaven. Second, you all have a common goal of existence; you all purpose to find the Father in heaven, thereby proving to the universe that you have become like him." 141:5.3 (1592.1)

When Simon Zelotes and Jesus were alone, Simon asked the Master:

"Why is it that I could not persuade him? Why did he so resist me and so readily lend an ear to you?"

Jesus answered: "Simon, Simon, how many times have I instructed you to refrain from all efforts to take something *out* of the hearts of those who seek salvation? How often have I told you to labor only to put something *into* these hungry souls? Lead men into the kingdom, and the great and living truths of the kingdom will presently drive out all serious error. When you have presented to mortal man the good news that God is his Father, you can the easier persuade him that he is in reality a son of God. And having done that, you have brought the light of salvation to the one who sits in darkness. Simon, when the Son of Man came first to you, did he come denouncing Moses and the prophets and proclaiming a new and better way of life? No. I came not to take away that which you had from your forefathers but to show you the perfected vision of that which your fathers saw only in part. Go then, Simon, teaching and preaching the kingdom, and when you have a man safely and securely within the kingdom, then is the time, when such a one shall come to you with inquiries, to impart instruction having to do with the progressive advancement of the soul within the divine kingdom." 141:6.2 (1592.4)

There was in Jerusalem in attendance upon the Passover festivities one Jacob, a wealthy Jewish trader from Crete, and he came to Andrew making request to see Jesus privately. Andrew arranged this secret meeting with Jesus at Flavius's home the evening of the next day. This man could not comprehend the Master's teachings, and he came because he desired to inquire more fully about the kingdom of God. Said Jacob to Jesus:

"But, Rabbi, Moses and the olden prophets tell us that Yahweh is a jealous God, a God of great wrath and fierce anger. The prophets say he hates evildoers and takes vengeance on those who obey not his law. You and your disciples teach us that God is a kind and compassionate Father who so loves all men that he would welcome them into this new kingdom of heaven, which you proclaim is so near at hand." 142:2.1 (1597.1)

When Jacob finished speaking, Jesus replied: "Jacob, you have well stated the teachings of the olden prophets who taught the children of their generation in accordance with the light of their day. Our Father in Paradise is changeless. But the concept of his nature has enlarged and grown from the days of Moses down through the times of Amos and even to the generation of the prophet Isaiah. And now have I come in the flesh to reveal the Father in new glory and to show forth his love and mercy to all men on all worlds. As the gospel of this kingdom shall spread over the world with its message of good cheer and good will to all men, there will grow up improved and better relations among the families of all nations. As time passes, fathers and their children will love each other more, and thus will be brought about a better understanding of the love of the Father in heaven for his children on earth. Remember, Jacob, that a good and true father not only loves his family as a whole—as a family—but he also truly loves and affectionately cares for each *individual* member." 142:2.2 (1597.2)

One of the great sermons which Jesus preached in the temple this Passover week was in answer to a question asked by one of his hearers, a man from Damascus. This man asked Jesus:

"But, Rabbi, how shall we know of a certainty that you are sent by God, and that we may truly enter into this kingdom which you and your disciples declare is near at hand?"

And Jesus answered: 142:5.1 (1601.1)

"As to my message and the teaching of my disciples, you should judge them by their fruits. If we proclaim to you the truths of the spirit, the spirit will witness in your hearts that our message is genuine. Concerning the kingdom and your assurance of acceptance by the heavenly Father, let me ask what father among you who is a worthy and kindhearted father would keep his son in anxiety or suspense regarding his status in the family or his place of security in the affections of his father's heart? Do you earth fathers take pleasure in torturing your children with uncertainty about their place of abiding love in your human hearts? Neither does your Father in heaven leave his faith children of the spirit in doubtful uncertainty as to their position in the kingdom. If you receive God as your Father, then indeed and in truth are you the sons of God. And if you are sons, then are you secure in the position and standing of all that concerns eternal and divine sonship. If you believe my words, you thereby believe in Him who sent me, and by thus believing in the Father, you have made your status in heavenly citizenship sure. If you do the will of the Father in heaven, you shall never fail in the attainment of the eternal life of progress in the divine kingdom. 142:5.2 (1601.2)

"The Supreme Spirit shall bear witness with your spirits that you are truly the children of God. And if you are the sons of God, then have you been born of the spirit of God; and whosoever has been born of the spirit has in himself the power to overcome all doubt, and this is the victory that overcomes all uncertainty, even your faith. 142:5.3 (1601.3) (Continued next page)

"Said the Prophet Isaiah, speaking of these times: 'When the spirit is poured upon us from on high, then shall the work of righteousness become peace, quietness, and assurance forever.' And for all who truly believe this gospel, I will become surety for their reception into the eternal mercies and the everlasting life of my Father's kingdom. You, then, who hear this message and believe this gospel of the kingdom are the sons of God, and you have life everlasting; and the evidence to all the world that you have been born of the spirit is that you sincerely love one another." 142:5.4 (1601.4)

Upon being presented by Flavius, Nicodemus said:

"Rabbi, we know that you are a teacher sent by God, for no mere man could so teach unless God were with him. And I am desirous of knowing more about your teachings regarding the coming kingdom." 142:6.3 (1602.2)

Jesus answered Nicodemus: "Verily, verily, I say to you, Nicodemus, except a man be born from above, he cannot see the kingdom of God." Then replied Nicodemus: "But how can a man be born again when he is old? He cannot enter a second time into his mother's womb to be born." 142:6.4 (1602.3)

Jesus said: "Nevertheless, I declare to you, except a man be born of the spirit, he cannot enter into the kingdom of God. That which is born of the flesh is flesh, and that which is born of the spirit is spirit. But you should not marvel that I said you must be born from above. When the wind blows, you hear the rustle of the leaves, but you do not see the wind—whence it comes or whither it goes—and so it is with everyone born of the spirit. With the eyes of the flesh you can behold the manifestations of the spirit, but you cannot actually discern the spirit." 142:6.5 (1602.4)

Nicodemus replied: "But I do not understand—how can that be?" Said Jesus: "Can it be that you are a teacher in Israel and yet ignorant of all this? It becomes, then, the duty of those who know about the realities of the spirit to reveal these things to those who discern only the manifestations of the material world. But will you believe us if we tell you of the heavenly truths? Do you have the courage, Nicodemus, to believe in one who has descended from heaven, even the Son of Man?" 142:6.6 (1602.5)

And Nicodemus said:

"But how can I begin to lay hold upon this spirit which is to remake me in preparation for entering into the kingdom?"

Jesus answered: "Already does the spirit of the Father in heaven indwell you. If you would be led by this spirit from above, very soon would you begin to see with the eyes of the spirit, and then by the wholehearted choice of spirit guidance would you be born of the spirit since your only purpose in living would be to do the will of your Father who is in heaven. And so finding yourself born of the spirit and happily in the kingdom of God, you would begin to bear in your daily life the abundant fruits of the spirit." 142:6.7 (1602.6)

After the busy period of teaching and personal work of Passover week in Jerusalem, Jesus spent the next Wednesday at Bethany with his apostles, resting. That afternoon, Thomas asked a question which elicited a long and instructive answer. Said Thomas:

"Master, on the day we were set apart as ambassadors of the kingdom, you told us many things, instructed us regarding our personal mode of life, but what shall we teach the multitude? How are these people to live after the kingdom more fully comes? Shall your disciples own slaves? Shall your believers court poverty and shun property? Shall mercy alone prevail so that we shall have no more law and justice?"

Jesus and the twelve spent all afternoon and all that evening, after supper, discussing Thomas's questions. For the purposes of this record we present the following summary of the Master's instruction: 142:7.1 (1603.2)

Jesus sought first to make plain to his apostles that he himself was on earth living a unique life in the flesh, and that they, the twelve, had been called to participate in this bestowal experience of the Son of Man; and as such coworkers, they, too, must share in many of the special restrictions and obligations of the entire bestowal experience. There was a veiled intimation that the Son of Man was the only person who had ever lived on earth who could simultaneously see into the very heart of God and into the very depths of man's soul. 142:7.2 (1603.3)

Very plainly Jesus explained that the kingdom of heaven was an evolutionary experience, beginning here on earth and progressing up through successive life stations to Paradise. In the course of the evening he definitely stated that at some future stage of kingdom development he would revisit this world in spiritual power and divine glory. 142:7.3 (1603.4)

He next explained that the "kingdom idea" was not the best way to illustrate man's relation to God; that he employed such figures of speech because the Jewish people were expecting the kingdom, and because John had preached in terms of the coming kingdom. Jesus said: "The people of another age will better understand the gospel of the kingdom when it is presented in terms expressive of the family relationship—when man understands religion as the teaching of the fatherhood of God and the brotherhood of man, sonship with God." Then the Master discoursed at some length on the earthly family as an illustration of the heavenly family, restating the two fundamental laws of living: the first commandment of love for the father, the head of the family, and the second commandment of mutual love among the children, to love your brother as yourself. And then he explained that such a quality of brotherly affection would invariably manifest itself in unselfish and loving social service. 142:7.4 (1603.5)

Following that, came the memorable discussion of the fundamental characteristics of family life and their application to the relationship existing between God and man. Jesus stated that a true family is founded on the following seven facts: 142:7.5 (1603.6)

1. *The fact of existence.* The relationships of nature and the phenomena of mortal likenesses are bound up in the family: Children inherit certain parental traits. The children take origin in the parents; personality existence depends on the act of the parent. The relationship of father and child is inherent in all nature and pervades all living existences. 142:7.6 (1604.1)
2. *Security and pleasure.* True fathers take great pleasure in providing for the needs of their children. Many fathers are not content with supplying the mere wants of their children but enjoy making provision for their pleasures also. 142:7.7 (1604.2)
3. *Education and training.* Wise fathers carefully plan for the education and adequate training of their sons and daughters. When young they are prepared for the greater responsibilities of later life. 142:7.8 (1604.3)
4. *Discipline and restraint.* Farseeing fathers also make provision for the necessary discipline, guidance, correction, and sometimes restraint of their young and immature offspring. 142:7.9 (1604.4)
5. *Companionship and loyalty.* The affectionate father holds intimate and loving intercourse with his children. Always is his ear open to their petitions; he is ever ready to share their hardships and assist them over their difficulties. The father is supremely interested in the progressive welfare of his progeny. 142:7.10 (1604.5) (Continued next page)

6. *Love and mercy.* A compassionate father is freely forgiving; fathers do not hold vengeful memories against their children. Fathers are not like judges, enemies, or creditors. Real families are built upon tolerance, patience, and forgiveness. 142:7.11 (1604.6)

7. *Provision for the future.* Temporal fathers like to leave an inheritance for their sons. The family continues from one generation to another. Death only ends one generation to mark the beginning of another. Death terminates an individual life but not necessarily the family. 142:7.12 (1604.7)

For hours the Master discussed the application of these features of family life to the relations of man, the earth child, to God, the Paradise Father. And this was his conclusion: "This entire relationship of a son to the Father, I know in perfection, for all that you must attain of sonship in the eternal future I have now already attained. The Son of Man is prepared to ascend to the right hand of the Father, so that in me is the way now open still wider for all of you to see God and, ere you have finished the glorious progression, to become perfect, even as your Father in heaven is perfect." 142:7.13 (1604.8)

Although Jesus discoursed for several hours, Thomas was not yet satisfied, for he said:

"But, Master, we do not find that the Father in heaven always deals kindly and mercifully with us. Many times we grievously suffer on earth, and not always are our prayers answered. Where do we fail to grasp the meaning of your teaching?" 142:7.16 (1605.1)

Jesus replied: "Thomas, Thomas, how long before you will acquire the ability to listen with the ear of the spirit? How long will it be before you discern that this kingdom is a spiritual kingdom, and that my Father is also a spiritual being? Do you not understand that I am teaching you as spiritual children in the spirit family of heaven, of which the fatherhead is an infinite and eternal spirit? Will you not allow me to use the earth family as an illustration of divine relationships without so literally applying my teaching to material affairs? In your minds cannot you separate the spiritual realities of the kingdom from the material, social, economic, and political problems of the age? When I speak the language of the spirit, why do you insist on translating my meaning into the language of the flesh just because I presume to employ commonplace and literal relationships for purposes of illustration? My children, I implore that you cease to apply the teaching of the kingdom of the spirit to the sordid affairs of slavery, poverty, houses, and lands, and to the material problems of human equity and justice. These temporal matters are the concern of the men of this world, and while in a way they affect all men, you have been called to represent me in the world, even as I represent my Father. You are spiritual ambassadors of a spiritual kingdom, special representatives of the spirit Father. By this time it should be possible for me to instruct you as full-grown men of the spirit kingdom. Must I ever address you only as children? Will you never grow up in spirit perception? Nevertheless, I love you and will bear with you, even to the very end of our association in the flesh. And even then shall my spirit go before you into all the world." 142:7.17 (1605.2)

Said Philip: "Master, these Greeks and Romans make light of our message, saying that such teachings are fit for only weaklings and slaves. They assert that the religion of the heathen is superior to our teaching because it inspires to the acquirement of a strong, robust, and aggressive character. They affirm that we would convert all men into enfeebled specimens of passive nonresisters who would soon perish from the face of the earth. They like you, Master, and freely admit that your teaching is heavenly and ideal, but they will not take us seriously.

They assert that your religion is not for this world; that men cannot live as you teach. And now, Master, what shall we say to these gentiles?" 143:1.2 (1607.4)

After Jesus had heard similar objections to the gospel of the kingdom presented by Thomas, Nathaniel, Simon Zelotes, and Matthew, he said to the twelve: 143:1.3 (1607.5)

"I have come into this world to do the will of my Father and to reveal his loving character to all mankind. That, my brethren, is my mission. And this one thing I will do, regardless of the misunderstanding of my teachings by Jews or gentiles of this day or of another generation. But you should not overlook the fact that even divine love has its severe disciplines. A father's love for his son oftentimes impels the father to restrain the unwise acts of his thoughtless offspring. The child does not always comprehend the wise and loving motives of the father's restraining discipline. But I declare to you that my Father in Paradise does rule a universe of universes by the compelling power of his love. Love is the greatest of all spirit realities. Truth is a liberating revelation, but love is the supreme relationship. And no matter what blunders your fellow men make in their world management of today, in an age to come the gospel which I declare to you will rule this very world. The ultimate goal of human progress is the reverent recognition of the fatherhood of God and the loving materialization of the brotherhood of man. 143:1.4 (1608.1)

"But who told you that my gospel was intended only for slaves and weaklings? Do you, my chosen apostles, resemble weaklings? Did John look like a weakling? Do you observe that I am enslaved by fear? True, the poor and oppressed of this generation have the gospel preached to them. The religions of this world have neglected the poor, but my Father is no respecter of persons. Besides, the poor of this day are the first to heed the call to repentance and acceptance of sonship. The gospel of the kingdom is to be preached to all men—Jew and gentile, Greek and Roman, rich and poor, free and bond—and equally to young and old, male and female. 143:1.5 (1608.2)

"Because my Father is a God of love and delights in the practice of mercy, do not imbibe the idea that the service of the kingdom is to be one of monotonous ease. The Paradise ascent is the supreme adventure of all time, the rugged achievement of eternity. The service of the kingdom on earth will call for all the courageous manhood that you and your coworkers can muster. Many of you will be put to death for your loyalty to the gospel of this kingdom. It is easy to die in the line of physical battle when your courage is strengthened by the presence of your fighting comrades, but it requires a higher and more profound form of human courage and devotion calmly and all alone to lay down your life for the love of a truth enshrined in your mortal heart. 143:1.6 (1608.3)

"Today, the unbelievers may taunt you with preaching a gospel of nonresistance and with living lives of nonviolence, but you are the first volunteers of a long line of sincere believers in the gospel of this kingdom who will astonish all mankind by their heroic devotion to these teachings. No armies of the world have ever displayed more courage and bravery than will be portrayed by you and your loyal successors who shall go forth to all the world proclaiming the good news—the fatherhood of God and the brotherhood of men. The courage of the flesh is the lowest form of bravery. Mind bravery is a higher type of human courage, but the highest and supreme is uncompromising loyalty to the enlightened convictions of profound spiritual realities. And such courage constitutes the heroism of the God-knowing man. And you are all God-knowing men; you are in very truth the personal associates of the Son of Man." 143:1.7 (1608.4)

At one of the evening conferences, Andrew asked Jesus:

"Master, are we to practice self-denial as John taught us, or are we to strive for the self-control of your teaching? Wherein does your teaching differ from that of John?"

Jesus answered: "John indeed taught you the way of righteousness in accordance with the light and laws of his fathers, and that was the religion of self-examination and self-denial. But I come with a new message of self- forgetfulness and self-control. I show to you the way of life as revealed to me by my Father in heaven. 143:2.2 (1609.3) (Continued next page)

"Verily, verily, I say to you, he who rules his own self is greater than he who captures a city. Self-mastery is the measure of man's moral nature and the indicator of his spiritual development. In the old order you fasted and prayed; as the new creature of the rebirth of the spirit, you are taught to believe and rejoice. In the Father's kingdom you are to become new creatures; old things are to pass away; behold I show you how all things are to become new. And by your love for one another you are to convince the world that you have passed from bondage to liberty, from death into life everlasting. 143:2.3 (1609.4)

"By the old way you seek to suppress, obey, and conform to the rules of living; by the new way you are first *transformed* by the Spirit of Truth and thereby strengthened in your inner soul by the constant spiritual renewing of your mind, and so are you endowed with the power of the certain and joyous performance of the gracious, acceptable, and perfect will of God. Forget not—it is your personal faith in the exceedingly great and precious promises of God that ensures your becoming partakers of the divine nature. Thus by your faith and the spirit's transformation, you become in reality the temples of God, and his spirit actually dwells within you. If, then, the spirit dwells within you, you are no longer bondslaves of the flesh but free and liberated sons of the spirit. The new law of the spirit endows you with the liberty of self-mastery in place of the old law of the fear of self-bondage and the slavery of self-denial. 143:2.4 (1609.5)

"Many times, when you have done evil, you have thought to charge up your acts to the influence of the evil one when in reality you have but been led astray by your own natural tendencies. Did not the Prophet Jeremiah long ago tell you that the human heart is deceitful above all things and sometimes even desperately wicked? How easy for you to become self-deceived and thereby fall into foolish fears, divers lusts, enslaving pleasures, malice, envy, and even vengeful hatred! 143:2.5 (1609.6)

"Salvation is by the regeneration of the spirit and not by the self-righteous deeds of the flesh. You are justified by faith and fellowshipped by grace, not by fear and the self-denial of the flesh, albeit the Father's children who have been born of the spirit are ever and always *masters* of the self and all that pertains to the desires of the flesh. When you know that you are saved by faith, you have real peace with God. And all who follow in the way of this heavenly peace are destined to be sanctified to the eternal service of the ever-advancing sons of the eternal God. Henceforth, it is not a duty but rather your exalted privilege to cleanse yourselves from all evils of mind and body while you seek for perfection in the love of God. 143:2.6 (1610.1)

"Your sonship is grounded in faith, and you are to remain unmoved by fear. Your joy is born of trust in the divine word, and you shall not therefore be led to doubt the reality of the Father's love and mercy. It is the very goodness of God that leads men into true and genuine repentance. Your secret of the mastery of self is bound up with your faith in the indwelling spirit, which ever works by love. Even this saving faith you have not of yourselves; it also is the gift of God. And if you are the children of this living faith, you are no longer the bondslaves of self but rather the triumphant masters of yourselves, the liberated sons of God. 143:2.7 (1610.2)

"If, then, my children, you are born of the spirit, you are forever delivered from the self-conscious bondage of a life of self-denial and watchcare over the desires of the flesh, and you are translated into the joyous kingdom of the spirit, whence you spontaneously show forth the fruits of the spirit in your daily lives; and the fruits of the spirit are the essence of the highest type of enjoyable and ennobling self-control, even the heights of terrestrial mortal attainment—true self-mastery." 143:2.8 (1610.3)

The water of Jacob's well was less mineral than that from the wells of Sychar and was therefore much valued for drinking purposes. Jesus was thirsty, but there was no way of getting water from the well. When, therefore, a woman of Sychar came up with her water pitcher and prepared to draw from the well, Jesus said to her, "Give me a drink." This woman of Samaria knew Jesus was a Jew by his appearance and dress, and she surmised that he was a Galilean Jew from his accent. Her name was Nalda and she was a comely creature. She was much surprised to have a Jewish man thus speak to her at the well and ask for water, for it was not deemed proper in those days for a self- respecting man to speak to a woman in public, much less for a Jew to converse with a Samaritan. Therefore Nalda asked Jesus,

"How is it that you, being a Jew, ask for a drink of me, a Samaritan woman?"

Jesus answered: "I have indeed asked you for a drink, but if you could only understand, you would ask me for a draught of the living water." Then said Nalda: "But, Sir, you have nothing to draw with, and the well is deep; whence, then, have you this living water? Are you greater than our father Jacob who gave us this well, and who drank thereof himself and his sons and his cattle also?" 143:5.2 (1612.5)

Jesus replied: "Everyone who drinks of this water will thirst again, but whosoever drinks of the water of the living spirit shall never thirst. And this living water shall become in him a well of refreshment springing up even to eternal life." Nalda then said: "Give me this water that I thirst not, neither come all the way hither to draw. Besides, anything which a Samaritan woman could receive from such a commendable Jew would be a pleasure." 143:5.3 (1613.1)

By this time Nalda was sobered, and her better self was awakened. She was not an immoral woman wholly by choice. She had been ruthlessly and unjustly cast aside by her husband and in dire straits had consented to live with a certain Greek as his wife, but without marriage. Nalda now felt greatly ashamed that she had so unthinkingly spoken to Jesus, and she most penitently addressed the Master, saying: "My Lord, I repent of my manner of speaking to you, for I perceive that you are a holy man or maybe a prophet." And she was just about to seek direct and personal help from the Master when she did what so many have done before and since—dodged the issue of personal salvation by turning to the discussion of theology and philosophy. She quickly turned the conversation from her own needs to a theological controversy. Pointing over to Mount Gerizim, she continued:

"Our fathers worshiped on this mountain, and yet *you* would say that in Jerusalem is the place where men ought to worship; which, then, is the right place to worship God?" 143:5.5 (1613.3)

Jesus perceived the attempt of the woman's soul to avoid direct and searching contact with its Maker, but he also saw that there was present in her soul a desire to know the better way of life. After all, there was in Nalda's heart a true thirst for the living water; therefore he dealt patiently with her, saying: "Woman, let me say to you that the day is soon coming when neither on this mountain nor in Jerusalem will you worship the Father. But now you worship that which you know not, a mixture of the religion of many pagan gods and gentile philosophies. The Jews at least know whom they worship; they have removed all confusion by concentrating their worship upon one God, Yahweh. But you should believe me when I say that the hour will soon come—even now is—when all sincere worshipers will worship the Father in spirit and in truth, for it is just such worshipers the Father seeks. God is spirit, and they who worship him must worship him in spirit and in truth. Your salvation comes not from knowing how others should worship or where but by receiving into your own heart this living water which I am offering you even now." 143:5.6 (1613.4)

On the evening that Nalda drew the crowd out from Sychar to see Jesus, the twelve had just returned with food, and they besought Jesus to eat with them instead of talking to the people, for they had been without food all day and were hungry. But Jesus knew that darkness would soon be upon them; so he persisted in his determination to talk to the people before he sent them away. When Andrew sought to persuade him to eat a bite before speaking to the crowd, Jesus said, "I have meat to eat that you do not know about." When the apostles heard this, they said among themselves:

"Has any man brought him aught to eat? Can it be that the woman gave him food as well as drink?"

When Jesus heard them talking among themselves, before he spoke to the people, he turned aside and said to the twelve: "My meat is to do the will of Him who sent me and to accomplish His work. You should no longer say it is such and such a time until the harvest. Behold these people coming out from a Samaritan city to hear us; I tell you the fields are already white for the harvest. He who reaps receives wages and gathers this fruit to eternal life; consequently the sowers and the reapers rejoice together. For herein is the saying true: 'One sows and another reaps.' I am now sending you to reap that whereon you have not labored; others have labored, and you are about to enter into their labor." This he said in reference to the preaching of John the Baptist. 143:6.1 (1615.2)

John had now been in prison a year and a half, and most of this time Jesus had labored very quietly; so it was not strange that John should be led to wonder about the kingdom.

John's friends interrupted Jesus' teaching to say to him: **"John the Baptist has sent us to ask—are you truly the Deliverer, or shall we look for another?"** 144:8.2 (1626.7)

Jesus paused to say to John's friends: "Go back and tell John that he is not forgotten. Tell him what you have seen and heard, that the poor have good tidings preached to them." And when Jesus had spoken further to the messengers of John, he turned again to the multitude and said: "Do not think that John doubts the gospel of the kingdom. He makes inquiry only to assure his disciples who are also my disciples. John is no weakling. Let me ask you who heard John preach before Herod put him in prison: What did you behold in John—a reed shaken with the wind? A man of changeable moods and clothed in soft raiment? As a rule they who are gorgeously appareled and who live delicately are in kings' courts and in the mansions of the rich. But what did you see when you beheld John? A prophet? Yes, I say to you, and much more than a prophet. Of John it was written: 'Behold, I send my messenger before your face; he shall prepare the way before you.' 144:8.3 (1626.8)

"Verily, verily, I say to you, among those born of women there has not arisen a greater than John the Baptist; yet he who is but small in the kingdom of heaven is greater because he has been born of the spirit and knows that he has become a son of God." 144:8.4 (1627.1)

Meanwhile, early Sunday morning, other crowds of afflicted souls and many curiosity seekers began to gather about the house of Zebedee. They clamored to see Jesus. Andrew and the apostles were so perplexed that, while Simon Zelotes talked to the assembly, Andrew, with several of his associates, went to find Jesus. When Andrew had located Jesus in company with the three, he said:

"Master, why do you leave us alone with the multitude? Behold, all men seek you; never before have so many sought after your teaching. Even now the house is surrounded by those who have come from near and far because of your mighty works. Will you not return with us to minister to them?" 145:5.5 (1635.4)

When Jesus heard this, he answered: "Andrew, have I not taught you and these others that my mission on earth is the revelation of the Father, and my message the proclamation of the kingdom of heaven? How is it, then, that you would have me turn aside from my work for the gratification of the curious and for the satisfaction of those who seek for signs and wonders? Have we not been among these people all these months, and have they flocked in multitudes to hear the good news of the kingdom? Why have they now come to besiege us? Is it not because of the healing of their physical bodies rather than as a result of the reception of spiritual truth for the salvation of their souls? When men are attracted to us because of extraordinary manifestations, many of them come seeking not for truth and salvation but rather in quest of healing for their physical ailments and to secure deliverance from their material difficulties. 145:5.6 (1635.5)

"All this time I have been in Capernaum, and both in the synagogue and by the seaside have I proclaimed the good news of the kingdom to all who had ears to hear and hearts to receive the truth. It is not the will of my Father that I should return with you to cater to these curious ones and to become occupied with the ministry of things physical to the exclusion of the spiritual. I have ordained you to preach the gospel and minister to the sick, but I must not become engrossed in healing to the exclusion of my teaching. No, Andrew, I will not return with you. Go and tell the people to believe in that which we have taught them and to rejoice in the liberty of the sons of God, and make ready for our departure for the other cities of Galilee, where the way has already been prepared for the preaching of the good tidings of the kingdom. It was for this purpose that I came forth from the Father. Go, then, and prepare for our immediate departure while I here await your return." 145:5.7 (1635.6)

On the second evening at Ramah, Thomas asked Jesus this question:

"Master, how can a new believer in your teaching really know, really be certain, about the truth of this gospel of the kingdom?" 146:3.3 (1641.5)

And Jesus said to Thomas: "Your assurance that you have entered into the kingdom family of the Father, and that you will eternally survive with the children of the kingdom, is wholly a matter of personal experience—faith in the word of truth. Spiritual assurance is the equivalent of your personal religious experience in the eternal realities of divine truth and is otherwise equal to your intelligent understanding of truth realities plus your spiritual faith and minus your honest doubts. 146:3.4 (1641.6)

"The Son is naturally endowed with the life of the Father. Having been endowed with the living spirit of the Father, you are therefore sons of God. You survive your life in the material world of the flesh because you are identified with the Father's living spirit, the gift of eternal life. Many, indeed, had this life before I came forth from the Father, and many more have received this spirit because they believed my word; but I declare that, when I return to the Father, he will send his spirit into the hearts of all men. 146:3.5 (1642.1)

"While you cannot observe the divine spirit at work in your minds, there is a practical method of discovering the degree to which you have yielded the control of your soul powers to the teaching and guidance of this indwelling spirit of the heavenly Father, and that is the degree of your love for your fellow men. This spirit of the Father partakes of the love of the Father, and as it dominates man, it unfailingly leads in the directions of divine worship and loving regard for one's fellows. At first you believe that you are sons of God because my teaching has made you more conscious of the inner leadings of our Father's indwelling presence; but presently the Spirit of Truth shall be poured out upon all flesh, and it will live among men and teach all men, even as I now live among you and speak to you the words of truth. And this Spirit of Truth, speaking for the spiritual endowments of your souls, will help you to know that you are the sons of God. It will unfailingly bear witness with the Father's indwelling presence, your spirit, then dwelling in all men as it now dwells in some, telling you that you are in reality the sons of God. 146:3.6 (1642.2)

"Every earth child who follows the leading of this spirit shall eventually know the will of God, and he who surrenders to the will of my Father shall abide forever. The way from the earth life to the eternal estate has not been made plain to you, but there is a way, there always has been, and I have come to make that way new and living. He who enters the kingdom has eternal life already—he shall never perish. But much of this you will the better understand when I shall have returned to the Father and you are able to view your present experiences in retrospect." 146:3.7 (1642.3)

The apostles were somewhat restless under the restrictions imposed by Jesus, and John, the youngest of the twelve, was especially restive under this restraint. He had brought Jesus to the pool thinking that the sight of the assembled sufferers would make such an appeal to the Master's compassion that he would be moved to perform a miracle of healing, and thereby would all Jerusalem be astounded and presently be won to believe in the gospel of the kingdom. Said John to Jesus:

"Master, see all of these suffering ones; is there nothing we can do for them?"

And Jesus replied: "John, why would you tempt me to turn aside from the way I have chosen? Why do you go on desiring to substitute the working of wonders and the healing of the sick for the proclamation of the gospel of eternal truth? My son, I may not do that which you desire, but gather together these sick and afflicted that I may speak words of good cheer and eternal comfort to them." 147:3.2 (1649.2)

In speaking to those assembled, Jesus said: "Many of you are here, sick and afflicted, because of your many years of wrong living. Some suffer from the accidents of time, others as a result of the mistakes of their forebears, while some of you struggle under the handicaps of the imperfect conditions of your temporal existence. But my Father works, and I would work, to improve your earthly state but more especially to insure your eternal estate. None of us can do much to change the difficulties of life unless we discover the Father in heaven so wills. After all, we are all beholden to do the will of the Eternal. If you could all be healed of your physical afflictions, you would indeed marvel, but it is even greater that you should be cleansed of all spiritual disease and find yourselves healed of all moral infirmities. You are all God's children; you are the sons of the heavenly Father. The bonds of time may seem to afflict you, but the God of eternity loves you. And when the time of judgment shall come, fear not, you shall all find, not only justice, but an abundance of mercy. Verily, verily, I say to you: He who hears the gospel of the kingdom and believes in this teaching of sonship with God, has eternal life; already are such believers passing from judgment and death to light and life. And the hour is coming in which even those who are in the tombs shall hear the voice of the resurrection." 147:3.3 (1649.3)

On the evening of this same Sabbath day, at Bethany, while Jesus, the twelve, and a group of believers were assembled about the fire in Lazarus's garden, Nathaniel asked Jesus this question: "Master, although you have taught us the positive version of the old rule of life, instructing us that we should do to others as we wish them to do to us, I do not fully discern how we can always abide by such an injunction. Let me illustrate my contention by citing the example of a lustful man who thus wickedly looks upon his intended consort in sin.

"How can we teach that this evil-intending man should do to others as he would they should do to him?" 147:4.1 (1650.2)

When Jesus heard Nathaniel's question, he immediately stood upon his feet and, pointing his finger at the apostle, said: "Nathaniel, Nathaniel! What manner of thinking is going on in your heart? Do you not receive my teachings as one who has been born of the spirit? Do you not hear the truth as men of wisdom and spiritual understanding? When I admonished you to do to others as you would have them do to you, I spoke to men of high ideals, not to those who would be tempted to distort my teaching into a license for the encouragement of evil-doing." 147:4.2 (1650.3)

When the Master had spoken, Nathaniel stood up and said: "But, Master, you should not think that I approve of such an interpretation of your teaching. I asked the question because I conjectured that many such men might thus misjudge your admonition, and I hoped you would give us further instruction regarding these matters." And then when Nathaniel had sat down, Jesus continued speaking: "I well know, Nathaniel, that no such idea of evil is approved in your mind, but I am disappointed in that you all so often fail to put a genuinely spiritual interpretation upon my commonplace teachings, instruction which must be given you in human language and as men must speak. Let me now teach you concerning the differing levels of meaning attached to the interpretation of this rule of living, this admonition to 'do to others that which you desire others to do to you': 147:4.3 (1650.4)

"1. *The level of the flesh.* Such a purely selfish and lustful interpretation would be well exemplified by the supposition of your question. 147:4.4 (1650.5)

"2. *The level of the feelings.* This plane is one level higher than that of the flesh and implies that sympathy and pity would enhance one's interpretation of this rule of living. 147:4.5 (1650.6)

"3. *The level of mind.* Now come into action the reason of mind and the intelligence of experience. Good judgment dictates that such a rule of living should be interpreted in consonance with the highest idealism embodied in the nobility of profound self-respect. 147:4.6 (1650.7)

"4. *The level of brotherly love.* Still higher is discovered the level of unselfish devotion to the welfare of one's fellows. On this higher plane of wholehearted social service growing out of the consciousness of the fatherhood of God and the consequent recognition of the brotherhood of man, there is discovered a new and far more beautiful interpretation of this basic rule of life. 147:4.7 (1651.1)

"5. *The moral level.* And then when you attain true philosophic levels of interpretation, when you have real insight into the *rightness* and *wrongness* of things, when you perceive the eternal fitness of human relationships, you will begin to view such a problem of interpretation as you would imagine a high- minded, idealistic, wise, and impartial third person would so view and interpret such an injunction as applied to your personal problems of adjustment to your life situations. 147:4.8 (1651.2)

"6. *The spiritual level.* And then last, but greatest of all, we attain the level of spirit insight and spiritual interpretation which impels us to recognize in this rule of life the divine command to treat all men as we conceive God would treat them. That is the universe ideal of human relationships. And this is your attitude toward all such problems when your supreme desire is ever to do the Father's will. I would, therefore, that you should do to all men that which you know I would do to them in like circumstances." 147:4.9 (1651.3)

When Simon and his friends who sat at meat with him heard these words, they were the more astonished, and they began to whisper among themselves,

"Who is this man that he even dares to forgive sins?"

And when Jesus heard them thus murmuring, he turned to dismiss the woman, saying, "Woman, go in peace; your faith has saved you." 147:5.5 (1652.2)

As Jesus arose with his friends to leave, he turned to Simon and said: "I know your heart, Simon, how you are torn betwixt faith and doubts, how you are distraught by fear and troubled by pride; but I pray for you that you may yield to the light and may experience in your station in life just such mighty transformations of mind and spirit as may be comparable to the tremendous changes which the gospel of the kingdom has already wrought in the heart of your unbidden and unwelcome guest. And I declare to all of you that the Father has opened the doors of the heavenly kingdom to all who have the faith to enter, and no man or association of men can close those doors even to the most humble soul or supposedly most flagrant sinner on earth if such sincerely seek an entrance." 147:5.6 (1652.3)

"It was the habit of Jesus two evenings each week to hold special converse with individuals who desired to talk with him, in a certain secluded and sheltered corner of the Zebedee garden. At one of these evening conversations in private Thomas asked the Master this question:

"Why is it necessary for men to be born of the spirit in order to enter the kingdom? Is rebirth necessary to escape the control of the evil one? Master, what is evil?"

When Jesus heard these questions, he said to Thomas: 148:4.1 (1659.8)

"Do not make the mistake of confusing *evil* with the *evil one,* more correctly the *iniquitous one.* He whom you call the evil one is the son of self-love, the high administrator who knowingly went into deliberate rebellion against the rule of my Father and his loyal Sons. But I have already vanquished these sinful rebels. Make clear in your mind these different attitudes toward the Father and his universe. Never forget these laws of relation to the Father's will: 148:4.2 (1660.1)

Evil is the unconscious or unintended transgression of the divine law, the Father's will. Evil is likewise the measure of the imperfectness of obedience to the Father's will. 148:4.3 (1660.2)

"Sin is the conscious, knowing, and deliberate transgression of the divine law, the Father's will. Sin is the measure of unwillingness to be divinely led and spiritually directed. 148:4.4 (1660.3)

"Iniquity is the willful, determined, and persistent transgression of the divine law, the Father's will. Iniquity is the measure of the continued rejection of the Father's loving plan of personality survival and the Sons' merciful ministry of salvation. 148:4.5 (1660.4)

"By nature, before the rebirth of the spirit, mortal man is subject to inherent evil tendencies, but such natural imperfections of behavior are neither sin nor iniquity. Mortal man is just beginning his long ascent to the perfection of the Father in Paradise. To be imperfect or partial in natural endowment is not sinful. Man is indeed subject to evil, but he is in no sense the child of the evil one unless he has knowingly and deliberately chosen the paths of sin and the life of iniquity. Evil is inherent in the natural order of this world, but sin is an attitude of conscious rebellion which was brought to this world by those who fell from spiritual light into gross darkness. 148:4.6 (1660.5)

"You are confused, Thomas, by the doctrines of the Greeks and the errors of the Persians. You do not understand the relationships of evil and sin because you view mankind as beginning on earth with a perfect Adam and rapidly degenerating, through sin, to man's present deplorable estate. But why do you refuse to comprehend the meaning of the record which discloses how Cain, the son of Adam, went over into the land of Nod and there got himself a wife? And why do you refuse to interpret the meaning of the record which portrays the sons of God finding wives for themselves among the daughters of men? 148:4.7 (1660.6)

"Men are, indeed, by nature evil, but not necessarily sinful. The new birth—the baptism of the spirit—is essential to deliverance from evil and necessary for entrance into the kingdom of heaven, but none of this detracts from the fact that man is the son of God. Neither does this inherent presence of potential evil mean that man is in some mysterious way estranged from the Father in heaven so that, as an alien, foreigner, or stepchild, he must in some manner seek for legal adoption by the Father. All such notions are born, first, of your misunderstanding of the Father and, second, of your ignorance of the origin, nature, and destiny of man. 148:4.8 (1660.7)

"The Greeks and others have taught you that man is descending from godly perfection steadily down toward oblivion or destruction; I have come to show that man, by entrance into the kingdom, is ascending certainly and surely up to God and divine perfection. Any being who in any manner falls short of the divine and spiritual ideals of the eternal Father's will is potentially evil, but such beings are in no sense sinful, much less iniquitous. 148:4.9 (1660.8)

"Thomas, have you not read about this in the Scriptures, where it is written: 'You are the children of the Lord your God.' 'I will be his Father and he shall be my son.' 'I have chosen him to be my son—I will be his Father.' 'Bring my sons from far and my daughters from the ends of the earth; even everyone who is called by my name, for I have created them for my glory.' 'You are the sons of the living God.' 'They who have the spirit of God are indeed the sons of God.' While there is a material part of the human father in the natural child, there is a spiritual part of the heavenly Father in every faith son of the kingdom." 148:4.10 (1661.1)

It was this same evening at Bethsaida that John also asked Jesus **why so many apparently innocent people suffered from so many diseases and experienced so many afflictions.**

In answering John's questions, among many other things, the Master said: 148:6.1 (1662.3)

"My son, you do not comprehend the meaning of adversity or the mission of suffering. Have you not read that masterpiece of Semitic literature—the Scripture story of the afflictions of Job? Do you not recall how this wonderful parable begins with the recital of the material prosperity of the Lord's servant? You well remember that Job was blessed with children, wealth, dignity, position, health, and everything else which men value in this temporal life. According to the time-honored teachings of the children of Abraham such material prosperity was all-sufficient evidence of divine favor. But such material possessions and such temporal prosperity do not indicate God's favor. My Father in heaven loves the poor just as much as the rich; he is no respecter of persons. 148:6.2 (1662.4)

"Although transgression of divine law is sooner or later followed by the harvest of punishment, while men certainly eventually do reap what they sow, still you should know that human suffering is not always a punishment for antecedent sin. Both Job and his friends failed to find the true answer for their perplexities. And with the light you now enjoy you would hardly assign to either Satan or God the parts they play in this unique parable. While Job did not, through suffering, find the resolution of his intellectual troubles or the solution of his philosophical difficulties, he did achieve great victories; even in the very face of the breakdown of his theological defenses he ascended to those spiritual heights where he could sincerely say, 'I abhor myself'; then was there granted him the salvation of a *vision of God.* So even through misunderstood suffering, Job ascended to the superhuman plane of moral understanding and spiritual insight. When the suffering servant obtains a vision of God, there follows a soul peace which passes all human understanding. 148:6.3 (1663.1)

"The first of Job's friends, Eliphaz, exhorted the sufferer to exhibit in his afflictions the same fortitude he had prescribed for others during the days of his prosperity. Said this false comforter: 'Trust in your religion, Job; remember that it is the wicked and not the righteous who suffer. You must deserve this punishment, else you would not be afflicted. You well know that no man can be righteous in God's sight. You know that the wicked never really prosper. Anyway, man seems predestined to trouble, and perhaps the Lord is only chastising you for your own good.' No wonder poor Job failed to get much comfort from such an interpretation of the problem of human suffering. 148:6.4 (1663.2)

"But the counsel of his second friend, Bildad, was even more depressing, notwithstanding its soundness from the standpoint of the then accepted theology. Said Bildad: 'God cannot be unjust. Your children must have been sinners since they perished; you must be in error, else you would not be so afflicted. And if you are really righteous, God will certainly deliver you from your afflictions. You should learn from the history of God's dealings with man that the Almighty destroys only the wicked.' 148:6.5 (1663.3)

"And then you remember how Job replied to his friends, saying: 'I well know that God does not hear my cry for help. How can God be just and at the same time so utterly disregard my innocence? I am learning that I can get no satisfaction from appealing to the Almighty. Cannot you discern that God tolerates the persecution of the good by the wicked? And since man is so weak, what chance has he for consideration at the hands of an omnipotent God? God has made me as I am, and when he thus turns upon me, I am defenseless. And why did God ever create me just to suffer in this miserable fashion?' 148:6.6 (1663.4)

"And who can challenge the attitude of Job in view of the counsel of his friends and the erroneous ideas of God which occupied his own mind? Do you not see that Job longed for a *human* God, that he hungered to commune with a divine Being who knows man's mortal estate and understands that the just must often suffer in innocence as a part of this first life of the long Paradise ascent? Wherefore has the Son of Man come forth from the Father to live such a life in the flesh that he will be able to comfort and succor all those who must henceforth be called upon to endure the afflictions of Job. 148:6.7 (1663.5)

"Job's third friend, Zophar, then spoke still less comforting words when he said: 'You are foolish to claim to be righteous, seeing that you are thus afflicted. But I admit that it is impossible to comprehend God's ways. Perhaps there is some hidden purpose in all your miseries.' And when Job had listened to all three of his friends, he appealed directly to God for help, pleading the fact that 'man, born of woman, is few of days and full of trouble.' 148:6.8 (1663.6)

"Then began the second session with his friends. Eliphaz grew more stern, accusing, and sarcastic. Bildad became indignant at Job's contempt for his friends. Zophar reiterated his melancholy advice. Job by this time had become disgusted with his friends and appealed again to God, and now he appealed to a just God against the God of injustice embodied in the philosophy of his friends and enshrined even in his own religious attitude. Next Job took refuge in the consolation of a future life in which the inequities of mortal existence may be more justly rectified. Failure to receive help from man drives Job to God. Then ensues the great struggle in his heart between faith and doubt. Finally, the human sufferer begins to see the light of life; his tortured soul ascends to new heights of hope and courage; he may suffer on and even die, but his enlightened soul now utters that cry of triumph, 'My Vindicator lives!' 148:6.9 (1664.1)

"Job was altogether right when he challenged the doctrine that God afflicts children in order to punish their parents. Job was ever ready to admit that God is righteous, but he longed for some soul-satisfying revelation of the personal character of the Eternal. And that is our mission on earth. No more shall suffering mortals be denied the comfort of knowing the love of God and understanding the mercy of the Father in heaven. While the speech of God spoken from the whirlwind was a majestic concept for the day of its utterance, you have already learned that the Father does not thus reveal himself, but rather that he speaks within the human heart as a still, small voice, saying, 'This is the way; walk therein.' Do you not comprehend that God dwells within you, that he has become what you are that he may make you what he is!" 148:6.10 (1664.2)

Then Jesus made this final statement: "The Father in heaven does not willingly afflict the children of men. Man suffers, first, from the accidents of time and the imperfections of the evil of an immature physical existence. Next, he suffers the inexorable consequences of sin—the transgression of the laws of life and light. And finally, man reaps the harvest of his own iniquitous persistence in rebellion against the righteous rule of heaven on earth. But man's miseries are not a *personal* visitation of divine judgment. Man can, and will, do much to lessen his temporal sufferings. But once and for all be delivered from the superstition that God afflicts man at the behest of the evil one. Study the book of *Job* just to discover how many wrong ideas of God even good men may honestly entertain; and then note how even the painfully afflicted Job found the God of comfort and salvation in spite of such erroneous teachings. At last his faith pierced the clouds of suffering to discern the light of life pouring forth from the Father as healing mercy and everlasting righteousness." 148:6.11 (1664.3)

The leader of the spying Pharisees, as Jesus stood talking to the people, induced a man with a withered hand to approach him and ask **if it would be lawful to be healed on the Sabbath day or should he seek help on another day.**

When Jesus saw the man, heard his words, and perceived that he had been sent by the Pharisees, he said: "Come forward while I ask you a question. If you had a sheep and it should fall into a pit on the Sabbath day, would you reach down, lay hold on it, and lift it out? Is it lawful to do such things on the Sabbath day?" And the man answered: "Yes, Master, it would be lawful thus to do well on the Sabbath day." Then said Jesus, speaking to all of them: "I know wherefore you have sent this man into my presence. You would find cause for offense in me if you could tempt me to show mercy on the Sabbath day. In silence you all agreed that it was lawful to lift the unfortunate sheep out of the pit, even on the Sabbath, and I call you to witness that it is lawful to exhibit loving-kindness on the Sabbath day not only to animals but also to men. How much more valuable is a man than a sheep! I proclaim that it is lawful to do good to men on the Sabbath day." And as they all stood before him in silence, Jesus, addressing the man with the withered hand, said: "Stand up here by my side that all may see you. And now that you may know that it is my Father's will that you do good on the Sabbath day, if you have the faith to be healed, I bid you stretch out your hand." 148:7.2 (1665.1)

And as this man stretched forth his withered hand, it was made whole. The people were minded to turn upon the Pharisees, but Jesus bade them be calm, saying: "I have just told you that it is lawful to do good on the Sabbath, to save life, but I did not instruct you to do harm and give way to the desire to kill." 148:7.3 (1665.2)

When the Pharisees from Jerusalem, together with other scribes and lawyers who sat with them, heard this pronouncement by Jesus, they began to say to themselves:

"How dare this man thus speak? Does he not understand that such words are blasphemy? Who can forgive sin but God?"

Jesus, perceiving in his spirit that they thus reasoned within their own minds and among themselves, spoke to them, saying: "Why do you so reason in your hearts? Who are you that you sit in judgment over me? What is the difference whether I say to this paralytic, your sins are forgiven, or arise, take up your bed, and walk? But that you who witness all this may finally know that the Son of Man has authority and power on earth to forgive sins, I will say to this afflicted man, Arise, take up your bed, and go to your own house." And when Jesus had thus spoken, the paralytic arose, and as they made way for him, he walked out before them all. And those who saw these things were amazed. 148:9.3 (1667.1)

When Jesus was visiting the group of evangelists working under the supervision of Simon Zelotes, during their evening conference Simon asked the Master:

"Why are some persons so much more happy and contented than others? Is contentment a matter of religious experience?"

Among other things, Jesus said in answer to Simon's question: 149:5.1 (1674.3)

"Simon, some persons are naturally more happy than others. Much, very much, depends upon the willingness of man to be led and directed by the Father's spirit which lives within him. Have you not read in the Scriptures the words of the wise man, 'The spirit of man is the candle of the Lord, searching all the inward parts'? And also that such spirit-led mortals say: 'The lines are fallen to me in pleasant places; yes, I have a goodly heritage.' 'A little that a righteous man has is better than the riches of many wicked,' for 'a good man shall be satisfied from within himself.' 'A merry heart makes a cheerful countenance and is a continual feast. Better is a little with the reverence of the Lord than great treasure and trouble therewith. Better is a dinner of herbs where love is than a fatted ox and hatred therewith. Better is a little with righteousness than great revenues without rectitude.' 'A merry heart does good like a medicine.' 'Better is a handful with composure than a superabundance with sorrow and vexation of spirit.' 149:5.2 (1674.4)

"Much of man's sorrow is born of the disappointment of his ambitions and the wounding of his pride. Although men owe a duty to themselves to make the best of their lives on earth, having thus sincerely exerted themselves, they should cheerfully accept their lot and exercise ingenuity in making the most of that which has fallen to their hands. All too many of man's troubles take origin in the fear soil of his own natural heart. 'The wicked flee when no man pursues.' 'The wicked are like the troubled sea, for it cannot rest, but its waters cast up mire and dirt; there is no peace, says God, for the wicked.' 149:5.3 (1674.5)

"Seek not, then, for false peace and transient joy but rather for the assurance of faith and the sureties of divine sonship which yield composure, contentment, and supreme joy in the spirit." 149:5.4 (1674.6)

It was at Gamala, during the evening conference, that Philip said to Jesus:

"Master, why is it that the Scriptures instruct us to 'fear the Lord,' while you would have us look to the Father in heaven without fear? How are we to harmonize these teachings?"

And Jesus replied to Philip, saying: 149:6.1 (1675.2)

"My children, I am not surprised that you ask such questions. In the beginning it was only through fear that man could learn reverence, but I have come to reveal the Father's love so that you will be attracted to the worship of the Eternal by the drawing of a son's affectionate recognition and reciprocation of the Father's profound and perfect love. I would deliver you from the bondage of driving yourselves through slavish fear to the irksome service of a jealous and wrathful King-God. I would instruct you in the Father-son relationship of God and man so that you may be joyfully led into that sublime and supernal free worship of a loving, just, and merciful Father-God. 149:6.2 (1675.3)

"The 'fear of the Lord' has had different meanings in the successive ages, coming up from fear, through anguish and dread, to awe and reverence. And now from reverence I would lead you up, through recognition, realization, and appreciation, to *love.* When man recognizes only the works of God, he is led to fear the Supreme; but when man begins to understand and experience the personality and character of the living God, he is led increasingly to love such a good and perfect, universal and eternal Father. And it is just this changing of the relation of man to God that constitutes the mission of the Son of Man on earth. 149:6.3 (1675.4)

"Intelligent children do not fear their father in order that they may receive good gifts from his hand; but having already received the abundance of good things bestowed by the dictates of the father's affection for his sons and daughters, these much loved children are led to love their father in responsive recognition and appreciation of such munificent beneficence. The goodness of God leads to repentance; the beneficence of God leads to service; the mercy of God leads to salvation; while the love of God leads to intelligent and freehearted worship. 149:6.4 (1675.5)

"Your forebears feared God because he was mighty and mysterious. You shall adore him because he is magnificent in love, plenteous in mercy, and glorious in truth. The power of God engenders fear in the heart of man, but the nobility and righteousness of his personality beget reverence, love, and willing worship. A dutiful and affectionate son does not fear or dread even a mighty and noble father. I have come into the world to put love in the place of fear, joy in the place of sorrow, confidence in the place of dread, loving service and appreciative worship in the place of slavish bondage and meaningless ceremonies. But it is still true of those who sit in darkness that 'the fear of the Lord is the beginning of wisdom.' But when the light has more fully come, the sons of God are led to praise the Infinite for what he *is* rather than to fear him for what he *does.* 149:6.5 (1675.6)

"When children are young and unthinking, they must necessarily be admonished to honor their parents; but when they grow older and become somewhat more appreciative of the benefits of the parental ministry and protection, they are led up, through understanding respect and increasing affection, to that level of experience where they actually love their parents for what they are more than for what they have done. The father naturally loves his child, but the child must develop his love for the father from the fear of what the father can do, through awe, dread, dependence, and reverence, to the appreciative and affectionate regard of love. 149:6.6 (1675.7)

"You have been taught that you should 'fear God and keep his commandments, for that is the whole duty of man.' But I have come to give you a new and higher commandment. I would teach you to 'love God and learn to do his will, for that is the highest privilege of the liberated sons of God.' Your fathers were taught to 'fear God—the Almighty King.' I teach you, 'Love God—the all-merciful Father.' 149:6.7 (1676.1)

"In the kingdom of heaven, which I have come to declare, there is no high and mighty king; this kingdom is a divine family. The universally recognized and unreservedly worshiped center and head of this far-flung brotherhood of intelligent beings is my Father and your Father. I am his Son, and you are also his sons. Therefore it is eternally true that you and I are brethren in the heavenly estate, and all the more so since we have become brethren in the flesh of the earthly life. Cease, then, to fear God as a king or serve him as a master; learn to reverence him as the Creator; honor him as the Father of your spirit youth; love him as a merciful defender; and ultimately worship him as the loving and all- wise Father of your more mature spiritual realization and appreciation. 149:6.8 (1676.2)

"Out of your wrong concepts of the Father in heaven grow your false ideas of humility and springs much of your hypocrisy. Man may be a worm of the dust by nature and origin, but when he becomes indwelt by my Father's spirit, that man becomes divine in his destiny. The bestowal spirit of my Father will surely return to the divine source and universe level of origin, and the human soul of mortal man which shall have become the reborn child of this indwelling spirit shall certainly ascend with the divine spirit to the very presence of the eternal Father. 149:6.9 (1676.3)

"Humility, indeed, becomes mortal man who receives all these gifts from the Father in heaven, albeit there is a divine dignity attached to all such faith candidates for the eternal ascent of the heavenly kingdom. The meaningless and menial practices of an ostentatious and false humility are incompatible with the appreciation of the source of your salvation and the recognition of the destiny of your spirit-born souls. Humility before God is altogether appropriate in the depths of your hearts; meekness before men is commendable; but the hypocrisy of self-conscious and attention-craving humility is childish and unworthy of the enlightened sons of the kingdom. 149:6.10 (1676.4)

"You do well to be meek before God and self-controlled before men, but let your meekness be of spiritual origin and not the self-deceptive display of a self-conscious sense of self-righteous superiority.

The prophet spoke advisedly when he said, 'Walk humbly with God,' for, while the Father in heaven is the Infinite and the Eternal, he also dwells 'with him who is of a contrite mind and a humble spirit.' My Father disdains pride, loathes hypocrisy, and abhors iniquity. And it was to emphasize the value of sincerity and perfect trust in the loving support and faithful guidance of the heavenly Father that I have so often referred to the little child as illustrative of the attitude of mind and the response of spirit which are so essential to the entrance of mortal man into the spirit realities of the kingdom of heaven. 149:6.11 (1676.5)

"Well did the Prophet Jeremiah describe many mortals when he said: 'You are near God in the mouth but far from him in the heart.' And have you not also read that direful warning of the prophet who said: 'The priests thereof teach for hire, and the prophets thereof divine for money. At the same time they profess piety and proclaim that the Lord is with them.' Have you not been well warned against those who 'speak peace to their neighbors when mischief is in their hearts,' those who 'flatter with the lips while the heart is given to double-dealing'? Of all the sorrows of a trusting man, none are so terrible as to be 'wounded in the house of a trusted friend.'" 149:6.12 (1677.1)

One evening at Shunem, after John's apostles had returned to Hebron, and after Jesus' apostles had been sent out two and two, when the Master was engaged in teaching a group of twelve of the younger evangelists who were laboring under the direction of Jacob, together with the twelve women, Rachel asked Jesus this question:

"Master, what shall we answer when women ask us, What shall I do to be saved?"

When Jesus heard this question, he answered: 150:5.1 (1682.3)

"When men and women ask what shall we do to be saved, you shall answer, Believe this gospel of the kingdom; accept divine forgiveness. By faith recognize the indwelling spirit of God, whose acceptance makes you a son of God. Have you not read in the Scriptures where it says, 'In the Lord have I righteousness and strength.' Also where the Father says, 'My righteousness is near; my salvation has gone forth, and my arms shall enfold my people.' 'My soul shall be joyful in the love of my God, for he has clothed me with the garments of salvation and has covered me with the robe of his righteousness.' Have you not also read of the Father that his name 'shall be called the Lord our righteousness.' 'Take away the filthy rags of self-righteousness and clothe my son with the robe of divine righteousness and eternal salvation.' It is forever true, 'the just shall live by faith.' Entrance into the Father's kingdom is wholly free, but progress—growth in grace—is essential to continuance therein. 150:5.2 (1682.4)

"Salvation is the gift of the Father and is revealed by his Sons. Acceptance by faith on your part makes you a partaker of the divine nature, a son or a daughter of God. By faith you are justified; by faith are you saved; and by this same faith are you eternally advanced in the way of progressive and divine perfection. By faith was Abraham justified and made aware of salvation by the teachings of Melchizedek. All down through the ages has this same faith saved the sons of men, but now has a Son come forth from the Father to make salvation more real and acceptable." 150:5.3 (1682.5)

The apostles and those who were with them, when they heard Jesus teach the people in this manner, were greatly perplexed; and after much talking among themselves, that evening in the Zebedee garden Matthew said to Jesus:

"Master, what is the meaning of the dark sayings which you present to the multitude? Why do you speak in parables to those who seek the truth?"

And Jesus answered: 151:1.3 (1689.1)

"In patience have I instructed you all this time. To you it is given to know the mysteries of the kingdom of heaven, but to the undiscerning multitudes and to those who seek our destruction, from now on, the mysteries of the kingdom shall be presented in parables. And this we will do so that those who really desire to enter the kingdom may discern the meaning of the teaching and thus find salvation, while those who listen only to ensnare us may be the more confounded in that they will see without seeing and will hear without hearing. My children, do you not perceive the law of the spirit which decrees that to him who has shall be given so that he shall have an abundance; but from him who has not shall be taken away even that which he has. Therefore will I henceforth speak to the people much in parables to the end that our friends and those who desire to know the truth may find that which they seek, while our enemies and those who love not the truth may hear without understanding. Many of these people follow not in the way of the truth. The prophet did, indeed, describe all such undiscerning souls when he said: 'For this people's heart has waxed gross, and their ears are dull of hearing, and their eyes they have closed lest they should discern the truth and understand it in their hearts.'" 151:1.4 (1689.2)

As Jesus paused for a moment to look over the congregation, one of the teachers from Jerusalem (a member of the Sanhedrin) rose up and asked:

"Do I understand you to say that you are the bread which comes down from heaven, and that the manna which Moses gave to our fathers in the wilderness did not?"

And Jesus answered the Pharisee, "You understood aright." Then said the Pharisee: "But are you not Jesus of Nazareth, the son of Joseph, the carpenter? Are not your father and mother, as well as your brothers and sisters, well known to many of us? How then is it that you appear here in God's house and declare that you have come down from heaven?" 153:2.10 (1711.2)

By this time there was much murmuring in the synagogue, and such a tumult was threatened that Jesus stood up and said: "Let us be patient; the truth never suffers from honest examination. I am all that you say but more. The Father and I are one; the Son does only that which the Father teaches him, while all those who are given to the Son by the Father, the Son will receive to himself. You have read where it is written in the Prophets, 'You shall all be taught by God,' and that 'Those whom the Father teaches will hear also his Son.' Everyone who yields to the teaching of the Father's indwelling spirit will eventually come to me. Not that any man has seen the Father, but the Father's spirit does live within man. And the Son who came down from heaven, he has surely seen the Father. And those who truly believe this Son already have eternal life. 153:2.11 (1711.3)

"I am this bread of life. Your fathers ate manna in the wilderness and are dead. But this bread which comes down from God, if a man eats thereof, he shall never die in spirit. I repeat, I am this living bread, and every soul who attains the realization of this united nature of God and man shall live forever. And this bread of life which I give to all who will receive is my own living and combined nature. The Father in the Son and the Son one with the Father—that is my life-giving revelation to the world and my saving gift to all nations." 153:2.12 (1711.4)

Then stood up another Pharisee, who said:

"Teacher, we would have you give us a predetermined sign which we will agree upon as establishing your authority and right to teach. Will you agree to such an arrangement?"

And when Jesus heard this, he said: "This faithless and sign-seeking generation seeks a token, but no sign shall be given you other than that which you already have, and that which you shall see when the Son of Man departs from among you." 153:4.5 (1714.4)

While pausing for lunch under the shadow of an overhanging ledge of rock, near Luz, Jesus delivered one of the most remarkable addresses which his apostles ever listened to throughout all their years of association with him. No sooner had they seated themselves to break bread than Simon Peter asked Jesus:

"Master, since the Father in heaven knows all things, and since his spirit is our support in the establishment of the kingdom of heaven on earth, why is it that we flee from the threats of our enemies? Why do we refuse to confront the foes of truth?"

But before Jesus had begun to answer Peter's question, Thomas broke in, asking: "Master, I should really like to know just what is wrong with the religion of our enemies at Jerusalem. What is the real difference between their religion and ours? Why is it we are at such diversity of belief when we all profess to serve the same God?" And when Thomas had finished, Jesus said: "While I would not ignore Peter's question, knowing full well how easy it would be to misunderstand my reasons for avoiding an open clash with the rulers of the Jews at just this time, still it will prove more helpful to all of you if I choose rather to answer Thomas's question. And that I will proceed to do when you have finished your lunch." 155:4.2 (1728.2)

One of the visiting Pharisees, mounting a lampstand, shouted out this question:

"You tell us that you are the bread of life. How can you give us your flesh to eat or your blood to drink? What avail is your teaching if it cannot be carried out?"

And Jesus answered this question, saying: "I did not teach you that my flesh is the bread of life nor that my blood is the water thereof. But I did say that my life in the flesh is a bestowal of the bread of heaven. The fact of the Word of God bestowed in the flesh and the phenomenon of the Son of Man subject to the will of God, constitute a reality of experience which is equivalent to the divine sustenance. You cannot eat my flesh nor can you drink my blood, but you can become one in spirit with me even as I am one in spirit with the Father. You can be nourished by the eternal word of God, which is indeed the bread of life, and which has been bestowed in the likeness of mortal flesh; and you can be watered in soul by the divine spirit, which is truly the water of life. The Father has sent me into the world to show how he desires to indwell and direct all men; and I have so lived this life in the flesh as to inspire all men likewise ever to seek to know and do the will of the indwelling heavenly Father." 153:3.2 (1712.2)

Then one of the Jerusalem spies who had been observing Jesus and his apostles, said: "We notice that neither you nor your apostles wash your hands properly before you eat bread. You must well know that such a practice as eating with defiled and unwashed hands is a transgression of the law of the elders. Neither do you properly wash your drinking cups and eating vessels.

"Why is it that you show such disrespect for the traditions of the fathers and the laws of our elders?"

And when Jesus heard him speak, he answered: "Why is it that you transgress the commandments of God by the laws of your tradition? The commandment says, 'Honor your father and your mother,' and directs that you share with them your substance if necessary; but you enact a law of tradition which permits undutiful children to say that the money wherewith the parents might have been assisted has been 'given to God.' The law of the elders thus relieves such crafty children of their responsibility, notwithstanding that the children subsequently use all such monies for their own comfort. Why is it that you in this way make void the commandment by your own tradition? Well did Isaiah prophesy of you hypocrites, saying: 'This people honors me with their lips, but their heart is far from me. In vain do they worship me, teaching as their doctrines the precepts of men.' 153:3.3 (1712.3)

"You can see how it is that you desert the commandment while you hold fast to the tradition of men. Altogether willing are you to reject the word of God while you maintain your own traditions. And in many other ways do you dare to set up your own teachings above the law and the prophets." 153:3.4 (1712.4)

Jesus then directed his remarks to all present. He said: "But hearken to me, all of you. It is not that which enters into the mouth that spiritually defiles the man, but rather that which proceeds out of the mouth and from the heart." But even the apostles failed fully to grasp the meaning of his words, for Simon Peter also asked him:

"Lest some of your hearers be unnecessarily offended, would you explain to us the meaning of these words?"

And then said Jesus to Peter: "Are you also hard of understanding? Know you not that every plant which my heavenly Father has not planted shall be rooted up? Turn now your attention to those who would know the truth. You cannot compel men to love the truth. Many of these teachers are blind guides. And you know that, if the blind lead the blind, both shall fall into the pit. But hearken while I tell you the truth concerning those things which morally defile and spiritually contaminate men. I declare it is not that which enters the body by the mouth or gains access to the mind through the eyes and ears, that defiles the man. Man is only defiled by that evil which may originate within the heart, and which finds expression in the words and deeds of such unholy persons. Do you not know it is from the heart that there come forth evil thoughts, wicked projects of murder, theft, and adulteries, together with jealousy, pride, anger, revenge, railings, and false witness? And it is just such things that defile men, and not that they eat bread with ceremonially unclean hands." 153:3.5 (1712.5)

On the evening of this same day Nathaniel asked Jesus:

"Master, why do we pray that God will lead us not into temptation when we well know from your revelation of the Father that he never does such things?"

Jesus answered Nathaniel: 156:5.3 (1738.2)

"It is not strange that you ask such questions seeing that you are beginning to know the Father as I know him, and not as the early Hebrew prophets so dimly saw him. You well know how our forefathers were disposed to see God in almost everything that happened. They looked for the hand of God in all natural occurrences and in every unusual episode of human experience. They connected God with both good and evil. They thought he softened the heart of Moses and hardened the heart of Pharaoh. When man had a strong urge to do something, good or evil, he was in the habit of accounting for these unusual emotions by remarking: 'The Lord spoke to me saying, do thus and so, or go here and there.' Accordingly, since men so often and so violently ran into temptation, it became the habit of our forefathers to believe that God led them thither for testing, punishing, or strengthening. But you, indeed, now know better. You know that men are all too often led into temptation by the urge of their own selfishness and by the impulses of their animal natures. When you are in this way tempted, I admonish you that, while you recognize temptation honestly and sincerely for just what it is, you intelligently redirect the energies of spirit, mind, and body, which are seeking expression, into higher channels and toward more idealistic goals. In this way may you transform your temptations into the highest types of uplifting mortal ministry while you almost wholly avoid these wasteful and weakening conflicts between the animal and spiritual natures. 156:5.4 (1738.3)

"But let me warn you against the folly of undertaking to surmount temptation by the effort of supplanting one desire by another and supposedly superior desire through the mere force of the human will. If you would be truly triumphant over the temptations of the lesser and lower nature, you must come to that place of spiritual advantage where you have really and truly developed an actual interest in, and love for, those higher and more idealistic forms of conduct which your mind is desirous of substituting for these lower and less idealistic habits of behavior that you recognize as temptation. You will in this way be delivered through spiritual transformation rather than be increasingly overburdened with the deceptive suppression of mortal desires. The old and the inferior will be forgotten in the love for the new and the superior. Beauty is always triumphant over ugliness in the hearts of all who are illuminated by the love of truth. There is mighty power in the expulsive energy of a new and sincere spiritual affection. And again I say to you, be not overcome by evil but rather overcome evil with good." 156:5.5 (1738.4)

Peter shuddered at the thought of the Master's dying—it was too disagreeable an idea to entertain—and fearing that James or John might ask some question relative to this statement, he thought best to start up a diverting conversation and, not knowing what else to talk about, gave expression to the first thought coming into his mind, which was:

"Master, why is it that the scribes say that Elijah must first come before the Messiah shall appear?"

And Jesus, knowing that Peter sought to avoid reference to his death and resurrection, answered: "Elijah indeed comes first to prepare the way for the Son of Man, who must suffer many things and finally be rejected. But I tell you that Elijah has already come, and they received him not but did to him whatsoever they willed." And then did the three apostles perceive that he referred to John the Baptist as Elijah. Jesus knew that, if they insisted on regarding him as the Messiah, then must John be the Elijah of the prophecy. 158:2.2 (1754.2)

They traveled on through Galilee until well past the time for their lunch, when they stopped in the shade to refresh themselves. And after they had partaken of food, Andrew, speaking to Jesus, said: **"Master, my brethren do not comprehend your deep sayings. We have come fully to believe that you are the Son of God, and now we hear these strange words about leaving us, about dying. We do not understand your teaching. Are you speaking to us in parables?** We pray you to speak to us directly and in undisguised form." 158:7.2 (1759.4)

In answer to Andrew, Jesus said: "My brethren, it is because you have confessed that I am the Son of God that I am constrained to begin to unfold to you the truth about the end of the bestowal of the Son of Man on earth. You insist on clinging to the belief that I am the Messiah, and you will not abandon the idea that the Messiah must sit upon a throne in Jerusalem; wherefore do I persist in telling you that the Son of Man must presently go to Jerusalem, suffer many things, be rejected by the scribes, the elders, and the chief priests, and after all this be killed and raised from the dead. And I speak not a parable to you; I speak the truth to you that you may be prepared for these events when they suddenly come upon us." And while he was yet speaking, Simon Peter, rushing impetuously toward him, laid his hand upon the Master's shoulder and said: "Master, be it far from us to contend with you, but I declare that these things shall never happen to you." 158:7.3 (1759.5)

Simon Peter was the apostle in charge of the workers at Hippos, and when he heard Jesus thus speak, he asked: **"Lord, how often shall my brother sin against me, and I forgive him? Until seven times?"**

And Jesus answered Peter: "Not only seven times but even to seventy times and seven. Therefore may the kingdom of heaven be likened to a certain king who ordered a financial reckoning with his stewards. And when they had begun to conduct this examination of accounts, one of his chief retainers was brought before him confessing that he owed his king ten thousand talents. Now this officer of the king's court pleaded that hard times had come upon him, and that he did not have wherewith to pay this obligation. And so the king commanded that his property be confiscated, and that his children be sold to pay his debt. When this chief steward heard this stern decree, he fell down on his face before the king and implored him to have mercy and grant him more time, saying, 'Lord, have a little more patience with me, and I will pay you all.' And when the king looked upon this negligent servant and his family, he was moved with compassion. He ordered that he should be released, and that the loan should be wholly forgiven. 159:1.4 (1763.1)

"And this chief steward, having thus received mercy and forgiveness at the hands of the king, went about his business, and finding one of his subordinate stewards who owed him a mere hundred denarii, he laid hold upon him and, taking him by the throat, said, 'Pay me all you owe.' And then did this fellow steward fall down before the chief steward and, beseeching him, said: 'Only have patience with me, and I will presently be able to pay you.' But the chief steward would not show mercy to his fellow steward but rather had him cast in prison until he should pay his debt. When his fellow servants saw what had happened, they were so distressed that they went and told their lord and master, the king. When the king heard of the doings of his chief steward, he called this ungrateful and unforgiving man before him and said: 'You are a wicked and unworthy steward. When you sought for compassion, I freely forgave you your entire debt. Why did you not also show mercy to your fellow steward, even as I showed mercy to you?' And the king was so very angry that he delivered his ungrateful chief steward to the jailers that they might hold him until he had paid all that was due. And even so shall my heavenly Father show the more abundant mercy to those who freely show mercy to their fellows. How can you come to God asking consideration for your shortcomings when you are wont to chastise your brethren for being guilty of these same human frailties? I say to all of you: Freely you have received the good things of the kingdom; therefore freely give to your fellows on earth." 159:1.5 (1763.2)

And then went Jesus over to Abila, where Nathaniel and his associates labored. Nathaniel was much bothered by some of Jesus' pronouncements which seemed to detract from the authority of the recognized Hebrew scriptures. Accordingly, on this night, after the usual period of questions and answers, Nathaniel took Jesus away from the others and asked:

"Master, could you trust me to know the truth about the Scriptures? I observe that you teach us only a portion of the sacred writings—the best as I view it—and I infer that you reject the teachings of the rabbis to the effect that the words of the law are the very words of God, having been with God in heaven even before the times of Abraham and Moses. What is the truth about the Scriptures?"

When Jesus heard the question of his bewildered apostle, he answered: 159:4.1 (1767.3)

"Nathaniel, you have rightly judged; I do not regard the Scriptures as do the rabbis. I will talk with you about this matter on condition that you do not relate these things to your brethren, who are not all prepared to receive this teaching. The words of the law of Moses and the teachings of the Scriptures were not in existence before Abraham. Only in recent times have the Scriptures been gathered together as we now have them. While they contain the best of the higher thoughts and longings of the Jewish people, they also contain much that is far from being representative of the character and teachings of the Father in heaven; wherefore must I choose from among the better teachings those truths which are to be gleaned for the gospel of the kingdom. 159:4.2 (1767.4)

"These writings are the work of men, some of them holy men, others not so holy. The teachings of these books represent the views and extent of enlightenment of the times in which they had their origin. As a revelation of truth, the last are more dependable than the first. The Scriptures are faulty and altogether human in origin, but mistake not, they do constitute the best collection of religious wisdom and spiritual truth to be found in all the world at this time. 159:4.3 (1767.5)

"Many of these books were not written by the persons whose names they bear, but that in no way detracts from the value of the truths which they contain. If the story of Jonah should not be a fact, even if Jonah had never lived, still would the profound truth of this narrative, the love of God for Nineveh and the so-called heathen, be none the less precious in the eyes of all those who love their fellow men. The Scriptures are sacred because they present the thoughts and acts of men who were searching for God, and who in these writings left on record their highest concepts of righteousness, truth, and holiness. The Scriptures contain much that is true, very much, but in the light of your present teaching, you know that these writings also contain much that is misrepresentative of the Father in heaven, the loving God I have come to reveal to all the worlds. 159:4.4 (1767.6)

"Nathaniel, never permit yourself for one moment to believe the Scripture records which tell you that the God of love directed your forefathers to go forth in battle to slay all their enemies—men, women, and children. Such records are the words of men, not very holy men, and they are not the word of God. The Scriptures always have, and always will, reflect the intellectual, moral, and spiritual status of those who create them. Have you not noted that the concepts of Yahweh grow in beauty and glory as the prophets make their records from Samuel to Isaiah? And you should remember that the Scriptures are intended for religious instruction and spiritual guidance. They are not the works of either historians or philosophers. 159:4.5 (1768.1)

"The thing most deplorable is not merely this erroneous idea of the absolute perfection of the Scripture record and the infallibility of its teachings, but rather the confusing misinterpretation of these sacred writings by the tradition-enslaved scribes and Pharisees at Jerusalem. And now will they employ both the doctrine of the inspiration of the Scriptures and their misinterpretations thereof in their determined effort to withstand these newer teachings of the gospel of the kingdom. Nathaniel, never forget, the Father does not limit the revelation of truth to any one generation or to any one people. Many earnest seekers after the truth have been, and will continue to be, confused and disheartened by these doctrines of the perfection of the Scriptures. 159:4.6 (1768.2)

"The authority of truth is the very spirit that indwells its living manifestations, and not the dead words of the less illuminated and supposedly inspired men of another generation. And even if these holy men of old lived inspired and spirit-filled lives, that does not mean that their *words* were similarly spiritually inspired. Today we make no record of the teachings of this gospel of the kingdom lest, when I have gone, you speedily become divided up into sundry groups of truth contenders as a result of the diversity of your interpretation of my teachings. For this generation it is best that we *live* these truths while we shun the making of records. 159:4.7 (1768.3)

"Mark you well my words, Nathaniel, nothing which human nature has touched can be regarded as infallible. Through the mind of man divine truth may indeed shine forth, but always of relative purity and partial divinity. The creature may crave infallibility, but only the Creators possess it. 159:4.8 (1768.4)

"But the greatest error of the teaching about the Scriptures is the doctrine of their being sealed books of mystery and wisdom which only the wise minds of the nation dare to interpret. The revelations of divine truth are not sealed except by human ignorance, bigotry, and narrow-minded intolerance. The light of the Scriptures is only dimmed by prejudice and darkened by superstition. A false fear of sacredness has prevented religion from being safeguarded by common sense. The fear of the authority of the sacred writings of the past effectively prevents the honest souls of today from accepting the new light of the gospel, the light which these very God-knowing men of another generation so intensely longed to see. 159:4.9 (1768.5)

"But the saddest feature of all is the fact that some of the teachers of the sanctity of this traditionalism know this very truth. They more or less fully understand these limitations of Scripture, but they are moral cowards, intellectually dishonest. They know the truth regarding the sacred writings, but they prefer to withhold such disturbing facts from the people. And thus do they pervert and distort the Scriptures, making them the guide to slavish details of the daily life and an authority in things nonspiritual instead of appealing to the sacred writings as the repository of the moral wisdom, religious inspiration, and the spiritual teaching of the God-knowing men of other generations." 159:4.10 (1769.1)

At Philadelphia, where James was working, Jesus taught the disciples about the positive nature of the gospel of the kingdom. When, in the course of his remarks, he intimated that some parts of the Scripture were more truth-containing than others and admonished his hearers to feed their souls upon the best of the spiritual food, James interrupted the Master, asking:

"Would you be good enough, Master, to suggest to us how we may choose the better passages from the Scriptures for our personal edification?"

And Jesus replied: "Yes, James, when you read the Scriptures look for those eternally true and divinely beautiful teachings, such as: 159:5.1 (1769.3)

"Create in me a clean heart, O Lord. 159:5.2 (1769.4)

"The Lord is my shepherd; I shall not want. 159:5.3 (1769.5)

"You should love your neighbor as yourself. 159:5.4 (1769.6)

"For I, the Lord your God, will hold your right hand, saying, fear not; I will help you. 159:5.5 (1769.7)

"Neither shall the nations learn war anymore." 159:5.6 (1769.8)

One of the apostles once asked:

"Master, what should I do if a stranger forced me to carry his pack for a mile?"

Jesus answered: "Do not sit down and sigh for relief while you berate the stranger under your breath. Righteousness comes not from such passive attitudes. If you can think of nothing more effectively positive to do, you can at least carry the pack a second mile. That will of a certainty challenge the unrighteous and ungodly stranger." 159:5.15 (1770.7)

The first afternoon that Jesus taught in the temple, a considerable company sat listening to his words depicting the liberty of the new gospel and the joy of those who believe the good news, when a curious listener interrupted him to ask:

"Teacher, how is it you can quote the Scriptures and teach the people so fluently when I am told that you are untaught in the learning of the rabbis?"

Jesus replied: "No man has taught me the truths which I declare to you. And this teaching is not mine but His who sent me. If any man really desires to do my Father's will, he shall certainly know about my teaching, whether it be God's or whether I speak for myself. He who speaks for himself seeks his own glory, but when I declare the words of the Father, I thereby seek the glory of him who sent me. But before you try to enter into the new light, should you not rather follow the light you already have? Moses gave you the law, yet how many of you honestly seek to fulfill its demands? Moses in this law enjoins you, saying, 'You shall not kill'; notwithstanding this command some of you seek to kill the Son of Man." 162:2.1 (1790.4)

When the crowd heard these words, they fell to wrangling among themselves. Some said he was mad; some that he had a devil. Others said this was indeed the prophet of Galilee whom the scribes and Pharisees had long sought to kill. Some said the religious authorities were afraid to molest him; others thought that they laid not hands upon him because they had become believers in him. After considerable debate one of the crowd stepped forward and asked Jesus,

"Why do the rulers seek to kill you?"

And he replied: "The rulers seek to kill me because they resent my teaching about the good news of the kingdom, a gospel that sets men free from the burdensome traditions of a formal religion of ceremonies which these teachers are determined to uphold at any cost. They circumcise in accordance with the law on the Sabbath day, but they would kill me because I once on the Sabbath day set free a man held in the bondage of affliction. They follow after me on the Sabbath to spy on me but would kill me because on another occasion I chose to make a grievously stricken man completely whole on the Sabbath day. They seek to kill me because they well know that, if you honestly believe and dare to accept my teaching, their system of traditional religion will be overthrown, forever destroyed. Thus will they be deprived of authority over that to which they have devoted their lives since they steadfastly refuse to accept this new and more glorious gospel of the kingdom of God. And now do I appeal to every one of you: Judge not according to outward appearances but rather judge by the true spirit of these teachings; judge righteously." 162:2.2 (1790.5)

Then said another inquirer: "Yes, Teacher, we do look for the Messiah, but when he comes, we know that his appearance will be in mystery. We know whence you are. You have been among your brethren from the beginning. The deliverer will come in power to restore the throne of David's kingdom.

"Do you really claim to be the Messiah?"

And Jesus replied: "You claim to know me and to know whence I am. I wish your claims were true, for indeed then would you find abundant life in that knowledge. But I declare that I have not come to you for myself; I have been sent by the Father, and he who sent me is true and faithful. By refusing to hear me, you are refusing to receive Him who sends me. You, if you will receive this gospel, shall come to know Him who sent me. I know the Father, for I have come from the Father to declare and reveal him to you." 162:2.3 (1791.1)

What really happened was this: Early the third morning of the feast, as Jesus approached the temple, he was met by a group of the hired agents of the Sanhedrin who were dragging a woman along with them. As they came near, the spokesman said:

"Master, this woman was taken in adultery—in the very act. Now, the law of Moses commands that we should stone such a woman. What do you say should be done with her?" 162:3.2 (1793.1)

It was the plan of Jesus' enemies, if he upheld the law of Moses requiring that the self-confessed transgressor be stoned, to involve him in difficulty with the Roman rulers, who had denied the Jews the right to inflict the death penalty without the approval of a Roman tribunal. If he forbade stoning the woman, they would accuse him before the Sanhedrin of setting himself up above Moses and the Jewish law. If he remained silent, they would accuse him of cowardice. But the Master so managed the situation that the whole plot fell to pieces of its own sordid weight. This woman, once comely, was the wife of an inferior citizen of Nazareth, a man who had been a troublemaker for Jesus throughout his youthful days. The man, having married this woman, did most shamefully force her to earn their living by making commerce of her body. He had come up to the feast at Jerusalem that his wife might thus prostitute her physical charms for financial gain. He had entered into a bargain with the hirelings of the Jewish rulers thus to betray his own wife in her commercialized vice. And so they came with the woman and her companion in transgression for the purpose of ensnaring Jesus into making some statement which could be used against him in case of his arrest. 162:3.3 (1793.2)

Jesus, looking over the crowd, saw her husband standing behind the others. He knew what sort of man he was and perceived that he was a party to the despicable transaction. Jesus first walked around to near where this degenerate husband stood and wrote upon the sand a few words which caused him to depart in haste. Then he came back before the woman and wrote again upon the ground for the benefit of her would-be accusers; and when they read his words, they, too, went away, one by one. And when the Master had written in the sand the third time, the woman's companion in evil took his departure, so that, when the Master raised himself up from this writing, he beheld the woman standing alone before him. Jesus said: "Woman, where are your accusers? did no man remain to stone you?" And the woman, lifting up her eyes, answered, "No man, Lord." And then said Jesus: "I know about you; neither do I condemn you. Go your way in peace." And this woman, Hildana, forsook her wicked husband and joined herself to the disciples of the kingdom. 162:3.5 (1793.4)

"Verily, verily, I say to you who believe the gospel that, if a man will keep this word of truth alive in his heart, he shall never taste death. And now just at my side a scribe says this statement proves that I have a devil, seeing that Abraham is dead, also the prophets. And he asks:

'Are you so much greater than Abraham and the prophets that you dare to stand here and say that whoso keeps your word shall not taste death? Who do you claim to be that you dare to utter such blasphemies?'

And I say to all such that, if I glorify myself, my glory is as nothing. But it is the Father who shall glorify me, even the same Father whom you call God. But you have failed to know this your God and my Father, and I have come to bring you together; to show you how to become truly the sons of God. Though you know not the Father, I truly know him. Even Abraham rejoiced to see my day, and by faith he saw it and was glad." 162:7.5 (1797.2)

As Martha busied herself with all these supposed duties, she was perturbed because Mary did nothing to help. Therefore she went to Jesus and said:

"Master, do you not care that my sister has left me alone to do all of the serving? Will you not bid her to come and help me?"

Jesus answered: "Martha, Martha, why are you always anxious about so many things and troubled by so many trifles? Only one thing is really worthwhile, and since Mary has chosen this good and needful part, I shall not take it away from her. But when will both of you learn to live as I have taught you: both serving in co-operation and both refreshing your souls in unison? Can you not learn that there is a time for everything—that the lesser matters of life should give way before the greater things of the heavenly kingdom?" 162:8.3 (1798.1)

One earnest disciple came to Jesus, saying:

"Master, I would be one of your new apostles, but my father is very old and near death; could I be permitted to return home to bury him?"

To this man Jesus said: "My son, the foxes have holes, and the birds of heaven have nests, but the Son of Man has nowhere to lay his head. You are a faithful disciple, and you can remain such while you return home to minister to your loved ones, but not so with my gospel messengers. They have forsaken all to follow me and proclaim the kingdom. If you would be an ordained teacher, you must let others bury the dead while you go forth to publish the good news." And this man went away in great disappointment. 163:2.2 (1801.5)

Another disciple came to the Master and said:

"I would become an ordained messenger, but I would like to go to my home for a short while to comfort my family."

And Jesus replied: "If you would be ordained, you must be willing to forsake all. The gospel messengers cannot have divided affections. No man, having put his hand to the plough, if he turns back, is worthy to become a messenger of the kingdom." 163:2.3 (1801.6)

Then Andrew brought to Jesus a certain rich young man who was a devout believer, and who desired to receive ordination. This young man, Matadormus, was a member of the Jerusalem Sanhedrin; he had heard Jesus teach and had been subsequently instructed in the gospel of the kingdom by Peter and the other apostles. Jesus talked with Matadormus concerning the requirements of ordination and requested that he defer decision until after he had thought more fully about the matter. Early the next morning, as Jesus was going for a walk, this young man accosted him and said:

"Master, I would know from you the assurances of eternal life. Seeing that I have observed all the commandments from my youth, I would like to know what more I must do to gain eternal life?"

In answer to this question Jesus said: "If you keep all the commandments—do not commit adultery, do not kill, do not steal, do not bear false witness, do not defraud, honor your parents—you do well, but salvation is the reward of faith, not merely of works. Do you believe this gospel of the kingdom?" And Matadormus answered: "Yes, Master, I do believe everything you and your apostles have taught me." And Jesus said, "Then are you indeed my disciple and a child of the kingdom." 163:2.4 (1801.7)

Then said the young man: "But, Master, I am not content to be your disciple; I would be one of your new messengers." When Jesus heard this, he looked down upon him with a great love and said: "I will have you to be one of my messengers if you are willing to pay the price, if you will supply the one thing which you lack." Matadormus replied: "Master, I will do anything if I may be allowed to follow you." Jesus, kissing the kneeling young man on the forehead, said: "If you would be my messenger, go and sell all that you have and, when you have bestowed the proceeds upon the poor or upon your brethren, come and follow me, and you shall have treasure in the kingdom of heaven." 163:2.5 (1802.1)

When Peter and the apostles heard these words, they were astonished exceedingly, so much so that Peter said:

"Who then, Lord, can be saved? Shall all who have riches be kept out of the kingdom?"

And Jesus replied: "No, Peter, but all who put their trust in riches shall hardly enter into the spiritual life that leads to eternal progress. But even then, much which is impossible to man is not beyond the reach of the Father in heaven; rather should we recognize that with God all things are possible." 163:3.2 (1803.4)

As they went off by themselves, Jesus was grieved that Matadormus did not remain with them, for he greatly loved him. And when they had walked down by the lake, they sat there beside the water, and Peter, speaking for the twelve (who were all present by this time), said:

"We are troubled by your words to the rich young man. Shall we require those who would follow you to give up all their worldly goods?"

And Jesus said: "No, Peter, only those who would become apostles, and who desire to live with me as you do and as one family. But the Father requires that the affections of his children be pure and undivided. Whatever thing or person comes between you and the love of the truths of the kingdom, must be surrendered. If one's wealth does not invade the precincts of the soul, it is of no consequence in the spiritual life of those who would enter the kingdom." 163:3.3 (1803.5)

And then said Peter,

"But, Master, we have left everything to follow you, what then shall we have?"

And Jesus spoke to all of the twelve: "Verily, verily, I say to you, there is no man who has left wealth, home, wife, brethren, parents, or children for my sake and for the sake of the kingdom of heaven who shall not receive manifold more in this world, perhaps with some persecutions, and in the world to come eternal life. But many who are first shall be last, while the last shall often be first. The Father deals with his creatures in accordance with their needs and in obedience to his just laws of merciful and loving consideration for the welfare of a universe. 163:3.4 (1804.1)

That evening a considerable company gathered about Jesus and the two apostles to ask questions, many of which the apostles answered, while others the Master discussed. In the course of the evening a certain lawyer, seeking to entangle Jesus in a compromising disputation, said:

"Teacher, I would like to ask you just what I should do to inherit eternal life?"

Jesus answered, "What is written in the law and the prophets; how do you read the Scriptures?" The lawyer, knowing the teachings of both Jesus and the Pharisees, answered: "To love the Lord God with all your heart, soul, mind, and strength, and your neighbor as yourself." Then said Jesus: "You have answered right; this, if you really do, will lead to life everlasting." 164:1.1 (1809.3)

But the lawyer was not wholly sincere in asking this question, and desiring to justify himself while also hoping to embarrass Jesus, he ventured to ask still another question. Drawing a little closer to the Master, he said,

"But, Teacher, I should like you to tell me just who is my neighbor?"

The lawyer asked this question hoping to entrap Jesus into making some statement that would contravene the Jewish law which defined one's neighbor as "the children of one's people." The Jews looked upon all others as "gentile dogs." This lawyer was somewhat familiar with Jesus' teachings and therefore well knew that the Master thought differently; thus he hoped to lead him into saying something which could be construed as an attack upon the sacred law. 164:1.2 (1809.4)

But Jesus discerned the lawyer's motive, and instead of falling into the trap, he proceeded to tell his hearers a story, a story which would be fully appreciated by any Jericho audience. Said Jesus: "A certain man was going down from Jerusalem to Jericho, and he fell into the hands of cruel brigands, who robbed him, stripped him and beat him, and departing, left him half dead. Very soon, by chance, a certain priest was going down that way, and when he came upon the wounded man, seeing his sorry plight, he passed by on the other side of the road. And in like manner a Levite also, when he came along and saw the man, passed by on the other side. Now, about this time, a certain Samaritan, as he journeyed down to Jericho, came across this wounded man; and when he saw how he had been robbed and beaten, he was moved with compassion, and going over to him, he bound up his wounds, pouring on oil and wine, and setting the man upon his own beast, brought him here to the inn and took care of him. And on the morrow he took out some money and, giving it to the host, said: 'Take good care of my friend, and if the expense is more, when I come back again, I will repay you.' Now let me ask you: Which of these three turned out to be the neighbor of him who fell among the robbers?" And when the lawyer perceived that he had fallen into his own snare, he answered, "He who showed mercy on him." And Jesus said, "Go and do likewise." 164:1.3 (1810.1)

As the Master stood there before the blind man, engrossed in deep thought, Nathaniel, pondering the possible cause of this man's blindness, asked:

"Master, who did sin, this man or his parents, that he should be born blind?" 164:3.2 (1811.3)

The rabbis taught that all such cases of blindness from birth were caused by sin. Not only were children conceived and born in sin, but a child could be born blind as a punishment for some specific sin committed by its father. 164:3.3 (1811.4)

Jesus decided to use this beggar in his plans for that day's work, but before doing anything for the blind man, Josiah by name, he proceeded to answer Nathaniel's question. Said the Master: "Neither did this man sin nor his parents that the works of God might be manifest in him. This blindness has come upon him in the natural course of events, but we must now do the works of Him who sent me, while it is still day, for the night will certainly come when it will be impossible to do the work we are about to perform. When I am in the world, I am the light of the world, but in only a little while I will not be with you." 164:3.7 (1812.1)

This was midwinter in Jerusalem, and the people sought the partial shelter of Solomon's Porch; and as Jesus lingered, the crowds asked him many questions, and he taught them for more than two hours. Some of the Jewish teachers sought to entrap him by publicly asking him:

"How long will you hold us in suspense? If you are the Messiah, why do you not plainly tell us?"

Said Jesus: "I have told you about myself and my Father many times, but you will not believe me. Can you not see that the works I do in my Father's name bear witness for me? But many of you believe not because you belong not to my fold. The teacher of truth attracts only those who hunger for the truth and who thirst for righteousness. My sheep hear my voice and I know them and they follow me. And to all who follow my teaching I give eternal life; they shall never perish, and no one shall snatch them out of my hand. My Father, who has given me these children, is greater than all, so that no one is able to pluck them out of my Father's hand. The Father and I are one." Some of the unbelieving Jews rushed over to where they were still building the temple to pick up stones to cast at Jesus, but the believers restrained them. 164:5.2 (1815.3)

As the apostles baptized believers, the Master talked with those who tarried. And a certain young man said to him:

"Master, my father died leaving much property to me and my brother, but my brother refuses to give me that which is my own. Will you, then, bid my brother divide this inheritance with me?"

Jesus was mildly indignant that this material-minded youth should bring up for discussion such a question of business; but he proceeded to use the occasion for the impartation of further instruction. Said Jesus: "Man, who made me a divider over you? Where did you get the idea that I give attention to the material affairs of this world?" And then, turning to all who were about him, he said: "Take heed and keep yourselves free from covetousness; a man's life consists not in the abundance of the things which he may possess. Happiness comes not from the power of wealth, and joy springs not from riches. Wealth, in itself, is not a curse, but the love of riches many times leads to such devotion to the things of this world that the soul becomes blinded to the beautiful attractions of the spiritual realities of the kingdom of God on earth and to the joys of eternal life in heaven. 165:4.1 (1821.1)

That evening after supper, when Jesus and the twelve gathered together for their daily conference, Andrew asked:

"Master, while we were baptizing the believers, you spoke many words to the lingering multitude which we did not hear. Would you be willing to repeat these words for our benefit?"

And in response to Andrew's request, Jesus said: 165:5.1 (1823.1)

"Yes, Andrew, I will speak to you about these matters of wealth and self-support, but my words to you, the apostles, must be somewhat different from those spoken to the disciples and the multitude since you have forsaken everything, not only to follow me, but to be ordained as ambassadors of the kingdom. Already have you had several years' experience, and you know that the Father whose kingdom you proclaim will not forsake you. You have dedicated your lives to the ministry of the kingdom; therefore be not anxious or worried about the things of the temporal life, what you shall eat, nor yet for your body, what you shall wear. The welfare of the soul is more than food and drink; the progress in the spirit is far above the need of raiment. When you are tempted to doubt the sureness of your bread, consider the ravens; they sow not neither reap, they have no storehouses or barns, and yet the Father provides food for every one of them that seeks it. And of how much more value are you than many birds! Besides, all of your anxiety or fretting doubts can do nothing to supply your material needs. Which of you by anxiety can add a handbreadth to your stature or a day to your life? Since such matters are not in your hands, why do you give anxious thought to any of these problems? 165:5.2 (1823.2)

As they sat thinking, Simon Peter asked:

"Do you speak this parable to us, your apostles, or is it for all the disciples?"

And Jesus answered: 165:6.1 (1824.4)

"In the time of testing, a man's soul is revealed; trial discloses what really is in the heart. When the servant is tested and proved, then may the lord of the house set such a servant over his household and safely trust this faithful steward to see that his children are fed and nurtured. Likewise, will I soon know who can be trusted with the welfare of my children when I shall have returned to the Father. As the lord of the household shall set the true and tried servant over the affairs of his family, so will I exalt those who endure the trials of this hour in the affairs of my kingdom. 165:6.2 (1824.5)

When Jesus would have risen to depart, one of the lawyers who was at the table, addressing him, said:

"But, Master, in some of your statements you reproach us also. Is there nothing good in the scribes, the Pharisees, or the lawyers?"

And Jesus, standing, replied to the lawyer: "You, like the Pharisees, delight in the first places at the feasts and in wearing long robes while you put heavy burdens, grievous to be borne, on men's shoulders. And when the souls of men stagger under these heavy burdens, you will not so much as lift with one of your fingers. Woe upon you who take your greatest delight in building tombs for the prophets your fathers killed! And that you consent to what your fathers did is made manifest when you now plan to kill those who come in this day doing what the prophets did in their day— proclaiming the righteousness of God and revealing the mercy of the heavenly Father. But of all the generations that are past, the blood of the prophets and the apostles shall be required of this perverse and self-righteous generation. Woe upon all of you lawyers who have taken away the key of knowledge from the common people! You yourselves refuse to enter into the way of truth, and at the same time you would hinder all others who seek to enter therein. But you cannot thus shut up the doors of the kingdom of heaven; these we have opened to all who have the faith to enter, and these portals of mercy shall not be closed by the prejudice and arrogance of false teachers and untrue shepherds who are like whited sepulchres which, while outwardly they appear beautiful, are inwardly full of dead men's bones and all manner of spiritual uncleanness." 166:1.5 (1826.2)

As Jesus and the twelve visited with the messengers of the kingdom at Gerasa, one of the Pharisees who believed in him asked this question:

"Lord, will there be few or many really saved?"

And Jesus, answering, said: 166:3.1 (1828.5)

"You have been taught that only the children of Abraham will be saved; that only the gentiles of adoption can hope for salvation. Some of you have reasoned that, since the Scriptures record that only Caleb and Joshua from among all the hosts that went out of Egypt lived to enter the promised land, only a comparatively few of those who seek the kingdom of heaven shall find entrance thereto. 166:3.2 (1828.6)

"You also have another saying among you, and one that contains much truth: That the way which leads to eternal life is straight and narrow, that the door which leads thereto is likewise narrow so that, of those who seek salvation, few can find entrance through this door. You also have a teaching that the way which leads to destruction is broad, that the entrance thereto is wide, and that there are many who choose to go this way. And this proverb is not without its meaning. But I declare that salvation is first a matter of your personal choosing. Even if the door to the way of life is narrow, it is wide enough to admit all who sincerely seek to enter, for I am that door. And the Son will never refuse entrance to any child of the universe who, by faith, seeks to find the Father through the Son. 166:3.3 (1828.7)

While most Palestinians ate only two meals a day, it was the custom of Jesus and the apostles, when on a journey, to pause at midday for rest and refreshment. And it was at such a noontide stop on the way to Philadelphia that Thomas asked Jesus:

"Master, from hearing your remarks as we journeyed this morning, I would like to inquire whether spiritual beings are concerned in the production of strange and extraordinary events in the material world and, further, to ask whether the angels and other spirit beings are able to prevent accidents." 166:4.1 (1830.1)

In answer to Thomas's inquiry, Jesus said: "Have I been so long with you, and yet you continue to ask me such questions? Have you failed to observe how the Son of Man lives as one with you and consistently refuses to employ the forces of heaven for his personal sustenance? Do we not all live by the same means whereby all men exist? Do you see the power of the spiritual world manifested in the material life of this world, save for the revelation of the Father and the sometime healing of his afflicted children? 166:4.2 (1830.2)

"All too long have your fathers believed that prosperity was the token of divine approval; that adversity was the proof of God's displeasure. I declare that such beliefs are superstitions. Do you not observe that far greater numbers of the poor joyfully receive the gospel and immediately enter the kingdom? If riches evidence divine favor, why do the rich so many times refuse to believe this good news from heaven? 166:4.3 (1830.3)

"The Father causes his rain to fall on the just and the unjust; the sun likewise shines on the righteous and the unrighteous. You know about those Galileans whose blood Pilate mingled with the sacrifices, but I tell you these Galileans were not in any manner sinners above all their fellows just because this happened to them. You also know about the eighteen men upon whom the tower of Siloam fell, killing them. Think not that these men who were thus destroyed were offenders above all their brethren in Jerusalem. These folks were simply innocent victims of one of the accidents of time. 166:4.4 (1830.4)

"There are three groups of events which may occur in your lives: 166:4.5 (1830.5)

> "1. You may share in those normal happenings which are a part of the life you and your fellows live on the face of the earth. 166:4.6 (1830.6)
>
> "2. You may chance to fall victim to one of the accidents of nature, one of the mischances of men, knowing full well that such occurrences are in no way prearranged or otherwise produced by the spiritual forces of the realm. 166:4.7 (1830.7)
>
> "3. You may reap the harvest of your direct efforts to comply with the natural laws governing the world. 166:4.8 (1830.8)

"There was a certain man who planted a fig tree in his yard, and when he had many times sought fruit thereon and found none, he called the vinedressers before him and said: 'Here have I come these three seasons looking for fruit on this fig tree and have found none. Cut down this barren tree; why should it encumber the ground?' But the head gardener answered his master: 'Let it alone for one more year so that I may dig around it and put on fertilizer, and then, next year, if it bears no fruit, it shall be cut down.' And when they had thus complied with the laws of fruitfulness, since the tree was living and good, they were rewarded with an abundant yield. 166:4.9 (1830.9)

"In the matter of sickness and health, you should know that these bodily states are the result of material causes; health is not the smile of heaven, neither is affliction the frown of God. 166:4.10 (1831.1)

"The Father's human children have equal capacity for the reception of material blessings; therefore does he bestow things physical upon the children of men without discrimination. When it comes to the bestowal of spiritual gifts, the Father is limited by man's capacity for receiving these divine endowments. Although the Father is no respecter of persons, in the bestowal of spiritual gifts he is limited by man's faith and by his willingness always to abide by the Father's will." 166:4.11 (1831.2)

Notwithstanding that this woman's affliction was wholly mental, her bowed-over form being the result of her depressed mind, the people thought that Jesus had healed a real physical disorder. Although the congregation of the synagogue at Philadelphia was friendly toward the teachings of Jesus, the chief ruler of the synagogue was an unfriendly Pharisee. And as he shared the opinion of the congregation that Jesus had healed a physical disorder, and being indignant because Jesus had presumed to do such a thing on the Sabbath, he stood up before the congregation and said:

"Are there not six days in which men should do all their work?

In these working days come, therefore, and be healed, but not on the Sabbath day." 167:3.2 (1836.1)

When the unfriendly ruler had thus spoken, Jesus returned to the speaker's platform and said: "Why play the part of hypocrites? Does not every one of you, on the Sabbath, loose his ox from the stall and lead him forth for watering? If such a service is permissible on the Sabbath day, should not this woman, a daughter of Abraham who has been bound down by evil these eighteen years, be loosed from this bondage and led forth to partake of the waters of liberty and life, even on this Sabbath day?" 167:3.3 (1836.2)

As they journeyed up the hills from Jericho to Bethany, Nathaniel walked most of the way by the side of Jesus, and their discussion of children in relation to the kingdom of heaven led indirectly to the consideration of the ministry of angels. Nathaniel finally asked the Master this question:

"Seeing that the high priest is a Sadducee, and since the Sadducees do not believe in angels, what shall we teach the people regarding the heavenly ministers?"

Then, among other things, Jesus said: 167:7.1 (1840.6)

"The angelic hosts are a separate order of created beings; they are entirely different from the material order of mortal creatures, and they function as a distinct group of universe intelligences. Angels are not of that group of creatures called 'the Sons of God' in the Scriptures; neither are they the glorified spirits of mortal men who have gone on to progress through the mansions on high. Angels are a direct creation, and they do not reproduce themselves. The angelic hosts have only a spiritual kinship with the human race. As man progresses in the journey to the Father in Paradise, he does traverse a state of being at one time analogous to the state of the angels, but mortal man never becomes an angel. 167:7.2 (1841.1)

"The angels never die, as man does. The angels are immortal unless, perchance, they become involved in sin as did some of them with the deceptions of Lucifer. The angels are the spirit servants in heaven, and they are neither all-wise nor all-powerful. But all of the loyal angels are truly pure and holy. 167:7.3 (1841.2)

"And do you not remember that I said to you once before that, if you had your spiritual eyes anointed, you would then see the heavens opened and behold the angels of God ascending and descending? It is by the ministry of the angels that one world may be kept in touch with other worlds, for have I not repeatedly told you that I have other sheep not of this fold? And these angels are not the spies of the spirit world who watch upon you and then go forth to tell the Father the thoughts of your heart and to report on the deeds of the flesh. The Father has no need of such service inasmuch as his own spirit lives within you. But these angelic spirits do function to keep one part of the heavenly creation informed concerning the doings of other and remote parts of the universe. And many of the angels, while functioning in the government of the Father and the universes of the Sons, are assigned to the service of the human races. When I taught you that many of these seraphim are ministering spirits, I spoke not in figurative language nor in poetic strains. And all this is true, regardless of your difficulty in comprehending such matters. 167:7.4 (1841.3)

Many of these angels are engaged in the work of saving men, for have I not told you of the seraphic joy when one soul elects to forsake sin and begin the search for God? I did even tell you of the joy in the *presence of the angels* of heaven over one sinner who repents, thereby indicating the existence of other and higher orders of celestial beings who are likewise concerned in the spiritual welfare and with the divine progress of mortal man. 167:7.5 (1841.4)

"Also are these angels very much concerned with the means whereby man's spirit is released from the tabernacles of the flesh and his soul escorted to the mansions in heaven. Angels are the sure and heavenly guides of the soul of man during that uncharted and indefinite period of time which intervenes between the death of the flesh and the new life in the spirit abodes." 167:7.6 (1841.5)

One evening Simon Zelotes, commenting on one of Jesus' statements, said:

"Master, what did you mean when you said today that many of the children of the world are wiser in their generation than are the children of the kingdom since they are skillful in making friends with the mammon of unrighteousness?"

Jesus answered: 169:2.1 (1853.4)

"Some of you, before you entered the kingdom, were very shrewd in dealing with your business associates. If you were unjust and often unfair, you were nonetheless prudent and farseeing in that you transacted your business with an eye single to your present profit and future safety. Likewise should you now so order your lives in the kingdom as to provide for your present joy while you also make certain of your future enjoyment of treasures laid up in heaven. If you were so diligent in making gains for yourselves when in the service of self, why should you show less diligence in gaining souls for the kingdom since you are now servants of the brotherhood of man and stewards of God? 169:2.2 (1853.5)

"You may all learn a lesson from the story of a certain rich man who had a shrewd but unjust steward. This steward had not only oppressed his master's clients for his own selfish gain, but he had also directly wasted and squandered his master's funds. When all this finally came to the ears of his master, he called the steward before him and asked the meaning of these rumors and required that he should give immediate accounting of his stewardship and prepare to turn his master's affairs over to another. 169:2.3 (1853.6)

"Now this unfaithful steward began to say to himself: 'What shall I do since I am about to lose this stewardship? I have not the strength to dig; to beg I am ashamed. I know what I will do to make certain that, when I am put out of this stewardship, I will be welcomed into the houses of all who do business with my master.' And then, calling in each of his lord's debtors, he said to the first, 'How much do you owe my master?' He answered, 'A hundred measures of oil.' Then said the steward, 'Take your wax board bond, sit down quickly, and change it to fifty.' Then he said to another debtor, 'How much do you owe?' And he replied, 'A hundred measures of wheat.' Then said the steward, 'Take your bond and write fourscore.' And this he did with numerous other debtors. And so did this dishonest steward seek to make friends for himself after he would be discharged from his stewardship. Even his lord and master, when he subsequently found out about this, was compelled to admit that his unfaithful steward had at least shown sagacity in the manner in which he had sought to provide for future days of want and adversity. 169:2.4 (1853.7)

"And it is in this way that the sons of this world sometimes show more wisdom in their preparation for the future than do the children of light. I say to you who profess to be acquiring treasure in heaven: Take lessons from those who make friends with the mammon of unrighteousness, and likewise so conduct your lives that you make eternal friendship with the forces of righteousness in order that, when all things earthly fail, you shall be joyfully received into the eternal habitations. 169:2.5 (1854.1)

"I affirm that he who is faithful in little will also be faithful in much, while he who is unrighteous in little will also be unrighteous in much. If you have not shown foresight and integrity in the affairs of this world, how can you hope to be faithful and prudent when you are trusted with the stewardship of the true riches of the heavenly kingdom? If you are not good stewards and faithful bankers, if you have not been faithful in that which is another's, who will be foolish enough to give you great treasure in your own name? 169:2.6 (1854.2)

"And again I assert that no man can serve two masters; either he will hate the one and love the other, or else he will hold to one while he despises the other. You cannot serve God and mammon." 169:2.7 (1854.3)

At the noon session of the Sanhedrin it was unanimously agreed that Jesus must be speedily destroyed, inasmuch as no friend of the Master attended this meeting. But they could not agree as to when and how he should be taken into custody. Finally they agreed upon appointing five groups to go out among the people and seek to entangle him in his teaching or otherwise to discredit him in the sight of those who listened to his instruction. Accordingly, about two o'clock, when Jesus had just begun his discourse on "The Liberty of Sonship," a group of these elders of Israel made their way up near Jesus and, interrupting him in the customary manner, asked this question:

"By what authority do you do these things? Who gave you this authority?" 173:2.2 (1891.3)

The rulers of the temple came before Jesus at this afternoon hour challenging not only his teaching but his acts. Jesus well knew that these very men had long publicly taught that his authority for teaching was Satanic, and that all his mighty works had been wrought by the power of the prince of devils. Therefore did the Master begin his answer to their question by asking them a counter-question. Said Jesus: "I would also like to ask you one question which, if you will answer me, I likewise will tell you by what authority I do these works. The baptism of John, whence was it? Did John get his authority from heaven or from men?" 173:2.4 (1892.1)

And when his questioners heard this, they withdrew to one side to take counsel among themselves as to what answer they might give. They had thought to embarrass Jesus before the multitude, but now they found themselves much confused before all who were assembled at that time in the temple court. And their discomfiture was all the more apparent when they returned to Jesus, saying: "Concerning the baptism of John, we cannot answer; we do not know." And they so answered the Master because they had reasoned among themselves: If we shall say from heaven, then will he say, Why did you not believe him, and perchance will add that he received his authority from John; and if we shall say from men, then might the multitude turn upon us, for most of them hold that John was a prophet; and so they were compelled to come before Jesus and the people confessing that they, the religious teachers and leaders of Israel, could not (or would not) express an opinion about John's mission. And when they had spoken, Jesus, looking down upon them, said, "Neither will I tell you by what authority I do these things." 173:2.5 (1892.2)

After speaking this parable, Jesus was about to dismiss the multitude when a sympathetic believer, making his way through the crowds toward him, asked:

"But, Master, how shall we know about these things? how shall we be ready for the king's invitation? what sign will you give us whereby we shall know that you are the Son of God?"

And when the Master heard this, he said, "Only one sign shall be given you." And then, pointing to his own body, he continued, "Destroy this temple, and in three days I will raise it up." But they did not understand him, and as they dispersed, they talked among themselves, saying, "Almost fifty years has this temple been in building, and yet he says he will destroy it and raise it up in three days." Even his own apostles did not comprehend the significance of this utterance, but subsequently, after his resurrection, they recalled what he had said. 173:5.4 (1895.2)

For several days Peter and James had been engaged in discussing their differences of opinion about the Master's teaching regarding the forgiveness of sin. They had both agreed to lay the matter before Jesus, and Peter embraced this occasion as a fitting opportunity for securing the Master's counsel. Accordingly, Simon Peter broke in on the conversation dealing with the differences between praise and worship, by asking:

"Master, James and I are not in accord regarding your teachings having to do with the forgiveness of sin. James claims you teach that the Father forgives us even before we ask him, and I maintain that repentance and confession must precede the forgiveness. Which of us is right? what do you say?" 174:1.1 (1898.1)

After a short silence Jesus looked significantly at all four and answered: "My brethren, you err in your opinions because you do not comprehend the nature of those intimate and loving relations between the creature and the Creator, between man and God. You fail to grasp that understanding sympathy which the wise parent entertains for his immature and sometimes erring child. It is indeed doubtful whether intelligent and affectionate parents are ever called upon to forgive an average and normal child. Understanding relationships associated with attitudes of love effectively prevent all those estrangements which later necessitate the readjustment of repentance by the child with forgiveness by the parent. 174:1.2 (1898.2)

"A part of every father lives in the child. The father enjoys priority and superiority of understanding in all matters connected with the child-parent relationship. The parent is able to view the immaturity of the child in the light of the more advanced parental maturity, the riper experience of the older partner. With the earthly child and the heavenly Father, the divine parent possesses infinity and divinity of sympathy and capacity for loving understanding. Divine forgiveness is inevitable; it is inherent and inalienable in God's infinite understanding, in his perfect knowledge of all that concerns the mistaken judgment and erroneous choosing of the child. Divine justice is so eternally fair that it unfailingly embodies understanding mercy. 174:1.3 (1898.3)

"When a wise man understands the inner impulses of his fellows, he will love them. And when you love your brother, you have already forgiven him. This capacity to understand man's nature and forgive his apparent wrongdoing is Godlike. If you are wise parents, this is the way you will love and understand your children, even forgive them when transient misunderstanding has apparently separated you. The child, being immature and lacking in the fuller understanding of the depth of the child-father relationship, must frequently feel a sense of guilty separation from a father's full approval, but the true father is never conscious of any such separation. Sin is an experience of creature consciousness; it is not a part of God's consciousness. 174:1.4 (1898.4)

"Your inability or unwillingness to forgive your fellows is the measure of your immaturity, your failure to attain adult sympathy, understanding, and love. You hold grudges and nurse vengefulness in direct proportion to your ignorance of the inner nature and true longings of your children and your fellow beings. Love is the outworking of the divine and inner urge of life. It is founded on understanding, nurtured by unselfish service, and perfected in wisdom." 174:1.5 (1898.5)

Tuesday morning, when Jesus arrived in the temple court and began to teach, he had uttered but few words when a group of the younger students from the academies, who had been rehearsed for this purpose, came forward and by their spokesman addressed Jesus: "Master, we know you are a righteous teacher, and we know that you proclaim the ways of truth, and that you serve only God, for you fear no man, and that you are no respecter of persons. We are only students, and we would know the truth about a matter which troubles us; our difficulty is this:

"Is it lawful for us to give tribute to Caesar? Shall we give or shall we not give?"

Jesus, perceiving their hypocrisy and craftiness, said to them: "Why do you thus come to tempt me? Show me the tribute money, and I will answer you." And when they handed him a denarius, he looked at it and said, "Whose image and superscription does this coin bear?" And when they answered him, "Caesar's," Jesus said, "Render to Caesar the things that are Caesar's and render to God the things that are God's." 174:2.2 (1899.2)

Before Jesus could get started with his teaching, another group came forward to question him, this time a company of the learned and crafty Sadducees. Their spokesman, drawing near to him, said:

"Master, Moses said that if a married man should die, leaving no children, his brother should take the wife and raise up seed for the deceased brother. Now there occurred a case where a certain man who had six brothers died childless; his next brother took his wife but also soon died, leaving no children. Likewise did the second brother take the wife, but he also died leaving no offspring. And so on until all six of the brothers had had her, and all six of them passed on without leaving children. And then, after them all, the woman herself died. Now, what we would like to ask you is this: In the resurrection whose wife will she be since all seven of these brothers had her?" 174:3.1 (1900.1)

Jesus knew, and so did the people, that these Sadducees were not sincere in asking this question because it was not likely that such a case would really occur; and besides, this practice of the brothers of a dead man seeking to beget children for him was practically a dead letter at this time among the Jews. Nevertheless, Jesus condescended to reply to their mischievous question. He said: "You all do err in asking such questions because you know neither the Scriptures nor the living power of God. You know that the sons of this world can marry and are given in marriage, but you do not seem to understand that they who are accounted worthy to attain the worlds to come, through the resurrection of the righteous, neither marry nor are given in marriage. Those who experience the resurrection from the dead are more like the angels of heaven, and they never die. These resurrected ones are eternally the sons of God; they are the children of light resurrected into the progress of eternal life. And even your Father Moses understood this, for, in connection with his experiences at the burning bush, he heard the Father say, 'I *am* the God of Abraham, the God of Isaac, and the God of Jacob.' And so, along with Moses, do I declare that my Father is not the God of the dead but of the living. In him you all do live, reproduce, and possess your mortal existence." 174:3.2 (1900.2)

Then came forward one of the groups of the Pharisees to ask harassing questions, and the spokesman, signaling to Jesus, said:

"Master, I am a lawyer, and I would like to ask you which, in your opinion, is the greatest commandment?"

Jesus answered: "There is but one commandment, and that one is the greatest of all, and that commandment is: 'Hear O Israel, the Lord our God, the Lord is one; and you shall love the Lord your God with all your heart and with all your soul, with all your mind and with all your strength.' This is the first and great commandment. And the second commandment is like this first; indeed, it springs directly therefrom, and it is: 'You shall love your neighbor as yourself.' There is no other commandment greater than these; on these two commandments hang all the law and the prophets." 174:4.2 (1901.2)

In order to avoid the crowds passing along the Kidron valley toward Gethsemane, Jesus and his associates were minded to climb up the western slope of Olivet for a short distance and then follow a trail over to their private camp near Gethsemane located a short distance above the public camping ground. As they turned to leave the road leading on to Bethany, they observed the temple, glorified by the rays of the setting sun; and while they tarried on the mount, they saw the lights of the city appear and beheld the beauty of the illuminated temple; and there, under the mellow light of the full moon, Jesus and the twelve sat down. The Master talked with them, and presently Nathaniel asked this question:

"Tell us, Master, how shall we know when these events are about to come to pass?" 176:0.2 (1912.2)

In answering Nathaniel's question, Jesus said: "Yes, I will tell you about the times when this people shall have filled up the cup of their iniquity; when justice shall swiftly descend upon this city of our fathers. I am about to leave you; I go to the Father. After I leave you, take heed that no man deceive you, for many will come as deliverers and will lead many astray. When you hear of wars and rumors of wars, be not troubled, for though all these things will happen, the end of Jerusalem is not yet at hand. You should not be perturbed by famines or earthquakes; neither should you be concerned when you are delivered up to the civil authorities and are persecuted for the sake of the gospel. You will be thrown out of the synagogue and put in prison for my sake, and some of you will be killed. When you are brought up before governors and rulers, it shall be for a testimony of your faith and to show your steadfastness in the gospel of the kingdom. And when you stand before judges, be not anxious beforehand as to what you should say, for the spirit will teach you in that very hour what you should answer your adversaries. In these days of travail, even your own kinsfolk, under the leadership of those who have rejected the Son of Man, will deliver you up to prison and death. For a time you may be hated by all men for my sake, but even in these persecutions I will not forsake you; my spirit will not desert you. Be patient! doubt not that this gospel of the kingdom will triumph over all enemies and, eventually, be proclaimed to all nations." 176:1.1 (1912.3)

Since Jerusalem was to become the cradle of the early gospel movement, Jesus did not want its teachers and preachers to perish in the terrible overthrow of the Jewish people in connection with the destruction of Jerusalem; wherefore did he give these instructions to his followers. Jesus was much concerned lest some of his disciples become involved in these soon-coming revolts and so perish in the downfall of Jerusalem. 176:1.3 (1913.2)

Then Andrew inquired:

"But, Master, if the Holy City and the temple are to be destroyed, and if you are not here to direct us, when should we forsake Jerusalem?"

Said Jesus: "You may remain in the city after I have gone, even through these times of travail and bitter persecution, but when you finally see Jerusalem being encompassed by the Roman armies after the revolt of the false prophets, then will you know that her desolation is at hand; then must you flee to the mountains. Let none who are in the city and around about tarry to save aught, neither let those who are outside dare to enter therein. There will be great tribulation, for these will be the days of gentile vengeance. And after you have deserted the city, this disobedient people will fall by the edge of the sword and will be led captive into all nations; and so shall Jerusalem be trodden down by the gentiles. In the meantime, I warn you, be not deceived. If any man comes to you, saying, 'Behold, here is the Deliverer,' or 'Behold, there is he,' believe it not, for many false teachers will arise and many will be led astray; but you should not be deceived, for I have told you all this beforehand." 176:1.4 (1913.3)

Even after this explicit warning, many of Jesus' followers interpreted these predictions as referring to the changes which would obviously occur in Jerusalem when the reappearing of the Messiah would result in the establishment of the New Jerusalem and in the enlargement of the city to become the world's capital. In their minds these Jews were determined to connect the destruction of the temple with the "end of the world." They believed this New Jerusalem would fill all Palestine; that the end of the world would be followed by the immediate appearance of the "new heavens and the new earth." And so it was not strange that Peter should say:

"Master, we know that all things will pass away when the new heavens and the new earth appear, but how shall we know when you will return to bring all this about?" 176:1.6 (1913.5)

When Jesus heard this, he was thoughtful for some time and then said: "You ever err since you always try to attach the new teaching to the old; you are determined to misunderstand all my teaching; you insist on interpreting the gospel in accordance with your established beliefs. Nevertheless, I will try to enlighten you." 176:1.7 (1914.1)

In further answer to Peter's question, Jesus said: "Why do you still look for the Son of Man to sit upon the throne of David and expect that the material dreams of the Jews will be fulfilled? Have I not told you all these years that my kingdom is not of this world? The things which you now look down upon are coming to an end, but this will be a new beginning out of which the gospel of the kingdom will go to all the world and this salvation will spread to all peoples. And when the kingdom shall have come to its full fruition, be assured that the Father in heaven will not fail to visit you with an enlarged revelation of truth and an enhanced demonstration of righteousness, even as he has already bestowed upon this world him who became the prince of darkness, and then Adam, who was followed by Melchizedek, and in these days, the Son of Man. And so will my Father continue to manifest his mercy and show forth his love, even to this dark and evil world. So also will I, after my Father has invested me with all power and authority, continue to follow your fortunes and to guide in the affairs of the kingdom by the presence of my spirit, who shall shortly be poured out upon all flesh. Even though I shall thus be present with you in spirit, I also promise that I will sometime return to this world, where I have lived this life in the flesh and achieved the experience of simultaneously revealing God to man and leading man to God. Very soon must I leave you and take up the work the Father has intrusted to my hands, but be of good courage, for I will sometime return. In the meantime, my Spirit of the Truth of a universe shall comfort and guide you. 176:2.3 (1914.4)

"You behold me now in weakness and in the flesh, but when I return, it shall be with power and in the spirit. The eye of flesh beholds the Son of Man in the flesh, but only the eye of the spirit will behold the Son of Man glorified by the Father and appearing on earth in his own name. 176:2.4 (1915.1)

"But the times of the reappearing of the Son of Man are known only in the councils of Paradise; not even the angels of heaven know when this will occur. However, you should understand that, when this gospel of the kingdom shall have been proclaimed to all the world for the salvation of all peoples, and when the fullness of the age has come to pass, the Father will send you another dispensational bestowal, or else the Son of Man will return to adjudge the age. 176:2.5 (1915.2)

"And now concerning the travail of Jerusalem, about which I have spoken to you, even this generation will not pass away until my words are fulfilled; but concerning the times of the coming again of the Son of Man, no one in heaven or on earth may presume to speak. But you should be wise regarding the ripening of an age; you should be alert to discern the signs of the times. You know when the fig tree shows its tender branches and puts forth its leaves that summer is near. Likewise, when the world has passed through the long winter of material-mindedness and you discern the coming of the spiritual springtime of a new dispensation, should you know that the summertime of a new visitation draws near. 176:2.6 (1915.3)

"But what is the significance of this teaching having to do with the coming of the Sons of God? Do you not perceive that, when each of you is called to lay down his life struggle and pass through the portal of death, you stand in the immediate presence of judgment, and that you are face to face with the facts of a new dispensation of service in the eternal plan of the infinite Father? What the whole world must face as a literal fact at the end of an age, you, as individuals, must each most certainly face as a personal experience when you reach the end of your natural life and thereby pass on to be confronted with the conditions and demands inherent in the next revelation of the eternal progression of the Father's kingdom." 176:2.7 (1915.4)

As they gathered about the campfire, some twenty of them, Thomas asked:

"Since you are to return to finish the work of the kingdom, what should be our attitude while you are away on the Father's business?"

As Jesus looked them over by the firelight, he answered: 176:3.1 (1916.1)

"And even you, Thomas, fail to comprehend what I have been saying. Have I not all this time taught you that your connection with the kingdom is spiritual and individual, wholly a matter of personal experience in the spirit by the faith-realization that you are a son of God? What more shall I say? The downfall of nations, the crash of empires, the destruction of the unbelieving Jews, the end of an age, even the end of the world, what have these things to do with one who believes this gospel, and who has hid his life in the surety of the eternal kingdom? You who are God-knowing and gospel-believing have already received the assurances of eternal life. Since your lives have been lived in the spirit and for the Father, nothing can be of serious concern to you. Kingdom builders, the accredited citizens of the heavenly worlds, are not to be disturbed by temporal upheavals or perturbed by terrestrial cataclysms. What does it matter to you who believe this gospel of the kingdom if nations overturn, the age ends, or all things visible crash, since you know that your life is the gift of the Son, and that it is eternally secure in the Father? Having lived the temporal life by faith and having yielded the fruits of the spirit as the righteousness of loving service for your fellows, you can confidently look forward to the next step in the eternal career with the same survival faith that has carried you through your first and earthly adventure in sonship with God. 176:3.2 (1916.2)

"Each generation of believers should carry on their work, in view of the possible return of the Son of Man, exactly as each individual believer carries forward his lifework in view of inevitable and ever-impending natural death. When you have by faith once established yourself as a son of God, nothing else matters as regards the surety of survival. But make no mistake! this survival faith is a living faith, and it increasingly manifests the fruits of that divine spirit which first inspired it in the human heart. That you have once accepted sonship in the heavenly kingdom will not save you in the face of the knowing and persistent rejection of those truths which have to do with the progressive spiritual fruit-bearing of the sons of God in the flesh. You who have been with me in the Father's business on earth can even now desert the kingdom if you find that you love not the way of the Father's service for mankind. 176:3.3 (1916.3)

"As individuals, and as a generation of believers, hear me while I speak a parable: There was a certain great man who, before starting out on a long journey to another country, called all his trusted servants before him and delivered into their hands all his goods. To one he gave five talents, to another two, and to another one. And so on down through the entire group of honored stewards, to each he intrusted his goods according to their several abilities; and then he set out on his journey. When their lord had departed, his servants set themselves at work to gain profits from the wealth intrusted to them. Immediately he who had received five talents began to trade with them and very soon had made a profit of another five talents. In like manner he who had received two talents soon had gained two more. And so did all of these servants make gains for their master except him who received but one talent. He went away by himself and dug a hole in the earth where he hid his lord's money. Presently the lord of those servants unexpectedly returned and called upon his stewards for a reckoning. And when they had all been called before their master, he who had received the five talents came forward with the money which had been intrusted to him and brought five additional talents, saying, 'Lord, you gave me five talents to invest, and I am glad to present five other talents as my gain.' And then his lord said to him: 'Well done, good and faithful servant, you have been faithful over a few things; I will now set you as steward over many; enter forthwith into the joy of your lord.' And then he who had received the two talents came forward, saying: 'Lord, you delivered into my hands two talents; behold, I have gained these other two talents.' And his lord then said to him: 'Well done, good and faithful steward; you also have been faithful over a few things, and I will now set you over many; enter you into the joy of your lord.' And then there came to the accounting he who had received the one talent. This servant came forward, saying, 'Lord, I knew you and realized that you were a shrewd man in that you expected gains where you had not personally labored; therefore was I afraid to risk aught of that which was intrusted to me. I safely hid your talent in the earth; here it is; you now have what belongs to you.' But his lord answered: 'You are an indolent and slothful steward. By your own words you confess that you knew I would require of you an accounting with reasonable profit, such as your diligent fellow servants have this day rendered. Knowing this, you ought, therefore, to have at least put my money into the hands of the bankers that on my return I might have received my own with interest.' And then to the chief steward this lord said: 'Take away this one talent from this unprofitable servant and give it to him who has the ten talents.' 176:3.4 (1916.4)

"To everyone who has, more shall be given, and he shall have abundance; but from him who has not, even that which he has shall be taken away. You cannot stand still in the affairs of the eternal kingdom. My Father requires all his children to grow in grace and in a knowledge of the truth. You who know these truths must yield the increase of the fruits of the spirit and manifest a growing devotion to the unselfish service of your fellow servants. And remember that, inasmuch as you minister to one of the least of my brethren, you have done this service to me. 176:3.5 (1917.1)

"And so should you go about the work of the Father's business, now and henceforth, even forevermore. Carry on until I come. In faithfulness do that which is intrusted to you, and thereby shall you be ready for the reckoning call of death. And having thus lived for the glory of the Father and the satisfaction of the Son, you shall enter with joy and exceedingly great pleasure into the eternal service of the everlasting kingdom." 176:3.6 (1917.2)

There stood Simon Peter, looking down into the upturned face of his Master. Jesus said nothing; it was not necessary that he should speak. His attitude plainly revealed that he was minded to wash Simon Peter's feet. Notwithstanding his frailties of the flesh, Peter loved the Master. This Galilean fisherman was the first human being wholeheartedly to believe in the divinity of Jesus *and* to make full and public confession of that belief. And Peter had never since really doubted the divine nature of the Master. Since Peter so revered and honored Jesus in his heart, it was not strange that his soul resented the thought of Jesus' kneeling there before him in the attitude of a menial servant and proposing to wash his feet as would a slave. When Peter presently collected his wits sufficiently to address the Master, he spoke the heart feelings of all his fellow apostles. 179:3.2 (1938.4)

After a few moments of this great embarrassment, Peter said,

"Master, do you really mean to wash my feet?"

And then, looking up into Peter's face, Jesus said: "You may not fully understand what I am about to do, but hereafter you will know the meaning of all these things." Then Simon Peter, drawing a long breath, said, "Master, you shall never wash my feet!" And each of the apostles nodded their approval of Peter's firm declaration of refusal to allow Jesus thus to humble himself before them. 179:3.3 (1939.1)

The dramatic appeal of this unusual scene at first touched the heart of even Judas Iscariot; but when his vainglorious intellect passed judgment upon the spectacle, he concluded that this gesture of humility was just one more episode which conclusively proved that Jesus would never qualify as Israel's deliverer, and that he had made no mistake in the decision to desert the Master's cause. 179:3.4 (1939.2)

As they all stood there in breathless amazement, Jesus said: "Peter, I declare that, if I do not wash your feet, you will have no part with me in that which I am about to perform." When Peter heard this declaration, coupled with the fact that Jesus continued kneeling there at his feet, he made one of those decisions of blind acquiescence in compliance with the wish of one whom he respected and loved. As it began to dawn on Simon Peter that there was attached to this proposed enactment of service some signification that determined one's future connection with the Master's work, he not only became reconciled to the thought of allowing Jesus to wash his feet but, in his characteristic and impetuous manner, said: "Then, Master, wash not my feet only but also my hands and my head." 179:3.5 (1939.3)

As the Master made ready to begin washing Peter's feet, he said: "He who is already clean needs only to have his feet washed. You who sit with me tonight are clean—but not all. But the dust of your feet should have been washed away before you sat down at meat with me. And besides, I would perform this service for you as a parable to illustrate the meaning of a new commandment which I will presently give you." 179:3.6 (1939.4)

But this teaching was too deep for many of the apostles, especially for Philip, who, after speaking a few words with Nathaniel, arose and said:

"Master, show us the Father, and everything you have said will be made plain." 180:3.8 (1947.7)

And when Philip had spoken, Jesus said: "Philip, have I been so long with you and yet you do not even now know me? Again do I declare: He who has seen me has seen the Father. How can you then say, Show us the Father? Do you not believe that I am in the Father and the Father in me? Have I not taught you that the words which I speak are not my words but the words of the Father? I speak for the Father and not of myself. I am in this world to do the Father's will, and that I have done. My Father abides in me and works through me. Believe me when I say that the Father is in me, and that I am in the Father, or else believe me for the sake of the very life I have lived—for the work's sake." 180:3.9 (1947.8)

As the Master paused for a moment, Judas Alpheus made bold to ask one of the few questions which either he or his brother ever addressed to Jesus in public. Said Judas:

"Master, you have always lived among us as a friend; how shall we know you when you no longer manifest yourself to us save by this spirit? If the world sees you not, how shall we be certain about you? How will you show yourself to us?" 180:4.4 (1948.5)

Jesus looked down upon them all, smiled, and said: "My little children, I am going away, going back to my Father. In a little while you will not see me as you do here, as flesh and blood. In a very short time I am going to send you my spirit, just like me except for this material body. This new teacher is the Spirit of Truth who will live with each one of you, in your hearts, and so will all the children of light be made one and be drawn toward one another. And in this very manner will my Father and I be able to live in the souls of each one of you and also in the hearts of all other men who love us and make that love real in their experiences by loving one another, even as I am now loving you." 180:4.5 (1949.1)

"Now that I am leaving you, seeing that the hour has come when I am about to go to the Father, I am surprised that none of you have asked me, 'Why do you leave us?'

Nevertheless, I know that you ask such questions in your hearts. I will speak to you plainly, as one friend to another. It is really profitable for you that I go away. If I go not away, the new teacher cannot come into your hearts. I must be divested of this mortal body and be restored to my place on high before I can send this spirit teacher to live in your souls and lead your spirits into the truth. And when my spirit comes to indwell you, he will illuminate the difference between sin and righteousness and will enable you to judge wisely in your hearts concerning them. 180:6.2 (1951.3)

"In just a little while I will leave you for a short time. Afterward, when you again see me, I shall already be on my way to the Father so that even then you will not see me for long." 180:6.5 (1952.1)

While he paused for a moment, the apostles began to talk with each other:

"What is this that he tells us? 'In just a little while I will leave you,' and 'When you see me again it will not be for long, for I will be on my way to the Father.' What can he mean by this 'little while' and 'not for long'?

We cannot understand what he is telling us." 180:6.6 (1952.2)

And since Jesus knew they asked these questions, he said: "Do you inquire among yourselves about what I meant when I said that in a little while I would not be with you, and that, when you would see me again, I would be on my way to the Father? I have plainly told you that the Son of Man must die, but that he will rise again. Can you not then discern the meaning of my words? You will first be made sorrowful, but later on will you rejoice with many who will understand these things after they have come to pass. A woman is indeed sorrowful in the hour of her travail, but when she is once delivered of her child, she immediately forgets her anguish in the joy of the knowledge that a man has been born into the world. And so are you about to sorrow over my departure, but I will soon see you again, and then will your sorrow be turned into rejoicing, and there shall come to you a new revelation of the salvation of God which no man can ever take away from you. And all the worlds will be blessed in this same revelation of life in effecting the overthrow of death. Hitherto have you made all your requests in my Father's name. After you see me again, you may also ask in my name, and I will hear you. 180:6.7 (1952.3) (Continued next page)

"Down here I have taught you in proverbs and spoken to you in parables. I did so because you were only children in the spirit; but the time is coming when I will talk to you plainly concerning the Father and his kingdom. And I shall do this because the Father himself loves you and desires to be more fully revealed to you. Mortal man cannot see the spirit Father; therefore have I come into the world to show the Father to your creature eyes. But when you have become perfected in spirit growth, you shall then see the Father himself." 180:6.8 (1952.4)

As John Zebedee stood there in the upper chamber, the tears rolling down his cheeks, he looked into the Master's face and said:

"And so I will, my Master, but how can I learn to love my brethren more?"

And then answered Jesus: "You will learn to love your brethren more when you first learn to love their Father in heaven more, and after you have become truly more interested in their welfare in time and in eternity. And all such human interest is fostered by understanding sympathy, unselfish service, and unstinted forgiveness. No man should despise your youth, but I exhort you always to give due consideration to the fact that age oftentimes represents experience, and that nothing in human affairs can take the place of actual experience. Strive to live peaceably with all men, especially your friends in the brotherhood of the heavenly kingdom. And, John, always remember, strive not with the souls you would win for the kingdom." 181:2.5 (1955.6)

Then spoke Matthew:

"But, Master, who will send us, and how shall we know where to go? Will Andrew show us the way?"

And Jesus answered: "No, Levi, Andrew will no longer direct you in the proclamation of the gospel. He will, indeed, continue as your friend and counselor until that day whereon the new teacher comes, and then shall the Spirit of Truth lead each of you abroad to labor for the extension of the kingdom. Many changes have come over you since that day at the customhouse when you first set out to follow me; but many more must come before you will be able to see the vision of a brotherhood in which gentile sits alongside Jew in fraternal association. But go on with your urge to win your Jewish brethren until you are fully satisfied and then turn with power to the gentiles. One thing you may be certain of, Levi: You have won the confidence and affection of your brethren; they all love you." (And all ten of them signified their acquiescence in the Master's words.) 181:2.13 (1957.3)

"Levi, I know much about your anxieties, sacrifices, and labors to keep the treasury replenished which your brethren do not know, and I am rejoiced that, though he who carried the bag is absent, the publican ambassador is here at my farewell gathering with the messengers of the kingdom. I pray that you may discern the meaning of my teaching with the eyes of the spirit. And when the new teacher comes into your heart, follow on as he will lead you and let your brethren see—even all the world—what the Father can do for a hated tax-gatherer who dared to follow the Son of Man and to believe the gospel of the kingdom. Even from the first, Levi, I loved you as I did these other Galileans. Knowing then so well that neither the Father nor the Son has respect of persons, see to it that you make no such distinctions among those who become believers in the gospel through your ministry. And so, Matthew, dedicate your whole future life service to showing all men that God is no respecter of persons; that, in the sight of God and in the fellowship of the kingdom, all men are equal, all believers are the sons of God." 181:2.14 (1958.1)

And then Jesus went over to Philip, who, standing up, heard this message from his Master: "Philip, you have asked me many foolish questions, but I have done my utmost to answer every one, and now would I answer the last of such questionings which have arisen in your most honest but unspiritual mind. All the time I have been coming around toward you, have you been saying to yourself,

'What shall I ever do if the Master goes away and leaves us alone in the world?'

O, you of little faith! And yet you have almost as much as many of your brethren. You have been a good steward, Philip. You failed us only a few times, and one of those failures we utilized to manifest the Father's glory. Your office of stewardship is about over. You must soon more fully do the work you were called to do—the preaching of this gospel of the kingdom. Philip, you have always wanted to be shown, and very soon shall you see great things. Far better that you should have seen all this by faith, but since you were sincere even in your material sightedness, you will live to see my words fulfilled. And then, when you are blessed with spiritual vision, go forth to your work, dedicating your life to the cause of leading mankind to search for God and to seek eternal realities with the eye of spiritual faith and not with the eyes of the material mind. Remember, Philip, you have a great mission on earth, for the world is filled with those who look at life just as you have tended to. You have a great work to do, and when it is finished in faith, you shall come to me in my kingdom, and I will take great pleasure in showing you that which eye has not seen, ear heard, nor the mortal mind conceived. In the meantime, become as a little child in the kingdom of the spirit and permit me, as the spirit of the new teacher, to lead you forward in the spiritual kingdom. And in this way will I be able to do much for you which I was not able to accomplish when I sojourned with you as a mortal of the realm. And always remember, Philip, he who has seen me has seen the Father." 181:2.20 (1960.1)

Then Nathaniel spoke, asking Jesus this question:

"I have listened to your teaching ever since you first called me to the service of this kingdom, but I honestly cannot understand the full meaning of all you tell us. I do not know what to expect next, and I think most of my brethren are likewise perplexed, but they hesitate to confess their confusion. Can you help me?"

Jesus, putting his hand on Nathaniel's shoulder, said: "My friend, it is not strange that you should encounter perplexity in your attempt to grasp the meaning of my spiritual teachings since you are so handicapped by your preconceptions of Jewish tradition and so confused by your persistent tendency to interpret my gospel in accordance with the teachings of the scribes and Pharisees. 181:2.23 (1961.2)

"I have taught you much by word of mouth, and I have lived my life among you. I have done all that can be done to enlighten your minds and liberate your souls, and what you have not been able to get from my teachings and my life, you must now prepare to acquire at the hand of that master of all teachers—actual experience. And in all of this new experience which now awaits you, I will go before you and the Spirit of Truth shall be with you. Fear not; that which you now fail to comprehend, the new teacher, when he has come, will reveal to you throughout the remainder of your life on earth and on through your training in the eternal ages." 181:2.24 (1961.3)

And then the Master, turning to all of them, said: "Be not dismayed that you fail to grasp the full meaning of the gospel. You are but finite, mortal men, and that which I have taught you is infinite, divine, and eternal. Be patient and of good courage since you have the eternal ages before you in which to continue your progressive attainment of the experience of becoming perfect, even as your Father in Paradise is perfect." 181:2.25 (1961.4)

Annas was considerably disturbed by Jesus' refusal to answer his questions, so much so that he said to him:

"Do you have no care as to whether I am friendly to you or not? Do you have no regard for the power I have in determining the issues of your coming trial?"

When Jesus heard this, he said: "Annas, you know that you could have no power over me unless it were permitted by my Father. Some would destroy the Son of Man because they are ignorant; they know no better, but you, friend, know what you are doing. How can you, therefore, reject the light of God?" 184:1.5 (1979.3)

The kindly manner in which Jesus spoke to Annas almost bewildered him. But he had already determined in his mind that Jesus must either leave Palestine or die; so he summoned up his courage and asked:

"Just what is it you are trying to teach the people? What do you claim to be?"

Jesus answered: "You know full well that I have spoken openly to the world. I have taught in the synagogues and many times in the temple, where all the Jews and many of the gentiles have heard me. In secret I have spoken nothing; why, then, do you ask me about my teaching? Why do you not summon those who have heard me and inquire of them? Behold, all Jerusalem has heard that which I have spoken even if you have not yourself heard these teachings." But before Annas could make reply, the chief steward of the palace, who was standing near, struck Jesus in the face with his hand, saying, "How dare you answer the high priest with such words?" Annas spoke no words of rebuke to his steward, but Jesus addressed him, saying, "My friend, if I have spoken evil, bear witness against the evil; but if I have spoken the truth, why, then, should you smite me?" 184:1.6 (1979.4)

As Pilate, trembling with fearful emotion, sat down by the side of Jesus, he inquired:

"Where do you come from? Really, who are you? What is this they say, that you are the Son of God?" 185:7.1 (1995.7)

But Jesus could hardly answer such questions when asked by a man-fearing, weak, and vacillating judge who was so unjust as to subject him to flogging even when he had declared him innocent of all crime, and before he had been duly sentenced to die. Jesus looked Pilate straight in the face, but he did not answer him. Then said Pilate: "Do you refuse to speak to me? Do you not realize that I still have power to release you or to crucify you?" Then said Jesus: "You could have no power over me except it were permitted from above. You could exercise no authority over the Son of Man unless the Father in heaven allowed it. But you are not so guilty since you are ignorant of the gospel. He who betrayed me and he who delivered me to you, they have the greater sin." 185:7.2 (1996.1)

The Crucifixion—Urantia's Greatest Tragedy

"The extraordinary and unusually cruel experience through which Jesus of Nazareth passed has caused Urantia to become locally known as 'the world of the cross.'" 20:6.6 (229.5)

	"The time has now come for the Son of Man to be glorified, and the Father shall be glorified in me. My friends, I am to be with you only a little longer. Soon you will seek for me, but you will not find me, for I am going to a place to which you cannot, at this time, come. But when you have finished your work on earth as I have now finished mine, you shall then come to me even as I now prepare to go to my Father. In just a short time I am going to leave you, you will see me no more on earth, but you shall all see me in the age to come when you ascend to the kingdom which my Father has given to me." 180:0.3 (1944.3)
Prior to the Crucifixion—Preparing the Apostles For Jesus' Leaving:	After Peter, James, John, and Matthew had asked the Master numerous questions, he continued his farewell discourse by saying: "And I am telling you about all this before I leave you in order that you may be so prepared for what is coming upon you that you will not stumble into serious error. The authorities will not be content with merely putting you out of the synagogues; I warn you the hour draws near when they who kill you will think they are doing a service to God. And all of these things they will do to you and to those whom you lead into the kingdom of heaven because they do not know the Father. They have refused to know the Father by refusing to receive me; and they refuse to receive me when they reject you, provided you have kept my new commandment that you love one another even as I have loved you. I am telling you in advance about these things so that, when your hour comes, as mine now has, you may be strengthened in the knowledge that all was known to me, and that my spirit shall be with you in all your sufferings for my sake and the gospel's. It was for this purpose that I have been talking so plainly to you from the very beginning. I have even warned you that a man's foes may be those of his own household. Although this gospel of the kingdom never fails to bring great peace to the soul of the individual believer, it will not bring peace on earth until man is willing to believe my teaching wholeheartedly and to establish the practice of doing the Father's will as the chief purpose in living the mortal life. 180:6.1 (1951.2) "Now that I am leaving you, seeing that the hour has come when I am about to go to the Father, I am surprised that none of you have asked me, Why do you leave us? Nevertheless, I know that you ask such questions in your hearts. I will speak to you plainly, as one friend to another. It is really profitable for you that I go away. If I go not away, the new teacher cannot come into your hearts. I must be divested of this mortal body and be restored to my place on high before I can send this spirit teacher to live in your souls and lead your spirits into the truth. And when my spirit comes to indwell you, he will illuminate the difference between sin and righteousness and will enable you to judge wisely in your hearts concerning them. 180:6.2 (1951.3)
	And since Jesus knew they asked these questions, he said: "Do you inquire among yourselves about what I meant when I said that in a little while I would not be with you, and that, when you would see me again, I would be on my way to the Father? I have plainly told you that the Son of Man must die, but that he will rise again. Can you not then discern the meaning of my words? You will first be made sorrowful, but later on will you rejoice with many who will understand these things after they have come to pass. A woman is indeed sorrowful in the hour of her travail, but when she is once delivered of her child, she immediately forgets her anguish in the joy of the knowledge that a man has been born into the world. And so are you about to sorrow over my departure, but I will soon see you again, and then will your sorrow be turned

	into rejoicing, and there shall come to you a new revelation of the salvation of God which no man can ever take away from you. And all the worlds will be blessed in this same revelation of life in effecting the overthrow of death. Hitherto have you made all your requests in my Father's name. After you see me again, you may also ask in my name, and I will hear you. 180:6.7 (1952.3)
	The Master had finished giving his farewell instructions and imparting his final admonitions to the apostles as a group. He then addressed himself to saying good-bye individually and to giving each a word of personal advice, together with his parting blessing. The apostles were still seated about the table as when they first sat down to partake of the Last Supper, and as the Master went around the table talking to them, each man rose to his feet when Jesus addressed him. 181:2.1 (1955.2)
Prior to the Crucifixion—Preparing the Apostles For Jesus' Leaving: (Continued)	The experience of parting with the apostles was a great strain on the human heart of Jesus; this sorrow of love bore down on him and made it more difficult to face such a death as he well knew awaited him. He realized how weak and how ignorant his apostles were, and he dreaded to leave them. He well knew that the time of his departure had come, but his human heart longed to find out whether there might not possibly be some legitimate avenue of escape from this terrible plight of suffering and sorrow. And when it had thus sought escape, and failed, it was willing to drink the cup. The divine mind of Michael knew he had done his best for the twelve apostles; but the human heart of Jesus wished that more might have been done for them before they should be left alone in the world. Jesus' heart was being crushed; he truly loved his brethren. He was isolated from his family in the flesh; one of his chosen associates was betraying him. His father Joseph's people had rejected him and thereby sealed their doom as a people with a special mission on earth. His soul was tortured by baffled love and rejected mercy. It was just one of those awful human moments when everything seems to bear down with crushing cruelty and terrible agony. 182:3.9 (1969.4) Jesus' humanity was not insensible to this situation of private loneliness, public shame, and the appearance of the failure of his cause. All these sentiments bore down on him with indescribable heaviness. In this great sorrow his mind went back to the days of his childhood in Nazareth and to his early work in Galilee. At the time of this great trial there came up in his mind many of those pleasant scenes of his earthly ministry. And it was from these old memories of Nazareth, Capernaum, Mount Hermon, and of the sunrise and sunset on the shimmering Sea of Galilee, that he soothed himself as he made his human heart strong and ready to encounter the traitor who should so soon betray him. 182:3.10 (1969.5) Before Judas and the soldiers arrived, the Master had fully regained his customary poise; the spirit had triumphed over the flesh; faith had asserted itself over all human tendencies to fear or entertain doubt. The supreme test of the full realization of the human nature had been met and acceptably passed. Once more the Son of Man was prepared to face his enemies with equanimity and in the full assurance of his invincibility as a mortal man unreservedly dedicated to the doing of his Father's will. 182:3.11 (1970.1)

Prior to the Crucifixion—Preparing the Apostles For Jesus' Leaving: (Continued)	Though Jesus knew that the plan for his death had its origin in the councils of the rulers of the Jews, he was also aware that all such nefarious schemes had the full approval of Lucifer, Satan, and Caligastia. And he well knew that these rebels of the realms would also be pleased to see all of the apostles destroyed with him. 183:0.4 (1971.4) Jesus sat down, alone, on the olive press, where he awaited the coming of the betrayer, and he was seen at this time only by John Mark and an innumerable host of celestial observers. 183:0.5 (1971.5)
Unjust Condemnation:	Here stood the Son of God incarnate as the Son of Man. He was arrested without indictment; accused without evidence; adjudged without witnesses; punished without a verdict; and now was soon to be condemned to die by an unjust judge who confessed that he could find no fault in him. If Pilate had thought to appeal to their patriotism by referring to Jesus as the "king of the Jews," he utterly failed. The Jews were not expecting any such a king. The declaration of the chief priests and the Sadducees, "We have no king but Caesar," was a shock even to the unthinking populace, but it was too late now to save Jesus even had the mob dared to espouse the Master's cause. 185:8.1 (1996.5)
Jesus' Majestic Attitude:	Throughout the whole sorrowful ordeal he bore himself with simple dignity and unostentatious majesty. He would not so much as cast reflections of insincerity upon his would-be murderers when they asked if he were "king of the Jews." With but little qualifying explanation he accepted the designation, knowing that, while they had chosen to reject him, he would be the last to afford them real national leadership, even in a spiritual sense. 186:2.8 (1999.8)
	By the time the soldiers were ready to depart with Jesus for Golgotha, they had begun to be impressed by his unusual composure and extraordinary dignity, by his uncomplaining silence. 186:4.3 (2001.6)
Jesus' Death Was of His Own Free Will:	What Jesus is now about to do, submit to death on the cross, he does of his own free will. In foretelling this experience, he said: "The Father loves and sustains me because I am willing to lay down my life. But I will take it up again. No one takes my life away from me—I lay it down of myself. I have authority to lay it down, and I have authority to take it up. I have received such a commandment from my Father." 187:0.3 (2004.3)
Just Before Nine O'clock This Friday Morning:	Before leaving the courtyard of the praetorium, the soldiers placed the crossbeam on Jesus' shoulders. It was the custom to compel the condemned man to carry the crossbeam to the site of the crucifixion. Such a condemned man did not carry the whole cross, only this shorter timber. The longer and upright pieces of timber for the three crosses had already been transported to Golgotha and, by the time of the arrival of the soldiers and their prisoners, had been firmly implanted in the ground. 187:1.1 (2004.5)

Just Before Nine O'clock This Friday Morning: (Continued)	These women of Jerusalem were indeed courageous to manifest sympathy for Jesus, for it was strictly against the law to show friendly feelings for one who was being led forth to crucifixion. It was permitted the rabble to jeer, mock, and ridicule the condemned, but it was not allowed that any sympathy should be expressed. Though Jesus appreciated the manifestation of sympathy in this dark hour when his friends were in hiding, he did not want these kindhearted women to incur the displeasure of the authorities by daring to show compassion in his behalf. Even at such a time as this Jesus thought little about himself, only of the terrible days of tragedy ahead for Jerusalem and the whole Jewish nation. 187:1.7 (2005.5)
	As the Master trudged along on the way to the crucifixion, he was very weary; he was nearly exhausted. He had had neither food nor water since the Last Supper at the home of Elijah Mark; neither had he been permitted to enjoy one moment of sleep. In addition, there had been one hearing right after another up to the hour of his condemnation, not to mention the abusive scourgings with their accompanying physical suffering and loss of blood. Superimposed upon all this was his extreme mental anguish, his acute spiritual tension, and a terrible feeling of human loneliness. 187:1.8 (2006.1)
	Shortly after passing through the gate on the way out of the city, as Jesus staggered on bearing the crossbeam, his physical strength momentarily gave way, and he fell beneath the weight of his heavy burden. The soldiers shouted at him and kicked him, but he could not arise. When the captain saw this, knowing what Jesus had already endured, he commanded the soldiers to desist. Then he ordered a passerby, one Simon from Cyrene, to take the crossbeam from Jesus' shoulders and compelled him to carry it the rest of the way to Golgotha. 187:1.9 (2006.2)
Shortly After Nine O'clock:	Before Jesus was put on his cross, the two brigands had already been placed on their crosses, all the while cursing and spitting upon their executioners. Jesus' only words, as they nailed him to the crossbeam, were, "Father, forgive them, for they know not what they do." He could not have so mercifully and lovingly interceded for his executioners if such thoughts of affectionate devotion had not been the mainspring of all his life of unselfish service. The ideas, motives, and longings of a lifetime are openly revealed in a crisis. 187:2.4 (2007.3)
	As Jesus saw his mother, with John and his brother and sister, he smiled but said nothing. Meanwhile the four soldiers assigned to the Master's crucifixion, as was the custom, had divided his clothes among them, one taking the sandals, one the turban, one the girdle, and the fourth the cloak. This left the tunic, or seamless vestment reaching down to near the knees, to be cut up into four pieces, but when the soldiers saw what an unusual garment it was, they decided to cast lots for it. Jesus looked down on them while they divided his garments, and the thoughtless crowd jeered at him. 187:2.8 (2007.7)
Before Eleven O'clock in the Morning:	At about half past nine o'clock this Friday morning, Jesus was hung upon the cross. Before eleven o'clock, upward of one thousand persons had assembled to witness this spectacle of the crucifixion of the Son of Man. Throughout these dreadful hours the unseen hosts of a universe stood in silence while they gazed upon this extraordinary phenomenon of the Creator as he was dying the death of the creature, even the most ignoble death of a condemned criminal. 187:3.1 (2008.2)

The Penitent Brigand:	This young man, the penitent brigand, had been led into a life of violence and wrongdoing by those who extolled such a career of robbery as an effective patriotic protest against political oppression and social injustice. And this sort of teaching, plus the urge for adventure, led many otherwise well-meaning youths to enlist in these daring expeditions of robbery. This young man had looked upon Barabbas as a hero. Now he saw that he had been mistaken. Here on the cross beside him he saw a really great man, a true hero. Here was a hero who fired his zeal and inspired his highest ideas of moral self-respect and quickened all his ideals of courage, manhood, and bravery. In beholding Jesus, there sprang up in his heart an overwhelming sense of love, loyalty, and genuine greatness.187:4.5 (2009.4)
Shortly Before One O'clock:	Although it was early in the season for such a phenomenon, shortly after twelve o'clock the sky darkened by reason of the fine sand in the air. The people of Jerusalem knew that this meant the coming of one of those hot-wind sandstorms from the Arabian Desert. Before one o'clock the sky was so dark the sun was hid, and the remainder of the crowd hastened back to the city. When the Master gave up his life shortly after this hour, less than thirty people were present, only the thirteen Roman soldiers and a group of about fifteen believers. These believers were all women except two, Jude, Jesus' brother, and John Zebedee, who returned to the scene just before the Master expired. 187:5.1 (2010.2)
Shortly After One O'clock in the Afternoon:	Shortly after one o'clock, amidst the increasing darkness of the fierce sandstorm, Jesus began to fail in human consciousness. His last words of mercy, forgiveness, and admonition had been spoken. His last wish— concerning the care of his mother—had been expressed. During this hour of approaching death the human mind of Jesus resorted to the repetition of many passages in the Hebrew scriptures, particularly the Psalms. The last conscious thought of the human Jesus was concerned with the repetition in his mind of a portion of the book of *Psalms* now known as the twentieth, twenty-first, and twenty-second Psalms. While his lips would often move, he was too weak to utter the words as these passages, which he so well knew by heart, would pass through his mind. Only a few times did those standing by catch some utterance, such as, "I know the Lord will save his anointed," "Your hand shall find out all my enemies," and "My God, my God, why have you forsaken me?" Jesus did not for one moment entertain the slightest doubt that he had lived in accordance with the Father's will; and he never doubted that he was now laying down his life in the flesh in accordance with his Father's will. He did not feel that the Father had forsaken him; he was merely reciting in his vanishing consciousness many Scriptures, among them this twenty-second Psalm, which begins with "My God, my God, why have you forsaken me?" And this happened to be one of the three passages which were spoken with sufficient clearness to be heard by those standing by. 187:5.2 (2010.3)
Just Before Three O'clock:	The sandstorm grew in intensity and the heavens increasingly darkened. Still the soldiers and the small group of believers stood by. The soldiers crouched near the cross, huddled together to protect themselves from the cutting sand. The mother of John and others watched from a distance where they were somewhat sheltered by an overhanging rock. When the Master finally breathed his last, there were present at the foot of his cross John Zebedee, his brother Jude, his sister Ruth, Mary Magdalene, and Rebecca, onetime of Sepphoris. 187:5.4 (2010.5)

Just Before Three O'clock: (Continued)	It was just before three o'clock when Jesus, with a loud voice, cried out, "It is finished! Father, into your hands I commend my spirit." And when he had thus spoken, he bowed his head and gave up the life struggle. When the Roman centurion saw how Jesus died, he smote his breast and said: "This was indeed a righteous man; truly he must have been a Son of God." And from that hour he began to believe in Jesus. 187:5.5 (2011.1)
	When these soldiers arrived at Golgotha, they did accordingly to the two thieves, but they found Jesus already dead, much to their surprise. However, in order to make sure of his death, one of the soldiers pierced his left side with his spear. Though it was common for the victims of crucifixion to linger alive upon the cross for even two or three days, the overwhelming emotional agony and the acute spiritual anguish of Jesus brought an end to his mortal life in the flesh in a little less than five and one-half hours. 187:5.8 (2011.4)
About Half Past Three O'clock:	In the midst of the darkness of the sandstorm, about half past three o'clock, David Zebedee sent out the last of the messengers carrying the news of the Master's death. The last of his runners he dispatched to the home of Martha and Mary in Bethany, where he supposed the mother of Jesus stopped with the rest of her family. 187:6.1 (2011.5)
The Burial of Jesus:	The rulers of the Jews had planned to have Jesus' body thrown in the open burial pits of Gehenna, south of the city; it was the custom thus to dispose of the victims of crucifixion. If this plan had been followed, the body of the Master would have been exposed to the wild beasts. 188:0.2 (2012.2)
	A crucified person could not be buried in a Jewish cemetery; there was a strict law against such a procedure. Joseph and Nicodemus knew this law, and on the way out to Golgotha they had decided to bury Jesus in Joseph's new family tomb, hewn out of solid rock, located a short distance north of Golgotha and across the road leading to Samaria. No one had ever lain in this tomb, and they thought it appropriate that the Master should rest there. Joseph really believed that Jesus would rise from the dead, but Nicodemus was very doubtful. These former members of the Sanhedrin had kept their faith in Jesus more or less of a secret, although their fellow Sanhedrists had long suspected them, even before they withdrew from the council. From now on they were the most outspoken disciples of Jesus in all Jerusalem. 188:1.2 (2013.1)
	At about half past four o'clock the burial procession of Jesus of Nazareth started from Golgotha for Joseph's tomb across the way. The body was wrapped in a linen sheet as the four men carried it, followed by the faithful women watchers from Galilee. The mortals who bore the material body of Jesus to the tomb were: Joseph, Nicodemus, John, and the Roman centurion. 188:1.3 (2013.2) They carried the body into the tomb, a chamber about ten feet square, where they hurriedly prepared it for burial. The Jews did not really bury their dead; they actually embalmed them. Joseph and Nicodemus had brought with them large quantities of

The Burial of Jesus: (Continued)	myrrh and aloes, and they now wrapped the body with bandages saturated with these solutions. When the embalming was completed, they tied a napkin about the face, wrapped the body in a linen sheet, and reverently placed it on a shelf in the tomb. 188:1.4 (2013.3) After placing the body in the tomb, the centurion signaled for his soldiers to help roll the doorstone up before the entrance to the tomb. The soldiers then departed for Gehenna with the bodies of the thieves while the others returned to Jerusalem, in sorrow, to observe the Passover feast according to the laws of Moses. 188:1.5 (2013.4)
Mission Completed:	It is of record that the divine Son of last appearance on your planet was a Paradise Creator Son who had completed six phases of his bestowal career; consequently, when he gave up the conscious grasp of the incarnated life on Urantia, he could, and did, truly say, "It is finished"—it was literally finished. His death on Urantia completed his bestowal career; it was the last step in fulfilling the sacred oath of a Paradise Creator Son. And when this experience has been acquired, such Sons are supreme universe sovereigns; no longer do they rule as vicegerents of the Father but in their own right and name as "King of Kings and Lord of Lords." With certain stated exceptions these sevenfold bestowal Sons are unqualifiedly supreme in the universes of their abode. Concerning his local universe, "all power in heaven and on earth" was relegated to this triumphant and enthroned Master Son. 21:4.5 (240.1)
Jesus' Death Was Not Planned By God:	It was man and not God who planned and executed the death of Jesus on the cross. True, the Father refused to interfere with the march of human events on Urantia, but the Father in Paradise did not decree, demand, or require the death of his Son as it was carried out on earth. It is a fact that in some manner, sooner or later, Jesus would have had to divest himself of his mortal body, his incarnation in the flesh, but he could have executed such a task in countless ways without dying on a cross between two thieves. All of this was man's doing, not God's. 186:5.2 (2002.3) The gospel of the good news that mortal man may, by faith, become spirit-conscious that he is a son of God, is not dependent on the death of Jesus. True, indeed, all this gospel of the kingdom has been tremendously illuminated by the Master's death, but even more so by his life. 186:5.4 (2002.5)
Jesus Did Not Die as a Sacrifice:	The salvation of God for the mortals of Urantia would have been just as effective and unerringly certain if Jesus had not been put to death by the cruel hands of ignorant mortals. If the Master had been favorably received by the mortals of earth and had departed from Urantia by the voluntary relinquishment of his life in the flesh, the fact of the love of God and the mercy of the Son—the fact of sonship with God—would have in no wise been affected. You mortals are the sons of God, and only one thing is required to make such a truth factual in your personal experience, and that is your spirit-born faith. 186:5.9 (2003.3) When once you grasp the idea of God as a true and loving Father, the only concept which Jesus ever taught, you must forthwith, in all consistency, utterly abandon all those primitive notions about God as an offended monarch, a stern and all-powerful ruler whose chief delight is to detect his subjects in wrongdoing and to see that they are adequately punished, unless some being almost equal to himself should volunteer

Jesus Did Not Die as a Sacrifice: (Continued)	to suffer for them, to die as a substitute and in their stead. The whole idea of ransom and atonement is incompatible with the concept of God as it was taught and exemplified by Jesus of Nazareth. The infinite love of God is not secondary to anything in the divine nature. 188:4.8 (2017.3)
	The cross is that high symbol of sacred service, the devotion of one's life to the welfare and salvation of one's fellows. The cross is not the symbol of the sacrifice of the innocent Son of God in the place of guilty sinners and in order to appease the wrath of an offended God, but it does stand forever, on earth and throughout a vast universe, as a sacred symbol of the good bestowing themselves upon the evil and thereby saving them by this very devotion of love. The cross does stand as the token of the highest form of unselfish service, the supreme devotion of the full bestowal of a righteous life in the service of wholehearted ministry, even in death, the death of the cross. And the very sight of this great symbol of the bestowal life of Jesus truly inspires all of us to want to go and do likewise. 188:5.9 (2019.2)
The Real Value of the Cross:	The sufferings of Jesus were not confined to the crucifixion. In reality, Jesus of Nazareth spent upward of twenty-five years on the cross of a real and intense mortal existence. The real value of the cross consists in the fact that it was the supreme and final expression of his love, the completed revelation of his mercy. 188:5.4 (2018.3)
	The triumph of the death on the cross is all summed up in the spirit of Jesus' attitude toward those who assailed him. He made the cross an eternal symbol of the triumph of love over hate and the victory of truth over evil when he prayed, "Father, forgive them, for they know not what they do." That devotion of love was contagious throughout a vast universe; the disciples caught it from their Master. The very first teacher of his gospel who was called upon to lay down his life in this service, said, as they stoned him to death, "Lay not this sin to their charge." 188:5.6 (2018.5)
	Make sure, then, that when you view the cross as a revelation of God, you do not look with the eyes of the primitive man nor with the viewpoint of the later barbarian, both of whom regarded God as a relentless Sovereign of stern justice and rigid law-enforcement. Rather, make sure that you see in the cross the final manifestation of the love and devotion of Jesus to his life mission of bestowal upon the mortal races of his vast universe. See in the death of the Son of Man the climax of the unfolding of the Father's divine love for his sons of the mortal spheres. The cross thus portrays the devotion of willing affection and the bestowal of voluntary salvation upon those who are willing to receive such gifts and devotion. There was nothing in the cross which the Father required—only that which Jesus so willingly gave, and which he refused to avoid. 188:5.11 (2019.4) If man cannot otherwise appreciate Jesus and understand the meaning of his bestowal on earth, he can at least comprehend the fellowship of his mortal sufferings. No man can ever fear that the Creator does not know the nature or extent of his temporal afflictions. 188:5.12 (2019.5) We know that the death on the cross was not to effect man's reconciliation to God but to stimulate man's *realization* of the Father's eternal love and his Son's unending mercy, and to broadcast these universal truths to a whole universe. 188:5.13 (2019.6)

The Resurrection— Urantia's Greatest Triumph

"In the vast court of the resurrection halls of the first mansion world of Satania, there may now be observed a magnificent material-morontia structure known as the 'Michael Memorial,' now bearing the seal of Gabriel. This memorial was created shortly after Michael departed from this world, and it bears this inscription: "In commemoration of the mortal transit of Jesus of Nazareth on Urantia." 188:3.11 (2015.7)

The Resurrection: Urantia's Greatest Triumph

<table>
<tr>
<td rowspan="3">Two Minutes Past
Three O'clock
Sunday Morning
April 9, A.D. 30:</td>
<td>SOON after the burial of Jesus on Friday afternoon, the chief of the archangels of Nebadon, then present on Urantia, summoned his council of the resurrection of sleeping will creatures and entered upon the consideration of a possible technique for the restoration of Jesus. These assembled sons of the local universe, the creatures of Michael, did this on their own responsibility; Gabriel had not assembled them. By midnight they had arrived at the conclusion that the creature could do nothing to facilitate the resurrection of the Creator. They were disposed to accept the advice of Gabriel, who instructed them that, since Michael had "laid down his life of his own free will, he also had power to take it up again in accordance with his own determination." Shortly after the adjournment of this council of the archangels, the Life Carriers, and their various associates in the work of creature rehabilitation and morontia creation, the Personalized Adjuster of Jesus, being in personal command of the assembled celestial hosts then on Urantia, spoke these words to the anxious waiting watchers: 189:0.1 (2020.1)

"Not one of you can do aught to assist your Creator-father in the return to life. As a mortal of the realm he has experienced mortal death; as the Sovereign of a universe he still lives. That which you observe is the mortal transit of Jesus of Nazareth from life in the flesh to life in the morontia. The spirit transit of this Jesus was completed at the time I separated myself from his personality and became your temporary director. Your Creator-father has elected to pass through the whole of the experience of his mortal creatures, from birth on the material worlds, on through natural death and the resurrection of the morontia, into the status of true spirit existence. A certain phase of this experience you are about to observe, but you may not participate in it. Those things which you ordinarily do for the creature, you may not do for the Creator. A Creator Son has within himself the power to bestow himself in the likeness of any of his created sons; he has within himself the power to lay down his observable life and to take it up again; and he has this power because of the direct command of the Paradise Father, and I know whereof I speak." 189:0.2 (2020.2)</td>
</tr>
<tr>
<td>At two forty-five Sunday morning, the Paradise incarnation commission, consisting of seven unidentified Paradise personalities, arrived on the scene and immediately deployed themselves about the tomb. At ten minutes before three, intense vibrations of commingled material and morontia activities began to issue from Joseph's new tomb, and at two minutes past three o'clock, this Sunday morning, April 9, A.D. 30, the resurrected morontia form and personality of Jesus of Nazareth came forth from the tomb. 189:1.1 (2020.4)</td>
</tr>
<tr>
<td>As far as we can judge, no creature of this universe nor any personality from another universe had anything to do with this morontia resurrection of Jesus of Nazareth. On Friday he laid down his life as a mortal of the realm; on Sunday morning he took it up again as a morontia being of the system of Satania in Norlatiadek. There is much about the resurrection of Jesus which we do not understand. But we know that it occurred as we have stated and at about the time indicated. We can also record that all known phenomena associated with this mortal transit, or morontia resurrection, occurred right there in Joseph's new tomb, where the mortal material remains of Jesus lay wrapped in burial cloths. 189:1.4 (2021.3)</td>
</tr>
</table>

Two Minutes Past Three O'clock Sunday Morning April 9, A.D. 30: (Continued)	Let us forever clarify the concept of the resurrection of Jesus by making the following statements: 189:1.6 (2021.5) 1. His material or physical body was not a part of the resurrected personality. When Jesus came forth from the tomb, his body of flesh remained undisturbed in the sepulchre. He emerged from the burial tomb without moving the stones before the entrance and without disturbing the seals of Pilate. 189:1.7 (2021.6) 2. He did not emerge from the tomb as a spirit nor as Michael of Nebadon; he did not appear in the form of the Creator Sovereign, such as he had had before his incarnation in the likeness of mortal flesh on Urantia. 189:1.8 (2021.7) 3. He did come forth from this tomb of Joseph in the very likeness of the morontia personalities of those who, as resurrected morontia ascendant beings, emerge from the resurrection halls of the first mansion world of this local system of Satania. And the presence of the Michael memorial in the center of the vast court of the resurrection halls of mansonia number one leads us to conjecture that the Master's resurrection on Urantia was in some way fostered on this, the first of the system mansion worlds. 189:1.9 (2021.8)
	Now is the mortal transit of Jesus—the morontia resurrection of the Son of Man—completed. The transitory experience of the Master as a personality midway between the material and the spiritual has begun. And he has done all this through power inherent within himself; no personality has rendered him any assistance. He now lives as Jesus of morontia, and as he begins this morontia life, the material body of his flesh lies there undisturbed in the tomb. The soldiers are still on guard, and the seal of the governor about the rocks has not yet been broken. 189:1.13 (2022.4)
Jesus' First Words of His Postmortal Career:	The first act of Jesus on arising from the tomb was to greet Gabriel and instruct him to continue in executive charge of universe affairs under Immanuel, and then he directed the chief of the Melchizedeks to convey his brotherly greetings to Immanuel. He thereupon asked the Most High of Edentia for the certification of the Ancients of Days as to his mortal transit; and turning to the assembled morontia groups of the seven mansion worlds, here gathered together to greet and welcome their Creator as a creature of their order, Jesus spoke the first words of the postmortal career. Said the morontia Jesus: "Having finished my life in the flesh, I would tarry here for a short time in transition form that I may more fully know the life of my ascendant creatures and further reveal the will of my Father in Paradise." 189:1.10 (2022.1)
At Ten Minutes Past Three O'clock:	At ten minutes past three o'clock, as the resurrected Jesus fraternized with the assembled morontia personalities from the seven mansion worlds of Satania, the chief of archangels—the angels of the resurrection—approached Gabriel and asked for the mortal body of Jesus. Said the chief of the archangels: "We may not participate in the morontia resurrection of the bestowal experience of Michael our sovereign, but we would have his mortal remains put in our custody for immediate dissolution. We do not propose to employ our technique of dematerialization; we merely wish to invoke the process of accelerated time. It is enough that we have seen the Sovereign live and die on Urantia; the hosts of heaven would be spared the memory of enduring the

At Ten Minutes Past Three O'clock: (Continued)	sight of the slow decay of the human form of the Creator and Upholder of a universe. In the name of the celestial intelligences of all Nebadon, I ask for a mandate giving me the custody of the mortal body of Jesus of Nazareth and empowering us to proceed with its immediate dissolution." 189:2.1 (2022.5) And when Gabriel had conferred with the senior Most High of Edentia, the archangel spokesman for the celestial hosts was given permission to make such disposition of the physical remains of Jesus as he might determine. 189:2.2 (2023.1) After the chief of archangels had been granted this request, he summoned to his assistance many of his fellows, together with a numerous host of the representatives of all orders of celestial personalities, and then, with the aid of the Urantia midwayers, proceeded to take possession of Jesus' physical body. This body of death was a purely material creation; it was physical and literal; it could not be removed from the tomb as the morontia form of the resurrection had been able to escape the sealed sepulchre. By the aid of certain morontia auxiliary personalities, the morontia form can be made at one time as of the spirit so that it can become indifferent to ordinary matter, while at another time it can become discernible and contactable to material beings, such as the mortals of the realm. 189:2.3 (2023.2) As they made ready to remove the body of Jesus from the tomb preparatory to according it the dignified and reverent disposal of near-instantaneous dissolution, it was assigned the secondary Urantia midwayers to roll away the stones from the entrance of the tomb. The larger of these two stones was a huge circular affair, much like a millstone, and it moved in a groove chiseled out of the rock, so that it could be rolled back and forth to open or close the tomb. When the watching Jewish guards and the Roman soldiers, in the dim light of the morning, saw this huge stone begin to roll away from the entrance of the tomb, apparently of its own accord—without any visible means to account for such motion—they were seized with fear and panic, and they fled in haste from the scene. The Jews fled to their homes, afterward going back to report these doings to their captain at the temple. The Romans fled to the fortress of Antonia and reported what they had seen to the centurion as soon as he arrived on duty. 189:2.4 (2023.3)
Discovery of the Empty Tomb:	The women who went on this mission of anointing Jesus' body were: Mary Magdalene, Mary the mother of the Alpheus twins, Salome the mother of the Zebedee brothers, Joanna the wife of Chuza, and Susanna the daughter of Ezra of Alexandria. 189:4.4 (2025.5) It was about half past three o'clock when the five women, laden with their ointments, arrived before the empty tomb. As they passed out of the Damascus gate, they encountered a number of soldiers fleeing into the city more or less panic-stricken, and this caused them to pause for a few minutes; but when nothing more developed, they resumed their journey. 189:4.5 (2025.6) They were greatly surprised to see the stone rolled away from the entrance to the tomb, inasmuch as they had said among themselves on the way out, "Who will help us roll away the stone?" They set down their burdens and began to look upon one another in fear and with great amazement. While they stood there, atremble with fear, Mary Magdalene ventured around the smaller stone and dared to enter the open

	sepulchre. This tomb of Joseph was in his garden on the hillside on the eastern side of the road, and it also faced toward the east. By this hour there was just enough of the dawn of a new day to enable Mary to look back to the place where the Master's body had lain and to discern that it was gone. In the recess of stone where they had laid Jesus, Mary saw only the folded napkin where his head had rested and the bandages wherewith he had been wrapped lying intact and as they had rested on the stone before the celestial hosts removed the body. The covering sheet lay at the foot of the burial niche. 189:4.6 (2025.7)
Discovery of the Empty Tomb: (Continued)	As these women sat there in the early hours of the dawn of this new day, they looked to one side and observed a silent and motionless stranger. For a moment they were again frightened, but Mary Magdalene, rushing toward him and addressing him as if she thought he might be the caretaker of the garden, said, "Where have you taken the Master? Where have they laid him? Tell us that we may go and get him." When the stranger did not answer Mary, she began to weep. Then spoke Jesus to them, saying, "Whom do you seek?" Mary said: "We seek for Jesus who was laid to rest in Joseph's tomb, but he is gone. Do you know where they have taken him?" Then said Jesus: "Did not this Jesus tell you, even in Galilee, that he would die, but that he would rise again?" These words startled the women, but the Master was so changed that they did not yet recognize him with his back turned to the dim light. And as they pondered his words, he addressed the Magdalene with a familiar voice, saying, "Mary." And when she heard that word of well-known sympathy and affectionate greeting, she knew it was the voice of the Master, and she rushed to kneel at his feet while she exclaimed, "My Lord, and my Master!" And all of the other women recognized that it was the Master who stood before them in glorified form, and they quickly knelt before him. 189:4.10 (2026.4) These human eyes were enabled to see the morontia form of Jesus because of the special ministry of the transformers and the midwayers in association with certain of the morontia personalities then accompanying Jesus. 189:4.11 (2027.1)
	After these women had recovered from the shock of their amazement, they hastened back to the city and to the home of Elijah Mark, where they related to the ten apostles all that had happened to them; but the apostles were not inclined to believe them. They thought at first that the women had seen a vision, but when Mary Magdalene repeated the words which Jesus had spoken to them, and when Peter heard his name, he rushed out of the upper chamber, followed closely by John, in great haste to reach the tomb and see these things for himself. 189:4.13 (2027.3)
	As Mary lingered after Peter and John had gone, the Master again appeared to her, saying: "Be not doubting; have the courage to believe what you have seen and heard. Go back to my apostles and again tell them that I have risen, that I will appear to them, and that presently I will go before them into Galilee as I promised." 189:5.4 (2027.8)

The Resurrection: Urantia's Greatest Triumph

The Dispensational Resurrection:	A little after half past four o'clock this Sunday morning, Gabriel summoned the archangels to his side and made ready to inaugurate the general resurrection of the termination of the Adamic dispensation on Urantia. When the vast host of the seraphim and the cherubim concerned in this great event had been marshaled in proper formation, the morontia Michael appeared before Gabriel, saying: "As my Father has life in himself, so has he given it to the Son to have life in himself. Although I have not yet fully resumed the exercise of universe jurisdiction, this self-imposed limitation does not in any manner restrict the bestowal of life upon my sleeping sons; let the roll call of the planetary resurrection begin." 189:3.1 (2024.3) The circuit of the archangels then operated for the first time from Urantia. Gabriel and the archangel hosts moved to the place of the spiritual polarity of the planet; and when Gabriel gave the signal, there flashed to the first of the system mansion worlds the voice of Gabriel, saying: "By the mandate of Michael, let the dead of a Urantia dispensation rise!" Then all the survivors of the human races of Urantia who had fallen asleep since the days of Adam, and who had not already gone on to judgment, appeared in the resurrection halls of mansonia in readiness for morontia investiture. And in an instant of time the seraphim and their associates made ready to depart for the mansion worlds. Ordinarily these seraphic guardians, onetime assigned to the group custody of these surviving mortals, would have been present at the moment of their awaking in the resurrection halls of mansonia, but they were on this world itself at this time because of the necessity of Gabriel's presence here in connection with the morontia resurrection of Jesus. 189:3.2 (2024.4)
David Zebedee Believed That Jesus Was Due to Arise:	From the tomb David and Joseph went immediately to the home of Elijah Mark, where they held a conference with the ten apostles in the upper chamber. Only John Zebedee was disposed to believe, even faintly, that Jesus had risen from the dead. Peter had believed at first but, when he failed to find the Master, fell into grave doubting. They were all disposed to believe that the Jews had removed the body. David would not argue with them, but when he left, he said: "You are the apostles, and you ought to understand these things. I will not contend with you; nevertheless, I now go back to the home of Nicodemus, where I have appointed with the messengers to assemble this morning, and when they have gathered together, I will send them forth on their last mission, as heralds of the Master's resurrection. I heard the Master say that, after he should die, he would rise on the third day, and I believe him." And thus speaking to the dejected and forlorn ambassadors of the kingdom, this self-appointed chief of communication and intelligence took leave of the apostles. On his way from the upper chamber he dropped the bag of Judas, containing all the apostolic funds, in the lap of Matthew Levi. 190:1.3 (2030.2)
About Half Past Nine O'clock:	It was about half past nine o'clock when the last of David's twenty-six messengers arrived at the home of Nicodemus. David promptly assembled them in the spacious courtyard and addressed them: 190:1.4 (2030.3) "Men and brethren, all this time you have served me in accordance with your oath to me and to one another, and I call you to witness that I have never yet sent out false information at your hands. I am about to send you on your last mission as volunteer messengers of the kingdom, and in so doing I release you from your oaths and

About Half Past Nine O'clock: (Continued)	thereby disband the messenger corps. Men, I declare to you that we have finished our work. No more does the Master have need of mortal messengers; he has risen from the dead. He told us before they arrested him that he would die and rise again on the third day. I have seen the tomb—it is empty. I have talked with Mary Magdalene and four other women, who have talked with Jesus. I now disband you, bid you farewell, and send you on your respective assignments, and the message which you shall bear to the believers is: 'Jesus has risen from the dead; the tomb is empty.'" 190:1.5 (2030.4)
	All this power which is inherent in Jesus—the endowment of life—and which enabled him to rise from the dead, is the very gift of eternal life which he bestows upon kingdom believers, and which even now makes certain their resurrection from the bonds of natural death. 190:0.2 (2029.2)

Morontia Appearances of Jesus

"The true evidences of the resurrection of Michael are spiritual in nature, albeit this teaching is corroborated by the testimony of many mortals of the realm who met, recognized, and communed with the resurrected morontia Master. He became a part of the personal experience of almost one thousand human beings before he finally took leave of Urantia." 189:2.9 (2024.2)

Morontia Appearances of Jesus

The First Morontia Appearance of Jesus	
Appeared To:	Five women: Mary Magdalene; Mary, mother of the Alpheus twins; Salome, mother of Zebedee brothers; Joanna, wife of Chuza; and Susanna, daughter of Ezra of Alexandria.
Where:	At the tomb, in the garden of Joseph of Arimathea.
When:	Sunday morning, April 9, A.D. 30, about 3:30 A.M.

It was about half past three o'clock when the five women, laden with their ointments, arrived before the empty tomb. As they passed out of the Damascus gate, they encountered a number of soldiers fleeing into the city more or less panic-stricken, and this caused them to pause for a few minutes; but when nothing more developed, they resumed their journey. 189:4.5 (2025.6)

As these women sat there in the early hours of the dawn of this new day, they looked to one side and observed a silent and motionless stranger. For a moment they were again frightened, but Mary Magdalene, rushing toward him and addressing him as if she thought he might be the caretaker of the garden, said, "Where have you taken the Master? Where have they laid him? Tell us that we may go and get him." When the stranger did not answer Mary, she began to weep. Then spoke Jesus to them, saying, "Whom do you seek?" Mary said: "We seek for Jesus who was laid to rest in Joseph's tomb, but he is gone. Do you know where they have taken him?" Then said Jesus: "Did not this Jesus tell you, even in Galilee, that he would die, but that he would rise again?" These words startled the women, but the Master was so changed that they did not yet recognize him with his back turned to the dim light. And as they pondered his words, he addressed the Magdalene with a familiar voice, saying, "Mary." And when she heard that word of well-known sympathy and affectionate greeting, she knew it was the voice of the Master, and she rushed to kneel at his feet while she exclaimed, "My Lord, and my Master!" And all of the other women recognized that it was the Master who stood before them in glorified form, and they quickly knelt before him. 189:4.10 (2026.4)

The Second Morontia Appearance of Jesus	
Appeared To:	Mary Magdalene
Where:	Near the tomb
When:	Sunday morning, April 9, A.D. 30

As Mary lingered after Peter and John had gone, the Master again appeared to her, saying: "Be not doubting; have the courage to believe what you have seen and heard. Go back to my apostles and again tell them that I have risen, that I will appear to them, and that presently I will go before them into Galilee as I promised." 189:5.4 (2027.8)

The Third Morontia Appearance of Jesus	
Appeared To:	James, Jesus' oldest brother
Where:	Bethany, in the garden of Lazarus, before the empty tomb of the resurrected brother of Martha and Mary.
When:	Sunday, about noon, April 9, A.D. 30

In the meantime, as they looked for James and before they found him, while he stood there in the garden near the tomb, he became aware of a near-by presence, as if someone had touched him on the shoulder; and when he turned to look, he beheld the gradual appearance of a strange form by his side. He was too much amazed to speak and too frightened to flee. And then the strange form spoke, saying: "James, I come to call you to the service of the kingdom. Join earnest hands with your brethren and follow after me." When James heard his name spoken, he knew that it was his eldest brother, Jesus, who had addressed him. They all had more or less difficulty in recognizing the morontia form of the Master, but few of them had any trouble recognizing his voice or otherwise identifying his charming personality when he once began to communicate with them. 190:2.3 (2032.1)

When James perceived that Jesus was addressing him, he started to fall to his knees, exclaiming, "My father and my brother," but Jesus bade him stand while he spoke with him. And they walked through the garden and talked for almost three minutes; talked over experiences of former days and forecast the events of the near future. As they neared the house, Jesus said, "Farewell, James, until I greet you all together." 190:2.4 (2032.2)

The Fourth Morontia Appearance of Jesus	
Appeared To:	His earthly family and their friends, twenty in all.
Where:	Home of Mary and Martha in Bethany
When:	Sunday, about 2 P.M., April 9, A.D. 30

And David did not long wait, for the fourth appearance of Jesus to mortal recognition occurred shortly before two o'clock in this very home of Martha and Mary, when he appeared visibly before his earthly family and their friends, twenty in all. The Master appeared in the open back door, saying: "Peace be upon you. Greetings to those once near me in the flesh and fellowship for my brothers and sisters in the kingdom of heaven. How could you doubt? Why have you lingered so long before choosing to follow the light of truth with a whole heart? Come, therefore, all of you into the fellowship of the Spirit of Truth in the Father's kingdom." As they began to recover from the first shock of their amazement and to move toward him as if to embrace him, he vanished from their sight. 190:2.6 (2032.4)

The Fifth Morontia Appearance of Jesus

Appeared To:	About twenty five women believers
Where:	Home of Joseph of Arimathea
When:	Sunday, about 4:15 P.M., April 9, A.D. 30

The fifth morontia manifestation of Jesus to the recognition of mortal eyes occurred in the presence of some twenty-five women believers assembled at the home of Joseph of Arimathea, at about fifteen minutes past four o'clock on this same Sunday afternoon. Mary Magdalene had returned to Joseph's house just a few minutes before this appearance. James, Jesus' brother, had requested that nothing be said to the apostles concerning the Master's appearance at Bethany. He had not asked Mary to refrain from reporting the occurrence to her sister believers. Accordingly, after Mary had pledged all the women to secrecy, she proceeded to relate what had so recently happened while she was with Jesus' family at Bethany. And she was in the very midst of this thrilling recital when a sudden and solemn hush fell over them; they beheld in their very midst the fully visible form of the risen Jesus. He greeted them, saying: "Peace be upon you. In the fellowship of the kingdom there shall be neither Jew nor gentile, rich nor poor, free nor bond, man nor woman. You also are called to publish the good news of the liberty of mankind through the gospel of sonship with God in the kingdom of heaven. Go to all the world proclaiming this gospel and confirming believers in the faith thereof. And while you do this, forget not to minister to the sick and strengthen those who are fainthearted and fear-ridden. And I will be with you always, even to the ends of the earth." And when he had thus spoken, he vanished from their sight, while the women fell on their faces and worshiped in silence. 190:3.1 (2033.1)

The Sixth Morontia Appearance of Jesus

Appeared To:	About forty Greek believers
Where:	Home of Flavius
When:	Sunday, about 4:30 P.M., April 9, A.D. 30

About half past four o'clock, at the home of one Flavius, the Master made his sixth morontia appearance to some forty Greek believers there assembled. While they were engaged in discussing the reports of the Master's resurrection, he manifested himself in their midst, notwithstanding that the doors were securely fastened, and speaking to them, said: "Peace be upon you. While the Son of Man appeared on earth among the Jews, he came to minister to all men. In the kingdom of my Father there shall be neither Jew nor gentile; you will all be brethren—the sons of God. Go you, therefore, to all the world, proclaiming this gospel of salvation as you have received it from the ambassadors of the kingdom, and I will fellowship you in the brotherhood of the Father's sons of faith and truth." And when he had thus charged them, he took leave, and they saw him no more. They remained within the house all evening; they were too much overcome with awe and fear to venture forth. Neither did any of these Greeks sleep that night; they stayed awake discussing these things and hoping that the Master might again visit them. Among this group were many of the Greeks who were at Gethsemane when the soldiers arrested Jesus and Judas betrayed him with a kiss. 190:4.1 (2033.4)

The Seventh Morontia Appearance of Jesus	
Appeared To:	To the brothers Cleopas and Jacob
Where:	On the road to Emmaus, about three miles from Jerusalem
When:	Sunday, a few minutes before 5:00 P.M., April 9, A.D. 30

On this Sunday afternoon, about three miles out of Jerusalem and a few minutes before five o'clock, as these two brothers trudged along the road to Emmaus, they talked in great earnestness about Jesus, his teachings, work, and more especially concerning the rumors that his tomb was empty, and that certain of the women had talked with him. Cleopas was half a mind to believe these reports, but Jacob was insistent that the whole affair was probably a fraud. While they thus argued and debated as they made their way toward home, the morontia manifestation of Jesus, his seventh appearance, came alongside them as they journeyed on. Cleopas had often heard Jesus teach and had eaten with him at the homes of Jerusalem believers on several occasions. But he did not recognize the Master even when he spoke freely with them. 190:5.2 (2034.3)

After walking a short way with them, Jesus said: "What were the words you exchanged so earnestly as I came upon you?" And when Jesus had spoken, they stood still and viewed him with sad surprise. Said Cleopas: "Can it be that you sojourn in Jerusalem and know not the things which have recently happened?" Then asked the Master, "What things?" Cleopas replied: "If you do not know about these matters, you are the only one in Jerusalem who has not heard these rumors concerning Jesus of Nazareth, who was a prophet mighty in word and in deed before God and all the people. The chief priests and our rulers delivered him up to the Romans and demanded that they crucify him. Now many of us had hoped that it was he who would deliver Israel from the yoke of the gentiles. But that is not all. It is now the third day since he was crucified, and certain women have this day amazed us by declaring that very early this morning they went to his tomb and found it empty. And these same women insist that they talked with this man; they maintain that he has risen from the dead. And when the women reported this to the men, two of his apostles ran to the tomb and likewise found it empty"—and here Jacob interrupted his brother to say, "but they did not see Jesus." 190:5.3 (2034.4)

As they walked along, Jesus said to them: "How slow you are to comprehend the truth! When you tell me that it is about the teachings and work of this man that you have your discussions, then may I enlighten you since I am more than familiar with these teachings. Do you not remember that this Jesus always taught that his kingdom was not of this world, and that all men, being the sons of God, should find liberty and freedom in the spiritual joy of the fellowship of the brotherhood of loving service in this new kingdom of the truth of the heavenly Father's love? Do you not recall how this Son of Man proclaimed the salvation of God for all men, ministering to the sick and afflicted and setting free those who were bound by fear and enslaved by evil? Do you not know that this man of Nazareth told his disciples that he must go to Jerusalem, be delivered up to his enemies, who would put him to death, and that he would arise on the third day? Have you not been told all this? And have you never read in the Scriptures concerning this day of salvation for Jew and gentile, where it says that in him shall all the families of the earth be blessed; that he will hear the cry of the needy and save the souls of the poor who seek him; that all nations shall call him blessed? That such a Deliverer shall be as the shadow of a great rock in a weary land. That he will feed the flock like a true shepherd, gathering the lambs in his arms and tenderly carrying them in his bosom. That he will open the eyes of the spiritually blind and bring the prisoners of despair out into full liberty and light; that all who sit in darkness shall see the great light of eternal salvation. That he will bind up the brokenhearted, proclaim liberty to the captives of sin, and open up the prison to those who are enslaved by fear and bound by evil. That he will comfort those who mourn and bestow upon them the joy of salvation in the place of sorrow and heaviness. That he shall be the desire of all nations and the everlasting joy of those who seek righteousness. That this Son of truth and righteousness shall rise upon the world with healing light and saving power; even that he will save his people from their sins; that he will really seek and save those who are lost. That he will not destroy the weak but minister salvation to all who hunger and thirst for righteousness. That those who believe in him shall have eternal life. That he will pour out his spirit upon all flesh, and that this Spirit of Truth shall be in each believer a well of water, springing up into everlasting life. Did you not understand how great was the gospel of the kingdom which this man delivered to you? Do you not perceive how great a salvation has come upon you?" 190:5.4 (2035.1)

By this time they had come near to the village where these brothers dwelt. Not a word had these two men spoken since Jesus began to teach them as they walked along the way. Soon they drew up in front of their humble dwelling place, and Jesus was about to take leave of them, going on down the road, but they constrained him to come in and abide with them. They insisted that it was near nightfall, and that he tarry with them. Finally Jesus consented, and very soon after they went into the house, they sat down to eat. They gave him the bread to bless, and as he began to break and hand to them, their eyes were opened, and Cleopas recognized that their guest was the Master himself. And when he said, "It is the Master —," the morontia Jesus vanished from their sight. 190:5.5 (2035.2)

The Eighth Morontia Appearance of Jesus

Appeared To:	Peter
Where:	In the garden of the home of Mark
When:	Sunday, about 8:30 P.M., April 9, A.D. 30

It was near half past eight o'clock this Sunday evening when Jesus appeared to Simon Peter in the garden of the Mark home. This was his eighth morontia manifestation. Peter had lived under a heavy burden of doubt and guilt ever since his denial of the Master. All day Saturday and this Sunday he had fought the fear that, perhaps, he was no longer an apostle. He had shuddered at the fate of Judas and even thought that he, too, had betrayed his Master. All this afternoon he thought that it might be his presence with the apostles that prevented Jesus' appearing to them, provided, of course, he had really risen from the dead. And it was to Peter, in such a frame of mind and in such a state of soul, that Jesus appeared as the dejected apostle strolled among the flowers and shrubs. 191:1.1 (2039.1)

When Peter thought of the loving look of the Master as he passed by on Annas's porch, and as he turned over in his mind that wonderful message brought him early that morning by the women who came from the empty tomb, "Go tell my apostles—and Peter"—as he contemplated these tokens of mercy, his faith began to surmount his doubts, and he stood still, clenching his fists, while he spoke aloud: "I believe he has risen from the dead; I will go and tell my brethren." And as he said this, there suddenly appeared in front of him the form of a man, who spoke to him in familiar tones, saying: "Peter, the enemy desired to have you, but I would not give you up. I knew it was not from the heart that you disowned me; therefore I forgave you even before you asked; but now must you cease to think about yourself and the troubles of the hour while you prepare to carry the good news of the gospel to those who sit in darkness. No longer should you be concerned with what you may obtain from the kingdom but rather be exercised about what you can give to those who live in dire spiritual poverty. Gird yourself, Simon, for the battle of a new day, the struggle with spiritual darkness and the evil doubtings of the natural minds of men." 191:1.2 (2039.2)

Peter and the morontia Jesus walked through the garden and talked of things past, present, and future for almost five minutes. Then the Master vanished from his gaze, saying, "Farewell, Peter, until I see you with your brethren." 191:1.3 (2039.3)

The Ninth Morontia Appearance of Jesus

Appeared To:	Ten of the Apostles
Where:	Upper chamber of Mark's home
When:	Sunday, shortly after 9 P.M., April 9, A.D. 30

Shortly after nine o'clock that evening, after the departure of Cleopas and Jacob, while the Alpheus twins comforted Peter, and while Nathaniel remonstrated with Andrew, and as the ten apostles were there assembled in the upper chamber with all the doors bolted for fear of arrest, the Master, in morontia form, suddenly appeared in the midst of them, saying: "Peace be upon you. Why are you so frightened when I appear, as though you had seen a spirit? Did I not tell you about these things when I was present with you in the flesh? Did I not say to you that the chief priests and the rulers would deliver me up to be killed, that one of your own number would betray me, and that on the third day I would rise? Wherefore all your doubtings and all this discussion about the reports of the women, Cleopas and Jacob, and even Peter? How long will you doubt my words and refuse to believe my promises? And now that you actually see me, will you believe? Even now one of you is absent. When you are gathered together once more, and after all of you know of a certainty that the Son of Man has risen from the grave, go hence into Galilee. Have faith in God; have faith in one another; and so shall you enter into the new service of the kingdom of heaven. I will tarry in Jerusalem with you until you are ready to go into Galilee. My peace I leave with you." 191:2.1 (2040.2)

When the morontia Jesus had spoken to them, he vanished in an instant from their sight. And they all fell on their faces, praising God and venerating their vanished Master. This was the Master's ninth morontia appearance. 191:2.2 (2040.3)

About midnight of this Monday the Master's morontia form was adjusted for transition to the second stage of morontia progression. When he next appeared to his mortal children on earth, it was as a second-stage morontia being. As the Master progressed in the morontia career, it became, technically, more and more difficult for the morontia intelligences and their transforming associates to visualize the Master to mortal and material eyes. 191:3.2 (2041.1)

Jesus made the transit to the third stage of morontia on Friday, April 14th; to the fourth stage on Monday, the 17th; to the fifth stage on Saturday, the 22nd; to the sixth stage on Thursday, the 27th; to the seventh stage on Tuesday, May 2nd; to Jerusem citizenship on Sunday, the 7th; and he entered the embrace of the Most Highs of Edentia on Sunday, the 14th [of May] 191:3.3 (2041.2).

In this manner did Michael of Nebadon complete his service of universe experience since he had already, in connection with his previous bestowals, experienced to the full the life of the ascendant mortals of time and space from the sojourn on the headquarters of the constellation even on to, and through, the service of the headquarters of the superuniverse. And it was by these very morontia experiences that the Creator Son of Nebadon really finished and acceptably terminated his seventh and final universe bestowal. 191:3.4 (2041.3)

The Tenth Morontia Appearance of Jesus	
Appeared To:	Abner, Lazarus, and one hundred and fifty associates, including more than fifty of the evangelistic corps
Where:	In the synagogue at Philadelphia
When:	Tuesday, shortly after 8:00 P.M. , April 11, A.D. 30

The meeting in the synagogue was just being opened by Abner and Lazarus, who were standing together in the pulpit, when the entire audience of believers saw the form of the Master appear suddenly. He stepped forward from where he had appeared between Abner and Lazarus, neither of whom had observed him, and saluting the company, said: 191:4.2 (2041.5)

"Peace be upon you. You all know that we have one Father in heaven, and that there is but one gospel of the kingdom—the good news of the gift of eternal life which men receive by faith. As you rejoice in your loyalty to the gospel, pray the Father of truth to shed abroad in your hearts a new and greater love for your brethren. You are to love all men as I have loved you; you are to serve all men as I have served you. With understanding sympathy and brotherly affection, fellowship all your brethren who are dedicated to the proclamation of the good news, whether they be Jew or gentile, Greek or Roman, Persian or Ethiopian. John proclaimed the kingdom in advance; you have preached the gospel in power; the Greeks already teach the good news; and I am soon to send forth the Spirit of Truth into the souls of all these, my brethren, who have so unselfishly dedicated their lives to the enlightenment of their fellows who sit in spiritual darkness. You are all the children of light; therefore stumble not into the misunderstanding entanglements of mortal suspicion and human intolerance. If you are ennobled, by the grace of faith, to love unbelievers, should you not also equally love those who are your fellow believers in the far-spreading household of faith? Remember, as you love one another, all men will know that you are my disciples. 191:4.3 (2041.6)

"Go, then, into all the world proclaiming this gospel of the fatherhood of God and the brotherhood of men to all nations and races and ever be wise in your choice of methods for presenting the good news to the different races and tribes of mankind. Freely you have received this gospel of the kingdom, and you will freely give the good news to all nations. Fear not the resistance of evil, for I am with you always, even to the end of the ages. And my peace I leave with you." 191:4.4 (2042.1)

When he had said, "My peace I leave with you," he vanished from their sight. With the exception of one of his appearances in Galilee, where upward of five hundred believers saw him at one time, this group in Philadelphia embraced the largest number of mortals who saw him on any single occasion. 191:4.5 (2042.2)

The next day, Wednesday, Jesus spent without interruption in the society of his morontia associates, and during the midafternoon hours he received visiting morontia delegates from the mansion worlds of every local system of inhabited spheres throughout the constellation of Norlatiadek. And they all rejoiced to know their Creator as one of their own order of universe intelligence. 191:4.7 (2042.4)

Jesus made the transit to the third stage of morontia on Friday, April 14; 191:3.3 (2041.2)

The Eleventh Morontia Appearance of Jesus	
Appeared To:	To the eleven Apostles
Where:	The Mark home at supper
When:	Sunday evening, a little after 6:00 P.M., April 16, A.D. 30

They were having their evening meal a little after six o'clock, with Peter sitting on one side of Thomas and Nathaniel on the other, when the doubting apostle said: "I will not believe unless I see the Master with my own eyes and put my finger in the mark of the nails." As they thus sat at supper, and while the doors were securely shut and barred, the morontia Master suddenly appeared inside the curvature of the table and, standing directly in front of Thomas, said: 191:5.2 (2042.6)

"Peace be upon you. For a full week have I tarried that I might appear again when you were all present to hear once more the commission to go into all the world and preach this gospel of the kingdom. Again I tell you: As the Father sent me into the world, so send I you. As I have revealed the Father, so shall you reveal the divine love, not merely with words, but in your daily living. I send you forth, not to love the souls of men, but rather to love men. You are not merely to proclaim the joys of heaven but also to exhibit in your daily experience these spirit realities of the divine life since you already have eternal life, as the gift of God, through faith. When you have faith, when power from on high, the Spirit of Truth, has come upon you, you will not hide your light here behind closed doors; you will make known the love and the mercy of God to all mankind. Through fear you now flee from the facts of a disagreeable experience, but when you shall have been baptized with the Spirit of Truth, you will bravely and joyously go forth to meet the new experiences of proclaiming the good news of eternal life in the kingdom of God. You may tarry here and in Galilee for a short season while you recover from the shock of the transition from the false security of the authority of traditionalism to the new order of the authority of facts, truth, and faith in the supreme realities of living experience. Your mission to the world is founded on the fact that I lived a God-revealing life among you; on the truth that you and all other men are the sons of God; and it shall consist in the life which you will live among men—the actual and living experience of loving men and serving them, even as I have loved and served you. Let faith reveal your light to the world; let the revelation of truth open the eyes blinded by tradition; let your loving service effectually destroy the prejudice engendered by ignorance. By so drawing close to your fellow men in understanding sympathy and with unselfish devotion, you will lead them into a saving knowledge of the Father's love. The Jews have extolled goodness; the Greeks have exalted beauty; the Hindus preach devotion; the faraway ascetics teach reverence; the Romans demand loyalty; but I require of my disciples life, even a life of loving service for your brothers in the flesh." 191:5.3 (2043.1)

When the Master had so spoken, he looked down into the face of Thomas and said: "And you, Thomas, who said you would not believe unless you could see me and put your finger in the nail marks of my hands, have now beheld me and heard my words; and though you see no nail marks on my hands, since I am raised in the form that you also shall have when you depart from this world, what will you say to your brethren? You will acknowledge the truth, for already in your heart you had begun to believe even when you so stoutly asserted your unbelief. Your doubts, Thomas, always most stubbornly assert themselves just as they are about to crumble. Thomas, I bid you be not faithless but believing—and I know you will believe, even with a whole heart." 191:5.4 (2043.2)

When Thomas heard these words, he fell on his knees before the morontia Master and exclaimed, "I believe! My Lord and my Master!" Then said Jesus to Thomas: "You have believed, Thomas, because you have really seen and heard me. Blessed are those in the ages to come who will believe even though they have not seen with the eye of flesh nor heard with the mortal ear." 191:5.5 (2043.3)

And then, as the Master's form moved over near the head of the table, he addressed them all, saying: "And now go all of you to Galilee, where I will presently appear to you." After he said this, he vanished from their sight. 191:5.6 (2043.4)

Jesus made the transit to . . . the fourth stage on Monday, the 17th; 191:3.3 (2041.2)

The Twelfth Morontia Appearance of Jesus

Appeared To:	Rodan and some eighty other believers, Greeks and Jews.
Where:	Alexandria, at the conclusion of the report by David's messenger regarding the crucifixion.
When:	Tuesday evening, about 8:30 P.M., April 18, A.D. 30.

While the eleven apostles were on the way to Galilee, drawing near their journey's end, on Tuesday evening, April 18, at about half past eight o'clock, Jesus appeared to Rodan and some eighty other believers, in Alexandria. This was the Master's twelfth appearance in morontia form. Jesus appeared before these Greeks and Jews at the conclusion of the report of David's messenger regarding the crucifixion. This messenger, being the fifth in the Jerusalem-Alexandria relay of runners, had arrived in Alexandria late that afternoon, and when he had delivered his message to Rodan, it was decided to call the believers together to receive this tragic word from the messenger himself. At about eight o'clock, the messenger, Nathan of Busiris, came before this group and told them in detail all that had been told him by the preceding runner. Nathan ended his touching recital with these words: "But David, who sends us this word, reports that the Master, in foretelling his death, declared that he would rise again." Even as Nathan spoke, the morontia Master appeared there in full view of all. And when Nathan sat down, Jesus said: 191:6.1 (2044.2)

"Peace be upon you. That which my Father sent me into the world to establish belongs not to a race, a nation, nor to a special group of teachers or preachers. This gospel of the kingdom belongs to both Jew and gentile, to rich and poor, to free and bond, to male and female, even to the little children. And you are all to proclaim this gospel of love and truth by the lives which you live in the flesh. You shall love one another with a new and startling affection, even as I have loved you. You will serve mankind with a new and amazing devotion, even as I have served you. And when men see you so love them, and when they behold how fervently you serve them, they will perceive that you have become faith-fellows of the kingdom of heaven, and they will follow after the Spirit of Truth which they see in your lives, to the finding of eternal salvation. 191:6.2 (2044.3)

"As the Father sent me into this world, even so now send I you. You are all called to carry the good news to those who sit in darkness. This gospel of the kingdom belongs to all who believe it; it shall not be committed to the custody of mere priests. Soon will the Spirit of Truth come upon you, and he shall lead you into all truth. Go you, therefore, into all the world preaching this gospel, and lo, I am with you always, even to the end of the ages." 191:6.3 (2044.4)

When the Master had so spoken, he vanished from their sight. 191:6.4 (2044.5)

The Thirteenth Morontia Appearance of Jesus	
Appeared To:	Ten of the Apostles
Where:	The shore of the Sea of Galilee, near the boat landing at Bethsaida
When:	Friday morning, 6:00 A.M., April 18, A.D. 30.

After the apostles had spent the afternoon and early evening of Thursday in waiting at the Zebedee home, Simon Peter suggested that they go fishing. When Peter proposed the fishing trip, all of the apostles decided to go along. All night they toiled with the nets but caught no fish. They did not much mind the failure to make a catch, for they had many interesting experiences to talk over, things which had so recently happened to them at Jerusalem. But when daylight came, they decided to return to Bethsaida. As they neared the shore, they saw someone on the beach, near the boat landing, standing by a fire. At first they thought it was John Mark, who had come down to welcome them back with their catch, but as they drew nearer the shore, they saw they were mistaken—the man was too tall for John. It had occurred to none of them that the person on the shore was the Master. They did not altogether understand why Jesus wanted to meet with them amidst the scenes of their earlier associations and out in the open in contact with nature, far away from the shut-in environment of Jerusalem with its tragic associations of fear, betrayal, and death. He had told them that, if they would go into Galilee, he would meet them there, and he was about to fulfill that promise. 192:1.2 (2045.7)

As they dropped anchor and prepared to enter the small boat for going ashore, the man on the beach called to them, "Lads, have you caught anything?" And when they answered, "No," he spoke again. "Cast the net on the right side of the boat, and you will find fish." While they did not know it was Jesus who had directed them, with one accord they cast in the net as they had been instructed, and immediately it was filled, so much so that they were hardly able to draw it up. Now, John Zebedee was quick of perception, and when he saw the heavy-laden net, he perceived that it was the Master who had spoken to them. When this thought came into his mind, he leaned over and whispered to Peter, "It is the Master." Peter was ever a man of thoughtless action and impetuous devotion; so when John whispered this in his ear, he quickly arose and cast himself into the water that he might the sooner reach the Master's side. His brethren came up close behind him, having come ashore in the small boat, hauling the net of fishes after them. 192:1.3 (2046.1)

By this time John Mark was up and, seeing the apostles coming ashore with the heavy-laden net, ran down the beach to greet them; and when he saw eleven men instead of ten, he surmised that the unrecognized one was the risen Jesus, and as the astonished ten stood by in silence, the youth rushed up to the Master and, kneeling at his feet, said, "My Lord and my Master." And then Jesus spoke, not as he had in Jerusalem, when he greeted them with "Peace be upon you," but in commonplace tones he addressed John Mark: "Well, John, I am glad to see you again and in carefree Galilee, where we can have a good visit. Stay with us, John, and have breakfast." 192:1.4 (2046.2)

As Jesus talked with the young man, the ten were so astonished and surprised that they neglected to haul the net of fish in upon the beach. Now spoke Jesus: "Bring in your fish and prepare some for breakfast. Already we have the fire and much bread." 192:1.5 (2046.3)

While John Mark had paid homage to the Master, Peter had for a moment been shocked at the sight of the coals of fire glowing there on the beach; the scene reminded him so vividly of the midnight fire of charcoal in the courtyard of Annas, where he had disowned the Master, but he shook himself and, kneeling at the Master's feet, exclaimed, "My Lord and my Master!" 192:1.6 (2046.4)

Peter then joined his comrades as they hauled in the net. When they had landed their catch, they counted the fish, and there were 153 large ones. And again was the mistake made of calling this another miraculous catch of fish. There was no miracle connected with this episode. It was merely an exercise of the Master's preknowledge. He knew the fish were there and accordingly directed the apostles where to cast the net. 192:1.7 (2046.5)

Jesus spoke to them, saying: "Come now, all of you, to breakfast. Even the twins should sit down while I visit with you; John Mark will dress the fish." John Mark brought seven good-sized fish, which the Master put on the fire, and when they were cooked, the lad served them to the ten. Then Jesus broke the bread and handed it to John, who in turn served it to the hungry apostles. When they had all been served, Jesus bade John Mark sit down while he himself served the fish and the bread to the lad. And as they ate, Jesus visited with them and recounted their many experiences in Galilee and by this very lake. 192:1.8 (2047.1)

This was the third time Jesus had manifested himself to the apostles as a group. When Jesus first addressed them, asking if they had any fish, they did not suspect who he was because it was a common experience for these fishermen on the Sea of Galilee, when they came ashore, to be thus accosted by the fish merchants of Tarichea, who were usually on hand to buy the fresh catches for the drying establishments. 192:1.9 (2047.2)

Jesus visited with the ten apostles and John Mark for more than an hour, and then he walked up and down the beach, talking with them two and two—but not the same couples he had at first sent out together to teach. All eleven of the apostles had come down from Jerusalem together, but Simon Zelotes grew more and more despondent as they drew near Galilee, so that, when they reached Bethsaida, he forsook his brethren and returned to his home. 192:1.10 (2047.3)

Before taking leave of them this morning, Jesus directed that two of the apostles should volunteer to go to Simon Zelotes and bring him back that very day. And Peter and Andrew did so. 192:1.11 (2047.4)

The Fourteenth Morontia Appearance of Jesus

Appeared To:	To the eleven Apostles
Where:	On a hill near Capernaum—The Mount of Ordination
When:	Saturday noon, April 22, A.D. 30

At noon on Saturday, April 22, the eleven apostles assembled by appointment on the hill near Capernaum, and Jesus appeared among them. This meeting occurred on the very mount where the Master had set them apart as his apostles and as ambassadors of the Father's kingdom on earth. And this was the Master's fourteenth morontia manifestation. 192:3.1 (2050.1)

At this time the eleven apostles knelt in a circle about the Master and heard him repeat the charges and saw him re-enact the ordination scene even as when they were first set apart for the special work of the kingdom. And all of this was to them as a memory of their former consecration to the Father's service, except the Master's prayer. When the Master—the morontia Jesus—now prayed, it was in tones of majesty and with words of power such as the apostles had never before heard. Their Master now spoke with the rulers of the universes as one who, in his own universe, had had all power and authority committed to his hand. And these eleven men never forgot this experience of the morontia rededication to the former pledges of ambassadorship. The Master spent just one hour on this mount with his ambassadors, and when he had taken an affectionate farewell of them, he vanished from their sight. 192:3.2 (2050.2)

Jesus made the transit to . . . the fifth stage on Saturday, the 22nd; to the sixth stage on Thursday, the 27th; 191:3.3 (2041.2)

The Fifteenth Morontia Appearance of Jesus

Appeared To:	More than five hundred from area of Capernaum
Where:	At Bethsaida, at the end of Peter's first public sermon since the resurrection.
When:	Saturday afternoon, 3:00 P.M., April 29th, A.D. 30

Accordingly, on Saturday, April 29, at three o'clock, more than five hundred believers from the environs of Capernaum assembled at Bethsaida to hear Peter preach his first public sermon since the resurrection. The apostle was at his best, and after he had finished his appealing discourse, few of his hearers doubted that the Master had risen from the dead. 192:4.2 (2050.5)

Peter ended his sermon, saying: "We affirm that Jesus of Nazareth is not dead; we declare that he has risen from the tomb; we proclaim that we have seen him and talked with him." Just as he finished making this declaration of faith, there by his side, in full view of all these people, the Master appeared in morontia form and, speaking to them in familiar accents, said, "Peace be upon you, and my peace I leave with you." When he had thus appeared and had so spoken to them, he vanished from their sight. This was the fifteenth morontia manifestation of the risen Jesus. 192:4.3 (2050.6)

Jesus made the transit to . . . the seventh stage on Tuesday, May 2; 191:3.3 (2041.2)

The Sixteenth Morontia Appearance of Jesus

Appeared To:	The eleven Apostles, the women's corps and their associates, and about fifty other leading disciples of the Master, including a number of Greeks.
Where:	Courtyard of Nicodemus in Jerusalem
When:	Friday night, about 9:00 P.M., May 5, A.D. 30

THE sixteenth morontia manifestation of Jesus occurred on Friday, May 5, in the courtyard of Nicodemus, about nine o'clock at night. On this evening the Jerusalem believers had made their first attempt to get together since the resurrection. Assembled here at this time were the eleven apostles, the women's corps and their associates, and about fifty other leading disciples of the Master, including a number of the Greeks. This company of believers had been visiting informally for more than half an hour when, suddenly, the morontia Master appeared in full view and immediately began to instruct them. Said Jesus: 193:0.1 (2052.1)

"Peace be upon you. This is the most representative group of believers—apostles and disciples, both men and women—to which I have appeared since the time of my deliverance from the flesh. I now call you to witness that I told you beforehand that my sojourn among you must come to an end; I told you that presently I must return to the Father. And then I plainly told you how the chief priests and the rulers of the Jews would deliver me up to be put to death, and that I would rise from the grave. Why, then, did you allow yourselves to become so disconcerted by all this when it came to pass? and why were you so surprised when I rose from the tomb on the third day? You failed to believe me because you heard my words without comprehending the meaning thereof. 193:0.2 (2052.2)

"And now you should give ear to my words lest you again make the mistake of hearing my teaching with the mind while in your hearts you fail to comprehend the meaning. From the beginning of my sojourn as one of you, I taught you that my one purpose was to reveal my Father in heaven to his children on earth. I have lived the God-revealing bestowal that you might experience the God-knowing career. I have revealed God as your Father in heaven; I have revealed you as the sons of God on earth. It is a fact that God loves you, his sons. By faith in my word this fact becomes an eternal and living truth in your hearts. When, by living faith, you become divinely God-conscious, you are then born of the spirit as children of light and life, even the eternal life wherewith you shall ascend the universe of universes and attain the experience of finding God the Father on Paradise. 193:0.3 (2052.3)

"I admonish you ever to remember that your mission among men is to proclaim the gospel of the kingdom—the reality of the fatherhood of God and the truth of the sonship of man. Proclaim the whole truth of the good news, not just a part of the saving gospel. Your message is not changed by my resurrection experience. Sonship with God, by faith, is still the saving truth of the gospel of the kingdom. You are to go forth preaching the love of God and the service of man. That which the world needs most to know is: Men are the sons of God, and through faith they can actually realize, and daily experience, this ennobling truth. My bestowal should help all men to know that they are the children of God, but such knowledge will not suffice if they fail personally to faith-grasp the saving truth that they are the living spirit sons of the eternal Father. The gospel of the kingdom is concerned with the love of the Father and the service of his children on earth. 193:0.4 (2052.4)

"Among yourselves, here, you share the knowledge that I have risen from the dead, but that is not strange. I have the power to lay down my life and to take it up again; the Father gives such power to his Paradise Sons. You should the rather be stirred in your hearts by the knowledge that the dead of an age entered upon the eternal ascent soon after I left Joseph's new tomb. I lived my life in the flesh to show how you can, through loving service, become God-revealing to your fellow men even as, by loving you and serving you, I have become God-revealing to you. I have lived among you as the Son of Man that you, and all other men, might know that you are all indeed the sons of God. Therefore, go you now into all the world preaching this gospel of the kingdom of heaven to all men. Love all men as I have loved you; serve your fellow mortals as I have served you. Freely you have received, freely give. Only tarry here in Jerusalem while I go to the Father, and until I send you the Spirit of Truth. He shall lead you into the enlarged truth, and I will go with you into all the world. I am with you always, and my peace I leave with you." 193:0.5 (2053.1)

When the Master had spoken to them, he vanished from their sight. It was near daybreak before these believers dispersed; all night they remained together, earnestly discussing the Master's admonitions and contemplating all that had befallen them. James Zebedee and others of the apostles also told them of their experiences with the morontia Master in Galilee and recited how he had three times appeared to them. 193:0.6 (2053.2)

Jesus made the transit to . . . Jerusem citizenship on Sunday, the 7th; 191:3.3 (2041.2)

The Seventeenth Morontia Appearance of Jesus	
Appeared To:	Nalda and seventy five Samaritan believers
Where:	Near Jacob's well at Sychar
When:	Sabbath afternoon, 4:00 P.M., May 13, A.D. 30

About four o'clock on Sabbath afternoon, May 13, the Master appeared to Nalda and about seventy-five Samaritan believers near Jacob's well, at Sychar. The believers were in the habit of meeting at this place, near where Jesus had spoken to Nalda concerning the water of life. On this day, just as they had finished their discussions of the reported resurrection, Jesus suddenly appeared before them, saying: 193:1.1 (2053.3)

"Peace be upon you. You rejoice to know that I am the resurrection and the life, but this will avail you nothing unless you are first born of the eternal spirit, thereby coming to possess, by faith, the gift of eternal life. If you are the faith sons of my Father, you shall never die; you shall not perish. The gospel of the kingdom has taught you that all men are the sons of God. And this good news concerning the love of the heavenly Father for his children on earth must be carried to all the world. The time has come when you worship God neither on Gerizim nor at Jerusalem, but where you are, as you are, in spirit and in truth. It is your faith that saves your souls. Salvation is the gift of God to all who believe they are his sons. But be not deceived; while salvation is the free gift of God and is bestowed upon all who accept it by faith, there follows the experience of bearing the fruits of this spirit life as it is lived in the flesh. The acceptance of the doctrine of the fatherhood of God implies that you also freely accept the associated truth of the brotherhood of man. And if man is your brother, he is even more than your neighbor, whom the Father requires you to love as yourself. Your brother, being of your own family, you will not only love with a family affection, but you will also serve as you would serve yourself. And you will thus love and serve your brother because you, being my brethren, have been thus loved and served by me. Go, then, into all the world telling this good news to all creatures of every race, tribe, and nation. My spirit shall go before you, and I will be with you always." 193:1.2 (2053.4)

These Samaritans were greatly astonished at this appearance of the Master, and they hastened off to the near-by towns and villages, where they published abroad the news that they had seen Jesus, and that he had talked to them. And this was the seventeenth morontia appearance of the Master. 193:1.3 (2054.1)

Jesus made the transit to the third stage of morontia on Friday, April 14;

- to the fourth stage on Monday, the 17th;
- to the fifth stage on Saturday, the 22nd;
- to the sixth stage on Thursday, the 27th;
- to the seventh stage on Tuesday, May 2;
- to Jerusem citizenship on Sunday, the 7th;
- and he entered the embrace of the Most Highs of Edentia on Sunday, the 14 . 191:3.3 (2041.2)

The Eighteenth Morontia Appearance of Jesus	
Appeared To:	Meeting of believers
Where:	Tyre, Phoenicia
When:	Tuesday evening, a little before 9:00 P.M., May 16, A.D. 30

The Master's eighteenth morontia appearance was at Tyre, on Tuesday, May 16, at a little before nine o'clock in the evening. Again he appeared at the close of a meeting of believers, as they were about to disperse, saying: 193:2.1 (2054.2)

"Peace be upon you. You rejoice to know that the Son of Man has risen from the dead because you thereby know that you and your brethren shall also survive mortal death. But such survival is dependent on your having been previously born of the spirit of truth-seeking and God-finding. The bread of life and the water thereof are given only to those who hunger for truth and thirst for righteousness—for God. The fact that the dead rise is not the gospel of the kingdom. These great truths and these universe facts are all related to this gospel in that they are a part of the result of believing the good news and are embraced in the subsequent experience of those who, by faith, become, in deed and in truth, the everlasting sons of the eternal God. My Father sent me into the world to proclaim this salvation of sonship to all men. And so send I you abroad to preach this salvation of sonship. Salvation is the free gift of God, but those who are born of the spirit will immediately begin to show forth the fruits of the spirit in loving service to their fellow creatures. And the fruits of the divine spirit which are yielded in the lives of spirit-born and God-knowing mortals are: loving service, unselfish devotion, courageous loyalty, sincere fairness, enlightened honesty, undying hope, confiding trust, merciful ministry, unfailing goodness, forgiving tolerance, and enduring peace. If professed believers bear not these fruits of the divine spirit in their lives, they are dead; the Spirit of Truth is not in them; they are useless branches on the living vine, and they soon will be taken away. My Father requires of the children of faith that they bear much spirit fruit. If, therefore, you are not fruitful, he will dig about your roots and cut away your unfruitful branches. Increasingly, must you yield the fruits of the spirit as you progress heavenward in the kingdom of God. You may enter the kingdom as a child, but the Father requires that you grow up, by grace, to the full stature of spiritual adulthood. And when you go abroad to tell all nations the good news of this gospel, I will go before you, and my Spirit of Truth shall abide in your hearts. My peace I leave with you." 193:2.2 (2054.3)

And then the Master disappeared from their sight. The next day there went out from Tyre those who carried this story to Sidon and even to Antioch and Damascus. Jesus had been with these believers when he was in the flesh, and they were quick to recognize him when he began to teach them. While his friends could not readily recognize his morontia form when made visible, they were never slow to identify his personality when he spoke to them. 193:2.3 (2054.4)

The Nineteenth Morontia Appearance of Jesus	
Appeared To:	The eleven Apostles
Where:	Western Slope of Mount Olivet, Jerusalem
When:	Thursday early morning, May 18, A.D. 30

Early Thursday morning, May 18, Jesus made his last appearance on earth as a morontia personality. As the eleven apostles were about to sit down to breakfast in the upper chamber of Mary Mark's home, Jesus appeared to them and said: 193:3.1 (2055.1)

"Peace be upon you. I have asked you to tarry here in Jerusalem until I ascend to the Father, even until I send you the Spirit of Truth, who shall soon be poured out upon all flesh, and who shall endow you with power from on high." Simon Zelotes interrupted Jesus, asking, "Then, Master, will you restore the kingdom, and will we see the glory of God manifested on earth?" When Jesus had listened to Simon's question, he answered: "Simon, you still cling to your old ideas about the Jewish Messiah and the material kingdom. But you will receive spiritual power after the spirit has descended upon you, and you will presently go into all the world preaching this gospel of the kingdom. As the Father sent me into the world, so do I send you. And I wish that you would love and trust one another. Judas is no more with you because his love grew cold, and because he refused to trust you, his loyal brethren. Have you not read in the Scripture where it is written: 'It is not good for man to be alone. No man lives to himself'? And also where it says: 'He who would have friends must show himself friendly'? And did I not even send you out to teach, two and two, that you might not become lonely and fall into the mischief and miseries of isolation? You also well know that, when I was in the flesh, I did not permit myself to be alone for long periods. From the very beginning of our associations I always had two or three of you constantly by my side or else very near at hand even when I communed with the Father. Trust, therefore, and confide in one another. And this is all the more needful since I am this day going to leave you alone in the world. The hour has come; I am about to go to the Father." 193:3.2 (2055.2)

When he had spoken, he beckoned for them to come with him, and he led them out on the Mount of Olives, where he bade them farewell preparatory to departing from Urantia. This was a solemn journey to Olivet. Not a word was spoken by any of them from the time they left the upper chamber until Jesus paused with them on the Mount of Olives. 193:3.3 (2055.3)

It was almost half past seven o'clock this Thursday morning, May 18, when Jesus arrived on the western slope of Mount Olivet with his eleven silent and somewhat bewildered apostles. From this location, about two thirds the way up the mountain, they could look out over Jerusalem and down upon Gethsemane. Jesus now prepared to say his last farewell to the apostles before he took leave of Urantia. As he stood there before them, without being directed they knelt about him in a circle, and the Master said: 193:5.1 (2057.3)

"I bade you tarry in Jerusalem until you were endowed with power from on high. I am now about to take leave of you; I am about to ascend to my Father, and soon, very soon, will we send into this world of my sojourn the Spirit of Truth; and when he has come, you shall begin the new proclamation of the gospel of the kingdom, first in Jerusalem and then to the uttermost parts of the world. Love men with the love wherewith I have loved you and serve your fellow mortals even as I have served you. By the spirit fruits of your lives impel souls to believe the truth that man is a son of God, and that all men are brethren. Remember all I have taught you and the life I have lived among you. My love overshadows you, my spirit will dwell with you, and my peace shall abide upon you. Farewell." 193:5.2 (2057.4)

When the morontia Master had thus spoken, he vanished from their sight. This so-called ascension of Jesus was in no way different from his other disappearances from mortal vision during the forty days of his morontia career on Urantia. 193:5.3 (2057.5)

The Spirit Of Truth

The Spirit Of Truth

<table>
<tr><td rowspan="5">Bestowal of the Spirit of Truth, About One O'clock:</td><td>Acting upon the instruction of Peter, John Mark and others went forth to call the leading disciples together at the home of Mary Mark. By ten thirty, one hundred and twenty of the foremost disciples of Jesus living in Jerusalem had forgathered to hear the report of the farewell message of the Master and to learn of his ascension. Among this company was Mary the mother of Jesus. She had returned to Jerusalem with John Zebedee when the apostles came back from their recent sojourn in Galilee. Soon after Pentecost she returned to the home of Salome at Bethsaida. James the brother of Jesus was also present at this meeting, the first conference of the Master's disciples to be called after the termination of his planetary career. 193:6.1 (2057.8)</td></tr>
<tr><td>Just about noon the apostles returned to their brethren in the upper chamber and announced that Matthias had been chosen as the new apostle. And then Peter called all of the believers to engage in prayer, prayer that they might be prepared to receive the gift of the spirit which the Master had promised to send. 193:6.6 (2058.5)</td></tr>
<tr><td>ABOUT one o'clock, as the one hundred and twenty believers were engaged in prayer, they all became aware of a strange presence in the room. At the same time these disciples all became conscious of a new and profound sense of spiritual joy, security, and confidence. This new consciousness of spiritual strength was immediately followed by a strong urge to go out and publicly proclaim the gospel of the kingdom and the good news that Jesus had risen from the dead. 194:0.1 (2059.1)

Peter stood up and declared that this must be the coming of the Spirit of Truth which the Master had promised them and proposed that they go to the temple and begin the proclamation of the good news committed to their hands. And they did just what Peter suggested. 194:0.2 (2059.2)</td></tr>
<tr><td>These believers felt themselves suddenly translated into another world, a new existence of joy, power, and glory. The Master had told them the kingdom would come with power, and some of them thought they were beginning to discern what he meant. 194:0.6 (2059.6)</td></tr>
<tr><td>The chief mission of this outpoured spirit of the Father and the Son is to teach men about the truths of the Father's love and the Son's mercy. These are the truths of divinity which men can comprehend more fully than all the other divine traits of character. The Spirit of Truth is concerned primarily with the revelation of the Father's spirit nature and the Son's moral character. The Creator Son, in the flesh, revealed God to men; the Spirit of Truth, in the heart, reveals the Creator Son to men. When man yields the "fruits of the spirit" in his life, he is simply showing forth the traits which the Master manifested in his own earthly life. When Jesus was on earth, he lived his life as one personality—Jesus of Nazareth. As the indwelling spirit of the "new teacher," the Master has, since Pentecost, been able to live his life anew in the experience of every truth-taught believer. 194:3.1 (2062.10)</td></tr>
</table>

The Spirit Of Truth

On the Day of Pentecost:	The apostles had been in hiding for forty days. This day happened to be the Jewish festival of Pentecost, and thousands of visitors from all parts of the world were in Jerusalem. Many arrived for this feast, but a majority had tarried in the city since the Passover. Now these frightened apostles emerged from their weeks of seclusion to appear boldly in the temple, where they began to preach the new message of a risen Messiah. And all the disciples were likewise conscious of having received some new spiritual endowment of insight and power. 194:1.1 (2060.1) It was about two o'clock when Peter stood up in that very place where his Master had last taught in this temple, and delivered that impassioned appeal which resulted in the winning of more than two thousand souls. The Master had gone, but they suddenly discovered that this story about him had great power with the people. No wonder they were led on into the further proclamation of that which vindicated their former devotion to Jesus and at the same time so constrained men to believe in him. Six of the apostles participated in this meeting: Peter, Andrew, James, John, Philip, and Matthew. They talked for more than an hour and a half and delivered messages in Greek, Hebrew, and Aramaic, as well as a few words in even other tongues with which they had a speaking acquaintance. 194:1.2 (2060.2)
	On the day of Pentecost the religion of Jesus broke all national restrictions and racial fetters. It is forever true, "Where the spirit of the Lord is, there is liberty." On this day the Spirit of Truth became the personal gift from the Master to every mortal. This spirit was bestowed for the purpose of qualifying believers more effectively to preach the gospel of the kingdom, but they mistook the experience of receiving the outpoured spirit for a part of the new gospel which they were unconsciously formulating. 194:3.5 (2063.3) Do not overlook the fact that the Spirit of Truth was bestowed upon all sincere believers; this gift of the spirit did not come only to the apostles. The one hundred and twenty men and women assembled in the upper chamber all received the new teacher, as did all the honest of heart throughout the whole world. This new teacher was bestowed upon mankind, and every soul received him in accordance with the love for truth and the capacity to grasp and comprehend spiritual realities. At last, true religion is delivered from the custody of priests and all sacred classes and finds its real manifestation in the individual souls of men. 194:3.6 (2063.4)
What Is The Spirit Of Truth?	Jesus continued to teach, saying: "When I have gone to the Father, and after he has fully accepted the work I have done for you on earth, and after I have received the final sovereignty of my own domain, I shall say to my Father: Having left my children alone on earth, it is in accordance with my promise to send them another teacher. And when the Father shall approve, I will pour out the Spirit of Truth upon all flesh. Already is my Father's spirit in your hearts, and when this day shall come, you will also have me with you even as you now have the Father. This new gift is the spirit of living truth. The unbelievers will not at first listen to the teachings of this spirit, but the sons of light will all receive him gladly and with a whole heart. And you shall know this spirit when he comes even as you have known me, and you will receive this gift in your hearts, and he will abide with you. You thus perceive that I am not going to leave you without help and guidance. I will not leave

What Is The Spirit Of Truth? (Continued)	you desolate. Today I can be with you only in person. In the times to come I will be with you and all other men who desire my presence, wherever you may be, and with each of you at the same time. Do you not discern that it is better for me to go away; that I leave you in the flesh so that I may the better and the more fully be with you in the spirit? 180:4.1 (1948.2) "In just a few hours the world will see me no more; but you will continue to know me in your hearts even until I send you this new teacher, the Spirit of Truth. As I have lived with you in person, then shall I live in you; I shall be one with your personal experience in the spirit kingdom. And when this has come to pass, you shall surely know that I am in the Father, and that, while your life is hid with the Father in me, I am also in you. I have loved the Father and have kept his word; you have loved me, and you will keep my word. As my Father has given me of his spirit, so will I give you of my spirit. And this Spirit of Truth which I will bestow upon you shall guide and comfort you and shall eventually lead you into all truth. 180:4.2 (1948.3)
What Is The Mission of The Spirit Of Truth?	Jesus lived on earth and taught a gospel which redeemed man from the superstition that he was a child of the devil and elevated him to the dignity of a faith son of God. Jesus' message, as he preached it and lived it in his day, was an effective solvent for man's spiritual difficulties in that day of its statement. And now that he has personally left the world, he sends in his place his Spirit of Truth, who is designed to live in man and, for each new generation, to restate the Jesus message so that every new group of mortals to appear upon the face of the earth shall have a new and up-to-date version of the gospel, just such personal enlightenment and group guidance as will prove to be an effective solvent for man's ever-new and varied spiritual difficulties. 194:2.1 (2060.6) The first mission of this spirit is, of course, to foster and personalize truth, for it is the comprehension of truth that constitutes the highest form of human liberty. Next, it is the purpose of this spirit to destroy the believer's feeling of orphanhood. Jesus having been among men, all believers would experience a sense of loneliness had not the Spirit of Truth come to dwell in men's hearts. 194:2.2 (2060.7)
Spirit Of Truth Will Live In Your Heart:	Jesus laid great emphasis upon what he called the two truths of first import in the teachings of the kingdom, and they are: the attainment of salvation by faith, and faith alone, associated with the revolutionary teaching of the attainment of human liberty through the sincere recognition of truth, "You shall know the truth, and the truth shall make you free." Jesus was the truth made manifest in the flesh, and he promised to send his Spirit of Truth into the hearts of all his children after his return to the Father in heaven. 141:7.6 (1593.7)
	Jesus continued to teach, saying: "When I have gone to the Father, and after he has fully accepted the work I have done for you on earth, and after I have received the final sovereignty of my own domain, I shall say to my Father: Having left my children alone on earth, it is in accordance with my promise to send them another teacher. And when the Father shall approve, I will pour out the Spirit of Truth upon all flesh. 180:4.1 (1948.2)

The Spirit Of Truth

What The Spirit Of Truth Does For Us:	Truth is living; the Spirit of Truth is ever leading the children of light into new realms of spiritual reality and divine service. You are not given truth to crystallize into settled, safe, and honored forms. Your revelation of truth must be so enhanced by passing through your personal experience that new beauty and actual spiritual gains will be disclosed to all who behold your spiritual fruits and in consequence thereof are led to glorify the Father who is in heaven. Only those faithful servants who thus grow in the knowledge of the truth, and who thereby develop the capacity for divine appreciation of spiritual realities, can ever hope to "enter fully into the joy of their Lord." What a sorry sight for successive generations of the professed followers of Jesus to say, regarding their stewardship of divine truth: "Here, Master, is the truth you committed to us a hundred or a thousand years ago. We have lost nothing; we have faithfully preserved all you gave us; we have allowed no changes to be made in that which you taught us; here is the truth you gave us." But such a plea concerning spiritual indolence will not justify the barren steward of truth in the presence of the Master. In accordance with the truth committed to your hands will the Master of truth require a reckoning. 176:3.7 (1917.3)
	"I am telling you these things while I am still with you that you may be the better prepared to endure those trials which are even now right upon us. And when this new day comes, you will be indwelt by the Son as well as by the Father. And these gifts of heaven will ever work the one with the other even as the Father and I have wrought on earth and before your very eyes as one person, the Son of Man. And this spirit friend will bring to your remembrance everything I have taught you." 180:4.3 (1948.4)
	"Now that I am leaving you, seeing that the hour has come when I am about to go to the Father, I am surprised that none of you have asked me, Why do you leave us? Nevertheless, I know that you ask such questions in your hearts. I will speak to you plainly, as one friend to another. It is really profitable for you that I go away. If I go not away, the new teacher cannot come into your hearts. I must be divested of this mortal body and be restored to my place on high before I can send this spirit teacher to live in your souls and lead your spirits into the truth. And when my spirit comes to indwell you, he will illuminate the difference between sin and righteousness and will enable you to judge wisely in your hearts concerning them. 180:6.2 (1951.3) "I have yet much to say to you, but you cannot stand any more just now. Albeit, when he, the Spirit of Truth, comes, he shall eventually guide you into all truth as you pass through the many abodes in my Father's universe. 180:6.3 (1951.4) "This spirit will not speak of himself, but he will declare to you that which the Father has revealed to the Son, and he will even show you things to come; he will glorify me even as I have glorified my Father. This spirit comes forth from me, and he will reveal my truth to you. Everything which the Father has in this domain is now mine; wherefore did I say that this new teacher would take of that which is mine and reveal it to you. 180:6.4 (1951.5)
	"The Father sent me into this world, but only a few of you have chosen fully to receive me. I will pour out my spirit upon all flesh, but all men will not choose to receive this new teacher as the guide and counselor of the soul. But as many as do

	receive him shall be enlightened, cleansed, and comforted. And this Spirit of Truth will become in them a well of living water springing up into eternal life. 181:1.4 (1954.1) "And now, as I am about to leave you, I would speak words of comfort. Peace I leave with you; my peace I give to you. I make these gifts not as the world gives—by measure—I give each of you all you will receive. Let not your heart be troubled, neither let it be fearful. I have overcome the world, and in me you shall all triumph through faith. I have warned you that the Son of Man will be killed, but I assure you I will come back before I go to the Father, even though it be for only a little while. And after I have ascended to the Father, I will surely send the new teacher to be with you and to abide in your very hearts. And when you see all this come to pass, be not dismayed, but rather believe, inasmuch as you knew it all beforehand. I have loved you with a great affection, and I would not leave you, but it is the Father's will. My hour has come. 181:1.5 (1954.2)
	This bestowal of the Son's spirit effectively prepared all normal men's minds for the subsequent universal bestowal of the Father's spirit (the Adjuster) upon all mankind. In a certain sense, this Spirit of Truth is the spirit of both the Universal Father and the Creator Son. 194:2.3 (2061.1)
What The Spirit Of Truth Does For Us: (Continued)	The coming of the Spirit of Truth on Pentecost made possible a religion which is neither radical nor conservative; it is neither the old nor the new; it is to be dominated neither by the old nor the young. The fact of Jesus' earthly life provides a fixed point for the anchor of time, while the bestowal of the Spirit of Truth provides for the everlasting expansion and endless growth of the religion which he lived and the gospel which he proclaimed. The spirit guides into *all* truth; he is the teacher of an expanding and always-growing religion of endless progress and divine unfolding. This new teacher will be forever unfolding to the truth-seeking believer that which was so divinely folded up in the person and nature of the Son of Man. 194:3.8 (2063.6) The manifestations associated with the bestowal of the "new teacher," and the reception of the apostles' preaching by the men of various races and nations gathered together at Jerusalem, indicate the universality of the religion of Jesus. The gospel of the kingdom was to be identified with no particular race, culture, or language. This day of Pentecost witnessed the great effort of the spirit to liberate the religion of Jesus from its inherited Jewish fetters. Even after this demonstration of pouring out the spirit upon all flesh, the apostles at first endeavored to impose the requirements of Judaism upon their converts. Even Paul had trouble with his Jerusalem brethren because he refused to subject the gentiles to these Jewish practices. No revealed religion can spread to all the world when it makes the serious mistake of becoming permeated with some national culture or associated with established racial, social, or economic practices. 194:3.9 (2064.1) The bestowal of the Spirit of Truth was independent of all forms, ceremonies, sacred places, and special behavior by those who received the fullness of its manifestation. When the spirit came upon those assembled in the upper chamber, they were simply sitting there, having just been engaged in silent prayer. The spirit was bestowed in the country as well as in the city. It was not necessary for the apostles to go apart to

What The Spirit Of Truth Does For Us: (Continued)	a lonely place for years of solitary meditation in order to receive the spirit. For all time, Pentecost disassociates the idea of spiritual experience from the notion of especially favorable environments. 194:3.10 (2064.2)
	The coming of the Spirit of Truth purifies the human heart and leads the recipient to formulate a life purpose single to the will of God and the welfare of men. The material spirit of selfishness has been swallowed up in this new spiritual bestowal of selflessness. Pentecost, then and now, signifies that the Jesus of history has become the divine Son of living experience. The joy of this outpoured spirit, when it is consciously experienced in human life, is a tonic for health, a stimulus for mind, and an unfailing energy for the soul. 194:3.19 (2065.7)
Now Man Is Subject to Threefold Guidance:	Since the bestowal of the Spirit of Truth, man is subject to the teaching and guidance of a threefold spirit endowment: the spirit of the Father, the Thought Adjuster; the spirit of the Son, the Spirit of Truth; the spirit of the Spirit, the Holy Spirit. 194:2.11 (2061.9)
Proof of Your Fellowship With The Spirit Of Truth:	Do not make the mistake of expecting to become strongly intellectually conscious of the outpoured Spirit of Truth. The spirit never creates a consciousness of himself, only a consciousness of Michael, the Son. From the beginning Jesus taught that the spirit would not speak of himself. The proof, therefore, of your fellowship with the Spirit of Truth is not to be found in your consciousness of this spirit but rather in your experience of enhanced fellowship with Michael. 194:2.4 (2061.2)

After Pentecost

After Pentecost

Peter's Mistake:	These men had been trained and instructed that the gospel which they should preach was the fatherhood of God and the sonship of man, but at just this moment of spiritual ecstasy and personal triumph, the best tidings, the greatest news, these men could think of was the *fact* of the risen Master. And so they went forth, endowed with power from on high, preaching glad tidings to the people—even salvation through Jesus—but they unintentionally stumbled into the error of substituting some of the facts associated with the gospel for the gospel message itself. Peter unwittingly led off in this mistake, and others followed after him on down to Paul, who created a new religion out of the new version of the good news. 194:0.3 (2059.3)
	And when all of this is taken into consideration, it is not difficult to understand how these men came to preach a *new gospel about Jesus* in the place of their former message of the fatherhood of God and the brotherhood of men. 194:0.7 (2059.7)
Paul's Influence:	Jesus lived a life which is a revelation of man submitted to the Father's will, not an example for any man literally to attempt to follow. This life in the flesh, together with his death on the cross and subsequent resurrection, presently became a new gospel of the ransom which had thus been paid in order to purchase man back from the clutch of the evil one—from the condemnation of an offended God. Nevertheless, even though the gospel did become greatly distorted, it remains a fact that this new message about Jesus carried along with it many of the fundamental truths and teachings of his earlier gospel of the kingdom. And, sooner or later, these concealed truths of the fatherhood of God and the brotherhood of men will emerge to effectually transform the civilization of all mankind. 194:2.8 (2061.6)
	Jesus founded the religion of personal experience in doing the will of God and serving the human brotherhood; Paul founded a religion in which the glorified Jesus became the object of worship and the brotherhood consisted of fellow believers in the divine Christ. In the bestowal of Jesus these two concepts were potential in his divine-human life, and it is indeed a pity that his followers failed to create a unified religion which might have given proper recognition to both the human and the divine natures of the Master as they were inseparably bound up in his earth life and so gloriously set forth in the original gospel of the kingdom. 196:2.6 (2092.4)
Stephen, Leader of the Greeks:	Stephen, the leader of the Greek colony of Jesus' believers in Jerusalem, thus became the first martyr to the new faith and the specific cause for the formal organization of the early Christian church. This new crisis was met by the recognition that believers could no longer go on as a sect within the Jewish faith. They all agreed that they must separate themselves from unbelievers; and within one month from the death of Stephen the church at Jerusalem had been organized under the leadership of Peter, and James the brother of Jesus had been installed as its titular head. 194:4.12 (2068.2)

After Pentecost

The Church at Jerusalem:	THE results of Peter's preaching on the day of Pentecost were such as to decide the future policies, and to determine the plans, of the majority of the apostles in their efforts to proclaim the gospel of the kingdom. Peter was the real founder of the Christian church; Paul carried the Christian message to the gentiles, and the Greek believers carried it to the whole Roman Empire. 195:0.1 (2069.1) Although the tradition-bound and priest-ridden Hebrews, as a people, refused to accept either Jesus' gospel of the fatherhood of God and the brotherhood of man or Peter's and Paul's proclamation of the resurrection and ascension of Christ (subsequent Christianity), the rest of the Roman Empire was found to be receptive to the evolving Christian teachings. Western civilization was at this time intellectual, war weary, and thoroughly skeptical of all existing religions and universe philosophies. The peoples of the Western world, the beneficiaries of Greek culture, had a revered tradition of a great past. They could contemplate the inheritance of great accomplishments in philosophy, art, literature, and political progress. But with all these achievements they had no soul-satisfying religion. Their spiritual longings remained unsatisfied. 195:0.2 (2069.2)
Compromises Made by Christianity:	Wisely or unwisely, these early leaders of Christianity deliberately compromised the *ideals* of Jesus in an effort to save and further many of his *ideas.* And they were eminently successful. But mistake not! these compromised ideals of the Master are still latent in his gospel, and they will eventually assert their full power upon the world. 195:0.12 (2070.8)
Hope of Unification:	No social system or political regime which denies the reality of God can contribute in any constructive and lasting manner to the advancement of human civilization. But Christianity, as it is subdivided and secularized today, presents the greatest single obstacle to its further advancement; especially is this true concerning the Orient. 195:10.7 (2084.7)
Hope of Modern Christianity:	If the Christian church would only dare to espouse the Master's program, thousands of apparently indifferent youths would rush forward to enlist in such a spiritual undertaking, and they would not hesitate to go all the way through with this great adventure. 195:10.10 (2085.2) The hope of modern Christianity is that it should cease to sponsor the social systems and industrial policies of Western civilization while it humbly bows itself before the cross it so valiantly extols, there to learn anew from Jesus of Nazareth the greatest truths mortal man can ever hear—the living gospel of the fatherhood of God and the brotherhood of man. 195:10.21 (2086.7)
	If Christianity could only grasp more of Jesus' teachings, it could do so much more in helping modern man to solve his new and increasingly complex problems. 195:10.19 (2086.5)

<table>
<tr><td rowspan="3">Reformation in the Church:</td><td>These various groupings of Christians may serve to accommodate numerous different types of would-be believers among the various peoples of Western civilization, but such division of Christendom presents a grave weakness when it attempts to carry the gospel of Jesus to Oriental peoples. These races do not yet understand that there is a religion of Jesus separate, and somewhat apart, from Christianity, which has more and more become a religion about Jesus. 195:10.15 (2086.1)</td></tr>
<tr><td>If the Christian church would only dare to espouse the Master's program, thousands of apparently indifferent youths would rush forward to enlist in such a spiritual undertaking, and they would not hesitate to go all the way through with this great adventure. 195:10.10 (2085.2)

Christianity is seriously confronted with the doom embodied in one of its own slogans: "A house divided against itself cannot stand." The non-Christian world will hardly capitulate to a sect-divided Christendom. The living Jesus is the only hope of a possible unification of Christianity. The true church—the Jesus brotherhood—is invisible, spiritual, and is characterized by unity, not necessarily by uniformity. Uniformity is the earmark of the physical world of mechanistic nature. Spiritual unity is the fruit of faith union with the living Jesus. The visible church should refuse longer to handicap the progress of the invisible and spiritual brotherhood of the kingdom of God. And this brotherhood is destined to become a living organism in contrast to an institutionalized social organization. It may well utilize such social organizations, but it must not be supplanted by them. 195:10.11 (2085.3)

But the Christianity of even the twentieth century must not be despised. It is the product of the combined moral genius of the God-knowing men of many races during many ages, and it has truly been one of the greatest powers for good on earth, and therefore no man should lightly regard it, notwithstanding its inherent and acquired defects. Christianity still contrives to move the minds of reflective men with mighty moral emotions. 195:10.12 (2085.4)</td></tr>
<tr><td>Someday a reformation in the Christian church may strike deep enough to get back to the unadulterated religious teachings of Jesus, the author and finisher of our faith. You may preach a religion about Jesus, but, perforce, you must live the religion of Jesus. In the enthusiasm of Pentecost, Peter unintentionally inaugurated a new religion, the religion of the risen and glorified Christ. The Apostle Paul later on transformed this new gospel into Christianity, a religion embodying his own theologic views and portraying his own personal experience with the Jesus of the Damascus road. The gospel of the kingdom is founded on the personal religious experience of the Jesus of Galilee; Christianity is founded almost exclusively on the personal religious experience of the Apostle Paul. Almost the whole of the New Testament is devoted, not to the portrayal of the significant and inspiring religious life of Jesus, but to a discussion of Paul's religious experience and to a portrayal of his personal religious convictions. The only notable exceptions to this statement, aside from certain parts of Matthew, Mark, and Luke, are the book of Hebrews and the Epistle of James. Even Peter, in his writing, only once reverted to the personal religious life of his Master. The New Testament is a superb Christian document, but it is only meagerly Jesusonian. 196:2.1 (2091.10)</td></tr>
</table>

Jesus and the Church:	Many earnest persons who would gladly yield loyalty to the Christ of the gospel find it very difficult enthusiastically to support a church which exhibits so little of the spirit of his life and teachings, and which they have been erroneously taught he founded. Jesus did not found the so-called Christian church, but he has, in every manner consistent with his nature, *fostered* it as the best existent exponent of his lifework on earth. 195:10.9 (2085.1)
The True Church:	Christianity is seriously confronted with the doom embodied in one of its own slogans: "A house divided against itself cannot stand." The non-Christian world will hardly capitulate to a sect-divided Christendom. The living Jesus is the only hope of a possible unification of Christianity. The true church—the Jesus brotherhood—is invisible, spiritual, and is characterized by *unity,* not necessarily by *uniformity.* Uniformity is the earmark of the physical world of mechanistic nature. Spiritual unity is the fruit of faith union with the living Jesus. The visible church should refuse longer to handicap the progress of the invisible and spiritual brotherhood of the kingdom of God. And this brotherhood is destined to become a *living organism* in contrast to an institutionalized social organization. It may well utilize such social organizations, but it must not be supplanted by them. 195:10.11 (2085.3)
The Original Gospel of the Kingdom:	Jesus does not require his disciples to believe in him but rather to believe *with* him, believe in the reality of the love of God and in full confidence accept the security of the assurance of sonship with the heavenly Father. The Master desires that all his followers should fully share his transcendent faith. Jesus most touchingly challenged his followers, not only to believe *what* he believed, but also to believe *as* he believed. This is the full significance of his one supreme requirement, "Follow me." 196:0.13 (2089.3)
	Jesus founded the religion of personal experience in doing the will of God and serving the human brotherhood; Paul founded a religion in which the glorified Jesus became the object of worship and the brotherhood consisted of fellow believers in the divine Christ. In the bestowal of Jesus these two concepts were potential in his divine-human life, and it is indeed a pity that his followers failed to create a unified religion which might have given proper recognition to both the human and the divine natures of the Master as they were inseparably bound up in his earth life and so gloriously set forth in the original gospel of the kingdom. 196:2.6 (2092.4) You would be neither shocked nor disturbed by some of Jesus' strong pronouncements if you would only remember that he was the world's most wholehearted and devoted religionist. He was a wholly consecrated mortal, unreservedly dedicated to doing his Father's will. Many of his apparently hard sayings were more of a personal confession of faith and a pledge of devotion than commands to his followers. And it was this very singleness of purpose and unselfish devotion that enabled him to effect such extraordinary progress in the conquest of the human mind in one short life. Many of his declarations should be considered as a confession of what he demanded of himself rather than what he required of all his followers. In his devotion to the cause of the kingdom, Jesus burned all bridges behind him; he sacrificed all hindrances to the doing of his Father's will. 196:2.7 (2093.1)

The Faith Which Jesus Desires For Us to Have:	Jesus did not cling to faith in God as would a struggling soul at war with the universe and at death grips with a hostile and sinful world; he did not resort to faith merely as a consolation in the midst of difficulties or as a comfort in threatened despair; faith was not just an illusory compensation for the unpleasant realities and the sorrows of living. In the very face of all the natural difficulties and the temporal contradictions of mortal existence, he experienced the tranquility of supreme and unquestioned trust in God and felt the tremendous thrill of living, by faith, in the very presence of the heavenly Father. And this triumphant faith was a living experience of actual spirit attainment. Jesus' great contribution to the values of human experience was not that he revealed so many new ideas about the Father in heaven, but rather that he so magnificently and humanly demonstrated a new and higher type of *living faith in God.* Never on all the worlds of this universe, in the life of any one mortal, did God ever become such a *living reality* as in the human experience of Jesus of Nazareth. 196:0.3 (2087.3)
	In the earthly life of Jesus, religion was a living experience, a direct and personal movement from spiritual reverence to practical righteousness. The faith of Jesus bore the transcendent fruits of the divine spirit. His faith was not immature and credulous like that of a child, but in many ways it did resemble the unsuspecting trust of the child mind. Jesus trusted God much as the child trusts a parent. He had a profound confidence in the universe—just such a trust as the child has in its parental environment. Jesus' wholehearted faith in the fundamental goodness of the universe very much resembled the child's trust in the security of its earthly surroundings. He depended on the heavenly Father as a child leans upon its earthly parent, and his fervent faith never for one moment doubted the certainty of the heavenly Father's overcare. He was not disturbed seriously by fears, doubts, and skepticism. Unbelief did not inhibit the free and original expression of his life. He combined the stalwart and intelligent courage of a full-grown man with the sincere and trusting optimism of a believing child. His faith grew to such heights of trust that it was devoid of fear. 196:0.11 (2089.1)
	You would be neither shocked nor disturbed by some of Jesus' strong pronouncements if you would only remember that he was the world's most wholehearted and devoted religionist. He was a wholly consecrated mortal, unreservedly dedicated to doing his Father's will. Many of his apparently hard sayings were more of a personal confession of faith and a pledge of devotion than commands to his followers. And it was this very singleness of purpose and unselfish devotion that enabled him to effect such extraordinary progress in the conquest of the human mind in one short life. Many of his declarations should be considered as a confession of what he demanded of himself rather than what he required of all his followers. In his devotion to the cause of the kingdom, Jesus burned all bridges behind him; he sacrificed all hindrances to the doing of his Father's will. 196:2.7 (2093.1)

<table>
<tr><td rowspan="2">Aim of Kingdom Believers:</td><td>Jesus' devotion to the Father's will and the service of man was even more than mortal decision and human determination; it was a wholehearted consecration of himself to such an unreserved bestowal of love. No matter how great the fact of the sovereignty of Michael, you must not take the human Jesus away from men. The Master has ascended on high as a man, as well as God; he belongs to men; men belong to him. How unfortunate that religion itself should be so misinterpreted as to take the human Jesus away from struggling mortals! Let not the discussions of the humanity or the divinity of the Christ obscure the saving truth that Jesus of Nazareth was a religious man who, by faith, achieved the knowing and the doing of the will of God; he was the most truly religious man who has ever lived on Urantia. 196:1.1 (2090.2)</td></tr>
<tr><td>It should not be the aim of kingdom believers literally to imitate the outward life of Jesus in the flesh but rather to share his faith; to trust God as he trusted God and to believe in men as he believed in men. Jesus never argued about either the fatherhood of God or the brotherhood of men; he was a living illustration of the one and a profound demonstration of the other. 196:1.5 (2091.1)</td></tr>
</table>

The Future

<table>
<tr><td rowspan="2">The Decline of Personal Religion:</td><td>The church, being an adjunct to society and the ally of politics, was doomed to share in the intellectual and spiritual decline of the so-called European "dark ages." During this time, religion became more and more monasticized, asceticized, and legalized. In a spiritual sense, Christianity was hibernating. Throughout this period there existed, alongside this slumbering and secularized religion, a continuous stream of mysticism, a fantastic spiritual experience bordering on unreality and philosophically akin to pantheism. 195:4.1 (2074.7)</td></tr>
<tr><td>During these dark and despairing centuries, religion became virtually secondhanded again. The individual was almost lost before the overshadowing authority, tradition, and dictation of the church. A new spiritual menace arose in the creation of a galaxy of "saints" who were assumed to have special influence at the divine courts, and who, therefore, if effectively appealed to, would be able to intercede in man's behalf before the Gods. 195:4.2 (2074.8)</td></tr>
<tr><td rowspan="2">The Modern Problems of Religion:</td><td>Religion is now confronted by the challenge of a new age of scientific minds and materialistic tendencies. In this gigantic struggle between the secular and the spiritual, the religion of Jesus will eventually triumph. 195:4.5 (2075.3)

The twentieth century has brought new problems for Christianity and all other religions to solve. The higher a civilization climbs, the more necessitous becomes the duty to "seek first the realities of heaven" in all of man's efforts to stabilize society and facilitate the solution of its material problems. 195:5.1 (2075.4)</td></tr>
<tr><td>Do not try to satisfy the curiosity or gratify all the latent adventure surging within the soul in one short life in the flesh. Be patient! be not tempted to indulge in a lawless plunge into cheap and sordid adventure. Harness your energies and bridle your passions; be calm while you await the majestic unfolding of an endless career of progressive adventure and thrilling discovery. 195:5.10 (2076.1)</td></tr>
<tr><td>The Problems of Materialism:</td><td>The violent swing from an age of miracles to an age of machines has proved altogether upsetting to man. The cleverness and dexterity of the false philosophies of mechanism belie their very mechanistic contentions. The fatalistic agility of the mind of a materialist forever disproves his assertions that the universe is a blind and purposeless energy phenomenon. 195:6.6 (2077.2)

The mechanistic naturalism of some supposedly educated men and the thoughtless secularism of the man in the street are both exclusively concerned with things; they are barren of all real values, sanctions, and satisfactions of a spiritual nature, as well as being devoid of faith, hope, and eternal assurances. One of the great troubles with modern life is that man thinks he is too busy to find time for spiritual meditation and religious devotion. 195:6.7 (2077.3)

Materialism reduces man to a soulless automaton and constitutes him merely an arithmetical symbol finding a helpless place in the mathematical formula of an unromantic and mechanistic universe. But whence comes all this vast universe of mathematics without a Master Mathematician? Science may expatiate on the conservation of matter, but religion validates the conservation of men's souls—it concerns their experience with spiritual realities and eternal values. 195:6.8 (2077.4)

Continued next page:</td></tr>
</table>

The Problems of Materialism: (Continued)	To say that mind "emerged" from matter explains nothing. If the universe were merely a mechanism and mind were unapart from matter, we would never have two differing interpretations of any observed phenomenon. The concepts of truth, beauty, and goodness are not inherent in either physics or chemistry. A machine cannot *know,* much less know truth, hunger for righteousness, and cherish goodness. 195:6.11 (2077.7)
	If men were only machines, they would react more or less uniformly to a material universe. Individuality, much less personality, would be nonexistent. 195:6.13 (2077.9)
	How foolish it is for material-minded man to allow such vulnerable theories as those of a mechanistic universe to deprive him of the vast spiritual resources of the personal experience of true religion. Facts never quarrel with real spiritual faith; theories may. Better that science should be devoted to the destruction of superstition rather than attempting the overthrow of religious faith—human belief in spiritual realities and divine values. 195:7.1 (2078.4)
	The inconsistency of the modern mechanist is: If this were merely a material universe and man only a machine, such a man would be wholly unable to recognize himself as such a machine, and likewise would such a machine-man be wholly unconscious of the fact of the existence of such a material universe. The materialistic dismay and despair of a mechanistic science has failed to recognize the fact of the spirit-indwelt mind of the scientist whose very supermaterial insight formulates these mistaken and self-contradictory *concepts* of a materialistic universe. 195:7.3 (2078.6)
	If this were only a material universe, material man would never be able to arrive at the concept of the mechanistic character of such an exclusively material existence. This very *mechanistic concept* of the universe is in itself a nonmaterial phenomenon of mind, and all mind is of nonmaterial origin, no matter how thoroughly it may appear to be materially conditioned and mechanistically controlled. 195:7.6 (2079.1)
	If the universe were only material and man only a machine, there would be no science to embolden the scientist to postulate this mechanization of the universe. Machines cannot measure, classify, nor evaluate themselves. Such a scientific piece of work could be executed only by some entity of supermachine status. 195:7.11 (2079.6).
	If man is only a machine, by what technique does this man come to *believe* or claim to *know* that he is only a machine? The experience of self-conscious evaluation of one's self is never an attribute of a mere machine. A self-conscious and avowed mechanist is the best possible answer to mechanism. If materialism were a fact, there could be no self-conscious mechanist. It is also true that one must first be a moral person before one can perform immoral acts. 195:7.13 (2079.8)
	Any scientific interpretation of the material universe is valueless unless it provides due recognition for the *scientist.* No appreciation of art is genuine unless it accords recognition to the *artist.* No evaluation of morals is worthwhile unless it includes the *moralist.* No

The Problems of Materialism: (Continued)	recognition of philosophy is edifying if it ignores the *philosopher,* and religion cannot exist without the real experience of the *religionist* who, in and through this very experience, is seeking to find God and to know him. Likewise is the universe of universes without significance apart from the I AM, the infinite God who made it and unceasingly manages it. 195:7.18 (2080.3) Mechanists—humanists—tend to drift with the material currents. Idealists and spiritists *dare* to use their oars with intelligence and vigor in order to modify the apparently purely material course of the energy streams. 195:7.19 (2080.4)
	The universe is not like the laws, mechanisms, and the uniformities which the scientist discovers, and which he comes to regard as science, but rather like the curious, thinking, choosing, creative, combining, and discriminating *scientist* who thus observes universe phenomena and classifies the mathematical facts inherent in the mechanistic phases of the material side of creation. Neither is the universe like the art of the artist, but rather like the striving, dreaming, aspiring, and advancing *artist* who seeks to transcend the world of material things in an effort to achieve a spiritual goal. 195:7.22 (2080.7) The scientist, not science, perceives the reality of an evolving and advancing universe of energy and matter. The artist, not art, demonstrates the existence of the transient morontia world intervening between material existence and spiritual liberty. The religionist, not religion, proves the existence of the spirit realities and divine values which are to be encountered in the progress of eternity. 195:7.23 (2080.8)
	Materialism denies God, secularism simply ignores him; at least that was the earlier attitude. More recently, secularism has assumed a more militant attitude, assuming to take the place of the religion whose totalitarian bondage it onetime resisted. Twentieth-century secularism tends to affirm that man does not need God. But beware! this godless philosophy of human society will lead only to unrest, animosity, unhappiness, war, and world-wide disaster. 195:8.5 (2081.5) Secularism can never bring peace to mankind. Nothing can take the place of God in human society. But mark you well! do not be quick to surrender the beneficent gains of the secular revolt from ecclesiastical totalitarianism. Western civilization today enjoys many liberties and satisfactions as a result of the secular revolt. The great mistake of secularism was this: In revolting against the almost total control of life by religious authority, and after attaining the liberation from such ecclesiastical tyranny, the secularists went on to institute a revolt against God himself, sometimes tacitly and sometimes openly. 195:8.6 (2081.6)
The Mistakes of Modern Religions:	But religious leaders are making a great mistake when they try to call modern man to spiritual battle with the trumpet blasts of the Middle Ages. Religion must provide itself with new and up-to-date slogans. Neither democracy nor any other political panacea will take the place of spiritual progress. False religions may represent an evasion of reality, but Jesus in his gospel introduced mortal man to the very entrance upon an eternal reality of spiritual progression. 195:6.10 (2077.6)
	Religion does need new leaders, spiritual men and women who will dare to depend solely on Jesus and his incomparable teachings. If Christianity persists in neglecting its spiritual mission while it continues to busy itself with social and material problems, the spiritual

<table>
<tr>
<td rowspan="4">The Mistakes of Modern Religions: (Continued)</td>
<td>renaissance must await the coming of these new teachers of Jesus' religion who will be exclusively devoted to the spiritual regeneration of men. And then will these spirit-born souls quickly supply the leadership and inspiration requisite for the social, moral, economic, and political reorganization of the world. 195:9.4 (2082.9)

The modern age will refuse to accept a religion which is inconsistent with facts and out of harmony with its highest conceptions of truth, beauty, and goodness. The hour is striking for a rediscovery of the true and original foundations of present-day distorted and compromised Christianity—the real life and teachings of Jesus. 195:9.5 (2083.1)</td>
</tr>
<tr>
<td>Selfish men and women simply will not pay such a price for even the greatest spiritual treasure ever offered mortal man. Only when man has become sufficiently disillusioned by the sorrowful disappointments attendant upon the foolish and deceptive pursuits of selfishness, and subsequent to the discovery of the barrenness of formalized religion, will he be disposed to turn wholeheartedly to the gospel of the kingdom, the religion of Jesus of Nazareth. 195:9.7 (2083.3)

The world needs more firsthand religion. Even Christianity—the best of the religions of the twentieth century—is not only a religion about Jesus, but it is so largely one which men experience secondhand. They take their religion wholly as handed down by their accepted religious teachers. What an awakening the world would experience if it could only see Jesus as he really lived on earth and know, firsthand, his life-giving teachings! Descriptive words of things beautiful cannot thrill like the sight thereof, neither can creedal words inspire men's souls like the experience of knowing the presence of God. But expectant faith will ever keep the hope-door of man's soul open for the entrance of the eternal spiritual realities of the divine values of the worlds beyond. 195:9.8 (2083.4)

Christianity has dared to lower its ideals before the challenge of human greed, war-madness, and the lust for power; but the religion of Jesus stands as the unsullied and transcendent spiritual summons, calling to the best there is in man to rise above all these legacies of animal evolution and, by grace, attain the moral heights of true human destiny. 195:9.9 (2083.5)</td>
</tr>
<tr>
<td>In winning souls for the Master, it is not the first mile of compulsion, duty, or convention that will transform man and his world, but rather the second mile of free service and liberty-loving devotion that betokens the Jesusonian reaching forth to grasp his brother in love and sweep him on under spiritual guidance toward the higher and divine goal of mortal existence. Christianity even now willingly goes the first mile, but mankind languishes and stumbles along in moral darkness because there are so few genuine second-milers—so few professed followers of Jesus who really live and love as he taught his disciples to live and love and serve. 195:10.5 (2084.5)</td>
</tr>
<tr>
<td>Ecclesiasticism is at once and forever incompatible with that living faith, growing spirit, and firsthand experience of the faith-comrades of Jesus in the brotherhood of man in the spiritual association of the kingdom of heaven. The praiseworthy desire to preserve traditions of past achievement often leads to the defense of outgrown systems of worship. The well-meant desire to foster ancient thought systems effectually prevents the sponsoring of new and adequate means and methods designed to satisfy the spiritual longings of the expanding and advancing minds of modern men. Likewise, the Christian churches of the twentieth century stand as great, but wholly unconscious, obstacles to the immediate advance of the real gospel—the teachings of Jesus of Nazareth. 195:10.8 (2084.8)</td>
</tr>
</table>

The Mistakes of Modern Religions: (Continued)	Many earnest persons who would gladly yield loyalty to the Christ of the gospel find it very difficult enthusiastically to support a church which exhibits so little of the spirit of his life and teachings, and which they have been erroneously taught he founded. Jesus did not found the so-called Christian church, but he has, in every manner consistent with his nature, *fostered* it as the best existent exponent of his lifework on earth. 195:10.9 (2085.1) If the Christian church would only dare to espouse the Master's program, thousands of apparently indifferent youths would rush forward to enlist in such a spiritual undertaking, and they would not hesitate to go all the way through with this great adventure. 195:10.10 (2085.2) Christianity is seriously confronted with the doom embodied in one of its own slogans: "A house divided against itself cannot stand." The non-Christian world will hardly capitulate to a sect-divided Christendom. The living Jesus is the only hope of a possible unification of Christianity. The true church—the Jesus brotherhood—is invisible, spiritual, and is characterized by *unity,* not necessarily by *uniformity.* Uniformity is the earmark of the physical world of mechanistic nature. Spiritual unity is the fruit of faith union with the living Jesus. The visible church should refuse longer to handicap the progress of the invisible and spiritual brotherhood of the kingdom of God. And this brotherhood is destined to become a *living organism* in contrast to an institutionalized social organization. It may well utilize such social organizations, but it must not be supplanted by them. 195:10.11 (2085.3)
	But there is no excuse for the involvement of the church in commerce and politics; such unholy alliances are a flagrant betrayal of the Master. And the genuine lovers of truth will be slow to forget that this powerful institutionalized church has often dared to smother newborn faith and persecute truth bearers who chanced to appear in unorthodox raiment. 195:10.13 (2085.5)
The Supremacy of Religion:	Personal, spiritual religious experience is an efficient solvent for most mortal difficulties; it is an effective sorter, evaluator, and adjuster of all human problems. Religion does not remove or destroy human troubles, but it does dissolve, absorb, illuminate, and transcend them. True religion unifies the personality for effective adjustment to all mortal requirements. Religious faith—the positive leading of the indwelling divine presence—unfailingly enables the God-knowing man to bridge that gulf existing between the intellectual logic which recognizes the Universal First Cause as *It* and those positive affirmations of the soul which aver this First Cause is *He,* the heavenly Father of Jesus' gospel, the personal God of human salvation. 196:3.1 (2093.6)
	The progressive comprehension of reality is the equivalent of approaching God. The finding of God, the consciousness of identity with reality, is the equivalent of the experiencing of self-completion—self-entirety, self-totality. The experiencing of total reality is the full realization of God, the finality of the God-knowing experience. 196:3.3 (2094.2) The full summation of human life is the knowledge that man is educated by fact, ennobled by wisdom, and saved—justified—by religious faith. 196:3.4 (2094.3) Physical certainty consists in the logic of science; moral certainty, in the wisdom of philosophy; spiritual certainty, in the truth of genuine religious experience. 196:3.5 (2094.4)

	Spiritual evaluation of life—worship. Only the spirit-indwelt man can realize the divine presence and seek to attain a fuller experience in and with this foretaste of divinity. 196:3.9 (2094.8)
	This profound experience of the reality of the divine indwelling forever transcends the crude materialistic technique of the physical sciences. You cannot put spiritual joy under a microscope; you cannot weigh love in a balance; you cannot measure moral values; neither can you estimate the quality of spiritual worship. 196:3.18 (2095.2) The Hebrews had a religion of moral sublimity; the Greeks evolved a religion of beauty; Paul and his conferees founded a religion of faith, hope, and charity. Jesus revealed and exemplified a religion of love: security in the Father's love, with joy and satisfaction consequent upon sharing this love in the service of the human brotherhood. 196:3.19 (2095.3)
The Supremacy of Religion: (Continued)	The exquisite and transcendent experience of loving and being loved is not just a psychic illusion because it is so purely subjective. The one truly divine and objective reality that is associated with mortal beings, the Thought Adjuster, functions to human observation apparently as an exclusively subjective phenomenon. Man's contact with the highest objective reality, God, is only through the purely subjective experience of knowing him, of worshiping him, of realizing sonship with him. 196:3.21 (2095.5) True religious worship is not a futile monologue of self-deception. Worship is a personal communion with that which is divinely real, with that which is the very source of reality. Man aspires by worship to be better and thereby eventually attains the *best*. 196:3.22 (2095.6) The idealization and attempted service of truth, beauty, and goodness is not a substitute for genuine religious experience—spiritual reality. Psychology and idealism are not the equivalent of religious reality. The projections of the human intellect may indeed originate false gods—gods in man's image—but the true God-consciousness does not have such an origin. The God-consciousness is resident in the indwelling spirit. Many of the religious systems of man come from the formulations of the human intellect, but the God-consciousness is not necessarily a part of these grotesque systems of religious slavery. 196:3.23 (2095.7)
	Religious insight possesses the power of turning defeat into higher desires and new determinations. Love is the highest motivation which man may utilize in his universe ascent. But love, divested of truth, beauty, and goodness, is only a sentiment, a philosophic distortion, a psychic illusion, a spiritual deception. Love must always be redefined on successive levels of morontia and spirit progression. 196:3.29 (2096.5) Art results from man's attempt to escape from the lack of beauty in his material environment; it is a gesture toward the morontia level. Science is man's effort to solve the apparent riddles of the material universe. Philosophy is man's attempt at the unification of human experience. Religion is man's supreme gesture, his magnificent reach for final reality, his determination to find God and to be like him. 196:3.30 (2096.6) In the realm of religious experience, spiritual possibility is potential reality. Man's forward spiritual urge is not a psychic illusion. All of man's universe romancing may not be fact, but much, very much, is truth. 196:3.31 (2096.7)

The Supremacy of Religion: (Continued)	Some men's lives are too great and noble to descend to the low level of being merely successful. The animal must adapt itself to the environment, but the religious man transcends his environment and in this way escapes the limitations of the present material world through this insight of divine love. This concept of love generates in the soul of man that superanimal effort to find truth, beauty, and goodness; and when he does find them, he is glorified in their embrace; he is consumed with the desire to live them, to do righteousness. 196:3.32 (2096.8) Be not discouraged; human evolution is still in progress, and the revelation of God to the world, in and through Jesus, shall not fail. 196:3.33 (2097.1) The great challenge to modern man is to achieve better communication with the divine Monitor that dwells within the human mind. Man's greatest adventure in the flesh consists in the well-balanced and sane effort to advance the borders of self-consciousness out through the dim realms of embryonic soul-consciousness in a wholehearted effort to reach the borderland of spirit-consciousness—contact with the divine presence. Such an experience constitutes God-consciousness, an experience mightily confirmative of the pre-existent truth of the religious experience of knowing God. Such spirit-consciousness is the equivalent of the knowledge of the actuality of sonship with God. Otherwise, the assurance of sonship is the experience of faith. 196:3.34 (2097.2) And God-consciousness is equivalent to the integration of the self with the universe, and on its highest levels of spiritual reality. Only the spirit content of any value is imperishable. Even that which is true, beautiful, and good may not perish in human experience. If man does not choose to survive, then does the surviving Adjuster conserve those realities born of love and nurtured in service. And all these things are a part of the Universal Father. The Father is living love, and this life of the Father is in his Sons. And the spirit of the Father is in his Sons' sons—mortal men. When all is said and done, the Father idea is still the highest human concept of God. 196:3.35 (2097.3)
Religion and Morality:	Even secular education could help in this great spiritual renaissance if it would pay more attention to the work of teaching youth how to engage in life planning and character progression. The purpose of all education should be to foster and further the supreme purpose of life, the development of a majestic and well-balanced personality. There is great need for the teaching of moral discipline in the place of so much self-gratification. Upon such a foundation religion may contribute its spiritual incentive to the enlargement and enrichment of mortal life, even to the security and enhancement of life eternal. 195:10.17 (2086.3)
	The all-consuming and indomitable spiritual faith of Jesus never became fanatical, for it never attempted to run away with his well-balanced intellectual judgments concerning the proportional values of practical and commonplace social, economic, and moral life situations. The Son of Man was a splendidly unified human personality; he was a perfectly endowed divine being; he was also magnificently co-ordinated as a combined human and divine being functioning on earth as a single personality. Always did the Master co-ordinate the faith of the soul with the wisdom-appraisals of seasoned experience. Personal faith, spiritual hope, and moral devotion were always correlated in a matchless religious unity of harmonious association with the keen realization of the reality and sacredness of all human loyalties—personal honor, family love, religious obligation, social duty, and economic necessity. 196:0.7 (2088.2)

	The human mind does not create real values; human experience does not yield universe insight. Concerning insight, the recognition of moral values and the discernment of spiritual meanings, all that the human mind can do is to discover, recognize, interpret, and *choose.* 196:3.10 (2094.9) The moral values of the universe become intellectual possessions by the exercise of the three basic judgments, or choices, of the mortal mind: 196:3.11 (2094.10) 1. Self-judgment—moral choice. 196:3.12 (2094.11) 2. Social-judgment—ethical choice. 196:3.13 (2094.12) 3. God-judgment—religious choice. 196:3.14 (2094.13)
	Unless a divine lover lived in man, he could not unselfishly and spiritually love. Unless an interpreter lived in the mind, man could not truly realize the unity of the universe. Unless an evaluator dwelt with man, he could not possibly appraise moral values and recognize spiritual meanings. And this lover hails from the very source of infinite love; this interpreter is a part of Universal Unity; this evaluator is the child of the Center and Source of all absolute values of divine and eternal reality. 196:3.16 (2094.15) Moral evaluation with a religious meaning—spiritual insight—connotes the individual's choice between good and evil, truth and error, material and spiritual, human and divine, time and eternity. Human survival is in great measure dependent on consecrating the human will to the choosing of those values selected by this spirit-value sorter—the indwelling interpreter and unifier. Personal religious experience consists in two phases: discovery in the human mind and revelation by the indwelling divine spirit. Through over-sophistication or as a result of the irreligious conduct of professed religionists, a man, or even a generation of men, may elect to suspend their efforts to discover the God who indwells them; they may fail to progress in and attain the divine revelation. But such attitudes of spiritual nonprogression cannot long persist because of the presence and influence of the indwelling Thought Adjusters. 196:3.17 (2095.1)
Religion and Morality: (Continued)	Every time man makes a reflective moral choice, he immediately experiences a new divine invasion of his soul. Moral choosing constitutes religion as the motive of inner response to outer conditions. But such a real religion is not a purely subjective experience. It signifies the whole of the subjectivity of the individual engaged in a meaningful and intelligent response to total objectivity—the universe and its Maker. 196:3.20 (2095.4)
	God is not the mere invention of man's idealism; he is the very source of all such superanimal insights and values. God is not a hypothesis formulated to unify the human concepts of truth, beauty, and goodness; he is the personality of love from whom all of these universe manifestations are derived. The truth, beauty, and goodness of man's world are unified by the increasing spirituality of the experience of mortals ascending toward Paradise realities. The unity of truth, beauty, and goodness can only be realized in the spiritual experience of the God-knowing personality. 196:3.24 (2095.8) Morality is the essential pre-existent soil of personal God-consciousness, the personal realization of the Adjuster's inner presence, but such morality is not the source of religious experience and the resultant spiritual insight. The moral nature is superanimal but subspiritual. Morality is equivalent to the recognition of duty, the realization of the existence

Religion and Morality (Continued)	of right and wrong. The moral zone intervenes between the animal and the human types of mind as morontia functions between the material and the spiritual spheres of personality attainment. 196:3.25 (2096.1) The evolutionary mind is able to discover law, morals, and ethics; but the bestowed spirit, the indwelling Adjuster, reveals to the evolving human mind the lawgiver, the Father-source of all that is true, beautiful, and good; and such an illuminated man has a religion and is spiritually equipped to begin the long and adventurous search for God.196:3.26 (2096.2) Morality is not necessarily spiritual; it may be wholly and purely human, albeit real religion enhances all moral values, makes them more meaningful. Morality without religion fails to reveal ultimate goodness, and it also fails to provide for the survival of even its own moral values. Religion provides for the enhancement, glorification, and assured survival of everything morality recognizes and approves. 196:3.27 (2096.3) Religion stands above science, art, philosophy, ethics, and morals, but not independent of them. They are all indissolubly interrelated in human experience, personal and social. Religion is man's supreme experience in the mortal nature, but finite language makes it forever impossible for theology ever adequately to depict real religious experience. 196:3.28 (2096.4)
The Future:	Religion is now confronted by the challenge of a new age of scientific minds and materialistic tendencies. In this gigantic struggle between the secular and the spiritual, the religion of Jesus will eventually triumph. 195:4.5 (2075.3)
	In confusion over man's origin, do not lose sight of his eternal destiny. Forget not that Jesus loved even little children, and that he forever made clear the great worth of human personality. 195:5.11 (2076.2) As you view the world, remember that the black patches of evil which you see are shown against a white background of ultimate good. You do not view merely white patches of good which show up miserably against a black background of evil. 195:5.12 (2076.3) When there is so much good truth to publish and proclaim, why should men dwell so much upon the evil in the world just because it appears to be a fact? The beauties of the spiritual values of truth are more pleasurable and uplifting than is the phenomenon of evil. 195:5.13 (2076.4)
	Scientists have unintentionally precipitated mankind into a materialistic panic; they have started an unthinking run on the moral bank of the ages, but this bank of human experience has vast spiritual resources; it can stand the demands being made upon it. Only unthinking men become panicky about the spiritual assets of the human race. When the materialistic-secular panic is over, the religion of Jesus will not be found bankrupt. The spiritual bank of the kingdom of heaven will be paying out faith, hope, and moral security to all who draw upon it "in His name." 195:6.1 (2076.6)
	No matter what the apparent conflict between materialism and the teachings of Jesus may be, you can rest assured that, in the ages to come, the teachings of the Master will fully triumph. In reality, true religion cannot become involved in any controversy with science; it is in no way concerned with material things. Religion is simply indifferent to, but sympathetic with, science, while it supremely concerns itself with the *scientist.* 195:6.2 (2076.7)

The Future

The Future: (Continued)	At the time of this writing the worst of the materialistic age is over; the day of a better understanding is already beginning to dawn. The higher minds of the scientific world are no longer wholly materialistic in their philosophy, but the rank and file of the people still lean in that direction as a result of former teachings. But this age of physical realism is only a passing episode in man's life on earth. Modern science has left true religion—the teachings of Jesus as translated in the lives of his believers—untouched. All science has done is to destroy the childlike illusions of the misinterpretations of life.195:6.4 (2076.9)
	The materialistic sociologist of today surveys a community, makes a report thereon, and leaves the people as he found them. Nineteen hundred years ago, unlearned Galileans surveyed Jesus giving his life as a spiritual contribution to man's inner experience and then went out and turned the whole Roman Empire upside down. 195:6.9 (2077.5)
	But even after materialism and mechanism have been more or less vanquished, the devastating influence of twentieth-century secularism will still blight the spiritual experience of millions of unsuspecting souls. 195:8.1 (2081.1)
	To the secularistic revolt you owe the amazing creativity of American industrialism and the unprecedented material progress of Western civilization. And because the secularistic revolt went too far and lost sight of God and *true* religion, there also followed the unlooked-for harvest of world wars and international unsettledness. 195:8.7 (2081.7)
	Do not overlook the value of your spiritual heritage, the river of truth running down through the centuries, even to the barren times of a materialistic and secular age. In all your worthy efforts to rid yourselves of the superstitious creeds of past ages, make sure that you hold fast the eternal truth. But be patient! when the present superstition revolt is over, the truths of Jesus' gospel will persist gloriously to illuminate a new and better way. 195:9.1 (2082.6) But paganized and socialized Christianity stands in need of new contact with the uncompromised teachings of Jesus; it languishes for lack of a new vision of the Master's life on earth. A new and fuller revelation of the religion of Jesus is destined to conquer an empire of materialistic secularism and to overthrow a world sway of mechanistic naturalism. Urantia is now quivering on the very brink of one of its most amazing and enthralling epochs of social readjustment, moral quickening, and spiritual enlightenment. 195:9.2 (2082.7)
	Ever bear in mind—God and men need each other. They are mutually necessary to the full and final attainment of eternal personality experience in the divine destiny of universe finality. 195:10.3 (2084.3)
	The call to the adventure of building a new and transformed human society by means of the spiritual rebirth of Jesus' brotherhood of the kingdom should thrill all who believe in him as men have not been stirred since the days when they walked about on earth as his companions in the flesh. 195:10.6 (2084.6)
	The great hope of Urantia lies in the possibility of a new revelation of Jesus with a new and enlarged presentation of his saving message which would spiritually unite in loving service the numerous families of his present-day professed followers. 195:10.16 (2086.2)

The Future: (Continued)	The time is ripe to witness the figurative resurrection of the human Jesus from his burial tomb amidst the theological traditions and the religious dogmas of nineteen centuries. Jesus of Nazareth must not be longer sacrificed to even the splendid concept of the glorified Christ. What a transcendent service if, through this revelation, the Son of Man should be recovered from the tomb of traditional theology and be presented as the living Jesus to the church that bears his name, and to all other religions! Surely the Christian fellowship of believers will not hesitate to make such adjustments of faith and of practices of living as will enable it to "follow after" the Master in the demonstration of his real life of religious devotion to the doing of his Father's will and of consecration to the unselfish service of man. Do professed Christians fear the exposure of a self-sufficient and unconsecrated fellowship of social respectability and selfish economic maladjustment? Does institutional Christianity fear the possible jeopardy, or even the overthrow, of traditional ecclesiastical authority if the Jesus of Galilee is reinstated in the minds and souls of mortal men as the ideal of personal religious living? Indeed, the social readjustments, the economic transformations, the moral rejuvenations, and the religious revisions of Christian civilization would be drastic and revolutionary if the living religion of Jesus should suddenly supplant the theologic religion about Jesus. 196:1.2 (2090.3)
	The common people heard Jesus gladly, and they will again respond to the presentation of his sincere human life of consecrated religious motivation if such truths shall again be proclaimed to the world. The people heard him gladly because he was one of them, an unpretentious layman; the world's greatest religious teacher was indeed a layman. 196:1.4 (2090.5)

The Religious Groups and Political Parties of Palestine

The Religious Groups and Political Parties of Palestine

Jesus' Attitude Toward the Various Groups:	In this time of waiting Jesus endeavored to teach his associates what their attitude should be toward the various religious groups and the political parties of Palestine. Jesus' words always were, "We are seeking to win all of them, but we are not of any of them." 137:7.5 (1534.4)
	All of these parties and sects, including the smaller Nazarite brotherhood, believed in the sometime coming of the Messiah. They all looked for a national deliverer. But Jesus was very positive in making it clear that he and his disciples would not become allied to any of these schools of thought or practice. The Son of Man was to be neither a Nazarite nor an Essene. 137:7.12 (1535.4)
	Jesus did not vehemently denounce even the Pharisees, as did John. He knew many of the scribes and Pharisees were honest of heart; he understood their enslaving bondage to religious traditions. Jesus laid great emphasis on "first making the tree good." He impressed the three [Peter, James, and John] that he valued the whole life, not just a certain few special virtues. 140:8.22 (1582.3)
Buddhism:	Ganid was shocked to discover how near Buddhism came to being a great and beautiful religion without God, without a personal and universal Deity. However, he did find some record of certain earlier beliefs which reflected something of the influence of the teachings of the Melchizedek missionaries who continued their work in India even to the times of Buddha. 131:3.1 (1446.3)
Confucianism:	Even the least God-recognizing of the world's great religions acknowledged the monotheism of the Melchizedek missionaries and their persistent successors. 131:9.1 (1452.5)
Essenes:	The Essenes were a true religious sect, originating during the Maccabean revolt, whose requirements were in some respects more exacting than those of the Pharisees. They had adopted many Persian beliefs and practices, lived as a brotherhood in monasteries, refrained from marriage, and had all things in common. They specialized in teachings about angels. 137:7.8 (1534.7)
	There was, throughout all these regions, a lingering belief in reincarnation. The older Jewish teachers, together with Plato, Philo, and many of the Essenes, tolerated the theory that men may reap in one incarnation what they have sown in a previous existence; thus in one life they were believed to be expiating the sins committed in preceding lives. The Master found it difficult to make men believe that their souls had not had previous existences. 164:3.4 (1811.5)

The Religious Groups and Political Parties of Palestine

Greeks:	Of the Greeks, Jesus said: "The Greeks and others have taught you that man is descending from godly perfection steadily down toward oblivion or destruction; I have come to show that man, by entrance into the kingdom, is ascending certainly and surely up to God and divine perfection. 148:4.9 (1660.8) Consider the Greeks, who have a science without religion, while the Jews have a religion without science. 155:1.4 (1726.1)
	The Greek mind was willing to borrow new and good ideas even from the Jews. 195:1.3 (2071.3)
	At the time Paul stood up in Athens preaching "Christ and Him Crucified," the Greeks were spiritually hungry; they were inquiring, interested, and actually looking for spiritual truth. Never forget that at first the Romans fought Christianity, while the Greeks embraced it, and that it was the Greeks who literally forced the Romans subsequently to accept this new religion, as then modified, as a part of Greek culture. 195:1.5 (2071.5) The Greek revered beauty, the Jew holiness, but both peoples loved truth. For centuries the Greek had seriously thought and earnestly debated about all human problems—social, economic, political, and philosophic—except religion. Few Greeks had paid much attention to religion; they did not take even their own religion very seriously. 195:1.6 (2071.6) The influence of Greek culture had already penetrated the lands of the western Mediterranean when Alexander spread Hellenistic civilization over the near-Eastern world. The Greeks did very well with their religion and their politics as long as they lived in small city-states, but when the Macedonian king dared to expand Greece into an empire, stretching from the Adriatic to the Indus, trouble began. The art and philosophy of Greece were fully equal to the task of imperial expansion, but not so with Greek political administration or religion. After the city-states of Greece had expanded into empire, their rather parochial gods seemed a little queer. The Greeks were really searching for one God, a greater and better God, when the Christianized version of the older Jewish religion came to them. 195:1.7 (2071.7)
	The Greeks, in contrast with the Jews and many other peoples, had long provisionally believed in immortality, some sort of survival after death, and since this was the very heart of Jesus' teaching, it was certain that Christianity would make a strong appeal to them. 195:2.8 (2073.3)
Herodians:	The angered Pharisees went away, and notwithstanding it was the Sabbath day, they hastened forthwith to Tiberias and took counsel with Herod [Antipas], doing everything in their power to arouse his prejudice in order to secure the Herodians as allies against Jesus. But Herod refused to take action against Jesus, advising that they carry their complaints to Jerusalem. 148:7.3 (1665.2)
	The Herodians were a purely political party that advocated emancipation from the direct Roman rule by a restoration of the Herodian dynasty. 137:7.10 (1535.2)

The Religious Groups and Political Parties of Palestine

Hebrew/Judaism:	The Jews were a part of the older Semitic race, which also included the Babylonians, the Phoenicians, and the more recent enemies of Rome, the Carthaginians. During the fore part of the first century after Christ, the Jews were the most influential group of the Semitic peoples, and they happened to occupy a peculiarly strategic geographic position in the world as it was at that time ruled and organized for trade. 121:2.1 (1333.3)
	Although Palestine was the home of Jewish religious culture and the birthplace of Christianity, the Jews were abroad in the world, dwelling in many nations and trading in every province of the Roman and Parthian states. 121:2.3 (1333.5)
	The centralization of the Jewish temple worship at Jerusalem constituted alike the secret of the survival of their monotheism and the promise of the nurture and sending forth to the world of a new and enlarged concept of that one God of all nations and Father of all mortals. The temple service at Jerusalem represented the survival of a religious cultural concept in the face of the downfall of a succession of gentile national overlords and racial persecutors. 121:2.6 (1333.8) The Jewish people of this time, although under Roman suzerainty, enjoyed a considerable degree of self-government and, remembering the then only recent heroic exploits of deliverance executed by Judas Maccabee and his immediate successors, were vibrant with the expectation of the immediate appearance of a still greater deliverer, the long-expected Messiah. 121:2.7 (1334.1)
	Throughout the whole wide world, no matter where the Jews found themselves dispersed by commerce or oppression, all with one accord kept their hearts centered on the holy temple at Jerusalem. Jewish theology did survive as it was interpreted and practiced at Jerusalem, notwithstanding that it was several times saved from oblivion by the timely intervention of certain Babylonian teachers. 121:6.8 (1339.4) As many as two and one-half million of these dispersed Jews used to come to Jerusalem for the celebration of their national religious festivals. And no matter what the theologic or philosophic differences of the Eastern (Babylonian) and the Urantia Western (Hellenic) Jews, they were all agreed on Jerusalem as the center of their worship and in ever looking forward to the coming of the Messiah. 121:6.9 (1339.5)
	The Jews entertained many ideas about the expected deliverer, and each of these different schools of Messianic teaching was able to point to statements in the Hebrew scriptures as proof of their contentions. In a general way, the Jews regarded their national history as beginning with Abraham and culminating in the Messiah and the new age of the kingdom of God. In earlier times they had envisaged this deliverer as "the servant of the Lord," then as "the Son of Man," while latterly some even went so far as to refer to the Messiah as the "Son of God." But no matter whether he was called the "seed of Abraham" or "the son of David," all were agreed that he was to be the Messiah, the "anointed one." Thus did the concept evolve from the "servant of the Lord" to the "son of David," "Son of Man," and "Son of God." 136:1.1 (1509.3)

Hinduism:	The Hindus likewise combined their multifarious deities into the "one spirituality of the gods" portrayed in the Rig-Veda, while the Mesopotamians reduced their gods to the more centralized concept of Bel-Marduk. The missionaries of Melchizedek carried the teachings of the one God with them wherever they journeyed. Much of this monotheistic doctrine, together with other and previous concepts, became embodied in the subsequent teachings of Hinduism. 131:4.1 (1447.5)
Jainism: (Suduanism)	The third group of religious believers who preserved the doctrine of one God in India—the survival of the Melchizedek teaching—were known in those days as the Suduanists. Latterly these believers have become known as followers of Jainism. 131:6.1 (1450.5)
Mithraism:	Moon worship preceded sun worship. Veneration of the moon was at its height during the hunting era, while sun worship became the chief religious ceremony of the subsequent agricultural ages. Solar worship first took extensive root in India, and there it persisted the longest. In Persia sun veneration gave rise to the later Mithraic cult. Among many peoples the sun was regarded as the ancestor of their kings. The Chaldeans put the sun in the center of "the seven circles of the universe." Later civilizations honored the sun by giving its name to the first day of the week. 85:5.2 (947.5) The sun god was supposed to be the mystic father of the virgin-born sons of destiny who ever and anon were thought to be bestowed as saviors upon favored races. These supernatural infants were always put adrift upon some sacred river to be rescued in an extraordinary manner, after which they would grow up to become miraculous personalities and the deliverers of their peoples. 85:5.3 (947.6)
	The Phrygian and Egyptian mysteries eventually gave way before the greatest of all the mystery cults, the worship of Mithras. The Mithraic cult made its appeal to a wide range of human nature and gradually supplanted both of its predecessors. Mithraism spread over the Roman Empire through the propagandizing of Roman legions recruited in the Levant, where this religion was the vogue, for they carried this belief wherever they went. And this new religious ritual was a great improvement over the earlier mystery cults. 98:5.1 (1082.2) The cult of Mithras arose in Iran and long persisted in its homeland despite the militant opposition of the followers of Zoroaster. But by the time Mithraism reached Rome, it had become greatly improved by the absorption of many of Zoroaster's teachings. It was chiefly through the Mithraic cult that Zoroaster's religion exerted an influence upon later appearing Christianity. 98:5.2 (1082.3) The Mithraic cult portrayed a militant god taking origin in a great rock, engaging in valiant exploits, and causing water to gush forth from a rock struck with his arrows. There was a flood from which one man escaped in a specially built boat and a last supper which Mithras celebrated with the sun-god before he ascended into the heavens. This sun-god, or Sol Invictus, was a degeneration of the Ahura-Mazda

Mithraism: (Continued)	deity concept of Zoroastrianism. Mithras was conceived as the surviving champion of the sun-god in his struggle with the god of darkness. And in recognition of his slaying the mythical sacred bull, Mithras was made immortal, being exalted to the station of intercessor for the human race among the gods on high. 98:5.3 (1082.4) The adherents of this cult worshiped in caves and other secret places, chanting hymns, mumbling magic, eating the flesh of the sacrificial animals, and drinking the blood. Three times a day they worshiped, with special weekly ceremonials on the day of the sun-god and with the most elaborate observance of all on the annual festival of Mithras, December twenty-fifth. It was believed that the partaking of the sacrament ensured eternal life, the immediate passing, after death, to the bosom of Mithras, there to tarry in bliss until the judgment day. On the judgment day the Mithraic keys of heaven would unlock the gates of Paradise for the reception of the faithful; whereupon all the unbaptized of the living and the dead would be annihilated upon the return of Mithras to earth. It was taught that, when a man died, he went before Mithras for judgment, and that at the end of the world Mithras would summon all the dead from their graves to face the last judgment. The wicked would be destroyed by fire, and the righteous would reign with Mithras forever. 98:5.4 (1082.5) At first it was a religion only for men, and there were seven different orders into which believers could be successively initiated. Later on, the wives and daughters of believers were admitted to the temples of the Great Mother, which adjoined the Mithraic temples. The women's cult was a mixture of Mithraic ritual and the ceremonies of the Phrygian cult of Cybele, the mother of Attis. 98:5.5 (1082.6)
	During the third century after Christ, Mithraic and Christian churches were very similar both in appearance and in the character of their ritual. A majority of such places of worship were underground, and both contained altars whose backgrounds variously depicted the sufferings of the savior who had brought salvation to a sin-cursed human race. 98:6.3 (1083.3) Always had it been the practice of Mithraic worshipers, on entering the temple, to dip their fingers in holy water. And since in some districts there were those who at one time belonged to both religions, they introduced this custom into the majority of the Christian churches in the vicinity of Rome. Both religions employed baptism and partook of the sacrament of bread and wine. The one great difference between Mithraism and Christianity, aside from the characters of Mithras and Jesus, was that the one encouraged militarism while the other was ultrapacific. Mithraism's tolerance for other religions (except later Christianity) led to its final undoing. But the deciding factor in the struggle between the two was the admission of women into the full fellowship of the Christian faith. 98:6.4 (1083.4) In the end the nominal Christian faith dominated the Occident. Greek philosophy supplied the concepts of ethical value; Mithraism, the ritual of worship observance; and Christianity, as such, the technique for the conservation of moral and social values. 98:6.5 (1083.5)
	The appealing teachings of the prevailing mystery cults, especially the Mithraic doctrines of redemption, atonement, and salvation by the sacrifice made by some god. 121:7.10 (1340.8)

The Religious Groups and Political Parties of Palestine

Nazarite:	**[Compilation of Urantia Book quotes]** Engedi, down by the Dead Sea, was the southern headquarters of the Nazarite brotherhood, and there John the Baptist was duly and solemnly inducted into this order for life. They had ceremonies and made vows to abstain from all intoxicating drinks, to let the hair grow, and to refrain from touching the dead even in one's own family. They made offerings which were required of those taking Nazarite vows. Samson and the prophet Samuel were Nazarites. A life Nazarite was looked upon as a sanctified and holy personality. The Jews regarded a Nazarite with almost the respect and veneration accorded the high priest, and this was not strange since Nazarites of lifelong consecration were the only persons, except high priests, who were ever permitted to enter the holy of holies in the temple. The Engedi colony included not only Nazarites of lifelong and time period consecration but numerous other ascetic herdsmen who congregated in this region with their herds and fraternized with the Nazarite brotherhood. They supported themselves by sheep raising and from gifts which wealthy Jews made to the order. John the Baptist was greatly influenced by the sacred writings of Isaiah and Malachi found at the Engedi home of the Nazarites included writings by. Abner was the acknowledged leader and head of the Engedi colony. Many of the Nazarite brotherhood believed in the sometime coming of the Messiah and became believers in Jesus, but the majority of these ascetic and eccentric men refused to accept him as a teacher sent from heaven because he did not teach fasting and other forms of self-denial.
Pharisees:	The scribes and rabbis, taken together, were called Pharisees. They referred to themselves as the "associates." In many ways they were the progressive group among the Jews, having adopted many teachings not clearly found in the Hebrew scriptures, such as belief in the resurrection of the dead, a doctrine only mentioned by a later prophet, Daniel. 137:7.6 (1534.5)
	The wealthy Pharisees were devoted to almsgiving, and they did not shun publicity regarding their philanthropy. Sometimes they would even blow a trumpet as they were about to bestow charity upon some beggar. It was the custom of these Pharisees, when they provided a banquet for distinguished guests, to leave the doors of the house open so that even the street beggars might come in and, standing around the walls of the room behind the couches of the diners, be in position to receive portions of food which might be tossed to them by the banqueters. 147:5.2 (1651.6)
	Jesus greatly enjoyed the keen sense of humor which these gentiles exhibited. It was the sense of humor displayed by Norana, the Syrian woman, as well as her great and persistent faith, that so touched the Master's heart and appealed to his mercy. Jesus greatly regretted that his people—the Jews—were so lacking in humor. He once said to Thomas: "My people take themselves too seriously; they are just about devoid of an appreciation of humor. The burdensome religion of the Pharisees could never have had origin among a people with a sense of humor. They also lack consistency; they strain at gnats and swallow camels." 156:2.8 (1736.5)

	The successful Roman state was based on: 71:1.13 (801.1) 1. The father-family. 71:1.14 (801.2) 2. Agriculture and the domestication of animals. 71:1.15 (801.3) 3. Condensation of population—cities. 71:1.16 (801.4) 4. Private property and land. 71:1.17 (801.5) 5. Slavery—classes of citizenship. 71:1.18 (801.6) 6. Conquest and reorganization of weak and backward peoples. 71:1.19 (801.7) 7. Definite territory with roads. 71:1.20 (801.8) 8. Personal and strong rulers. 71:1.21 (801.9) The great weakness in Roman civilization, and a factor in the ultimate collapse of the empire, was the supposed liberal and advanced provision for the emancipation of the boy at twenty-one and the unconditional release of the girl so that she was at liberty to marry a man of her own choosing or to go abroad in the land to become immoral. The harm to society consisted not in these reforms themselves but rather in the sudden and extensive manner of their adoption. The collapse of Rome indicates what may be expected when a state undergoes too rapid extension associated with internal degeneration. 71:1.22 (801.10)
Romans:	In the great monotheistic renaissance of Melchizedek's gospel during the sixth century before Christ, too few of the Salem missionaries penetrated Italy, and those who did were unable to overcome the influence of the rapidly spreading Etruscan priesthood with its new galaxy of gods and temples, all of which became organized into the Roman state religion. This religion of the Latin tribes was not trivial and venal like that of the Greeks, neither was it austere and tyrannical like that of the Hebrews; it consisted for the most part in the observance of mere forms, vows, and taboos. 98:3.2 (1080.4) Roman religion was greatly influenced by extensive cultural importations from Greece. Eventually most of the Olympian gods were transplanted and incorporated into the Latin pantheon. 98:3.3 (1080.5) The religious initiation of Roman youths was the occasion of their solemn consecration to the service of the state. Oaths and admissions to citizenship were in reality religious ceremonies. The Latin peoples maintained temples, altars, and shrines and, in a crisis, would consult the oracles. They preserved the bones of heroes and later on those of the Christian saints. 98:3.4 (1080.6)
	The emerging Roman state conquered politically but was in turn conquered by the cults, rituals, mysteries, and god concepts of Egypt, Greece, and the Levant. These imported cults continued to flourish throughout the Roman state up to the time of Augustus, who, purely for political and civic reasons, made a heroic and somewhat successful effort to destroy the mysteries and revive the older political religion. 98:3.6 (1080.8)

	One of the priests of the state religion told Augustus of the earlier attempts of the Salem teachers to spread the doctrine of one God, a final Deity presiding over all supernatural beings; and this idea took such a firm hold on the emperor that he built many temples, stocked them well with beautiful images, reorganized the state priesthood, re- established the state religion, appointed himself acting high priest of all, and as emperor did not hesitate to proclaim himself the supreme god. 98:3.7 (1081.1) This new religion of Augustus worship flourished and was observed throughout the empire during his lifetime except in Palestine, the home of the Jews. And this era of the human gods continued until the official Roman cult had a roster of more than two score self-elevated human deities, all claiming miraculous births and other superhuman attributes. 98:3.8 (1081.2)
	At this time the Roman Empire included all of southern Europe, Asia Minor, Syria, Egypt, and northwest Africa; and its inhabitants embraced the citizens of every country of the Eastern Hemisphere. 132:0.3 (1455.3)
	And these Romans were a great people. They could govern the Occident because they did govern themselves. Such unparalleled honesty, devotion, and stalwart self-control was ideal soil for the reception and growth of Christianity. 195:2.4 (2072.8)
Romans: (Continued)	It was easy for these Greco-Romans to become just as spiritually devoted to an institutional church as they were politically devoted to the state. The Romans fought the church only when they feared it as a competitor of the state. Rome, having little national philosophy or native culture, took over Greek culture for its own and boldly adopted Christ as its moral philosophy. Christianity became the moral culture of Rome but hardly its religion in the sense of being the individual experience in spiritual growth of those who embraced the new religion in such a wholesale manner. True, indeed, many individuals did penetrate beneath the surface of all this state religion and found for the nourishment of their souls the real values of the hidden meanings held within the latent truths of Hellenized and paganized Christianity. 195:2.5 (2072.9)
	The spiritual impetus of nominally accepting Hellenized Christianity came to Rome too late to prevent the well-started moral decline or to compensate for the already well-established and increasing racial deterioration. This new religion was a cultural necessity for imperial Rome, and it is exceedingly unfortunate that it did not become a means of spiritual salvation in a larger sense. 195:3.8 (2074.3) Even a good religion could not save a great empire from the sure results of lack of individual participation in the affairs of government, from overmuch paternalism, overtaxation and gross collection abuses, unbalanced trade with the Levant which drained away the gold, amusement madness, Roman standardization, the degradation of woman, slavery and race decadence, physical plagues, and a state church which became institutionalized nearly to the point of spiritual barrenness. 195:3.9 (2074.4)

The Religious Groups and Political Parties of Palestine

<table>
<tr><td rowspan="2">Sadducees:</td><td>The Sadducees consisted of the priesthood and certain wealthy Jews. They were not such sticklers for the details of law enforcement. The Pharisees and Sadducees were really religious parties, rather than sects. 137:7.7 (1534.6)</td></tr>
<tr><td>As they journeyed up the hills from Jericho to Bethany, Nathaniel walked most of the way by the side of Jesus, and their discussion of children in relation to the kingdom of heaven led indirectly to the consideration of the ministry of angels. Nathaniel finally asked the Master this question: "Seeing that the high priest is a Sadducee, and since the Sadducees do not believe in angels, what shall we teach the people regarding the heavenly ministers?" 167:7.1 (1840.6)</td></tr>
<tr><td rowspan="4">Samaritans:</td><td>In the very midst of Palestine there lived the Samaritans, with whom "the Jews had no dealings," notwithstanding that they held many views similar to the Jewish teachings. 137:7.11 (1535.3)</td></tr>
<tr><td>For more than six hundred years the Jews of Judea, and later on those of Galilee also, had been at enmity with the Samaritans. This ill feeling between the Jews and the Samaritans came about in this way: About seven hundred years B.C., Sargon, king of Assyria, in subduing a revolt in central Palestine, carried away and into captivity over twenty-five thousand Jews of the northern kingdom of Israel and installed in their place an almost equal number of the descendants of the Cuthites, Sepharvites, and the Hamathites. Later on, Ashurbanipal sent still other colonies to dwell in Samaria. 143:4.1 (1612.1)

The religious enmity between the Jews and the Samaritans dated from the return of the former from the Babylonian captivity, when the Samaritans worked to prevent the rebuilding of Jerusalem. Later they offended the Jews by extending friendly assistance to the armies of Alexander. In return for their friendship Alexander gave the Samaritans permission to build a temple on Mount Gerizim, where they worshiped Yahweh and their tribal gods and offered sacrifices much after the order of the temple services at Jerusalem. At least they continued this worship up to the time of the Maccabees, when John Hyrcanus destroyed their temple on Mount Gerizim. The Apostle Philip, in his labors for the Samaritans after the death of Jesus, held many meetings on the site of this old Samaritan temple. 143:4.2 (1612.2)</td></tr>
<tr><td>The antagonisms between the Jews and the Samaritans were time-honored and historic; increasingly since the days of Alexander they had had no dealings with each other. The twelve apostles were not averse to preaching in the Greek and other gentile cities of the Decapolis and Syria, but it was a severe test of their loyalty to the Master when he said, "Let us go into Samaria." But in the year and more they had been with Jesus, they had developed a form of personal loyalty which transcended even their faith in his teachings and their prejudices against the Samaritans. 143:4.3 (1612.3)</td></tr>
<tr><td>Jesus declared himself so fully to the Samaritans because he could safely do so, and because he knew that he would not again visit the heart of Samaria to preach the gospel of the kingdom. 143:6.5 (1616.1)</td></tr>
</table>

The Religious Groups and Political Parties of Palestine

Shinto:	Only recently had the manuscripts of this Far-Eastern religion been lodged in the Alexandrian library. It was the one world religion of which Ganid had never heard. This belief also contained remnants of the earlier Melchizedek teachings. 131:7.1 (1451.1)
Suduanism: (Jainism)	The third group of religious believers who preserved the doctrine of one God in India—the survival of the Melchizedek teaching—were known in those days as the Suduanists. Latterly these believers have become known as followers of Jainism. 131:6.1 (1450.5)
Taoism:	The messengers of Melchizedek penetrated far into China, and the doctrine of one God became a part of the earlier teachings of several Chinese religions; the one persisting the longest and containing most of the monotheistic truth was Taoism . . 131:8.1 (1451.4)
Zealots:	At about this time there was considerable agitation, especially at Jerusalem and in Judea, in favor of rebellion against the payment of taxes to Rome. There was coming into existence a strong nationalist party, presently to be called the Zealots. The Zealots, unlike the Pharisees, were not willing to await the coming of the Messiah. They proposed to bring things to a head through political revolt. 127:2.1 (1396.6)
	The Zealots were a group of intense Jewish patriots. They advocated that any and all methods were justified in the struggle to escape the bondage of the Roman yoke. 137:7.9 (1535.1)
Zoroastrianism:	Zoroaster was himself directly in contact with the descendants of the earlier Melchizedek missionaries, and their doctrine of the one God became a central teaching in the religion which he founded in Persia. Aside from Judaism, no religion of that day contained more of these Salem teachings. 131:5.1 (1449.4)
The Gentile Social Groups:	1. The aristocracy. The upper classes with money and official power, the privileged and ruling groups. 121:3.2 (1335.1) 2. The business groups. The merchant princes and the bankers, the traders—the big importers and exporters—the international merchants. 121:3.3 (1335.2) 3. The small middle class. Although this group was indeed small, it was very influential and provided the moral backbone of the early Christian church, which encouraged these groups to continue in their various crafts and trades. Among the Jews many of the Pharisees belonged to this class of tradesmen. 121:3.4 (1335.3) 4. The free proletariat. This group had little or no social standing. Though proud of their freedom, they were placed at great disadvantage because they were forced to compete with slave labor. The upper classes regarded them disdainfully, allowing that they were useless except for "breeding purposes." 121:3.5 (1335.4) 5. The slaves. Half the population of the Roman state were slaves; many were superior individuals and quickly made their way up among the free proletariat and even among the tradesmen. The majority were either mediocre or very inferior. 121:3.6 (1335.5)

The Religious Groups and Political Parties of Palestine

<table>
<tr><td>Gentile Philosophy:</td><td>
1. The Epicurean. This school of thought was dedicated to the pursuit of happiness. The better Epicureans were not given to sensual excesses. At least this doctrine helped to deliver the Romans from a more deadly form of fatalism; it taught that men could do something to improve their terrestrial status. It did effectually combat ignorant superstition. 121:4.2 (1335.11)
2. The Stoic. Stoicism was the superior philosophy of the better classes. The Stoics believed that a controlling Reason-Fate dominated all nature. They taught that the soul of man was divine; that it was imprisoned in the evil body of physical nature. Man's soul achieved liberty by living in harmony with nature, with God; thus virtue came to be its own reward. Stoicism ascended to a sublime morality, ideals never since transcended by any purely human system of philosophy. While the Stoics professed to be the "offspring of God," they failed to know him and therefore failed to find him. Stoicism remained a philosophy; it never became a religion. Its followers sought to attune their minds to the harmony of the Universal Mind, but they failed to envisage themselves as the children of a loving Father. 121:4.3 (1336.1)
3. The Cynic. Although the Cynics traced their philosophy to Diogenes of Athens, they derived much of their doctrine from the remnants of the teachings of Machiventa Melchizedek. Cynicism had formerly been more of a religion than a philosophy. At least the Cynics made their religio-philosophy democratic. In the fields and in the market places they continually preached their doctrine that "man could save himself if he would." They preached simplicity and virtue and urged men to meet death fearlessly. These wandering Cynic preachers did much to prepare the spiritually hungry populace for the later Christian missionaries. Their plan of popular preaching was much after the pattern, and in accordance with the style, of Paul's Epistles. 121:4.4 (1336.2)
4. The Skeptic. Skepticism asserted that knowledge was fallacious, and that conviction and assurance were impossible. It was a purely negative attitude and never became widespread. 121:4.5 (1336.3)
</td></tr>
<tr><td>Gentile Religions:</td><td>
1. The pagan cults. These were a combination of Hellenic and Latin mythology, patriotism, and tradition. 121:5.3 (1336.7)
2. Emperor worship. This deification of man as the symbol of the state was very seriously resented by the Jews and the early Christians and led directly to the bitter persecutions of both churches by the Roman government. 121:5.4 (1336.8)
3. Astrology. This pseudo science of Babylon developed into a religion throughout the Greco- Roman Empire. Even in the twentieth century man has not been fully delivered from this superstitious belief. 121:5.5 (1337.1)
4. The mystery religions. Upon such a spiritually hungry world a flood of mystery cults had broken, new and strange religions from the Levant, which had enamored the common people and had promised them individual salvation. These religions rapidly became the accepted belief of the lower classes of the Greco-Roman world. And they did much to prepare the way for the rapid spread of the vastly superior Christian teachings, which presented a majestic concept of Deity, associated with an intriguing theology for the intelligent and a profound proffer of salvation for all, including the ignorant but spiritually hungry average man of those days. 121:5.6 (1337.2)
</td></tr>
</table>

Jewish Celebrations—
Feasts of Commemoration

Jesus' Early Interest In Recurring Jewish Religious Feasts:	Having met John, who came from near Jerusalem, Jesus began to evince an unusual interest in the history of Israel and to inquire in great detail as to the meaning of the Sabbath rites, the synagogue sermons, and the recurring feasts of commemoration. His father explained to him the meaning of all these seasons. The first was the midwinter festive illumination, lasting eight days, starting out with one candle the first night and adding one each successive night; this commemorated the dedication of the temple after the restoration of the Mosaic services by Judas Maccabee. Next came the early springtime celebration of Purim, the feast of Esther and Israel's deliverance through her. Then followed the solemn Passover, which the adults celebrated in Jerusalem whenever possible, while at home the children would remember that no leavened bread was to be eaten for the whole week. Later came the feast of the first-fruits, the harvest ingathering; and last, the most solemn of all, the feast of the new year, the day of atonement. While some of these celebrations and observances were difficult for Jesus' young mind to understand, he pondered them seriously and then entered fully into the joy of the feast of tabernacles, the annual vacation season of the whole Jewish people, the time when they camped out in leafy booths and gave themselves up to mirth and pleasure. 123:3.5 (1359.6)
	Joseph saw how his son had sickened at the sight of the temple rites and wisely led him around to view the "Gate Beautiful," the artistic gate made of Corinthian bronze. But Jesus had had enough for his first visit at the temple. They returned to the upper court for Mary and walked about in the open air and away from the crowds for an hour, viewing the Asmonean palace, the stately home of Herod, and the tower of the Roman guards. During this stroll Joseph explained to Jesus that only the inhabitants of Jerusalem were permitted to witness the daily sacrifices in the temple, and that the dwellers in Galilee came up only three times a year to participate in the temple worship: at the Passover, at the feast of Pentecost (seven weeks after Passover), and at the feast of tabernacles in October. These feasts were established by Moses. They then discussed the two later established feasts of the dedication and of Purim. Afterward they went to their lodgings and made ready for the celebration of the Passover. 125:1.5 (1379.1)
Feast of the New Year: (SEPTEMBER)	Having met John, who came from near Jerusalem, Jesus began to evince an unusual interest in the history of Israel and to inquire in great detail as to the meaning of the Sabbath rites, the synagogue sermons, and the recurring feasts of commemoration. His father explained to him the meaning of all these seasons. The first was the midwinter festive illumination, lasting eight days, starting out with one candle the first night and adding one each successive night; this commemorated the dedication of the temple after the restoration of the Mosaic services by Judas Maccabee. Next came the early springtime celebration of Purim, the feast of Esther and Israel's deliverance through her. Then followed the solemn Passover, which the adults celebrated in Jerusalem whenever possible, while at home the children would remember that no leavened bread was to be eaten for the whole week. Later came the feast of the first-fruits, the harvest ingathering; and last, the most solemn of all, the feast of the new year, the day of atonement. 123:3.5 (1359.6)

	While some of these celebrations and observances were difficult for Jesus' young mind to understand, he pondered them seriously and then entered fully into the joy of the feast of tabernacles, the annual vacation season of the whole Jewish people, the time when they camped out in leafy booths and gave themselves up to mirth and pleasure. 123:3.5 (1359.6)
	Jesus planned to remain throughout the week of the feast of tabernacles with John. This feast was the annual holiday of all Palestine; it was the Jewish vacation time. Although Jesus did not participate in the merriment of the occasion, it was evident that he derived pleasure and experienced satisfaction as he beheld the lighthearted and joyous abandon of the young and the old. 134:9.4 (1495.1)
Feast of the Tabernacles: (OCTOBER)	**4. The Feast of Tabernacles** The presence of people from all of the known world, from Spain to India, made the feast of tabernacles an ideal occasion for Jesus for the first time publicly to proclaim his full gospel in Jerusalem. At this feast the people lived much in the open air, in leafy booths. It was the feast of the harvest ingathering, and coming, as it did, in the cool of the autumn months, it was more generally attended by the Jews of the world than was the Passover at the end of the winter or Pentecost at the beginning of summer. The apostles at last beheld their Master making the bold announcement of his mission on earth before all the world, as it were. 162:4.1 (1793.5) This was the feast of feasts, since any sacrifice not made at the other festivals could be made at this time. This was the occasion of the reception of the temple offerings; it was a combination of vacation pleasures with the solemn rites of religious worship. Here was a time of racial rejoicing, mingled with sacrifices, Levitical chants, and the solemn blasts of the silvery trumpets of the priests. At night the impressive spectacle of the temple and its pilgrim throngs was brilliantly illuminated by the great candelabras which burned brightly in the court of the women as well as by the glare of scores of torches standing about the temple courts. The entire city was gaily decorated except the Roman castle of Antonia, which looked down in grim contrast upon this festive and worshipful scene. And how the Jews did hate this ever-present reminder of the Roman yoke! 162:4.2 (1794.1) Seventy bullocks were sacrificed during the feast, the symbol of the seventy nations of heathendom. The ceremony of the outpouring of the water symbolized the outpouring of the divine spirit. This ceremony of the water followed the sunrise procession of the priests and Levites. The worshipers passed down the steps leading from the court of Israel to the court of the women while successive blasts were blown upon the silvery trumpets. And then the faithful marched on toward the Beautiful Gate, which opened upon the court of the gentiles. Here they turned about to face westward, to repeat their chants, and to continue their march for the symbolic water. 162:4.3 (1794.2) On the last day of the feast almost four hundred and fifty priests with a corresponding number of Levites officiated. At daybreak the pilgrims assembled from all parts of the city, each carrying in the right hand a sheaf of myrtle, willow, and palm branches, while in the left hand each one carried a branch of the paradise apple—the citron, or the "forbidden fruit." These pilgrims divided into three groups

Feast of the Tabernacles: (Continued)	for this early morning ceremony. One band remained at the temple to attend the morning sacrifices; another group marched down below Jerusalem to near Maza to cut the willow branches for the adornment of the sacrificial altar, while the third group formed a procession to march from the temple behind the water priest, who, to the sound of the silvery trumpets, bore the golden pitcher which was to contain the symbolic water, out through Ophel to near Siloam, where was located the fountain gate. After the golden pitcher had been filled at the pool of Siloam, the procession marched back to the temple, entering by way of the water gate and going directly to the court of the priests, where the priest bearing the water pitcher was joined by the priest bearing the wine for the drink offering. These two priests then repaired to the silver funnels leading to the base of the altar and poured the contents of the pitchers therein. The execution of this rite of pouring the wine and the water was the signal for the assembled pilgrims to begin the chanting of the Psalms from 113 to 118 inclusive, in alternation with the Levites. And as they repeated these lines, they would wave their sheaves at the altar. Then followed the sacrifices for the day, associated with the repeating of the Psalm for the day, the Psalm for the last day of the feast being the eighty-second, beginning with the fifth verse. 162:4.4 (1794.3)
Feast of Dedication: HANUKKAH (DECEMBER)	Having met John, who came from near Jerusalem, Jesus began to evince an unusual interest in the history of Israel and to inquire in great detail as to the meaning of the Sabbath rites, the synagogue sermons, and the recurring feasts of commemoration. His father explained to him the meaning of all these seasons. The first was the midwinter festive illumination, lasting eight days, starting out with one candle the first night and adding one each successive night; this commemorated the dedication of the temple after the restoration of the Mosaic services by Judas Maccabee. 123:3.5 (1359.6)
Feast of Purim: (MARCH)	Having met John, who came from near Jerusalem, Jesus began to evince an unusual interest in the history of Israel and to inquire in great detail as to the meaning of the Sabbath rites, the synagogue sermons, and the recurring feasts of commemoration. His father explained to him the meaning of all these seasons. The first was the midwinter festive illumination, lasting eight days, starting out with one candle the first night and adding one each successive night; this commemorated the dedication of the temple after the restoration of the Mosaic services by Judas Maccabee. Next came the early springtime celebration of Purim, the feast of Esther and Israel's deliverance through her. 123:3.5 (1359.6)
Passover: (APRIL)	Having met John, who came from near Jerusalem, Jesus began to evince an unusual interest in the history of Israel and to inquire in great detail as to the meaning of the Sabbath rites, the synagogue sermons, and the recurring feasts of commemoration. His father explained to him the meaning of all these seasons. The first was the midwinter festive illumination, lasting eight days, starting out with one candle the first night and adding one each successive night; this commemorated the dedication of the temple after the restoration of the Mosaic services by Judas Maccabee. Next came the early springtime celebration of Purim, the feast of Esther and Israel's deliverance through her. Then followed the solemn Passover, which the adults celebrated in Jerusalem whenever possible, while at home the children would remember that no leavened bread was to be eaten for the whole week. 123:3.5 (1359.6)

Passover: (APRIL) (Continued)	Women seldom went to the Passover feast at Jerusalem; they were not required to be present. Jesus, however, virtually refused to go unless his mother would accompany them. And when his mother decided to go, many other Nazareth women were led to make the journey, so that the Passover company contained the largest number of women, in proportion to men, ever to go up to the Passover from Nazareth. Ever and anon, on the way to Jerusalem, they chanted the one hundred and thirtieth Psalm. 125:0.2 (1377.2)
	That night they assembled for the Passover rites, eating the roasted flesh with unleavened bread and bitter herbs. Jesus, being a new son of the covenant, was asked to recount the origin of the Passover, and this he well did, but he somewhat disconcerted his parents by the inclusion of numerous remarks mildly reflecting the impressions made on his youthful but thoughtful mind by the things which he had so recently seen and heard. This was the beginning of the seven-day ceremonies of the feast of the Passover. 125:2.2 (1379.3) Even at this early date, though he said nothing about such matters to his parents, Jesus had begun to turn over in his mind the propriety of celebrating the Passover without the slaughtered lamb. He felt assured in his own mind that the Father in heaven was not pleased with this spectacle of sacrificial offerings, and as the years passed, he became increasingly determined someday to establish the celebration of a bloodless Passover. 125:2.3 (1379.4)
Pentecost: (JUNE)	The apostles had been in hiding for forty days. This day happened to be the Jewish festival of Pentecost, and thousands of visitors from all parts of the world were in Jerusalem. Many arrived for this feast, but a majority had tarried in the city since the Passover. Now these frightened apostles emerged from their weeks of seclusion to appear boldly in the temple, where they began to preach the new message of a risen Messiah. And all the disciples were likewise conscious of having received some new spiritual endowment of insight and power. 194:1.1 (2060.1)
	Pentecost was the great festival of baptism, the time for fellowshipping the proselytes of the gate, those gentiles who desired to serve Yahweh. It was, therefore, the more easy for large numbers of both the Jews and believing gentiles to submit to baptism on this day. In doing this, they were in no way disconnecting themselves from the Jewish faith. Even for some time after this the believers in Jesus were a sect within Judaism. All of them, including the apostles, were still loyal to the essential requirements of the Jewish ceremonial system. 194:1.5 (2060.5)

Gleanings About Jesus From Parts I-III of *The Urantia Book*

Revealing God:	INASMUCH as man's highest possible concept of God is embraced within the human idea and ideal of a primal and infinite personality, it is permissible, and may prove helpful, to study certain characteristics of the divine nature which constitute the character of Deity. The nature of God can best be understood by the revelation of the Father which Michael of Nebadon unfolded in his manifold teachings and in his superb mortal life in the flesh. The divine nature can also be better understood by man if he regards himself as a child of God and looks up to the Paradise Creator as a true spiritual Father. 2:0.1 (33.1) The nature of God can be studied in a revelation of supreme ideas, the divine character can be envisaged as a portrayal of supernal ideals, but the most enlightening and spiritually edifying of all revelations of the divine nature is to be found in the comprehension of the religious life of Jesus of Nazareth, both before and after his attainment of full consciousness of divinity. If the incarnated life of Michael is taken as the background of the revelation of God to man, we may attempt to put in human word symbols certain ideas and ideals concerning the divine nature which may possibly contribute to a further illumination and unification of the human concept of the nature and the character of the personality of the Universal Father. 2:0.2 (33.2)
	But the inhabitants of Urantia are to find deliverance from these ancient errors and pagan superstitions respecting the nature of the Universal Father. The revelation of the truth about God is appearing, and the human race is destined to know the Universal Father in all that beauty of character and loveliness of attributes so magnificently portrayed by the Creator Son who sojourned on Urantia as the Son of Man and the Son of God. 4:5.7 (60.6)
Jesus Speaking of the Living God:	Said Jesus: "My Father, who gave them to me, is greater than all; and no one is able to pluck them out of my Father's hand." As you glimpse the manifold workings and view the staggering immensity of God's well-nigh limitless creation, you may falter in your concept of his primacy, but you should not fail to accept him as securely and everlastingly enthroned at the Paradise center of all things and as the beneficent Father of all intelligent beings. There is but "one God and Father of all, who is above all and in all," "and he is before all things, and in him all things consist." 3:5.4 (51.3)
	This was midwinter in Jerusalem, and the people sought the partial shelter of Solomon's Porch; and as Jesus lingered, the crowds asked him many questions, and he taught them for more than two hours. Some of the Jewish teachers sought to entrap him by publicly asking him: "How long will you hold us in suspense? If you are the Messiah, why do you not plainly tell us?" Said Jesus: "I have told you about myself and my Father many times, but you will not believe me. Can you not see that the works I do in my Father's name bear witness for me? But many of you believe not because you belong not to my fold. The teacher of truth attracts only those who hunger for the truth and who thirst for righteousness. My sheep hear my voice and I know them and they follow me. And to all who follow my teaching I give eternal life; they shall never perish, and no one shall snatch them out of my hand. My Father, who has given me these children, is greater than all, so that no one is able to pluck them out of my Father's hand. The Father and I are one." 164:5.2 (1815.3)

Jesus' Concept of God:	In the study of the religious life of Jesus, view him positively. Think not so much of his sinlessness as of his righteousness, his loving service. Jesus upstepped the passive love disclosed in the Hebrew concept of the heavenly Father to the higher *active* and creature-loving affection of a God who is the Father of every individual, even of the wrongdoer. 5:4.15 (68.3)
	The doctrine of the total depravity of man destroyed much of the potential of religion for effecting social repercussions of an uplifting nature and of inspirational value. Jesus sought to restore man's dignity when he declared that all men are the children of God. 99:5.5 (1091.4)
Growing Appreciation of Our Creator Son:	Throughout your local universe experience the Creator Son, whose personality is comprehensible by man, must compensate for your inability to grasp the full significance of the more exclusively spiritual, but none the less personal, Eternal Son of Paradise. As you progress through Orvonton and Havona, as you leave behind you the vivid picture and deep memories of the Creator Son of your local universe, the passing of this material and morontia experience will be compensated by ever-enlarging concepts and intensifying comprehension of the Eternal Son of Paradise, whose reality and nearness will ever augment as you progress Paradiseward. 6:8.7 (80.4)
Personal Headquarters:	Salvington is the personal headquarters of Michael of Nebadon, but he will not always be found there. While the smooth functioning of your local universe no longer requires the fixed presence of the Creator Son at the capital sphere, this was not true of the earlier epochs of physical organization. A Creator Son is unable to leave his headquarters world until such a time as gravity stabilization of the realm has been effected through the materialization of sufficient energy to enable the various circuits and systems to counterbalance one another by mutual material attraction. 32:2.5 (359.2)
	Our Creator Son is the personification of the 611,121st original concept of infinite identity of simultaneous origin in the Universal Father and the Eternal Son. The Michael of Nebadon is the "only-begotten Son" personalizing this 611,121st universal concept of divinity and infinity. His headquarters is in the threefold mansion of light on Salvington. And this dwelling is so ordered because Michael has experienced the living of all three phases of intelligent creature existence: spiritual, morontial, and material. Because of the name associated with his seventh and final bestowal on Urantia, he is sometimes spoken of as Christ Michael. 33:1.1 (366.2)
Illuminated Plan For Mortal Survival:	But the evolution of a local universe is a long narrative. Papers dealing with the superuniverse introduce this subject, those of this section, treating of the local creations, continue it, while those to follow, touching upon the history and destiny of Urantia, complete the story. But you can adequately comprehend the destiny of the mortals of such a local creation only by a perusal of the narratives of the life and teachings of your Creator Son as he once lived the life of man, in the likeness of mortal flesh, on your own evolutionary world. 32:2.13 (360.2)

Master Son:	Upon the completion of the Creator Son's seventh and final creature bestowal, the uncertainties of periodic isolation terminate for the Divine Minister, and the Son's universe helper becomes forever settled in surety and control. It is at the enthronement of the Creator Son as a Master Son, at the jubilee of jubilees, that the Universe Spirit, before the assembled hosts, first makes public and universal acknowledgment of subordination to the Son, pledging fidelity and obedience. This event occurred in Nebadon at the time of Michael's return to Salvington after the Urantian bestowal. Never before this momentous occasion did the Universe Spirit acknowledge subordination to the Universe Son, and not until after this voluntary relinquishment of power and authority by the Spirit could it be truthfully proclaimed of the Son that "all power in heaven and on earth has been committed to his hand." 33:3.5 (368.5)
	The Master Son, Michael, is supremely concerned with but three things: creation, sustenance, and ministry. He does not personally participate in the judicial work of the universe. Creators never sit in judgment on their creatures; that is the exclusive function of creatures of high training and actual creature experience. 33:7.1 (372.5)
Jesus Referred to Angels:	After the second millennium of sojourn at seraphic headquarters the seraphim are organized under chiefs into groups of twelve (12 pairs, 24 seraphim), and twelve such groups constitute a company (144 pairs, 288 seraphim), which is commanded by a leader. Twelve companies under a commander constitute a battalion (1,728 pairs or 3,456 seraphim), and twelve battalions under a director equal a seraphic unit (20,736 pairs or 41,472 individuals), while twelve units, subject to the command of a supervisor, constitute a legion numbering 248,832 pairs or 497,664 individuals. Jesus alluded to such a group of angels that night in the garden of Gethsemane when he said: "I can even now ask my Father, and he will presently give me more than twelve legions of angels." 38:6.1 (421.4)
	Though serving under the direct supervision of the Infinite Spirit as personalized on Salvington, since the bestowal of Michael on Urantia, seraphim and all other local universe orders have become subject to the sovereignty of the Master Son. Even when Michael was born of the flesh on Urantia, there issued the superuniverse broadcast to all Nebadon which proclaimed, "And let all the angels worship him." All ranks of angels are subject to his sovereignty; they are a part of that group which has been denominated "his mighty angels." 38:6.3 (421.6)
	The Souls of Peace. The early millenniums of the upward strivings of evolutionary men are marked by many a struggle. Peace is not the natural state of the material realms. The world's first realize "peace on earth and good will among men" through the ministry of the seraphic souls of peace. Although these angels were largely thwarted in their early efforts on Urantia, Vevona, chief of the souls of peace in Adam's day, was left on Urantia and is now attached to the staff of the resident governor general. And it was this same Vevona who, when Michael was born, heralded to the worlds, as the leader of the angelic host, "Glory to God in Havona and on earth peace and good will among men." 39:5.5 (437.4)

Memorial to Michael:	These circular reservations of the Sons occupy an enormous area, and until nineteen hundred years ago there existed a great open space at its center. This central region is now occupied by the Michael memorial, completed some five hundred years ago. Four hundred and ninety-five years ago, when this temple was dedicated, Michael was present in person, and all Jerusem heard the touching story of the Master Son's bestowal on Urantia, the least of Satania. The Michael memorial is now the center of all activities embraced in the modified management of the system occasioned by Michael's bestowal, including most of the more recently transplanted Salvington activities. The memorial staff consists of over one million personalities. 46:5.19 (525.1)
What Jesus Did For Religion:	Jesus' life and teachings finally divested religion of the superstitions of magic, the illusions of mythology, and the bondage of traditional dogmatism. But this early magic and mythology very effectively prepared the way for later and superior religion by assuming the existence and reality of supermaterial values and beings. 103:9.4 (1141.2)
Our Contact With Michael:	But the fused individual is really one personality, one being, whose unity defies all attempts at analysis by any intelligence of the universes. And so, having passed the tribunals of the local universe from the lowest to the highest, none of which have been able to identify man or Adjuster, the one apart from the other, you shall finally be taken before the Sovereign of Nebadon, your local universe Father. And there, at the hand of the very being whose creative fatherhood in this universe of time has made possible the fact of your life, you will be granted those credentials which entitle you eventually to proceed upon your superuniverse career in quest of the Universal Father. 112:7.8 (1238.3)
	Before leaving the mansion worlds, all mortals will have permanent seraphic associates or guardians. And as you ascend the morontia spheres, eventually it is the seraphic guardians who witness and certify the decrees of your eternal union with the Thought Adjusters. Together they have established your personality identities as children of the flesh from the worlds of time. Then, with your attainment of the mature morontia estate, they accompany you through Jerusem and the associated worlds of system progress and culture. After that they go with you to Edentia and its seventy spheres of advanced socialization, and subsequently will they pilot you to the Melchizedeks and follow you through the superb career of the universe headquarters worlds. And when you have learned the wisdom and culture of the Melchizedeks, they will take you on to Salvington, where you will stand face to face with the Sovereign of all Nebadon. And still will these seraphic guides follow you through the minor and major sectors of the superuniverse and on to the receiving worlds of Uversa, remaining with you until you finally enseconaphim for the long Havona flight. 113:7.4 (1248.4)
After the Seven Bestowals:	Urantia is the sentimental shrine of all Nebadon, the chief of ten million inhabited worlds, the mortal home of Christ Michael, sovereign of all Nebadon, a Melchizedek minister to the realms, a system savior, an Adamic redeemer, a seraphic fellow, an associate of ascending spirits, a morontia progressor, a Son of Man in the likeness of mortal flesh, and the Planetary Prince of Urantia. And your record tells the truth when it says that this same Jesus has promised sometime to return to the world of his terminal bestowal, the World of the Cross. 119:8.8 (1319.1)

List of References to Jesus in Parts I-III

Paper:Section.Paragraph (page number.paragraph)				
1:6.3 (30.2)	16:9.6 (196.2)	33:3.5 (368.5)	43:4.7 (490.2)	53:1.6 (602.3)
1:6.8 (30.7)	20:5.5 (228.2)	33:3.6 (369.1)	43:4.9 (490.4)	53:2.3 (602.6)
1:7.1 (31.1)	20:6.1 (228.5)	33:4.7 (370.4)	43:5.6 (491.2)	53:3.3 (603.4)
2:0.1 (33.1–3)	20:6.2 (229.1)	33:5.2 (370.7)	45:1.11 (510.9)	53:4.5 (605.2)
2:1.7 (34.6)	20:6.3 (229.2)	33:6.1 (371.3)	45:2.3 (511.3)	53:5.2 (605.6)
2:5.10 (40.2)	20:6.6 (229.5)	33:7.1 (372.5)	45:3.7 (512.7)	53:5.4 (605.8)
2:6.2 (40.6)	20:10.3 (232.6)	34:7.6 (382.6)	45:3.22 (513.3)	53:5.6 (606.2)
2:6.4 (41.2)	21:4.5 (240.1)	35:0.1 (384.1)	45:4.11 (514.1)	53:6.3 (606.6)
3:3.2 (49.1)	21:6.4 (242.3)	37:2.6 (407.6)	45:4.16 (514.6)	53:7.1 (607.2)
3:5.4 (51.3)	27:0.2 (298.2)	37:3.4 (409.1)	46:0.1 (519.1)	53:7.4 (607.5)
4:5.6 (60.5)	28:6.18 (316.5)	37:3.4 (409.2)	46:5.19 (525.1)	53:7.14 (609.2)
4:5.7 (60.6)	30:4.11 (341.1)	37:5.1 (410.4)	46:5.32 (527.1)	53:8.1 (609.4)
5:4.5 (67.3)	30:4.17 (341.7)	38:0.1 (418.1)	46:8.1 (528.7)	53:8.6 (610.2)
5:4.5 (67.4)	30:4.28 (343.3)	38:6.1 (421.4)	47:0.1 (530.1)	53:9.1 (610.6)
5:4.5 (67.5)	32:0.3 (357.3)	38:6.3 (421.6)	48:6.26 (553.7)	53:9.2 (611.1)
5:4.5 (67.6)	32:2.1 (358.3)	39:5.5 (437.4)	49:5.26 (567.6)	53:9.3 (611.2)
5:4.13 (68.1)	32:2.5 (359.2)	40:6.5 (448.4)	50:6.5 (578.5)	53:9.5 (611.4)
5:4.13 (68.2)	32:2.13 (360.2)	40:7.2 (448.9)	51:3.9 (584.2)	54:4.2 (616.1)
5:4.13 (68.3)	33:1.1 (366.2)	40:10.14 (454.3)	52:5.2 (595.7)	54:4.5 (616.4)
7:5.4 (86.5)	33:1.4 (367.1)	41:10.5 (466.4)	52:5.5 (596.3)	54:5.6 (617.6)
7:7.6 (89.5)	33:1.5 (367.2)	43:1.6 (486.5)	52:5.5 (596.3)	55:10.10 (635.1)
13:1.8 (145.3)	33:3.2 (368.2)	43:3.8 (489.3)	52:7.1 (598.4)	55:11.7 (635.9)
56:8.4 (644.2)	77:8.1 (864.2)	94:6.1 (1033.4)	99:5.10 (1091.9)	104:1.11 (1144.8)
56:10.14 (647.5)	80:7.7 (895.7)	94:7.8 (1036.2)	99:5.11 (1091.10)	104:1.12 (1144.9)

Paper:Section.Paragraph (page number.paragraph)				
57:3.8 (654.1)	83:6.3 (927.4)	94:10.3 (1038.7)	100:2.7 (1096.4)	104:2.5 (1146.1)
57:3.9 (654.2)	83:8.3 (929.6)	94:12.7 (1041.5)	100:4.4 (1098.1)	106:2.6 (1165.3)
57:3.11 (654.4)	87:7.6 (966.1)	95:3.1 (1045.4)	100:5.10 (1100.1)	108:4.1 (1190.2)
57:8.6 (660.8)	91:6.6 (999.9)	95:5.2 (1047.2)	100:5.11 (1100.2)	108:4.2 (1190.3)
65:5.4 (736.7)	91:7.2 (1000.3)	95:5.3 (1047.3)	100:7.1 (1101.5) to 100:7.18 (1103.6)	109:6.4 (1200.4)
66:8.6 (753.2)	92:1.5 (1004.3)	95:7.2 (1050.7)		112:7.8 (1238.3)
67:3.1 (756.2)	92:4.8 (1008.1)	95:7.3 (1051.1)	101:6.5 (1112.1)	113:1.1 (1241.3&4)
67:8.1 (761.8)	92:5.13 (1010.1)	96:0.2 (1052.2)	101:6.8 (1112.4)	113:7.4 (1248.4)
68:3.5 (766.6)	92:7.12 (1013.7)	96:1.10 (1053.8)	101:6.16 (1113.5)	114:0.8 (1250.8)
71:6.1 (805.5)	93:0.2 (1014.2)	96:5.1 (1057.6)	101:6.17 (1113.6)	114:1.1 (1250.12)
74:2.6 (830.1)	93:1.2 (1014.4)	97:0.2 (1062.2)	102:3.10 (1122.6)	114:1.2 (1251.1)
75:2.2 (840.4)	93:2.7 (1016.1)	97:7.5 (1068.5)	102:4.1 (1123.1)	114:2.1 (1251.4–6)
76:5.3 (852.2)	93:3.2 (1016.4)	97:7.9 (1069.4)	102:6.7 (1125.2)	114:2.6 (1252.4)
76:5.7 (853.1)	93:3.7 (1017.1)	97:8.4 (1071.2)	102:8.7 (1128.3)	114:3.5 (1253.3–4)
76:6.2 (853.3)	93:4.15 (1018.4)	97:10.8 (1076.5)	103:4.4 (1133.4)	114:7.16 (1259.1)
77:6.6 (863.1)	93:7.3 (1022.1)	98:0.1 (1077.1)	103:5.2 (1133.7)	117:1.8 (1279.6)
77:7.2 (863.3)	93:9.11 (1024.2)	98:6.4 (1083.4)	103:5.6 (1134.4)	117:3.4 (1281.5–6)
77:7.5 (863.6)	93:10.4 (1024.6)	98:7.2 (1084.1)	103:9.4 (1141.2)	117:5.4 (1286.2)
77:7.6 (863.7)	93:10.5 (1025.1)	98:7.11 (1084.10)	104:1.8 (1144.5)	117:6.3 (1288.2)
77:7.7 (863.8)	94:4.1 (1031.2)	98:7.12 (1085.1)	104:1.10 (1144.7)	Papers 119

Comparison of Part IV of *The Urantia Book* to the Four Gospels of Christianity

Note: The original version of this manuscript included this section. However, in 1983, eight years after the publication of the original Part IV Study Aid, Duane Faw published a significantly more extensive comparison of *The Urantia Book* and the Christian Bible. Rather than attempt to duplicate that significant material here, we encourage you to refer to "*Paramony—Paralleling and Harmonizing The Bible and The Urantia Book*" by Duane Faw. While it is out of print at the time of this writing, new and used copies are available on Amazon.com and CosmicCreations.BIZ.

www.ingramcontent.com/pod-product-compliance
Ingram Content Group UK Ltd.
Pitfield, Milton Keynes, MK11 3LW, UK
UKHW051206260726
13967UKWH00011B/3142